Inside Windows 95

Jim Boyce

Paul J. Sanna

Rob Tidrow

Jonathan J. Chau

Scott Fuller

Kevin Pagan

Russell Jacobs

R. James Ruehlin

New Riders

New Riders Publishing, Indianapolis, Indiana

Inside Windows 95

By Jim Boyce, Paul J. Sanna, Rob Tidrow, Jonathan J. Chau, Scott Fuller, Kevin Pagan, Russell Jacobs, and R. James Ruehlin

Published by:
New Riders Publishing
201 West 103rd Street
Indianapolis, IN 46290 USA

Printed in the United States of America 1 2 3 4 5 6 7 8 9 0

```
Inside Windows 95/Jim Boyce…[et al.].
       p.    cm.
     Includes index.
     ISBN 1-56205-375-2
     1. Microsoft Windows 95.
     2. Operating systems (Computers)
   I. Boyce,Jim, 1958-
QA76.76.O63I563   1995
005.4'469--dc20
                                   95-36607
                                      CIP
```

Warning and Disclaimer

Publisher	*Don Fowley*
Associate Publisher	*Tim Huddleston*
Marketing Manager	*Ray Robinson*
Acquisitions Manager	*Jim LeValley*
Managing Editor	*Tad Ringo*

Product Development Specialist
Emmett Dulaney

Acquisitions Editor
Alan Harris

Software Specialist
Steve Weiss

Development Editor
Ian Sheeler

Production Editor
John Kane

Copy Editors
Phil Worthington
Amy Bezek
Sarah Kearns
Cliff Shubs

Technical Editor
Karen Saint Rain

Assistant Marketing Manager
Tamara Apple

Acquisitions Coordinator
Stacey Beheler

Publisher's Assistant
Karen Opal

Cover Designer
Sandra Stevenson-Schroeder

Book Designer
Kim Scott

Manufacturing Coordinator
Paul Gilchrist

Production Manager
Kelly Dobbs

Production Team Supervisor
Laurie Casey

Graphics Image Specialists
Clint Lahnen, Dennis Sheehan

Production Analysts
Angela D. Bannan
Bobbi Satterfield
Mary Beth Wakefield

Production Team
Elaine Brush, Angela Calvert, Kim Cofer, Kevin Foltz, David Garratt, Mike Henry, Aleata Howard, Aren Howell, Shawn MacDonald, Joe Millay, Erika Millen, Kim Mitchell, Erich J. Richter, Christine Tyner, Beth Rago, Tim Taylor, Karen Walsh

Indexer
Chris Cleveland

About the Authors

Jim Boyce, the lead author for *Inside Windows 95*, is a contributing editor and columnist for *WINDOWS* magazine, a columnist for *CADENCE* magazine, and a regular contributor to other computer publications. He has been involved with computers since the late seventies, and has used computers as a user, programmer, and systems manager in a variety of capacities. He has a wide range of experience in the DOS, Windows, and Unix environments. Jim has authored and coauthored over two dozen books on computers and software. You can contact Jim at the address 76516.3403@compuserve.com.

Paul J. Sanna was born in Greenwich, Connecticut, and attended DePauw University in Greencastle, Indiana, before graduating from Boston University with a bachelors degree in English. He began working with computers in 1985, working for a market analysis company that tracked the aerospace industry. For the last six years, Paul has worked for a software development company in Stamford, Connecticut, in the development department, where his focus has been on the company's line of Windows-based, client/server accounting and financial reporting. Paul lives in Bethel, Connecticut, with his wife, Andrea, and their twin daughters, Rachel and Allison. Apart from his family, his free time is spent watching New York Giants football and finding someone willing to play golf with a novice.

Rob Tidrow has edited and contributed to the development of several popular New Riders Publishing titles, including *Understanding Windows 95, Inside Novell NetWare, Inside Windows 3.1, Inside Microsoft Access,* and *Technology Edge: A Guide to Field Computing.* He also is co-author of *AutoCAD Student Workbook,* also by New Riders Publishing. Rob has created technical documentation and instructional programs for use in a variety of industrial settings. He resides in Indianapolis with his wife and two boys, Adam and Wesley.

Jonathan J. Chau is a freelance writer and consultant, specializing in PC operating systems, including Windows NT, OS/2, and Windows 95.

Scott M. Fuller is president of IDEAS, a computer consulting group specializing in law firms. Mr. Fuller has an extensive background in system design, operations, operations management, and technical training for a wide variety of clients. He has contributed to several books, including *Learn Windows 95 in a Day, Upgrade to Windows 95 Quick & Easy, Learn Timeslips in a Day, Learn CompuServe in a Day,* and *Learn Prodigy in a Day.*

Kevin D. Pagan is an attorney specializing in civil trial law. Mr. Pagan has a bachelor's degree in accounting and is currently a member of both the Texas Bar Association and the American Bar Association. He is the co-author of *Learn Timeslips in a Day* and *Learn CompuServe in a Day.*

Russ Jacobs is a software developer for the technical development division of The Prudential in Roseland, New Jersey. He also is president of Software Alchemy, a company specializing in the development and writing of technical books. As a member of IBM's Best Team, Team OS/2, and president of the Northern New Jersey OS/2 Users Group, Russ often speaks about software design and development. Russ is a lead beta tester for IBM, Microsoft, and Borland. Russ has edited or developed over 20 titles for Que and has been a contributing author for titles for Que and R&D Publishing.

Jim Ruehlin is a user interface designer and software engineer. He has worked for hardware and software manufacturers, and has written a technical column for the *San Diego Daily Transcript.* Jim has been writing code since he learned BASIC when he was 16, and holds a Bachelor of Arts degree in cognitive science from the University of California at San Diego. He currently lives in San Diego with three computers and a web browser.

Trademark Acknowledgments

Contents at a Glance

Part V: Integration and Automation

Part VI: Messaging and Communications

Part VII: Sharing Resources and Using the Internet

Part VIII: Appendix

Table of Contents

4   Adding and Configuring New Hardware   103

Part III: Windows 95 Architecture and Optimization

Part IV: Putting Windows 95 to Work

17 Installing and Uninstalling Applications 509

18 Running Applications 531

23 Working with Multimedia Audio and CD-ROM 621

Part V: Integration and Automation

24 Exchanging Data between Applications 639

Part VI: Messaging and Communications

Part VII: Sharing Resources and Using the Internet

34   Network Concepts and Configuration   911

Part VIII: Appendix

A Other Sources of Information   1017

Index   1021

Introduction

Welcome to *Inside Windows 95,* your complete guide to Microsoft Windows 95. With the release of Windows 95, Microsoft has introduced an entirely new operating system for the PC. The result is a faster, more useful environment for your applications than DOS or even Windows 3.*x* ever provided. With this new operating system come new features, new accessories, and a completely redesigned interface.

Inside Windows 95 is written for the computer-literate user who is migrating from DOS or another operating system to Windows 95, or upgrading from Windows 3.*x* to Windows 95. Within the pages of this book you will find solid explanations of core Windows 95 features, along with expert tips and tricks for optimizing your system and Windows 95. If you require an entry-level book on Windows 95, consult *Understanding Windows 95,* also from New Riders Publishing.

Who Should Read This Book?

Inside Windows 95 is written for the experienced Windows 3.*x* or Windows 95 user who wants to learn more about Windows 95. This book assumes you have some Windows experience and want to know more about Windows 95's architecture, core features, and internal functions.

You can learn how to apply Windows 95's latest enhancements to your own computer work without relearning Windows concepts and functions you already know through your own experience. Specifically, this book makes the following assumptions about your Windows skill level:

◆ You are familiar with the mouse and mouse actions

◆ You know how to use dialog boxes and other Windows interface objects

◆ You understand the concept of windowed applications, and you know how to control program windows (minimize, maximize, resize, move, and so on)

◆ You know how to start and run applications in Windows

◆ You have some background knowledge in operating a PC

How This Book Is Structured

Inside Windows 95 is designed as a reference to help experienced computer users find information quickly. To make finding the information easier, the book is divided into parts, each of which covers a specific group of Windows 95 concepts and features.

Part One: Overview and Setup

Part One introduces the Windows 95 environment and explores the options you have for installing and configuring Windows 95. Within the four chapters in Part One are a tour of Windows 95, a detailed discussion of setup and configuration issues, tips on troubleshooting installation and Windows 95 startup, and an explanation of hardware detection and adding new hardware.

Part Two: Working in Windows 95

The Windows 95 GUI (graphical user interface) is different from the interface in Windows 3.*x*. The Windows 95 interface offers better ease-of-use, enhanced power and flexibility, and improved program and document management. Within Part Two's six chapters, you learn about the new Windows 95 interface and how to use it, as well as the new file/folder paradigm employed by Windows 95 and how to manage files and directories in Windows 95. Other chapters explain fonts, printing, interface customization, and the use of Accessibility Options.

Part Three: Windows 95 Architecture and Optimization

Part Three offers a deeper look into some of Windows 95's key components. The first of six chapters in Part Three explains the Windows 95 architecture, providing a detailed look into the inner workings of the operating system to help you understand performance issues and how Windows 95 differs from previous operating systems and environments. Other chapters provide a detailed look at system selection and hardware upgrades, the Registry, and how to optimize physical and virtual memory. You also learn about the disk utilities in Windows 95 and how to apply them to optimize your system's disk storage space. Part Three also explores ways to improve and enhance your Windows 95 environment through Microsoft Plus! for Windows 95, an add-on for Microsoft Windows 95.

Part Four: Putting Windows 95 to Work

Part Four helps you begin to apply some of the new, powerful features in Windows 95. The seven chapters in this part explain how to install and uninstall applications, work with Windows applications, create and use a Briefcase for file synchronization, and use new features in Windows 95 that support expanded multimedia capabilities. Part Four also explores how to use and create your own Windows 95 Help files, integrate DOS applications and tools in your Windows 95 environment, and ensure data security through the Backup utility.

Part Five: Integration and Automation

Windows 95 improves on the data sharing capabilities in Windows 3.x by expanding OLE support to almost all facets of the Windows 95 interface. Part Six explains in detail how to perform static and dynamic data exchanges between Windows applications using the Clipboard, Object Linking and Embedding (OLE), and Dynamic Data Exchange (DDE). You also learn in Part Six how to exchange data between the Windows and DOS environments.

Part Six: Messaging and Communications

One of the most significant additions to Windows 95 is its many features that enable faster and easier data communications. In addition to a new 32-bit communications program, Windows 95 includes an Exchange e-mail client that integrates all your messaging functions, from faxing to e-mail. Windows 95 includes Exchange service providers for Microsoft Fax, Microsoft Mail, CompuServe Mail, and Internet mail, and all these providers are explored in detail in Part Seven. *Inside Windows 95* also devotes chapters to Microsoft's new online service, the Microsoft Network (MSN), and to using Windows 95 as a remote access client and server.

Part Seven: Sharing Resources and Using the Internet

Networking is considerably improved and simplified in Windows 95. Part Seven provides a detailed look at configuring and using Windows 95's network features, starting with an in-depth look at network concepts. Also covered in detail are peer-to-peer networking with Windows 95, TCP/IP and Internet access, and Internet utilities.

Conventions Used in This Book

Throughout this book, certain conventions are used to help you distinguish the various elements of Windows 95, DOS, their system files, and sample data. Before you look ahead, you should spend a moment examining the following conventions:

- ◆ Shortcut keys normally are found in the text where appropriate. As an example, Ctrl+V is the shortcut key for the Paste command.

- ◆ When you see a plus sign (+) between key names, you should hold down the first key while pressing the second key, then release both keys. Shift+F12, for example, is a shortcut key for the Print command.

- ◆ On-screen, Windows 95 underlines the letters of some menu names, file names, and option names. The underlined letter is the letter you can type to choose that command or option. In this book, such letters are displayed in bold, underlined, blue type, such as <u>**F**</u>ile.

- ◆ Information you type is in **boldface.** This applies to individual letters and numbers, as well as to text strings. This convention does not apply to special keys, such as Enter, Esc, and Ctrl.

- ◆ New terms appear in *italics*.

- ◆ Text that is displayed on-screen but is not part of Windows 95 or a Windows application—such as command prompts and messages—appears in a `special typeface`.

- ◆ At times, a line of programming code or screen output might be too long to fit on one line in the book. In these instances, the line will break to a second line, and that second line will begin with a code continuation character: ➥.

Notes, Tips, and Stops

Inside Windows 95 features many special sidebars, which are set apart from the normal text by icons. Three different types of sidebars are used: Notes, Tips, and Stops:

Note Notes include extra information that you should find useful, but which complements the discussion at hand instead of being a part of it.

Notes might describe special situations that result from unusual circumstances. These sidebars tell you what to expect or what steps to take when such situations occur. Notes also might tell you how to avoid problems with your software and hardware.

Tip Tips provide you with quick instructions for getting the most from your Windows 95 system. A Tip might show you how to conserve memory in some setups, how to speed up a procedure, or how to perform one of many time-saving and system-enhancing techniques.

Stop Stops inform you when a procedure might be dangerous; that is, when you run the risk of losing data, locking your system, or even damaging your hardware. Stops generally tell you how to avoid such losses or describe the steps you can take to remedy them.

These sidebars enhance the possibility that *Inside Windows 95* will be able to answer your most pressing questions about Windows 95 use, architecture, and performance. Although Notes, Tips, and Stops do not condense an entire section into a few steps, these snippets will point you in new directions for solutions to your needs and problems.

New Riders Publishing

The staff of New Riders Publishing is committed to bringing you the very best in computer reference material. Each New Riders book is the result of months of work by authors and staff who research and refine the information contained within its covers.

As part of this commitment to you, the NRP reader, New Riders invites your input. Please let us know if you enjoy this book, if you have trouble with the information and examples presented, or if you have a suggestion for the next edition.

Please note, though: New Riders staff cannot serve as a technical resource for Windows 95 or for related questions about software- or hardware-related problems. Please refer to the documentation that accompanies Windows 95 or to the applications' Help systems.

If you have a question or comment about any New Riders book, there are several ways to contact New Riders Publishing. We will respond to as many readers as we can. Your name, address, and phone number will never become part of a mailing list or be used for any purpose other than to help us continue to bring you the best books possible. You can write us at the following address:

> New Riders Publishing
> Attn: Associate Publisher
> 201 W. 103rd Street
> Indianapolis, IN 46290

If you prefer, you can fax New Riders Publishing at (317) 581-4670.

To send NRP mail from CompuServe, use the following address:

> 74507,3713

To send mail from the Internet, use the following address:

> edulaney@mcp.com

New Riders Publishing is an imprint of Macmillan Computer Publishing. To obtain a catalog or information, or to purchase any Macmillan Computer Publishing book, call (800) 428-5331.

Thank you for selecting *Inside Windows 95*!

Part I

Overview and Setup

A Tour of Windows 95

W indows 95 is the most significant software release since Windows 3.0 spurred the inevitable shift from character-based DOS to graphical user interfaces for PCs. Windows 3.*x* brought the point-and-click ease of use to the PC that Apple Macintosh users had long enjoyed, and Windows 95 further simplifies using a PC. Unlike Windows 3.*x*, however, Windows 95 no longer relies on DOS—Windows 95 is a complete, 32-bit operating system that no longer is hobbled by the limited capabilities of the original DOS operating system.

The new features and capabilities in Windows 95 do more than just make it easier to use your PC and access network resources; Windows 95's multitasking, multithreading, and 32-bit device support provide a much higher performance level for your PC.

This chapter provides a quick tour of Windows 95, giving you an overview of Windows 95's new features and capabilities. The chapter covers the following topics:

◆ A tour of Windows 95's key user features

◆ A brief overview of Windows 95 architectural elements

◆ An overview of multitasking, multithreading, and other performance improvements in Windows 95

◆ A visual tour of Windows 95

Note   If you are a new PC user or have just made the move from DOS to Windows 95, *Understanding Windows 95*, also from New Riders Publishing, will give you a good introduction to using Windows 95. *Understanding Windows 95* provides a tutorial look at the features in Windows 95 that are most important to the average user.

The most obvious features in Windows 95 are the changes to the user interface from the Windows 3.*x* interface. The following section gives you a brief look at only the most prominent features of the new interface. All aspects of the Windows 95 interface are covered in detail in Chapters 5 and 6.

Exploring the Windows 95 Interface

The Windows 95 interface is similar to Windows 3.*x*, but Windows 95 introduces numerous changes that make using the PC easier. The new interface also makes it much easier to access resources locally and on the network. Gone, for example, is the Windows Program Manager, which has been replaced by a more integrated Windows desktop (see fig. 1.1).

Figure 1.1

The Windows desktop.

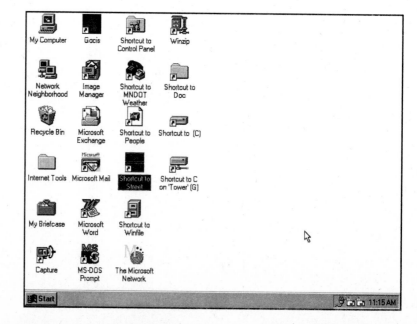

Overview of the Windows 95 Desktop

In Windows 3.*x*, Program Manager is the default mechanism for organizing your applications and providing quick access to those applications, as well as to your documents and your PC's resources. Although Program Manager is included with Windows 95, Program Manager no longer starts by default when Windows boots. Instead, the Windows 95 desktop integrates many of the features found in Program Manager.

 Tip   When you upgrade an existing Windows 3.*x* installation to Windows 95, Setup gives you the option of converting all your existing Program Manager groups to Windows 95 folders. Refer to Chapter 2, "Setting Up and Booting Windows 95," for more information on setting up Windows 95 and converting your existing Program Manager groups.

Instead of organizing objects such as applications and documents in group windows, the new Windows 95 desktop enables you to create folders to contain objects. *Folders* are really nothing more than directories that are represented on the desktop as either an icon or as a window. When the folder is closed, it is represented as an icon on the desktop. When the folder is open, it appears as a typical window with a border, scroll bars, title bar, and menu (see fig. 1.2). Inside the window are icons for the applications, documents, and other folders (subdirectories) contained in the folder.

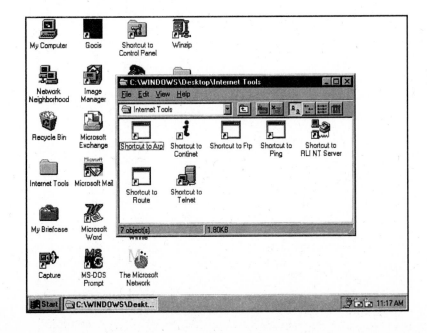

Figure 1.2

A folder opened on the desktop.

Tip   Because a folder can contain other folders, the Windows 95 desktop provides a much better means of organizing the objects with which you work on a regular basis. In essence, folders are like group windows that can contain other (nested) groups.

You also can create shortcuts to objects. A *shortcut* is a special type of file—a visual pointer to an object—that is represented by an icon, just like folders, applications, documents, and other objects. You might create a shortcut on the desktop to your word processor, for example, but the application's executable file resides in its own folder, not in the desktop directory. When you double-click on the shortcut's icon, Windows 95 reads information from the shortcut's file to locate the application with which the shortcut is associated. Windows 95 then starts the application based on the information it finds in the shortcut file.

Windows 95 also includes a few special folders that do not represent directories; instead, they contain other objects. The following list describes these special folders:

◆ **My Computer.** This object contains icons for all disks connected to the PC, including local disks and remote network disks that are mapped to local drive letters. My Computer also contains icons for the Control Panel folder, Fonts folder, Printers folder, and Dial-Up Networking folder.

◆ **Network Neighborhood.** If your PC is connected to a network, the Network Neighborhood appears on the desktop. The Network Neighborhood folder contains icons of each of the other PCs in your workgroup, as well as an icon labeled Entire Network that enables you to browse for network resources outside of your workgroup.

◆ **Control Panel.** The Control Panel folder contains objects you can use to control the way Windows 95 appears and functions. This is similar to the Windows 3.*x* Control Panel.

◆ **Printers.** The Printers folder displays icons for all printers installed on your system, including local and network printers. You can control a printer's properties and its print queue through the Printers folder.

◆ **Fonts.** The Fonts folder displays all the fonts installed on your system.

The desktop also includes the Recycle Bin, which actually is a temporary directory where deleted objects are stored. The desktop also includes all folders created on the desktop, and a Briefcase, which you can use to synchronize files on two computers. You will read more about these objects and folders in upcoming chapters.

Tip   You can create shortcuts on the desktop to folders. If you work often with a folder on drive C that contains the majority of your documents, for example, create a shortcut on the desktop to the folder. When you open the folder, its contents are immediately available to you—you can double-click on a document icon in the folder to start the document's parent application and open the document.

The Taskbar

Another important feature of the Windows 95 desktop is the Taskbar. The Taskbar includes a Start button (see fig. 1.3) that gives you access to a hierarchical menu. You can use this menu to start applications, open documents, open the Control Panel, access the Explorer, and access other standard objects.

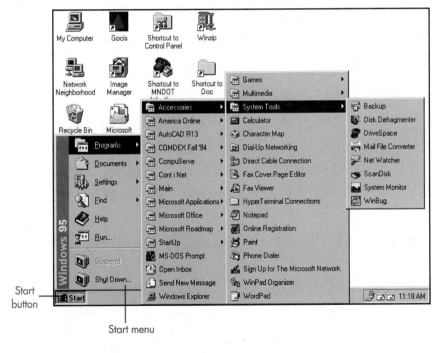

Figure 1.3

The Start menu provides quick access to programs, documents, and other objects.

The Taskbar acts as a task-switcher, enabling you to switch between running applications. Running applications appear as buttons on the Taskbar. To switch to a particular program, you just click on its button, and that application then moves to the foreground.

The Taskbar also displays status information. The clock, for example, appears in the Taskbar. If your PC uses power-saving features, the Taskbar includes an indicator showing whether your PC is running on AC or battery power, as well as an indicator of battery condition. Other informational indicators also appear on the Taskbar from time to time, and you will read about these additional indicators in later chapters.

 Tip   You can relocate the Taskbar to any of the four sides of the display just by dragging it into position. You also can set the Taskbar to automatically hide when you are not using it. When hidden, the Taskbar reappears when you move the cursor to the edge of the display where the Taskbar is located.

Understanding Explorer

Also central to the new Windows 95 interface is Explorer, which provides a consistent mechanism for viewing files, folders, and objects. In some ways, Explorer is like the Windows 3.x File Manager, which enables you to view directories and their contents as a hierarchical tree. Explorer extends those capabilities, however, giving you a view of all objects to which your PC has access, including network printers and directories, local printers, Exchange (the common e-mail and information client in Windows 95), and other resources. Figure 1.4 shows Explorer. To start Explorer, choose Start, Programs, and Windows Explorer.

Figure 1.4

Explorer provides access to all of your PC's resources.

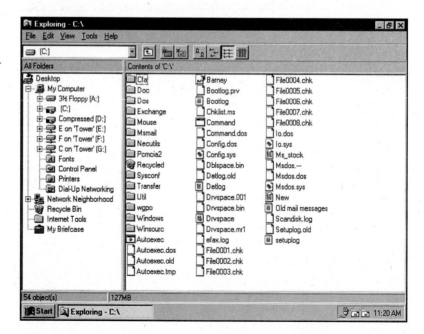

The left pane in Explorer shows the desktop, which comprises your PC's local disks, the Fonts folder, the Control Panel folder, the Printers folder, and the Dial-Up Networking folder. The desktop also includes the Network Neighborhood if your PC is connected to a network. The Network Neighborhood provides quick access to all other workstations, servers, and shared resources (such as printers) available on the network.

Selecting an object from the left pane causes the contents of the selected object to be displayed in the right pane. Double-clicking on the icon of one of your PC's local hard disks, for example, displays the contents of that hard disk in Explorer's right pane. As with the Windows 3.*x* File Manager, you can use Explorer to open applications and documents, manage files and directories, print documents, and perform other common tasks.

Explorer Windows on the Desktop

Although Explorer exists as an application, the Explorer interface also extends onto the Windows 95 desktop, providing a common interface for displaying objects such as folders. A typical folder window (see fig. 1.5) includes a title bar, a menu, and an optional toolbar and status bar.

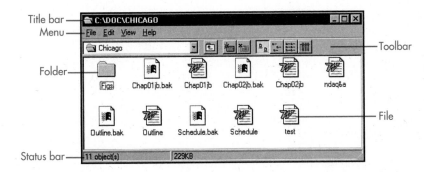

Figure 1.5

A typical folder window.

You can control the way in which a folder window displays the objects contained in the folder. By default, the objects appear as large icons, just like the program and document items in a Program Manager group. You can display the objects as small icons, a simple list, or a detailed list. You also can control the types of files that are displayed in a folder. These options are explored in more detail in Chapter 6, "Managing Files and Folders."

Exploring Windows 95's New Features

The new Windows 95 interface is significant in its own right for making your PC easier to use and improving your productivity. The new interface, however, is just one part of the picture. In addition to its new interface, Windows 95 contains a wealth of new features that add to its capability. Most of these new features are made possible by the fact that Windows 95 is a complete operating system that no longer requires DOS. All functions that previously were handled by DOS have been improved and incorporated in Windows 95.

This section briefly examines most of these new features. Performance improvements, such as Windows 95's new flat memory structure, are described later in this chapter.

Making Windows 95 Easier to Use

Windows 95 includes many new features aimed at making the PC easier to use and expanding your PC's capabilities. Some of these new features include the following:

◆ **Long file names.** Windows 95 now supports file names of up to 255 characters. File names can include multiple periods, spaces, and other punctuation symbols not allowed in DOS 8.3 (eight-character file name and three-character extension) file-name format. A Windows 95 application must be written to use long file names, however; existing Windows 3.*x* applications do not support long file names.

◆ **Plug and Play.** Windows 95 supports Plug and Play, which simplifies the task of installing new hardware in a PC. With many peripherals, you can simply turn off the PC, install the hardware, then restart the PC. Windows 95 automatically configures the new hardware and loads any necessary drivers. If you plug a new PCMCIA modem into your notebook PC, for example, Windows 95 recognizes the new modem and automatically installs support for the modem.

◆ **Quick access to documents and other objects.** Windows 95 keeps track of documents you work with and adds their paths to a special Documents menu within the Start menu (see fig. 1.6). Rather than open the source application and then hunt for the document to open, you can simply click on the document's name in the Documents menu, and Windows 95 opens the source application and the document file automatically.

◆ **Improved accessories.** Many of the accessory programs included with Windows 3.*x,* such as Paintbrush and Write, have been improved or replaced by new applications in Windows 95. Windows 95 also includes new accessories.

◆ **Add New Hardware wizard.** Windows 95 includes a wizard called Add New Hardware that automates much of the task of adding new hardware to your PC. This wizard helps you install hardware that doesn't support Plug and Play, enabling Windows 95 to automatically install the hardware with little or no intervention from you.

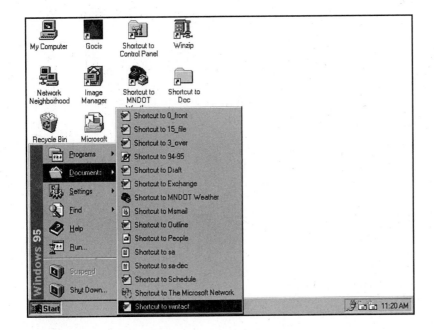

Figure 1.6

The Documents menu gives you quick access to recently used documents and other objects.

Using long file names and other issues dealing with files and folders are explored in Chapter 6. Plug and Play, adding new hardware, and controlling hardware are covered in Chapter 4. The Documents menu and other interface shortcuts are explored in Chapters 5 and 6.

New System Tools and Utilities

Windows 95 includes many new tools to provide a better Help system, to make it easier to locate and preview documents, and to manage your files and disks. A few of these new utilities include the following:

◆ **New Help system.** The Help system in Windows 95 has been completely rewritten. Help now includes an improved organizational structure, an expanded index, and a much-improved search engine.

◆ **Find.** The Start menu gives you access to a Find utility that enables you to search your PC or entire network for a file, folder, or other computer.

◆ **Viewers.** Windows 95 includes a selection of file viewers that enable you to preview a document without opening the document's source application. You also can view the contents of executable files and other types of files using these file viewers.

◆ **Disk tools.** Windows 95 includes a set of Windows-based utility programs for managing your disks and files. These utilities include DriveSpace (compress disks and manage compressed disks; see fig. 1.7), ScanDisk (disk scanning and repair; see fig. 1.8), Disk Defragmenter (defragment a disk to improve its performance), Backup (backup and restore files to disk or tape), and other utilities to monitor your PC's performance and access to your PC by other users on the network.

Figure 1.7

DriveSpace enables you to almost double the capacity of your PC's hard disks.

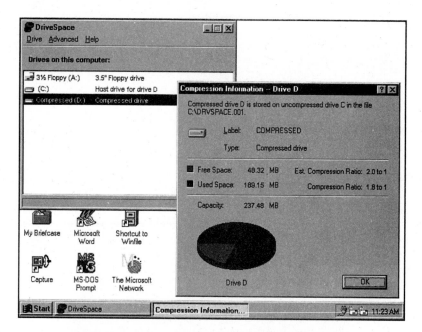

Figure 1.8

ScanDisk enables Windows 95 to find and repair problems with your files and disks.

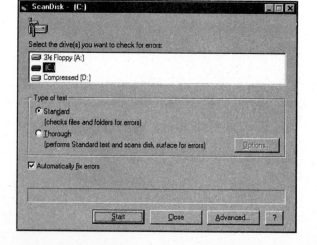

The new Windows 95 Help system is covered in Chapter 20. Using the Find utility and working with file viewers are covered in Chapter 7. Managing disks is explained in Chapter 15. Monitoring performance and controlling network access are covered in Chapters 34 and 35.

Communications Tools

Windows 95 integrates data communication at the system level, providing numerous features to support e-mail, Internet access, faxing, and access to online services. Windows 95 also provides a front end for Microsoft's new online service, The Microsoft Network.

◆ **Exchange.** A key feature in Windows 95's communications capability is Exchange, the e-mail client bundled with Windows 95 (see fig. 1.9). Exchange provides a common e-mail front end for Microsoft Mail, CompuServe, the Internet, At Work Fax, and other e-mail applications that support the Mail API (MAPI). Exchange adds many new features to the mail capability in Windows 95, including rich text messages, message filters, and remote mail.

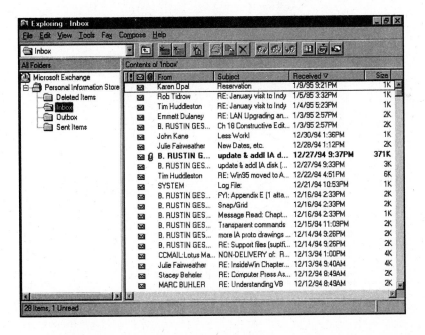

Figure 1.9

Exchange provides a common e-mail system.

◆ **TCP/IP and Internet tools.** Windows 95 includes a 32-bit TCP/IP protocol stack and tools such as FTP, Telnet, Arp, Ping, and Route, for use on the Internet. In addition, the Exchange e-mail client includes an Internet provider that enables you to use Exchange to send and retrieve e-mail on the Internet.

◆ **At Work Fax.** Bundled with Windows 95 is a new version of At Work Fax, Microsoft's fax send/receive utility. At Work Fax is integrated with the Exchange mail client. You can send and receive faxes as easily as you send e-mail messages.

◆ **The Microsoft Network.** Microsoft has become an online service provider with its new online service called The Microsoft Network (MSN). MSN offers file libraries, special-interest forums, product support, news, and other information services (see fig. 1.10).

Figure 1.10

The Microsoft Network offers a range of online information services.

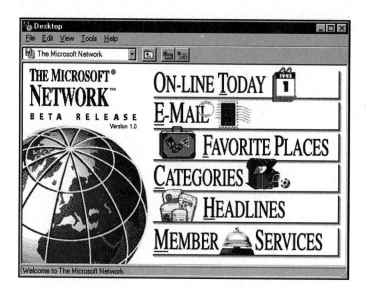

General data communications issues and The Microsoft Network are covered in Chapters 28 and 32. E-mail and Exchange are explored in Chapters 29 and 30. At Work Fax is explained in Chapter 31. TCP/IP and Internet issues are explored in Chapters 36 and 37.

Improved Networking

Windows 95 improves and expands on the networking features in Windows for Workgroups to provide easy, peer-to-peer networking. Windows 95 also includes network client software to enable it to work seamlessly in Novell NetWare and Microsoft networks, as well as with other network operating systems. The following are some of the networking improvements in Windows 95:

◆ **Network Neighborhood.** Integrated with the Windows 95 desktop is the Network Neighborhood, a special folder that gives you quick access to network resources. The Network Neighborhood folder displays an icon for each of the nodes in your workgroup. Double-clicking on a node's icon displays a folder containing that node's shared resources. The Network Neighborhood folder also contains an Entire Network icon that you can use to locate resources on the network that are outside of your workgroup.

◆ **Multiple network support.** Windows 95 supports multiple networks, enabling you to view and use resources provided by different types of servers. You can, for example access resources on NetWare servers and NT servers at the same time.

◆ **Client for NetWare.** Windows 95 includes a Novell NetWare client that provides full NetWare client support under Windows 95. The NetWare client enables you to use command-line server utilities such as FILER and SYSCON from the command prompt. You also can browse and connect to NetWare servers from Windows 95.

◆ **User-level security.** Windows 95 supports user-level security, which enables a PC that is sharing some of its resources to do so on a user-by-user basis. User authentication is handled by a Windows NT or Novell NetWare security server.

◆ **Multiple user profiles.** Multiple users can work with the same PC, but each can have a personal desktop configuration and other settings. Windows 95 automatically configures itself when the user logs on.

◆ **Remote administration.** PCs running Windows 95 can be administered remotely over a LAN or through remote access.

◆ **UNC resource naming.** It no longer is necessary to map local drive IDs to remote network drives. Instead, the Universal Naming Convention (UNC) name can be specified. Instead of mapping a remote disk to drive ID F, for example, you can simply access the drive by its name, such as \\SERVER\APPS.

Networking is a major feature in Windows 95. Many aspects of Windows 95 networking are covered in Parts Six and Seven.

Support for Portables

Windows 95 includes many features for users who have portable PCs or who work from home or other remote sites. These features include the following:

◆ **Support for docking configurations.** Windows 95 automatically reconfigures your notebook PC when you dock it into a docking station.

◆ **Briefcase.** The Briefcase, a new utility in Windows 95, enables you to synchronize files on two computers. The Briefcase automatically updates the multiple copies of the files to ensure that all copies are the most current.

◆ **Power management.** Windows 95 includes full support for power management on notebooks and on power-saving desktop PCs. The Taskbar displays a power-source indicator, as well as a battery status indicator when the PC is running on battery power.

◆ **Dial-Up Networking.** Windows 95 includes software that enables a Windows 95 workstation to serve as both a remote access services (RAS) server and client (see fig. 1.11). A Windows 95 PC can dial into a RAS server (NT Server, Windows 95 server, or other appropriate RAS server) to access resources on the RAS server as well as on the network to which the server is connected. Dial-Up Networking is a key aspect of remote mail and other Windows 95 networking features.

Figure 1.11

A Windows 95 PC can act as a RAS server and a RAS client.

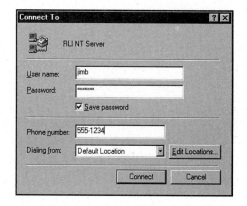

◆ **Direct cable connection.** Windows 95 supports a direct null-modem serial connection between two PCs. This enables you to transfer files quickly and easily between the two PCs, such as a notebook and desktop PC. The direct cable connection also enables you to create a mini-network without installing a network adapter in either PC.

◆ **Deferred printing.** In Windows 95, you can print even when your PC does not have immediate access to a printer. The document is placed in the print queue and is printed when the printer is connected to the PC or becomes available across the network.

Support for docking configurations and other issues for portable PC users are covered in Chapters 4 and 12. RAS is explained in detail in Chapter 33. Direct cable connections are explored in Chapter 34. Printing issues, including deferred printing, are described in Chapter 8.

Exploring Performance and the Windows 95 Architecture

It isn't necessary to fully understand the architecture of Windows 95 in order to use it. But understanding some of the most important aspects of the Windows 95 architecture can help you understand how Windows 95 differs significantly from previous versions and how you can best use Windows 95 to your advantage. It would require many chapters to explore the Windows 95 architecture in detail, so this chapter only describes in brief the most prominent aspects of the Windows 95 architecture. These and other facets of the Windows 95 architecture are explored in greater depth in Chapter 11, "Understanding the Windows 95 Architecture."

A Complete Operating System

Unlike previous versions of Windows, Windows 95 is a complete, 32-bit operating system. Previous versions of Windows actually are *operating environments* that run as applications under the DOS operating system. Although these previous versions of Windows expand the capabilities of the PC, they still are limited by the capabilities (and lack thereof) of DOS. Windows 3.*x*, for example, is constrained by the 1 MB conventional memory limitations of DOS.

Windows 95 eliminates the need for DOS. Windows 95 not only includes all the core functionality of DOS, but improves on that core by replacing old 16-bit DOS components with 32-bit, protected-mode alternatives. Instead of relying on DOS to provide such services as disk I/O, Windows 95 handles all aspects of hardware and software performance. DOS programs and commands are replaced in Windows 95 by Windows-specific versions. These commands can be found in the \Windows\Command folder. Using DOS commands and running DOS applications is explained in Chapter 21, "Integrating Windows and DOS."

32-Bit File System

All disk services, which in Windows 3.*x* were handled primarily by DOS, now are handled exclusively by Windows (a necessity, because DOS might no longer even be present on the machine). By replacing the old DOS disk services with 32-bit counterparts, Windows significantly improves disk performance—the processor no longer has to switch from protected mode to real mode in order to process disk I/O requests. In addition, the Windows disk services support a variety of storage devices, including CD-ROM drives. This expanded device support improves the performance of devices that were relatively slow under Windows 3.*x* even with the addition of 32-bit file and disk access in Windows for Workgroups.

Note Windows and Windows for Workgroups versions 3.1 and 3.11 include various levels of 32-bit disk and file access. In many situations, particularly those involving DOS-based applications, these versions of Windows are forced to pass disk I/O tasks on to DOS services, reducing disk performance. By completely replacing DOS, Windows 95 enables even older DOS applications to benefit from improved disk access.

By providing a full range of disk I/O services, the new Windows file system eliminates the need for real-mode device drivers that were required with previous versions of DOS and Windows. The CD driver MSCDEX, for example, which was required with DOS to access CD-ROM drives, is no longer required in Windows 95. Instead, Windows 95 uses its own 32-bit CD-ROM file system to access and read the CD.

Tip The new Windows 95 installable file system also makes possible the use of long file names, which are discussed earlier in this chapter and in detail in Chapter 6, "Managing Files and Folders."

Device Drivers

Most devices require a *driver,* which essentially is a miniprogram that provides a set of core services that manage and provide access to the device. In DOS, device drivers typically are loaded into memory during boot. This means these device drivers are always in memory, even when they are not needed.

Windows 3.*x* improved device support by allowing for *virtual device drivers,* which are 32-bit, protected-mode drivers. Virtual device drivers enable more than one application to access the resource being controlled by the virtual device driver. Virtual device drivers also provide better performance than DOS-based real-mode drivers because they are 32-bit and operate in protected-mode.

The primary disadvantage to virtual device drivers in Windows 3.*x* is the same as with DOS device drivers—the drivers are loaded statically when Windows starts and always consume memory, even when not in use. Windows 95 improves virtual device driver support by enabling these device drivers to be loaded dynamically. If a virtual device driver is not being used, Windows 95 can remove the device driver from memory to free that memory for other use. When the device driver is once again needed, Windows 95 loads it again. This capability to dynamically load and unload device drivers improves Windows 95's memory use over that of Windows 3.*x*.

Multitasking and Multithreading

Another significant improvement in Windows 95 over Windows 3.*x* is in multitasking and multithreading. *Multitasking* is the capability of an operating system or operating environment to run multiple programs at one time. In Windows, for example, you can open word processing, spreadsheet, database, and graphics applications at the same time. You don't have to close a program to use another—you simply switch from one program to another.

Windows 3.*x*'s multitasking is *non-preemptive,* or *cooperative.* This means that Windows 3.*x* can't preempt, or take away, processor control from an application. If an application takes control of the processor and doesn't give up that control, no other application can gain control of the processor and execute. Cooperative multitasking in Windows 3.*x* is therefore limited by the design of the applications you run—a poorly written application could effectively eliminate multitasking by hogging the processor.

Windows 95 overcomes that limitation by providing *preemptive multitasking.* This means that Windows 95 retains full control of the processor and is able to preempt an application's access to the processor. When another application requires the use of the processor, Windows 95 takes control of the processor from the running application and shifts that access to the second application. Preemptive multitasking, therefore, enables applications to work more smoothly together and eliminates the problem of an ill-behaved application taking full control of the system.

Note To retain compatibility in Windows 95, Win16 applications (16-bit applications written for Windows 3.*x*) still run using cooperative multitasking. Win32 applications (32-bit applications written specifically for Windows 95), however, support preemptive multitasking. Therefore, it still is possible for an ill-behaved Win16 application to affect the performance of other Win16 applications, and to a degree, the performance of Win32 applications. Win16 applications do, however, take advantage of some of the preemptive multitasking capabilities of system-level services such as printing and communications.

In addition to preemptive multitasking, Windows 95 also provides *multithreaded execution,* or *multithreading,* which enhances Windows 95's multitasking capability. A Win32 application is called a *process,* and a process consists of at least one *thread of execution.* Each thread is a unit of code that can request a time slice from Windows. An application, therefore, can be broken up into multiple threads, each of which can use a time slice.

By contrast, in cooperative multitasking, each application requests a time slice to use. Each thread then executes until its time slice is used up. Breaking up an application into multiple threads makes the application more responsive, and applications operate together more smoothly. Instead of applications running one after the other, each taking its turn at the processor, individual threads have their turn at the processor. The result is a much smoother background operation of applications.

 Note   Disregarding the hype you will hear to the contrary, Windows 95 does not support *true multitasking*. In Windows 95, applications still must share the processor on a one-at-a-time basis. The processor switches between tasks so rapidly, however, that applications seem to be running at the same time. True multitasking, in which applications really do run concurrently, is only possible on multiple-processor systems (computers that contain more than one CPU). Windows 95 does not support multiple processors.

System Robustness

Robustness typically refers to an operating system's capability to survive component failures, ill-behaved applications, and applications that fail. Windows 95 provides a more robust operating system than Windows 3.*x*, primarily because of the separation of applications. Each Win32 application runs in its own memory address space, which effectively isolates it from other applications. If a Win32 application fails, Windows can remove it from memory without affecting other applications.

Windows 95 also provides better protection from errant Win16 applications. Even though all Win16 applications share a common memory address space (just as they do in Windows 3.*x*), they are separated from all Win32 applications, which have their own memory address space. If a Win16 application fails, Windows 95 is much less likely to fail or gradually degenerate.

Expanded Resource Support

Resources such as icons, windows, and various other data elements require a small amount of memory to enable Windows to manage them. In Windows 3.*x*, the amount of resource memory was limited to two 16-bit, 64 KB blocks of memory. As more and more resources were used, the amount of resource memory naturally decreased. Eventually, Windows 3.*x* reached a point at which it could not open any additional applications or documents because there was not enough resource memory left to accommodate the additional resources. This inability to open applications often happened when the system had plenty of free RAM.

Microsoft has reengineered resource memory in Windows 95. The majority of objects have been moved to new 32-bit heaps, which are effectively unlimited. For compatibility, however, some objects still are stored in the 16-bit heap. Although continuing to rely on the 16-bit heap still imposes a limit on the amount of resource memory available to applications, the limits are substantially higher. The result is that you can run many more applications under Windows 95 than you previously could under Windows 3.*x*.

Note The changes described briefly in the previous sections are only some of the significant changes in Windows 95 over DOS and Windows 3.*x*. Many of these additional changes are explored in Chapter 11, "Understanding the Windows 95 Architecture."

A Visual Tour of Windows 95

The features described in the previous sections are just some of the main features in Windows 95. The following visual tour of Windows 95 points out some of these features as well as many others. If you have some experience with Windows 3.*x*, this visual tour also helps you understand some of the changes in Windows 95 from previous versions of Windows.

Figure 1.12 shows the Windows 95 interface, including the desktop, the Start button, and the Taskbar. You can customize each of these items to add commands and access to applications.

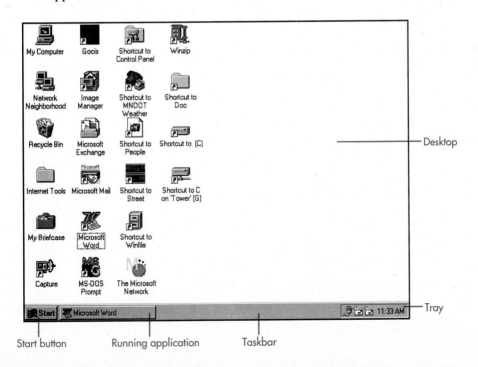

Figure 1.12

The Windows desktop, Taskbar, and Start button.

The My Computer folder gives you quick access to your entire PC, as well as to the Control Panel folder, Printers folder, and Dial-Up Networking folder (see fig. 1.13). This organizes all your PC's resources, whether local or remote, into a single folder.

Figure 1.13

My Computer displays all your PC's resources in a single folder.

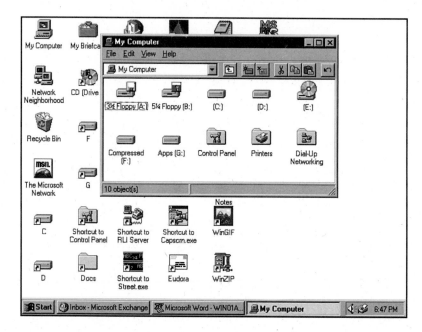

Just as the My Computer folder organizes all of your local resources into a single folder, the Network Neighborhood folder provides quick access to the entire network (see fig. 1.14). The Network Neighborhood folder contains icons for all the PCs in your workgroup. Clicking on a computer's icon displays icons for all of the resources, including printers, that the computer is sharing. You also can choose the Entire Network icon to access network resources that are located on PCs in other workgroups.

You can customize the Taskbar, controlling the way it appears on the desktop. You also can add commands to the Start menu to provide quick access to applications and documents (see fig. 1.15).

Right-clicking on an object displays a context menu that enables you to set properties for the selected object. Right-clicking on the desktop, for example, displays property sheets you can use to set the display's colors, screen saver, resolution, and other settings (see fig. 1.16). Right-clicking on a folder or program icon displays property sheets for that item (see fig. 1.17).

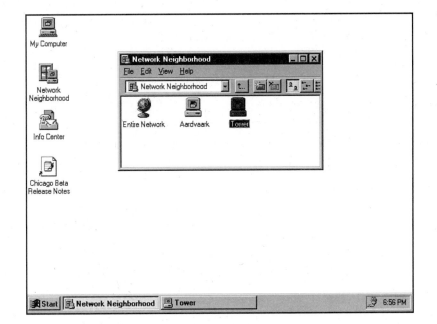

Figure 1.14

The Network Neighborhood folder gives you quick access to all network resources.

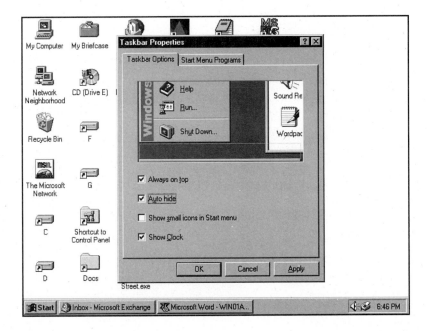

Figure 1.15

Right-click on the Taskbar to set properties for the Start menu and Taskbar.

Figure 1.16

Right-click on the desktop to display property sheets for the display.

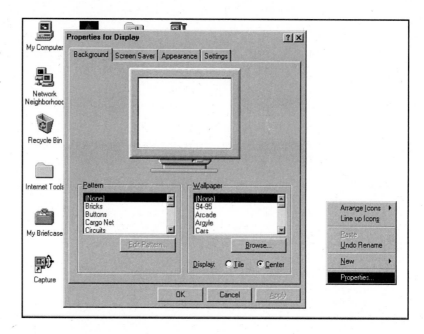

Figure 1.17

Right-click on an object to open a context menu and set the object's properties.

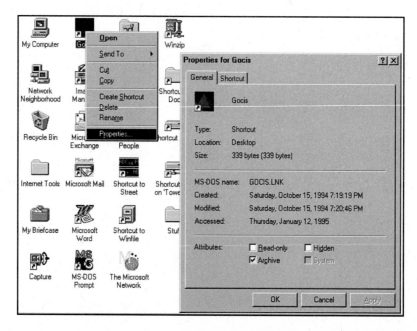

Windows 95's Explorer is tightly integrated into the Windows interface (see fig. 1.18). Explorer gives you a view of all your PC's resources, making it easy to manage files, start applications, open documents, and perform other common tasks.

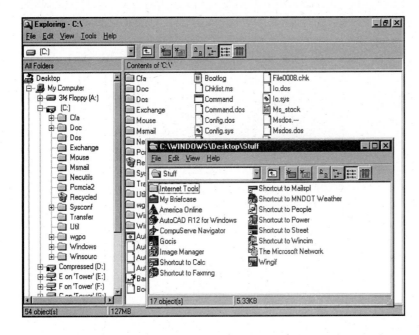

Figure 1.18

Many character-istics of Explorer carry over into folder windows.

You can create shortcuts on the desktop to disks and folders, which gives you quick access to your applications, documents, and other files (see fig. 1.19). You even can create shortcuts to remote network folders without mapping a local drive ID to the remote folder.

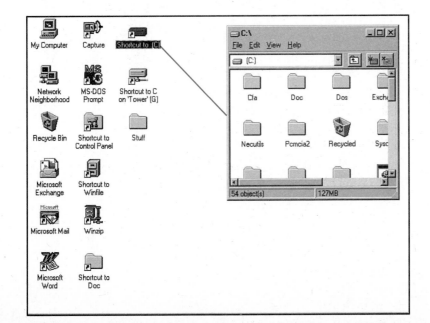

Figure 1.19

You can create shortcuts on the desktop to disks and folders.

Windows includes a wide range of accessory programs for word processing, data communications, managing personal information such as phone numbers and addresses, and much more. Figures 1.20 through 1.23 show a few of Windows 95's accessory programs.

Figure 1.20

WordPad enables you to create and edit ASCII and formatted text files and Word for Windows documents.

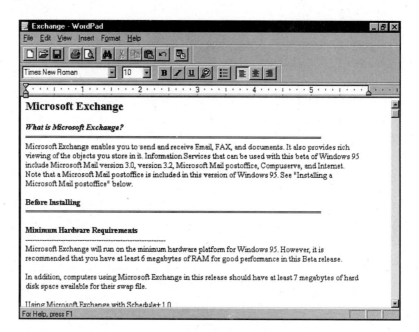

Figure 1.21

HyperTerminal provides data communications capability.

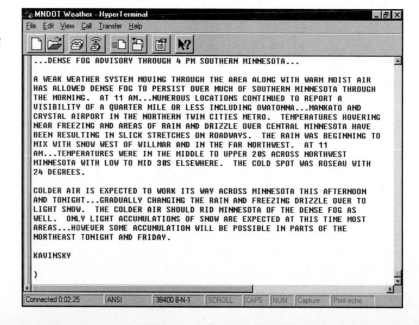

Figure 1.22

Paint enables you to create and edit bitmaps.

Figure 1.23

You can use the Phone Dialer to track addresses and phone numbers.

Windows 95 offers many features for users who need to work from outside the office, such as at home or on business trips. One such feature is Dial-Up Networking, which you can use to connect from a remote site to the LAN resources at your office (see fig. 1.24).

The Control Panel gives you nearly complete control over your PC (see fig. 1.25).

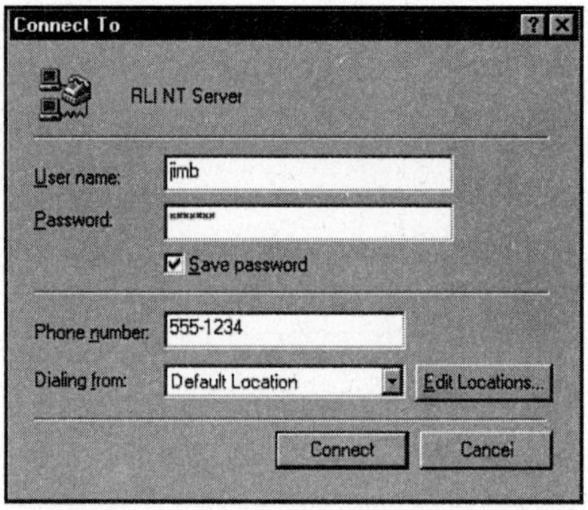

Figure 1.24

Dial-Up Networking enables you to connect to a remote PC or network to access remote resources.

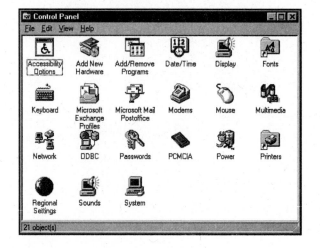

Figure 1.25

Use the Control Panel to control and configure your PC.

Windows 95 includes a number of features to make the PC easier to use for people with disabilities (see fig. 1.26).

Exchange provides an integrated e-mail system for your LAN, CompuServe, the Internet, faxing, and other e-mail and messaging systems (see fig. 1.27).

The Briefcase is a special folder you can use to synchronize files on two PCs (see fig. 1.28). The Briefcase is particularly useful for people who work outside the office and need to ensure that files on their notebook or home PCs are up-to-date with their office PCs.

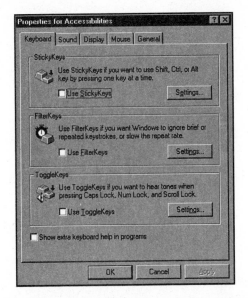

Figure 1.26

The Windows 95 Accessibility features are designed to assist people with disabilities.

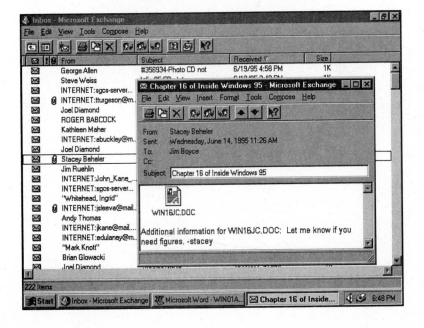

Figure 1.27

Exchange provides full e-mail and fax capability.

Figure 1.28

*The Briefcase
enables you to
synchronize files
on two PCs.*

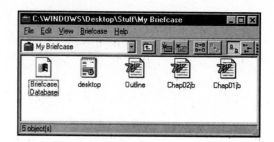

CHAPTER

2

Setting Up and Booting Windows 95

As with previous versions of Windows, installing and configuring Windows 95 is relatively simple. A little careful planning and preparation on your part will help ensure a quick and trouble-free installation. This chapter explains the process for installing Windows 95 on a stand-alone PC and performing local installations on networked PCs. The chapter covers the following topics:

◆ Overview of the Windows 95 setup process

◆ Planning and preparing to install Windows 95

◆ Running Setup and specifying Setup options

◆ Configuring network settings

◆ Completing the setup process

◆ Understanding and controlling the boot process

◆ Understanding the effects of Setup on DOS

◆ Understanding the effects of Setup on System.ini and Win.ini

This chapter primarily addresses two types of readers: users who want to install Windows 95 on a single PC, and system administrators who need to install Windows 95 in a stand-alone configuration on one or more PCs. Chapter 3, "Troubleshooting Setup and Startup," will help you troubleshoot your Windows 95 installation, if necessary.

If you already know what you need to install Windows 95 and want to get started right away, turn to the section "Running Setup" later in this chapter. If you are not familiar with installing Windows 95, the next section helps you understand how you can install Windows 95 on your PC. Understanding the setup process helps you determine the best method to use to install Windows 95 in a stand-alone configuration.

Note   Unless otherwise specified, throughout the book, the term "Windows 3.x" refers equally to Windows and Windows for Workgroups versions 3.1 and 3.11. It does not, however, include Windows 3.0.

Overview of Setup

As with its predecessors, Windows 95 uses a program called Setup that enables you to install and configure Windows 95 on a PC. An installation in which you place Windows 95 on the PC's hard disk is called a *stand-alone* installation. Or, you can install a shared copy of Windows, which enables Windows 95 to run on the PC by using a set of shared files located on a network server—called a *shared installation*. This chapter describes the overall Setup process and explains how to perform a stand-alone installation.

Requirements for Setup

Two different versions of the Windows 95 product are available: a full version and an upgrade version. The upgrade version is intended for PCs that already contain a copy of Windows 3.x (including Windows 3.0), Windows NT, or OS/2. Because previous versions of Windows rely on the DOS operating system, these systems also contain a working copy of DOS. You can't use the upgrade version to install Windows 95 on a PC unless that PC contains a copy of one of the other operating systems previously mentioned.

The full Windows 95 version is intended for PCs that contain a DOS operating system but not a copy of a previous version of Windows, as well as for PCs that have no operating system at all installed. Therefore, you must have the full version before you can install Windows 95 on a new, unpartitioned, unformatted hard disk. The full version includes a boot disk that enables Setup to boot the PC and then partition and

format the hard disk for Windows 95. When you start Setup from the boot disk, it also can read your PC's CD-ROM drive to enable you to install Windows 95 from CD.

Hardware and Operating System Requirements

Windows 95 requires a minimum hardware configuration, described in the following list:

◆ 386 or higher PC-compatible CPU, although adequate performance requires a 486 or better

◆ A minimum of 4 MB of RAM (more is strongly recommended)

◆ 10 MB to 40 MB of free disk space, depending on the installation options (see the list in the section "Planning and Preparing for the Installation" for more detailed disk space requirements)

◆ VGA or better display

◆ FAT file system (Windows 95 will not install in an NTFS or HPFS partition)

◆ For installation on a compressed disk, at least 3 MB of available uncompressed space

If you install the upgrade version of Windows 95, in addition to the minimum hardware described in the preceding list, the PC must contain a bootable version of MS-DOS 3.2 or later, or an OEM version of DOS that supports disk partitions of 32 MB or more, and it must contain Windows 3.*x*. Or, it must contain Windows NT or OS/2.

If you use the full version of Windows 95, the PC does not need to have an operating system. If the system contains Windows NT or OS/2, however, you must be able to dual-boot the system (boot to DOS, not Windows NT or OS/2), because Windows 95 Setup is a Win16 application that you have to run from real-mode DOS or Windows 3.*x* (except Windows 3.0).

 Note　If the PC contains an operating system not yet mentioned here, such as Unix, you still can install Windows 95. To do so, however, you must install Windows 95 into a FAT disk partition. To boot a particular operating system after you install Windows 95, use the FDISK utility (available in both Unix and Windows 95) to make the operating system's partition active, then restart the system.

In addition to the operating system requirements described previously, the hard disk on which you plan to install Windows 95 must use the FAT file system—you can't

install Windows 95 in a Windows NT NTFS or OS/2 HPFS partition. Windows 95 Setup does recognize and support disks that have been compressed with Double-Space, DriveSpace, Stacker 3.0 or 4.*x*, or SuperStor; however, you must have at least 3 MB of uncompressed space available before you can install Windows 95. Windows 95 does support FAT partitions created using FDISK on removable drives, including those from Iomega and Bernoulli.

 Stop   If your PC contains an NTFS or HPFS file system in addition to a FAT partition, and you install Windows 95 into the FAT partition, Windows 95 cannot read the files in the NTFS or HPFS partitions. Windows 95 supports only FAT partitions.

For more information on installing Windows 95 on PCs that contain Windows NT or OS/2, refer to the sections "Installing on PCs with Windows NT" and "Installing on PCs with OS/2" later in this chapter.

 Tip   If your disk has been partitioned using Disk Manager (Dmdrvr.bin), SpeedStor (Sstor.sys), or Golden Bow Vfeature, Setup converts these partitions to standard FAT partitions.

Understanding the Setup Process

You can use Setup to install Windows in stand-alone and shared configurations, locally or across the network, and to reinstall, repair, or update an existing Windows 95 installation. You also can use the Add/Remove Programs control in the Control Panel (see fig. 2.1) to add and remove Windows components and Windows applications, and to create a Windows boot disk. Upgrading and repairing Windows 95 and creating a boot disk are explained in Chapter 3, "Troubleshooting Setup and Startup."

Setup performs many different tasks in stand-alone and shared installations, described in the following list:

◆ **Hardware detection.** Setup automatically attempts to detect your PC's hardware and configure installation options.

◆ **Verify system requirements.** Setup determines whether you actually can install Windows 95 on your PC, which includes checking the amount of available disk space on the target disk.

◆ **Install files.** Setup copies all necessary drivers, applications, and other files required to run Windows 95 on your PC, based on what you select during Setup.

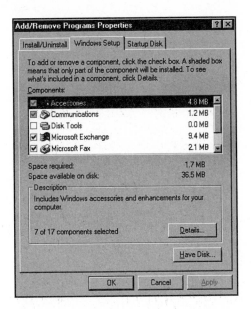

Figure 2.1

Use the Add/ Remove Programs object in Control Panel to add or remove Windows 95 features.

◆ **Configure Windows 95.** Setup automatically configures Windows 95 to work with your PC's hardware.

◆ **Configure the network.** If you install Windows 95 on a networked PC, Setup installs and configures the necessary networking components.

◆ **Install and configure printers.** Setup installs and configures printer drivers for the printers available to your PC.

◆ **Convert existing Windows 3.x environment.** If you upgrade an existing copy of Windows 3.*x* to Windows 95, Setup imports all your Windows 3.*x* program groups, and creates equivalent shortcuts and makes them available in the Start menu. Setup also imports settings from Win.ini and System.ini into the Windows 95 Registry, and migrates your existing Windows applications to the Windows 95 environment so that these applications can run under Windows 95.

Stop   You must install Windows 95 over your existing copy of Windows 3.x if you want to be able to run your Windows applications under Windows 95. If you install Windows 95 to a new directory, and keep your existing Windows 3.x installation, you still have to reinstall the majority of your Windows applications under Windows 95 before they run properly in Windows 95.

Before you plan on installing Windows 95, you need to understand a few key points about Windows 95 so you can integrate Windows 95 with your existing operating system and applications. The next section explains these key points.

Understanding Windows 95 Boot Options

You can install Windows 95 on a PC as that PC's sole operating system—Windows 95 does not require DOS. When you turn on a PC on which Windows 95 is the sole operating system, the full Windows 95 operating system, complete with graphical user interface (GUI), automatically boots. On such a system, you also can boot Windows 95 to a command line that resembles the DOS command line. In fact, you can run DOS programs and execute various DOS commands (Windows 95 includes updated versions of many DOS commands previously included with DOS) from the Windows 95 command line. If you have booted the system to the Windows 95 command prompt, just enter **WIN** at the Windows 95 command line to start the GUI and load the full Windows 95 operating system.

This Windows 95 command-line environment (essentially a limited stand-alone DOS session), does not represent the entire Windows 95 operating system. The majority of drivers load during boot of the GUI. If you don't run MSCDEX or an equivalent CD-ROM driver, for example, you cannot access the CD-ROM drive from the Windows 95 command line. These driver limitations do not apply to DOS sessions you open within Windows 95—such DOS sessions have full access to all hardware and network resources available to Windows applications. DOS sessions that you run under Windows 95 also benefit from the performance advantages, such as improved disk I/O, that are inherent in the Windows 95 operating system.

 Tip   To enable multiboot, which you can use to boot operating systems other than Windows 95 (such as DOS and Windows NT), you must edit the hidden file Msdos.sys located in the root directory of your boot disk. Refer to the section "Booting Your System" later in this chapter for instructions on modifying Msdos.sys to enable multiboot.

Windows 95 also supports multiboot options on PCs that contain other operating systems, such as previous versions of DOS, Windows NT, or OS/2. Whether you can use multiboot depends on how you install Windows 95. The following sections explain your options for installing Windows 95 on PCs that already have operating systems.

Installing Over MS-DOS and Windows 3.x

If you install Windows 95 on a PC that contains a previous version of DOS, Setup replaces some of the existing DOS files and renames others. If you install Windows 95 into a new directory (and don't upgrade an existing Windows installation), you can boot your previous version of DOS. If you upgrade your existing version of Windows to Windows 95, you cannot boot your old version of DOS. This is not a problem, however, because the DOS core included in Windows 95 is fully compatible with the DOS environment it replaces. For a more complete explanation of how Setup effects an existing DOS installation, see the section "The Effects of Setup on DOS" later in this chapter.

Installing on PCs with Windows NT

If you have a PC that contains Windows NT, you can retain Windows NT on the system and also install Windows 95 as long as the system has a FAT partition to accommodate Windows 95. How you install Windows 95, however, depends on how you installed Windows NT and whether you have a copy of Windows 3.*x* on the system. The following list summarizes your installation options based on possible configurations:

◆ **Windows NT only.** Although you can install Windows 95 into the same directory as Windows NT, doing so causes problems with NT. Windows 95 rewrites the Windows 3.*x* DLLs in the \Windows\System directory so that Windows 95 can run Win16 and Win32 (16-bit and 32-bit) Windows applications. Windows NT relies on the old DLLs to run Win16 applications. Installing Windows 95 in the same directory as Windows NT prevents Windows NT from properly running some Win16 applications. Windows 95 also relocates the screen fonts to the \Windows\Fonts directory, which forces Windows NT to use a different system font, one that does not display properly in many dialog boxes. You therefore should install Windows 95 into its own directory.

◆ **Windows NT and Windows 3.x sharing a directory.** If you have Windows 3.*x* and Windows NT in the same directory, you can't update your existing copy of Windows 3.*x* to Windows 95. Instead, you must install Windows 95 into a new directory. You also have to reinstall each of your Windows applications to use them under Windows 95.

◆ **Windows NT and Windows 3.x in separate directories.** If you have Windows NT and Windows 3.*x* in separate directories, you can upgrade your existing copy of Windows 3.*x* to Windows 95. Or, you can choose to install Windows 95 in a new directory. If you install Windows 95 in a new directory, however, you must reinstall all your Windows applications separately before they can run properly under Windows 95.

Tip

In general, the only Windows applications that will not run properly without being reinstalled under Windows 95 are those that use DLLs in the Windows or Windows\System folders, or which place special settings in System.ini or Win.ini. If an application is self-contained in its own directory, and doesn't store any of its settings in System.ini or Win.ini, it probably will run fine under Windows 95 without requiring reinstallation. Unfortunately, the majority of common productivity applications don't fall into the latter category.

When you install Windows 95 on a system that contains Windows NT, Setup retains the Windows NT Boot Loader. When the system boots, the NT Boot Loader enables you to select from Windows NT or DOS. Selecting MS-DOS boots Windows 95. If you prefer, you can use the Windows NT System icon in the Control Panel to modify the boot message to reference Windows 95 rather than MS-DOS.

To install Windows 95 on a system that contains Windows NT, boot the system to MS-DOS and run Setup. During the installation process, Setup reboots your PC, and the Windows NT Boot Loader again appears. Again select MS-DOS to enable Setup to complete the installation and configuration process. After you properly set up Windows 95, you can boot whichever operating system you need.

Tip   Before you begin to install, boot Windows NT, open the Control Panel, and choose the System icon. In the System dialog box, select MS-DOS from the **S**tartup drop-down list, then choose OK. The NT Boot Loader then automatically boots MS-DOS rather than Windows NT, which enables the Windows 95 Setup process to complete without requiring you to monitor the system and manually boot MS-DOS for the second Setup pass. After Windows 95 is fully installed and working, you can boot Windows NT again and use the System icon to specify whether you want to boot Windows NT or Windows 95 (selecting MS-DOS causes the NT Boot Loader to boot Windows 95 automatically).

Installing on PCs with OS/2

If your PC contains a working copy of OS/2, you also can install Windows 95 on the system, provided that the system contains a FAT partition to accommodate Windows 95. To install Windows 95 on a system that contains OS/2, first verify that you have an OS/2 boot disk—you need the boot disk before you can boot OS/2 and restore the OS/2 Boot Manager after you install Windows 95. Next, boot the system to DOS. If your OS/2 PC is not configured to enable dual-boot (booting DOS or OS/2), you need to reconfigure it so that it does before you can install Windows 95. After you configure the system for dual-boot (check your OS/2 documentation to learn how to do that), boot the PC to DOS and run Setup to install Windows 95.

Note   *Dual-boot,* in OS/2 terms, simply involves placing both sets of bootable files (those for OS/2 and for any other operating system) in the same bootable partition. You then make one set active, and that is the operating system that boots whenever you start up the computer until the other set is made active.

During installation, Setup warns you before it disables the OS/2 Boot Manager. Go ahead and let Setup remove the Boot Manager and complete the installation. Setup does not affect any other OS/2 files. After Windows 95 is installed and working properly, use the OS/2 boot disk to reboot the system. Then run Fdisk (OS/2 version) and restore the OS/2 Boot Manager.

Summarizing Your Options

You should base your installation of Windows 95 on the information provided in the previous sections. The following list summarizes your options for installing Windows 95 based on your PC's current configuration and describes which version of Windows 95 (full or upgrade) you need to use:

◆ **DOS only and no existing Windows 3.x, or new system with no operating system.** Version: Full. After you install, you can boot Windows 95 or your previous version of DOS (Windows 95 is the default).

◆ **DOS and Windows 3.x, existing Windows 3.x directory.** Version: Upgrade. If you install Windows 95 in your current Windows directory, Setup migrates all existing program groups, applications, and special drivers to Windows 95. You do not need to reinstall your Windows applications to run them under Windows 95. However, you cannot boot your previous version of DOS (unless you boot the PC from a floppy disk).

◆ **DOS and Windows 3.x, new directory.** Version: Upgrade. If you install Windows 95 into a new directory, Setup does not update your existing copy of Windows 3.x. None of your current Windows 3.x settings, groups, or drivers migrate to Windows 95. You have to reinstall any Windows applications that you want to run under Windows 95. You can boot Windows 95 or your previous version of DOS.

◆ **Windows NT.** Version: Upgrade. Your PC must have a FAT disk partition that contains enough space to accommodate Windows 95 and its swap file. Space requirements vary according to how many Windows 95 components you install, but ranges from 20–100 MB. Although you can install Windows 95 into your existing Windows NT directory, you really should avoid doing so. Install Windows 95 into a new directory. You have to reinstall any Windows applications that you want to run under Windows 95. Setup maintains the Windows NT Boot Loader, which enables you to boot Windows NT or Windows 95.

◆ **OS/2.** Version: Full. Your PC must have a FAT disk partition that contains enough space to accommodate Windows 95 and its swap file. You must install Windows 95 into a new directory and reinstall any Windows applications that you want to run under Windows 95. Setup does not maintain the OS/2 Boot Manager, but after Windows 95 installs, you can boot the system with your OS/2 boot disk, then run OS/2 Fdisk to restore the Boot Manager.

Planning and Preparing for the Installation

Before you run Setup to install Windows 95, you should do some planning to ensure that your PC is capable of running Windows 95 and is optimized for it. You also should make sure that you know what effects installing Windows 95 will have on your current operating system and applications. If you do not, read the previous sections of this chapter to make sure you understand how to install Windows 95 to best accommodate your existing applications and the way you work.

After you decide which way to install Windows 95, you should optimize your system accordingly before you run Setup. Optimizing and preparing the system includes four basic steps, described briefly in the following sections.

Back Up Important Files

First, you should back up your important files. Although you probably will not have any problems when you install Windows 95, you still need to back up your system in case something unforeseen does happen to cause data loss. At the very least, back up your document files.

Note   Windows 95 includes a new Backup utility, and it might not be compatible with your existing backup software. Therefore, after you back up your files to tape, you should retain your existing backup software so that you can read the backup copies in the future. To convert your backed-up files to Windows 95 Backup format, install Windows 95 (including Backup), restore the backed-up files to the system, then use Windows 95 Backup to back them up again.

Archive and Delete Files

Scan your system for files you don't need. Archive the files you want to keep but don't need on the system, then delete those files from the system. Depending on your system's configuration, you might archive files to a network server, floppy disk, or tape. Just be sure to keep your archive copies in a safe place in case you need them later. If you use a backup program to archive the files, be sure to retain a copy of that backup program so that you can restore the archived files later.

In addition to archiving files that do not have to be on the system, delete other files that are no longer useful to make as much free space as possible available on the disk. The following list offers some tips on which files you might be able to delete:

◆ **TMP and other temporary files.** If you currently are running Windows, exit Windows and delete all files in the Windows temporary directory. If you're not sure which directory Windows uses for temporary files, the SET TEMP statement in Autoexec.bat just happens to specify the location of the temporary directory.

Note   You should exit Windows and delete the files in the TEMP directory instead of attempting to delete the files from Windows. As it works, Windows creates temporary files in the TEMP directory, and deleting these files with Windows running could cause Windows to hang.

◆ **BAK and other backup files.** Many applications create backup copies of documents when you save the document. Although many applications use a file extension of BAK for backup files, you should check your document directory for additional backup files that you can delete.

◆ **Old DOS files.** If you have upgraded your copy of DOS, your system might still contain your old DOS files. Check for a directory name similar to OLD_DOS.1 in the root directory of the drive that contains your current DOS files. You can erase the files in the old DOS directory.

Tip   Setup will detect an old DOS directory during Windows 95 installation, and can delete those files for you if you instruct it to. So, you can delete the files before you run Setup, or you can let Setup handle it for you.

◆ **Old applications and documents.** If you have applications or documents on your system that you don't use, archive or delete them.

◆ **Unused Windows 3.x components.** In Windows 3.*x*, run Windows Setup from the Main group. Choose Options, Add/Remove Windows Components. Setup displays a dialog box from which you can delete README files, accessories, games, screen savers, and multimedia files (including wallpaper bitmaps) from your current Windows 3.*x* installation. Delete the files you don't use. Windows 95 Setup lets you choose which new Windows 95 features you want Setup to install, and you can omit whichever options you won't use.

Archiving and deleting files ensures a maximum amount of disk space to accommodate Windows 95. Reducing the number of files on the disk also can improve file access time, although often the improvement is negligible.

configuration process in a general way. For detailed technical information on network driver, protocol, client, and service options, refer to Chapter 34, "Network Concepts and Configuration."

If you currently use real-mode drivers for your network adapter, for example, consider switching to protected-mode drivers for better performance. If yours is a common network adapter, the chances are very good that Windows 95 includes a new protected-mode driver for the adapter.

Figure 2.4 shows the Network property sheet that you can use to specify the installed drivers and other network settings for your PC. The Configuration page enables you to add and remove drivers and protocols, specify logon method, and control print and file sharing options. The Identification page enables you to specify the computer name, workgroup, and description for your PC. The Access Control page enables you to specify whether your PC makes its resources available on a share-level or user-level basis (explained later in this section).

Figure 2.4

The Configuration page of the Network property sheet.

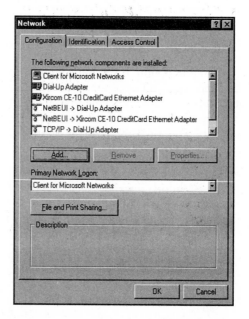

Specifying Driver and Protocol Settings

During installation, Setup detects your existing network settings and drivers and attempts to automatically install the appropriate drivers and protocols. If the PC contains a network adapter for which no settings exist (a new PC, for example), Setup attempts to detect the card's manufacturer and model so that it can install the correct set of drivers, protocols, and client software. If you use the Custom option during Setup, you can modify these settings prior to completing the installation process.

Tip　If Setup properly detected your existing network configuration and settings, and you only want to add additional network services, you can skip to the section "Adding Adapters, Protocols, Clients, and Services."

The Configuration page (refer to figure 2.4) enables you to specify the clients, adapters, logon method, and file and print sharing capabilities of your PC. Use the Configuration page to accomplish the tasks described in the following list:

◆ Specify which network adapter(s) is installed in your PC and control(s) the adapter's settings

◆ Add client software to enable your PC to access network resources (such as adding a NetWare client to enable the PC to access a NetWare server)

◆ Add a network protocol (such as NetBEUI or TCP/IP) and bind it to an adapter

◆ Specify adapter and protocol settings

◆ Specify the logon method

◆ Control file and print sharing options

To change the settings of an already installed adapter, select the adapter from the list of installed components, then choose Properties. Or, simply double-click on the adapter in the list. Both of these actions display the property sheet for the adapter, as shown in figure 2.5.

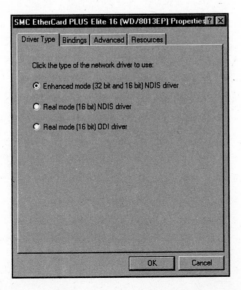

Figure 2.5

Property sheet for a typical network adapter.

The Driver Type page enables you to specify whether the adapter uses a 32-bit protected-mode NDIS driver, a 16-bit NDIS real-mode driver, or a 16-bit ODI driver. If one of these three types of drivers is unavailable for the adapter, the option button associated with that driver type will be disabled (dimmed). The following list explains each of these three driver types:

◆ **Enhanced-mode (32-bit and 16-bit) NDIS driver.** This option installs a combination of 16-bit and 32-bit NDIS 3.1 drivers. It includes the 16-bit driver primarily to enable Windows 95 to provide network services when Windows 95 runs in fail-safe mode. Windows 95 does not support NDIS 3.0, but does include NDIS 3.1 drivers to replace all previous NDIS 3.0 drivers.

◆ **Real-mode (16-bit) NDIS driver.** This option installs a 16-bit, real-mode NDIS 2.*x* driver.

◆ **Real-mode (16-bit) ODI driver.** This option installs a 16-bit, real-mode Open Datalink Interface (ODI) driver.

The Bindings page (see fig. 2.6) enables you to bind specific protocols to a network adapter. Suppose that you use a physical network adapter to connect to a local LAN, and that the LAN uses the standard NetBEUI protocol. You also use a virtual dial-up network adapter to connect to the Internet, which requires a TCP/IP protocol. Using the Bindings page, you would bind the NetBEUI protocol to the physical LAN adapter, and the TCP/IP protocol to the virtual dial-up adapter.

Figure 2.6

Use the Bindings page to bind a protocol to an adapter.

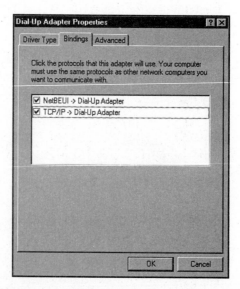

Tip   You can bind multiple protocols to a network adapter. For example, you might connect through a virtual dial-up adapter to a remote Windows NT server to access the resources on the server's LAN. The remote LAN has a physical connection to the Internet, so you also might want to use it to connect to the Internet. You would bind the NetBEUI protocol to the dial-up adapter so that you could access the LAN, and bind a TCP/IP protocol to the same dial-up adapter so that you could access the Internet.

In addition to the Driver Type and Bindings pages, the property sheet for an adapter might also include an Advanced page. The Advanced page enables you to specify advanced settings for the adapter. These advanced settings vary from one adapter to another. Usually, you should be able to use the default Advanced settings for an adapter. If the adapter seems to be working improperly, check with your adapter documentation to see if you need to modify any of the adapter's advanced settings.

Many network adapters also include a Resources page, as shown in figure 2.7. The Resources page enables you to specify the system resources that the adapter uses, typically including the adapter's I/O base address, interrupt request (IRQ) line, and RAM buffer address range. The *I/O base address* is the memory address by which the operating system communicates with the adapter. The adapter uses the *IRQ line*—the hardware line over which peripherals get the attention of the microprocessor—to signal the CPU when the adapter needs servicing by the CPU. The *RAM buffer address range* is a block of RAM that the adapter uses to buffer network I/O. The physical configuration of the adapter determines these three settings.

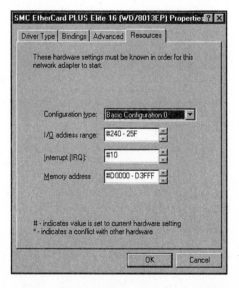

Figure 2.7

The Resources page for a network adapter.

With many adapters, you must use jumpers or switches on the adapter to manually set the I/O base address, IRQ, and RAM base address. Other adapters are *software-configured*, which means that you don't have to set jumpers or switches on the adapter to specify its settings. Instead, you specify the settings in the Resources page, and Windows 95 configures the network adapter.

Tip Some network adapters use a combination of manual and software configuration. You can configure the card manually by setting jumpers and switches on the adapter, or you can set a jumper on the adapter to enable the adapter to be software-configured. For ease in reconfiguring your system in the future, set up your network adapter to enable software configuration.

Check your adapter's manual to determine the correct settings to use for I/O base address, IRQ, and RAM address range. If you're not sure what settings to use for your network adapter, accept the defaults that Setup offers. The most likely problem you encounter if the settings conflict with another device is that you can't access the network. After completing the installation process, you can turn off the system, remove the network adapter, and use the adapter manual as a reference to verify its settings. Then, reinstall the adapter and power up the system to check the network. If the settings you accepted in Setup don't match the settings on the adapter, open Control Panel, choose Network, and modify the adapter settings. Reboot the system and test the network again.

For detailed information on configuring network adapters, and configuring and troubleshooting other LAN components, refer to Chapter 34, "Network Concepts and Configuration."

Adding Adapters, Protocols, Clients, and Services

During Windows 95 installation you might want to add an additional adapter, protocol, client, or service to your Windows 95 network configuration. When Setup displays the Network property sheet, click on the Add button to display a dialog box from which you can select one of the following four selections:

◆ **Adapter.** Choose this option to install a driver for a new network adapter. The adapter can be a physical adapter installed in the PC or a virtual adapter, such as the Microsoft Dial-Up Adapter, which enables you to use remote access services (RAS, also called Dial-Up Networking) on your PC and connect to a remote network. (Refer to Chapter 33, "Using Remote Access Services," for more information on RAS and the Dial-Up Adapter.)

◆ **Protocol.** This option enables you to add a network protocol and bind the protocol to a selected adapter. If you want to add TCP/IP to your physical LAN adapter to provide Internet access services, for example, you would add the

TCP/IP protocol. If you want to add the capability to connect to a NetWare server, you probably want to add the IPX/SPX-compatible protocol.

◆ **Client.** Client software enables your PC to access file and printer resources on the network. To enable your PC to access resources on a NetWare server, for example, you must add the Microsoft Client for NetWare Networks or one of the other NetWare clients provided with Windows 95.

◆ **Service.** As well as providing access to files and printers, network services provide additional network access and control features. For example, Windows 95 includes network services for backup across the network, using a remote registry, managing network printers, monitoring network performance, and performing other services.

To add a network component, choose Add in Setup's Network Configuration dialog box. In the Select Network Component Type dialog box, choose the type of network component you want to add, then choose the Add button. Setup provides a list of vendors for the options for which it includes support. Select the appropriate vendor, then select the desired adapter, protocol, client, or service from the list. If you have a driver disk provided by a vendor, choose the Have Disk button to install the network component from the driver disk. Whether you add a component included with Windows 95 or a component acquired from a vendor-supplied disk, the prompts in the dialog boxes are self-explanatory, and you should have no problem installing the component. If you need help with technical aspects of network setup, refer to Chapter 34, "Network Concepts and Configuration."

Specifying Identification Settings

The Identification page of the Network property sheet (see fig. 2.8) enables you to specify the name of your PC, the workgroup in which the PC is a member, and an optional description for your PC.

The computer name is the name by which other computers on the network know your PC (as listed). It also is the name by which other users can access the resources that your PC shares. Suppose that your PC's name is FRED and that you share your drive C using the share name DRIVE-C. Other users can connect to your drive C by specifying the share name \\FRED\DRIVE-C.

Computer names are limited to 15 characters, and can't contain spaces. If you need to use a space for readability, use the hyphen or underscore character. Also, computer names must be unique not only within a workgroup, but also across the network. Computer names are not case-sensitive. You can use the following special characters in a computer name:

! @ # $ % ^ & ( ) - _ ' { } . ~

Figure 2.8

*Use the
Identification
page to specify ID
information about
your PC.*

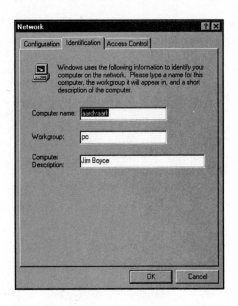

 Note   Refer to Chapter 35, "Sharing Resources in Windows 95," for more information on computer names, share names, and sharing resources such as disks and printers.

The workgroup name you specify in the Identification page is the name of the workgroup to which your PC belongs. A *workgroup* is a group of computers with which you connect most often to exchange e-mail, share resources, and share other information. Workgroups are purely a logical entity—workgroups provide a means for logically grouping computers together, but belonging to a particular workgroup doesn't entail any physical requirements. In fact, you can dial into a LAN from a remote site and become a member of a workgroup on the remote LAN. Belonging to a workgroup does not prevent you from accessing resources shared by other workgroups—you can easily access the resources shared by any computer on your network, regardless of the workgroup in which the remote PC belongs.

Workgroup names are limited to 15 characters. As with computer names, the workgroup name cannot include spaces. Workgroup names are not case-sensitive. In short, the same naming conventions apply to workgroup names as to computer names.

The Computer Description field in the Identification page enables you to specify an optional description for your computer. This optional description offers additional information about your PC to other users browsing for information on the LAN. The description is limited to 48 characters. The description can contain spaces, but not commas.

Specifying Access Control Settings

The Access Control page of the Network property sheet (see fig. 2.9) specifies how access to your PC's shared resources is handled.

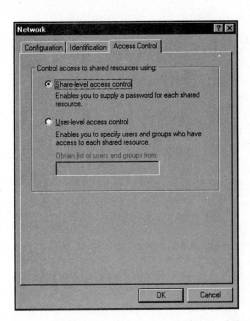

Figure 2.9

The Access Control page.

The two options in the Access Control page are described in the following list:

◆ **Share-level access control.** Access to your shared resources is provided solely based on password protection of the shared resource. You supply a password for the resource when you share it, and any user who supplies the correct password can access the shared resource. Each shared folder can have a full-access password and a read-only password, enabling you to give some users full access to the resource while limiting access to other users.

◆ **User-level access control.** Use this option to provide access to your PC's resources based on the security provided by a security server such as an NT domain server or NetWare bindery server. This option enables you to provide customized access to resources on a user-by-user basis.

Whether you choose share-level or user-level access depends on the degree of control you want to exercise over the resources your PC shares. If restricting access to full or read-only based on passwords is acceptable, choose share-level access control. If you need to provide customized, user-by-user access, choose user-level access control. User-level access control, however, must be supported by a security server on your network. A Windows 95 node cannot act as a security server for user-level access control. The Access Control List (ACL) does reside on the local Windows 95 node, however, and you can add and remove users from the ACL and specify access control rights.

Specifying the Logon Method

The Configuration page of the Network property sheet (refer to figure 2.4) includes the Primary Network Logon drop-down list, which enables you to specify the way in which you will be logged on to the network. The options provided in the list vary according to the types of clients you install. If you use the Client for Microsoft Networks, for example, this client will appear in the list. Selecting the client as the logon method causes Windows 95 to use the security method provided by the client to log you on to the network. If you use the Client for Microsoft Networks, for example, Windows 95 prompts you for the name of a Windows NT domain server and attempts to validate your logon name and password with the domain server. If the domain server can't be found, Windows 95 logs you onto the network without domain validation.

If you choose Windows Logon from the Primary Network Logon drop-down list, Windows 95 logs you onto your PC and to the network if available, but doesn't display an error message if the network is not available. This logon method is useful if your network is sometimes unavailable when you attempt to log on (such as when you work on a portable PC not connected to the LAN). For more information on controlling the way Windows 95 maintains network resource information and attempts to reconnect to resources when you log on, refer to Chapter 35, "Sharing Resources in Windows 95."

Specifying Sharing Options

The File and Print Sharing button in the Configuration page enables you to specify whether your PC will share its local printer and file resources with other users on the network. Choosing the File and Print Sharing button displays the File and Print Sharing dialog box shown in figure 2.10.

Figure 2.10

The File and Print Sharing dialog box.

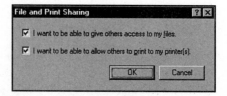

To enable or disable access to your local disks and printers, simply place a check in or clear the appropriate check box.

Note   These two options control resource access globally on your PC. If you want to limit access to specific users, turn on the two options in the File and Print Sharing dialog box, then use user-level access (explained previously, in the "Specifying Access Control Settings" section). To limit access based on password protection, use user-level access (also explained previously).

Completing the Setup Process

After Setup copies files to your system, Setup reboots the system to complete the installation process. During this final phase of installation, Setup migrates your existing Windows 3.*x* environment, if any, to Windows 95. Setup integrates custom settings in your Win.ini and System.ini files into the system registry and converts your existing Program Manager groups and objects to Windows 95 folders and shortcuts.

Tip   During installation, Setup might detect standard Windows 3.*x* DLLs that have been modified from their originals by various applications that you have installed on your computer. Setup will ask you if it should restore the original DLLs. In general, your programs should continue to run correctly without restoring the originals. And, restoring the original DLLs could cause the programs to stop working.

To access the objects previously contained in your Program Manager groups, click on the Start button on the Taskbar, then choose Programs. Each of your Program Manager groups appears as a selection in the Programs menu. Selecting an item from the menu opens a submenu that contains the objects formerly part of the group. Select the object with which you want to work, and Windows 95 opens the object.

If you prefer to continue to work with Program Manager during a transition from Windows 3.*x* to Windows 95, you can. Windows 95 includes an updated version of Program Manager designed to work with Windows 95 (see fig. 2.11). To run Program Manager, choose Start, then **R**un, and in the Run dialog box, type **PROGMAN** in the **O**pen combo box, then choose OK.

New Riders Publishing
INSIDE
SERIES

Figure 2.11

Windows 95 includes a version of Program Manager to help during your transition from Windows 3.x.

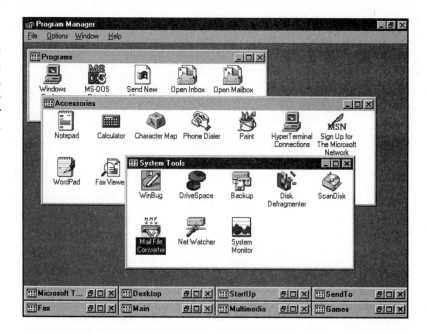

Tip
If you want Program Manager to start automatically when you boot Windows 95, but you also want to maintain the new Windows 95 shell, create a shortcut to Program Manager in the Startup folder. Use the following steps to create a shortcut in Startup for Program Manager:

1. Choose Start, **S**ettings, **T**askbar.

2. Choose the Start Menu Programs tab.

3. Choose the **A**dd button, then in the **C**ommand line text box of the Create Shortcut dialog box, enter **C:\Windows\progman**, substituting the proper path to your Windows directory for C:\Windows. If you prefer, you can choose the **B**rowse button and browse in the Windows folder for the Progman object.

4. Choose the **N**ext button to display the Select Program Folder dialog box. Scroll through the list of folders and choose Startup, then click on **N**ext.

5. In the dialog box labeled Select a Title for the Program, type **Program Manager** (or whatever title you want to use), then click on the Finish button. Windows 95 automatically creates a shortcut to Progman in the Startup folder.

During Windows 95 installation, you can specify that Setup install Program Manager as the default shell. When Setup prompts you to verify your equipment settings (display, machine, mouse, and so on), look at the bottom of the list Setup provides. The last item enables you to specify Windows 95 or Program Manager as the user interface.

When you're ready to turn off the computer, choose Start, then Shutdown, then Shut down the computer.

Booting Your System

All you have to do to boot Windows 95 on your system is turn on the computer—Windows 95 boots automatically. You can, however, control the way the system boots.

Four function keys provide quick access to the boot options you can use when the computer starts. Pressing F4 during display of the boot message Starting Windows 95 boots your previous version of DOS, if one exists on your system. (See the following section "Using Multiboot and Booting to DOS" for more information on booting to DOS.) Pressing F5 causes Windows 95 to bypass your configuration files, Config.win and Autoexec.win, when booting the system. Pressing F6 causes Windows 95 to boot in fail-safe mode, with network support if possible. The fourth option enables you to view a list of boot options.

To view a list of boot options, turn on the PC, and during display of Starting Windows 95, press F8. You should see a menu similar to the following:

```
1. Normal
2. Logged (\BOOTLOG.TXT)
3. Safe mode
4. Safe mode with network support
5. Step-by-step confirmation
6. Command prompt only
7. Safe mode command prompt only
```

Tip You can press F8 or any of the other boot function keys any time after the PC completes its Power On Self Test (POST). You do not have to wait until you see Starting Windows 95. If your PC contains a SCSI host adapter, for example, you can press the boot function key when you see the message that indicates that the SCSI BIOS is loading.

The following list explains the options listed in the boot menu:

◆ **Normal.** This option starts the full Windows operating system and GUI.

◆ **Logged (\BOOTLOG.TXT).** This option boots the full Windows 95 operating system and GUI, but also creates a boot log in the root directory of the boot disk. The boot log file, Bootlog.txt, is useful for identifying and troubleshooting startup problems.

◆ **Safe mode.** This option boots a minimal Windows 95 operating system and excludes the majority of drivers, except those required to boot the system (such as disk drivers). This mode uses a standard VGA display driver to help overcome startup problems caused by an incompatible or improperly configured display driver. Use safe mode when you suspect that a driver is causing a startup problem.

◆ **Safe mode with network support.** This option boots a minimal Windows 95 operating system similar to safe mode, but loads real-mode support for your network. This mode enables you to bypass some of your drivers, but still retain network access.

◆ **Step-by-step confirmation.** This option is similar to the single-step boot option MS-DOS offers. Windows 95 steps through each statement in your Config.win and Autoexec.win files, enabling you to accept or reject each line. This option is particularly useful for troubleshooting problems caused by drivers or other statements in either file.

◆ **Command prompt only.** This option boots the Windows 95 command line, but does not boot the GUI or full set of drivers. If you rely on the 32-bit Windows 95 CD-ROM driver to access your CD-ROM drive, for example, you cannot use the CD-ROM drive from this command prompt because the driver does not load until the full operating system and GUI load. Booting to the command line enables you to boot a minimal operating system quickly to perform file maintenance and troubleshooting. The range of commands available with this option is similar to a standard DOS operating system command-line environment, and you also can execute DOS programs.

◆ **Safe mode command prompt only.** This option boots a minimal operating system similar to the Safe mode option, except the system boots to a command prompt rather than to a GUI. Only critical drivers load, and a standard VGA driver is used to overcome potential display problems.

Tip   If you boot the system to a command prompt, you can start the GUI and full operating system by entering **WIN** at the command prompt.

Using Multiboot and Booting to DOS

If you install Windows 95 on a system that already contains a working copy of DOS, and you install Windows 95 into a new directory (not into an existing Windows 3.*x* directory), you can boot your system to Windows 95 or to your previous version of DOS.

When you install Windows 95, Setup disables the multiboot option that allows you to boot your previous version of DOS. To enable multiboot, you must edit the hidden file Msdos.sys, located in the root directory of your boot disk. Add the setting `BootMulti=1` to the `[Options]` section of Msdos.sys to enable multiboot on your system.

Msdos.sys is a system, hidden, read-only file. Before you can edit the file, you must change these attributes. You can easily change the attributes of the file in Windows 95. To do so from a folder, open the folder for the root directory of your boot disk (such as C:\). Choose <u>V</u>iew, <u>O</u>ptions, then select the View tab. Click on the <u>S</u>how all files option button, then choose OK. The folder displays all files, including the hidden Msdos.sys file. Right-click on the Msdos.sys icon, then choose <u>P</u>roperties. Clear the check boxes labeled <u>R</u>ead-only, Ar<u>c</u>hive, and Hi<u>d</u>den, then choose OK. You now can use Notepad or WordPad to edit the file. After you edit the file, restore the read-only, archive, and hidden properties.

Tip   If you prefer, you can change the attributes of Msdos.sys from the command line. Enter the command **ATTRIB -S -H -R MSDOS.SYS** at the command line to change the attributes of Msdos.sys and make it possible to edit the file. After you modify and save the file, enter the command **ATTRIB +S +H +R MSDOS.SYS** to reassign the proper attributes to the file.

After you add the setting `BootMulti=1` to the `[Options]` section of Msdos.sys, reboot the system. When you see the prompt `Starting Windows 95`, press F4 to boot your previous version of DOS. Or, if you press F8, a new option appears at the end of the Windows 95 boot list, labeled `Previous version of MS-DOS`. Selecting this option boots your previous version of DOS.

Tip   To boot Windows 95 after you boot the computer to your previous version of DOS, simply reboot the computer by pressing Ctrl+Alt+Del, or press the computer's reset button.

For additional information on how Windows 95 and MS-DOS coexist on your system, refer to Chapter 21, "Integrating Windows and DOS."

Understanding the Boot Files

In many respects, Windows 95 is similar to DOS in the way it boots the PC. Windows 95 uses a group of system files to control the boot process. The following list explains the Windows 95 startup files:

◆ **Io.sys.** This file provides a minimal real-mode operating system to enable the system to boot. This version of Io.sys replaces the IO.SYS and MSDOS.SYS files previously used with DOS. Io.sys also sets various settings previously defined in Config.sys.

◆ **Msdos.sys.** This file is included for compatibility with *legacy applications* (applications written for DOS and Windows 3.*x*). In addition, it can contain a variety of settings for controlling the boot process.

◆ **Config.sys.** You can use this file to load real-mode drivers, specify the operating system settings that various applications require, and override settings set by Io.sys. This file is not required to run Windows 95. If your system contains a bootable version of DOS, the system contains two separate Config.* files, one for Windows 95 and the other for DOS (explained later in this section).

◆ **Autoexec.bat.** You can use this file to load real-mode drivers and applications, specify a PATH and other operating system settings, and specify settings that applications require. If your system contains a bootable version of DOS, the system contains two separate Autoexec.* files, one for Windows 95 and the other for DOS.

◆ **Bootlog.txt.** This file is created if you select option 2 (Logged) from the boot menu. Windows creates a text file, named Bootlog.txt, that contains information about the initialization of the system. By examining the Bootlog.txt file, you can identify the cause of a failed boot.

The following sections explain the Windows 95 boot files.

Understanding Io.sys

Io.sys is a binary file that processes the other boot files—Msdos.sys, Config.sys, and Autoexec.bat—and then starts Windows 95. You cannot Modify Io.sys to control the way Windows 95 boots, but understanding the function that Io.sys performs can help you modify the boot process in other ways.

 Note If your system contains a bootable version of MS-DOS, during DOS boot the Io.sys file is renamed Io.win, and the file Io.dos, which is the old Io.sys file for DOS, is renamed Io.sys to enable DOS to boot. For systems that run PC DOS, the DOS version of this file is named Ibmbio.com.

Io.sys loads a selection of drivers and specifies a variety of default settings, including the following:

◆ **Himem.sys.** This driver provides extended memory management for the real-mode Windows 95 command-line environment and single-application DOS mode. It also allocates to Windows 95 all extended memory. Windows 95, when it is running, takes over the functions provided by Himem.sys. You can place an entry for Himem.sys in Config.sys to override the default settings provided by Io.sys for Himem.sys.

◆ **Ifshlp.sys.** This is the Installable File System Helper, which loads device drivers and enables the real-mode environment to perform a full range of disk I/O calls. Until Ifshlp.sys is loaded, only minimal disk I/O services, provided through Io.sys, are available. This file is loaded by Io.sys only if Ifshlp.sys is found on the system. Windows 95 takes over the functions provided by Ifshlp.sys when the full operating system (GUI) is running.

◆ **Setver.exe.** This program responds to operating system version queries from applications. For some DOS applications to run correctly, the application must run under a specific version of DOS. Setver.exe enables you to "fool" applications into thinking they are running on a specific version of DOS by having Setver.exe report a specific DOS version number to the application.

◆ **Dblspace.bin or Drvspace.bin.** If your system uses DoubleSpace or DriveSpace disk compression (included with MS-DOS 6.*x*), Io.sys loads the appropriate driver. DoubleSpace and DriveSpace enable you to compress your disks to store more data on them. Windows 95 includes a new version of DriveSpace that enables you to compress your drives—you don't need a previous version of MS-DOS to use DriveSpace.

◆ **dos=high,umb.** This setting directs the system to load DOS into the UMA and provide memory management of the UMA.

◆ **files=60.** This setting specifies the number of file handle buffers to be created to handle files opened by standard DOS I/O calls. This setting does not affect files opened by Windows 95 and is provided primarily for compatibility with older applications.

◆ **buffers=30.** This setting specifies a number of file buffers to create to handle file I/O generated by Io.sys file calls. This setting is not required by Windows 95.

◆ **stacks=9,256.** This setting specifies the number and size of stack frames. The setting is not required by Windows 95 and is included only for compatibility with older applications.

◆ **lastdrive=z.** This setting specifies the last drive letter that the system can assign a drive. If Setup finds this setting in Config.sys during installation, Setup moves the setting to the Registry. This setting is not required for Windows 95, but is provided for compatibility with older applications.

◆ **shell=command.com /p.** This setting specifies the command-line interpreter, the program that provides the Windows 95 command line.

◆ **fcbs=4.** This setting specifies the file control blocks to be created. The setting is not required by Windows 95, but is provided for compatibility with older applications.

Tip

The settings that Io.sys provides serve primarily for compatibility with older applications and in general are not required by Windows 95. For this reason, the settings are not given detailed coverage in *Inside Windows 95*. For detailed information on the settings described in the previous list, refer to *Inside MS-DOS 6.22*, also from New Riders Publishing.

Although you can't modify Io.sys, you can override its default settings by adding appropriate statements in Config.sys. To override the default Himem.sys settings, for example, include the setting for Himem.sys in Config.sys.

Note

If you specify values for FILES, BUFFERS, or STACKS in Config.sys, the values must be equal to or greater than the default values Io.sys specifies. The default settings are FILES=60, BUFFERS=30, and STACKS=9,256. These settings are not required by Windows 95, but are provided for compatibility with legacy applications.

Io.sys does not load Emm386.exe. If you need to provide memory management of the UMA for real-mode drivers or applications that you run from the Windows 95 command line (without the full operating system started), use the Config.sys file to load Emm386.exe.

If your system doesn't require real-mode drivers, and you do not need to run DOS applications from the Windows 95 command line (without the full operating system started), you probably do not need to use a Config.sys file—the drivers and settings provided by Io.sys are adequate.

Understanding Msdos.sys

The Msdos.sys file also supports other settings that control the way in which Windows 95 boots. Unlike Io.sys, the Msdos.sys file is a text-only file that you can modify. Msdos.sys consists of two standard sections, [Options] and [Paths]. The [Paths] section includes settings that specify paths to various Windows files, including the Registry. The [Options] section can contain a variety of settings that enable you to control the way in which your PC boots.

Tip In order to edit Msdos.sys, you must first change its file attributes. The section "Using Multiboot and Booting to DOS" earlier in this chapter explains how to change file attributes.

The following list explains the settings for the `[Paths]` section of Msdos.sys:

◆ **WinDir=*path*.** This value lists the path you specified for the Windows 95 directory during Setup.

◆ **WinBootDir=*path*.** By default, this entry is set to the same path you specified during Setup for the location of the Windows 95 directory. This setting specifies the location of the files necessary to boot Windows 95.

◆ **HostWinBootDrv=*path*.** This setting specifies the location of the the root directory of the boot disk.

The `[Options]` section of Msdos.sys supports numerous settings that control the way Windows boots. The settings for the `[Options]` section also enable you to control other aspects of the Windows 95 startup process. The settings for the `[Options]` section are explained in the following list:

◆ **BootDelay=*n*.** *n* specifies the delay in seconds that Windows 95 pauses to display the `Starting Windows 95` boot message before it begins to boot the operating system. The default value is 2. Setting `BootKeys=0` causes Windows 95 to ignore this delay setting. Increasing the value of this setting gives you more time to press a boot function key.

◆ **BootFailSafe=1 or 0.** Set to `0`, Windows 95 does not use fail-safe boot. Set to 1 enables fail-safe boot, but does not cause the system to boot in fail-safe mode—a value of 1 only makes fail-safe boot available at boot time. Press F6 or F8 during boot to select fail-safe mode.

◆ **BootGUI=1 or 0.** Set to 1 (the default), Windows automatically boots the Windows 95 GUI and full operating system. Set this to `0` to boot to the real-mode Windows 95 command prompt. Creating an empty Win.bat file in the boot directory has the same effect as setting `BootGUI=0`. If you create an empty Win.bat file, however, you can't start Windows from the command prompt in the root directory, because Win.bat takes precedence over Win.com (which starts Windows).

◆ **BootKeys=1 or 0.** A value of 1 for this setting enables the F4, F5, F6, and F8 keys during boot. Specify a value of `0` for this setting to disable the boot keys.

◆ **BootMenu=1 or 0.** Specifying a value of 1 causes the boot menu to be displayed automatically—you don't have to press F8 to display the menu. The default value is `0`, which causes the boot menu to appear only if you press F8 during boot. Use the `BootMenuDelay` setting to specify the amount of time the boot menu displays before the default menu option executes.

◆ **BootMenuDefault=#.** This option specifies the default boot menu item. The default is `1`, `Normal`, when the system is booting normally. The default is `4`, `Safe mode with network support`, when Windows boots using fail-safe. Specify a different number to change the default. This setting works in conjunction with `BootMenuDelay` and `BootMenu`.

◆ **BootMenuDelay=#.** This setting specifies the number of seconds the boot menu displays before the default item executes. This setting affects only the boot sequence when the boot menu displays automatically because of `BootMenu=1`. If you press a boot function key during boot, the menu appears until you select a menu option, regardless of the amount of time that passes.

◆ **BootMulti=1 or 0.** A setting of `1` enables you to boot your previous version of DOS, and a setting of `0` disables multiboot. If `BootMulti=1`, you can press F4 or select option 8 from the boot menu to boot your previous version of DOS. See the section "Using Multiboot and Booting to DOS" earlier in this chapter for more information on booting your system to DOS.

◆ **BootWarn=1 or 0.** Specifying a setting of `0` disables the fail-safe menu and warning. A value of `1` is the default, which enables the fail-safe menu and warning.

◆ **BootWin=1 or 0.** Specifying a value of `1` (the default) causes Windows 95 to be booted automatically as the operating system. A setting of `0` causes your previous version of DOS to be booted automatically (similar to pressing F4 during boot) rather than Windows 95.

◆ **DblSpace=1 or 0.** A value of `0` for this setting disables loading of Dblspace.bin. A value of `1` (the default) enables Windows 95 to load Dblspace.bin when required.

◆ **DoubleBuffer=1 or 0.** Specifying a value of `1` directs Windows 95 to use double-buffering for SCSI host adapters installed in the system. Double-buffering is required by many SCSI host adapters to ensure proper I/O. If your PC contains a SCSI host adapter that requires double-buffering, Setup includes the setting `DoubleBuffer=1` automatically in Msdos.sys. Refer to Chapter 15, "Optimizing Data Storage," for information regarding double-buffering.

◆ **DrvSpace=1 or 0.** A value of `0` for this setting disables loading of Drvspace.bin. A value of `1` (the default) enables Windows 95 to load Drvspace.bin when required.

◆ **LoadTop=1 or 0.** This setting controls whether Windows 95 loads Command.com or Drvspace.bin in the UMA, or above 640 KB. Specify a value of 0 for Windows 95 to load these files in conventional memory below 640 KB. Loading these files below 640 KB can eliminate conflict with NetWare or other drivers and applications that require loading at a specific memory address range that could conflict with these files.

◆ **Logo=1 or 0.** A value of 0 disables display of the animated Windows 95 logo during boot, which can eliminate problems with some third-party memory managers during boot. If you use a third-party memory manager and your system hangs during display of the animated Windows 95 logo, add the setting Logo=0 to the [Options] section of Msdos.sys.

◆ **Network=1 or 0.** Specify a value of 0 to prevent network components from being loaded. Specifying a value of 1 (the default) enables fail-safe mode to load real-mode network drivers.

To incorporate any of the settings explained in the preceding list, change the attributes of Msdos.sys to make it editable, add the settings, restore the previous file attributes, then reboot the system.

Understanding Config.sys and Autoexec.bat

Config.sys serves to load device drivers and specify settings that control the way in which Windows 95 uses system hardware. You don't need Config.sys to run Windows 95—you need Config.sys only if your PC requires real-mode drivers or you need to override certain Io.sys settings.

Windows 95 includes 32-bit drivers to support most hardware. If you have some hardware in your system that a new Windows 95 32-bit driver doesn't support, you can load the real-mode driver supplied with the device in Config.sys. If you have a sound card for which Windows 95 has no driver, for example, you can load the driver provided with the sound card in Config.sys.

Tip If your system contains a bootable version of DOS, you have two Config.* files on the system. The working copy is always named Config.sys. When the system boots to Windows 95, the file Config.win is renamed Config.sys. When the system boots to DOS, the file Config.dos is renamed to Config.sys. Windows 95 handles this renaming automatically.

Similar to Config.sys, Autoexec.bat serves to specify settings and load drivers, although Autoexec.bat primarily controls the software environment rather than hardware. You can use Autoexec.bat to automatically execute programs and load drivers during startup. Unless you have to load the drivers before starting the full Windows 95 operating system, however, you don't need Autoexec.bat. If you want to start an application automatically when the GUI and full operating system start, you can place the application in the Startup folder. Windows 95 automatically starts all applications in the Startup folder as soon as you log on to Windows.

The last of the boot files, Bootlog.txt, is explained in Chapter 3, "Troubleshooting Setup and Startup." Other aspects of Config.sys and Autoexec.bat are explained in the following section.

The Effects of Setup on DOS

When you install Windows 95 on a system that contains a working copy of DOS, Setup makes numerous modifications to your existing DOS files. This section explains those modifications.

Changes to Config.sys

Setup scans your PC's Config.sys file and removes references to drivers or settings that Io.sys handles. Setup also removes references to statements in Config.sys no longer required due to functions Windows 95 provides, such as disk caching. Table 2.1 lists drivers and settings that Setup removes from or converts to comment lines in Config.sys.

TABLE 2.1
Settings Removed from Config.sys by Setup

Astcache.sys	Cache-at.sys	Cache-em.sys	Cache.exe
Cache.sys	Cacher.sys	Cemm.exe	Cemmp.exe
Delpurge.exe	Delwatch.exe	Diskmap.exe	Diskopt.exe
Emmdrv.sys	Emmxma.sys	Enhdisk.sys	Fast512.sys
Fastdisk.sys	Fastopen	Fastopen.exe	Fastopen.exe
Flash.exe	Hardrive.sys	Hidos.sys	Hpcache.sys
Hyper dkx.exe	Hyper286.exe	Hyper386.exe	Hyperdkc.exe
Hyperdke.exe	Ibmcache.sys	Icache.sys	Ifshlp.sys
Kboard.sys	Lock.exe	Login.exe	Mcache.sys
Memmax.exe	Mlpart.sys	Ncache.exe	Olicache.sys
Password.exe	Pc-cache.com	Pc-kwik.exe	Pckwik.sys

Pckwin.sys	Qcache.exe	Qcache.win	Rendir.exe
Scplus.exe	Script.exe	Share	Share.com
Share.exe	Shelldrv.sys	Smartdrv.exe	Smartdrv.sys
Spooler.sys	Superon.bat	Superpck.exe	Superpck.exe
Taskmax.exe	Touch.exe	Xdel.exe	Xdir.exe
Xdisk.sys	Xma2ems.sys	Xmaem.sys	Zcache.sys
Zspool.sys			

If you decide to edit Config.sys yourself, do not add references to SmartDrive or other disk cache utilities. Windows 95 includes its own built-in disk cache. You also do not need to add a mouse driver to Config.sys for DOS applications that you run under Windows 95—Windows 95 provides support for the mouse in DOS applications through its own mouse driver.

Tip   If you add a statement in Config.sys for Himem.sys in order to override the settings for Himem.sys provided in Io.sys, and your PC has over 16 MB of RAM, you must add the /e switch to the himem.sys command line to enable Himem to control memory above 16 MB.

You should not have to modify Config.sys. Its primary purpose is to provide compatibility for applications that require it, and to enable you to load real-mode drivers and override certain Io.sys defaults.

Changes to Autoexec.bat

In addition to modifying Config.sys, Setup also modifies Autoexec.bat if it exists on your system when you install Windows 95. (Setup does not create an Autoexec.bat file if one does not exist.) Typically, Autoexec.bat is used to start applications and set system environment settings, such as PATH, at system startup. Many of the functions commonly performed by Autoexec.bat are handled in Windows 95 by Io.sys, including the following:

◆ **Real-mode network startup.** This statement starts the real-mode network redirector by binding the real-mode network components to the appropriate adapters and validating the binding. Errors are logged in Ndislog.txt.

◆ **Path.** Io.sys sets the path to include the Windows and Windows\Command folders. This is equivalent to an Autoexec.bat setting of PATH=C:\WINDOWS;C:\WINDOWS\COMMAND. If you add a PATH statement in Autoexec.bat to place additional folders on the path, be sure to start the PATH statement with the Windows and Windows\Command folders. Do not include directories that contain a previous version of Windows, if any, in the PATH statement.

◆ **Prompt.** Io.sys sets the command-line prompt to the equivalent of PROMPT=PG. This setting causes the command prompt to display the current drive and directory, followed by a chevron, as in C:\WINDOWS>. If you want a different prompt, place the statement in Autoexec.bat. If you want the prompt to appear in DOS, edit the file Autoexec.dos. To set the prompt for use on the Windows command line, add the appropriate prompt setting to Autoexec.win. Or, simply boot the operating system for which you want to set the prompt, then modify Autoexec.bat to include the appropriate prompt statement.

◆ **Temporary directory.** Io.sys sets the temporary directory environment variables TMP and TEMP to point to the \Windows\Temp folder. Both variables specify the location of the directory in which Windows creates temporary files. Both settings are provided for compatibility. To specify a different location for the temporary directory, add a setting for TEMP in the Autoexec.bat file.

◆ **Setting comspec.** Io.sys sets the location of the command interpreter with a setting equivalent to COMPSEC=C:\WINDOWS\COMMAND\COMMAND.COM. Enter an appropriate setting in Autoexec.bat if you want to specify a different location for the command interpreter under Windows 95.

Setup makes numerous changes to Autoexec.bat. Table 2.2 lists the statements and settings that Setup removes from Autoexec.bat.

TABLE 2.2
Lines Removed from Autoexec.bat by Setup

=ascsi	cache	cache-at	cache-em
delpurge	delq	delwatch	diskmap
diskopt	dosshell	eraq	fast512
fastopen	flash	hyper286	hyper386
hyperdkc	hyperdke	hyperdkx	ibmcache
icache	lock	login	mcache
memmax	ncache	password	pc-cache
pc-kwik	pckwin	qcache	rendir
scplus	script	setcfg	share
smartdrv	superon	superpck	taskmax
touch	UnSet=compsec	win	xdel
xdir	zcache		

Tip　If you need to connect to a network server prior to starting Windows 95, you can create a batch file that accomplishes the connection, then add the batch file to the Windows 95 Startup folder.

Changes to Other DOS Files

If you upgrade your existing Windows 3.*x* installation to Windows 95, Setup makes numerous other changes to your existing DOS files. Many of these changes are to protect your data—the file and disk commands included with DOS do not support long file names, and using them on folders and files that use long file names destroys the long file names. Some of the other changes owe to the fact that Windows 95 replaces many of the functions performed by DOS commands and utilities, making these command and utilities obsolete. Table 2.3 lists MS-DOS files that Setup deletes.

TABLE 2.3
MS-DOS Files Deleted by Setup

Ansi.sys	Attrib.exe	Chkdsk.exe	Choice.exe
Country.sys	Debug.exe	Defrag.exe	Deltree.exe
Diskcopy.exe	Display.sys	Doskey.com	D??space.bin
D??space.exe	D??space.sys	Edit.com	Edit.hlp
Ega.cpi	Emm386.exe	Fc.exe	Fdisk.exe
Find.exe	Format.com	Help.com	Help.hlp
Keyb.com	Keyboard.sys	Label.exe	Mem.exe
Mode.exe	More.com	Move.com	Mscdex.exe
Msd.exe	Networks.txt	Nlsfunc.exe	Os2.txt
Ramdrive.sys	Readme.txt	Scandisk.exe	Scandisk.ini
Setver.exe	Share.exe	Smartdrv.exe	Sort.exe
Start.exe	Subst.exe	Sys.com	Xcopy.exe

Setup also deletes a variety of files from previous versions of DOS. Table 2.4 lists the files from versions of MS-DOS prior to 5.0 that Setup deletes.

TABLE 2.4
Files Deleted by Setup from Pre-5.0 Versions of MS-DOS

Append.com	Asgnpart.com	Backup.exe	Bootf.com
Cache.sys	Cemm.exe	Cemmp.exe	Chkdsk.exe
Cmpqadap.com	Compact.exe	Configur.com	Debug.exe
Detect.com	Diskcomp.exe	Diskcopy.exe	Diskinit.com
Diskinit.exe	Dosutil.meu	Dskscan.exe	Dsksetup.com
Edlin.exe	Emm386.sys	Enhdisk.sys	Fastopen.exe
Fastart.exe	Fdisk.com	Filesys.exe	For150.exe
Format.exe	Gdu.exe	Graftabl.exe	Graphics.exe
Hardrive.sys	Hpcache.com	Hpdcache.com	Ifsfunc.exe
Indskbio.sys	Install.exe	Keyb32.com	Keybchf.com
Keybchg.com	Keybda.com	Keybfr.com	Keybfr.exe
Keybgk.com	Keybgr.com	Keybgr.exe	Keybit.com
Keybit.exe	Keybno.com	Keybsp.com	Keybsv.exe
Keybsw.com	Keybuk.com	Keybuk.exe	Keybus.com
Label.exe	Mode.exe	Mvbuild.exe	Pamcode.com
Paminstl.com	Part.exe	Password.exe	Prep.exe
Print.exe	Recover.exe	Restore.exe	Select.com
Select.dat	Select.exe	Select.hlp	Select.prt
Select1.dat	Select2.dat	Setup.exe	Shell.clr
Shell.hlp	Shell.meu	Shellb.com	Shellc.exe
Tree.exe	Vdisk.sys	Xmaem.sys	Zcache.sys
zspool.com			

Setup also deletes files on systems that contain versions of DOS other than MS-DOS (OEM versions of DOS, for example). Table 2.5 lists files that Setup deletes on these types of systems.

TABLE 2.5
Non-MS-DOS Files Deleted by Setup

Delpurge.exe	Delwatch.exe	Diskmap.exe	Diskopt.exe
Dosbook.exe	Hidos.sys	Lock.exe	Login.exe

Memmax.exe	Password.exe	Rendir.exe	Setup.exe
Sys.com	Taskmax.exe	Taskmax.ini	Touch.exe
Uninstal.exe	Xdel.exe	Xdir.exe	

Understanding Changes to System.ini and Win.ini

Setup modifies System.ini and Win.ini if you upgrade an existing Windows 3.*x* installation to Windows 95. Setup makes these changes because the majority of functions these two files handle are now performed by Windows 95's Registry. The System.ini and Win.ini files are maintained primarily for compatibility with Windows 3.*x* applications. For example, Setup relocates all settings in the [Network drivers] section of System.ini to the Registry. Setup also moves the *lanabase* setting from the [nwblink] section of System.ini to the Registry.

Setup Changes to System.ini

Setup deletes some settings from the [386Enh] section of System.ini entirely. These settings are as follows:

◆ `device=*vfd`

◆ `device=*configmg`

◆ `device=serial.386`

◆ `device=isapnp.386`

◆ `device=wshell.386`

◆ `device=lpt.386`

◆ `device=pagefile.386`

◆ `timercriticalsection=`

Setup also adds new settings to System.ini and modifies existing settings to enable Windows 3.*x* applications to take advantage of Windows 95 features. Following is a list of the settings that Setup adds to the [boot] section of System.ini:

◆ `comm.drv=comm.drv`

◆ `dibeng.drv=dibeng.dll`

◆ `gdi.exe=gdi.exe`

◆ `sound.drv=sound.drv`

◆ `user.exe=user.exe`

Setup also makes numerous modifications to the [386Enh] section of System.ini. Most of these changes deal with virtual device drivers. Setup relocates the following settings from the [386Enh] section of System.ini to the Registry:

◆ `Network=`

◆ `Network3=`

◆ `SecondNet=`

◆ `Transport=`

◆ `V86ModeLANAs=`

Setup adds a large number of settings to the [386Enh] section. The vast majority of these new settings are for virtual device drivers provided by Windows 95. Adding these device drivers to the System.ini file enables Windows 3.*x* applications to access these drivers. Table 2.6 lists the new settings added to the [386Enh] section of System.ini by Setup.

TABLE 2.6
Settings Added to [386Enh] by Setup

device=*biosxlat	device=*combuff	device=*dosmgr
device=*dynapage	device=*ifsmgr	device=*int13
device=*ios	device=*pageswap	device=*parity
device=*perf	device=*reboot	device=*shell
device=*spooler	device=*v86mmgr	device=*vcache
device=*vcd	device=*vcdfsd	device=*vcomm
device=*vcond	device=*vdef	device=*vdmad
device=*vfat	device=*vfbackup	device=*vmcpd
device=*vmpoll	device=*vpicd	device=*vsd

device=*vshare	device=*vtd	device=*vtdapi
device=*vwin32	device=*vxdldr	maxbps=270
shellname=krnl386.exe		

Setup Changes to Win.ini

Setup also makes changes to your existing Win.ini file. The changes relate primarily to font and desktop settings. Table 2.7 lists the settings that Setup relocates from Win.ini to the Registry.

TABLE 2.7
Win.ini Settings Moved to the Registry

Beep	BorderWidth	BorderWidth
CaptionHeight	CaptionWidth	CursorBlinkRate
DoubleClickSpeed	KeyboardDelay	KeyboardSpeed
MenuHeight	MenuWidth	MinArrange
MinHorzGap	MinVertGap	MinWidth
MouseSpeed	MouseThreshold1	MouseThreshold2
ScreenSaveActive	ScreenSaveTimeOut	ScrollHeight
ScrollWidth	SmCaptionHeight	SmCaptionWidth
SwapMouseButtons		

C H A P T E R

3

Troubleshooting Setup and Startup

Chapter 2 explains the Windows 95 setup and installation process. In most cases, you should have no problems installing and starting Windows 95. As you will soon learn, Windows 95 makes it much easier to overcome and fix the problems when they do occur. This chapter explains general troubleshooting techniques and how specifically to troubleshoot Setup and system boot by covering the following topics:

◆ Troubleshooting Setup

◆ Troubleshooting startup

◆ Creating and using a startup disk

◆ General troubleshooting techniques and tips

◆ Sources of information for troubleshooting

In addition to techniques you can use to troubleshoot Setup and startup, you also will find information at the end of this chapter that will help you locate information about known bugs, new and updated Windows 95 files, and other sources of information that are helpful in troubleshooting your system.

Troubleshooting Setup

To troubleshoot Setup, you first need an understanding of the process Setup uses to install Windows 95 on your system; then you can begin to troubleshoot specific problems. Chapter 2, "Setting Up and Booting Windows 95," explains the Setup process in general; the following section explains the Setup process in more detail.

Understanding the Setup Process

Windows 95 Setup goes through a number of different phases to install Windows 95. These include the following:

- ◆ Initial configuration and detection

- ◆ Hardware and system detection

- ◆ Startup disk and file extraction

- ◆ System configuration and Setup completion

The following sections detail these four Setup phases, explaining their purpose and outlining potential problems.

Initial Configuration and Detection

The Setup wizard automates much of the Setup process, prompting you for information as necessary to determine the options you want to use to install Windows 95. These initial configuration steps enable Setup to determine which support files it requires to run, which files to copy to your system, and which Windows 95 utilities and applications to install. This phase of the Setup process involves the following:

- ◆ **Detecting previous version of Windows.** If you start Setup from the DOS prompt, Setup scans the computer's local hard disk to determine if a previous version of Windows is installed. If Setup locates a previous version of Windows, it prompts you to exit Setup and run Setup from within Windows. You can

continue to run Setup from DOS, or exit and run Setup from Windows. Functionally, there is no difference between the two methods. If you experience a problem running Setup from DOS, try running it from Windows instead. If you experience a problem running Setup from Windows, exit Windows and try running Setup from DOS.

◆ **Minimum hardware configuration.** After scanning for a previous version of Windows, Setup checks your hardware to determine if your computer is capable of running Windows 95, checking for adequate CPU, memory, and available hard disk space. See table 3.1 for minimum hardware requirements for running Windows 95.

◆ **Existing operating system.** Setup checks your computer to verify that it contains an existing operating system that is compatible with Windows 95. For DOS systems, the operating system must be MS-DOS 3.2 or higher, or an equivalent OEM version of DOS (PC DOS, DR DOS, and so on) that supports disk partitions larger than 32 MB. Other compatible operating systems include Windows and Windows for Workgroups 3.*x* (which includes DOS), OS/2, and Windows NT.

◆ **Extended memory support.** Setup checks your system to determine if an extended memory manager, such as Himem.sys, is present. If Setup can't locate an extended memory manager, it loads its own extended memory manager.

◆ **TSR check.** Setup scans your system for TSRs, drivers, and other memory-resident programs that are not compatible with Setup. If any incompatible programs are found, Setup displays a warning message, giving you the opportunity to exit Setup and remove the incompatible program from your Config.sys and/or Autoexec.bat file before running Setup again.

◆ **Install minimal Windows shell.** If you start Setup from Windows, the Windows-based portion of Setup starts. If you start Setup from DOS, Setup copies a minimal Windows configuration in order to run the remainder of Setup, which is a Windows-based program. Up to this point in the Setup process, the processor is running in real mode.

◆ **Enable standard mode.** If you start Setup from DOS, Setup switches the processor into Standard mode and makes the computer's extended memory available.

◆ **Retrieve user information.** Setup begins requesting information from you about your Windows 95 installation, including the directory in which you want Windows 95 installed, and the options to install.

TABLE 3.1
Windows 95 Minimum Hardware Requirements

Item	Minimum Requirements
CPU	80386 or higher (or equivalent compatible non-Intel CPU).
Hard disk	Varies with installation option, but ranges from 10 MB to more than 80 MB for a local installation. Shared network installations require roughly 2.5 MB of free disk space.
RAM	4 MB is the minimum, although systems with only 4 MB will not perform well. Consider 8 MB to be a practical minimum for running Windows 95.
Video subsystem	VGA minimum, SuperVGA recommended.

Hardware and System Detection

After the initial configuration phase, Setup begins the hardware and system detection phase. As a part of this phase, Setup checks the system for existing software components such as existing Windows drivers. Setup also performs hardware detection to determine the internal and peripheral components for which it must install support.

 Note Setup prompts you before it begins hardware detection, giving you the option of bypassing hardware detection. If you bypass hardware detection, you must manually specify and configure hardware components and settings.

On computers that do not have a Plug and Play BIOS (referred to as *legacy systems*), Setup scans the system's interrupts, I/O ports, and memory locations for hardware components that Setup can detect based on its internal database of hardware profiles. Setup also checks legacy systems for Plug and Play–compliant devices, which even on legacy systems are capable of providing their model and configuration information to Setup. On Plug and Play systems, Setup checks for installed Plug and Play device support, as well as connected Plug and Play peripherals.

Although Setup often can detect a conflict and step you through resolving the conflict, Setup sometimes will hang due to a conflict between devices or other problems in detecting a certain item. If Setup hangs, the status indicator will stop moving and there will be no disk activity for an extended period of time. You then can reboot the system and Setup will restart automatically, giving you the option of using Safe Recovery. Safe Recovery enables you to bypass the hardware detection phase and specify hardware settings manually. Manual hardware configuration is explained later in the section "Overcoming Hardware Conflicts."

Startup Disk and File Extraction

After the configuration and detection phases are complete, Setup begins copying files from the distribution file sets to your system as required based on your hardware and software selections. If during initial configuration you directed Setup to create a startup disk, Setup copies to your system the minimum files required for the startup disk, then creates it. (For more information on creating and using a startup disk, refer to the section "Creating and Using a Startup Disk" later in this chapter.)

After creating the startup disk, Setup continues the file extraction process, copying all required files from the distribution disks, CD, or shared network folder to your computer or home directory (in the case of shared network installations). Setup then adds settings to the Registry to support your hardware and software selections.

System Configuration and Setup Completion

After Setup completes the file copy process, Setup incorporates your existing Win.ini and System.ini settings, as appropriate, into the Registry. Setup also replaces many of your existing MS-DOS files with updated versions that are compatible with Windows 95 (particularly with Windows 95's long file names). A number of DOS files are deleted, some are renamed, and others are replaced. For more information on how Setup affects DOS, refer to the section "The Effects of Setup on DOS" in Chapter 2.

In addition to modifying your DOS files during the final configuration phase, Setup also uses a set of wizards to step you through the process of configuring various options such as printers, the Exchange mail client, and other options. Many of these options are configured automatically without any input from you.

When the installation and configuration process is complete, Setup modifies the boot sector of the drive and creates Io.sys, which replaces the original DOS IO.SYS and MSDOS.SYS files (on DOS systems). The existing IO.SYS and MSDOS.SYS files are renamed Io.dos and Msdos.dos. Setup then reboots the system.

After the system reboots, Setup combines individual VxDs (virtual device drivers) to create Vmm32.vxd. The individual device drivers are determined by the hardware and software selections you make during the setup process. Setup also renames a few of the temporary files it uses during the setup process (Arial.win, User32.tmp, and Logo.sys) to their new file names, then backs up the old Registry file (copying System.dat to System.da0) and renames the new Registry file (from System.new to System.dat).

Next, Setup processes the RunOnce key in the Registry to complete the installation and configuration process. This process includes configuring MIDI and PCMCIA devices and configuring software options such as printer drivers, Exchange, and the Control Panel. Hardware vendors also can add to the RunOnce key to cause their custom setup processes to run automatically during Setup. To complete the installation process, Setup converts Windows 3.*x* program groups to Windows 95 folders, creating shortcuts in the Programs menu to each program group and objects they contain.

Understanding Hardware Detection

As mentioned previously, Windows 95 divides devices into two types: Plug and Play and legacy. Setup uses two methods to detect the hardware in your PC. On systems with a Plug and Play BIOS, Setup polls the system for installed Plug and Play devices. Setup also can identify Plug and Play devices on legacy systems that don't have a Plug and Play BIOS.

To identify legacy devices, Windows 95 Setup divides hardware into different classes. Sound cards fall into one class, SCSI host adapters fall into another, and so on. Setup uses these class distinctions to simplify hardware detection and reduce the possibility of hardware conflicts during detection.

Setup uses an internal list of devices and their signatures to detect hardware based on classification. Setup scans ROM strings, configuration files, and device drivers in memory to detect the signatures of various devices. These signature hints enable Setup to scan your system for various types of devices with relatively little chance of locking up the system during the detection phase, because the hints narrow the list of possible devices and help avoid the possibility that Setup might direct a driver to poll the wrong device. If no hints are found for a particular class of device, Setup skips detection for the entire class. If Setup finds no hint of a sound card, for example, it does not perform hardware detection to locate and identify a sound card. Microsoft uses the term *safe detection* to describe Setup's capability to perform detection through hints rather than direct hardware access.

Setup provides safe detection for the following four classes of devices:

◆ Network adapters

◆ SCSI host adapters

◆ Sound cards

◆ Proprietary CD-ROM adapters

Setup scans memory for Lsl.com and Ipx.com to determine whether to scan for network settings, and also scans the Windows, Windows for Workgroups, and LAN Manager directories for Protocol.ini. If Setup locates Protocol.ini, Setup extracts network settings from the file.

Most SCSI host adapters do not require a driver in Config.sys (pre-Windows 95) in order to support a SCSI hard disk. Device drivers are typically required, however, to

support other SCSI devices such as tape drives, CD-ROM drives, scanners, and other devices. Therefore, Setup scans the ROM address space for hint strings that indicate the presence of a SCSI host adapter to provide support for SCSI hard disks. Setup also scans Config.sys to provide support for other SCSI devices.

Proprietary CD-ROM adapters typically require a device driver installed in Config.sys, so Setup scans Config.sys to locate hints for safe detection of these adapters. Windows 95 supports proprietary CD-ROM adapters from Mitsumi, SONY, and Panasonic.

Sound cards are one type of device for which Setup relies heavily on safe detection. Rather than poll I/O addresses for sound cards, Setup instead scans Config.sys and System.ini for sound card hints. If Setup finds no sound-related device drivers or other hints in Config.sys or System.ini, Setup skips detection of sound cards altogether.

Now that you have some background in the Setup process and in how Setup detects hardware, you're ready to begin troubleshooting your Setup problems. The following section explains how to use Safe Recovery to troubleshoot and overcome a failed installation.

Using Safe Recovery

When Setup experiences a problem, it attempts to automatically correct or compensate for the problem. How Setup proceeds after a failed setup attempt depends on when the failure occurred. Regardless of when the problem occurs, Setup relies on two log files that it creates during installation to determine the cause of the failure and overcome the problem. These log files—Setuplog.txt and Detlog.txt—are described in the following sections.

Setuplog.txt and Failures Prior to Hardware Detection

If the failure occurs prior to the hardware detection phase, Setup reads the file Setuplog.txt to determine the point at which the problem occurred. Setuplog.txt is an ASCII (text-only) file to which Setup writes status information during the installation process. When a failure occurs and you restart Setup, Setup scans Setuplog.txt to identify processes that started but did not complete. The processes that failed are skipped. Although it is possible that Setup could fail multiple times, the fact that Setup skips failed processes on subsequent tries ensures that the installation process always progresses, even though some items might not be installed completely. The end result is that Windows 95 often can install basic support and run, enabling you to incorporate the skipped items manually. Unfortunately, Setup does not inform you of which items it has skipped.

 Note   Setup creates Setuplog.txt in the root directory of the boot disk.

If you experience a problem with Setup, check your system for a copy of Setuplog.txt and scan the file to determine if you can identify the point or points at which Setup failed. If you were able to install a minimal Windows 95 configuration and boot without support for certain devices, you can open Notepad or WordPad in Windows 95 to read Setuplog.txt. If Setup was unable to install a minimal working copy of Windows 95, you should be able to boot your system to DOS and use the EDIT command to read the file. If you are unable to boot the system from the hard disk, you can boot using a DOS system disk.

The following list explains the majority of sections you might find in a Setuplog.txt file:

◆ **[Choose Directory].** This section specifies the installation directory, information about the Windows 95 source files and directories, the type of installation you selected (typical, custom, and so on), and other general information about the Setup prior to the detection phase.

◆ **[FileCopy].** This section provides a lengthy list of the files that were copied to your system during Setup.

◆ **[OptionalComponents].** This section lists the optional components and which ones were installed. A value of 1 for a component, such as "Calculator"=1, indicates that the component was installed. A value of zero indicates that the component was not installed.

◆ **[Restart].** This section lists processes that Setup performed after it restarted the system.

◆ **[System].** This section lists your system hardware configuration, such as display type, keyboard type, and so forth.

◆ **[NameAndOrg].** This section contains the user and organization names that were entered during Setup.

◆ **[Destination].** This section lists paths that Setup uses to track file destinations.

◆ **[Setup].** This section contains a variety of settings that specify options selected during Setup.

◆ **[Network].** This section contains settings that indicate network setup options that were specified.

◆ **[Started].** This section contains messages and options generated during the initial startup phase of Setup.

◆ **[Detection].** This section contains status information and messages regarding the initial detection phase.

In addition to the sections described in the previous list, the Setuplog.txt file also can contain additional sections and settings. If you scan through Setlog.txt, you will notice that the entries in the file follow the logical progression of the Setup process, with initial Setup actions appearing near the top of the file and actions that occur near the end of the Setup process appearing near the end of the file.

Detlog.txt and Failures during Hardware Detection

During the hardware detection phase, Setup creates and writes to a hidden file name Detlog.txt, storing in Detlog.txt the hardware that was detected and the parameters for each device. The Detlog.txt file also is modified when you use the Device Manager or Add New Hardware wizard from the Control Panel. Detlog.txt, therefore, serves as a common hardware detection log for each of the functions that adds hardware support for Windows 95. If a Detlog.txt file already exists, it is renamed Detlog.old, and a new Detlog.txt file is created. Setup creates the Detlog.txt file in the root directory of the boot disk.

Note Hardware detection occurs only if you specify the auto-detection option in the Add New Hardware wizard or in Setup. Otherwise, a device must be added manually. Windows 95 updates the Detlog.txt file only if automatic detection takes place.

Although Setup can track and overcome hardware detection errors, Setup doesn't use Detlog.txt for that purpose. Instead, Detlog.txt serves only as a log that you can use to identify hardware detection problems. If a detection error occurs, Setup creates a binary file named Detcrash.log and reads Detcrash.log in subsequent installation attempts to overcome the hardware detection problem.

If your system locks up during the hardware detection phase, Setup will bypass the failed device during the next installation attempt. If you want to track down the source of the problem, you can boot the system to DOS and scan Detlog.txt for possible problems. Table 3.2 describes settings you will find in a typical Detlog.txt file.

TABLE 3.2
Detlog.txt Settings

Setting	Function
Parameters	Lists command-line switches that were used to start Setup
WinVer	Lists DOS and Windows versions detected by Setup
AvoidMem	Specifies upper memory blocks that Setup avoids during detection

continues

TABLE 3.2, CONTINUED
Detlog.txt Settings

Setting	Function
LogCrash	Specifies whether or not a valid Detcrash.log file was found
DetectClass:Skip	Indicates that Setup Class found no hints for a class of devices and is skipping the class
Detected	Lists a component that was detected
UserOverride	Records classes that you directed Setup to skip during installation

In addition to the settings in table 3.2, the Detlog.txt file also can contain other settings. The Detlog.txt file, for example, will contain numerous QueryIOMem statements that indicate calls performed by Setup to detect various components. These QueryIOMem entries also include information about the result of the call (whether the device was detected).

Verifying and Updating Your Windows 95 Installation

In previous versions of Windows, the loss or corruption of a single system could require that you completely reinstall Windows. Windows 95, however, includes a much better mechanism for recovering from damaged or overwritten files.

If you run Setup on a computer on which Windows 95 has already been successfully installed, Setup detects the existing copy of Windows 95 and displays a dialog box inquiring whether you want to perform a complete setup or simply verify your current Windows 95 installation. If you indicate that you want to verify your current installation, Setup runs through the installation process, but instead of recopying all the operating system components and files, Setup verifies the files. If a file is corrupted or is a different version, Setup recopies the file from the distribution disks or CD.

Tips for Specific Setup Problems

The following sections provide tips for overcoming specific problems during Setup that are not discussed specifically in the previous sections.

Setup Will Not Start

This problem is generally due to a lack of sufficient free RAM. Setup requires a minimum of 420 KB of free conventional memory. Issue the MEM /C command at the DOS prompt to determine the amount of free conventional memory. If your

system has less than 420 KB free, check Config.sys and Autoexec.bat for device drivers and TSRs that you can eliminate to acquire enough memory to run Setup. In general, you need to retain your extended memory manager (such as Himem.sys) and any device drivers that are required for your system to recognize critical devices such as CD-ROM drives (if installing from CD). If necessary, eliminate device drivers for nonessential devices such as sound cards.

You have the following three options for eliminating the unnecessary device drivers and TSRs from memory:

◆ Delete their entries from Config.sys and Autoexec.bat and reboot

◆ Comment their entries in Config.sys and Autoexec.bat and reboot

◆ Simply reboot and bypass the entries in Config.sys and Autoexec.bat

To comment an entry in Config.sys or Autoexec.bat, place a semicolon at the beginning of the line. To single-step through the boot process and bypass specific device drivers and TSRs, reboot the system and press F8 when you see the message Starting MS-DOS (MS-DOS 6.*x*).

Note   If you are using a version of DOS prior to 6.*x*, you must comment out the lines in Config.sys and Autoexec.bat—these versions of DOS do not support single-step boot.

If you don't have any device drivers in Config.sys or Autoexec.bat that are required to access critical hardware, such as a CD-ROM drive, you can bypass your Config.sys and Autoexec.bat files altogether. Setup will load its own extended memory driver and continue with the installation process. To bypass your startup files with MS-DOS 6.*x*, press F5 when you see the message Starting MS-DOS. With earlier versions of DOS, rename Config.sys and Autoexec.bat to Config.old and Autoexec.old, then reboot.

Other problems starting Setup include the lack of available extended memory and the inability to access the source disk (floppy or CD). Windows 95 requires a minimum of 3 MB of extended memory, which means that the absolute minimum amount of RAM required in a system to run Setup is 4 MB. If your PC contains less than 4 MB of RAM, you will not be able to run Setup or use Windows 95. Also, verify that you can access the drive you are using to install Windows 95.

Error B1

If you receive the B1 error during Setup, you are installing Windows 95 on a 386 PC with a B1 step CPU. The B1 step chip, manufactured prior to April 1987, contains a bug that causes incorrect 32-bit math operations, rendering the chip unusable for Windows 95. You could replace the CPU with a later 386 chip, but upgrading to a faster processor is a much more effective solution. Refer to Chapter 12, "Selecting and Upgrading Hardware," for a discussion of system processor upgrades.

Problems during File Copy

If Setup experiences problems while in the file copy phase (copying files from the distribution disk or CD to your hard disk), the problem could be due to virus protection software. If you are running virus software, disable it and retry Setup. If your PC has virus protection built into the BIOS, run the PC's BIOS setup program and disable virus protection, then run Setup.

Incorrect DOS Version

If you receive an error similar to `Incorrect DOS version`, verify that you are running MS-DOS 3.2 or later, or the equivalent OEM version of DOS as discussed previously in this chapter. This problem also can be caused by 386MAX. If you are running the 386MAX memory manager on your system, disable 386MAX in Config.sys and Autoexec.bat, reboot, and retry Setup.

Standard Mode: Fault in MS-DOS Extender

This error generally is the result of a memory conflict. To overcome the problem, remove EMM386 from your Config.sys file and reboot, then restart Setup. Or, run Setup from Windows 3.*x*.

Cannot Open File *.Inf

If you receive an error message similar to this one, you might need to free some additional memory. Exit Windows 3.*x,* remove SmartDrive from Config.sys and Autoexec.bat, then reboot the system. Restart Windows and reattempt to run Windows 95 Setup. If the problem persists, make sure you are not running any other programs in Windows when you try to run Setup. Also remove other nonessential programs and TSRs from Config.sys and Autoexec.bat.

No Valid Boot Partition

If Setup generates the error message `Setup unable to find valid boot partition`, you either do not have a valid, bootable partition on your hard disk, or your disk compression software has hidden the boot drive. If you're using compression software, make sure you have not mapped a network drive to the ID of the host disk for the compressed logical drive. Also, verify that you have a valid boot partition—if you can boot the PC from the hard disk, you do.

Troubleshooting Startup

After you get Windows 95 installed, you should have no problem starting Windows 95. If Windows 95 fails to start, however, you can use some common troubleshooting techniques, such as scanning the Bootlog.txt file to locate the source of the problem.

The first time it boots after Setup, Windows 95 creates a hidden file called Bootlog.txt in the root directory of the boot disk. Windows 95 writes initialization and completion status information for all aspects of the startup process to Bootlog.txt. On subsequent boots, however, Windows 95 does not write to Bootlog.txt automatically—you must direct it to do so.

To cause Windows 95 to write to Bootlog.txt during the startup process, press F8 when the system begins to boot. This displays the boot menu. Then, select option 2 (Logged) from the menu, and Windows 95 will create a Bootlog.txt file as it boots. If you are starting Windows 95 from the command prompt, enter **WIN /B** to start Windows 95 and to have Windows 95 create a Bootlog.txt file.

Windows 95 logs the initialization of each process with an entry such as `Loading`, `LoadStart`, `*INIT`, or a similar indicator that a process has been started. The completion of a process is marked by an entry containing a string such as `SUCCESS` or `DONE`. Each process should therefore be marked by a pair of entries, one for the initialization and another for the completion of the process. The first two lines in a typical Bootlog.txt file, for example, are the following:

```
Loading Device = C:\WINDOWS\HIMEM.SYS
LoadSuccess   = C:\WINDOWS\HIMEM.SYS
```

The trick to using Bootlog.txt to locate startup problems is to search the file for processes for which there is a startup entry but no completion entry. If you find an entry that reads `Loading Device = C:\WINDOWS\DBLBUFF.SYS` but there is no entry that reads `LoadSuccess = C:\WINDOWS\DBLBUFF.SYS`, double-buffering for your SCSI hard disk failed to load, indicating a possible problem with the SCSI subsystem.

Tips for Specific Startup Problems

This section of the chapter describes possible problems you might encounter during Windows 95 startup and offers suggestions for overcoming those problems.

System Hangs after Setup

If Windows 95 hangs the first time it tries to boot after installation, the problem could lie in Windows 95's capability to detect ISA-based adapters that support a limited Plug and Play capability. Windows 95 uses a software module referred to as the *ISA enumerator* to detect these devices, but the detection process can be hung by the ISA enumerator attempting to access a port that is in use by another device. If Windows 95 hangs the first time it tries to boot, boot the system to DOS, remove the line `device=ISAPNP.386` from System.ini, and attempt to reboot Windows 95.

System Registry File Missing

The Registry comprises two files: System.dat and User.dat. When the Registry is modified, Windows 95 makes a backup copy of the two Registry files, naming them System.da0 and User.da0. If a problem occurs with the Registry files during startup (files are corrupted or missing), Windows 95 attempts to restore the backup (.da0) files to create a working Registry. If Windows 95 is unable to restore the files, Windows 95 starts in Safe Mode and displays a dialog box you can use to initiate the Registry recovery.

 Tip   If you receive a Registry error message during startup, boot to the command line and check the Msdos.sys file for the setting WinDir. Verify that WinDir points to the directory where the Registry files are located. If the WinDir setting is blank or missing, correct the setting and resave the file. Then, reboot the system.

Without a valid Registry, Windows 95 will be capable of only very limited functionality. If Windows 95 is unable to recover the Registry from the backup files, you must either copy the Registry file(s) from a backup set to the directory specified by the WinDir setting in Msdos.sys or run Setup again to enable Setup to create a new Registry.

For more information on using, backing up, and restoring the Registry, refer to Chapter 13, "Working with the Registry and Ini Files."

Disabling Virus Protection in the BIOS

If your system BIOS includes a virus protection feature that prevents applications from writing to the boot sector of the hard disk, you will experience problems with Setup failing near the end of the installation process and with Windows 95 not starting properly. Run your BIOS setup program and disable virus protection until you have Windows 95 installed and working properly. Then, reenable your BIOS virus protection and retest Windows 95 to verify that it works properly.

Problems with VxDs

During installation, Setup copies a number of individual VxDs to the file Vmm32.vxd in the \Windows\System folder. A missing or damaged VxD, whether an individual VxD or one included in Vmm32.vxd, can cause Windows 95 to abort startup. Typically, you will see a message informing you of which VxD caused the problem. One solution is to run Setup again and choose the Verify option. Setup will restore the VxD.

You also can simply copy the VxD to the \Windows\System\Vmm32 folder. Then, add an entry to the [386Enh] section of System.ini that reads **device=*file.vxd***, where *file.vxd* is the name of the VXD you copied. If two instances of the same VxD are loaded, the second one takes precedence over the first and intercepts and handles all calls to the VxD. Therefore, if a copy of a VxD in Vmm32.vxd is damaged, copying the individual VxD file to the \Windows\System\Vmm32 folder can overcome the problem. Running Setup again and performing a verify operation, however, is preferable because other files could have been damaged.

Creating and Using a Startup Disk

During the installation process, Setup gives you the option of creating a startup disk. This startup disk is a bootable Windows 95 disk containing a selection of utility files and programs such as Fdisk, ScanDisk, Edit, and so on.

 Tip It's important that you create a startup disk to enable you to boot the computer if your hard disk fails or your Windows 95 startup files become corrupted.

Hopefully, you created a startup disk when you installed Windows 95. If you did not create a startup disk and Windows 95 is running properly, you can create one yourself. To create a startup disk, open the Control Panel and choose the Add/Remove Programs icon. Then click on the Startup Disk tab from the Add/Remove Programs property sheet to display the Startup Disk property page (see fig. 3.1). Choose the <u>C</u>reate Disk button to direct Windows 95 to create a startup disk.

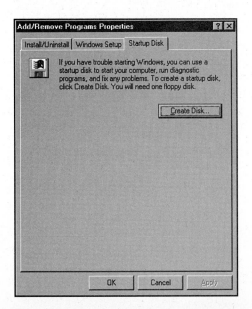

Figure 3.1

The Startup Disk property page.

General Troubleshooting Techniques

In addition to the specific solutions outlined in the previous sections, a number of general troubleshooting techniques exist that can help you overcome a variety of problems with Windows 95. The following sections discuss general troubleshooting and offer some tips to help you get your system back in working condition.

Boyce's Corollary to Murphy's Law

Unless you've been living in a vacuum, you know that Murphy's Law states "Anything that can go wrong will go wrong." PCs are subject to Boyce's Corollary to Murphy's Law, which is this:

> Your PC will continue to work just fine until you start fiddling with it and screw it up.

Although PC hardware degrades over time, the actual possibility that some part of your computer will fail (excluding wear-and-tear components such as the floppy disk or hard disk) is relatively remote. By far the most common causes of problems with the PC working properly are the result of a change you have made to the system, either directly or indirectly by adding a new piece of hardware, adding software, reconfiguring drivers, and so on.

Whatever the cause of your PC's problem, following some general steps will generally help you resolve the problem and get your PC working again. As you are trouble-shooting, keep the following ideas in mind:

◆ The problem is likely being caused by a change that you or someone else has made to the system.

◆ If the problem is caused by a hardware failure, you should be able to not only identify the problem, but to fix it.

◆ The problem might be the result of more than one cause. Don't assume that fixing one problem will solve the entire problem.

◆ You should follow some specific steps and procedures to troubleshoot the problem.

The last point in the previous list is perhaps the most important to effective trouble-shooting. A methodical approach generally brings results. The following sections explain some of the procedures and techniques you should use when troubleshooting a problem in Windows 95.

Using Backups

The Registry consists of two files—User.dat and System.dat. These Registry files generally reside in the Windows directory or in the directory specified by the WinDir setting in the Msdos.sys file (which is located in the root directory of the boot disk). If you have configured Windows 95 to support multiple desktop configurations, however, a unique User.dat file resides in each user's profile directory. If your user name is fredf, for example, your User.dat file resides in the \Windows\Profiles\fredf folder. In all cases, however, only one System.dat file is used.

Windows 95 automatically maintains a backup of your Registry files in User.da0 and System.da0. When a Registry problem occurs, Windows 95 can restore the Registry files from the backups. Even though Windows 95 maintains backup copies of the Registry files, you should consider backing up the Registry files on your own. Rather than simply back up the latest Registry files, however, you also should back up the previous Registry files in case a change that was made in the new Registry is the cause of the problem. If a problem does occur and Windows 95 is unable to successfully restore the Registry, you can boot the computer to the command prompt and restore the backup files yourself.

The method you use to back up your Registry files depends entirely on your preferences and whether you perform regular backups of other files. If nothing else, back up your Registry files to a floppy disk at least once a week and always before you begin installing new hardware or software.

Using System Logs

Although few people do so, it is a good idea to maintain a set of logs for your computer. These logs should list the hardware installed in your PC, the settings of each hardware component, changes you have made to the hardware or software configuration, and any other changes, however minor, that you make to your system. When a problem occurs, you can scan the log to identify a related change that might be causing the problem.

Tip Although you could easily keep a log on your PC as a Notepad or WordPad file, you should also keep a hard copy of the log in case you are unable to boot your system to read the log.

Using Startup Switches

Windows 95 supports a number of command-line switches you can include with the WIN command to start Windows 95 with various options enabled and disabled for troubleshooting purposes. To start Windows 95 with a command-line switch, first boot the system to the command prompt. To do so, press the F8 key while the system is booting (any time after the PC completes the power-on self test). When the boot menu appears, select option 6, "Command prompt only," to boot Windows 95 to the command prompt, then enter **WIN /D** followed by the appropriate switch as described in the following sections. For example, you would enter **WIN /D:F** to start Windows 95 with 32-bit disk access turned off.

◆ **:F.** Turns off 32-bit disk access. Using this switch is similar to the setting 32BitDiskAccess=FALSE in the [386Enh] section of System.ini. Turning off 32-bit disk access is necessary with drives that are not compatible with Windows 95's 32-bit disk access.

◆ **:M.** Enables Safe Mode and is similar to selecting option 3, "Safe Mode," from the boot menu or pressing F5 during the boot process.

◆ **:N.** Enables Safe Mode with networking support and is similar to selecting option 4, "Safe mode with network support," from the boot menu or pressing F6 during the boot process.

◆ **:S.** Prevents Windows 95 from using ROM address space between F000:0000 and 1 MB for a break point. This switch is equivalent to the setting SystemROMBreakPoint=FALSE in the [386Enh] section of System.ini.

◆ **:V.** Specifies that the ROM routine will handle interrupts from the hard disk controller, and is equivalent to a setting of VirtualHDIRQ=FALSE in the [386Enh] section of System.ini.

◆ **:X.** Excludes all of the UMA range from Windows 95's use, and is equivalent to the setting EMMExclude=A000-FFFF in the [386Enh] section of System.ini. This switch can help you identify memory conflicts in the UMA between devices.

Using Safe Mode

To provide a means of overcoming a variety of potential problems, Windows 95 includes a Safe Mode, which boots a minimal operating system environment. By eliminating the majority of drivers, Safe Mode typically enables you to at least boot your system so that you can run Setup or the Control Panel to correct the problem. If your network adapter is improperly configured, for example, Safe Mode enables you to boot the machine and use the Control Panel to remove and add drivers and configuration settings as necessary.

Windows 95 actually supports two Safe Modes: one without network support, and one with network support. If you are experiencing a network problem, you should use Safe Mode without network support. If the problem is not related to the network, you

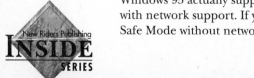

can boot using Safe Mode with network support in order to access a server and driver files as necessary to correct your problem.

To boot Safe Mode without network support, press F5 during the boot process or press F8 to display the boot menu and choose option 3, "Safe mode." To boot Safe Mode with network support, press F6 at the beginning of the boot process or press F8 to display the boot menu, then choose option 4, "Safe mode with network support."

When Windows 95 boots using Safe Mode, only the minimum drivers required to get Windows 95 up and running are loaded. Windows 95 also uses a standard VGA driver to enable you to boot the system when a video driver is the problem.

Using Single-Step Boot

Windows 95 eliminates much of the need for a Config.sys file or loading real mode drivers in Config.sys, but some devices still require real mode drivers. If you believe that a real mode driver is causing your Windows 95 problem, you can single-step through the boot process to possibly identify errors that occur when the driver is loaded.

To single-step through the boot process, press F8 at the beginning of the boot process to display the boot menu, then choose option 5, "Step-by-step confirmation." Windows 95 displays each line of your Config.sys and Autoexec.bat files in turn, enabling you to confirm the execution of each one. You also can bypass entries in Config.sys and Autoexec.bat that you feel might be causing the problem. If you bypass an entry and Windows 95 boots and runs normally, it is a good indication that the bypassed driver is the cause of the problem.

Using a Clean Boot

If you are an experienced DOS user, you probably are familiar with the term *clean boot,* which means to bypass the Config.sys and Autoexec.bat files altogether during boot. In DOS 6.*x,* you accomplish a clean boot by pressing F5 during the boot process. In Windows 95, there actually are two ways to perform a clean boot. Booting Windows 95 in Safe Mode bypasses the Config.sys and Autoexec.bat files, effectively performing a clean boot.

You might, however, want to bypass your Config.sys and Autoexec.bat files and boot Windows 95 in normal mode to retain network support or other normal Windows 95 features that are not available in Safe Mode. In this situation, you need to rename your Config.sys and Autoexec.bat files so that they will be bypassed during boot. For example, rename Config.sys to Config.old and Autoexec.bat to Autoexec.old, then reboot the system.

Note If you boot your system to DOS to rename the Config.sys and Autoexec.bat files, you must rename Config.win and Autoexec.win. These two files are renamed Config.sys and Autoexec.bat when you boot Windows 95. The Config.sys and Autoexec.bat files you see when you boot the system to DOS are the DOS configuration files that are stored in Config.dos and Autoexec.dos when the system is booted to Windows 95.

Using the Startup Disk

The startup disk, which you can create during Windows 95 installation or after installation through the Control Panel, provides a means to boot your system from a set of known, good files. To boot from the startup disk, simply insert the startup disk in your PC's boot floppy disk and reset the computer. The Windows 95 command line will boot from the floppy.

After the system is booted, you can use the tools on the floppy disk to begin trouble-shooting and clearing up your computer's problems. The startup disk includes ScanDisk, Fdisk, and other utility programs you can use to fix disk and other types of problems.

Tip If your computer's boot sector becomes damaged for some reason (such as a virus infection), you can re-create the master boot record using the Fdisk program on the startup disk. Write-protect the startup disk to avoid possible virus infection, then boot the system using the startup disk. Make the hard disk active, then, at the command prompt, enter **A:FDISK /MBR**. Remove the startup disk and reboot the system.

Sources of Information for Troubleshooting

Many other good sources of information can help you identify and overcome a variety of problems with your computer. The following list describes just a few of these resources:

◆ **Microsoft Knowledgebase.** The Microsoft Knowledgebase is a database of over 40,000 technical documents maintained by Microsoft that detail bugs and answers to questions about Microsoft products. You can gain access to the Microsoft Knowledgebase on CompuServe (GO MSKB), and on the Internet at Microsoft's World Wide Web server, www.microsoft.com.

◆ **Microsoft Connection.** The Microsoft Connection (GO MICROSOFT) is a collection of forums on CompuServe that offer information, files, and interaction with users of various Microsoft products around the world.

◆ **Microsoft Internet Services.** In addition to the Knowledgebase, Microsoft provides access to a wide variety of information and services on the Internet at the web site www.microsoft.com. These services include information about Microsoft products, sales, and technical support.

◆ *Keeping Your PC Alive, Special Edition.* This book from New Riders Publishing gives the layman the skills necessary to troubleshoot and repair a wide variety of typical computer problems. The book also covers hardware upgrades, enabling the average user to install almost any new component, including CPU upgrades.

Adding and Configuring New Hardware

I n previous versions of DOS and Windows, adding new hardware to your computer was often a hit-and-miss experience that required considerable trial and error and hardware and software reconfiguration. Unfortunately, the process often exceeded the average user's knowledge and capabilities. Although the same process isn't perfect in Windows 95, it is significantly simpler. You often can simply install the device and turn on the PC, and Windows 95 automatically installs support for the device. This automatic installation works for many devices without Plug and Play BIOS support.

This chapter explains the processes you use to install and configure support for new hardware in your PC, and covers the following topics:

◆ Understanding driver and configuration issues

◆ Understanding and using automatic configuration

◆ Installing and configuring hardware manually

◆ Configuring and using PCMCIA devices

◆ Controlling devices with the Device Manager

◆ Using multiple hardware profiles

◆ Using real mode and Windows 3.*x* drivers

◆ Overcoming device conflicts

You perform most Windows 95 hardware and software configuration tasks through the Control Panel, using the System object and Add New Hardware object. The following sections explain how to use these objects, as well as automatic methods for configuring hardware.

Understanding Hardware Configuration Issues

Windows 95 includes features that simplify the task of installing and configuring new hardware. First and foremost is Windows 95's support for automatic installation and configuration of hardware, both for *Plug and Play systems* (those that contain a Plug and Play BIOS) and for *legacy systems* (computers that have standard BIOS, not designed for Plug and Play). Automatic installation and configuration, as well as Plug and Play, are explained in more detail in the section "Understanding and Using Automatic Configuration" later in this chapter. For now, just understand that in many situations, Windows 95 can automatically install support for a majority of common adapters and peripherals. This capability brings installation of new hardware and peripherals well within the reach and capabilities of the typical user.

In addition to supporting automatic installation and configuration for many devices, Windows 95 also provides wizards to automate installation and configuration of devices that Windows 95 can't install and configure automatically. Installing a modem, for example, is as simple as selecting a few choices in the modem installation wizard. In most cases, Windows 95 can detect your modem to determine its manufacturer and type (see fig. 4.1).

Windows 95 also provides a wizard that steps you through installing devices that Windows 95 can't install by itself. The Add New Hardware wizard (see fig. 4.2) enables you to let Windows 95 attempt to detect the new hardware, or you can manually specify the device manufacturer and type.

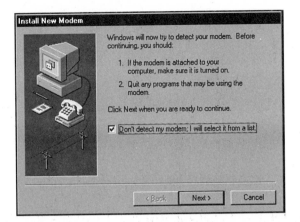

Figure 4.1

The Install New Modem wizard automates modem configuration.

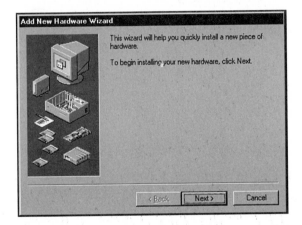

Figure 4.2

The Add New Hardware wizard steps you through installing a device.

As well as making it easier for you to install and configure devices such as CD-ROM drives, sound cards, and video adapters, Windows 95 also makes it much simpler to install printers, particularly across the network. To install support for a network printer, you often can just drag the printer's icon from the Network Neighborhood folder to your desktop. Windows 95 automatically copies the necessary driver files from the server to which the printer is connected. (For more information about installing and using printers, refer to Chapter 8, "Printing and Managing Printers.")

The following sections briefly explain some of the other improvements in Windows 95 for hardware configuration and support.

Better Device Management

Windows 95 improves your ability to view, manage, and modify drivers and hardware configuration settings. The Device Manager, which you access by using the System object in the Control Panel, provides a unified mechanism for managing your drivers and hardware settings. The Device Manager is explored in detail later in this chapter in the section "Controlling Devices with the Device Manager."

Improved Driver Structure

A major improvement in Windows 95 over previous versions of Windows and DOS is a shift from monolithic vendor-supplied drivers to minidrivers that are a part of the Windows 95 operating system. Instead of relying on a hardware manufacturer to supply a unique driver for each device, Microsoft has expanded the minidriver concept used in Windows 3.*x* for printers to many other types of devices in Windows 95. Windows 95 includes minidrivers for modems, display adapters, mice, printers, and other classes of devices. These additional minidrivers simplify writing device drivers for Windows 95, and enable better driver performance through the use of 32-bit minidrivers.

32-Bit System Drivers

Although Windows 95's minidrivers provide better performance for peripheral devices, Windows 95's system virtual device drivers provide overall improved hardware performance. Microsoft replaces many of the system drivers found in previous versions of Windows and DOS with 32-bit virtual device drivers to improve performance. These new device drivers including the following:

- ◆ Virtual FAT file system
- ◆ SmartDrive disk cache
- ◆ CD-ROM file system
- ◆ Network clients, protocols, and services
- ◆ PCMCIA driver
- ◆ Virtual Share (vshare) driver to replace Share.exe
- ◆ Drivers for hard disks, including SCSI devices
- ◆ DriveSpace support (which includes DoubleSpace support)

Many of these items are described in detail in other chapters.

Support for PCMCIA Devices

The proliferation of notebook computers has pushed PCMCIA support up into the important issue class. Windows 95 includes excellent support for PCMCIA devices on notebooks as well as on desktop systems (which use PCMCIA docking modules). Windows 95 supports PCMCIA devices through included 32-bit device drivers and Card and Socket Services.

Windows 95 supports hot-swapping and auto-configuration of PCMCIA devices. You can remove and insert PCMCIA devices without powering down the system or shutting down Windows 95. You can plug in a modem, for example, and Windows 95 automatically configures the modem so that you can begin using it. Inserting a network adapter causes Windows 95 to automatically make the network available and updates the interface to show available network resources.

Support for Docking Stations

Windows 95 provides support for *hot docking,* or dynamically docking and undocking a notebook computer from a docking station without shutting down Windows 95 or powering down the PC. Windows 95 automatically resolves potential conflicts when you dock and undock the computer, such as open remote files, pending print jobs, establishing and disconnecting network services, changes in display resolution, and other issues.

Dynamically Loaded Device Drivers

To improve memory performance, Windows 95 supports dynamically loadable device drivers, which enables Windows 95 to load a device driver when it is needed and remove the driver from memory when the driver is not needed. The PCMCIA drivers, for example, are dynamic and loaded only when a device is inserted into a socket. When the device is removed, its driver is removed from memory. This dynamic device driver design also is implemented with other Windows 95 device drivers.

Getting Ready to Install New Devices

Now that you have some background in the performance and structural changes in Windows 95 that relate to hardware installation and configuration, you're ready to begin installing and managing your hardware. The following section explains how to take advantage of Plug and Play and Windows 95's support for automatic installation of non–Plug and Play devices.

Understanding and Using Automatic Configuration

Windows 95 automates hardware installation and configuration in many instances, providing support for Plug and Play and automatic installation of non–Plug and Play devices (such as standard ISA adapters). By far, Plug and Play is one of the most significant usability improvements in Windows 95 for the average user. The following section explains Plug and Play and how you can take advantage of it.

Understanding Plug and Play

Plug and Play refers to a set of industry specifications that define mechanisms by which the computer's operating system (in this case, Windows 95) can detect and configure hardware. The majority of hardware manufacturers now design their adapters and peripherals to support Plug and Play. Systems and hardware not designed to support Plug and Play are referred to as *legacy* systems and hardware.

Installing legacy hardware in legacy systems is often confusing and difficult for the average user. With adapters, for example, you often must manually configure settings on the adapter. Specifying settings that work properly in your system requires that you know the settings that other devices use and which settings the new device can use. Conflicting settings often severely upsets the system or the hardware.

Installing and configuring new hardware in a true Plug and Play system, however, is almost effortless. You simply install the device, and the Plug and Play BIOS, in conjunction with Windows 95, detects the hardware, configures it using settings that do not conflict with other devices, and installs the necessary driver support for the device. Essentially, the device configures itself.

Although systems that have Plug and Play BIOSs are only now becoming more common, you still can take advantage of Plug and Play to an extent on legacy systems. As explained in more detail in the section "Understanding Hardware Detection" in Chapter 3, Windows 95 Setup searches in memory, ROM, and configuration files for hints of legacy devices for which it can automatically install support. Setup often can automatically detect and install support for a device, even if it is not Plug and Play compliant.

A number of different types of devices are common in today's PCs, and many of these types of devices can support Plug and Play. The following sections explain some of the issues relating to these device types.

ISA Devices

ISA stands for Industry Standard Architecture. The ISA bus and its associated devices were introduced in the IBM AT. The vast majority of PCs in use today contain ISA buses, although the number of new systems that contain PCI local buses is gradually overtaking the number of ISA bus systems.

Windows 95 can automatically detect and install support for many ISA devices through hints and autodetection features built into Windows 95. In addition, legacy ISA devices and Plug and Play devices can coexist in standard ISA-based systems with or without a Plug and Play BIOS.

EISA Devices

EISA stands for Enhanced Industry Standard Architecture. The EISA bus is an extension of the ISA bus. EISA devices typically are software-configurable, similar to today's new Plug and Play devices. Windows 95 supports automatic detection and configuration of EISA devices, although Windows 95 does not allocate resources to the EISA devices. Instead, Windows 95 reads the EISA device's resource requirements from the device's nonvolatile RAM where its configuration information is stored. EISA systems can contain ISA, EISA, and Plug and Play devices.

SCSI Devices

SCSI stands for Small Computer Standard Interface. Common SCSI devices include hard disks, tape drives, CD-ROM drives, and scanners. The SCSI subsystem enables multiple devices to be daisy-chained together on a single SCSI host adapter. The host adapter connects the SCSI devices to the PC's bus, enabling the devices to communicate with the CPU.

Legacy SCSI host adapters and devices require manual configuration of device IDs and manual bus termination. Plug and Play SCSI host adapters and devices can be configured and terminated automatically.

PCMCIA Devices

PCMCIA stands for Personal Computer Memory Card International Association. PCMCIA devices are credit card–sized adapters that install in special PCMCIA bus slots, usually in notebook and other portable computers. PCMCIA adapters are now available for desktop systems, enabling you to use PCMCIA devices in desktop computers.

The Windows 95 32-bit PCMCIA drivers and Card and Socket Services support Plug and Play for PCMCIA devices, including automatic detection and configuration and *hot-swapping* (removing and installing PCMCIA devices while the system is powered up and Windows 95 is running). If your PCMCIA device requires a manufacturer-supplied real-mode driver, many Plug and Play PCMCIA features will not be available for the device.

For more information on using PCMCIA devices, read the section "Configuring and Using PCMCIA Devices" later in this chapter.

VESA Local Bus and PCI Local Bus Devices

VESA stands for Video Electronic Standards Association. The VESA local (VL) bus provides a high-speed direct connection between the CPU and the VL device, enabling faster performance than possible using a standard ISA bus. VL bus devices are limited primarily to video adapters, although some VL bus disk adapters are available. VL bus devices are treated like legacy ISA devices in Windows 95.

The PCI (Peripheral Component Interconnect) bus also is a high-speed bus, similar to the VL bus, that provides direct connection between the CPU and peripheral devices for increased performance. The PCI bus is used in most Pentium-based and PowerPC-based systems. PCI bus devices are handled similarly to EISA-based devices—Windows 95 does not configure PCI devices, but instead reads the resource requirements from the device's nonvolatile RAM.

Installing a Plug and Play Device

Installing a Plug and Play device is truly a simple task: turn off the computer, install the device, then turn on the computer. If the system contains a Plug and Play BIOS, the BIOS recognizes the new device, as does Windows 95. Windows 95 then configures the device so that it doesn't conflict with any other devices and installs support for the device so that you can begin using it. Even if the system does not contain a Plug and Play BIOS, Windows 95 usually can properly detect, configure, and install support for the device. If the driver is not already installed, Windows 95 prompts you to insert the Windows 95 disk (or CD) that contains the driver.

Note Automatic detection and configuration of Plug and Play devices, as well as many legacy devices, occurs automatically when Windows 95 starts. After you install the device and turn on the computer, you see the standard Windows 95 logon dialog box. After you supply a valid logon name and password, Windows 95 displays a dialog box that informs you it has detected new hardware and will install support for it. If Windows 95 is unable to complete the configuration and installation process on its own, a hardware setup wizard appears to step you through installing the device.

Installing and Configuring Hardware Manually

In some cases, you must manually configure and install a device if you want to use it with Windows 95. Even so, the process is relatively simple. If you install a legacy device that Windows 95 can detect, Windows 95 probably can complete the installation process on its own, prompting you for a driver disk if necessary.

Sometimes Windows 95 can detect that a new device has been installed, but cannot correctly detect the device type or install support for the device. Sometimes Windows 95 cannot detect the device at all. Either way, you can use the Add New Hardware wizard to install support for the new device.

After you install or attach the device, start Windows 95 and open the Control Panel. Choose the Add New Hardware icon to start the Add New Hardware wizard, then click on the Next button. At this point, you must choose whether you want Windows 95 to try to detect the new device (see fig. 4.3). Because Windows 95 did not detect and install the device automatically, the wizard probably will not be able to detect the device. Choose the Yes option button if you want the wizard to try to detect the device, or choose the No button if you want to manually specify the device manufacturer and model.

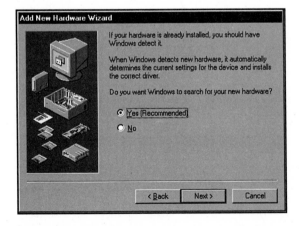

Figure 4.3

The initial dialog box of the Add New Hardware wizard.

If you choose Yes, the hardware wizard attempts to detect the new hardware installed in your PC. At the completion of the hardware detection, the wizard pauses to let you view the hardware it found. To do so, choose the Details button in the wizard's dialog box to view the list of detected devices (see fig. 4.4). Click on the Finish button to enable the wizard to install support for all devices in the list.

Figure 4.4

*The Add New
Hardware wizard
can display a list
of detected
devices.*

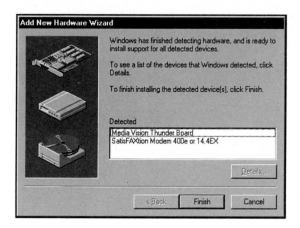

 Tip   Although you can't select only some devices from the detection list, you can use the
Device Manager to remove devices after the wizard completes the installation.

If you choose No to prevent the wizard from attempting to detect the hardware, a
dialog box appears, as shown in figure 4.5. From the hardware list, choose the type of
device you want to install. Then, click on Next. The wizard displays a hardware
selection dialog box (see fig. 4.6) you can use to specify the manufacturer and model
of the device you are installing.

Figure 4.5

*Choose the type of
hardware you are
installing.*

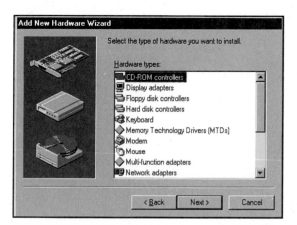

After you select the device you want to install, click on the Next button to enable the
wizard to install the necessary drivers for the device. If the device manufacturer and
model aren't listed, but the device includes a driver disk, choose Have Disk. The
wizard prompts you to insert the driver disk so that it can copy the driver files to your
PC and configure the device.

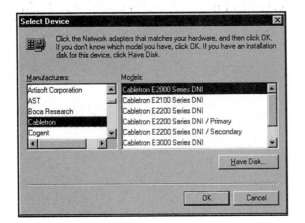

Figure 4.6

Specify the manufacturer and model of the device.

Depending on the device, the wizard might also prompt you to supply resource information about the device (see fig. 4.7). Resource information often includes IRQ, DMA, or I/O address range information. Specify the correct settings, then click on Next and follow the prompts to complete the installation. Before you can use some devices, you have to restart Windows 95; when the wizard completes the installation process, Windows 95 displays a prompt asking if you want to restart the system.

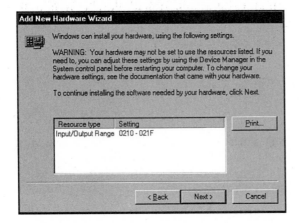

Figure 4.7

Specify resource information about the device.

Note Although you can install nearly any device using the Add New Hardware wizard, you also can install some types of devices using other objects in the Control Panel. The Modems object enables you to add a new modem, for example, and the Network object enables you to add a new adapter (although Windows 95 probably automatically recognizes the adapter when you start up the system after you

continues

install it). For more information on installing and configuring modems, refer to Chapter 28, "Modems and Data Communications." For information on installing and configuring network adapters, refer to Chapter 2, "Setting Up and Booting Windows 95," and Chapter 34, "Network Concepts and Configuration."

Configuring and Using PCMCIA Devices

If your PC includes PCMCIA slots, Setup should automatically detect and install support for PCMCIA devices. If Windows 95 detects PCMCIA slots in your PC, the PCMCIA object appears in the Control Panel and a PCMCIA object also appears in the Device Manager (choose the System object in Control Panel to access the Device Manager). Setup also runs the PCMCIA wizard the first time you start Windows 95 to configure the PCMCIA drivers.

To enable PCMCIA support if Setup cannot do so automatically, run the PCMCIA wizard (choose the PCMCIA object in the Control Panel or choose the PCMCIA controller object in the Device Manager).

 Note   Windows 95 supports Intel-compatible and Databook-compatible PCMCIA sockets for full Plug and Play performance, and also supports the use of real-mode drivers for other types of PCMCIA sockets and devices.

The PCMCIA wizard adds 32-bit PCMCIA driver support for the PCMCIA devices, and removes (comments out) any real-mode PCMCIA drivers from the Config.sys file. To determine whether Windows 95 supports your PCMCIA controller, open the Control Panel and start the Add New Hardware wizard. When prompted whether you want the wizard to detect hardware, choose No. Choose PCMCIA socket from the Hardware types list, then click on Next. Windows 95 displays a list of the manufacturers and models supported by Windows 95 drivers (see fig. 4.8). This is a list of PCMCIA controllers, not PCMCIA devices. After the controller is working properly, Windows 95 should be able to automatically detect and install the drivers for the individual PCMCIA cards.

If your PCMCIA controller is not supported by a 32-bit Windows driver, you must use the real-mode drivers for the PCMCIA controller supplied with the PC or controller device (and in some cases, provided with the PCMCIA devices). In the case of PCMCIA network adapters, the PCMCIA socket driver and network driver both must be Plug and Play–compatible to work properly. If you use an NDIS 3.1 network driver, you must use the 32-bit Windows 95 PCMCIA socket driver. If you use a real-mode network driver, you must use a real-mode socket driver.

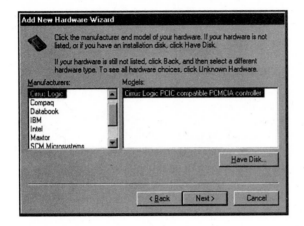

Figure 4.8

Some of the PCMCIA controller devices supported by Windows 95.

Using the 32-Bit PCMCIA Drivers

If your PC contains a PCMCIA controller, Setup should automatically detect it during installation. To configure your PC to use the Windows 95 32-bit PCMCIA socket driver, run the PCMCIA wizard in the Control Panel, or double-click on the PCMCIA object in the Device Manager. The PCMCIA wizard installs the 32-bit drivers and comments out the real-mode drivers in the Config.sys file. Then restart the system so that the new drivers can take effect.

To verify that enhanced PCMCIA support is enabled, open the Device Manager and choose the PCMCIA object, then click on the General tab to display the General property page (see fig. 4.9). A check beside a hardware profile in the Device Usage list indicates that enhanced PCMCIA support is enabled.

Specifying PCMCIA Controller and Device Settings

Windows 95 uses a common set of configuration settings for the PCMCIA slots when you use the drivers supplied with Windows 95, which works well for most devices. These settings include IRQ and memory window (RAM address range) settings. Some devices, however, require settings different from what Windows 95 uses. If your PCMCIA device(s) does not work, changing the memory window and/or the IRQ of the device might overcome the problem.

To specify new settings for the memory window, open the Control Panel and choose the PCMCIA icon to display the PC Card property sheet. Click on the Global Settings tab to display the Global Settings property page, shown in figure 4.10.

Figure 4.9

The General property page for a PCMCIA controller.

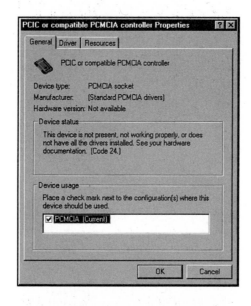

Figure 4.10

The Global Settings property page for PCMCIA devices.

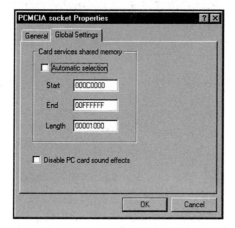

If the Automatic selection check box is enabled, Windows 95 automatically assigns values for the memory window. To specify a different value, clear the Automatic selection check box, then enter different start and end values in the Start and End text boxes based on the requirements specified in the documentation for your PCMCIA devices. Choose OK to apply the changes.

To change the resources (IRQ and I/O port settings) that the PCMCIA controller uses, choose the System object in the Control Panel, then click on the Device Manager tab to display the Device Manager property page. Locate the PCMCIA controller in the Device Manager's hardware list, then double-click on the PCMCIA controller or select it and choose Properties. Windows 95 displays a property sheet for the PCMCIA controller; click on the Resources tab to display the Resources property page shown in figure 4.11.

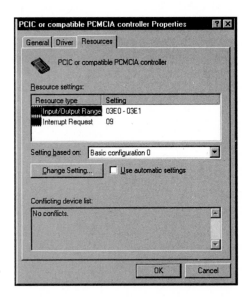

Figure 4.11

The Resources property page for a PCMCIA controller.

You can choose from six basic configurations by selecting an option from the Setting based on drop-down list. If none of the six configurations matches your hardware requirements, select the resource you would like to change from the Resource settings list, then choose the Change Setting button. A dialog box appears in which you can change the setting for the device (see fig. 4.12).

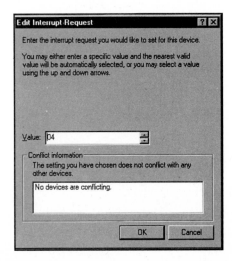

Figure 4.12

Specify the IRQ in the Edit Interrupt Request dialog box.

You also can change the settings of individual PCMCIA devices. Double-click on the PCMCIA device in the Device Manager, or select the device and choose P<u>r</u>operties. Windows 95 displays a typical property page for the device. Choose the Resources tab, then choose the <u>S</u>et Configuration Manually button to display a property page. Specify the correct IRQ and memory settings for the device, then choose OK to apply the changes.

Hot-Swapping PCMCIA Devices

If your PCMCIA controller and devices use the 32-bit drivers provided by Windows 95, you can *hot-swap* PCMCIA devices, which means you can insert and remove PCMCIA devices without shutting down Windows 95 or powering down your PC. If you want to temporarily remove your network adapter to use a modem, for example, you can leave Windows 95 running.

Before you remove a device, however, you should shut down the device to ensure that it is not actively using resources that could become corrupted (such as an open file) or cause the system to lock up. To stop a PCMCIA device, choose the PCMCIA object in the Control Panel to display the Socket Status dialog box. Select the device you want to stop, then choose <u>S</u>top. Windows 95 displays a message indicating when you can remove the device.

 Tip   You don't need to do a thing before you insert a PCMCIA card in a socket. Simply verify that any necessary cables are attached to the card, then insert the card in its socket. If the device has previously been used in the computer, Windows 95 loads the device drivers for the device and enables the device. If the device has not been used before, Windows 95 detects the device and installs support for it automatically, prompting you for the location of the Windows 95 distribution disks or CD, if necessary. If you use real-mode PCMCIA controller drivers, however, automatic detection and installation probably will not work and you will have to use the Add New Hardware wizard to manually add the device driver.

Controlling Devices with the Device Manager

The Device Manager, which is a property page on the System property sheet, enables you to view and control the devices installed in your PC. Device Manager enables you to change drivers for a device, remove devices from the system, print a summary of a device or all devices in the PC, and print a system summary. The following sections explain these uses.

Viewing and Changing Device Properties

To view and change the properties of a device or class, open the Control Panel and choose the System object. Click on the Device Manager tab to display the Device Manager property page, similar to the one shown in figure 4.13.

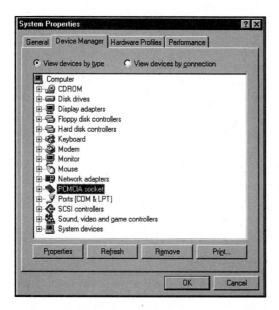

Figure 4.13

The Device Manager property page.

By default, the Device Manager shows the devices in your PC organized by device class as a hierarchical tree, as shown in figure 4.13. To view the devices in a particular class, click on the plus sign (+) next to the class name to expand its branch, as shown in figure 4.14. To collapse the branch, click on the minus sign (–) beside the class name.

A device's branch shows the devices that fall under that class. In the Disk drives branch, for example, all the disk drives listed are installed in your PC (refer to figure 4.14 for an example). To view the properties of a particular device, open the branch in which the device is located, then double-click on the device or select it and choose Properties. The resulting property sheet naturally varies from one device type to another because of the differences between devices. Some devices have a single property page, but others have several.

All devices have a General property page that provides general information about the device (such as manufacturer), its driver, and whether the device is working properly. Most devices also have additional pages that enable you to view and set various properties for the device. For example, figure 4.15 shows the Settings property page for a hard disk drive, figure 4.16 shows the Driver page for a video adapter, and figure 4.17 shows the Resources page for a hard disk controller. These all are fairly typical representations of device property pages.

Figure 4.14

The Disk drives branch expanded in the Device Manager.

Figure 4.15

The Settings property page for a hard disk.

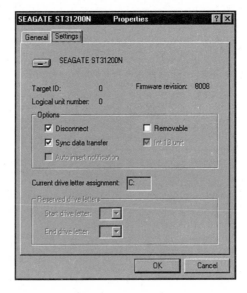

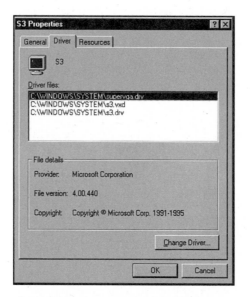

Figure 4.16

The Driver page for a video adapter.

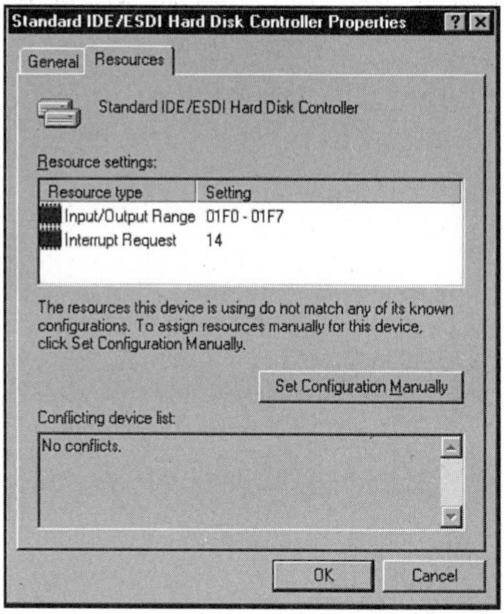

Figure 4.17

The Resources page for a hard disk controller.

Later sections of this chapter discuss changes you might want to make to specific devices. The following sections explain changes you can make to devices in general.

Changing Drivers

If you want or need to change the driver for a device, you can use the Device Manager. If the device supports a driver change, the device's property sheet includes a Driver page similar to the one shown in figure 4.18.

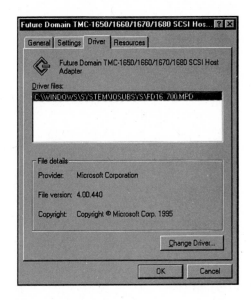

Figure 4.18

A typical Driver property page.

The Driver property page lists the current driver(s) for the device, as well as other information about the driver files. To change drivers, choose the Change Driver button to display the Select Device dialog box shown in figure 4.19. From the Models list, select the device model for which you want to install support. If the device you want to use is not listed, choose the Show all devices option button. If you have a driver disk supplied by the device's manufacturer, choose the Have Disk button. Windows 95 then prompts you to insert the driver disk or specify the path to its location. After you locate and select the appropriate device, choose OK and follow the prompts to complete the driver installation process.

Changing Device Resource Assignments

You might need to change the resources a device uses to overcome a resource conflict or to make a resource available for a new device you install. For example, you might need to change the IRQ a device uses because it conflicts with another device. If a device supports resource changes, the device includes a Resources property page similar to the one shown in figure 4.20.

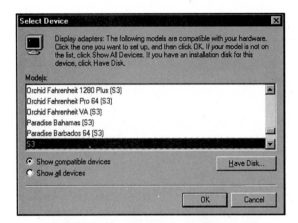

Figure 4.19

The Select Device dialog box.

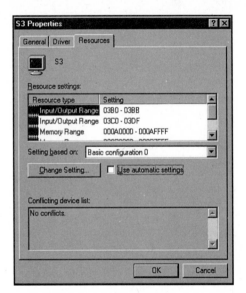

Figure 4.20

A typical device Resources property page.

To change resources for a device, first open its Resources page. If the Resources page includes a Set Configuration Manually button, click on it to display additional controls on the property page that enable you to change resources for the device. Next, clear the Use automatic settings check box to enable the resource controls on the property page.

Windows 95 provides multiple basic configurations for many types of devices. These basic configurations are nothing more than common combinations of IRQ, I/O, and DMA settings (where appropriate) for that type of device. You can select a configuration from the drop-down list, which changes the resources displayed in the Resource settings list. When you find the set of resources values that work for your device, choose OK to apply the changes.

To specify a combination of settings that differs from the predefined basic configurations, choose the setting in the <u>R</u>esource settings list, then choose the <u>C</u>hange Setting button. Windows 95 displays a message if you can't change the setting. Otherwise, a dialog box appears that enables you to specify a new value for the resource setting (see fig. 4.21). Specify a new value, then choose OK to make the change take effect.

Figure 4.21

A dialog box for changing IRQ values.

Removing a Device

Sometimes you have to remove a driver. Windows 95 might incorrectly install two copies of a device, for example, and you need to remove the duplicate. Or, you might remove a component from your system and/or replace it with another device, and then you don't need the old driver anymore.

To remove a device, choose the System object in the Control Panel, then click on the Device Manager tab to display the Device Manager property page. Select the device you want to remove, then choose <u>R</u>emove. If you select a device class from the tree, the entire class and all of its devices are removed. If you open a class and select an individual device, then choose <u>R</u>emove, only the selected device is removed. In many cases, removing a device requires restarting Windows 95, and you are prompted to do so when necessary.

Setting Specific Device Properties

Detailing every setting of every possible device type is impractical. Instead, the following sections provide an overview of the settings for common devices that you are most likely to need or want to change. The following sections do not cover changing drivers or resource settings, because these two topics are covered earlier in the chapter, in the sections "Changing Drivers" and "Changing Device Resource Assignments." Changing modem and COM port properties is explained in Chapter 28, "Modems and Data Communications."

Changing CD-ROM Settings

The Settings property page for a CD-ROM drive (see fig. 4.22) typically shows the SCSI logical unit number, defined by the SCSI host adapter, and the device ID, defined by the hardware settings on the CD-ROM drive itself. The only settings you might need or want to change on the CD-ROM Settings property page are the following:

◆ **Auto insert notification.** This check box, if enabled, causes Windows 95 to receive notification when you insert a CD into the drive. If you insert an audio CD, Windows 95 opens the CD Player and begins to play the CD. If you insert a program CD, Windows 95 starts the program, but only if the CD supports the Windows 95 AutoPlay feature. AutoPlay has no effect on data or program CDs not specifically developed for Windows 95 AutoPlay.

◆ **Start drive letter.** This setting specifies the beginning drive letter that Windows 95 reserves for removable devices such as CD-ROM drives. The value of this setting defaults to the first drive letter available after your last hard disk drive letter.

◆ **End drive letter.** This setting specifies the ending drive letter that Windows 95 reserves for removable devices. Increase the value of this setting if you want to make additional drive IDs available for removable drives.

Note Typically, you need not change any settings for a hard disk drive or a floppy disk drive.

Figure 4.22

The Settings property page for a CD-ROM drive.

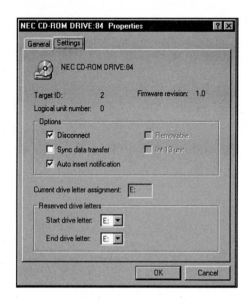

Setting SCSI Host Adapter Properties

If your SCSI host adapter requires or can use optional command-line switches to enable special options or features, you can use the Device Manager to add those command-line switches. In the Device Manager, choose the SCSI host adapter from the SCSI controllers class, then choose Properties. Click on the Settings tab to display the Settings property page shown in figure 4.23. Enter the command-line switches in the Adapter settings text box, then choose OK.

Figure 4.23

The Settings property page for a SCSI host adapter.

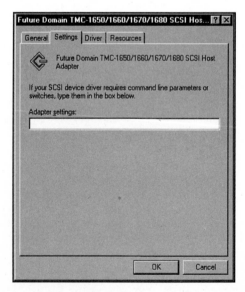

Note The command-line switches supported by a SCSI host adapter driver depend solely on the host adapter.

Setting System Device Properties

You usually do not have to change any of the settings for the devices listed in the System class. In certain situations, however, you might need or want to make some changes to improve performance. The following sections explain some of the changes you can make to common System class devices in the Device Manager.

Changing DMA Settings

The direct memory access (DMA) controller device in the system class includes two groups of settings you can use to control how Windows 95 handles DMA. Figure 4.24 shows the Settings property page for the direct memory access control device, which you can access by double-clicking on the direct memory access controller object in the System devices class.

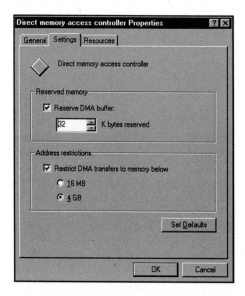

Figure 4.24

The Settings property page of the direct memory access controller.

The first of these groups, Reserved memory, enables you to specify an amount of RAM to use as a DMA buffer. This setting can be required to increase the DMA buffer size for your network adapter to function properly if you use real-mode network drivers, and also can help overcome problems with other devices that require DMA buffering. To increase the DMA buffer size, place a check in the Reserve DMA buffer check box, then specify the size of the buffer in kilobytes with the associated increment control.

The Address restrictions group on the Settings property page enables you to restrict the memory area in which DMA transfers occur. To set a transfer limit, enable the check box in the Address restrictions group, then choose either the 16 MB or 4 GB option.

Changing Floating-Point Coprocessor Settings

The Numeric data processor device in the System devices class refers to your PC's math coprocessor, sometimes referred to as a *floating-point unit*, or FPU. In 386 and earlier Intel-compatible processors, the FPU is separate from the CPU. In 486- and Pentium-based CPUs (excluding the 486SX), the FPU is an integral part of the CPU. The FPU designed for the 486SX CPU is a separate chip usually referred to as the 487.

The FPU handles the majority of the floating-point math operations in your PC. By performing the calculations in hardware rather than in software, the FPU significantly speeds the performance of applications that rely on math operations (if the application can take advantage of the FPU). Some applications actually require the presence of an FPU to run.

Early versions of the Pentium suffer from a bug in the FPU that results in math errors. The Settings page of the numeric data processor's property sheet (see fig. 4.25) enables you to control whether Windows 95 uses the FPU in your system. Windows 95 performs a set of diagnostics on the FPU to determine whether it functions correctly. You can use the three option buttons in the Settings group to control whether Windows 95 uses the FPU. If you turn off the FPU, Windows 95 handles math operations in software rather than hardware. This slows down performance but ensures that an FPU error does not affect the accuracy of your applications.

Printing System and Device Summaries

A useful feature of the Device Manager is the capability to print system and device summaries. A system summary includes information about your system, such as the processor type, BIOS information, machine type, Windows version, and bus type. The system summary also includes a summary of your system's IRQ, I/O port, UMA (upper memory area), and DMA usage. To print a system summary, open the Device Manager, choose the Print button to display the Print dialog box (see fig. 4.26), then choose the System summary option.

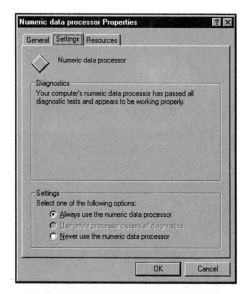

Figure 4.25

The Settings property page for the math coprocessor.

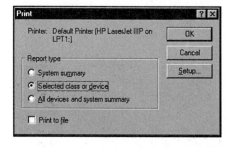

Figure 4.26

The Print dialog box for printing system and device summaries.

If you select a device class from the Device Manager's list before you choose the Print button, you can choose the Selected class or device option from the Print dialog box. This option prints a report of the selected class, including the resources (IRQ, DMA, I/O port) and drivers each device in the class uses. If you select a single device in a class, this option prints a similar report of only the selected device.

The All devices and system summary option in the Print dialog box prints a system summary and a report for all classes and devices in your system.

 Tip   You can choose the Print to file check box to print the report to a file rather than the printer. The file contains embedded printer codes for the selected printer. To print a report to an ASCII file without printer codes, use the Add Printer wizard in the

continues

Printers folder to add the Generic / Text Only printer, then print your reports to that printer. You can connect the Generic / Text Only printer to the FILE: port or enable the Print to file check box in the Print dialog box to direct the output to a file.

Using Multiple Hardware Profiles

Windows 95 enables you to maintain multiple hardware profiles and choose from those profiles when you boot the system. Each profile references its own set of devices (many of which are naturally duplicated in each profile), and you can enable or disable a device for a specific profile. When Windows 95 starts, it loads only the device drivers for the devices in the selected profile.

Tip   If Windows 95 can't determine which profile your PC should use when the PC boots, Windows 95 displays a menu that enables you to choose which profile you want to use to boot the PC.

Windows 95 automatically recognizes most docking stations and supports hot docking, which enables you to dock and undock your notebook computer without shutting down Windows 95 or powering down the system. For this reason, multiple hardware profiles generally are not required to support docking stations. In some cases, however, you might need to create and use profiles to support your docking station. You also might want to create multiple hardware profiles in situations in which you use a device only occasionally, and that device puts an abnormal load on the system or conflicts with other devices. In the case of a device conflict, you can remove one of the conflicting devices from each of the profiles, eliminating the conflict. (The ideal solution, however, would be to resolve the conflict within the profile by changing the resource requirements of the devices.)

Tip   Although Windows 95 does not store different resource settings for a device in different profiles, you can add multiple instances of a device, specifying different resource settings for each one. You then can enable one instance for one profile, and a different instance for another profile. The methods for using different resource settings for a device are explained later in the section "Using Different Resource Settings."

Creating a Hardware Profile

You cannot directly create a hardware profile. Instead, you must copy an existing profile, giving it a new name. You then can add or remove devices as necessary from your hardware profiles. To copy a profile, open the Control Panel, choose the System object, then click on the Hardware Profiles tab to display the Hardware Profiles property page shown in figure 4.27.

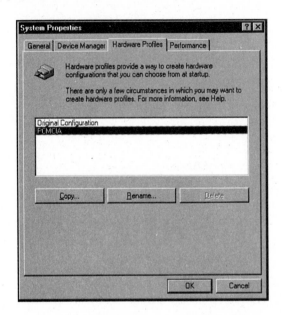

Figure 4.27

The Hardware Profiles property page.

Select from the list in the Hardware Profiles property page the profile you want to copy. By default, your system includes a hardware profile named Original Configuration. Then choose Copy. Windows 95 displays a simple dialog box you can use to enter a name for the new profile. Specify the name of your choice and choose OK. If, later, you want to rename any profile, just select the profile and choose Rename. Windows 95 prompts you for a new name.

When you create a profile, Windows 95 places all the devices in the source profile in the new profile. You then must modify the profiles, adding or removing devices as necessary. To modify a profile, open the Device Manager property page. Then, select the device you want to add or remove from a profile and display its property sheet. If the device can be removed from the selected profile, the General property page for the device includes a Device usage group that lists all the defined hardware profiles (see fig. 4.28). Beside each profile name is a check box. If the check box is enabled for a profile, the selected device driver will be used in that profile. If the check box is cleared, the device will not be used in that profile. Simply enable or clear the check boxes as necessary, then choose OK.

Figure 4.28

The Device usage group in a General property page.

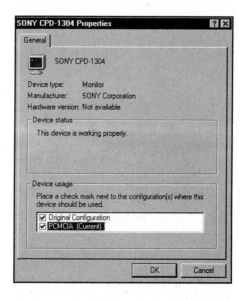

Tip   To add a device to a profile when the device is not yet installed on the system, first run the Add New Hardware wizard to install the device. Then, open the Hardware Profiles property page and add or remove the device in the appropriate profiles.

When you remove a device in Device Manager, Windows 95 displays the Confirm Device Removal dialog box (see fig. 4.29), which enables you to remove a device from all configurations or only a specific configuration.

Figure 4.29

The Confirm Device Removal dialog box.

Using Different Resource Settings

You cannot maintain different sets of resource settings from one profile to another for the same instance of a device. You can, however, add multiple instances of a device, then apply different resource settings to each instance. Then, you can add and remove instances of the driver from various profiles to achieve the end result of maintaining different resource settings for the same physical device.

To install multiple instances of a device, run the Add New Hardware wizard in the Control Panel and choose manual installation (bypass hardware detection). Use the process described previously in this chapter to install another copy of the device, then use the Device Manager to set its resource properties as necessary. Next, use the Hardware Profiles property page to add and remove devices from each profile as necessary.

Using Real-Mode and Windows 3.x Drivers

Windows 95 includes 32-bit protected-mode drivers for a wide variety of hardware, and in most cases, you won't have to use older 16-bit real-mode drivers for the devices in your PC. In certain cases in which Windows 95 doesn't include a 32-bit driver for a device, you can use another driver for a compatible device. In some situations, however, you have to continue to use the real-mode drivers that came with the device until the manufacturer makes a Windows 95 driver available for the device.

Generally, Windows 95 leaves real-mode drivers in place for devices during Setup if Setup cannot provide protected-mode driver support for the device. In these situations, the drivers are usually loaded in the Config.sys or Autoexec.bat file. If you need to use a real-mode driver for a device, you can install the driver in two ways. The first method is to use the Add New Hardware wizard to install the device. Direct the wizard not to detect the device, and when the wizard displays the manufacturer and model dialog box, choose the Have Disk button. Specify the path to the driver disk that was supplied with the device, then follow the remaining prompts to complete the installation process.

If the device includes a device driver disk but doesn't support automatic installation by Windows 95, you still can add support for the device. Copy the driver file(s) from the driver disk to your computer, then modify your Config.sys and Autoexec.bat files as necessary to add entries for the driver file(s) according to the device's documentation.

Note If you boot the system to DOS to modify the Config.sys and Autoexec.bat files, remember that Windows 95 actually maintains two sets of configuration files. When the system is booted to DOS, the Windows 95 Config.sys and Autoexec.bat files, if any, are named Config.win and Autoexec.win. If you boot the system to the Windows 95 command line, however, the correct files to edit are Config.sys and Autoexec.bat.

Overcoming Device Conflicts

If two devices attempt to use the same resources, such as IRQ, DMA channel, or I/O addresses, a *device conflict* occurs. Device conflicts sometimes are relatively harmless. You can share IRQ values between two COM ports, for example, as long as you don't try to use the two ports at the same time. With other types of devices, however, a device conflict can cause the system to hang or even refuse to boot.

Note EISA and MCA bus systems are capable of sharing interrupts in hardware.

If you use true Plug and Play systems and devices, device conflicts should not occur because the system can automatically detect available resources and assign them to a new device. When you use devices that do not support Plug and Play, or you use some Plug and Play devices on a legacy system, device conflict still can be a problem.

The best solution to device conflicts is to avoid them. Before you install a new device, open the Device Manager property page and print a system and device summary for the system. Check the printout to determine available resources for the new device, then configure the device for those available resources. After you install the device, use the Device Manager to apply the correct resource settings to the device if the Add New Hardware wizard can't detect or set the correct resources.

Windows 95 also provides an automated tool to help you troubleshoot device conflicts. You can access the Hardware Conflict Troubleshooter from the Windows 95 Help index. To open the Troubleshooter, choose Start, then Help, or press Win+F1 on the Microsoft Natural Keyboard. In the Contents pane, choose the Troubleshooting topic, then choose "If you have a hardware conflict" from the Troubleshooting tree to open the Troubleshooter (see fig. 4.30).

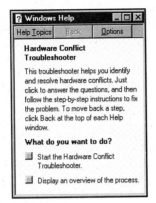

Figure 4.30

The Hardware Conflict Troubleshooter.

Click on the button labeled Start the Hardware Conflict Troubleshooter. The Troubleshooter then steps you through troubleshooting the device conflict. Follow the prompts to identify and correct the problem.

Part II

Working in Windows 95

Working in Windows 95

The Windows 95 graphical user interface (GUI) is very different from the Windows 3.*x* interface. The new Windows 95 interface improves the usability of your PC and simplifies a variety of tasks. Accessing network resources in Windows 95, for example, is significantly easier than in Windows 3.*x*.

This chapter examines the Windows 95 interface and explores the ways in which you can use Windows 95 to perform common tasks, such as starting applications and working with documents. The chapter includes the following topics:

◆ Working with the Windows 95 desktop

◆ Introducing Explorer

◆ Working with folders

◆ Working with applications and documents

◆ Using the keyboard

◆ Using and creating shortcuts

◆ Customizing the Taskbar and Start menu

◆ Starting applications automatically

◆ Using the Recycle Bin

Inside Windows 95 targets intermediate to advanced users, so this chapter assumes you have a handle on mouse fundamentals. Experience with Windows 3.*x* or a GUI, such as those found in OS/2 and many versions of Unix, is helpful but not necessary.

Tip   This chapter doesn't cover basic user interface concepts, such as moving the mouse pointer, types of mouse pointers, or working with menus and dialog boxes. If you need a complete explanation of these topics, refer to *Understanding Windows 95,* from New Riders Publishing.

Some of the interface components and concepts in this chapter are explained in brief just to give you an overview of the Windows 95 interface. Where appropriate, these concepts are covered in greater detail elsewhere in *Inside Windows 95.*

Working with the Windows 95 Desktop

The Windows 95 interface consists of two key features—the desktop and the Taskbar (see fig. 5.1). The *desktop* essentially is a blank surface on which all other Windows components appear. The *Taskbar* provides various status information about your PC and enables you to start applications and switch among running applications.

Figure 5.1

The Windows 95 desktop and Taskbar.

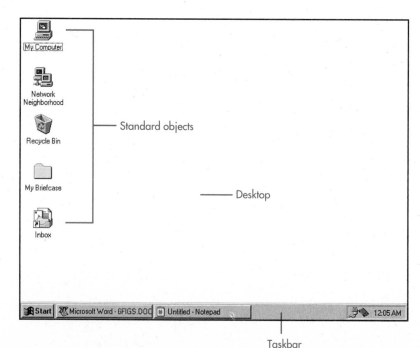

The Windows 95 default desktop includes My Computer, Network Neighborhood, and the Recycle Bin, among other objects. Before you read about these objects, you need a brief introduction to folders. Later sections explain folders in more detail.

Understanding Folders

The objects on the desktop named My Computer, Network Neighborhood, and Recycle Bin are examples of folders. *Folders* provide a uniform means of organizing and displaying information. If you have used any recent operating system such as DOS (including Windows 3.*x*), Unix, or OS/2, you no doubt are quite familiar with the concept of directories. *Directories* enable you to organize the data on your disks in a meaningful way. The Windows files, for example, reside in a number of different directories, usually all under the main \Windows directory.

Folders resemble directories in many ways. In fact, one type of Windows 95 folder is nothing more than a graphical representation of a directory on a disk. The objects that appear in the folder window are equivalent to the files that reside in the directory. Figure 5.2 shows this type of folder window.

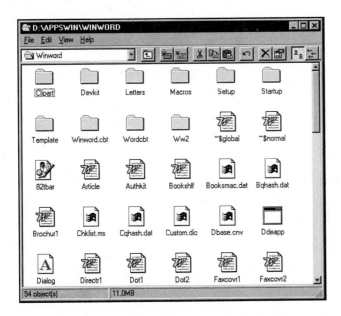

Figure 5.2

An open disk folder.

Windows 95 supports special folders that don't reference a directory on the disk, but rather, contain other types of objects. These folders are actually container objects for applications and other objects not necessarily related to files. The My Computer folder is an example of this type of folder.

The relationship between folders and directories is explained in greater detail in the section "Working with Folders" later in this chapter.

Using the My Computer Folder

My Computer provides quick access to all resources on your PC, including your local hard disk, remote disks mapped to drive IDs on your PC, the Control Panel, the Printers folder, and the Dial-Up Networking folder. Figure 5.3 shows the contents of My Computer on a typical PC.

Figure 5.3

My Computer provides quick access to your PC's resources.

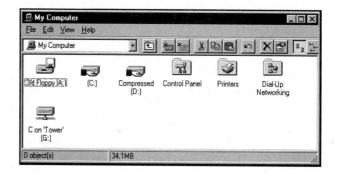

All the disk resources available to your PC, locally or through disk mappings to remote network disks, appear in My Computer. To view the contents of a local hard disk, for example, just open My Computer and double-click on the disk's icon. Depending on how you configure your folder windows (explained in "Working with Folders" later in this chapter), the contents of the open folder change to show the contents of the newly selected object, or a new folder window appears on the desktop to show the contents of the selected object. If you double-click on the drive C icon, for example, the contents of drive C appear in the new folder window (see fig. 5.4)

Besides displaying an icon for each local floppy and hard disk drive, My Computer displays an icon for each remote network drive mapped to a logical drive ID on your PC. If you connect logical drive F to a remote server, for example, My Computer displays an icon for drive F. Selecting the network drive's icon opens a window that displays the contents of the remote disk, just as opening a local drive displays its contents.

My Computer also contains three other folders, explained in the following list:

◆ **Control Panel.** This folder provides a variety of tools you can use to control the way your PC, its components, and Windows 95 operate, as well as to control the appearance and behavior of the Windows 95 interface. The Control Panel folder calls heavily upon the Control Panel application in Windows 3.*x*.

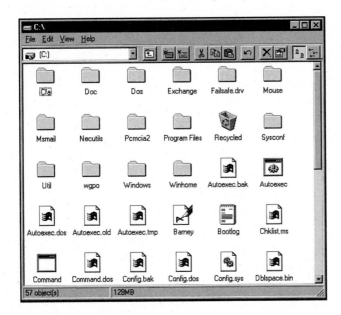

Figure 5.4

The contents of drive C displayed in a folder window.

◆ **Printers.** The Printers folder gives you quick access to all printers available to your PC, including remote network printers. An icon represents each printer, and double-clicking on the icon opens a queue window you can use to set printer options and monitor print jobs.

◆ **Dial-Up Networking.** The Dial-Up Networking folder contains objects that enable you to use remote access services (RAS) to connect your PC to a remote PC or network. You can use RAS, for example, to connect your notebook PC to the office LAN when you're out of town or at home.

Inside Windows 95 covers the Control Panel whenever appropriate throughout the book. Chapter 9, "Personalizing Windows," discusses customizing the Windows 95 interface and includes an exploration of many of the controls in the Control Panel folder.

Chapter 8, "Printing and Managing Printers," explores the Printers folder, explaining how to print, specify printer options, control the print queue, and other printing issues.

Chapter 33, "Using Remote Access Services," explains the Dial-Up Networking folder and RAS in detail. If you think you might want to provide or use remote services, Dial-Up Networking can help you provide remote e-mail, LAN access, and other workgroup services.

Tip   Renaming My Computer on your system is easy. For example, you might prefer a name like "PC" or your PC's network machine name. To change the name of the My Computer folder (or any other folder), click once on the folder to select it. Then click once on the title text below the icon. This highlights the current folder name, and you can enter the new name. You can include spaces and punctuation characters in the folder name. Refer to Chapter 6, "Managing Files and Folders," for more information on using long file names to name files and folders.

Using the Network Neighborhood Folder

The Network Neighborhood (see fig. 5.5) provides quick access to the PCs and printers on your network. The Network Neighborhood folder displays the resources available in your workgroup; the Entire Network folder, whose icon appears in the Network Neighborhood folder, gives you access to the resources shared by servers and PCs outside your workgroup.

Figure 5.5

The Network Neighborhood folder provides quick access to network resources.

As you learn in more detail in Part Seven, Windows 95's strategy for providing access to network resources, such as files and printers, makes accessing and using those resources much easier. The Network Neighborhood icon is a key element of that strategy. When you open Network Neighborhood, you see icons for each of the computers that are part of your workgroup, with the name of each computer under its icon. To view the resources a particular computer shares, simply double-click on its icon, and an open folder (a folder window) appears on the desktop displaying the resources the selected computer shares (see fig. 5.6). Shared disk resources appear as folders, with the name of the share serving as the name of the folder. Shared printers appear as printer folders with the printer's share name serving as the folder name.

This method of resource access is so easy because you no longer have to associate a local drive ID with each shared disk resource you want to access. You simply open the remote computer's folder, open the shared folder to display its contents, then choose the application or file you want to use. This can save time when you want to access a single file or application on a server you seldom use.

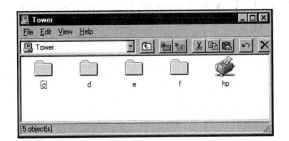

Figure 5.6

A folder showing the resources shared by a remote PC.

Tip

You can easily create a shortcut on the desktop to a remote computer or its shared resources. When you need to access the remote computer's shared resources, you simply open the shortcut folder, and the resources are immediately available. Creating shortcuts is covered later in this chapter, in the section "Creating and Using Shortcuts."

Quick access to network resources carries over into the standard file dialog boxes. If you choose **F**ile, **O**pen to display an application's Open dialog box, you can enter a UNC name to a resource, instead of first having to associate a drive ID with the remote disk. To open a file named **report** in a shared directory named **docs** on a server name **fred**, for example, you would enter **\\fred\docs\report** in the File Name text box.

If you are not familiar with networks and resources, Chapter 34, "Network Concepts and Configuration," helps give an idea of the impact networking has on day-to-day computing. Chapter 35, "Sharing Resources in Windows 95," explains resource sharing in detail.

Using the Start Menu

One key use of your computer is to run applications and create and manage documents. As with Windows 3.*x*, Windows 95 makes opening applications and documents easy. Windows 95 adds flexibility in letting you customize the way you access your frequently used applications and documents.

At the bottom of the desktop is the Taskbar (see fig. 5.7). You use the Taskbar to start applications, open documents, and manage running applications. The Taskbar also serves as a status bar.

At the left of the Taskbar is the Start button, which when clicked opens the Start menu (refer to figure 5.7). Until you customize the desktop, the Start menu is the primary mechanism you use to start applications and open documents. The Start menu includes a set of standard menu items, discussed in the following sections.

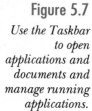

Figure 5.7

Use the Taskbar to open applications and documents and manage running applications.

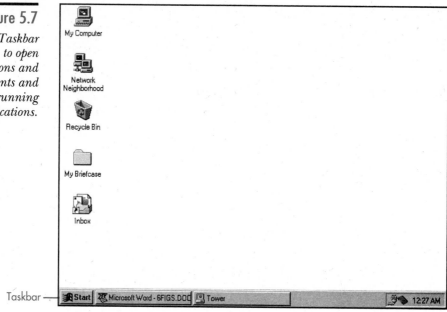

Taskbar ———

Using the Programs Menu Item

The <u>P</u>rograms menu item displays a hierarchical menu of program groups, such as Accessories and Startup. If you upgrade a copy of Windows 3.*x* to Windows 95, Setup migrates all your Program Manager groups to items in the <u>P</u>rograms menu. To open a program, select the menu item for the appropriate group from the <u>P</u>rograms menu. A menu of the objects in the group appears, and then to start the application, you just select its menu item.

Tip   You don't have to click on a menu to open the menu. Just move the cursor over the menu item to highlight the item, then let the cursor rest on the item for a second. The menu opens automatically. If you prefer, you can click on the menu to open it immediately.

Similar to Windows 3.*x*, Windows 95 includes a set of accessory programs for doing simple word processing, maintaining addresses and phone numbers, and performing other common tasks. You can find these accessories in the <u>P</u>rograms, Accessories menu (see fig. 5.8). For example, to start WordPad, a simple word processor, choose Start, <u>P</u>rograms, Accessories, and then WordPad.

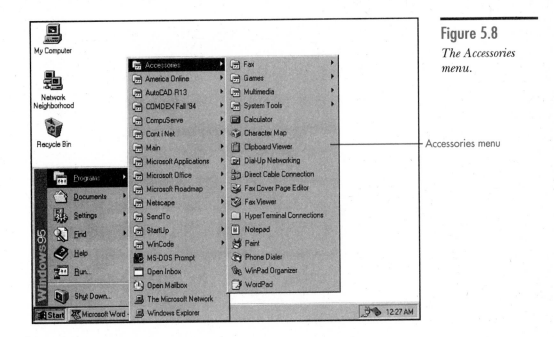

Figure 5.8

The Accessories menu.

Accessories menu

Note WordPad takes the place of the Windows 3.x Write application. WordPad can open documents in ASCII (text only), Microsoft Word, RTF, and Windows Write formats, and it can write documents in ASCII, Microsoft Word, and RTF formats.

The Accessories menu also contains other menus, including the following:

◆ **Fax.** The Fax menu includes items for using Microsoft Fax, which is included with Windows 95. Microsoft Fax enables you to send and receive faxes using a fax-modem on your PC or one shared on the network. For information on using Microsoft Fax, refer to Chapter 31, "Using Microsoft Fax."

◆ **Games.** The Games menu contains items for a variety of games included in Windows 95. If you're addicted to Windows Solitaire in Windows 3.x, try Windows 95's FreeCell.

◆ **Multimedia.** The Multimedia menu includes items that enable you to work with multimedia, including a volume control, the Media Player, a CD Player, and Sound Recorder. For information on using multimedia in Windows 95, refer to Chapter 23, "Working with Multimedia Audio and CD-ROM."

◆ **System Tools.** The System menu gives you access to a selection of system utility applications. These applications enable you to compress your hard disk, defragment and repair files on the hard disk, back up files, and monitor your PC's performance. Chapter 15, "Optimizing Data Storage," covers the disk utility applications.

The Programs menu is not limited to only those items it contains when you first install Windows 95. When you install a new application, a menu item is added to the Programs menu. If you install Microsoft Office, for example, a menu item named Microsoft Office appears in the Programs menu. The Microsoft Office menu then lists all applications you install as part of Microsoft Office. For more information on installing applications, refer to Chapter 17, "Installing and Uninstalling Applications."

 Tip

The Setup application for many Windows 3.x applications communicates with the Windows 3.x Program Manager to create a program group for the new application. If you install a Windows 3.x application under Windows 95, Windows 95 intercepts those calls and instead creates a folder to contain the new application's objects. Windows 95 also adds an entry in the Programs menu for the new application.

Using the Documents Menu

The Start menu contains a **D**ocuments menu that gives you quick access to documents with which you have recently worked (see fig. 5.9). If you double-click on a document in a folder, for example, the document's parent application opens and loads the selected document. The name of the selected document is then added to the **D**ocuments menu. If later you want to open the document again, just choose Start, **D**ocuments, then choose the document from the menu. The **D**ocuments menu keeps track of the last 15 documents you open.

 Note

In addition to tracking documents, the Documents menu also keeps track of disk folders that you open.

Using the Settings Menu

The **S**ettings menu gives you access to the Control Panel, Printers folder, and Taskbar. Choosing the **C**ontrol Panel item in the **S**ettings menu opens the Control Panel. Another way you can open the Control Panel is to open the My Computer folder and choose the Control Panel folder. The objects in the Control Panel are explained throughout *Inside Windows 95*.

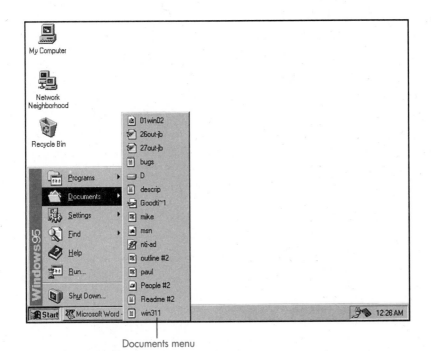

Figure 5.9

The Documents menu gives you quick access to recently opened documents.

Documents menu

Choosing the Printers menu item in the Settings menu opens the Printers folder. As explained earlier in the section on My Computer, the Printers folder contains icons for each of the printers available to your PC. You can open the Printers folder from My Computer as well. Chapter 8, "Printing and Managing Printers," explains printing and working with the Printers folder.

Choosing the Taskbar menu item in the Settings menu opens a dialog box you can use to customize the Start menu and Taskbar. These topics are explained in the section "Customizing the Taskbar and Start Menu" later in this chapter.

Using the Find Menu

The Find menu item in the Start menu enables you to search for files on your PC or on the network, search for computers on the network, and search the Microsoft Network online service for topics. Find is excellent for tracking down information and eliminates the need to open Explorer (or File Manager, as in Windows 3.*x*) to search for a file. Find's capability for locating computers and information on the Microsoft Network adds to its usefulness.

Chapter 6, "Managing Files and Folders," covers using Find to locate files and folders, and Chapter 35, "Sharing Resources in Windows 95," explains using Find to locate computers on the network. Chapter 32, "Using the Microsoft Network," covers finding information on the Microsoft Network.

Using the Help Menu

As with Windows 3.*x*, Windows 95 has an extensive Help system. If you need help using Windows 95, choose Start, then **H**elp. Windows 95 displays a dialog box (similar to the one shown in figure 5.10) that you can use to search the Help index for Windows 95 and get information about specific topics. For more information on using and customizing Help, and on creating your own Help files, refer to Chapter 20, "Using and Building Windows Help."

Figure 5.10

Windows 95 includes an extensive online Help system.

 Tip   For help using a Windows application, choose an appropriate selection from the application's **H**elp menu.

Using the Run Menu

The **R**un menu item enables you to start applications that do not appear elsewhere in the Programs menu or on the desktop. Choosing **R**un from the Start menu is similar to choosing **F**ile, **R**un from Program Manager's menu or from File Manager's menu. The Run dialog box in Windows 95 (see fig. 5.11), however, has some improvements over the old Windows 3.*x* Run dialog box.

Figure 5.11

You can use the Run dialog box to start applications.

To run an application, enter the path to its executable file in the **O**pen combo box. Run maintains a list of the applications that you have opened recently by using the Run dialog box. If you have opened the application recently, open the drop-down list to see if the application's path appears in the list. Select the application, then choose OK. If you don't know the path to the application, or prefer not to type the path, choose the **B**rowse button and use the Browse dialog box (see fig. 5.12) to locate the application's executable file.

Shutting Down the PC

In addition to items that enable you to open applications and documents, the Start menu also includes an item you use to shut down your PC. Rather than simply shut off your PC after you finish using it, you should use the Sh**u**t Down item in the Start menu to shut down Windows and your PC. When you choose Sh**u**t Down, Windows 95 displays the Shut Down Windows dialog box, shown in figure 5.13. The four option buttons in the dialog box are described in the following list:

◆ **S**hut down the computer. Choose this option when you want to shut down Windows and turn off your PC. Windows 95 will close open files and prepare your system for a safe shutdown.

◆ **R**estart the computer. Choose this option to restart the computer if you experience a problem in Windows 95, or if you have made a Windows 95 configuration change and need to restart Windows 95 for the change to take effect. This is similar to resetting the PC, except that Windows 95 first closes all files and prepares the PC to be shut down before resetting.

◆ **Restart the computer in MS-DOS mode.** Choose this option if you want to restart the PC with a real-mode MS-DOS operating system to run a DOS application that does not run well under Windows 95.

◆ **Close all programs and log on as a different user.** Choose this option to log off of Windows, close all programs, and log on using a different user ID. If you share a PC with another user, you should choose this option when you are finished using the PC. Windows 95 will restart with a logon dialog box displayed so that the next user can log on to the system.

Figure 5.13

Use the Shut Down Windows dialog box to shut down your PC.

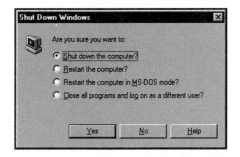

Tip   If your PC supports power-saving features and power management is enabled, the Start menu includes a Suspend menu item. Choose Suspend to suspend the PC. Press the Resume button on the keyboard to wake up the PC.

Using the Taskbar

The Taskbar, on which you find the Start menu, serves as a task switcher and status bar. The Taskbar enables you to switch quickly and easily among your running applications and control the way those running applications appear on the desktop.

By default, you can always see the Taskbar located at the bottom of the desktop. You can configure the Taskbar, however, to appear at the right, left, or top of the desktop. You also can configure the Taskbar to hide automatically when not in use. When the Taskbar is hidden, moving the cursor to the edge of the desktop at which the Taskbar is located brings it back into view. The section "Customizing the Start Menu and Taskbar" later in this chapter explains how to change the location and behavior of the Taskbar.

All running applications appear as buttons in the Taskbar. A foreground application's button appears pressed. Background applications' buttons appear raised. To switch to a particular application, simply click on its button in the Taskbar, and the application moves to the foreground. To use the Taskbar to open an application's Control menu, right-click on the application's button in the Taskbar. The Control menu appears near the application's button.

Tip   If you prefer a quicker method of switching programs than the Taskbar, hold down Alt and press Tab, then release Tab but keep Alt down. A small dialog box appears, containing icons for all open applications, folders, and other objects. Continue to hold down Alt, and press Tab to cycle through the icons and choose the icon for the object you want to use. When the icon for what you want is highlighted, release Alt. That application moves to the foreground. Other keyboard shortcuts are explained later in the section "Using the Keyboard."

Cascading and Tiling Applications

The Taskbar can help you quickly organize all open windows on the desktop. Assume you have a couple folder windows and an application window open, and you want to view all of them. Just right-click on the Taskbar and choose Tile Horizontally or Tile Vertically. Windows 95 arranges the open windows on your desktop, as shown in figures 5.14 and 5.15.

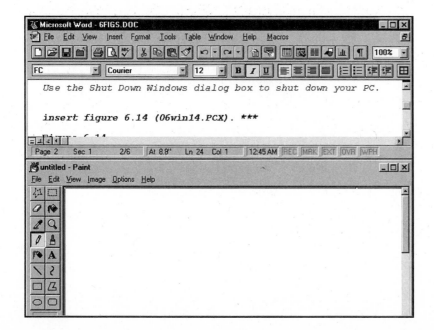

Figure 5.14

Windows tiled horizontally.

Figure 5.15

Windows tiled vertically.

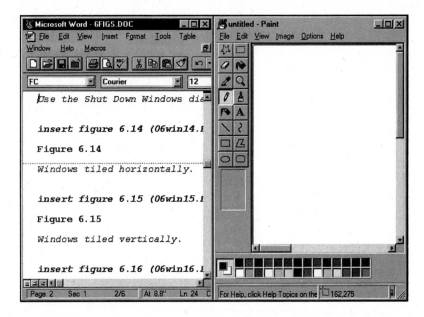

Another arrangement method is to *cascade* all open windows, so that the windows overlap one on top of the other (see fig. 5.16). To cascade all open windows, right-click on the Taskbar and choose <u>C</u>ascade.

Figure 5.16

All open windows cascaded on the desktop.

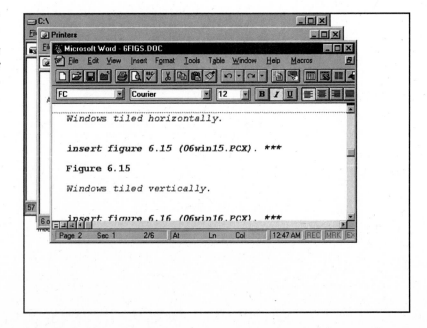

Note   When you choose Tile **H**orizontally, Tile **V**ertically, or **C**ascade, Windows 95 organizes only the windows currently open on the desktop. Minimized windows are not affected.

After you tile or cascade the windows on the desktop, you can switch back to the original view. Assume you have three open windows, all of them maximized (which means you can see only one). You right-click on the Taskbar and choose Tile **H**orizontally. A few minutes later, you want to maximize them all again, returning them to the arrangement you had before you tiled them. After you tile or cascade windows with the Taskbar, a menu item labeled either **U**ndo Cascade or **U**ndo Tile appears in the Taskbar's object menu. Choose this menu item to restore the windows to their original locations and states.

Minimizing All Windows

When you work with more than one application or window, minimizing all the windows so that you can work with shortcuts and other objects on the desktop can eat up time. If you're running four maximized applications, for example, you have to minimize each one so that you can access your shortcuts and other objects on the desktop. To overcome this problem, Windows 95 includes the **M**inimize All Windows item, which you can find in the Taskbar's context menu. To minimize all windows and provide clear access to the desktop, right-click on the Taskbar, then choose **M**inimize All Windows. All open windows instantly minimize.

Tip   If you are using a Microsoft Natural Keyboard, hold down the Windows key and press M to minimize all applications.

Working with Status Indicators

At the right edge of the Taskbar (if your Taskbar is at the bottom of the desktop) is the tray, which contains various status indicators. For example, the current time appears at the far right of the tray (see fig. 5.17). If you place the cursor over the time indicator, a *ToolTip* (a small text box) appears at the cursor to display the day and date. Other status indicators behave the same way—rest the cursor on the indicator for a second, and a ToolTip appears with additional status information.

Other status indicators can appear in the tray, depending on your system's configuration. If your system contains PCMCIA devices, for example, a status indicator for the PCMCIA slots appears in the tray. If power management is enabled, a battery indicator appears in the tray to indicate remaining battery charge. When you use Dial-Up Networking to connect to a remote LAN or PC, a modem indicator appears in the tray, indicating modem activity.

Figure 5.17

Status indicators appear in the Taskbar.

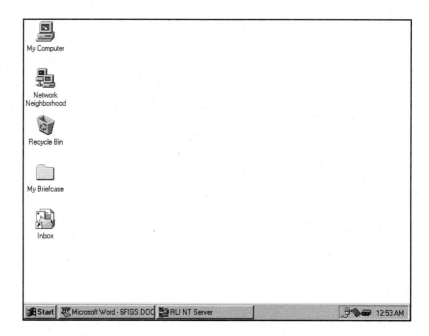

Double-clicking on a status indicator in the Taskbar typically provides additional information about the selected item. Double-clicking on the time indicator, for example, opens the Day/Time Properties dialog box (see fig. 5.18), which you can use to set the system's date, time, and time zone. Double-clicking on the modem status indicator opens a dialog box similar to the one shown in figure 5.19, which shows you the status of the modem and information about bytes transferred.

Figure 5.18

The Day/Time Properties dialog box.

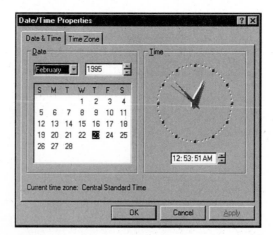

New Riders Publishing
INSIDE SERIES

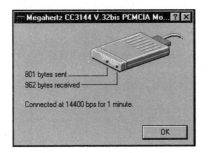

Figure 5.19

The modem status dialog box.

Tip   When you have unread mail in your inbox, an envelope icon appears in the tray. Double-clicking on the envelope opens the Inbox so that you can read the new message(s).

Now that you have had a general introduction to the Windows 95 interface, you're ready to examine some of the interface components in more detail and learn to customize them to your needs. The following section explains the use of folders in more detail, including how to open applications and documents from a folder.

Working with Folders

You read earlier in this chapter that folders are a major component of the Windows 95 interface. *Folders* are really nothing more than standard windows that serve as containers for objects such as files. When you open a folder, it looks like a window. When you close a folder, it looks like a folder icon. Folders can contain files, other folders, and other types of objects.

A key point to understand about folders is that they actually come in two basic types—those that Windows 95 uses to display the contents of a directory and those, like the Control Panel, that actually are applications that present their information in a standard folder window. As a user, however, the distinction between these two types of folders is transparent—you work with the contents of either type of folder in the same way.

Another key point about folders lies in their relationship to directories. A standard folder is nothing more than a graphical mechanism for displaying the contents of a directory. Microsoft has just changed some terminology in Windows 95—what was called a directory in the DOS and Windows 3.*x* realm now is called a folder. Therefore, a folder can contain other folders, just as a directory can contain subdirectories. When you open a folder, you see the contents of the directory it represents—the files that reside in the directory appear as icons in the folder window. Any subdirectories appear in the folder as additional folders.

Note   Throughout *Inside Windows 95*, the terms *directory* and *folder* are used interchangeably. Some folders, however, such as the Control Panel and Printers folders, are *not* directories. These special folders are actually applications that appear and function like a standard folder.

A folder window is very similar to other application windows: it has a border, menu, title bar, control menu, and other controls. Figure 5.20 shows a typical folder window.

Figure 5.20

A typical folder with its components labeled

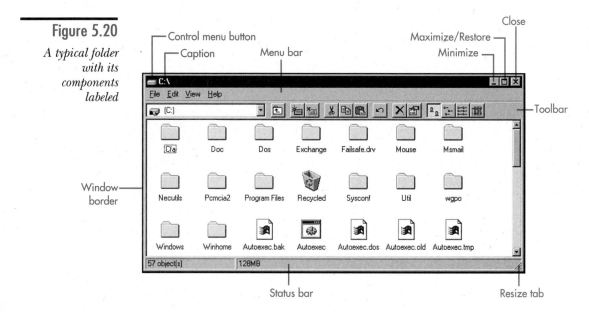

The following section explains how to turn on some of the optional components shown in figure 5.20.

Controlling a Folder's Appearance

Windows 95 lets you do quite a bit to modify the appearance of a folder. By default, folder windows do not contain a toolbar, although they do contain a menu bar. To display a folder's toolbar, choose View, Toolbar. A folder's toolbar contains a number of tools you can use to select a folder, move up to the current folder's parent folder, change the way information appears in the folder, and control the folder in other ways. Figure 5.21 identifies the tools in a folder's toolbar. You also can determine a folder tool's function by resting the cursor on the tool for a second and reading the resulting ToolTip.

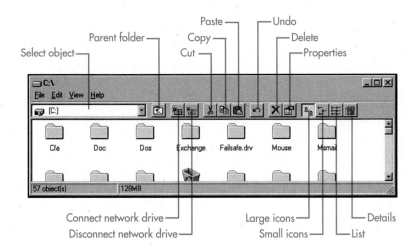

Figure 5.21

Use a folder's toolbar to control the appearance and function of the folder window.

The following list explains the function of the tools in a folder's toolbar:

◆ **Select object.** Use this drop-down list to select the object you want to view in the folder window. For example, you can choose a disk or directory, or another type of object, such as the Control Panel, Printers folder, Network Neighborhood, and so on.

◆ **Parent folder.** Click on this button to view the contents of the folder's parent folder. For example, if you view the contents of a directory, choose this button to view the contents of the parent directory. This is similar to selecting the double dots (..) in a File Manager window in Windows 3.*x*.

◆ **Connect network drive.** Click on this button to associate a remote network disk resource with a logical drive ID on your PC. When you click on this button, a dialog box appears that you can use to specify the drive ID (drive letter) and the path to the remote resource. You also can browse for the resource if you don't know its UNC path name.

◆ **Disconnect network drive.** Click on this button to disconnect a remote network drive from a local logical drive ID.

◆ **Cut.** Click on this button to cut the selected object(s) from the folder and place them on the Clipboard.

◆ **Copy.** Click on this button to copy the selected object(s) to the Clipboard.

◆ **Paste.** Click on this button to paste the contents of the Clipboard to the folder.

◆ **Undo.** Click on this button to undo the previous action.

- ◆ **Delete.** Click on this button to delete the selected object(s).

- ◆ **Properties.** Click on this button to set the properties of the selected object(s).

- ◆ **Show large icons.** Click on this button to view the contents of the folder as large icons with a description under each icon.

- ◆ **Show small icons.** Click on this button to view the contents of the folder as small icons with a description to the right of each icon.

- ◆ **Show list.** Click on this button to view the contents of the folder as a list. This view is similar to the small icons view except for the way in which the objects are arranged in the window.

- ◆ **Show details.** Click on this button to view the contents of the folder as a detailed list. A detailed list of files, for example, contains the file name, size, type, and modification date.

To display a folder's status bar, choose <u>V</u>iew, Status <u>B</u>ar. The status bar displays information about objects currently selected in the folder.

Tip   To rename a folder or file, just click on the object to select it, then click on the object's description (which appears underneath the object's icon). Type the new name, then press Enter. If you change the name of a folder, you actually change the name of the directory it represents. (This association between folder name and directory name doesn't have any bearing or relationship to the names of special folder objects, such as My Computer.)

Selecting Objects in a Folder

If you are experienced with Windows 3.*x* or other GUIs, selecting and working with objects in a folder will be second-nature to you. To open an application or a document, just double-click on its icon. If you double-click on a document, and the document type is properly associated with its parent application, the application opens and displays the selected document.

Tip   If you have installed an application under Windows 95, the application's document type(s) should be properly registered with Windows. See Chapter 6, "Managing Files and Folders," for more information on registering file types with Windows.

In addition to selecting and working with a single object, you can select and work with multiple objects. You can use a boundary box, for example, to select multiple objects.

New Riders Publishing
INSIDE
SERIES

To do so, place the cursor in a blank area of the folder background (not on an icon), then drag the cursor. As you drag the cursor, a dashed box appears (see fig. 5.22). Enclose in the box all objects you want to select. You also can use the mouse and keyboard in combination to choose multiple objects. Hold the Ctrl key and click on objects to select them one at a time. Hold the Shift key and click objects to select a range of objects.

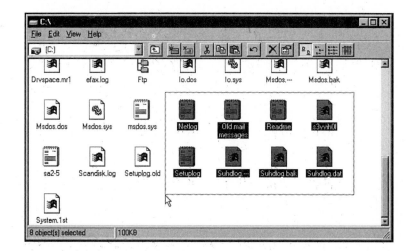

Figure 5.22

You can use a box to select multiple objects.

What you do with multiple objects after you select them depends on the types of objects. You can select multiple application icons, for example, then press Enter to open all of them. If you select only documents, pressing Enter opens the parent application(s) for the documents and loads the documents into the application(s). If you want to delete multiple objects, use your preferred selection method, then press Del.

 Tip   To open multiple applications using the mouse, select the application's icons, then hold down the Ctrl key and double-click on a blank area of the folder background (not on an icon).

For information on using the keyboard to select and open objects, refer to the section "Using the Keyboard" later in this chapter.

Creating Your Own Folders

Sooner or later you will want to create your own folders. Creating a folder is easy: right-click in the object where you want to create the new folder, then choose New, Folder from the resulting menu. Windows 95 creates a new folder with the name New

Folder. Select the folder, then click on its name to highlight the text. Enter the name you want for the folder.

To create a folder inside another folder, for example, right-click on the blank background anywhere inside the folder. Then, choose <u>N</u>ew, <u>F</u>older. To create a folder on the desktop, right-click on the desktop and choose <u>N</u>ew, <u>F</u>older.

When you create new folders, however, remember that you actually are creating directories. If you create a folder named Frannie's Weekly Reports in the C:\ folder, you're actually creating a directory named Frannie's Weekly Reports in the root directory of drive C. If you create a folder on the desktop, you're creating a directory in the C:\Windows\Desktop directory.

 Tip   You probably guessed from the previous paragraph that you can name a folder using long file names. You also can name files using long file names. For more information on long file names, read Chapter 6, "Managing Files and Folders."

Copying and Moving Objects

In Windows 3.*x* Program Manager, you can copy and move objects between program groups simply by dragging the objects' icons from one group window to another. The same ease of use holds true in Windows 95—you can move an object from one folder to another simply by dragging the object from the first folder and dropping it in the second folder. If you want to move a document file, for example, open the folder that currently contains the file, then open the folder in which you want to place the file. Then, just drag the file's icon from one folder to another. The file moves accordingly.

You also can copy objects between folders. To copy an object, hold down the Ctrl key while you drag the object from its original folder to its new folder, then release the object. Windows creates a copy of the object in the second folder.

 Tip   You also can copy objects between folders using the Clipboard. Select one or more objects in a folder, then press Ctrl+C to copy a list of the items to the Clipboard. Then, open the folder in which you want to copy the objects and press Ctrl+V to copy them to the folder. If you want to move the objects rather than copy them, select the objects and press Ctrl+X, then open the folder in which you want to place them and choose Ctrl+V. Using the Clipboard to copy and move objects enables you to copy and move objects without keeping both the source and destination folders open at the same time.

Another method for moving and copying objects gives you other options. You can use the right mouse button (called *right-dragging*), rather than the left button, to drag an

object. When you right-drag an object from one location to another and then release the object, Windows displays a menu similar to the one shown in figure 5.23. This menu gives you the option of moving or copying the object. You also can create a shortcut to the object. Shortcuts are explained later in this chapter, in the section "Creating and Using Shortcuts."

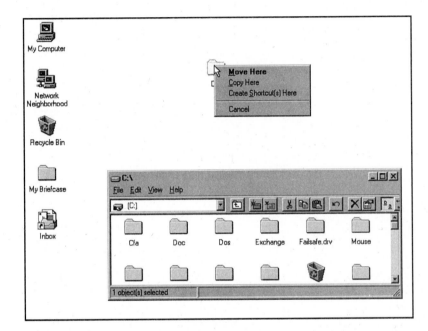

Figure 5.23

A special menu appears when you right-drag an object to a new location.

Tip   To copy or move multiple objects, select the objects, right-drag one of the objects to the new location, then choose, according to your need, **M**ove Here, **C**opy Here, or Create **S**hortcut(s) Here.

You can read more about copying and moving objects in Chapter 6, "Managing Files and Folders."

Setting Object Properties

A critical concept in Windows 95 is that almost all objects have properties associated with them; for example, a file's properties include its type, name, size, modification date, attributes, and other information. You can easily change some of these properties, such as the file's attributes. You can't change certain others, however, such as the time the file was created—you can only view these properties.

Other objects also have properties. The desktop, for example, has many different properties that you can view and set. These properties include the screen saver, color scheme, video drivers, resolution, and much more. (See Chapter 9, "Personalizing Windows 95," for an explanation of how to set the desktop's properties and customize Windows 95 in other ways.)

The easiest way to view an object's properties is to right-click on the object, which brings up a context menu for the object (see fig. 5.24). The contents of the context menu vary according to the type of object selected, but there are many similarities between context menus for various types of objects. This section explains the Properties item in the context menu. Other context menu items are explained elsewhere in this chapter and in other chapters.

Figure 5.24

Use the context menu to work with an object and set its properties.

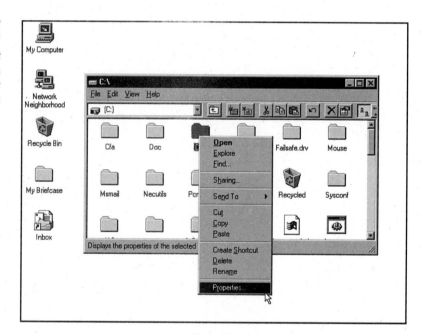

After you choose Properties from an object's context menu, one or more property sheets appear on the display to enable you to view and set the object's properties. Figure 5.25 shows the property sheet for a typical file, and figure 5.26 shows the property sheet for the desktop. You can use the controls in the object's property sheet to set the object's properties as appropriate.

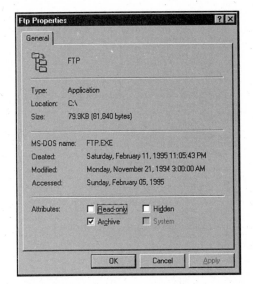

Figure 5.25

The property sheets for a typical file.

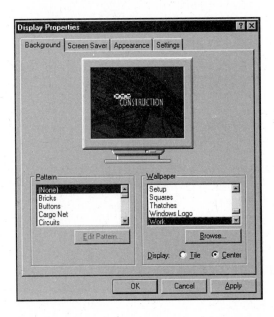

Figure 5.26

Property sheet for the desktop.

Introducing Explorer

You can use folders for most application and document accessing that you do regularly. You can copy, move, find, and delete objects easily. Sometimes, however, you need a broader picture of your PC's resources, or you need to see a hierarchical view of those resources.

Windows 95 includes an application called Explorer that provides that hierarchical view of your PC's resources (see fig. 5.27). If you have used File Manager in Window 3.*x,* Explorer should seem fairly familiar to you. You can open multiple copies of Explorer to view the objects in different folders or on different computers.

Figure 5.27

Explorer enables you to browse and manage your PC's resources.

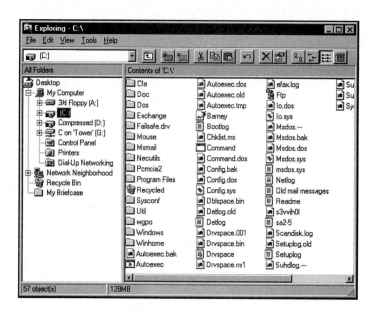

To open Explorer, choose Start, <u>P</u>rograms, and select Windows Explorer. If you want to open a full Explorer view of a folder—on the desktop or in another folder—hold down the Shift key and double-click on the folder. Explorer opens with selected folder contents on display.

For detailed information on using Explorer, refer to Chapter 6, "Managing Files and Folders."

Creating and Using Shortcuts

In addition to containing files, folders, and special objects such as the Control Panel, a folder can contain a shortcut. (You also can place a shortcut on the desktop.) A *shortcut* is a special type of file linked to another object. You can think of a shortcut as a pointer to an object—when you double-click on the shortcut, Windows 95 checks the contents of the shortcut file to determine the object with which the shortcut is linked. Then, Windows 95 opens that object. If you create a shortcut on the desktop to the Control Panel, for example, double-clicking on the Control Panel shortcut opens the Control Panel.

Shortcuts are extremely useful, and are the primary mechanism you use to customize your desktop to give yourself quick access to the applications and documents you use most often. Do you need to open files from a particular disk and folder? Create a shortcut on the desktop to that folder. Do you often access files in a particular volume on a server? Create a shortcut on the desktop to that volume. Do you use one or two applications often and want to have quick access to them? Create shortcuts on the desktop to the applications' executable files.

Tip   You don't need to map a local drive letter to a remote disk resource to open that resource. You can use the remote computer's UNC path name to create a shortcut to another user's machine or a server. When you double-click on the shortcut icon, a folder opens displaying the resources that the remote computer shares, including all disk shares and shared printers.

Creating Shortcuts

You can create a shortcut in a folder, on the desktop, or in the Start menu. There are a few different ways to create shortcuts, the easiest of which is to right-drag the object for which you want a shortcut into the location where you want the shortcut created. To create a shortcut on the desktop to drive C, for example, open My Computer, then right-drag the C drive icon onto the desktop. When you release the icon, Windows 95 displays a pop-up menu with two items: Create $\underline{S}$hortcut(s) Here, and Cancel. Choose Create $\underline{S}$hortcut(s) Here to create a shortcut to drive C. When you double-click on the shortcut icon, Windows 95 opens a folder that displays the contents of drive C. Figure 5.28 shows various shortcuts on the desktop.

To create a shortcut in a folder, right-drag the object into the folder, release the object, and choose Create $\underline{S}$hortcut(s) Here. To create a shortcut of an object *in* a folder, right-click on the object and choose Create $\underline{S}$hortcut. Windows 95 creates a shortcut in the folder to the selected object. You then can drag the shortcut into another folder or onto the desktop to relocate the shortcut.

Tip   Some objects can't be moved or copied, but you can create a shortcut to the object. For example, you can't copy the Control Panel onto the desktop, but you can create a shortcut on the desktop to the Control Panel. Windows 95 prevents you from copying entire disks to your desktop—if you right-drag a disk icon from My Computer to the desktop, for example, the only choice that appears in the object menu is Create $\underline{S}$hortcut(s) Here.

An important point to understand about copying, moving, and shortcuts is this: you can copy or move a file onto the desktop, just as you can create a shortcut on the

Figure 5.28

*Various shortcuts
on the desktop.*

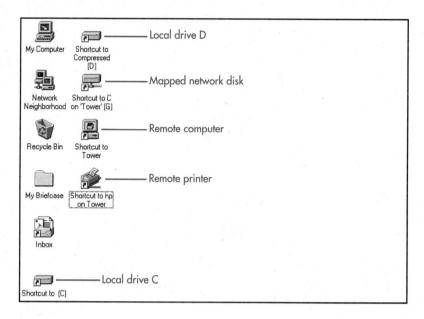

desktop to that file. If you copy a file to the desktop, you actually copy it to the \Windows\Desktop directory. If you move the file to the desktop, you move it to the \Windows\Desktop directory. The same holds true for folders—if you copy or move a folder to the desktop, you move or copy an entire directory and all of its contents (including subdirectories) to the \Windows\Desktop directory. You probably won't want to copy or move objects to the desktop very often. Instead, you'll want to create shortcuts on the desktop to those objects.

Stop   Take care that you don't move objects from remote network computers to your own computer, unless you're absolutely sure you want to remove the object from the remote PC and place it on your PC. It's easy to move an important file from another computer onto yours, then accidentally delete it from your PC. To be safe, create a shortcut to the file instead of moving or copying it.

To help you understand the ways in which you can create shortcuts, the following list summarizes the three most common methods:

◆ **Right-drag an object.** If you right-drag an object and drop it on the desktop or in a folder, Windows 95 displays a menu of options for copying, moving, or creating a shortcut for the object. Choose the Create Shortcut(s) Here item from the menu.

◆ **Right-click on the object.** This displays the context menu for the object. Choose the Create Shortcut item from the context menu to create the shortcut for the object in the same location (folder or desktop) as the original object. After you create the shortcut, left-drag it to move it to the desktop or to the folder of your choice.

◆ **Right-click on the desktop or in a folder.** This displays the context menu for the desktop or for the folder. Choose New, Shortcut. Windows creates a new, "empty" shortcut. The description is highlighted, so type a description for the shortcut and press Enter. Then, right-click on the shortcut to display its context menu. Choose Properties, then click on the Shortcut tab to display the Shortcut property page. In the Link To text box, specify the name of the program file, document file, or directory to which you want the shortcut to reference. If the object is a program, you might also want to specify its working directory, assign it a hot key, and specify the default type of window for it to use. Use the controls in the Shortcut property sheet to set these properties.

Creating Shortcuts to Network Resources

If you work regularly with certain network resources, you should consider creating shortcuts on the desktop or in a folder to those remote network resources. If you often use applications on a particular server, for example, you can create a shortcut on the desktop to the server. When you double-click on the shortcut icon, a folder window opens displaying the resources that the server shares.

The easiest way to create a shortcut to another user's computer or to a server is through the Network Neighborhood folder. Open Network Neighborhood and locate the computer for which you want to create a shortcut. When you locate the computer, right-drag its icon onto your desktop, then choose Create Shortcut(s) Here.

Tip If you often print to a particular network printer, consider creating a shortcut on the desktop to that printer. When you need to manage print jobs on that printer, you can double-click on the shortcut icon to quickly open a queue folder for the printer. For more information on working with network printers, refer to Chapter 8, "Printing and Managing Printers," and Chapter 35, "Sharing Resources in Windows 95."

Setting a Shortcut's Properties

As with most other types of objects in Windows 95, shortcuts have various properties associated with them. By changing a shortcut's properties, you control the way in which the shortcut functions.

To change a shortcut's properties, right-click on the shortcut's icon to display its context menu, then choose Properties. Shortcut property sheets include two property pages, General and Shortcut. The General property page provides information about the shortcut file, such as its name, modification date, and other file-related information. As with other files, you can set the file attributes of the shortcut file using the General page of the Shortcut property sheets.

The Shortcut page of the Shortcut property sheets (see fig. 5.29) enables you to set properties that control the way the shortcut works. For example, you can associate the shortcut with a different file, specify a startup directory, assign a shortcut key to the shortcut, and change the icon associated with the shortcut.

Figure 5.29

*The Shortcut page
of the Shortcut
property sheet.*

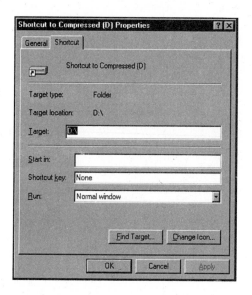

To associate the shortcut with a different file, enter the path to the particular file in the Target text box. If you move the file with which the shortcut is associated to a different directory, for example, specify the new path to the file in the Target text box.

To specify a startup directory (a directory that becomes active when you open the object associated with the shortcut), enter the path to the startup directory in the Start in text box. If you create a shortcut to your word processor, for example, and want a specific document directory to be active when you start the word processor, enter the path to the document directory in the Start in text box.

You also can assign a keyboard shortcut to a program shortcut. Assume that you create a shortcut to your word processor and you want the word processor to open whenever you press Ctrl+Alt+W or another key sequence of your choice. To assign the

keyboard shortcut to the program shortcut, click in the Shortcut key text box, then press the key combination you want assigned to the shortcut. Whenever you press this key combination, the shortcut activates and opens its associated file.

To control the way a shortcut opens its associated file, select one of the three options from the Run drop-down list. You can open the object in a normal window, maximized, or minimized. If you have programs that you want to have available in the Taskbar, for example, but don't want to use them as soon as you double-click on their shortcuts, select the Minimized option from the Run drop-down list.

 Tip   If you're familiar with Windows 3.x, you can see similarities between a shortcut's properties and a Program Manager program item's properties. They essentially perform the same functions, enabling you to control the way an application or document opens.

Finding the Original Copy

Shortcuts are files that contain information that link them to other files. Somewhere along the line, you might need to find the file with which a shortcut is associated. You might have a shortcut on the desktop to an application, for example, and want to browse for other files in the same directory—but you don't know the original file's location.

To quickly find the file with which a shortcut is associated, right-click on the shortcut's icon to display its context menu, then choose Properties. When the property sheet appears, click on the Shortcut tab to show the Shortcut page. Next, choose the Find Target button. Windows 95 opens a window that displays the contents of the folder in which the original file resides.

Customizing the Taskbar and Start Menu

As with most aspects of Windows 95, you can control the appearance and behavior of the Taskbar and Start menu to suit your preferences. You can add new items to the Start menu to enable you to access applications and documents quickly, and you can relocate the Taskbar if you want it somewhere other than at the bottom of the display. The next section explains how to customize the Taskbar.

Customizing the Taskbar

By default, the Taskbar appears at the bottom of the desktop with the Start button at the left of the Taskbar and the tray at the right. You can easily change the location of the Taskbar so that it resides at the right, left, or top of the desktop rather than at the bottom. To relocate the Taskbar, just drag it from its current location to its new location at one edge of the desktop. When the Taskbar is near its new location, Windows 95 shows an outline of the Taskbar in its new location. Release the mouse button and the Taskbar moves to the new location. Figure 5.30 shows the Taskbar located at the right edge of the display.

Figure 5.30

The Taskbar can be relocated to any edge of the desktop.

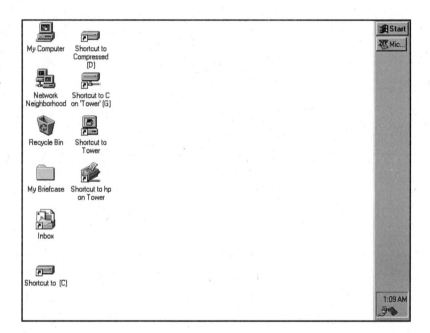

 Tip   To drag the Taskbar, place the tip of the mouse pointer on any blank area of the Taskbar, hold down the left button, and drag the Taskbar to its new location.

When you move the Taskbar to the left or right edges of the desktop, the Start button moves to the top of the Taskbar. The tray is located at the bottom of the Taskbar. The buttons of any running programs appear horizontally below the Start button.

In addition to controlling the location of the Taskbar, you can change how and when it appears on the desktop. By default, the Taskbar is always visible. If you prefer, you can hide the Taskbar to keep it from covering parts of your application windows when

you're not using the Taskbar. To set the Taskbar's properties, right-click on the Taskbar, then choose P̲roperties. Or, choose Start, then T̲askbar. Either method displays the Taskbar property sheet, shown in figure 5.31.

Figure 5.31

The Taskbar property sheet.

The Taskbar Options page includes four check boxes that control the way the Taskbar appears and functions:

◆ **Always on t̲op.** If you enable this option, the Taskbar always appears on top of any window or other object on the desktop. Enabling this option gives you access to the Taskbar even when an application or other window might otherwise cover it up.

◆ **Au̲to hide.** Enable this check box if you want the Taskbar to hide itself when you are not using it. When the Taskbar is hidden, it appears as a thin line at whichever edge of the display you have positioned it. To view the Taskbar, just move the mouse pointer onto the line, and the Taskbar appears. If your Taskbar is hidden at the bottom of the display, for example, just move the mouse pointer to the very bottom of the display.

◆ **Show s̲mall icons in Start menu.** This check box controls whether the Start menu uses small or large icons beside each Start menu item. Enable this option to use small icons; disable the option to use large icons (the default).

◆ **Show C̲lock.** Enable this option if you want the time to appear in the status area of the Taskbar. Disable this option if you don't want the time to show in the Taskbar.

Customizing the Start Menu

You can add your own items to the Start menu to make the items easily accessible. You also can remove items from the Start menu. For example, you can remove a program folder from the Programs menu without actually deleting the folder or its contents, which enables you to minimize the number of items on the Programs menu without deleting the objects it references.

Adding an item to the Start menu only requires that you place a shortcut to the item or the item itself in the appropriate folder under the \Windows\Start Menu folder. All you have to do to delete an item is remove the object from the appropriate directory under \Windows\Start Menu.

 Note   If your system is configured to provide a separate desktop and environment for each user, the start menu items are located in \Windows\Profiles*user*\Start Menu, where *user* is the Windows logon name of a particular user. For the purposes of this chapter, the Start menu items are assumed to be in \Windows\Start Menu. For more information on configuring Windows 95 to support multiple users and desktops, refer to Chapter9, "Personalizing Windows 95."

When you choose Start, Windows 95 displays in the Start menu all the objects contained in the \Windows\Start Menu folder. Any new items you add to the folder automatically appear in the Start menu. If you add a shortcut to the \Windows\Start Menu\Programs folder, for example, that shortcut appears in the Programs menu.

Although you can add and remove items from the Start menu manually, Windows 95 automates the process to simplify it. Essentially, this automation consists of a wizard that automates creating and deleting shortcuts. To add an item to the Start menu, choose Start, Settings, Taskbar, or right-click on the Taskbar and choose Properties. When Windows 95 displays the property sheet for the Taskbar, click on the Start Menu Programs tab to display the property page shown in figure 5.32.

To add an item to the Start menu, choose Add. Windows 95 displays the Create Shortcut dialog box shown in figure 5.33. In the Command line text box, enter the path to the file or other object for which you want to create a shortcut, or choose the Browse button to browse for the object. After you locate the object and its entry appears in the Command line text box, choose Next.

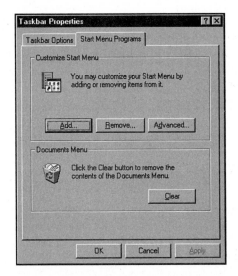

Figure 5.32

The Start Menu Programs property page.

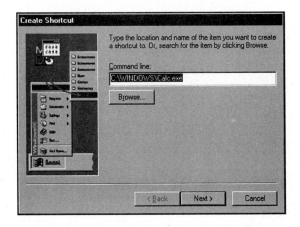

Figure 5.33

The Create Shortcut dialog box.

Windows 95 then displays the Select Program Folder dialog box (see fig. 5.34), which provides a hierarchical view of the folders referenced in the Start menu. Locate the folder in which you want to place the new shortcut, then click on Next to return to the Create Shortcut dialog box. If you like your selections, choose Finish. Windows 95 creates the shortcut in the specified directory, which causes it to be displayed in the appropriate place in the Start menu.

Figure 5.34

The Select Program Folder dialog box.

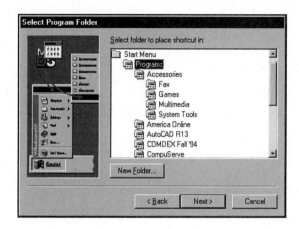

To remove an item from the Start menu, display the Start Menu Programs page, then choose **R**emove. Windows 95 displays the Remove Shortcuts/Folders dialog box. Locate the folder or shortcut you want to remove, then choose **R**emove. Windows 95 removes the selected folder or shortcut.

Stop   If your Start Menu folder contains folders in addition to shortcuts to folders, removing a folder removes all objects it contains, just like deleting a directory and its contents. Be certain you really want to remove a folder before you remove it from the Start Menu.

If you do remove a folder, then realize you didn't want to, look in the Recycle Bin for the folder. Move the folder from the Recycle Bin back into its original location in the Start Menu folder.

The A**d**vanced button in the Start Menu Programs property page provides a nonautomated method for creating, moving, and deleting shortcuts. Essentially, all the A**d**vanced button does is open the Explorer with the Start Menu folder displayed in Explorer. You then can use Explorer to create, remove, and move shortcuts and folders in and out of the Start Menu folder.

Using Quick Viewers

Windows 95 includes a selection of file viewing utilities called Quick Viewers. *Quick Viewers* enable you to view the contents of a document without opening the document's parent application; for example, you can view the contents of a Microsoft Word document without opening Word.

To preview a document using a Quick Viewer, select the document in a folder or in Explorer, then choose File, Quick View. Or, right-click on the document icon and choose Quick View from the context menu.

If the Quick View item doesn't appear in the File menu or context menu, the system doesn't contain a Quick Viewer for the selected document type. Or, a proper association doesn't exist between the document type and the appropriate viewer. The Quick Viewer document associations are stored in the Registry in \HKEY_CLASSES_ROOT\QuickView. For more information on the Registry, read Chapter 13, "Working with the Registry and Ini Files."

When you choose Quick View, Windows 95 opens a viewer appropriate to the selected document type. Figure 5.35, for example, shows a Microsoft Word document displayed by a Quick Viewer.

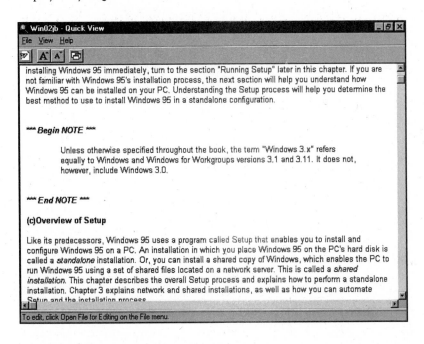

Figure 5.35

A Word document displayed in a Quick Viewer window.

You can use a Quick Viewer to view the contents of a document, but you can't edit the document. To edit the document, choose File, Open File for Editing. Or, click on the Open File for Editing button on the Quick Viewer toolbar. Windows 95 opens the source application and loads the selected document.

Starting Applications Automatically

You might have some applications or documents you use every time you turn on your PC. So that you can have those applications or documents open and ready when your PC boots, Windows 95 includes a Startup folder. All items in the Startup folder open automatically as soon as Windows 95 boots and you log on. If you place a shortcut to your spreadsheet application in the Startup folder, for example, the spreadsheet program opens as soon as Windows 95 starts.

 Note The Startup folder in Windows 95 is very similar to the Startup program group in Windows 3.x.

To start an object automatically when Windows 95 starts, simply create a shortcut for the object in the Startup folder. You can open the Startup folder and right-drag an object into the folder to create the shortcut, use the Create Shortcut wizard (choose Start, Settings, Taskbar), or use any other method for creating shortcuts. However, you should avoid copying objects to the Startup folder to make them start automatically. For example, don't copy your spreadsheet program's executable file to the Startup folder. Instead, use a shortcut to the spreadsheet application. Using shortcuts rather than duplicating objects can save a considerable amount of disk space.

 Tip You can bypass the Startup folder during startup so that its contents do not start automatically. If you are not using a network or user profiles (Windows 95 does not display a logon dialog box), press and hold down the Shift key while Windows 95 is starting. When the desktop appears, release the Shift key. If you are using a network or user profiles, enter your user name and password when the logon dialog box appears. Then, press and hold down the Shift key, then choose OK to begin startup and logon. When the desktop appears, release the Shift key.

Changing the Startup Group

You can specify a different folder as your startup folder. To specify a different folder, first open the Registry Editor. Open HKey_Current_User\Software\ Microsoft\ Windows\CurrentVersion\Explorer\Shell Folders. Or, choose Edit, Search, and search for the string Startup. Edit the Startup value to point to the folder you want to use as your startup folder. The next time you start Windows 95, the objects in the specified folder will start automatically.

Using the Keyboard

If you don't like to use a mouse, your mouse quits working, or you simply prefer to use the keyboard for certain tasks, some keyboard shortcuts can help you navigate in Windows 95. The following list provides some tips on using the keyboard rather than the mouse to do a variety of tasks in Windows 95:

◆ **Opening a menu.** Usually, one character in each menu name is underlined. To open a menu, hold down the Alt key and press the underlined letter. To open the File menu, for example, press Alt+F. If you prefer, you can press and release the Alt key, then press and release the underlined letter—it works the same as pressing the keys together. A third method is to press and release the Alt key, then use the right- or left-arrow key to highlight a menu name. When the menu is highlighted, press the down-arrow key to open the menu.

◆ **Selecting menu items.** After you open a menu, you can select items from the menu by using the arrow keys to move the selection highlight through the menu. To open a cascade menu, highlight the menu, then press the right-arrow key. After you highlight the command you want, press Enter.

◆ **Using keyboard shortcuts.** Some commands in a menu have keyboard shortcuts listed beside them. The Open command in WordPad's File menu, for example, includes a Ctrl+O shortcut. You can press this shortcut to issue the File, Open command without even opening the menu.

◆ **Using control menus.** Each program and folder window includes a control menu that you can use to control the window's state (normal, minimized, maximized), close the window, and display the Taskbar. To open a program or folder's control menu, press Alt+Spacebar. Each document window also includes its own control menu. To open a document's control menu, press Alt, then press the down-arrow key.

◆ **Resizing and moving a window.** To resize or move a window with the keyboard, open the window's control menu and choose the Size or Move commands. Then, use the arrow keys to move and resize the window.

◆ **Opening and using the Taskbar.** To open the Taskbar and display the Start menu, press Ctrl+Esc. To select a running program from the Taskbar, press Ctrl+Esc to open the Taskbar, then press Esc to close the Start menu. Press Tab, then use the arrow keys to select a program from the Taskbar.

◆ **Switching between applications and folder windows.** To switch between running applications, hold down the Alt key and press Tab. While you continue to hold down the Alt key, a small dialog box appears in the middle of the display; it contains an icon for each of the running applications or open folders. Press Tab to highlight the application or folder you want to use, then release the Alt key. To cancel selecting an application in this way, press Esc, then release the Alt key.

◆ **Switching between applications and folders (including dialog boxes).** In addition to pressing Alt+Tab to switch between running programs, you also can press Alt+Esc. Pressing Alt+Esc does not display a dialog box that enables you to choose the application you want to use; instead, Windows 95 immediately switches to the next application in sequence. If the Taskbar is not hidden, Alt+Esc also cycles through the applications in the Taskbar in addition to open windows. The primary advantage of using Alt+Esc is that Alt+Esc switches to open dialog boxes (such as many in the Control Panel) that Alt+Tab ignores.

◆ **Moving around in a dialog box or property sheet.** To move from one control to another in a dialog box or property sheet, just press Tab. To switch from one property sheet to another, use the left- and right-arrow keys, the Home key, and the End key.

Using a Microsoft Natural Keyboard

Microsoft has incorporated support into Windows 95 for the Microsoft Natural Keyboard, incorporating special shortcut keys you can enter on the keyboard to quickly access Windows 95 features and control the Windows 95 interface. The following list explains these shortcuts:

◆ **Applications key.** Press the Apps key to display the context menu of the current window.

◆ **Windows key.** Press the Win key to open the Start menu.

◆ **Windows+R.** Press this combination to display the Run dialog box.

◆ **Windows+M.** Use this key combination to minimize all open windows.

◆ **Windows+Shift+M.** This key combination corresponds to Undo Minimize All, restoring previously minimized applications to windows.

◆ **Windows+F1.** This key combination opens Windows 95 Help.

◆ **Windows+E.** Use this key combination to open Explorer with My Computer displayed in the Explorer window.

◆ **Windows+F.** This combination opens the Find dialog box to locate files.

◆ **Windows+Ctrl+F.** This combination opens the Find Computer dialog box.

◆ **Windows+Tab.** Press this combination to activate objects on the Taskbar, and when the object is selected (its button is pressed), press Enter to activate the object.

◆ **Windows+Break.** Press this combination to display the System property page.

Using the Recycle Bin

Previous versions of DOS and Windows include an UNERASE feature that enable you to retrieve files you had erased. Windows 95 includes something similar, called the *Recycle Bin,* a standard folder in which Windows 95 places files that you delete. The Recycle Bin appears as a trashcan icon on the desktop. When you have items in the Recycle Bin, the icon appears as a trashcan with papers in it. An empty trashcan icon indicates an empty Recycle Bin.

When you delete one or more files, Windows 95 places the files in the Recycle Bin, instead of immediately deleting them. The files remain in the Recycle Bin until you empty it. To empty the objects from the Recycle Bin, right-click on the Recycle Bin icon, then choose Empty Recycle Bin. Windows 95 prompts you to verify that you really want to delete the items in the Recycle Bin. If you choose Yes, Windows 95 empties the Recycle Bin, permanently deleting the objects it contains. Choose No to cancel the operation. If the Recycle Bin is open in a window, choose File, Empty Recycle Bin, to empty the Recycle Bin.

By default, Windows 95 places deleted objects in the Recycle Bin, but you can control how Windows 95 handles objects that you delete from each disk. To specify how the Recycle Bin is used, right-click on the Recycle Bin icon and choose Properties. Windows 95 displays the property sheet shown in figure 5.36.

Tip To immediately delete items even when the Recycle Bin is configured to store deleted files, hold down the Shift key when you delete the objects. Instead of moving to the Recycle Bin, the items are immediately deleted.

Figure 5.36

*Property sheet for
the Recycle Bin.*

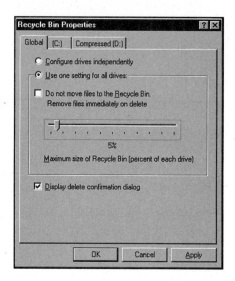

The following list explains the controls in the Global property page for the Recycle
Bin:

◆ **Configure drives independently.** Choose this option button if you want to
separately configure the way each disk is handled for file deletion. For example,
if you want files deleted from drive C to be placed in the Recycle Bin but files
from drive D to be immediately deleted, choose this option. You then can use
the drive pages of the Recycle Bin properties to control how each drive is
handled.

◆ **Use one setting for all drives.** Choose this option button if you want all
drives handled in the same way. To place deleted files from all disks in the
Recycle Bin, for example, choose this option. Also choose this option if you
want all files immediately deleted regardless of the disk from which they are
deleted (see following option).

◆ **Do not move files to the Recycle Bin.** Enable this option if you want all
files immediately deleted, bypassing the Recycle Bin. Use this setting in conjunction with the option Use one setting for all drives to cause Windows 95 to bypass
the Recycle Bin for all disks.

◆ **Maximum size of the Recycle Bin.** Use this slider to control the amount of
disk space that Windows 95 allocates to the Recycle Bin. To optimize the
amount of space available on your disk, set this control to a minimum setting.
The size is a percentage of total disk space, so the same percentage setting will
indicate different amounts of disk space with drives of different sizes.

◆ **Display delete confirmation dialog box.** Enable this option if you want Windows 95 to display a confirmation dialog box before it deletes items. If you do not want to confirm file deletions, disable this option.

Note　Windows 95 dynamically resizes the Recycle Bin folder as necessary. Therefore, specifying a size with the **M**aximum size of Recycle Bin doesn't automatically allocate a specific amount of space to the Recycle Bin—it simply sets a maximum amount of space that can be used in the Recycle Bin to store deleted files. If Recycle Bin is empty, no disk space is used other than the space used by the Recycle Bin folder itself (which is minimal).

In addition to the Global page, the Recycle Bin property sheet includes pages for each of the hard disks in your system. If you choose the option **C**onfigure drives independently, the controls in the disk sheets are enabled, which enables you to control how the Recycle Bin handles files that are deleted from each disk. Figure 5.37 shows a typical disk page.

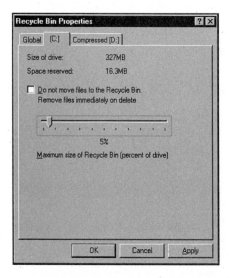

Figure 5.37

A typical Recycle Bin disk property page.

The settings you can specify on each disk property page match corresponding settings on the Global page. The only difference is that the settings on the disk pages apply only to their associated disks—settings on the Global page apply to all disks.

Tip　Each disk contains a Recycled folder. When you delete one or more files from drive C, the files are placed in the Recycled folder on drive C. Files deleted from other drives are placed in the Recycled folders on those drives. The Recycled folder is located in the root directory of a disk.

Managing Files and Folders

Much of the work you do on your PC probably involves files in one way or another. Many people find and manage document files every day. Windows 95 provides a program called Explorer that you use to view and manage your files, as well as other objects on your PC. You also can manage your PC's file system with the Windows File Manager, folder windows, and other methods. This chapter examines Explorer and other file-related issues, including the following topics:

- ◆ Using Explorer

- ◆ Using File Manager

- ◆ Formatting disks

- ◆ Copying and moving files

- ◆ Creating and working with folders

- ◆ Searching for files and folders

- ◆ Using long file names

- ◆ Managing files from the command line

You can perform most file and disk management tasks without opening Explorer—you can simply open a folder window and perform the task. If you work with a large number of objects or want to copy or delete entire folders, however, using Explorer often is more practical.

Explorer is only one method for managing files and folders—this chapter focuses on file management tasks rather than on Explorer. The following section provides an overview of Explorer to help you understand how it works and how to use it effectively. Later sections explain how to perform various tasks, using a variety of methods, including Explorer, to format disks and manage files and folders. This chapter treats Explorer as one tool among many that you can use to manage your files and folders, instead of focusing on it as a file management application.

Introducing Explorer

As you might have read in Chapter 5, "Working in Windows 95," the Windows 95 Explorer is an application provided in Windows 95 that you can use to view and manage the resources on your PC. Explorer provides a view of other objects, including the desktop, Printers folder, Control Panel, Network Neighborhood, Dial-Up Networking folder, Recycle Bin, Briefcase, and any other objects on your Windows 95 desktop, doing more than just showing you a view of your PC's disks. Figure 6.1 shows the Explorer window with these objects displayed in the Tree pane of the Explorer window.

Figure 6.1

Explorer provides a view of all your PC's resources.

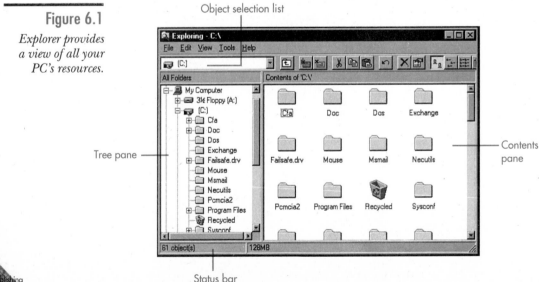

Tip   To run Explorer, choose Start, Programs, and Windows Explorer. To open an Explorer window of a folder, hold down the Shift key and double-click on the folder's icon. If you have a shortcut on the desktop to a folder, for example, you can open an Explorer window of that folder by holding down the Shift key and double-clicking on the shortcut icon.

Examining the Explorer Window

By default, the Explorer window includes two panes. The left pane, the Tree pane, arranges the resources on your desktop in a hierarchical tree that includes all objects on the desktop. Selecting an object from the tree displays its contents in the Contents pane.

How the objects appear in the Contents pane depends on which view options you select. You can display the objects as large icons, small icons, a simple list, or a detailed list by choosing one of the four options from the View menu or by choosing a view option from the toolbar. If you select the large or small icon view, a labeled icon represents each item. If you select the List option, the Contents pane displays a small icon for each object to indicate its type, along with a description (see fig. 6.2). The description for folders is the folder's name, and the description for files is the file's long file name (explained later in this chapter) or, if the file doesn't have a long file name, its short file name.

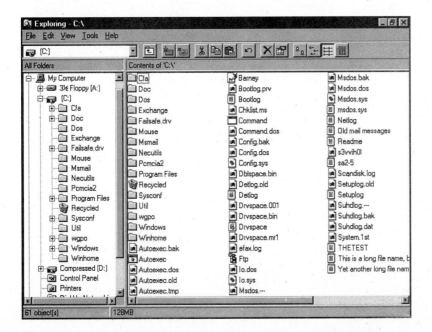

Figure 6.2

Objects displayed as a list in Explorer.

You also can display a detailed list of the objects in the selected folder by choosing
<u>V</u>iew, <u>D</u>etails or by clicking on the Details button on the toolbar. In addition to
displaying an icon and description for each object, Explorer displays the object's type
and the date the object was last modified (see fig. 6.3).

Figure 6.3

*A detailed list in
Explorer.*

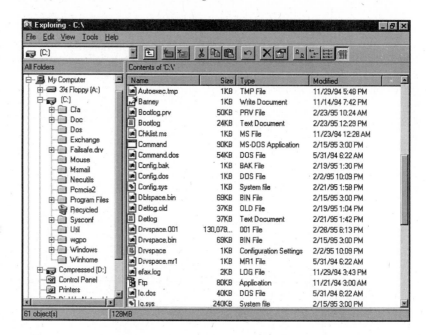

The Explorer window looks and functions much like any folder window. You can use
the <u>V</u>iew menu to turn on or off the toolbar and status bar, and to control other
options.

Opening Objects in Explorer

Objects in Explorer's tree include a small plus sign (+) beside them if they contain
additional folders (refer to figure 6.1). To expand a folder to show its subfolders,
click on the plus sign. After you expand a folder to show its subfolders, the plus sign
switches to a minus sign (–). To collapse a folder, click on the minus sign. Collapsing
a folder makes it possible to view more objects in the tree, which is useful when you
want to copy or move objects between different folders and can't otherwise see both
folders in the tree. Collapsing folders also simplifies the entire tree view, reducing
clutter and making locating objects easier.

 Tip   You can expand and collapse an object by double-clicking on it in the tree.

To view the contents of a folder, click on the folder name or icon in the tree. The Contents pane changes to display the contents of the folder. If the selected folder contains other folders, their icons appear in the Contents pane, even if the folder is not expanded in the tree (see fig. 6.4).

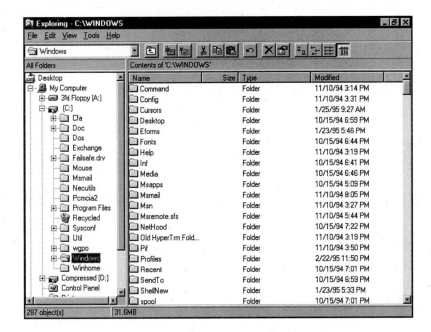

Figure 6.4

The Contents pane displays all subfolders and other objects in the folder.

To open an object inside a folder, double-click on the object or select the object with the arrow keys and press Enter. If the object is an application, Explorer starts the application. If the object is a document, Explorer starts the document's parent application and loads the document into the application. If you attempt to open a document that has no application association, Explorer issues the Open With dialog box (see fig. 6.5), which prompts you to specify the application you want to use to open the document. Select the application you want to use to open the document, then choose OK.

Tip

Enable the Always use this program to open this file check box if you want to associate the selected document type with the application. This places an entry for the document in the Registry, and enables Windows 95 to use the same application in the future to open documents of the same type without any input from you.

Figure 6.5

Use the Open With dialog box to specify which application to use to open a document.

You also can use the context menu to open an object. Right-click on an object, select it, or use the cursor keys and press Shift+F10 to open the context menu. If Windows recognizes the object type, the first menu item in the context menu is **O**pen. Choose **O**pen to open the document. If Windows 95 does not recognize the document type, the first item in the context menu is **O**pen With. Choose **O**pen With to display the Open With dialog box, and specify the application you want to use to open the document.

 Tip   Because Explorer windows are just like other folder windows, you have the same options for controlling the appearance of the Explorer window as you do with folder windows. To set Explorer's view options, choose **V**iew, **O**ptions. For information on setting folder options, refer to Chapter 5, "Working in Windows 95."

Jumping to a Specific Folder

You can open a folder in Explorer simply by selecting it from the Tree or Contents panes. Sometimes, however, this method for opening a folder is impractical. For example, the folder you want to open might be buried deep in the tree.

Rather than burrow your way through the tree to find a folder, you can jump directly to the folder. To do so, choose **T**ools, **G**o To or press Ctrl+G to display the Go To Folder dialog box (see fig. 6.6). Enter the path to the folder you want to view in Explorer; for example, enter **C:\Windows** in the text area of the combo box to view the Windows folder. You also can use the drop-down list to select most recently used objects.

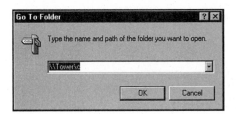

Figure 6.6

The Go To Folder dialog box.

The objects listed in the Go To Folder dialog box's drop-down list are the same objects that appear in the Run dialog box (choose Start, Run). The drop-down list in the Go To Folder dialog box usually displays a list of files rather than folders. Selecting a file from the list and choosing OK causes Explorer to display the folder that contains the specified file. Explorer does not open the file, however.

Tip　The list in the Run dialog box and Go To Folder dialog boxes are the same, so maybe you have realized that you can "run" a folder to open it. A quick way to open a folder window is to choose Start, Run, specify the name of the folder in the Run dialog box, and choose OK. To open the C:\Windows\Start Menu\Programs folder, for example, enter **c:\windows\start menu\programs** in the Run dialog box.

Shortcuts for Using Explorer

Explorer includes many shortcuts keystrokes you can use to simplify working with Explorer. The shortcut keys are described in the following list:

◆ **F4.** Opens the select object drop-down list, after which you can use the arrow keys to select an object to view in Explorer.

◆ **F5.** Refreshes the view.

◆ **F6.** Switches between the Tree and Contents panes.

◆ **Ctrl+G.** Shortcut to the Go To command; similar to choosing Tools, Go To.

◆ **Ctrl+Z.** Issues the Edit, Undo command.

◆ **Ctrl+A.** Selects all objects in the Contents pane.

◆ **Backspace.** Moves the view to the parent folder.

◆ ***.** (On the numeric keypad.) Expands all folders under the selection in the tree.

◆ **+.** (On the numeric keypad.) Expands the tree of the current selection.

◆ **-.** (On the numeric keypad.) Collapses the current selection's tree.

◆ **Right arrow.** With tree active, expands current selection's tree, if not already expanded; if already expanded, moves to the first child object in the selection.

◆ **Left arrow.** With tree active, collapses the current selection, if expanded; if not expanded, moves to the current object's parent.

◆ **Ctrl+arrow.** Scrolls the tree without moving the current selection.

Using Explorer Command Switches

As with many Windows applications, Explorer supports *command-line switches,* which are optional parameters you include on the command line to start Explorer set with certain options. The syntax for the Explorer command line follows:

```
explorer [/n] [/e][,/root,object][[,/select],subobject]
```

The command-line switches in the preceding syntax example are as follows:

◆ **/n.** Explorer always opens a new window, even if the specified folder is already open (see the /root switch).

◆ **/e.** Explorer uses Windows Explorer view. If you specify a folder with the /root option and do not specify the /e option, Explorer opens a standard folder window rather than the Explorer window.

◆ **/root,object.** Specifies the object to use as the root in the Tree pane. By default, the desktop is the root object. To open an explorer view of only one folder on a disk, specify the drive letter and folder path in place of *object.* To open Explorer with only the Windows directory displayed, for example, use **/root,c:\windows** for this option.

◆ **/select.** This option specifies that the parent folder specified by the /root option is opened. If you also include the *subobject* option, Explorer selects the specified object in the Contents pane but does not open the object. To open \Windows as the root with the Command folder selected but not opened, use the command line **Explorer /e,/root,c:\windows,/select,Command.**

◆ **subobject.** Specifies the object to open in the Contents pane. To open the Command folder, for example, use the command line **Explorer /e,/root,c:\windows,Command.**

Getting Quick Access to Explorer

If you use Explorer a lot, consider creating a shortcut on the desktop to Explorer (shortcuts are explained in Chapter 5, "Working in Windows 95"). You also might want to assign a shortcut key that enables you to load Explorer with a quick keystroke. You can't assign a shortcut keystroke directly to Explorer's executable file (Explorer.exe), but you can assign a shortcut keystroke to your Explorer shortcut. After you create the shortcut on the desktop to Explorer, select the shortcut and open its context menu (Shift+F10 or right-click). In the Shortcut page of the property sheets for the shortcut, click in the Shortcut key text box, then press the shortcut key sequence you want to assign to Explorer, such as Ctrl+Alt+X. Then, whenever you need to open Explorer, just press Ctrl+Alt+X (or whatever shortcut key sequence you assign to the shortcut).

Before a shortcut keystroke can work, however, the shortcut has to be in the \Windows\Desktop folder, or, if you use multiple user profiles, in the \Windows\Profiles\user\Desktop folder.

Tip You can use Explorer command-line switches to control the way in which Explorer opens, including the object that appears by default in the Explorer window. In addition to assigning a shortcut key to the Explorer shortcut, you might want to include command-line switches in the shortcut's command-line entry. In fact, you can create multiple shortcuts to Explorer, each with different startup options and shortcut keys. For example, you might assign Shift+Ctrl+Alt+C to a drive C Explorer shortcut, and Shift+Ctrl+Alt+D to a drive D Explorer shortcut.

Summarizing Explorer

Explorer is tightly integrated with the Windows 95 environment. Although Explorer is a separate program, you can consider Explorer to encompass the entire desktop. When you open a folder on the desktop, you see information presented in the same way that the information is presented in Explorer. Explorer simply gives you a much broader view than a folder window of your PC's resources.

The following sections examine common file and folder management tasks and describe various methods you can use to accomplish the tasks. The tasks are explained using non-Explorer methods, then, usually, using an Explorer method as well.

Understanding and Using Long File Names

Before you begin creating, copying, and renaming objects, you should understand Windows 95's long file names. Versions of DOS and Windows prior to Windows 95 support file names in what is referred to as *8.3 format*. The file's name consist of no more than eight characters and can be followed by a file extension of no more than three characters. The name and extension are separated by a period. A valid file name in 8.3 format, for example, is Myreport.doc.

Windows 95 adds support for long file names. Applications written to do so now can work with primary file names of up to 255 characters. Rather than name a file Myreport.doc, for example, you can create a file named First Quarter Sales and Analysis - Midwest. Long file names enable you to use much more descriptive, easier-to-understand file names than you can in 8.3 format.

Because only programs designed specifically for Windows 95 support long file names, each file also includes a short file name, called an *alias*, in 8.3 format. Aliases enable programs that do not support long file names to continue working with files that have long file names. When you create a file that has a long file name, Windows 95 automatically generates an 8.3 alias for the file using the first six characters of the long file name, a tilde (~), and a number. Programs that don't support long file names see this 8.3 alias as the file's name.

The following are important points to keep in mind when you deal with file names in Windows 95:

- **Not all programs support long file names.** If you use a Windows 3.*x* or DOS program, it can't recognize long file names. If you open a file that has a long file name while using such a program, then resave the file, you could lose the long file name.

- **Long file names can include additional characters not allowed in 8.3 format names.** In addition to the characters you can use in an 8.3 format file name ($ % ' - _ @ ~ ` ! ( ) ^ # &), you can include the following characters in long file names: + , ; = [ ]. You can place any number of periods in a long file name (assuming you don't exceed the 255-character maximum).

- **You can't specify the 8.3 alias.** Windows 95 automatically generates 8.3 aliases when you create a file. You can't specify the 8.3 alias assigned to a file.

- **Some utility programs can destroy long file names.** Backup and restore programs not designed to support long file names destroy long file names.

◆ **Long names transported to other systems might not be visible.** If you copy a file that has a long file name to a system that does not support long file names, only the 8.3 alias is visible to the destination system.

◆ **Maximum path length is 260 characters, including NULL.** Although you can use up to 255 characters for long file names, you should generally try to use no more than 70 or 80 characters in a file name. Because the path is limited to 260 characters, using a smaller long file name leaves space for path information to accompany the file name when you need to copy or move a file.

To be recognized as an 8.3 file name, the file name must consist of eight or fewer characters, only valid 8.3 characters, no more than a three-character extension, and only uppercase letters. Any file name that includes lowercase letters is treated as a long file name, regardless of length. In addition, lowercase characters are retained in the long file name—not converted to uppercase. Even so, the Windows 95 file system is not case-sensitive. You can't save a file named "This Is a Test" in a folder that already contains a file named "this IS a TEST". File system searches are not case-sensitive. Performing a Find operation on the string "try*.doc" would locate the files TRY.DOC and TryIt.doc.

Using Long File Names in Applications

Only specifically designed applications can recognize and support long file names. To meet Microsoft's Windows 95 compatibility requirements, applications marketed as being compatible with Windows 95 must recognize and support long file names. Therefore, any Windows 95 application should support long file names. Windows 3.*x* and MS-DOS applications, however, do not support long file names.

Even though MS-DOS and Windows 3.*x* applications don't support long file names, you typically can load and modify a file that has a long file name while using a Windows 3.*x* or MS-DOS application without losing the long file name, even if you modify the file outside of Windows 95. If you boot your system to a previous version of DOS, run Windows 3.*x*, and edit the file, for example, the long file name still is intact and visible when you open the file again in Windows 95. Whether an application preserves the long file names, however, depends on the method the application uses to store the file. You can use the following simple test to determine whether you can use an older application to work on long file name documents outside of Windows 95:

1. Create and save a document with a long file name in a Windows 95 application that is compatible with the older application (the two applications must be able to read the same file).

2. Boot the system to your previous version of MS-DOS (and Windows 3.*x* if appropriate) and load the older application in question.

3. Open the file that has the long file name and resave it.

4. Reboot the system to Windows 95 and verify whether the file has retained the long file name.

Windows 95 also provides compatibility between older applications and long file names when you run the application under Windows 95. Most applications that you run under Windows 95, therefore, should not destroy long file names. Nevertheless, you should run a test to determine whether the application destroys long file names. Create a document that has a long file name using a compatible application, open the document in the older application and resave it, then determine whether the long file name is still intact.

Stop   The ability to run older MS-DOS and Windows 3.x applications on files that have long file names without destroying the file names doesn't apply to most backup, disk utility, and antivirus applications. In general, these types of applications destroy long file names, although the files and their data are left unaffected.

Using Long File Names at the Command Prompt

Windows 95 updates many of your command-line applications (DOS commands) to support long file names. The COPY command, for example, enables you to copy a file that has a long file name. This long file name support is available from command-line sessions that you start under Windows 95 and when you boot the PC to the command line rather than to the GUI.

To use a long file name at the command prompt, simply type it as you would a short file name. If the file name contains special characters, such as spaces, however, you must include the file name in quotation marks. The following is an example of using the COPY command to copy a file with a long file name that contains spaces:

```
copy "This is a long file name.txt" "Yet another long file name.txt"
```

By default, the Windows 95 command prompt environment uses a keyboard buffer of 127 characters, which limits the length of long file names you can use at the command prompt. If you copy a file that has a long file name to the root directory of a floppy disk for example, the long file name is limited to 119 characters—127 minus 4 characters for "copy" and another two characters for the floppy disk ID, such as "A:". Decrease the limit by 2 more if you need to enclose the long file name in quotation marks—one character for each quotation mark.

You can, however, increase the size of the keyboard buffer by using the SHELL command. To increase the size of the keyboard buffer to its maximum of 255 characters, use the /u switch along with SHELL. Edit Config.sys and add or modify the SHELL statement using the /u switch and keyboard buffer size as in the following example:

```
shell=c:\windows\command.com /u:255
```

After you modify the keyboard buffer, save the changes to Config.sys and reboot the PC. The Windows 95 command line and MS-DOS sessions that you create under Windows 95 then uses the increased keyboard buffer size.

 Note   When Windows 95 exits to single-application MS-DOS Mode, the system uses only the real-mode FAT (file allocation table) file system. You can't see long file names created in Windows 95 or from the Windows 95 command line during MS-DOS Mode. You can, however, still see the 8.3 aliases of the files that have long file names.

Disabling Long File Names

Generally you shouldn't experience any problems using long file names. After you use long file names, you start to wonder how you got along without them and how you could handle the constraints of the 8.3 file naming system. If, by some unlikely chance, you decide that using long file names disturbs the use of your system or applications, you can disable Windows 95's use of long file names. To disable long file names, follow these steps:

1. First remove the long file names by using the LFNBK (Long File Name BacKup) utility.

2. Run the Registry Editor (Regedit) and locate the Registry key `Hkey_Local_Machine\System\CurrentControlSet\Control\FileSystem`.

3. Set the value of `Win31FileSystem` to **01**.

4. Shut down and restart the computer.

 Tip   You can direct Setup to disable long file names when you install Windows 95. For information on using Setup and disabling long file names during Setup, refer to Chapter 2, "Setting Up and Booting Windows 95."

Examining NTFS, HPFS, and FAT Issues

Windows 95 nodes can access files stored on Windows NT NTFS volumes and LAN Manager and OS/2 HPFS volumes located on remote computers, although Windows 95 can't read NTFS or HPFS volumes on a local disk. To some degree, long file name compatibility exists between Windows 95 and these other systems, although some limitations (described in the following sections) apply to accessing long file names on FAT volumes from operating systems other than Windows 95.

Windows NT 3.1

Windows NT 3.1 does not support long file names on FAT partitions. Therefore, computers that run Windows NT 3.1 can't see long file names created on Windows 95 computers, nor long file names created by Windows 95 on the Windows NT 3.1 computer's local FAT volumes (which could occur on computers that dual-boot Windows NT 3.1 and Windows 95). Windows NT 3.1 also destroys long file names in a local FAT volume.

Windows NT 3.1 NTFS volumes, however, do support long file names. Windows 95 nodes that run a protected-mode network client can view long file names in the NTFS volumes of Windows NT 3.1 servers. Windows 95 nodes that run real-mode network clients, however, can see only the 8.3 file-name aliases in the NTFS volume.

Windows NT 3.5

Windows NT 3.5 uses the same mechanism to support long file names on FAT volumes as does Windows 95, so Windows 95 and Windows NT 3.5 nodes can access long file names on a FAT drive without problems. Therefore, a computer can dual-boot Windows NT 3.5 and Windows 95 and still enable both operating systems to see and work with long file names on a local FAT volume. As well, Windows 95 nodes can view the long file names in NTFS and FAT volumes on Windows NT 3.5 servers.

HPFS and HPFS/386 Volumes

LAN Manager OS/2-based systems support HPFS and HPFS/386 file systems, as do systems upgraded from OS/2 to Windows NT. These file systems support long file names of up to 254 characters. As with NTFS volumes, Windows 95 nodes that run protected-mode network clients can view the long file names in HPFS and HPFS/386 volumes. Windows 95 nodes that run real-mode network clients can view only the 8.3 aliases for the files in the HPFS and HPFS/386 volumes.

Creating Folders and Documents

Windows 95 provides a selection of methods you can use to create new folders and documents. This section of the chapter includes a discussion of why you would want to create these types of items, and provides a description of the many methods you can use to create them.

Creating Folders

As you probably know, a folder that you create in Windows 95 is really nothing more than a directory. Although you can use the MKDIR or MD commands at the command prompt to create a directory (folder), you probably would find that creating folders in Windows 95 is easier.

The easiest way to create a folder is to right-click where you want the folder created, then choose New, Folder. Windows 95 creates a new folder named New Folder and highlights the folder name so you can immediately enter a new name for the folder. If you right-click on the desktop, the folder is created on the desktop in the \Windows\Desktop folder, or in the \Windows\Profiles*user*\Desktop folder if you configure Windows 95 to provide unique desktop environments. If you right-click in an open folder, the new folder is created in the open folder (creating a subdirectory).

 Tip   To use the keyboard to create a folder on the desktop, make sure that no open folder window is in the foreground, then press Shift+F10 to display the desktop's context menu. Choose New, Folder, to create the folder on the desktop. To create a folder in a folder window, choose File, New, Folder.

You use a similar method in Explorer to create a folder. Just right-click on the folder in which you want the new folder created, then choose New, Folder. Or, select the parent folder (or the desktop) and choose File, New, Folder.

Creating New Documents

If you have used Windows 3.*x* or DOS applications, you probably are used to creating documents from within an application; for example, you create the data in the application, then choose File, Save As to save the document to disk. In Windows 95 you can start a new document without first opening the parent application for the document.

If you right-click on the desktop or in a folder and choose New, a list of document types appears (see fig. 6.7). The menu lists all document types of OLE-aware applications properly registered in Windows 95. To create a new document, simply select it from the list of document types. Windows 95 creates a new document in the currently opened folder or on the desktop, depending on where you right-click.

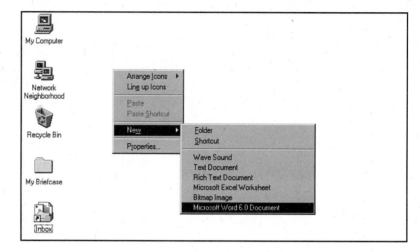

Figure 6.7

You can create a new document without opening the parent application.

As when you create a new folder, Windows 95 automatically assigns a name to the new document. If you create a new Word for Windows 6.0 document, for example, Windows 95 names the new file New Microsoft Word 6.0 Document. The name is automatically highlighted, so you can immediately enter a document name of your choice. If a document already exists with the name Windows 95 would otherwise assign, a number is added to the end of the new document name, such as New Microsoft Word 6.0 Document #2.

When you use the preceding method to create a new document, Windows 95 does not automatically open the parent application. To edit the document, double-click on its icon, or select the icon and press Enter.

Tip   Instead of right-clicking, you can choose File, New and then select the document type to create. Or, you can just press Shift+F10 to open the folder's or desktop's context menu.

Sending Objects

Windows 95 enables you to send objects to a floppy disk, Microsoft Fax, your Briefcase, an e-mail recipient, other disk locations, and printers, all with unbegrudging ease. You can right-click on a file, for example, then choose Send To and select the

floppy disk to which you want to send the file (see fig. 6.8). Windows 95 then copies the file to the floppy disk. Using the Send To method is simpler than opening My Computer and dragging the file to the floppy disk icon, because it eliminates the need to open My Computer to make the floppy drive icon available.

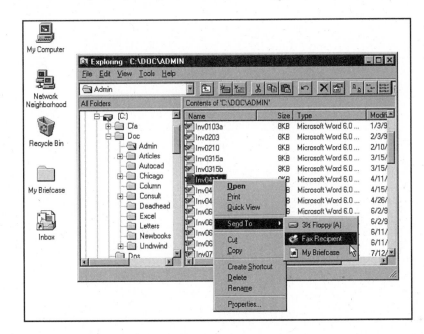

Figure 6.8

Right-click on an object and choose Send To to send the object to floppy, fax, e-mail, or Briefcase.

To use Send To, right-click on an object such as a file, folder, or shortcut in a folder, in an Explorer window, or on the desktop. From the context menu, choose Send To, followed by the destination of the object. If Microsoft Fax and a Briefcase are configured on your system, they appear in the Send To menu along with any floppy drive(s) in your system.

Tip An alternative method of using Send To is to select the object and choose File, Send To. Or, select the object and press Shift+F10 to display its context menu.

Windows 95 adds only your PC's floppy disks, Briefcase, Mail, and Fax to the Send To menu, but you easily can add other items to the menu. To do so, just create shortcuts in the \Windows\SendTo folder for each of the locations to which you want to be able to send objects. Any shortcuts that appear in the \Windows\SendTo folder automatically appear on the Send To menu.

For example, if you want to be able to print a document by selecting it and choosing Send To, then selecting a printer from the menu, add shortcuts in \Windows\SendTo for all your printers. Or, you might want to create shortcuts in \Windows\SendTo to a selection of remote network folders.

The following list explains how Windows 95 handles an object going to some of the possible destinations:

◆ **Floppy disk, or local or remote hard disk.** Windows 95 handles a Send To a floppy as a standard file copy. If you send a folder to a floppy, all files and subfolders in the folder are copied to the floppy disk.

◆ **Fax recipient.** Windows 95 starts a wizard that steps you through creating a fax. You then use Exchange to send the fax.

◆ **Mail recipient.** Windows 95 opens a new message composition window and attaches the selected object to the message.

◆ **Briefcase.** Choosing this option is similar to choosing the Floppy item, inasmuch as Windows 95 simply copies the object. The difference is that Windows 95 copies the object(s) to the Briefcase rather than to the floppy disk.

◆ **Printer.** Windows 95 opens the source application for the document, then prints it to the selected printer. This is similar to dragging a document onto a printer icon in the Printers folder or onto a printer shortcut.

You can find more information about copying and moving objects in the section "Copying, Moving, and Renaming Objects" later in this chapter. For more information on sending a fax, refer to Chapter 31, "Using Microsoft Fax." For detailed information on using a Briefcase, refer to Chapter 19, "Creating and Using a Briefcase." For information regarding setting up, using, and managing printers, refer to Chapter 8, "Printing and Managing Printers."

Formatting and Labeling Disks

As with previous versions of MS-DOS and Windows, Windows 95 offers a few different methods for formatting and labeling disks, some of which are very similar, if not identical, to the methods used in MS-DOS and Windows 3.x. A significant difference, however, is that you now can format a disk in Windows 95 as you work on other tasks. You naturally do experience some performance degradation in your other applications during formatting, but the extent of the performance hit depends on your PC's CPU type and speed.

Note   You cannot format a disk that contains open files, including the disk that Windows 95 currently is using, such as the disk from which you run Windows 95. You also cannot format compressed drives or drives currently hosting a compressed drive. To format a drive hosting a compressed drive, back up the compressed drive (if you want to keep its files), unmount the compressed drive, then format the host disk. To format a compressed drive, use DriveSpace (for DriveSpace volumes) or your compression software's management program.

To format a disk, open My Computer and right-click on the disk's icon, then choose Format. Or, select the disk's icon and press Shift+F10, then choose Format. If Windows 95 can format the disk, a dialog box similar to the one shown in figure 6.9 appears. If Windows 95 can't format the disk for any reason previously explained, Windows 95 displays an error message to explain why it can't reformat the drive.

Figure 6.9

The Format dialog box.

You can choose one of the following options to define how to reformat the disk:

◆ **Quick (erase).** Choose this option to delete the files from a previously formatted disk. This option is faster than the Full option, but does not ensure that any new bad sectors are identified.

◆ **Full.** Choose this option to perform a full sector-by-sector format of the disk. This option is necessary for disks being formatted for the first time, and you should choose this option if you want to verify the identifications and exclusion of bad sectors on the disk.

◆ **Copy system files only.** Choose this option to copy the system files to the disk, making a previously formatted disk bootable.

In addition to specifying the type of format to perform, you also must specify the capacity of the disk to be formatted. The Capacity drop-down list enables you to choose the capacity for which you want the drive formatted. For 3.5-inch disks, for example, the Capacity drop-down list includes 1.44 MB and 720 KB selections. 5.25-inch disks include selections for 1.2 MB and 360 KB formats. If you format a hard disk, the hard disk's total formatted capacity automatically appears in the list—you can't change capacity on a hard disk, but you can use DriveSpace to double its capacity. For information on using DriveSpace, refer to Chapter 15, "Optimizing Data Storage."

Besides formatting the disk, you can add a label to it. A disk's label appears in directory listings and in Windows 3.x-style drive selection list boxes. Figure 6.10, for example, shows a hard disk labeled "apps" in Word for Windows' Open dialog box.

Figure 6.10

A hard disk labeled "apps" in a drive selection box.

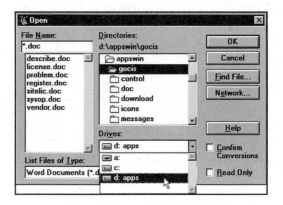

Unfortunately, disk labels have not seen the same increase in length as file names in Windows 95. Disk labels are limited to no more than 11 characters. If you format a disk that has previously been formatted and labeled, the disk's current label appears in the Label text box (of the Format dialog box). You can use the existing label, enter a new label, or clear the text box to use no label at all. You also can enable the No label check box to specify that you want the disk to have no label.

If you enable the Display summary when finished check box, Windows 95 displays a status dialog box (see fig. 6.11) after it finishes formatting, and it provides information about the amount of free space on the disk, number of bad sectors, and more.

If you want to create a bootable disk, enable the Copy system files check box. In addition to formatting the disk, Windows 95 then copies the necessary boot files to the disk to enable the disk to be used to boot the PC. This is similar to the Copy system files only option button, except you use the Copy system files only option for already-formatted disks—you use the Copy system files check box to create a boot disk from an unformatted disk.

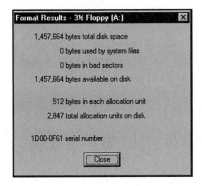

After you specify the necessary settings, choose §tart to begin formatting. Here, you can switch away from the Format dialog box to other applications and continue working during the format.

You also can use the FORMAT command at the command prompt to format a disk. Generally, formatting a disk from the GUI is as easy, or easier, than using the FORMAT command, particularly for new users. You might need to use the FORMAT command, however, to format the hard disk on which you intend to install Windows 95. For more information on preparing a disk to install Windows 95, refer to Chapter 2, "Setting Up and Booting Windows 95." You can enter **FORMAT** /? at the command prompt to obtain a listing of FORMAT command syntax and options, assuming FORMAT.COM is in the current directory. You can find FORMAT.COM in the \Windows\Command directory.

Note   For information about partitioning a disk or formatting a disk to install Windows 95, refer to Chapter 15, "Optimizing Data Storage."

In addition to formatting a disk through the disk's context menu in My Computer, you can format a disk in Explorer. Select the disk you want to format, then press Shift+F10 to display the disk's context menu, or right-click on the disk's icon. From the context menu, choose For**m**at to format the disk.

Tip   You can right-click on a disk shortcut icon to format the disk associated with the shortcut.

Copying, Moving, and Renaming Objects

Much file and folder management you do probably includes copying and moving objects between disks and folders, and renaming objects. This section explains how you can perform these types of actions in Windows 95.

Copying and Moving Files and Folders

During the course of a normal week, it's a sure bet that you often copy files from folder to folder or from one disk to another. If you want to back up a couple document files, for example, you probably copy them from the hard disk to a floppy disk or to a network disk. Moving a file is similar to copying it, except the original is deleted after it copies to its new location.

Chapter 5, "Working in Windows 95," explains how to copy and move objects simply by dragging them from one folder to another. One of the easiest methods of copying or moving a selection of files is to drag their icons to their destination. More often than not, using Explorer is the easiest way to accomplish this, because Explorer enables you to see both the source folder and destination folder in one window. After you open Explorer, locate and select the files you want to copy or move. Then, click on one of the files and drag the files to the folder or disk to which you want to copy the files. Whether the drag acts as a copy or a move depends on the relationship between the source and destination folders. The following list explains the relationship:

- ◆ **Same disk.** Dragging files or folders within the same disk moves them. Holding down Ctrl while dragging the files copies them.

- ◆ **Different disk.** Dragging files or folders from one disk to a different disk copies the files. Holding down Shift while dragging the files moves them.

If you want to be able to choose whether to move or copy the files, right-drag the files to their destination. This opens a menu that gives you the option of moving or copying the files, or creating shortcuts to the files.

Tip   You can select multiple files and folders in the Contents pane, enabling you to copy or move a selection of folders and files. Hold down the Shift key while clicking to select a range of files or folders, and hold down the Ctrl key while clicking to select objects one at a time.

Often, however, you can't see both the destination folder in the tree and the source folder. The destination folder might be far removed in the folder structure from the source folder, or located on another disk. The solution is to first locate the destination folder, expanding its parent folder if necessary. You only have to display the folder in the tree—you don't have to actually open the destination folder. Then, scroll through the tree to locate and open the source folder. Select in the Contents pane all files and folders you want to copy, then scroll through the Tree pane to locate the destination folder. Drag the files from the Contents pane and drop them on the destination folder.

Note Copying a folder adds it as a folder to the structure of the destination folder. Dragging the folder \Harry to the folder \Fiddlesticks creates a folder named \Fiddlesticks\Harry. All of the files and folders in \Harry are duplicated in \Fiddlesticks\Harry.

If you need to see the contents of the source and destination folders, or you want to open multiple source or destination folders, one instance of Explorer doesn't do the trick. This isn't a problem, however, because you can open as many instances of Explorer as you need. Just choose Start, Programs, Windows Explorer as many times as you want instances of Explorer on the desktop. Next, select a different view in each instance. Then, select and copy files between Explorer windows as necessary.

Tip Dragging a folder to copy it also copies all files and other folders contained in that folder. To copy the Windows folder and all its subfolders and files, for example, you simply would drag the Windows folder to a new location. Before you copy a folder, make sure you really want to copy all its files and folders, too.

Using the Clipboard to Copy Files and Folders

Dragging files and folders between folder windows and Explorer windows is just one method of copying files. If you look in Explorer's File menu, you might be surprised not to find a Copy command, even if you have selected one or more files or folders. This doesn't mean that you can't use the menus or keyboard to copy files—the capability does exist, but it might not be where you expect to find it.

If you select one or more files or folders, then open the Edit menu, you find the Copy command enabled. To copy files using the menu, select the files or folders you want to copy, then choose Edit, Copy or press Ctrl+C. Explorer copies the files and folders to the Clipboard. Then, select the destination to which you want the folders copied and choose Edit, Paste or press Ctrl+V. Explorer copies the files to the destination.

Note   Explorer does not actually copy the files or folders to the Clipboard. In fact, copying
the actual files to the Clipboard would often be impractical—the contents of the
Windows folder and all its subfolders, for example, would scarcely fit on the
Clipboard. Explorer instead simply copies the names of the selected objects to the
Clipboard in a variety of special list-based formats. When you choose Edit, Paste
or press Ctrl+V, Explorer looks at the contents of the Clipboard, determines that a
file list exists in the Clipboard, then copies the files to the destination based on that
list.

You also can use the Clipboard to move files. Instead of copying the file and folder list
to the Clipboard, however, you cut the objects, then paste them into their new
location. Unlike a typical cut operation, which actually removes the original to the
Clipboard, Explorer treats the operation differently. When you select folders and
files, then choose Edit, Cut or press Ctrl+X, Explorer dims the selected objects to
indicate that they have been cut. The files and folders are removed, however, only if
you select a destination and choose Edit, Paste or press Ctrl+V. If you perform any
other operation, Explorer just "un-dims" the files and does nothing with them.

To use the Clipboard to move files, therefore, first select the files and folders you
want to move. Choose Edit, Cut or press Ctrl+X to cut the file list to the Clipboard.
Then select the destination folder and choose Edit, Paste or press Ctrl+V. Explorer
copies the files to the new location and deletes the original copies.

Tip   You do not have to use Explorer to copy or move files with the Clipboard. You can
open a folder window, select objects, then cut, copy, and paste between folder
windows.

Renaming Files, Folders, and Disks

Renaming a file or folder is a simple process in Windows 95, one you can perform
equally well in a folder window, on the desktop, or in Explorer. To rename a folder or
file in any of these locations, simply select the object and click on its title, which
highlights it. Type a new title and press Enter to change the title. If you have trouble
selecting and highlighting the name, right-click on the object and choose Rename
from its context menu, which also highlights the name, and then you can enter a new
name.

Tip   To use the keyboard to rename an object, select the object and press Shift+F10 to
open its context menu. Then choose Rename.

Like files and folders, disks have names—a disk's label is its name. Unlike files and folders, however, you can't click on a disk's description and change the disk's label. To change a disk's label, first select the disk's icon, in My Computer or in Explorer. Open the disk's property sheet by pressing Alt+Enter. Or, open the disk's context menu by pressing Shift+F10 or by right-clicking on the icon and choosing Properties. Windows displays the property sheet shown in figure 6.12. In the Label text box on the General page, enter up to 11 characters for the disk's label. Then, choose OK or Apply to make the name change take effect.

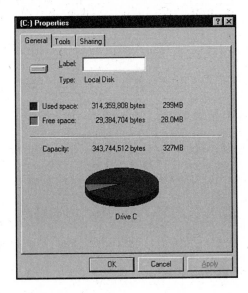

Figure 6.12

The General property page for a disk.

Searching for Files and Folders

Windows 95 includes an integrated search tool called Find that helps you locate files, folders, computers on the network, and topics on the Microsoft Network. This chapter covers using Find to locate files and folders; Chapter 35, "Sharing Resources in Windows 95," explains how to use Find to locate computers on the network. Chapter 32, "Using the Microsoft Network," explains how to use Find to locate topics on MSN.

Before you begin reading about Find, however, you need to understand wild cards. The following section explains the changes to wild-card pattern matching in Windows 95. Even if you are familiar with wild cards in previous versions of DOS or Windows, you should read the following section to understand the changes to wild cards in Windows 95.

Understanding and Using Wild Cards

Windows 95 supports using wild cards to control pattern matching in file names. Wild cards help you locate files by name or by extension, quickly and easily. The two wild-card characters that Windows 95 supports are the asterisk (*) and the question mark (?). You use the asterisk to represent multiple characters, and the question mark to represent single characters. Aside from a few exceptions, you can use a combination of wild-card characters whenever you specify a file or folder name during a file open or search procedure.

To list or find all files whose names start with the letter G, for example, specify **G*.*** as the file name. This will find file names such as "goofy.doc", "glad you called", "gadflies.xls", and "Good Golly, Miss Molly.wav". To list or find all files that have a file extension of doc, specify a file name of ***.doc**. This will find files with names such as "alpha.doc", "bravo.doc", "charlie.doc", "delta echo foxtrot.doc", and any other file that has a doc extension.

If you need to refine the search a little, you can use the question mark rather than the asterisk. To list all files whose names begin with any letter and have the characters "older" as the rest of the file name, specify **?older.***. This will find files with names such as "colder.doc", "bolder.txt", and "holder.wav". To find a file that has a name such as "holder of the keys", you could specify a file string of **?older*.***.

The way in which Windows 95 differs from previous versions of DOS and Windows lies in the use of the asterisk. Previously, DOS and Windows would recognize only the first asterisk and ignore any characters that followed it, up to the period that separated the file name and extension. For example, entering ***older.doc** would list all files with a doc extension, regardless of their names. This was equivalent to specifying ***.doc**, because the system ignored the characters that formed "older".

Windows 95, however, does not ignore the characters that follow an asterisk, and you can use multiple asterisks and question marks in a specification to further define the pattern matching. A valid search specification would be ***older*.***. Files found with this specification might include "bolder21.mid", "its colder in here", "solder is hot.wav", and so on. Windows 95 would find *any* file that contains the string "older". The specification **?rouch*.*** might locate the files "grouch.zip", "crouch.down.now", "zrouch33", and so on. Remember, the question mark represents only one character, so a file named "what a grouch" will not be found. To find such a file, use the string ***grouch*.***.

Now that you have some background in pattern matching and wild cards, you're ready to start finding those files and folders you've been missing.

Finding Files and Folders

You can access Find from the Start menu or from Explorer. To access Find from the Start menu, choose Start, Find, then Files or Folders. To access Find from Explorer, choose Tools, Find, then Files or Folders. Windows 95 displays the Find dialog box shown in figure 6.13.

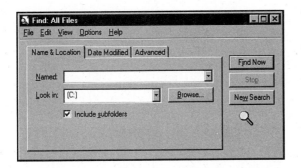

Figure 6.13

Locate files and folders with the Find dialog box.

Enter a name specification in the Named combo box, or use the drop-down list portion of the combo box to select a name pattern you have entered previously. To specify the disk or folder in which Find should search for the files or folders, choose an object from the Look in combo box or type a location, such as **C:**. If you want Find to search all folders in the disk or folder you specify in the Look in combo box, enable the Include subfolders check box. When you're satisfied with your search criteria, choose Find Now. Find expands the dialog box to include a search results list (see fig. 6.14), and any files or folders that match the search criteria appear in the results list.

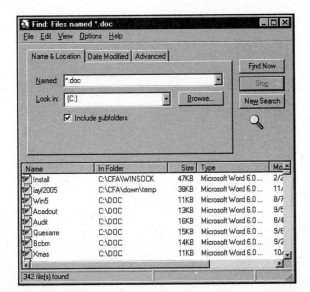

Figure 6.14

The Find dialog box expanded to show the results list.

Tip To select a path or object to search, choose **B**rowse. Use the resulting Browse dialog box to choose the object or path you want to include in the search.

You should understand that the search results list is dynamic, not just a static list of files found. If you want to start an application or open a document you find from doing a search, simply double-click on its name in the results list. Or, if you want to delete or rename a file or folder, just click on it and delete or rename it as you would in Explorer. You also can copy and move files from the results list. As you would with a folder window or Explorer window, select the files and drag them to their destination using the Shift key to move the files or the Ctrl key to copy the files. Or, you can select the files in the results list, then press Ctrl+C to copy them to the Clipboard, or Ctrl+X to cut them to the Clipboard. Then paste the files and/or folders into their new locations.

If you want to clear the search results list and begin a new search, choose the Ne**w** Search button.

Searching by Modification Date

By default, Find searches for all files and folders that match your search pattern. You can, however, limit the search to only those files or folders modified during a certain time period. To search based on modification date, click on the Date Modified tab. The Find dialog box changes as shown in figure 6.15.

Figure 6.15

The Date Modified page of the Find dialog box.

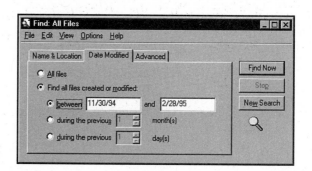

To include all files in the search, choose the **A**ll files option button. To limit the file search, choose the Find all files created or **m**odified option. Then, use one of the following three options to control the search:

◆ **b**etween. Use this option and the accompanying text boxes to specify a range of dates to include in the search. Any file or folder modified during the time defined by the specified range is included in the search.

◆ **during the previous month(s).** Use this option and the accompanying increment control to specify a number of previous months to include in the search. Any file or folder modified within the specified previous month range is included in the search.

◆ **during the previous day(s).** Use this option and the accompanying increment control to specify a number of past days to include in the search. Any file or folder modified within the specified number of days past is included in the search.

When your settings in the Name & Location page and Date Modified page suit your search needs, choose Find Now to initiate the search.

Using Advanced Options

The Advanced page of the Find dialog box enables you to refine your search even further. You can use the Advanced page to specify the types of files to be included in the search, specify that the file must contain specific text to be included in the search, and specify an upper or lower file size limit. The following list explains these items:

◆ **Of type.** Use this drop-down list to specify the type of file for which you want to search. The drop-down list includes all file types registered with Windows 95.

◆ **Containing text.** Specify a text string in this text box to have Find search for documents that contain the string. If you want to search for a letter to a Mr. Frazzle, for example, enter **Frazzle** in this text box.

◆ **Size is.** Choose **at least** from this drop-down list to specify a minimum file size criteria for the search, then use the KB increment control to specify the minimum size. Choose **at most** from this drop-down list to specify a maximum file size criteria for the search, and use the KB increment control to specify the maximum size. If you use the **at least** option, Find includes in the search all files that have a file size of at least the amount you specify with the **KB** option. If you use the **at most** option, Find includes in the search all files that have a file size of no more than the amount you specify with the **KB** option.

When you are satisfied with your search criteria, choose Find Now to initiate the search.

Using Other Search Options

The Options menu includes two options you can use to further refine your search. The Case Sensitive option causes Find to treat your search string as case sensitive; for example, the string "FindMe" would not be treated as equal to "findme" or "FINDME". The Case Sensitive option applies to text within a file if you use the

Containing text option—it has no effect on file names, because Windows 95 does not treat file names as being case-sensitive.

The Save Results option in the Options menu causes Find to create an icon on the desktop that contains the results of the search (see fig. 6.16). You can select the icon to open a Find dialog box with the save results displayed in the results list. Enabling the Save Results option causes Find to save the results automatically. You also can choose File, Save Search to save the contents of the results window to the desktop.

Figure 6.16

Search results saved on the desktop.

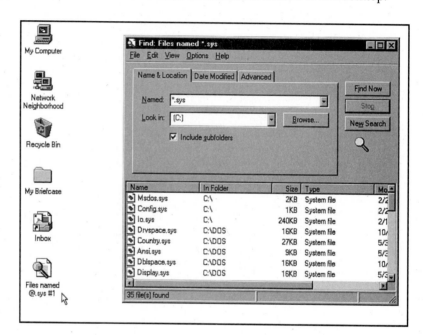

Viewing and Setting Disk and File Properties

As with nearly all other objects in Windows 95, disks have various properties associated with them. In fact, if you have read the sections in this chapter on formatting and labeling disks, you already know about one disk property—the disk label. In addition to its label, a disk has other properties, some of which you can modify, and others that you can only view.

Viewing a Disk's Properties

To view a disk's properties, right-click on the disk's icon in My Computer or in Explorer, then choose Properties. Or, select the disk's icon and press Alt+Enter. Windows 95 displays a property sheet similar to the one shown in figure 6.17.

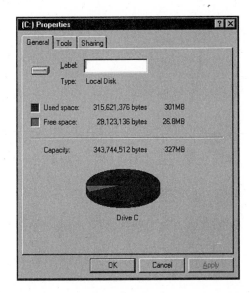

Figure 6.17

The property sheet for a disk.

The General property page shows the amount of space used on the disk, the amount of space available, the total capacity of the disk, and the disk's label. You can change a local disk's label by entering a new label in the Label text box. You can't change remote network disks' labels, however.

The only general property you can change about a disk is its label. The capacity, space used, and space available properties simply indicate the disk's capacity—you can't affect the disk's capacity by changing any of its properties. There are, however, two other property pages for a disk.

The Tools page enables you to open a variety of disk optimization tools to increase the performance of the selected disk. For more information on optimizing a disk, refer to Chapter 15, "Optimizing Data Storage."

The Sharing page enables you to share a local disk with other users on the network. For information on sharing disks and other resources, refer to Chapter 35, "Sharing Resources in Windows 95."

Files also have properties.

Viewing and Setting File and Folder Properties

You can view and set file properties in much the same way you view and set disk properties. Select the file or folder, then press Alt+Enter to display its property sheets. Or, right-click on the object and choose Properties. The property sheets for a typical file are shown in figure 6.18. The General property page for a folder is essentially identical to the General property page for a file. Folders have an additional property page named Sharing, which enables you to share the folder with other users on the network (fig. 6.19).

Figure 6.18

The General property page for a file.

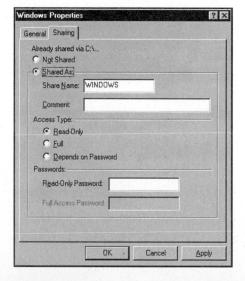

Figure 6.19

The Sharing property page for a folder.

Changing File Attributes

The only properties you can change for a file are its attributes. The file attributes, which appear on the General property page, are explained in the following list:

◆ **Read-only.** You cannot delete or modify a file for which the read-only attribute is enabled.

◆ **Hidden.** Enabling a file's hidden attribute hides it from normal view. To enable display of hidden files and folders in a folder window or Explorer, choose View, Options, View, and Show all files.

◆ **Archive.** The archive attribute specifies whether you should archive the file during a backup. Some backup applications use the archive attribute to determine whether a file has been backed up since it was last modified.

◆ **System.** System files are files that Windows 95 requires as part of the core operating system.

If an attribute check box is enabled (contains a check), that attribute is enabled for the file. If the check box is clear, the attribute is not set. If multiple files are selected, the check box might be solid gray. This indicates that only some of the selected files have this attribute.

To change a file or folder's attributes, simply enable and clear the attribute check boxes as necessary.

Viewing Version Information

Windows application and support files include version and copyright information embedded within the file. You can view these file properties in the Version property page for the file. To view the version information, select the file and press Alt+Enter to display its property sheets. Then click on the Version tab to display the Version page (see fig. 6.20).

To view a particular property, select an item from the Item name list. The associated version information appears in the Value list.

Note You can't change version information for a file—you can only view the information.

Version information can be extremely useful for identifying out-of-date files, replacing old files with new versions, and avoiding having to replace new files with old files. When you install a Windows application, however, Setup generally displays a message when it is about to replace a newer version of a file with an older version, giving you the option of keeping the newer file or replacing it with the older version. You should nearly always keep the newer version of the file.

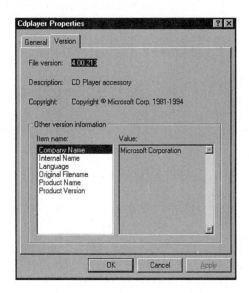

Using File Manager

In addition to Explorer, Windows 95 includes an updated version of File Manager, the file and directory management program included with Windows 3.*x.* Figure 6.21 shows the File Manager window.

If you have experience using Windows 3.*x,* you probably know about File Manager. Only minor changes have been made to File Manager, and these only so that it has the same look and feel as other Windows 95 applications.

To run File Manager in Windows 95, choose Start, **R**un and enter **winfile** in the **O**pen combo box. Or, locate and open the file Winfile.exe in the Windows folder. If you use File Manager often, consider creating a shortcut on the desktop to File Manager.

Unless you are very comfortable using File Manager, you probably will use the methods in Windows 95 and Explorer in particular to manage your files and folders. Therefore, this chapter assumes you already know how to use File Manager and doesn't cover it.

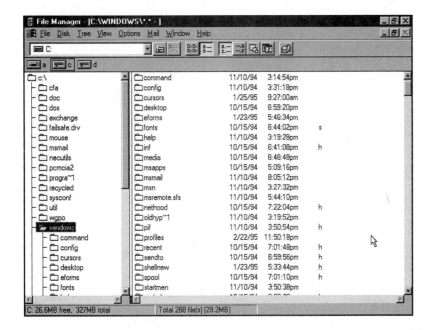

Figure 6.21

Windows 95 includes an updated version of File Manager.

Managing Files from the Command Line

You probably will perform most of your file and folder management tasks from the Windows 95 GUI, using folder windows or Explorer. If you often work from a DOS VM (DOS session), or you have many years of experience using DOS, you might prefer to perform some of your file and folder maintenance from the command prompt. Because Windows 95 incorporates a DOS environment, it includes most of the DOS file and directory commands included with previous versions of DOS. The syntax for the majority of these commands is identical or very similar to their DOS counterparts. For help with the syntax of a command, enter the command at the command prompt, followed by the /? switch, as in the following example:

```
XCOPY /?
```

CHAPTER

7

Working with Fonts

In the early days of the PC, before Windows became popular and DOS-based character-mode applications were the norm rather than the exception, your ability to use different fonts in an application was typically very limited. Although you could change the size of text, word processing applications usually offered no more than one or two fonts. The introduction of TrueType fonts in Windows 3.1 increased your ability to work with many different fonts considerably. Today, you can choose from literally thousands of different fonts to use in your applications and documents, although only a handful of those thousands of fonts are included with Windows 95.

This chapter examines fonts and explains your options in Windows 95 for using and managing them. The topics covered in this chapter are

- ◆ Understanding fonts

- ◆ Viewing and managing fonts

- ◆ Installing new fonts

- ◆ Removing fonts

If you only want to know how to view, manage, add, and remove fonts, you can skip to the section "Viewing and Managing Fonts." Using fonts effectively, however, requires a basic understanding of fonts and how they work in Windows 95. The following section provides an overview of the different types of fonts available in Windows 95.

Understanding Fonts

Generally, the term *font* is used interchangeably with *typeface*, even though the two are different. A *typeface* is the basic design of a character set, defined by the shape of the characters. Each typeface is identified by a name, such as Arial, Times New Roman, and so on. A *font* is a complete set of characters of a given typeface at a particular point size and style. All the characters in the Arial typeface at 12 points in bold, for example, constitute a font. All the characters in the Arial typeface at 14 points constitute a different font from the same character set in 12 points.

 Note   A *font family* is the entire range of sizes and styles of a single typeface.

Many different types of fonts exist, and Windows 95 uses many of them. The following list explains the most common types of fonts:

- **Bitmap or raster fonts.** These fonts are created using patterns of pixels to define the shape and size of the characters. Each character requires a unique bitmap to define the character in each point size and style. Each bitmap or raster font file contains one set of characters in the given size and style. Defining two different font sizes, therefore, requires two separate font files. Defining a bold font requires yet another font file. These types of fonts are often referred to as *screen fonts*. You cannot download screen fonts to a printer, which typically results in a comparable printer font that looks somewhat different from a screen font, and printed output that looks different from its representation on the display.

- **TrueType fonts.** These fonts are often referred to as *outline fonts*. TrueType fonts are generated from an outline, which is a set of instructions that define the contours of the characters. Because the font is defined by its contour, only one font file is required to define the font in a given style. A single font file can define a set of TrueType characters in a size range from 2 points to nearly 700 points. TrueType fonts are compatible with nearly all types of devices, including displays and printers.

- **Vector fonts.** These are scalable fonts that consists of line segments and dots. Vector fonts are often used for output to plotters and some types of printers. Vector fonts don't offer the same quality of output as TrueType fonts.

◆ **Device-specific fonts.** These fonts are specific to a certain device, such as a printer. You install the fonts in the printer's firmware or download them to the printer on a per-job basis. PostScript fonts are considered to be device-specific fonts.

Each of the types of fonts used in Windows 95 has different applications and advantages. Because of their versatility and scalability without loss of resolution or quality, TrueType fonts are the most commonly used fonts in Windows 95. The following section explains TrueType fonts in more detail.

Understanding TrueType Fonts

Windows 95 includes TrueType fonts to support five different font families: Arial, Times New Roman, Courier New, Symbol, and Wingding. In addition to these standard Windows 95 TrueType fonts, many applications include their own fonts. Many other TrueType fonts are available commercially, as shareware, or as freeware, making literally thousands of different fonts available for use in Windows 95.

TrueType fonts offer a number of advantages over other types of fonts, most notably in quality and scalability. The following list explains the major advantages of TrueType fonts:

◆ **Ease of use.** Using TrueType fonts requires little knowledge or effort on your part. You can use TrueType fonts in a document simply by choosing the desired font characteristics from a standard dialog box. Installing and removing TrueType fonts also is very easy in Windows 95.

◆ **Identical screen and printer output.** One of the most important advantages of using TrueType fonts is that the appearance of the characters on the display almost exactly matches the output of the characters on the printer. This uniformity typically is referred to as *what-you-see-is-what-you-get*, or *WYSIWYG* (pronounced *wiz-ee-wig*), enabling you to see on-screen exactly how the output will look on paper.

Note Because of differences in dot pitch between monitors and printers, some slight differences exist between the appearance of characters on the display and on the printed page. These differences, however, are minimal.

◆ **Scalability.** TrueType fonts are outline fonts. The shape of the characters in a typeface in a given style are defined mathematically. Because the characters are defined by their contours rather than based on a static bitmap image, TrueType fonts can be scaled from a minimum of 2 points to a maximum of about 700 points without diminishing resolution or quality—unlike screen fonts, which are limited to the sizes their font files define. You also can rotate TrueType fonts without losing resolution or quality, although the capability to rotate TrueType fonts depends on the application, not on Windows 95.

◆ **Portability.** TrueType fonts are portable between various printers, which means that a document prints the same regardless of the printer type or model. You don't have to worry about whether you have a printer font that matches the font you're using in the document, because the application and the printer use the same font. You also can port TrueType fonts between operating systems. You can use the TrueType fonts you use in Windows 95 on a Macintosh system as well, for example, which means that a document looks the same even when you move it from a Windows 95 environment to a Macintosh environment.

 Note   TrueType fonts are not supported on plotters. Plotters typically require printer or special plotter fonts.

◆ **Minimal storage requirements.** A single TrueType font file defines a font for all type sizes. TrueType fonts require much less disk space and fewer files to store the same range of font sizes as equivalent bitmap fonts.

◆ **Not application-specific.** Any Windows application that supports the Windows 95 universal printer drivers can use TrueType fonts. In addition, many DOS word processing applications can use TrueType fonts, as can Macintosh applications.

In Windows 3.*x*, TrueType fonts did offer certain disadvantages, chief among them being the amount of memory they consumed even when you weren't using them. If you installed 30 fonts, Windows 3.*x* needed memory to manage each of them in every Windows session, even if you used only one font regularly. Windows 95, however, handles TrueType fonts much more efficiently, resulting in a much smaller memory footprint to support the installed fonts. You can install an unlimited number of TrueType fonts, and use almost 1,000 TrueType fonts in one document.

 Tip   In Windows 3.*x*, installed fonts were listed in the Win.ini file. Because of the size limitations inherent in Ini files, the number of font entries also was so limited, imposing a limit on the number of fonts you could install. In Windows 95, TrueType fonts are stored in the Registry. If you use a Windows 3.*x* application that installs fonts, and therefore, adds entries to Win.ini for the new fonts, Windows 95 automatically moves the font entries to the Registry. When a Windows 3.*x* application requests an enumeration of fonts, Windows 95 supplies a font list from the Registry. The shift of TrueType fonts from Win.ini to the Registry, therefore, is transparent to the user.

How Windows 95 Renders TrueType Fonts

The process Windows 95 uses to display TrueType fonts is not as simple as you might assume. A request from an application for a character goes to the GDI, which passes the request to the TrueType rasterizer. The TrueType rasterizer converts the TrueType outline definition of the character to a bitmap. The TrueType rasterizer then returns the bitmap to the GDI, which passes the bitmap to the display driver to display on-screen. This process occurs for every character. Figure 7.1 illustrates the process as a request from Word for Windows for a character.

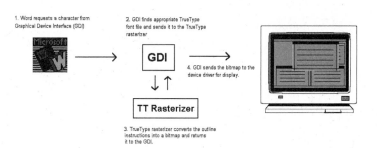

Figure 7.1

The process used to render a single TrueType character.

If the resolution of the screen and printer matched, the same bitmaps returned by the rasterizer could be used on the screen and on the printer. Screen resolution and printer resolution differ, however, and even 300-dpi (dots-per-inch) printers often don't have the necessary resolution to define a character accurately. A lowercase *m*, for example, might have different widths for each of its legs because of the lack of resolution of the output device.

To overcome the inability to directly map a character outline to an output device, TrueType fonts use *hints*, which are instructions that optimize the appearance of the character by changing its outline to suit the output device. Hinting distorts the outline of the character so that the resulting character on the output device more closely matches the original outline.

Tip
Hinting is most important on displays and printers with relatively low dpi resolution. Printers with resolutions of 600 dpi and higher can render characters accurately with fewer hints.

When you print a document that contains TrueType fonts, the way in which the fonts are rendered depend on the printer you use. On LaserJet and compatible printers, TrueType generates LaserJet soft fonts and downloads the characters to the printer. Unlike with other types of soft fonts that require that you download the entire font file to the printer, you only have to download the characters required to print the document. The characters then print as text, rather than graphics.

On PostScript printers, TrueType fonts 14 points and smaller download as Type 3 (bitmap) fonts, which download faster than outline fonts. For larger character sizes, TrueType downloads Type 1 (outline) fonts for each size required in the document. The printer then renders the characters based on the downloaded outlines.

On dot-matrix printers, TrueType fonts are sent to the printer as graphics. Although printing TrueType fonts on a dot-matrix printer generally is a slow process, the resulting print quality is generally very good.

Understanding Raster Fonts

Earlier in this chapter you read that raster fonts (bitmap fonts) are created using patterns of pixels to define the shape and size of the characters. Each character requires a unique bitmap to define the character in each point size and style. Windows 95 includes raster fonts in different sizes to match specific video display resolutions. The raster fonts for an EGA display, for example, have a height to width ratio of 96×72. VGA raster fonts, however, have a height to width ratio of 96×96. The raster fonts included with Windows 95 are MS Sans Serif, MS Serif, Courier, System, and Terminal.

Raster font files typically contain multiple sizes of a particular typeface. In general, Windows 95 can render raster fonts in even multiples of the fonts' defined sizes. The MS Serif font, for example, includes 8, 10, 12, and 14 point sizes. Windows 95 can render the MS Serif in multiple sizes such as 16, 20, 24, 28, and so on.

 Tip Scaling of raster fonts works best for normal fonts. If you scale bold, italic, or underline fonts too large, the result is jagged characters.

You can use raster fonts in a document and print them on many types of printers. To print a particular raster font, however, the resolution and aspect ratio of the font must match the resolution and aspect ratio of the printer. If a particular raster font does not appear in the Fonts dialog box in your application, even though the font is installed, the font probably doesn't match the resolution and aspect ratio of the selected printer. Changing the printer's resolution or selecting a printer with the same resolution and aspect ratio as the raster font should make the font available in the application's Font dialog box.

 Tip If you need to use a particular raster font on a printer, but the installed raster font doesn't match the printer's resolution, you might be able to install a different raster font that does match the printer's resolution. The raster font files are stored in cabinet 6, or the file Win95_06.cab. To extract the files from the cabinet to the fonts

directory, open a DOS session and enter **extract *source*\win95_06.cab
*.fon *Windows*\Fonts**, where *source* defines the location of the cabinet and
Windows defines the location of your Windows directory. To extract from a floppy
disk in drive A to a Windows directory located on drive C, for example, use the
command **extract a:win95_06.cab *.fon c:\windows\fonts**. Then, open
the Fonts folder and install the files as described later in this chapter in the section
"Installing and Removing Fonts."

Understanding Vector Fonts

You create vector fonts by using points and vectors, much like the way a plotter plots a
drawing by moving a pen between points. To some degree, vector fonts are similar to
TrueType fonts—neither type of font relies on bitmaps, but rather, on mathematical
definitions. And like TrueType fonts, vector fonts can be scaled to any size. Vector
fonts typically are used on plotters.

Vector fonts do have some drawbacks, however. First, vector fonts consist of GDI calls
and are time-consuming to generate. And although you can scale vector fonts, the
results are not as good as with TrueType fonts. Unless you send output to a plotter,
consider using TrueType fonts rather than vector fonts.

Using Screen and Printer Fonts

In addition to being categorized in Windows 95 as TrueType, raster, or vector, fonts
also are categorized by intended output device, or as *screen* or *printer* fonts. As their
names imply, Windows 95 uses screen fonts to represent characters on-screen, and
printer fonts to create characters on a printer. TrueType fonts serve as both screen
fonts and printer fonts.

Printer fonts are divided into three types, as described in the following list:

- ◆ **Printable screen fonts.** These are screen fonts that also can be rendered on
  the printer.

- ◆ **Device fonts.** These fonts are stored in the printer, in its hardware or in a font
  cartridge.

- ◆ **Downloadable soft fonts.** These fonts are downloaded from your hard disk
  to the printer's memory per need.

TrueType fonts are identified in font selection dialog boxes by a special TT icon, and
printer fonts are sometimes identified by a printer icon (see fig. 7.2). In other
applications, only TrueType fonts are identified by icon in the Font dialog boxes—
other types of fonts such as printer fonts have no icon associated with them.

Figure 7.2

*TrueType fonts
are identified by a
TT icon, and
printer fonts are
sometimes
identified by a
printer icon.*

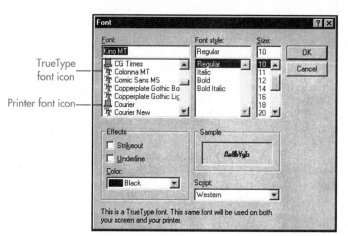

To use a particular font in a document, simply select it from the Font dialog box and specify any settings, such as bold, italic, and so on. When you're ready to print the document, you might need to download the font or specify other options to control the way the printer handles the fonts. The section "Controlling Fonts for Printing" later in this chapter explains how to download and control fonts during printing.

Viewing and Managing Fonts

Windows 95 provides access and control over fonts through the Fonts folder, which you access from the Control Panel. The Fonts folder itself is the \Windows\Fonts directory. Opening the Fonts folder displays a folder window similar to the one shown in figure 7.3. By default, the Fonts folder shows an icon for each of the fonts in the Fonts folder. TrueType fonts are represented by a TrueType icon. Screen and printer fonts are represented by an "A" icon.

To view a sample of a font, double-click on the font's icon, or select the icon and press Enter. Windows 95 displays a window that contains sample text in various sizes and other information about the font (see fig. 7.4). To print a page of sample text in the selected font, choose the **P**rint button. After you view the sample, choose **D**one to close the window.

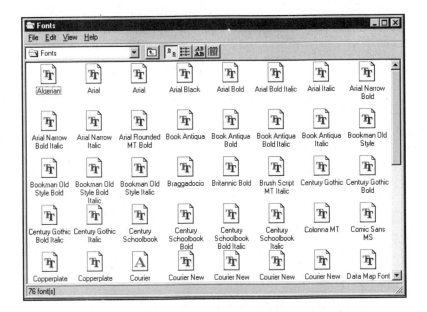

Figure 7.3
The Fonts folder.

Figure 7.4
*A font window
showing sample
text and
information
about a font.*

Each of the icons in the Fonts folder simply represents a font file in the \Windows\Fonts directory. You can select a font and press Alt+Enter, or choose Properties from a font's context menu to display a standard file properties page for the font file (see fig. 7.5).

Figure 7.5

A typical file property page for a font file.

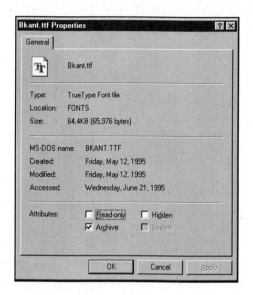

Controlling the Fonts Folder

As with other types of folders, you can control the appearance of the Fonts folder and change the way in which the fonts appear in the folder. The view options for the Fonts folder are somewhat different, however, from a typical folder window. The View menu contains the Large Icons, List, and Details commands found in other folder windows. These commands display the icons as large icons, a simple list, or a detailed list, respectively, just like any other folder that displays files.

The command List Fonts by Similarity in the View menu enables you to organize the view in the Fonts folder window to show fonts according to their similarity to one another. You can sort the fonts according to their similarity to the Arial font, for example. The fonts appear in the folder as a simple list with a description of the degree of similarity to the selected font. Fonts are listed in descending order of similarity—fonts that are most similar in appearance are listed at the top of the list (see fig. 7.6). To view a particular font, just double-click on its name in the list.

The List Fonts by Similarity command enables you to locate fonts that share the same general appearance. If a particular font isn't quite what you want but is very similar, sort the Fonts window by similarity to locate all other fonts that have a similar appearance. After you display the fonts by similarity, you can choose a different font from

the drop-down list in the Font folder's toolbar. The list then re-sorts to show the degree of similarity to the newly selected font. To switch back to an icon, list, or detail view, choose View, followed by the appropriate view option.

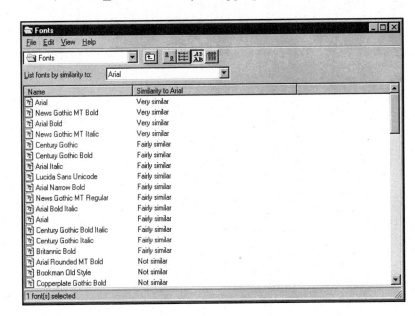

Figure 7.6

Fonts displayed by similarity.

Simplifying the Fonts Folder

If you have many fonts installed in the Fonts folder, you might want to simplify the view to include only one reference to each font family. Rather than display separate icons for Arial, Arial Bold, and Arial Italic, for example, the Fonts folder can display a single icon to represent the entire Arial family. To hide font variations and display a single icon for each font family, choose View, Hide Variations. Figure 7.7 shows a Fonts folder for which the Hide Variations option is enabled.

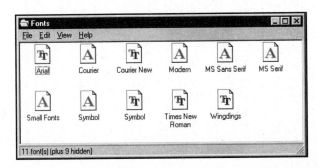

Figure 7.7

Fonts folder with variations (bold, italic, etc.) hidden.

Tip   Dragging a font's icon from the Fonts folder moves or copies the font file, depending on how you drag the font. This behavior is identical to any folder that represents files in a directory.

Installing and Removing Fonts

Although you easily can copy new font files to the Fonts folder, simply copying the files doesn't make those fonts available in your applications. Instead, you must install the fonts, which adds the new fonts to the Registry and thus makes the fonts available to your applications.

To install a font, open the Fonts folder and choose File, Install New Font. Windows 95 opens an Add Fonts dialog box (see fig. 7.8) that you use to locate the font files for the fonts you want to install. When you select a directory, Windows 95 scans the directory and lists in the List of fonts list any font files that it finds. You can select one or more font files to install. To select all font files, choose the Select All button.

Figure 7.8

The Add Fonts dialog box.

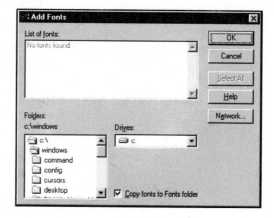

You can use the Copy fonts to Fonts folder check box to control whether the font files are copied to the \Windows\Fonts folder. If you enable this check box, the font files are copied from their source location to the \Windows\Fonts folder, and references to the new fonts are added in the Registry. If the check box is cleared, the font files remain in their source location, but the font references still are added to the Registry.

 Tip   If you install fonts from a network server, you might want to leave the font files on the server to conserve disk space on your computer. Windows 95 then can read the font files from the server whenever necessary.

After you select the fonts you want to install and specify whether the associated font files should be copied to your local Fonts folder, choose OK. Windows 95 installs the fonts, and you can begin using them in your applications.

With Windows 3.*x*, the primary disadvantage of installing numerous fonts is the amount of resource memory required to maintain the fonts even when they are not being used. Windows 95 significantly reduces the memory requirements for installing and using a large number of fonts, making retaining a large number of fonts on your PC much more practical.

If you never use certain fonts on your system, or you run very low on disk space, you might want to remove some of the fonts. You remove a font in the same way you remove a file from a folder. Select the font(s) you want to remove, then choose File, Delete, or simply press the Del key. Windows 95 deletes the font files and removes the font from the Registry.

Using Special Characters

Although using special characters in a document is not directly related to fonts, the font you use does have some bearing on the types of special characters available to you. This section explains how you can insert special characters not available from the keyboard in a document.

In many applications, you can hold down the Alt key and press a sequence of keys on the numeric keypad to insert special characters. Holding down the Alt key and pressing 0181 inserts the µ character, for example. The value 0181 corresponds to the character's ASCII value.

Remembering more than just a few ASCII values can prove rather difficult, so Windows 95 provides a much easier method to enable you to insert special characters and symbols in a document. Located in the Accessories menu is the Character Map application, a simple utility that displays all the characters in a given font and enables you to easily copy characters from the Character Map to the Clipboard. After you transfer the character to the Clipboard, copying the character from the Clipboard to a document is a simple matter.

To use the Character Map, choose Start, Programs, Accessories, and Character Map. The Character Map appears on the desktop, as shown in figure 7.9.

To insert one or more characters from the Character Map, select a font from the Font drop-down list to display all the characters available in that font. Then, select a character and choose Select, or double-click on the character, to place the character in the Characters to copy text box. When you're ready to copy the characters to the Clipboard, choose Copy. Then open the document in which you want to use the characters and press Ctrl+V or choose Edit, Paste.

Figure 7.9

*The Character
Map application.*

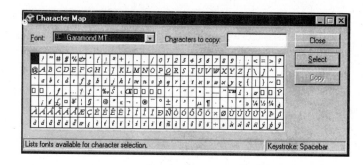

Tip   The characters in the Character Map can be difficult to read because of their small size. Click on a character and hold down the mouse button to view an enlarged copy of the character.

When you select a character from the Character map, the character's key sequence appears in the lower right corner of the Character Map's status line. If you prefer, you can switch to the application in which you want to use the character and enter the key sequence to insert the character, instead of using the Clipboard.

Controlling Fonts for Printing

Using special characters and various fonts in a document typically is only part of the picture—often, you need to print those documents and want to have the fonts print as they appear in the document. Printing documents with a variety of fonts often requires some additional effort beyond just issuing the print job. You might have to download fonts to the printer or perform other tasks before you can print the document. This section of the chapter explains the most important issues relating to printing and fonts. For more detailed information about printing and managing printers, refer to Chapter 8, "Printing and Managing Printers."

Printers vary from one model and manufacturer to another, but the options for managing fonts for the printer are much the same, regardless of printer model. Most font options apply to laser printers and PostScript printers. Other types of printers have few, if any, options you can set to control how the printer handles different fonts.

Any printer that uses a Windows 95 universal printer driver can print TrueType fonts. This means that you can print a document that uses any of the fonts installed on your system and the results are identical to the document as it appears on-screen. In general, only two options control the way a printer handles TrueType fonts, and these appear in the printer's Fonts property page, as follows:

◆ **Download TrueType as Bitmap Soft Fonts.** This option causes the TrueType fonts to be downloaded to the printer as soft fonts. The printer then renders the fonts. This option can speed up printing when you print documents that contain only a few fonts, but can slow printing if you print a document that contains many different fonts or documents that contain complex graphics.

◆ **Print TrueType as Graphics.** This option causes the fonts to be rendered on the computer and printed as graphics, speeding up printing when numerous fonts or complex graphics are included in the document. In addition, this option enables you to clip text with graphics, preventing parts of characters overlaid by graphics or only partially on the page from being printed. Some printers also include an option to download TrueType fonts as outline fonts to the printer.

PostScript printers offer additional options for controlling fonts and printing. These options define how the PostScript and TrueType fonts are handled, including whether TrueType fonts map to PostScript fonts installed on the printer. Figure 7.10 shows a typical Fonts property page for a PostScript printer.

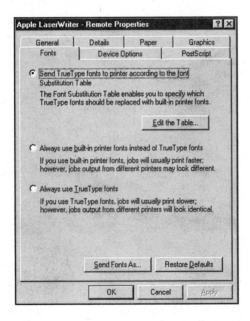

Figure 7.10

A typical Fonts property page.

The following list explains the options on the Fonts property page:

◆ **Send TrueType fonts to printer according to the font Substitution Table.** This option offers the most control over how the printer handles TrueType fonts. You can modify a table of all installed fonts to specify whether a given font is downloaded as outlines or mapped to a specific font that resides in the printer.

◆ **Always use built-in printer fonts instead of TrueType fonts.** This option causes PostScript fonts rather than TrueType fonts to be used. A font-matching algorithm matches the TrueType font as closely as possible with one of the printer's PostScript fonts. This often speeds up printing by eliminating the time and overhead required to download the TrueType fonts, but results in differences between the document's appearance on-screen and on the printed page.

◆ **Always use TrueType fonts.** This option causes TrueType fonts to be printed on the printer even if a corresponding or similar PostScript font is available. Using this option can add a small amount of time to the print job, but results in identical output on the screen and printer.

Even though the options described in the previous list are fairly common, remember that options can vary from one printer to another. The options might vary somewhat for your printer.

Printing and Managing Printers

L ike Windows 3.*x* before it, Windows 95 supports a truly impressive array of printers from numerous manufacturers. Windows 95 makes getting the most out of your printer easier than did Windows 3.*x*. One quite welcome feature, for example, is the ease with which you can configure a remote network printer for use on your computer. You don't even need a driver for the printer—Windows 95 copies the driver from the remote computer to which the printer is connected. Windows 95 also offers expanded drag-and-drop printing, improved queue management, and many other new printing features.

This chapter explains how to set up, configure, use, and manage local and remote printers. The topics covered include the following:

◆ Setting up and configuring printers

◆ Printing from Windows applications

◆ Printing from the desktop

◆ Using deferred printing

◆ Using the Extended Capabilities Port (ECP)

◆ Printing from DOS applications

◆ Controlling a printer's queue

◆ Using PostScript printers

◆ Setting advanced printing options

◆ Using image color matching

◆ Printing in Novell NetWare environments

◆ Using DEC PrintServer for Windows 95

◆ Troubleshooting printer problems

This chapter aims to help you begin printing as soon as possible. The first few sections explain how to set up and configure a printer, and print from Windows applications. Later sections explain some more complex printer issues, such as setting up and using print server hardware and software.

Setting Up a Local Printer

When you run Setup to install Windows 95, Setup migrates all your existing printers to the Windows 95 environment, copying to your system any new Windows 95 drivers necessary to support your installed printers. Therefore, you might have to do nothing more to begin printing under Windows 95 than configure the printers' settings. If you do have to install a new printer driver, however, the process is simple. This section explains how to install a local printer (one connected to your PC). The section "Setting Up a Network Printer" later in this chapter explains how to set up printers for use across the network.

 Note If you have Windows 3.*x* experience and have installed printers, you shouldn't have any trouble installing a printer under Windows 95. Just run the Add Printer wizard, which is located in the Printers folder. You then might want to skip to the section "Setting Printer Options" later in this chapter to learn about the differences in how you configure a printer in Windows 95 versus Windows 3.*x*.

The Printers folder, located in My Computer, gives you access to all your installed printers. The Printers folder also contains a wizard that helps you install a local or remote printer. Open the Printers folder in My Computer and select the Add Printer

icon. The Add Printer wizard starts and displays an informational message about the Add Printer wizard. Click on Next to continue.

Add Printer then prompts you to choose how the printer is connected to your computer. Choose the **L**ocal printer option to install a driver for a printer connected to your PC, or choose **R**emote printer to install a remote network printer. Choose the **L**ocal printer option, then click on Next.

The Add Printer wizard then provides a list of printers, separated by manufacturer, that Windows 95 supports (see fig. 8.1). From the **M**anufacturers list, choose the manufacturer of the printer you want to install. Then, from the **P**rinters list, choose the model of printer connected to your PC. If you can't find the exact model in the list, check your printer manual to see if your printer is compatible with one of the printers shown in the list.

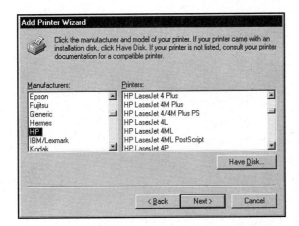

Figure 8.1

Select the printer's manufacturer and model.

Note   You should try to use a driver included with Windows 95 unless none of them will work for your printer. If your printer includes a disk that contains printer drivers for Windows 3.*x* or Windows 95, choose the Have **D**isk button, and the Add Printer wizard steps you through adding a driver from the disk. If you don't have a driver disk, and can't find your printer model or manufacturer listed, determine if your printer is compatible with one of the printers supported by Windows 95. Then, select the compatible printer from the **M**anufacturers and **P**rinters lists.

After you choose a printer model and click on Next, Add Printer prompts you to select the port to which the printer is connected (see fig. 8.2). The following section helps delineate your port choices.

Figure 8.2

Select the port to which the printer is connected.

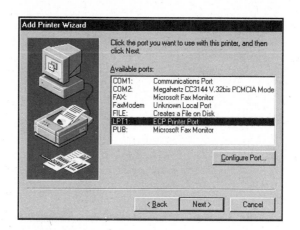

Using a COM or LPT Port

The ports listed in the Add Printer Wizard dialog box include your PC's local serial (COM) ports and local physical parallel (LPT) ports. The name of any driver already associated with a COM port appears beside the COM port in the list. If you've configured a modem to use COM2, for example, the modem's name appears beside COM2 in the list. If no device is associated with the port, the title Communications Port appears beside the port name.

Most printers use an LPT port (explained next), but some output devices include support for both COM and LPT ports. Many of the HP LaserJet printers, for example, include both a COM and an LPT port, which enables you to connect the printer to both port types. Some output devices don't support LPT ports. Many plotters, for example, include a COM port and an HPIB (Hewlett-Packard Interface Bus) port, but not an LPT port.

If you need to connect your output device to a COM port, you should verify that no other devices use that COM port. Sometimes, however, you can connect your printer to the same COM port assigned to another device, but that capability depends on the type of device. If the other device is another printer or a modem, for example, you should be able to associate and use your new printer with the same COM port without any problems. However, this assumes that you use an external serial port switch to connect all the devices to the COM port. Otherwise, you have to disconnect one device from the port and connect the other whenever you want to use it.

If you decide to use a COM port for your output device, you need to configure the settings for the port. To do so, select the port you plan to use, then choose the Configure Port button. Add Printer then displays a property sheet for the port, as shown in figure 8.3.

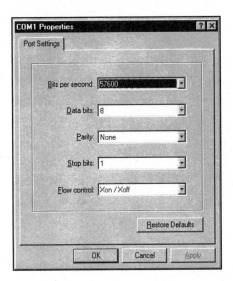

Figure 8.3

Specify settings for the COM port on its properties page.

The following list explains the settings on the COM port property sheet:

◆ **Bits per second.** Select a bits-per-second (bps) rate for the device. This setting specifies the speed at which data courses through the port. The appropriate setting depends on the capability of the device you attach to the port. The higher the setting, the faster the output goes to the device, so check the manual for the output device to determine the correct setting.

◆ **Data bits.** This setting specifies the number of data bits in one data word. Generally, the correct value is 8 or 7, depending on the device. Check the manual for the device to determine the correct setting. If you're not sure, try the default setting of 8. If that doesn't work, try 7.

◆ **Parity.** This setting defines the type of parity checking mechanism the port uses to validate data between the PC and the output device. The available settings are even, odd, none, mark, and space. Choose the appropriate setting according to your output device (refer to the device's manual).

◆ **Stop bits.** This setting specifies the number of stop bits included in each data word, and actually is a timing mechanism. Use the setting your output device's manual recommends.

◆ **Flow control.** This setting specifies the type of mechanism that controls data flow between the PC and the output device. Use the setting your output device's manual recommends.

◆ **Restore defaults.** Choose this button if you want to restore all the settings in the property sheet to their default values.

Generally, the default settings do work, but you might want to increase the bps rate to speed up printing. For a detailed explanation of all these settings, refer to Chapter 28, "Modems and Data Communications."

If your printer is connected to one of your PC's LPT ports, select an appropriate LPT port from the list. Note that the dialog box lists only the LPT ports present in your system. Windows 95 can, however, address *virtual* LPT ports from LPT1 through LPT9. These virtual ports do not physically exist in your PC, but Windows 95 can treat them as local ports for associating remote network printers with logical LPT ports on your PC. Using virtual LPT ports is explained later in the section "Setting Up a Network Printer."

When you set up a local printer to use an LPT port, you must specify the physical port to which the printer is connected. Nothing can prevent you from specifying the same LPT port for more than one printer. For example, you might have two or three printers connected to an LPT switch box that in turn is connected to your LPT1 port. When you need to use a particular printer, you select it in Windows 95, change the printer switch to the appropriate printer, and print.

LPT ports have only one port setting to configure in the Add Printer dialog box. Choose an LPT port, then choose Configure Port. Add Printer calls up the dialog box shown in figure 8.4.

Figure 8.4

The Configure LPT Port dialog box.

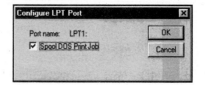

The Spool DOS Print Job check box enables you to determine whether print jobs that originate from DOS applications are spooled through the same 32-bit print spooler that the Windows 95 applications use. This option is enabled by default, because spooling DOS print jobs through the Windows 95 spooler results in better background printing for the application and eliminates device conflicts between DOS applications and Windows 95 applications, which might otherwise attempt to access the port at the same time. Therefore, you should leave this option enabled unless you experience problems printing from the DOS application and determine that the problem lies in the DOS application's inability to use the Windows 95 spooler (unlikely).

Using the FILE: Port

The port selection list in the Add Printer wizard includes a port named FILE:. This entry does not reference a physical port, but rather, enables you to direct a print job to a file. The resulting file contains not only the document data, but also printer control commands. You then can use the COPY command from a command prompt to send the file to the printer. Or, you might be using a third-party print spooler that requires you to place the print jobs in a spool directory. Associating a printer driver with the FILE: port enables you to do that.

Tip   If you want to print data to an ASCII text file, install and use the Generic/Text Only printer.

When you print to a printer associated with the FILE: port, Windows 95 issues a Print To File dialog box similar to the one shown in figure 8.5. This dialog box is similar to a typical Save As dialog box, and includes controls you can use to select the disk, folder, and file name by which to save the file. After you enter a file name and choose OK, the file prints to the file rather than to a printer.

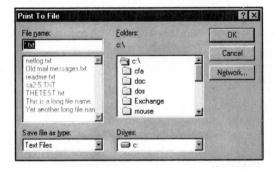

Figure 8.5

The Print To File dialog box.

Using Other Ports

You probably can see other port entries in the Add Printer dialog box than just the COM, LPT, and FILE: port entries. You use the FAX: and PUB: ports, for example, to configure a printer driver for Microsoft Fax. Using Microsoft Fax is explained in Chapter 31.

In addition to the Microsoft Fax ports, you might see other ports listed in the Add Printer dialog box. If you have installed WinFAX, for example, a port entry named FaxModem probably appears in the dialog box. An entry for ECP appears in the dialog box if your system contains an Extended Capabilities Port (ECP). The section "Using the Extended Capabilities Port" later in this chapter discusses the ECP.

Completing the Setup Process

After you specify the port to which your printer is connected, Add Printer prompts you for a name for the printer (see fig. 8.6). This name appears under the printer's icon in the Printers folder. The dialog box also includes a prompt that asks whether you want to use this new printer as the default Windows printer. If you choose Yes, the printer becomes the default Windows printer. Unless you choose a different printer in the Windows application, the application prints to the default printer. If you click on the Printer button in Word for Windows' toolbar, for example, output automatically directs to the default printer.

Figure 8.6

Specify a name for the printer and whether you want it to be the default printer.

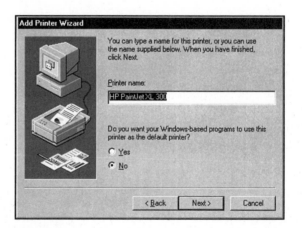

Next, Add Printer asks you if you want to print a test page. You always can benefit from printing a test page to verify that the printer is connected and configured properly. Choose Yes to print a test page, or No to skip printing the test page, then click on Finish to complete the printer setup process. Add Printer then copies the necessary drivers from the Windows 95 CD or distribution disks and add an icon to the Printers folder for the new printer.

Setting Up a Network Printer

Setting up a network printer in Windows 3.*x* can be confusing if you're not a computer expert. Not only must you have the correct drivers for the remote printer, but you also have to associate a local printer port with the remote printer, a task that typically involves using both the Control Panel and Print Manager. Windows 95, however, makes the process almost automatic. And unlike Windows 3.*x*, Windows 95 does not require that you have a driver for the network printer. Windows 95 simply copies the driver and any other required files across the network from the computer

that shares the remote printer. This makes quickly installing and beginning to use a network printer possible, even if you don't have the driver on your computer or the Windows 95 distribution disks (or CD).

Understanding Point and Print Setup

Automatic setup of network printers is called *Point and Print* in Windows 95. Windows 95's Point and Print attempts to determine the type of printer you want to install and copies the necessary driver and support files from the computer sharing the printer, from another location on the network, or from a local source (Windows 95 CD or disks). The files required for a particular printer are defined in the Windows 95 Inf files.

If Windows 95 can't determine from the server which printer you are installing, or if the print server doesn't support Point and Print, you can use the Add Printer wizard to install printer support for the remote printer. If the print server supports UNC names, you don't have to associate the remote printer with any of the PC's local printer ports. If the print server doesn't support UNC names, however, you can easily associate one of the local PC's printer ports with the network printer. This local port can be a virtual port, which means it does not have to physically exist in the PC. If you have only one printer port in the PC, LPT1, you still can associate LPT2 through LPT9 with the remote printer.

Windows 95, Windows NT, and Novell NetWare servers all support Point and Print. You can automatically set up across the network printers shared by servers running any of these three operating systems.

Setting Up a Network Printer

Windows 95 provides more than one method for setting up network printers, all of which are designed to simplify the process so that a user can install support for a network printer as easily as possible, without assistance from a network administrator. One of the easiest ways to install support for a network printer is simply to print to the printer—Windows 95 automatically detects the absence of the required printer driver and installs the necessary files.

You can install support for a network printer in a variety of ways. The following list explains two of the most common ways:

◆ **Drag a document to the printer's icon.** Open the Network Neighborhood folder and choose the computer to which the remote printer is connected. The computer's resource window shows icons for the computer's shared disk resources and printers. Drag a document onto the printer's icon to make Windows 95 install the necessary printer drivers and print the document to the printer.

◆ **Double-click on the printer's icon.** Locate and double-click on the printer's icon in the Network Neighborhood. Windows 95 automatically installs support for the printer, prompting you for information such as the name by which you want the printer shown on your PC, whether to print a test page, and other minor details.

You also can use the Add Printer wizard to set up a network printer. Open the Printers folder and start the Add Printer wizard. When Windows 95 prompts you to choose between a local and remote network printer, choose the Network printer option, then click on Next. Windows 95 then prompts you for the path name of the shared printer. In the Network path or queue name text box, enter the path to the shared printer. The path consists of the name of the computer sharing the printer, and the name by which the printer is shared. To specify a printer shared as hpnetprint on a computer named aardvaark, for example, enter **\\aardvaark\hpnetprint**. If you don't know the name of the printer, choose the Browse button. Windows 95 provides a Browse for Printer dialog box that you can use to browse the network for the printer (see fig. 8.7).

Figure 8.7

The Browse for Printer dialog box.

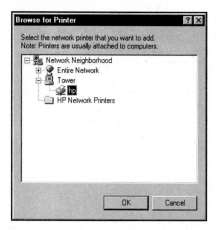

The Browse for Printer dialog box resembles the Network Neighborhood, showing all the computers in your workgroup in an expandable tree. To view the printers connected to a particular computer, click on the + sign beside the computer's name. To locate a printer connected to a computer outside your workgroup, expand the Entire Network branch, then locate the computer and printer you want to use. After you find the printer, select it and choose OK. The Add Printer wizard returns to the Add Printer dialog box. The rest of the printer setup process is similar to setting up a local printer. Work through the Add Printer wizard to complete the printer setup process. After you finish, Windows 95 adds an icon in the Printers folder for the network printer. You then can print to the network printer as if it were connected locally to your PC.

Later sections of this chapter explain network-related issues for printing to NetWare servers.

After you configure a printer, be it local or remote, you probably need to set a few options for the printer to control the way it prints. The following section examines the most common types of settings you can specify for various printers.

Setting Printer Options

Most printers enable you to control a wide range of options that define how the printer functions, including the amount of memory installed in it, the paper source it uses, the port to which it is connected, how it handles graphics and fonts, and much more. These options vary from printer to printer, but many are common to all printers. You use the Printers folder to set these options globally for a printer. You can override most of the settings when you print a document, however, by specifying options in the application's Print dialog box.

To set a printer's options, open the Printers folder, select the printer, and open its context menu (right-click on the printer and choose Properties, or press Shift+F10). Windows 95 then displays a set of property pages for the printer. Figure 8.8 shows the property pages for a typical printer, the HP LaserJet IIIP.

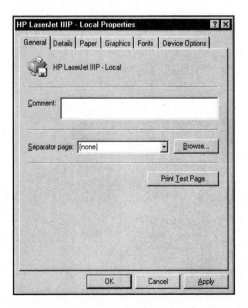

Figure 8.8

Property pages for an HP LaserJet IIIP.

The General, Details, and Sharing property pages apply to most printers (a Sharing page appears only if your computer is connected to a network). The following sections explain these and other property pages individually. Because covering all the printers that Windows 95 supports is impossible, the following sections use common printers to explain various settings. For specific help with settings for your printer, click on the question mark button on the property sheet, then click on the setting control about which you need information. Windows 95 displays a small text box that contains a description of the control's function. Or, consult your printer manual for more information.

Setting General Properties

The General property page, shown in figure 8.8, contains only a few controls. The Comments text box enables you to enter a comment for the printer. You can enter any information you like in the Comments text box, but one typical use is to provide information about the printer for other users who access the printer across the network. For example, you might enter the office location of the printer so that other users know its location.

Using a Separator Page

The Separator page combo box enables you to print a job separator page between each print job. Separator pages help you organize your own print jobs if you print many different documents to the printer. Separator pages also help separate print jobs that other users on the network print to your printer. You can choose from three standard options: None, Full, and Simple. If you select None, no separator page prints between print jobs. The Full option creates a graphical separator page that contains the document name, user name, and print date and time. The Simple option creates a text-only printout of the same information that prints when you use Full option.

 Tip   You can assign a separator page only on a printer connected to your PC. You can't assign a separator page on a remote network printer. For more information on sharing printers and other resources, refer to Chapter 35, "Sharing Resources in Windows 95."

Besides the None, Full, and Simple separator page options, you can use any Windows metafile (WMF file) as a separator page. This enables you to use a custom image for the separator page that might include your company logo or other information. Choose the Browse button to search for a WMF file, or enter the path to the file in the text box area of the Separator page combo box.

Note Although you can use a custom WMF file as a separator page, Windows 95 does not include any other information on the page; for example, your custom separator page does not include user, document, or time-printed information. If you specify a separator page on a shared network printer, consider using the Full option or the Simple option to be sure to include user information on the separator page, enabling you to route the completed print jobs to their intended recipients.

Setting Port Properties

The Details property page (see fig. 8.9) contains settings that enable you to control port, driver, and spooler settings. The Print to the following port drop-down list box enables you to select the port you want to associate with the printer driver. If you want to switch the printer from LPT1 to LPT2, for example, select LPT2 from the drop-down list. Or, you can select a network printer path from the drop-down list to associate the printer driver with a printer located elsewhere on the network.

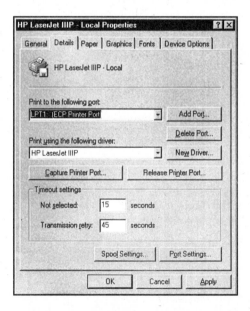

Figure 8.9

The Details property page for a printer.

The Add Port and Delete Port buttons enable you to make additional local and remote ports available to your printers, and to remove existing ports. Typically, Windows 95 automatically recognizes new physical ports. If you install a new I/O adapter that contains a second LPT port, for example, Windows 95 recognizes the new port as soon as you turn on and boot the system. However, you might want to add a new network printer to your list of available ports. To do so, choose Add Port, which displays the Add Port dialog box (see fig. 8.10).

Figure 8.10

The Add Port dialog box.

To add a network printer, choose the **N**etwork option button. In the accompanying text box, enter the path to the network printer resource. The path must include the remote computer's name and the name of its shared printer. To specify a printer share named *netprint* on a computer named *horatio,* enter **\\horatio\netprint** in the text box. Or, choose the **B**rowse button to search the network for a printer.

To add a different type of port, choose the **O**ther option button, then select a port from the accompanying list. To add a local printer port, for example, select Local Port from the list, then choose OK. Windows 95 then prompts you for the name of the port you want to add. Specify the port name, then choose OK.

To delete a port, choose the **D**elete port button from the Details property page. Windows 95 displays a list of the available ports. Select the port you want to delete, then choose OK.

You also can set various properties for a selected COM or LPT port. To set port properties, choose the P**o**rt Settings button. If you select an LPT port, Windows 95 calls up the dialog box shown in figure 8.11. If you select a COM port, Windows 95 displays the dialog box shown in figure 8.12.

Figure 8.11

The configuration dialog box for an LPT port.

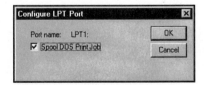

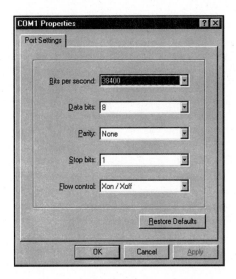

Figure 8.12

The configuration dialog box for a COM port.

The $\underline{S}$pool DOS Print Job check box in the Configure LPT Port dialog box enables you to control whether print jobs that DOS applications generate are spooled or sent directly to the printer. If you want superior printing performance, you should configure the port to enable spooling of print jobs from DOS applications. If the DOS application cannot print correctly through the spooler for some reason, turn off this option.

The COM*x* Properties dialog box (refer to figure 8.12) enables you to specify settings for a COM port. These settings are typical for a COM port, regardless of the type of device connected to the port. Chapter 28, "Modems and Data Communications," covers these settings in detail.

Capturing and Releasing Ports

If the network client you use doesn't support UNC names, you must associate a local LPT port with the remote printer. Associating a local printer port with a remote network printer is called *capturing* the port. If you print from DOS applications, you also might need to capture local ports for remote network printers. The DOS applications then can print to the remote printers as if they were connected to local LPT ports.

You can capture any LPT port, physical or virtual. If your PC contains only one LPT port, for example, that port probably is configured as LPT1. However, you can capture ports LPT2 through LPT9, associating them with remote network printers. The printer isn't connected locally to the PC, so it doesn't matter that the port the network printer captures isn't present on the computer. The port simply serves as a logical object Windows 95 can use to control the printer internally. And you can assign the same LPT port to more than one printer, just as you can when you use local printer ports. As long as you don't try to print to two printers that share a printer port at the same time, duplicating ports shouldn't cause any problems.

Tip   If your PC contains physical LPT ports, don't capture those ports for network printers—just use the first available virtual LPT port.

To capture a port for a remote network printer, first use one of the methods described earlier in this chapter to install the printer. Then, call up the printer's Details property page and choose the <u>C</u>apture Printer Port button. Windows 95 displays the Capture Printer Port dialog box, as shown in figure 8.13.

Figure 8.13

The Capture Printer Port dialog box.

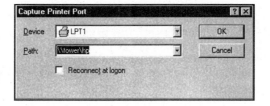

From the <u>D</u>evice drop-down list, select the port ID that you want to associate with the remote network printer. Then, use the <u>P</u>ath combo box to specify the path to the network printer. You can manually enter a path in the text box portion of the combo box, or use the drop-down list to select a previously used path.

By default, Windows 95 does not automatically capture the port and assign it to the remote network printer each time you log on. If you want the port to be associated with the remote printer each time you log on to Windows 95, thereby making the printer available automatically, enable the Reconnect at logon check box. Windows 95 then automatically associates the selected port with the remote printer each time you log on to Windows 95.

Tip   You can capture multiple printer ports for a remote printer, although doing so seldom is necessary. For example, you can capture LPT2 and LPT3 for the same printer. Applications that print to either port have their output redirected to the same remote printer. In addition, capturing a port for a remote printer does not affect the existing UNC connection. An application still can print to the printer using its UNC name rather than the captured port. A Windows application, for example, would print using the UNC name, whereas a DOS application would print through the captured port.

You sometimes have to disconnect a remote network printer from a local LPT port, or *release* the port. To release a port, display the printer's Details property page and choose the Release Printer Port button. Windows 95 displays the Release Printer Port dialog box, shown in figure 8.14. From the Printer list, select the printer port you want to release and choose OK.

Figure 8.14

The Release Printer Port dialog box.

Changing and Adding Drivers

The Details property page also enables you to change the driver associated with a printer so that you can change driver types without changing other information such as port settings, and enables you to provide support for a different printer type without running through the entire process of installing a new printer.

You can use a currently installed driver or install a new driver. To associate an existing driver with the printer, simply select the appropriate driver from the Print using the following driver drop-down list. To add a new driver, choose the New driver button. Adding a new driver from here on out is the same as when you use the Add Printer wizard to install a driver.

Specifying Timeout Settings

If you select a local printer port for the printer, you enable the two controls in the Timeout settings group: Not selected and Transmission retry. The Not selected setting specifies the amount of time Windows 95 waits for the printer to acknowledge that it's online before Windows 95 generates an error message. The default setting is 15 seconds. Increase this setting if the printer typically is not yet available after 15 seconds (if you wait until after you issue the print job before turning on the printer, for example).

The Transmission retry setting specifies the amount of time Windows 95 waits for the printer to come back online and accept more data after the printer's buffer fills, an error occurs, or in other situations. The default is 45 seconds. You might want to increase this setting for PostScript printers, which typically take longer to return online because of additional printer setup and font downloading that occurs during a print job. You also might want to increase this setting if you print large print jobs to non-PostScript printers.

Note Only the Transmission retry setting applies to printers connected to COM ports. The Not selected setting does not apply to printers connected to COM ports.

Specifying Spool Settings

You can specify a number of settings that control the way data spools to the print queue, which enables you to balance system response against print speed. To specify spool settings, choose the Spool Settings button from the Details property page to display the Spool Settings dialog box (see fig. 8.15).

Figure 8.15

The Spool Settings dialog box.

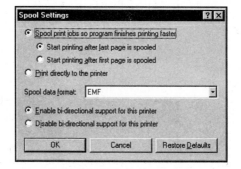

Spooling enables Windows 95 to provide better application response during printing. With a typical spooler, a print job is created as a series of temporary files on disk. The operating system—here, Windows 95—then takes over sending these temporary files to the printer, working as a background task. By separating the sending of the data to the printer from the source application, the application becomes available to you much more quickly to enable you to continue using the application after you issue a print job. The application completes the print job very quickly.

Spooling typically provides the best overall performance because you can continue to use your computer while print jobs are completed. If you need to print a 200-page document, for example, you don't have to wait until each of those 200 pages prints before you can resume using your computer. In a select few situations, however, turning off spooling is beneficial. For example, you might have to turn off spooling if your disk is nearly full and doesn't have sufficient space to accommodate the temporary print files.

Four settings in the Spool Settings dialog box enable you to control whether print jobs go directly to the printer or spool to disk, and if they spool, when spooling actually begins. The four settings are explained in the following list:

◆ **Spool print jobs so program finishes printing faster.** Choose this option button to enable spooling, which causes print jobs to spool to disk, then print to the printer as a background task. If you enable this setting, you can use the following two settings to specify when spooling begins:

◆ **Start printing after last page is spooled.** If you choose this option, Windows 95 does not begin sending data to the printer until the last page spools to disk. Choosing this option can return control of the application to you more quickly because Windows 95 isn't trying to spool data to disk and send data to the printer at the same time. Instead, all the data spools to disk, control of the application returns to you, and the printing begins in the background.

◆ **Start printing after first page is spooled.** If you want the job to begin printing immediately, choose this option. Windows 95 spools the first page to disk, then begins sending that page to the printer. At the same time, it continues spooling the additional pages to disk.

◆ **Print directly to the printer.** Choose this option to disable spooling. If you enable this option, Windows 95 sends print jobs directly to the printer, instead of spooling them to disk. You don't regain control of the application until the entire print job goes to the printer's buffer. You can speed the printing process slightly by disabling spooling, but you still can't use your PC during the print job.

Understanding Enhanced Metafile Format

One major change in Windows 95 printing is the format in which data is sent from the spooler to the printer. In Windows 3.*x*, the printer driver sent raw printer data to the printer. In Windows 95, you can use enhanced metafile format (EMF), rather than raw format, to send the data to non-PostScript printers.

Metafiles contain graphical data and are a common file format for Windows drawing applications. Unlike bitmaps, which define an image as a series of dots, metafiles define an image as a collection of graphical objects, such as lines and circles. The advantage metafiles offer over bitmapped images is that you can scale and resize metafiles without affecting the image quality. Although some restrictions do apply to resizing, scaling, clipping, and other actions on standard metafiles, transformed metafiles come out as much better images than do transformed bitmapped images.

EMF improves on the Windows 3.*x* metafile format, adding new features to the metafile format to make it much more useful and remove the restrictions for scaling and sizing that previously hindered the use of standard Windows 3.*x* metafiles. Although EMF was developed primarily to overcome the limitations in standard metafiles for developers of drawing applications, EMF enhances printing in Windows 95.

Before you can truly understand EMF, you need to understand the function that the Graphical Device Interface (GDI) performs in Windows 95. The GDI is a core Windows 95 component that handles most graphical I/O in Windows 95, from painting the screen to sending output to printers. The GDI supports a variety of drawing commands for rendering graphical objects and text. EMF files use those same drawing commands. In fact, a metafile really amounts to being little more than a file that contains the GDI commands, palette, and other information needed to render the image defined by the GDI commands.

When you print from a Windows application, the printer driver filters the data through the GDI. The GDI renders the data in the background and sends it to the print spooler. Figure 8.16 shows the flow of data from an application to a printer.

Figure 8.16
Data flow from an application to the printer.

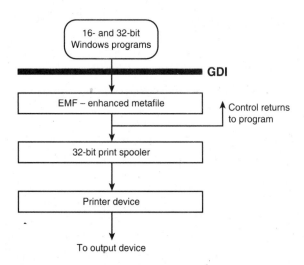

The EMF format enables the GDI to process and send the data to the spooler more quickly because the EMF format is native to the GDI—instead of converting the data from the application to raw printer format, the GDI simply generates the GDI drawing commands necessary to render the print job on the printer. This decrease in rendering time returns control of the application to you more quickly.

Note If you print to a printer attached to a Windows 95 server, the EMF rendering occurs on the server rather than on the client computer that generated the print job. This reduces the client computer's workload, further increasing the benefit of using EMF. If you print to a server running Windows NT or Novell NetWare, EMF rendering occurs locally on the client computer and the rendered data is then sent to the server. When you print to a local printer, all rendering naturally occurs on the local computer.

The Spool data format drop-down list on the Spool Settings dialog box enables you to specify the data format that Windows 95 uses to send data to the print spooler. You can choose RAW, to direct Windows 95 to send the information to the printer in raw format, or EMF, to direct Windows 95 to send the data to the spooler in enhanced metafile format.

Using Bidirectional Support

Many newer computers include *bidirectional* printer ports that enable information to flow, not only from the computer to the output device (such as a printer), but also from the printer to the computer. Bidirectional ports provide three main benefits, described in the following list:

◆ **Simplified installation.** Windows 95 can query the printer to determine its model and configuration, enabling Windows 95 to automatically configure the printer properly during installation.

◆ **Device configuration identification.** Windows 95's capability for querying the printer about device configuration issues, such as amount of memory and fonts installed, enables it to display and manage printer configuration information.

◆ **Device status updates.** Because the printer can send information to Windows 95, a bidirectional port enables the printer to inform Windows 95 about printer conditions, such as out of paper or toner, paper jams, and so forth, which enables Windows 95 to bring these problems to the user's attention.

If your PC contains a bidirectional parallel port, you can choose the E nable bi-directional support for this printer option button to enable bidirectional support for the printer. Or, you can choose the Di sable bi-directional support for this printer option button to disable bidirectional support.

Note Even if your LPT ports support bidirectional transfer, they might not be configured as such. Run your system's BIOS setup program and check the port settings to determine if the ports are configured for bidirectional use. You need make no changes in Windows 95 other than to enable bidirectional support for the printer, as specified previously in this section.

Setting Sharing Properties

The Sharing page of a printer's property sheet enables you to share the printer with other users on the network. To share a printer, first configure all its other settings and print a test page to verify that it is working properly. Then, display the Sharing page of the printer's property sheets. Choose the Shared As option button to enable sharing, then enter a name for the printer in the Share Name text box. This name appears to other users when they browse the network for resources. You also can add an optional comment in the Comment text box. The comment appears as additional information in the Network Neighborhood folder if the user configures the folder for a detailed view.

Tip   To protect the printer with a password to restrict use of the printer, enter a password in the Password text box. Any user who tries to access the printer must answer a prompt to enter the password.

Chapter 35, "Sharing Resources in Windows 95," offers a detailed explanation of sharing resources and using shared resources.

Setting Other Properties

You also can set properties for a printer other than those described in the previous sections. These options vary from printer to printer, but many types of settings are common among most printers. The property sheets for a printer, therefore, often include pages that enable you to control options for graphics, fonts, device settings (such as memory installed in the printer), and other settings. The most common property pages are described in the following list:

◆ **Paper.** Use the Paper property page to specify the type of paper, the default paper tray or bin, number of copies to print, printable area, and output mode (landscape or portrait).

◆ **Graphics.** Use the Graphics property page to specify settings that control the way the printer handles graphics. Typical settings include printer resolution, intensity (darkness), and how the printer dithers images.

◆ **Fonts.** This property page enables you to specify the font cartridges installed in the printer, download fonts to the printer, and install new fonts. You also can specify how the printer handles TrueType fonts, either printing the fonts as graphics or as fonts downloaded to the printer. For more information on TrueType fonts, refer to Chapter 7, "Working with Fonts."

◆ **Device Options.** The Device Options page contains settings that enable you to control various printer properties, such as the amount of memory installed in the printer. These settings vary from one printer to another.

Tip

Jobs typically print faster if you set the printer to download TrueType fonts to the printer (use soft fonts) rather than print the fonts as graphics. If you use many different fonts scattered throughout the document, however, printing the TrueType fonts as soft fonts can increase printing time because of the excessive font downloading that has to occur. In such a situation, printing the TrueType fonts as graphics can actually decrease printing time.

Setting PostScript Properties

PostScript printers include options that other types of printers don't require. These PostScript-only settings are scattered throughout the PostScript printer's property sheet, although PostScript printers also include a PostScript property page (see fig. 8.17).

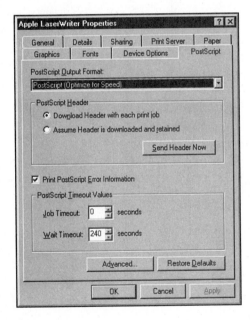

Figure 8.17

The PostScript property page.

The following list explains some of the most common settings that apply to PostScript printers.

◆ **PostScript Output Format.** Unlike Windows 3.*x*, Windows 95 supports a selection of different PostScript formats. Use this drop-down list to select a format that suits your situation.

◆ **PostScript Header.** Each PostScript print job requires that header information be sent to the printer to configure the printer for page layout and other characteristics. If the header information doesn't change from one print job to another, you don't need to download the header for each job. The PostScript Header group contains the following controls:

    ◆ **Download Header with each print job.** Choose this option if you want the header information to download to the printer for each print job.

    ◆ **Assume Header is downloaded and retained.** Choose this option to prevent the header from being downloaded for each print job.

    ◆ **Send Header Now.** Choose this button to download the header to the printer immediately.

◆ **Print PostScript Error Information.** PostScript printers can report various errors that Windows 95 can't recognize. Choose this option if you have printer problems and want a printout of the errors, if any.

◆ **PostScript Timeout Values.** These values are similar to the Timeout values you set for the printer's LPT port. They include the following settings:

    ◆ **Job Timeout.** This setting specifies the amount of time a print job can take to transmit from the computer to the printer before the printer terminates the print job. Increase the setting for large, complex print jobs, or specify a setting of 0 to cause the printer to wait indefinitely.

    ◆ **Wait Timeout.** This setting specifies the amount of time that the printer waits for the computer to send additional data before it terminates the print job. Large, complex jobs might require a higher setting, or specify a value of 0 to cause the printer to wait indefinitely.

Printing from Windows Applications

Printing from a Windows application is relatively simple. Each Windows application that supports printing includes a Print command in its File menu. When you choose Print, a Print dialog box similar to the ones shown in figures 8.18 and 8.19 appears. Figure 8.18 shows the standard Windows 95 Print dialog box, and figure 8.19 shows a typical application-derived Print dialog box, which in this example is from Word for Windows. The controls in the Print dialog box vary from one application to another, but are very similar.

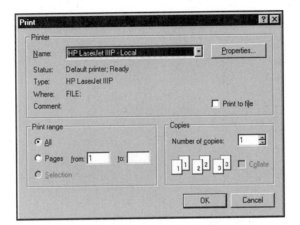

Figure 8.18

A standard Windows 95 Print dialog box.

Figure 8.19

The Word for Windows Print dialog box.

One printer in Windows 95 is always the default printer. Windows 95 uses the default printer to print a document unless you specify a different printer. If you click on the printer button in an application's toolbar, for example, the application typically sends the current document to the default printer without prompting you for any additional information. To specify a different printer, choose File, Print, then select the printer from the Name drop-down list. Some of the options in the Print dialog box then change to reflect the change in printers.

Note   Some applications change the default printer when you select a different printer. Most applications, however, simply print to the selected printer without changing the default printer. If you print from an application that changes the default printer each time you select a different printer, you can easily restore the original default printer. After you issue the print job, choose File, Print again, select the printer you want to assign as the default printer, then cancel the print job. You also can set the default printer from the Printers folder. Select the printer you want to assign as the default printer, display its context menu, then choose Set As Default.

Setting Printer Options for a Document

You can set options globally for a printer by using its properties in the Printers folder. You also can set properties for the printer per the document. After you choose File, Print (activating the Print dialog box), choose the Properties button to display a set of property pages for the printer (see fig. 8.20). These property pages comprise a subset of all the printer's property pages, showing the properties that you can set on a per-document basis.

Figure 8.20

Property pages for setting printer properties for a document.

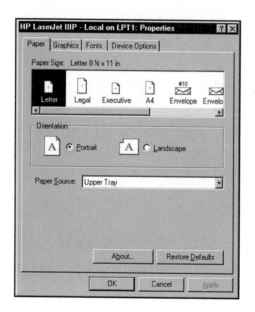

If you need to change a property not made available in these property pages, cancel the print job, then open the Printers folder and set the printer's properties as necessary.

Printing from the Desktop

In addition to printing a document from an application as described in the previous section, Windows 95 provides the capability to print documents directly from the desktop. This capability simplifies printing a document. You can use one of four primary methods to print documents from the desktop. All these methods are similar, and are described in the following sections.

Printing from the Context Menu

Using the document's context menu is one of the easiest ways to print a document. You can open the folder that contains the document, right-click on the document's icon to display its context menu, then choose Print. Windows 95 opens the document's parent application, prints the document to the default printer, then closes the document. If the parent application is open before you initiate the print job, Windows 95 does not close the application, but it does close the document. If the application is not open before you issue the print job, Windows 95 closes the application after the job spools.

 Note If the document resides on the desktop, you print in the same way. Select the document and display its context menu, then choose Print.

 Tip If you select a document type that is not associated with an OLE-compliant application, the Print command will not appear in the document's context menu. You will have to open the document and print it manually.

Printing with Drag-and-Drop

Another method for printing from the desktop is to drag a document onto a printer. Open the folder that contains the document, then drag the document from the folder to a printer in the Printers folder or to a printer shortcut, on the desktop or in a folder. Windows 95 opens the parent application, prints the document to the default printer, then closes the document.

You also can drag a document into a printer queue window to print the document. For example, open the Printers folder, double-click on a printer icon to open its queue window, and then drag a document from the desktop or a folder into the queue window. The document prints on the selected printer.

 Tip You can't drag and drop an object onto a button on the Taskbar. If you drag the object over the button and hold the object over the button for a second, however, the application that the button represents opens on the desktop and you can drag the object into it. Therefore, you can open a printer's queue window and minimize it, and place the queue on the Taskbar. Then, drag a document onto the queue's button and hold it over the button for a second. When the queue window opens on the desktop, drag the document into the queue window and release the document to print it. You can use this same method to open a document. Rather than drag the document onto a printer queue, drag it onto an application.

Printing with Send To

The third method of printing from the desktop relies on the Send To menu. One of the menu items in a context menu is Se<u>n</u>d To. Choosing Se<u>n</u>d To displays a list of the objects in the \Windows\SendTo folder or, if Windows is configured to support multiple desktops, the \Windows\Profiles*user*\SendTo folder. To use the Se<u>n</u>d To menu to enable printing, simply place shortcuts to printers in the \Windows\SendTo or \Windows\Profiles*user*\SendTo folder. Next, select a document and open its context menu. Then, choose Se<u>n</u>d To, followed by the shortcut for the printer to which you want to send the document. Windows 95 opens the parent application, prints the document to the selected printer, then closes the document.

Printing from a Folder

In addition to using a document's object menu, drag-and-drop, or Send To to print a document, you can start a print job from a folder window. Simply select the document, then choose <u>F</u>ile, <u>P</u>rint. Windows 95 opens the document's parent application, prints the document, and closes the document.

Using Deferred Printing

Windows 95 adds new features for printing, one of those being deferred printing. *Deferred printing* enables you to issue a print job even when the printer you want to use is offline. You can print to a network printer from your notebook computer, for example, even when your PC is not connected to the network. After you bring your PC back into the office, you can connect to the network, and the queue begins to send the print jobs to the printer. Essentially, deferred printing simply means that the queue is placed offline until the printer becomes available.

For the most part, Windows 95 automatically handles deferred printing. After you boot Windows 95, the operating system determines the available printers. The icons of any printers not available across the network are dimmed in the Printers folder, indicating offline printers. If you print to an unavailable printer, the print job spools to the queue, where the job remains until the printer and queue are back online.

You also can manually place a queue offline, enabling you to use deferred printing even if the printer is available. You also have to place a queue offline if the printer becomes unavailable after you boot Windows 95. To place a queue offline, open the Printers folder and select the printer whose queue you want to place offline. Open the printer's context menu, then choose <u>W</u>ork Offline. Any jobs you send to the printer's queue are held in the queue until you place the queue back online. To place the queue back online, open the printer's context menu and clear the <u>W</u>ork Offline option.

During your PC's boot, Windows 95 detects the offline queues and prompts you to specify whether you want to begin printing the jobs in the queue. You can choose <u>Y</u>es to place the queue back online and begin printing the jobs, <u>N</u>o to leave the queue offline, or Cancel to cancel the print jobs. Therefore, when you bring your notebook into the office, connect it to the network, and boot the system, Windows 95 should automatically place the queue back online and begin printing the jobs in the queue.

 Tip Deferred printing is not limited to Windows 95 applications. Any Windows application, 16-bit or 32-bit, can use deferred printing, because the same spooler handles all printing. DOS applications also can use deferred printing if the printer is configured to spool DOS print jobs (explained earlier in this chapter in the section "Setting Up a Local Printer").

Using Deferred Printing for Local Printers

If you open the context menu for a local printer, you might notice the absence of a <u>W</u>ork Offline command in the menu. Nevertheless, you can defer printing on local printers. You might wonder, however, why you would want to do so. Well, assume you have a docking station in your office for your notebook computer, and that you have a printer connected to the docking station. When you remove your notebook from the office, you don't have your local printer any more. You still can print to the local printer's queue while the printer is unavailable, then place the queue back online when you dock the notebook.

To defer printing on a local printer, open the printer's context menu and choose P<u>a</u>use Printing. Print to the printer as if it were available. You can shut down the PC with the jobs pending in the queue, and when you boot the PC again, those jobs still are held in the queue. As it does with network printers, Windows 95 detects the pending jobs in the local printer's queue at startup and asks you if you want to begin printing the pending jobs. Verify that the printer is connected and turned on, then choose <u>Y</u>es to begin printing. Choose <u>N</u>o to leave the queue in its offline state and retain the jobs in the queue. Choose Cancel to clear the queue of all pending print jobs.

Using the Extended Capabilities Port

Many newer PCs include an enhanced parallel port, called an Extended Capabilities Port (ECP). The ECP supports bidirectional communication and increased through-put. These capabilities not only enable faster printing, but also make it practical to use some of the new devices, such as CD-ROM drives and sound adapters, that use a parallel port interface.

Generally, enabling the ECP on a PC requires changing BIOS settings. For example, your BIOS might enable you to configure the port as a standard unidirectional LPT port, bidirectional LPT port, or ECP. Before Windows 95 can recognize your ECP, you must first change the BIOS settings for the port to enable it as an ECP. The way in which you perform BIOS setup varies from one PC to another (depending on the BIOS type and manufacturer). Check your system manual to determine how to run your PC's BIOS setup program and enable ECP support for the port.

Tip On some systems, you enter BIOS setup by pressing F1 after the power-on self test (POST) finishes. On other systems, pressing the Del key after the POST enters the BIOS setup program. And on other machines, pressing Ctrl+Alt+Esc from the DOS prompt enters BIOS setup.

To provide ECP support in Windows 95, first run your BIOS setup program and enable the ECP. As the BIOS setup program runs, note the base address, IRQ, and DMA values for the ECP. You need these settings to configure the ECP in Windows 95.

After you configure the ECP in the system BIOS, start Windows 95 and open the Control Panel. Choose the System icon, then click on the Device Manager tab to display the Device Manager property page (see fig. 8.21). Your Device Manager page will resemble the one shown in figure 8.21, but you'll see differences owing to the hardware installed on your PC.

Figure 8.21

The Device Manager property page.

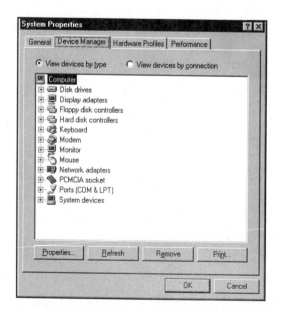

Expand the tree labeled Ports (COM and LPT) to list the installed ports. Then, remove the existing LPT port for which you want to enable the ECP. If you want to enable the ECP for LPT1, for example, remove LPT1. Removing the LPT port is necessary because the LPT port shares the same settings as the ECP (because they are the same physical port).

After you remove the LPT port, restart the PC. Windows 95 doesn't automatically recognize the ECP and install a driver for it the way it does with some other types of hardware. Instead, you must open the Control Panel and use the Add New Hardware wizard to add the ECP. Double-click on the Add New Hardware icon, then click on Next to display the dialog box shown in figure 8.22.

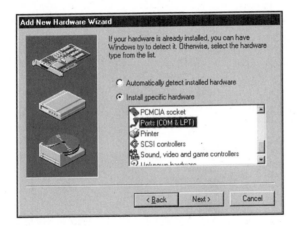

Figure 8.22

Select the ECP port to install using the Add New Hardware wizard.

Although you can direct Windows 95 to automatically detect the hardware in your PC, it might not detect the ECP. To save the time Windows 95 takes to search your PC for installed and new devices, choose the Install specific hardware option. Then, scroll through the accompanying list, select the Ports (COM & LPT) option, and click on Next. The Add New Hardware wizard displays a new dialog box, shown in figure 8.23, that you can use to select the type of port to install. Select (standard port types) from the Manufacturers list, select ECP Printer Port from the Models list, and click on Next.

The Add New Hardware wizard then displays a dialog box that lists the resource requirements for the ECP. These are the same base address, IRQ, and DMA channel resource settings you need to note during BIOS setup when you configure the PC to use the ECP. You can't use the wizard to specify new settings—instead, you can use the Device Manager to change the settings before you reboot the PC. To complete the process so that you can open the Device Manager and change the settings, click on Next, then Finish. Windows 95 displays a message that you must shut down the computer to install the new hardware and asks if you want to shut down the computer now. Choose No.

Figure 8.23

*Select ECP
Printer Port from
the Models list.*

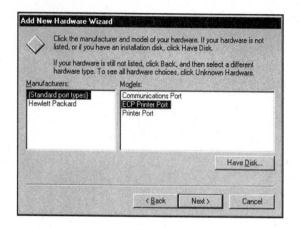

To specify the proper settings for the ECP, open the Control Panel and choose the System icon, then click on the Device Manager tab. Expand the Ports (COM and LPT) branch, select the ECP Printer Port item, then choose Properties. Windows 95 displays a set of property pages for the ECP port. Click on the Resources tab to display the Resources property page (see fig. 8.24).

Figure 8.24

*The Resources
page in the ECP
Printer Port
property sheet.*

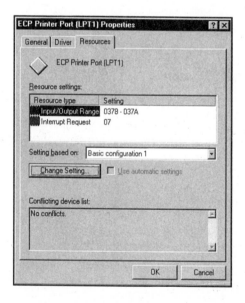

Windows 95 includes four basic configurations for ECPs, but you can modify any of the four to suit the requirements of your hardware. If your ECP doesn't require a DMA channel but does require an IRQ, for example, start with basic configuration 1, which includes settings for address range and IRQ. Next, choose the setting from the

Resource settings list that you need to change to accommodate your ECP, then choose the Change Setting button. Windows 95 displays a dialog box, similar to the one shown in figure 8.25, that you can use to specify the new setting. Choose the setting that matches your hardware, then choose OK. Repeat the process for the base address range, IRQ, and DMA, as applicable. After you specify the correct settings, choose OK to close the ECP Printer Port property sheets.

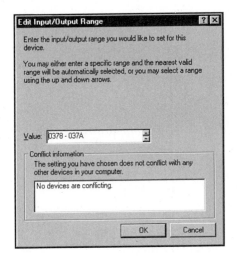

Figure 8.25

Specify the settings that apply to your ECP.

After you close the ECP Printer Port property sheets, Windows 95 asks if you want to shut down the computer. Choose Yes to shut down the computer, then restart the PC after it shuts down all the way. After Windows 95 boots, the ECP is enabled and ready for use in Windows 95. Other than associating the ECP with the driver for the printer connected to the port, you need make no additional changes to begin using the ECP. Refer to the section "Setting Up a Local Printer" earlier in this chapter for more information on configuring ports and printer drivers.

Printing from DOS Applications

In Windows 3.*x*, DOS applications did not use the Windows spooler and sometimes caused conflicts with Windows applications that attempted to use the printer while the DOS application was printing. In Windows 95, however, DOS applications can spool their print jobs through the Windows 95 spooler, which offers some strong advantages.

First, spooling DOS application print jobs through the Windows 95 spooler results in smoother printing and multitasking performance. You no longer have to wait for the

DOS application's job to finish printing before you can begin working in another application. Instead, the job spools from the DOS application to the print queue, just as it does for Windows 95 applications. This restores control of the PC to you more rapidly.

Spooling DOS print jobs through a common spooler also eliminates conflicts between DOS applications and Windows 95 applications that attempt to print at the same time. You can open a DOS application and start a print job, for example, then switch to a Windows application and start a second print job. Both are spooled to the queue without conflict. Therefore, you no longer have to configure Windows to give control of the printer port to Windows 95 or to DOS—both environments can have equal access to the print spooler.

Spooling DOS application print jobs is enabled by default. If you have a DOS application that can't print properly through the Windows 95 spooler, you can disable DOS spooling. To do so, open the Printers folder and display the context menu for any printer connected to the port for which you want to disable spooling. Choose Properties to display the printer's property sheet, then click on the Details tab. Choose the Port Settings button to display the Configure LPT Port dialog box, clear the Spool DOS Print Job check box, then choose OK to close the dialog box, and OK again to close the printer's property sheet.

Note Even though DOS applications use the Windows 95 spooler, DOS applications do not use Windows 95 printer drivers. You must continue to use the printer drivers supplied with your DOS applications. Also, DOS applications do not take advantage of EMF format spooling. The primary advantages of spooling DOS print jobs to the Windows 95 spooler are the elimination of device conflicts and improved multitasking.

Capturing Ports for Printers in DOS

You can capture a port for a remote network printer using the method explained earlier in this chapter in the section "Capturing and Releasing Ports." Capturing a port is necessary if your network client doesn't support UNC path names.

You also can capture ports from the DOS command line. To capture a printer port, open a DOS session and enter the command **NET USE LPTn:** *server**printer*, where LPTn: is the name of the port you want to capture and *server**printer* is the path to the printer. To capture LPT1: for a printer named Laser on a computer named PrintServer, for example, use the command **NET USE LPT1: \\\\PRINTSERVER\\ LASER**. On NetWare systems, use the command **CAPTURE LPTn:**.

Controlling a Printer's Queue

Previous sections of this chapter deal primarily with installing and configuring printers and various methods for printing from Windows and DOS applications. Your control over the printer and print jobs doesn't end when you start printing in an application. You can view and manage the print queue, giving you control over such things as the order in which jobs print. The following sections explain how to view and manage a printer's queue, and explain the differences in control you have over local printers versus network printers.

Viewing the Queue

Viewing a printer's queue is simple—just open the Printers folder and double-click on the printer whose queue you want to view. Or, select the printer and press Enter. A window similar to the one shown in figure 8.26 appears.

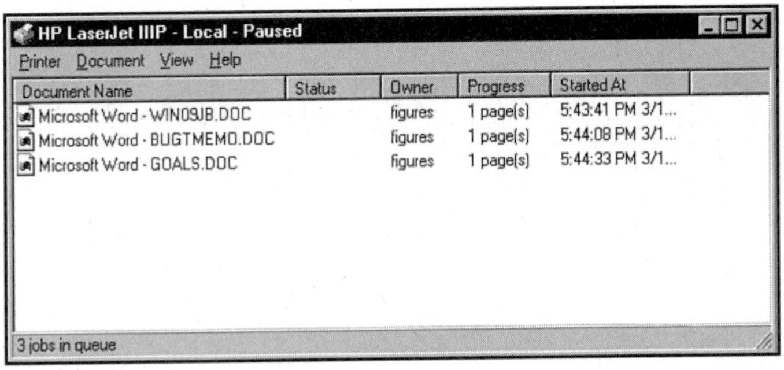

Figure 8.26

A typical queue window showing jobs pending.

The queue window lists all the pending jobs, as well as the current job (the one currently being sent to the printer). The queue lists various information about each print job, including the user who initiated the job, the status of the job, its size, and other information. The jobs are listed in the order in which they are sent to the printer, with the currently printing job at the top of the list.

Changing Queue Priority

Occasionally, you might decide to move a print job located low in the queue to higher in the queue to make it print sooner. Assume you have a number of jobs pending. You realize that you need to print a copy of a report for a meeting scheduled in 10 minutes. You can print the report, then open the queue and move the report from the bottom of the queue to the top to make it print after the current job finishes. To change job order in the queue, simply drag the job into its new position and release it.

Pausing and Canceling Print Jobs

In addition to changing queue order, you sometimes will want to pause printing and cancel print jobs. Consider the previous example of an urgently needed report: What if the current print job still has 50 pages to print? Even if you move the report near the top of the queue so that it prints next, printing the 50 pages of the current job, plus your report document probably will take longer than the 10 minutes you have left before the meeting. Therefore, you need to pause the current print job and cancel it so you can print your report.

To pause a print job, select the job from the queue window, then choose Document, Pause Printing. Windows 95 pauses the print job, but any pages already sent to the printer's buffer still print.

Unfortunately, you can't pause a job that's printing, move another job ahead of it to print, then resume the paused job. If you pause the current job, the effect is the same as pausing the queue altogether—none of the other jobs can print until you resume or cancel the paused job. You can, however, pause jobs not currently printing. If you pause a few jobs in the middle of the queue, any jobs higher in the queue will print. Then, jobs lower in the queue than the paused jobs will print. If you make no other changes to the queue, all the nonpaused pending jobs will print, leaving only the paused jobs in the queue.

Pausing, Resuming, and Purging the Printer

Sometimes you need to pause the entire queue rather than just one print job; for example, you might want to pause printing if the printer runs out of toner (or the equivalent for non–laser printers) or jams before the job finishes. To pause the queue, choose Printer, Pause Printing. Any pages already in the printer's queue still print, but no other pages are sent to the printer. To pause the pages in the buffer, place the printer offline.

To resume printing, first place the printer online. Then, choose Printer, then Pause Printing to remove the check from the Pause Printing menu item.

If you want to remove all print jobs from the queue, choose Printer, Purge Print Jobs. All pending print jobs are removed from the queue, and are not sent to the printer.

Controlling a Network Printer Queue

You can view and manage the queue of a network printer in much the same way as a local printer. Some restrictions, however, do impede your ability to manage jobs in a network queue.

When you open the printer's queue window, you see all the print jobs pending for the printer, regardless of who originated each one. You can pause and cancel your own print jobs, but you can't pause or cancel other users' print jobs. Unlike in a local queue, you can't change the order of print jobs in the queue whether the jobs you want to change are your own or another user's. To effectively move one or more of your print jobs to a lower position in the queue, simply pause the job(s). As jobs continue to be sent to the printer, those below your paused jobs in the queue "jump over" your jobs and are printed. Also, you can't pause or unpause the printer, nor purge the queue.

The person who logs on to the computer to which the printer is attached can manage the queue in all ways. If your printer is shared on the network, for example, you can move print jobs around in the queue, pause jobs, and cancel jobs, even if other users initiate those jobs. You also can pause and resume the printer, and purge the queue.

Note Before you cancel other users' print jobs or purge the queue, note the users' names and the descriptions of their print jobs. Then, you should send an e-mail message to those users to inform them that you are canceling their print jobs.

Using Image Color Matching

Windows 95 includes support for Image Color Matching (ICM), which enables applications to provide consistency between the colors of objects on the display and the color of those objects after they're printed. ICM enables you to see on the display the color output that will be rendered on the printer.

ICM is based on technology that Microsoft has licensed from Eastman Kodak, and relies on color format standards defined by InterColor 3.0, a standard developed by a consortium of companies that include Eastman Kodak, Microsoft, Apple Computer, Sun Microsystems, Silicon Graphics, and others. InterColor 3.0 provides for standard and consistent definition of color properties of display and output devices across vendors and platforms.

ICM relies on color profiles that define the color properties of monitors, printers, scanners, and other output devices. The manufacturer of the ICM-compliant device provides ICM profiles. Windows 95 places the ICM profiles in the \Windows\System\Color folder when you install support for the device during setup.

To use ICM during printing, you must set the appropriate printer properties. (Naturally, only color printers offer support for ICM.) To control ICM properties for a printer, first open the printer's property sheet. Then, choose the Graphics tab to display the Graphics property page. If the printer supports ICM, the Graphics property page will be similar to the one shown in figure 8.27.

Figure 8.27

The Graphics property page of an ICM-compliant printer.

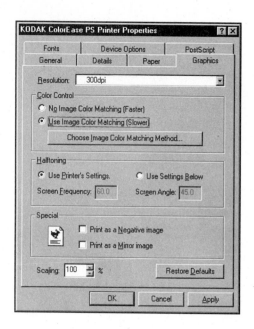

 Note   The description of ICM options in this section are based on the Kodak ColorEase PostScript printer. Other output devices naturally have different capabilities and corresponding options. Therefore, the options for a particular output device will differ somewhat from those described in this section. The Kodak ColorEase example simply gives you a general understanding of ICM capabilities in Windows 95.

If color matching doesn't affect a job you are about to print, you can turn off color matching. To turn off color matching, choose the No Image Color Matching option button. If you do want to use ICM, choose the Use Image Color Matching option button. Because of the additional overhead and color matching computation, printing is slower.

If you decide to use ICM, you can specify a few options that control the way ICM matches and renders the colors of the output. After you choose Use Image Color Matching, choose the Choose Image Color Matching Method button. Windows 95 displays a dialog box similar to the one shown in figure 8.28.

The controls in the Image Color Matching Method group enable you to control where the color matching takes place. The options are explained by descriptions in the dialog box. The following list provides an overview of these three options:

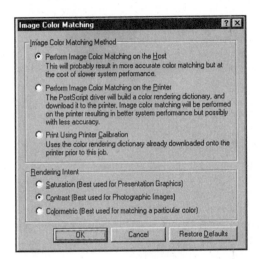

Figure 8.28

*Set ICM options
in the Image
Color Matching
dialog box.*

◆ **Perform Image Color Matching on the Host.** Choose this option to have color matching performed by the input device (essentially, on the computer). Choosing this option generally results in the best color matching, although processing time increases.

◆ **Perform Image Color Matching on the Printer.** Choose this option to perform color matching on the printer. Overall performance increases, but the color match isn't likely to be as accurate.

◆ **Print Using Printer Calibration.** Choose this option if you have previously downloaded a color dictionary with the Perform Image Color Matching on the Printer option. Performance improves even further because you eliminate the processing time required to define the color dictionary and download it to the printer. Color accuracy is the same as with the Perform Image Color Matching on the Printer option.

You also can control the rendering process to tailor it to specific end results. The options in the Rendering Intent group in the Image Color Matching dialog box control the color output. Each of the three options in the Rendering Intent group includes a description that explains the option's purpose. Choose the Saturation option to optimize the output for color saturation, which generally is ideal for presentation graphics. Choose the Contrast option to optimize the output for contrast, which generally is ideal for reproducing photographic images. If color accuracy is most important, choose the Colormetric option.

Printing in Novell NetWare Environments

The Microsoft Client for NetWare Networks integrates in NetWare environments the Point and Print features described earlier in this chapter (in the section "Understanding Point and Print Setup"). The result is support for all of the new Windows 95 printing features for network nodes running the Client for NetWare Networks. In addition, Windows 95 includes a 32-bit service, called Microsoft Print Agent for NetWare, that enables NetWare servers to despool print jobs from a server print queue to a client node running Microsoft Print Agent for NetWare. This service can take the place of dedicated PCs running PSERVER to accomplish the same task. The following section explains how to configure a NetWare print server. Later sections explain how to configure and use Microsoft Print Agent for NetWare.

Configuring Point and Print under NetWare

Windows 95 can store the Point and Print information for a printer in the NetWare Bindery, enabling clients to take advantage of Point and Print printer installation. To configure Point and Print support on a NetWare server, you must run the Client for NetWare Networks on a Windows 95 node, and you must have administrator privileges for the server to which the printer is connected.

After you log on to a server from a Windows 95 node with administrator privileges, open the Network Neighborhood and locate the server that provides Point and Print support. Open the server's window, then choose the printer for which you want to install Point and Print support. The printer's queue window opens.

From the printer's queue window, choose Point and Print Setup, then choose Set Printer Model from the context menu, which brings up the Select Printer dialog box. Select the manufacturer and model of the printer, then choose OK. Then, open the context menu again and choose Set Driver Path. Enter the UNC path to the directory in which to store the drivers, then choose OK.

Unlike the previous steps, the next step is not automated. You must ensure that the driver and support files are available in the directory you specified in the previous step. To do so, open the file Msprint.inf and locate the printer model for which you are installing Point and Print support. The entry for the printer includes a list of all required files. If these files are not available in the directory you specified as the driver path, manually copy the files from the Windows 95 distribution disks or CD to the driver directory.

Tip   If you install shared files on the server to enable shared network installation of Windows 95, simply reference the shared Windows 95 directory as the driver path.

Using Point and Print under NetWare

After you install Point and Print support for a printer, clients can use Point and Print installation to install support for the network printer on their nodes. There is no difference in the methods you use to install a network printer on a NetWare client node from the methods you use on a Microsoft client node. From the client node, simply locate the printer's server in Network Neighborhood, then double-click on the printer's icon in the server's folder window. Windows 95 starts the Add Printer wizard, steps you through installing the printer, and copies the files from the directory that the server's driver path specifies (explained in the previous section) to the client node. You also can install a printer by dragging its icon from the server folder window to your Printers folder, which also causes the Add Printer wizard to run.

Using Microsoft Print Agent for NetWare

Windows 95 includes a 32-bit service, named Microsoft Print Agent for NetWare, that serves as a background PSERVER utility, despooling print jobs from a NetWare server's queue. This offloads much of the overhead involved in managing the queue and print jobs from the server to the computer running Print Agent for NetWare.

Currently, DOS-based PSERVER requires a dedicated PC running only PSERVER to despool print jobs from the server—you can't use the computer running PSERVER for any other purposes. Unlike DOS-based PSERVER, Print Agent for NetWare runs as a background Windows 95 task, despooling print jobs from the NetWare server while the computer serves for other tasks (such as for a regular user workstation). The trade-off, however, between DOS-based PSERVER and Print Agent for NetWare is that a computer running PSERVER can support multiple printers, but Print Agent for NetWare can support only a single printer. Because the Print Agent for NetWare can operate as a background task on a user's machine, however, you can distribute printers currently served by a single dedicated PSERVER node to multiple user nodes.

Installing Print Agent for NetWare

Microsoft Print Agent for NetWare is included on the Windows 95 CD in the \Admin\Nettools\Prtagent directory. Before you install Print Agent for NetWare, first install the Client for NetWare Networks if it is not already installed. Verify that your NetWare access is functioning correctly on the client computer and that you can connect to the NetWare server.

To install Print Agent for NetWare, open the Control Panel and choose the Network icon. In the Configuration page of the Network property sheet, choose the **A**dd button to display the Select Network Component Type dialog box. Choose Service, then choose **A**dd to display the Select Network Service dialog box (see fig. 8.29).

Figure 8.29

The Select Network Service dialog box.

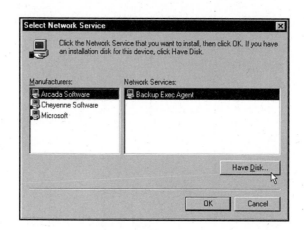

In the Select Network Service dialog box, choose Have **D**isk. Windows 95 prompts you for the path to the disk or directory that contains the files for the service you want to install. Specify the \Admin\Nettools\Prtagent directory on the CD, or the equivalent directory on a server if you have copied the Admin files to the server, then choose OK. Windows 95 then displays a new Select Network Service dialog box in which the Print Agent for NetWare service appears (see fig. 8.30). Select the service, then choose OK. Windows 95 installs the necessary files from the CD and also installs additional support files from the Windows 95 distribution directory (which could be on the CD, on a server, or from the Windows 95 disks). Follow the prompts Windows 95 provides to complete the installation process. Windows 95 prompts you to restart the computer so that the changes can take effect.

Configuring Print Agent for NetWare

There are no configurable properties in the Control Panel for the Print Agent for NetWare service. Instead, you configure the service for the printer on the local computer that will despool jobs from the NetWare server queue. To configure Print Agent for NetWare for a local printer, open the Printers folder and select the local printer that will service the network queue. Then, open the printer's context menu and click on the Print Server tab to display the Print Server property page shown in figure 8.31.

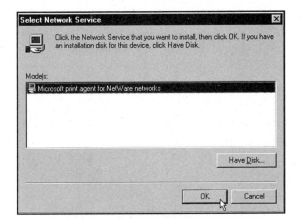

Figure 8.30

Choose the Print Agent for NetWare from the dialog box.

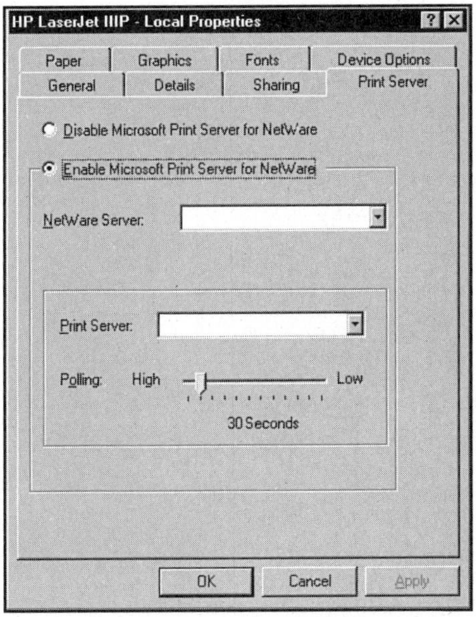

Figure 8.31

The Print Server property page.

Next, choose the Enable Microsoft Print Agent for NetWare option button. Print Agent for NetWare then enumerates the NetWare servers on the network for which you have sufficient access privileges based on the user ID by which you are logged on to the network. From the NetWare Server drop-down list, select the NetWare server whose queue you want to use Print Agent for NetWare to service. The available print server(s) on the selected NetWare server then appear in the Print Server list.

Next, use the Polling slider control to adjust the frequency at which Print Agent for NetWare will poll the server's print queue. You can adjust the setting from a minimum of 15 seconds to a maximum of 3 minutes. A longer setting results in better workstation performance, and a shorter setting results in better queue and printing performance. When your settings are correct, choose OK.

 Note The workstation on which Print Agent for NetWare runs does not have to run the File and Printer Sharing for NetWare service.

Personalizing Windows 95

Windows 95 is a very rich environment that offers numerous ways to customize the interface and the operating system. This chapter explains the many ways you can change Windows 95's appearance and operation. The chapter covers the following topics:

- ◆ Personalizing the desktop and display

- ◆ Setting time and date options

- ◆ Setting keyboard options

- ◆ Setting mouse options

- ◆ Specifying regional settings

- ◆ Setting security options

- ◆ Setting power management options

- ◆ Setting network options

- ◆ Supporting multiple users and configurations

Most of the changes in look and function you can make to Windows 95 are simple to do. Most users like to customize the interface. The next section examines the many ways you can change the interface to affect the way Windows 95 looks and functions.

Personalizing the Desktop and Display

You can easily change colors and other aspects of the Windows 95 interface. Windows 95 also makes changing display resolution and other operating system parameters much easier than in Windows 3.*x*. One of the most significant changes from Windows 3.*x* is that Windows 95 enables you to maintain multiple desktop configurations. Windows 95 can maintain a unique desktop for each user, which makes possible sharing a single PC and at the same time providing a unique, custom desktop among multiple users. You can find an explanation of multiple user profiles in the section "Supporting Multiple Configurations and Users" later in this chapter. First you should learn about the changes you can make to the user interface, because those potential changes apply to both single- and multiple-user profiles.

Changing Background and Wallpaper

You can change two aspects of the desktop—the background and wallpaper. Most users do want to change the background.

Changing the Background Pattern

The *background* is a pattern you can apply to the Windows 95 desktop. Figure 9.1 shows the Cargo Net background, one of the many predefined patterns you can use. You also can create your own patterns. You are restricted to two colors for the desktop pattern—black and the color of the desktop.

Tip Because the pattern is applied as black on top of the desktop color, specifying a background color of black causes a black-on-black pattern, which is invisible.

To specify a predefined background pattern, right-click on the Windows 95 desktop and choose Properties to display the property sheet for the desktop (see fig. 9.2). Or, with no items selected on the desktop, press Shift+F10 to display the property sheet.

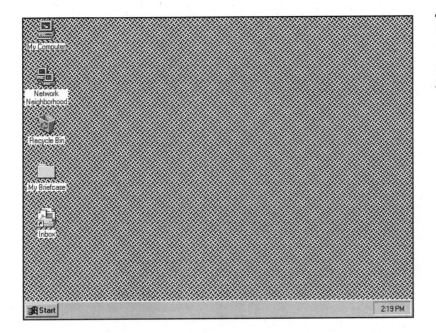

Figure 9.1

The Cargo Net background pattern.

Tip   You also can open the Display property sheet by choosing the Display icon from the Control Panel.

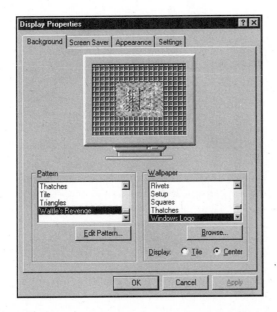

Figure 9.2

The Display property sheet.

The Background page of the Display property sheet enables you to choose from Windows 95's predefined background patterns, edit an existing pattern, or create a new pattern. To use an existing pattern, simply select a pattern from the **P**attern list box. Windows 95 then displays a sample of the pattern. Choose OK or **A**pply to apply the pattern to the desktop.

If you want to edit an existing pattern or create a new pattern, first choose a pattern from the list, then choose the **E**dit Pattern button. Windows 95 provides a Pattern Editor dialog box (see fig. 9.3) that you can use to modify the pattern. Click on the squares in the **P**attern box to change the pattern. After you establish a pattern that satisfies you, choose **D**one to save the modified pattern. Or, enter a new name in the **N**ame combo box, then choose **A**dd to add the new pattern.

Figure 9.3

The Pattern Editor dialog box.

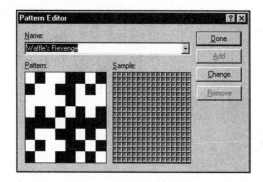

Using Wallpaper

Besides adding a background pattern to the desktop, you can apply a wallpaper image. The wallpaper image appears on top of the desktop pattern. If the wallpaper covers the entire desktop, it also hides any existing pattern. Figure 9.4 shows a wallpaper image on top of a desktop pattern.

Wallpaper really amounts to nothing more than a bitmap image applied to the desktop. You can use any bitmap (BMP) or Device-Independent Bitmap (DIB) file, therefore, as wallpaper. You also can use *RLE (Run-Length Encoded)* files, a type of compressed bitmap file.

To assign a bitmap as wallpaper, open the Display property sheet. On the Background page, select a bitmap from the **W**allpaper list. This list references all the bitmap files in the Windows directory. Or, click on the **B**rowse button to choose a bitmap from a different disk or directory.

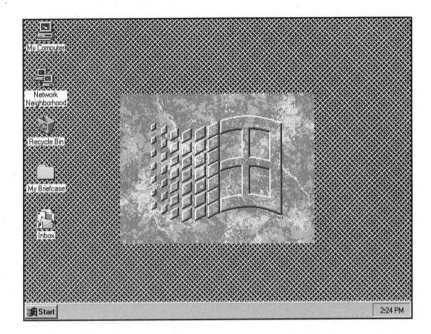

Figure 9.4

A wallpaper image on top of a desktop pattern.

If the bitmap image is small, you probably want to tile the image across the desktop, as shown later in figure 9.5. If you have a large bitmap image, such as a photograph, you probably want to center it, as shown previously in figure 9.4. Choose the Center or Tile option accordingly.

 Tip The Registry contains a handful of settings you can use to control wallpaper, in the key HKEY_CURRENT_USER/Control Panel/desktop. The values for TileWallpaper and WallpaperStyle essentially have the same effect. A value of 1 for either setting tiles the wallpaper, and a value of 0 for either setting centers the wallpaper. You can give either setting values other than 0 or 1—even numbers have the same effect as 0, and odd numbers have the same effect as 1.

Fine-Tuning Wallpaper Position

Regardless of whether you tile or center a wallpaper image, you can control the exact position of the image on the desktop. By default, Windows 95 centers the wallpaper exactly in the middle of the desktop. If you use the Tile option, Windows 95 places the first instance of the image in the upper left corner of the display, then tiles the images from that first instance.

If the desktop resolution is an even multiple of the wallpaper bitmap's size, then the image fits evenly on the display. For example, assume that you tile a bitmap that is 320 pixels wide by 240 pixels tall on a standard VGA display of 640×480 pixels. You get a 2×2 pattern of images. The lower right image fits exactly in the right corner of the display (see fig. 9.5).

Figure 9.5

Wallpaper tiled evenly on the desktop.

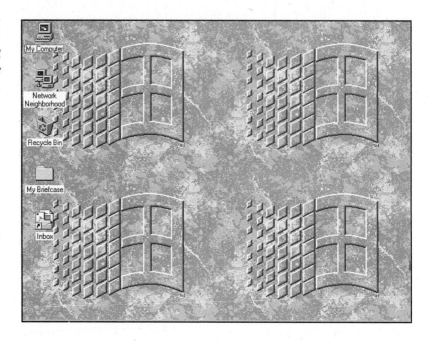

If the desktop resolution is not an even multiple of the bitmap's size, the wallpaper will not tile evenly on the desktop. The tiles at the right and bottom of the desktop are incomplete, as you can see in figure 9.6.

Two solutions can work to make the image tile evenly on the desktop—you can crop the image so that its size is an even divisor of the desktop, or you can shift the starting point of the first tile. Two Registry settings in HKEY_CURRENT_USER/Control Panel/desktop enable you to control the wallpaper's horizontal and vertical positions: WallpaperOriginX and WallpaperOriginY. WallpaperOriginX specifies a horizontal position for the left edge of the bitmap, and WallpaperOriginY specifies the position of the top edge of the wallpaper bitmap.

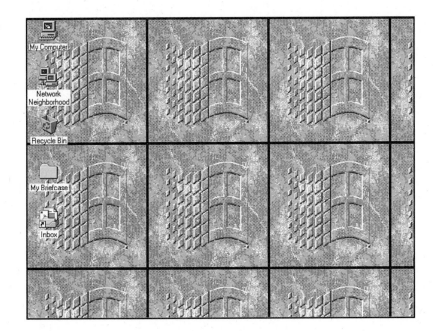

Figure 9.6

Wallpaper tiled unevenly on the desktop.

Note The WallpaperOriginX and WallpaperOriginY settings do not exist in the Registry by default. You must add the settings as explained later in this section.

If you want to center a tiled pattern on the desktop, you first need to figure out the horizontal and vertical amounts by which an even-tiled pattern is less than the desktop size. Assume you have a bitmap that's 200×200 and your desktop is 640×480. The bitmap's horizontal size is a multiple of 600, which gives you a horizontal remainder of 40 (640 – 600), so you need to shift the image 20 pixels horizontally (half of the remainder, 40) to center the pattern horizontally. The bitmap's vertical size is a multiple of 400, which gives you a remainder of 80 (480 – 400), so you need to shift the image 40 pixels vertically (half of 80) to center the image vertically. Set WallpaperOriginX to 20 for your horizontal shift and set WallpaperOriginY to 40 for your vertical shift. Figure 9.7 shows the results of the shift.

Figure 9.7

A 200×200 bitmap centered on a 640×480 desktop.

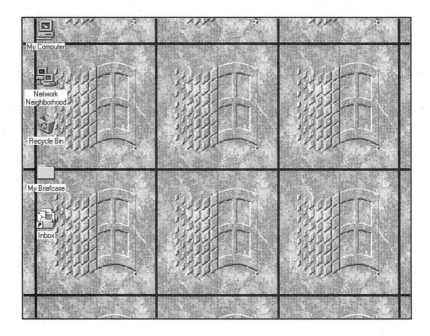

To change or add Registry settings, choose Start, then <u>R</u>un, enter **regedit** in the <u>O</u>pen combo box, and choose OK. Open the appropriate key in the Registry by selecting it from the tree. Locate the setting you want to change, then double-click on the setting in the right pane or select it and press Enter. Enter the new value for the setting and choose OK. Figure 9.8 shows the WallpaperOriginX value being changed.

If your Registry does not contain the WallpaperOriginX and WallpaperOriginY strings, you must add them. To do so, open the Registry Editor as explained previously. Open the key HKEY_CURRENT_USER/Control Panel/desktop. This key contains the strings TileWallpaper, Wallpaper, and a few others. Next, choose <u>E</u>dit, <u>N</u>ew, <u>S</u>tring Value. Registry Editor creates a string entry with a name similar to New Value #1 and highlights the name. Type the name WallpaperOriginX, then press Enter. Next, double-click on the newly created string or choose <u>E</u>dit, <u>M</u>odify to display the Edit String dialog box. Enter in the <u>V</u>alue Data text box the value you need to use to shift the wallpaper horizontally, then choose OK. Repeat this process to create and set the WallpaperOriginY value.

You can use the WallpaperOriginX and WallpaperOriginY settings to shift a centered wallpaper image, just as you can shift a tiled pattern. Figure 9.9 shows a wallpaper image that has been shifted to the lower right corner of the display by setting WallpaperOriginX and WallpaperOriginY to nonzero values.

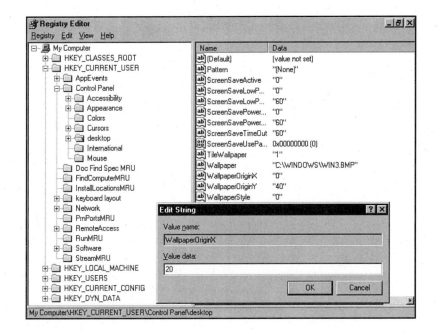

Figure 9.8

*The
WallpaperOriginX
value being
changed in the
Registry.*

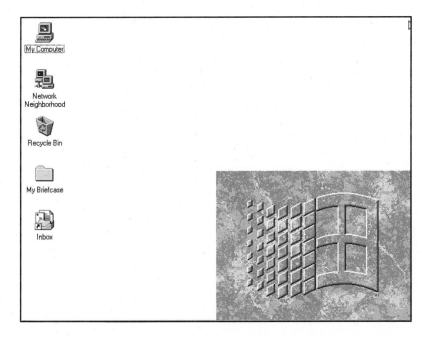

Figure 9.9

*A wallpaper
image shifted to
the lower right
corner of the
desktop.*

Using a Screen Saver and Energy-Saving Features

The Screen Saver property page of the Display property sheet (see fig. 9.10) enables you to configure Windows 95 to use a screen saver and to configure your monitor's energy-saving features (if any). Screen savers came into being to prevent *burn-in,* which occurs when the same image remains on the display for an extended period of time. Most of today's computer monitors are not susceptible to burn-in and don't require a screen saver. But, screen savers have become a novel way to personalize your PC, and they offer an additional layer of security for your PC. You can configure the screen saver to have a password, then engage the screen saver when you need to leave your PC unattended. To turn off the screen saver and regain access to the PC, you or anyone else must enter the correct password.

Figure 9.10

The Screen Saver property page.

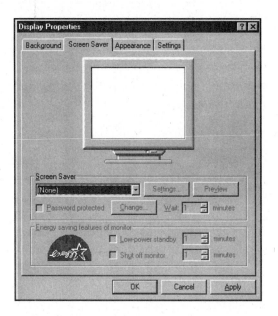

Windows 95 includes a selection of screen savers. To view a screen saver, choose one from the Screen Saver drop-down list in the Screen Saver property page. A sample appears in the sample display. To view a sample of the screen saver on the entire display, choose the Preview button. Move the mouse or press Esc to cancel the preview and return to the property page.

Use the Wait spin control to specify the amount of time in minutes that you want to pass before the screen saver engages. If the screen saver engages and you have not set a password, moving the mouse or pressing any key on the keyboard turns off the screen saver and returns you to Windows.

Most of the screen savers supplied with Windows 95 include settings you can use to control the way the screen saver functions. After you select a screen saver, choose the Settings button to specify settings for the screen saver. The settings vary from one screen saver to the next. Figure 9.11 shows a typical dialog box for specifying screen saver settings.

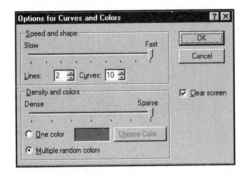

Figure 9.11

One of the screen saver setup dialog boxes.

To password-protect your PC, place a check in the **P**assword protected check box in the Screen Saver property sheet. Then, choose the **C**hange button to specify a password. Choose a password that you can remember easily but which other users would have difficulty guessing.

Tip If you forget your password and the screen saver engages, turn off the computer, then restart it (be aware that you might lose data in documents you haven't saved— always save your documents before you leave your system for any period of time). When Windows 95 restarts, display the property sheet for the desktop and choose the Screen Saver page. Clear the **P**assword protected check box, then choose OK. If you want to reinstate a screen saver and password, open the Screen Saver property page, enable the **P**assword protected check box, and choose **C**hange to specify a new password.

Setting Monitor Power-Saving Options

If your PC supports power management for your monitor, the Screen Saver property page includes options that enable Windows 95 to reduce or turn off power to the PC's monitor. The **L**ow-power standby check box, if enabled, causes Windows 95 to reduce power to the monitor after the specified amount of time passes. The Sh**u**t off monitor check box, if enabled, causes Windows 95 to turn off power to the monitor after the specified amount of time passes. If your PC doesn't support power management for the monitor, these check boxes are disabled (dimmed) on the Screen Saver property page.

Changing Interface Colors and Fonts

Windows 95 gives you a lot of control over its desktop's appearance. The Appearance property page (see fig. 9.12) enables you to change the color, size, and font of almost any component of the Windows 95 interface; you can change desktop colors, icon title fonts, scroll bar sizes, and much more. The Appearance property page enables you to select from predefined color schemes or create your own.

Figure 9.12

You can change interface color, size, and font with the Appearance property page.

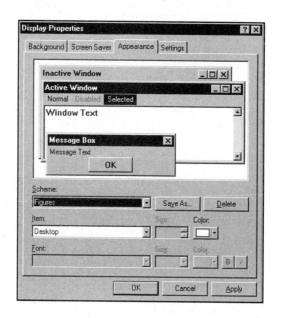

The simplest way to change interface properties is to choose a predefined scheme from the Scheme drop-down list box to provide a starting point. Then, use the other controls on the Appearance property page to customize individual settings. You can use the Bold and Italic buttons to apply character formatting to some of the font options. As you make changes to various components, the sample components showing in the upper half of the property page change accordingly. You also can click on a component in the sample to select it and display its current settings. After you configure the display according to your preferences, choose OK or Apply to apply the changes.

Tip

Most interface changes are purely aesthetic and don't affect your productivity in Windows 95. Other changes, however, can make Windows 95 easier to use. If you have trouble using the scroll bars, for example, making the scroll bars larger might make them easier for you to use. Making the icon font size larger makes the icon descriptions on the desktop and in folder Windows easier to read, particularly on higher-resolution displays.

You also can use the Registry Editor to change interface components. All component settings are stored in the Registry under HKEY_CURRENT_USER/Control Panel; the desktop colors settings, for example, are stored in HKEY_CURRENT_USER/Control Panel/Colors (see fig. 9.13). Most other settings for font and object size are stored in HKEY_CURRENT_USER/Control Panel/desktop/WindowMetrics. Generally, using the Appearance property page is easier for changing interface characteristics. Modifying the settings directly in the Registry, however, enables you to control settings individually that you can control only as groups if you use the Appearance property page. You can adjust the colors for each of the parts of command buttons separately in the Registry, for example, but only as a group from the property page.

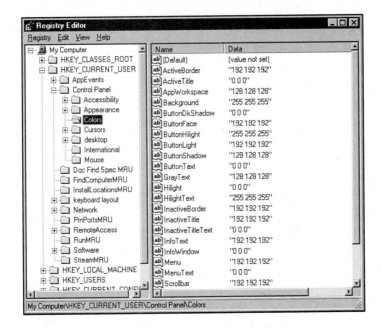

Figure 9.13

Desktop color settings in the Registry.

Changing Display Driver Settings

Other changes you can use the Settings property page to make to the Windows 95 interface are display resolution, number of colors supported, and monitor type (see fig. 9.14).

Figure 9.14

*The Settings page
of the Display
property sheet.*

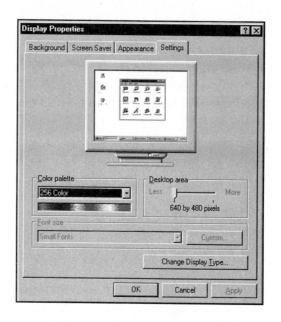

Changing Display Resolution

The **D**esktop area slider enables you to control the Windows 95 display's resolution, and the available settings depend on the capabilities of the display driver for which Windows 95 is configured. Setting the display to a higher resolution gives you more room to work on the display by reducing the relative size of all objects on the display. You can fit more cells of a spreadsheet into a window, for example, because the relative size of the font used in each cell is smaller than on a lower-resolution display.

To change display resolution, choose the resolution you want to use with the **D**esktop area slider. The first time you change to a particular resolution, you'll probably need to restart Windows 95 before the change can take effect. Unlike Windows 3.*x*, however, Windows 95 can change resolution without restarting if you select a resolution that has been used on the computer before. In such a case, Windows 95 simply changes resolution and asks you if you want to continue to use the new resolution. If you choose **Y**es, the change remains in effect and you can continue working at the new resolution. If you answer **N**o, Windows 95 switches back to the previous resolution.

 Tip The maximum resolution Windows 95 can use depends on the combination of display adapter, video driver, and monitor you use. The display adapter, for example, might be capable of supporting a higher display resolution than the monitor. Also, high-resolution displays can be difficult to read on some monitors due to the size and sharpness of the image. Experiment with display resolution until you find one that suits your monitor and your ability to read the display.

Changing Color Density

The Color palette drop-down list, which varies according to the installed video driver, enables you to specify how many colors the display driver uses. Increasing the number of colors often gives you better-looking images and a wider choice of colors, but also requires more memory and can slow down performance. Also, supporting a large number of colors generally is important only when you use applications for creating, viewing, or editing graphics images. If optimizing speed and memory are your primary concerns, use the minimum number of colors and lowest practical resolution. If you have a relatively fast computer, however, you might hardly even notice the decrease in performance that using a high-resolution, high-color display can cause. Experiment with the settings to find the combination that suits your situation.

 Note   To change the number of colors you want your display driver to use, choose an option from the Color palette drop-down list. You have to restart Windows 95 before the change can take effect—Windows 95 can't change the color palette on the fly the way it sometimes can change the resolution.

If the current Windows 95 display driver supports font size selection, the Font size drop-down list and Custom button are enabled on the Settings property page. These two controls enable you to control the overall size of the system font, which Windows 95 uses for such things as menus, buttons, dialog boxes, and other general text that contributes to the Windows 95 interface. You can select a font size from the Font size drop-down list, or choose Custom to use the Custom Font Size dialog box to specify a custom size (see fig. 9.15).

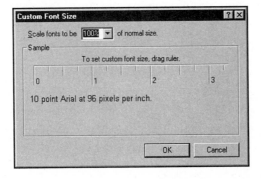

Figure 9.15

The Custom Font Size dialog box.

Changing the font size is particularly useful if you use a high-resolution mode and have trouble reading the text on the display (a typical problem on 14-inch monitors).

If you use a standard VGA display at a resolution of 640×480, consider reducing the size of the system font to reduce the amount of display space required for dialog boxes, menus, and other components. Although changing font size isn't as effective as changing resolution to give you more room on the desktop, it can help.

Changing the Display Type

You can choose the Change Display Type button on the Settings property page to bring up the Change Display Type dialog box (see fig. 9.16) and specify the type of display adapter and monitor your PC uses.

Figure 9.16

The Change Display Type dialog box.

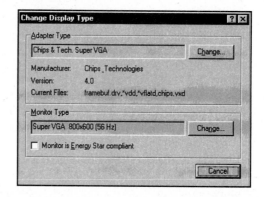

You sometimes need to change the adapter type to take advantage of some of the graphic adapter's capabilities, such as high-resolution modes. Setting the monitor type correctly enables special features for the monitor. If you can't find your monitor in the list, choose (Standard monitor types) from the Manufacturers list, then choose the appropriate generic monitor type from the Models list.

Setting Date and Time Options

On Windows 3.*x* and DOS systems, you can set the system date and time by using the BIOS setup program, the DOS command line, or the Control Panel. In Windows 95, you use the Date/Time object in the Control Panel to set the system time, date, and time zone. Choosing the Date/Time object opens the Date/Time property sheet (see fig. 9.17).

The Date & Time property controls are self-explanatory. Use them to set the current month, day, year, and time. As you change settings, the calendar and clock on the property page change accordingly.

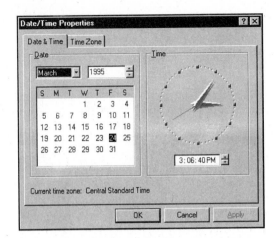

Figure 9.17

The Date & Time page of the Date/ Time property sheet.

The Time Zone property page (see fig. 9.18) enables you to specify the time zone in which your PC is located. You also can configure Windows 95 to automatically adjust for daylight saving time by enabling the Automatically adjust clock for daylight saving changes check box.

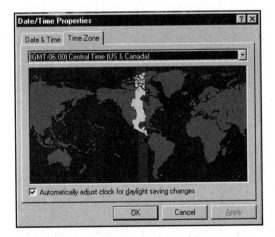

Figure 9.18

The Time Zone property page.

Setting Keyboard Options

The Keyboard item in the Control Panel enables you to control various options for your keyboard, such as key response and repeat rate. Choosing the Keyboard item displays the Keyboard property sheet, as shown in figure 9.19.

Figure 9.19

The Keyboard property sheet.

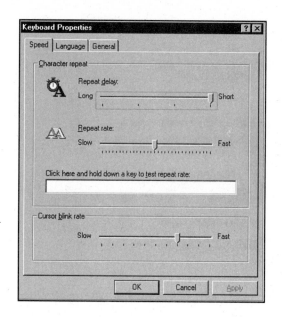

Setting Keyboard Response

The Speed property page enables you to control your keyboard's responsiveness. You can use the Repeat delay control to specify the amount of time a key must be held down for Windows 95 to begin repeating the character, and the Repeat rate control to specify how rapidly Windows 95 repeats the character. After you use the Repeat delay and Repeat rate controls to specify settings, click in the associated text box, then press and hold a key to test the repeat delay and rate.

Tip   The Cursor blink rate control enables you to specify the rate at which the text cursor blinks. Increasing the value can make finding the cursor easier in some applications.

Setting Language Options

The Language property page (see fig. 9.20) enables you to install support for multiple languages and keyboard layouts so that you can quickly switch between languages and keyboard layouts as you work.

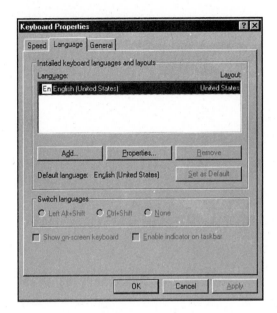

Figure 9.20

The Language property page.

Use the A**d**d button if you want to add new languages and/or keyboard layouts to your Windows 95 environment. To specify the keyboard layout for a particular language, select the language and choose the **P**roperties button. Windows 95 issues a simple dialog box you can use to specify the keyboard layout to associate with the language.

The Switch languages group in the Language property page contains three options you can use to control your ability to switch languages with a keystroke. Pressing the selected keystroke causes Windows 95 to cycle to the next installed language while you work, which makes possible switching almost instantly to a different language and keyboard layout. In addition, you can check the **E**nable indicator on taskbar check box to display a language indicator in the Taskbar's tray (status area). Clicking on the language indicator in the tray displays a pop-up menu of installed languages (see fig. 9.21), and you can switch to a language simply by choosing it from the menu.

Figure 9.21

Choose the language indicator on the tray to choose a language.

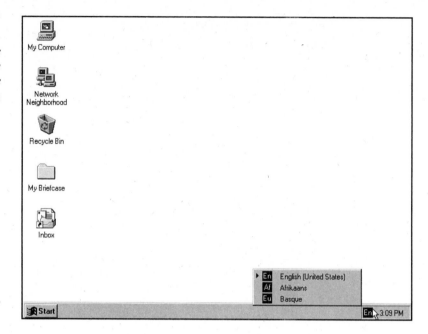

Changing Keyboard Type

The General keyboard property page enables you to specify the type of keyboard attached to your computer. To change keyboard drivers, choose the **C**hange button on the General property page. Choose the manufacturer and model from the resulting dialog box.

Setting Mouse Options

The Mouse object in the Control Panel enables you to change various settings that affect the mouse and screen pointers. You can use the Buttons property page, shown in figure 9.22, to shift the left and right buttons and change the double-click speed. If you have trouble clicking fast enough for Windows 95 to recognize a double-click, try reducing the double-click speed setting. Test the setting by double-clicking on the Test area box—a jack-in-the-box pops up or down if Windows 95 recognizes your mouse action as a double-click.

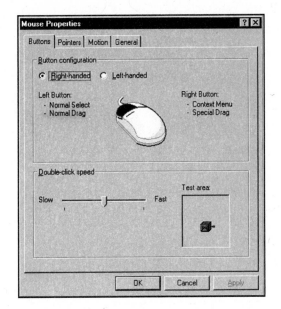

Figure 9.22

The Buttons page of the Mouse property sheet.

Tip Some three-button mice, such as those from Logitech, enable you to use a single click of the middle button as a double-click. You need modify a setting in the Registry to configure Windows 95 to recognize a single click of the middle button as a double-click event. To program the Logitech mouse's middle button, open the Registry key HKEY_LOCAL_MACHINE/SOFTWARE/Logitech/MOuseware/ MouseMan/0000 and set DoubleClick to 001. If you are using a different three-button mouse, search the Registry for the string DoubleClick or check the mouse's documentation to determine how to program the middle button for a double-click.

Setting Pointer Options

The Pointers property page (see fig. 9.23) enables you to customize the pointers that Windows 95 uses for various actions. You can choose from predefined schemes or create your own pointer schemes.

To use a predefined scheme, select one from the Scheme drop-down list. You then can choose OK or Apply to apply the new pointer scheme or further customize your pointers. To specify a pointer for a particular action, select the action from the pointer list, then choose Browse. Windows 95 gives you a standard Browse dialog box you can use to locate standard cursor files (*.cur) and animated cursor files (*.ani).

Figure 9.23

*The Pointers
property page.*

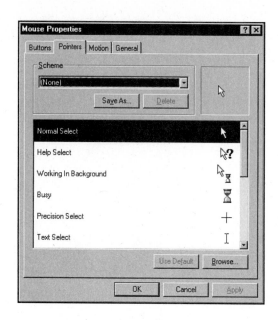

Note If you select the (None), 3D Pointers, Windows Standard (large), or Windows Standard (extra large) predefined schemes from the **S**chemes drop-down list, you lose your default animated cursors (assuming your computer supports animated cursors). Selecting the (None) option doesn't restore the animated cursors. To restore the animated cursors, set the Working in Background pointer to c:\windows\system\appstart.ani and the Busy pointer to c:\windows\system\hourglas.ani. Windows 95 changes the pointers after you choose OK or **A**pply. Or, you can open the Registry Editor and locate HKEY_CURRENT_USER/Control Panel/Cursors. Set the value of AppStarting to **c:\windows\system\appstart.ani** and set the value of Wait to **c:\windows\system\hourglas.ani**. If you change pointers by editing the Registry, however, you have to restart the computer or log on as a different user before the change takes effect.

Controlling Mouse Motion

The Motion page (see fig. 9.24) enables you to control the mouse's responsiveness and turn on or off pointer trails. Use the Pointer speed slider control to control the acceleration of the mouse. Slide the control toward Slow to slow down the pointer's motion or toward Fast to speed up the pointer's motion.

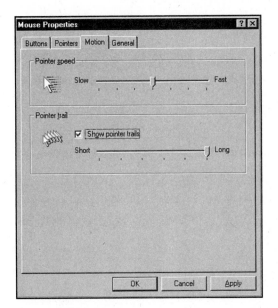

Figure 9.24

The Motion page of the Mouse property sheet.

The Pointer trail group enables you to turn on and off pointer trails. When you turn on pointer trails, ghost pointers shadow the real pointer as you move it on the display, creating a trail of pointers. Turning on pointer trails comes in particularly handy on monochrome and passive-matrix LCD displays, on which finding the pointer often proves annoyingly difficult. To turn on pointer trails, enable the Show pointer trails check box. Then, use the associated slider control to control the relative appearance of the pointer trail. Sliding the control to the left results in fewer ghost pointer images, and sliding the control to the right increases the number of ghost pointer images. After you arrange the settings to your liking, choose OK or Apply to actualize the change.

Changing Mouse Types

As with other hardware components, the General page of the Mouse property sheet enables you to specify the type of mouse connected to your computer. This setting should be correct from the original Windows 95 installation Setup performed. If you install a new mouse or want to use a different driver, however, you can choose the Change button on the General page to initiate a dialog box from which you can choose a different manufacturer and model of mouse. Choosing a new mouse causes Windows 95 to install a new driver for the selected mouse.

Specifying Regional Settings

The Regional Settings object in the Control Panel enables you to customize your Windows 95 settings for specific countries. Choosing the Regional Settings icon opens the Regional Settings property sheet, shown in figure 9.25. The regional settings include format for date, time, currency, and other country-specific settings.

Figure 9.25

The Regional Settings property sheet.

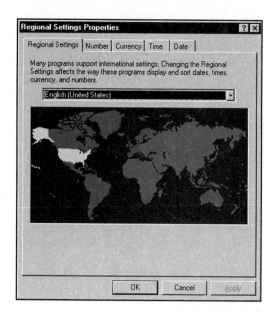

You can set a wide variety of settings at one time by selecting a country from the drop-down list on the Regional Settings page. Selecting a country loads a settings scheme for the selected country. You then can use the other Regional Settings property pages to view and modify individual settings.

Tip   You can select a country from the global map on the Regional Settings page. The bright green area shows the currently selected country. The dark green areas represent countries supported by another set of regional settings. The aqua-colored countries do not have predefined settings, although you can select a country that has similar settings and modify individual settings as needed.

To set individual settings, choose the appropriate property page. The settings on each property page are self-explanatory and you should have no trouble choosing the settings you need.

Setting Security Options

The Passwords object in the Control Panel enables you to control various security settings for your PC. Choosing the Passwords icon displays the Passwords property sheet shown in figure 9.26.

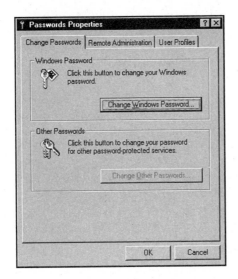

Figure 9.26

The Passwords property sheet.

The Change Passwords page enables you to change the password you use to log on to Windows 95. If you choose the Change Windows Password button, Windows 95 displays a dialog box in which you can enter your current password and a new password (see fig. 9.27). Simply enter your old password and new password in the appropriate text boxes.

Figure 9.27

The Change Windows Password dialog box.

If you use your computer to access other password-protected services, such as a Windows NT domain or NetWare server, clicking on the Change Windows Password button issues a dialog box similar to the one shown in figure 9.28. If you have the same password for the domain or server as you have as your Windows 95 logon password, choose from the dialog box the service for which you want to change passwords. Windows 95 changes the password, not only for Windows 95 logon, but also for the other selected services.

Figure 9.28

Choose a service for which you want to change passwords.

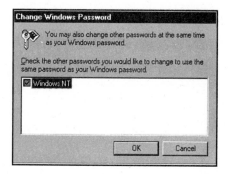

Tip   To specify a logon method, choose the Network object in Control Panel to open the Network property sheet. Select your network client from the list of installed clients, adapters, services, and protocols, then choose Properties. Windows 95 displays a property page you can use to specify logon parameters for the client. Figure 9.29 shows the logon parameters for the Client for Microsoft Networks. For more information on configuring network settings, refer to Chapter 2, "Setting Up and Booting Windows 95," and Chapter 34, "Network Concepts and Configuration."

Figure 9.29

Logon parameters for the Client for Microsoft Networks.

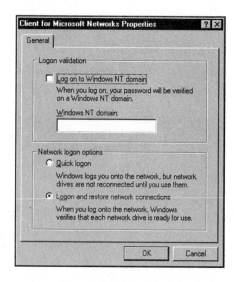

You also can change the passwords of other password-protected services separately from your Windows 95 password. To do so, choose the Change Other Passwords button from the Change Passwords property page. Windows 95 displays a dialog box similar to the one shown in 9.27, in which you can specify the service for which you want to change passwords.

Note   The Remote Administration page enables you to configure your PC to be managed remotely by an administrator. The User Profiles page enables you to configure your PC to support multiple user profiles. User profiles enable each user of a PC to have a unique desktop environment. Profiles also enable you to maintain different desktop environments for yourself, each tailored to different uses. User profiles are explained later in this chapter, in the section "Supporting Multiple Configurations and Users."

Setting Power Management Options

Most notebook PCs and an increasing number of desktop PCs support some level of power management that enables Windows 95 to shut down the PC's resources—including hard disk, display, and even the CPU—after the system has been idle for a specified amount of time or at your direction. If your PC is configured to support power management (generally configured in the BIOS setup program), you can use the Power object in the Control Panel to control power management on your PC. Choosing the Power icon brings up the Power property sheet, shown in figure 9.30.

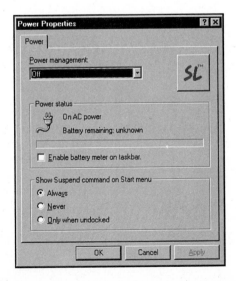

Figure 9.30

The Power property sheet.

The Power property sheet indicates whether the PC is running on AC power or its battery (in the case of a notebook PC). Use the Power management drop-down list to select the power management method you want to use or to turn off power management. The primary difference between the Standard and Advanced options is that the Advanced option provides additional controls that enable you to delay the power-down of devices until the system is idle. Otherwise, devices are powered down after their associated activity time-out value comes to pass. To specify power management options for a computer with an SL processor, choose the SL button. A dialog box similar to the one shown in figure 9.31 should appear.

Figure 9.31

The SL Enhanced Options dialog box.

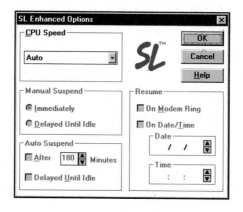

The following list explains the control groups in the SL Enhanced Options dialog box.

◆ **CPU Speed.** This drop-down list enables you to control CPU management. Select Auto if you want the CPU to run at full speed but also to power down whenever possible to conserve power. Choose 10%, 25%, or 50% to run the CPU at a specific reduced speed. Choose 100% to run the CPU at full speed and prevent it from powering down.

◆ **Manual Suspend.** The two settings in this group enable you to control the way the system powers down when you press the Suspend button, close the display (on a notebook PC), or choose the Suspend button in the Start menu. Choose the Immediately option in the Manual Suspend group if you want the PC to suspend immediately when you press the PC's Suspend button or close the display. Windows 95 suspends all applications, even those currently processing. Choose the Delayed Until Idle option to cause Windows 95 to wait for all applications to finish processing before it powers down the PC. Windows 95 thinks some applications are processing when they actually are just waiting for input, so the system might not enter suspend mode if you're running such an application and you've selected the Delayed Until Idle option.

◆ **Auto Suspend.** This option controls how the system powers down automatically after a specified period of time with no keyboard or mouse activity. The After option enables you to specify an amount of time after which the system powers down automatically. The Delayed Until Idle option causes the system to power down automatically only if no applications are active. These settings don't affect the screen, hard disk, or other devices individually. Instead, they control shutdown of the entire system, including the CPU.

◆ **Resume.** These settings control how the system resumes after being suspended. The On Modem Ring option, if enabled, causes the system to resume if a call comes in to a line that is connected to the PC's modem. The On Date/Time option enables you to specify a specific date and time at which the system will resume.

Supporting Multiple Configurations and Users

Windows 95 includes a feature not found in Windows 3.x that makes it much easier for multiple users to share a single PC. This feature, called *user profiles,* also enables a user to have the same desktop configuration regardless of the network node from which the user logs on to the network. You also might want to use multiple configurations, even if you are the only person using the PC. When writing this book, for example, I used two configurations: one for regular work (writing) and another with a simplified desktop configuration for capturing figures.

Tip
If your children use your PC at home, profiles can help you make it easier for them to use the PC without getting into areas or running applications they shouldn't be running. You can configure a unique desktop environment for each child that contains only those objects to which they should have access. For instructions on how to restrict user access, refer to the section "Applying User Restrictions" later in this chapter.

Profiles work in conjunction with the Windows 95 logon process. When you log on, Windows 95 builds your desktop environment from the shortcuts and other objects stored in a profile that matches your logon name. If your logon name is freddy, for example, Windows 95 uses the shortcuts and other objects in the \Windows\Profiles\freddy folder. The desktop, for example, is based on the objects in \Windows\Profiles\freddy\desktop. If you don't use profiles, this information comes instead from the \Windows\desktop folder.

To configure your PC to support multiple user profiles, open the Control Panel, choose the Passwords icon, then click on the User Profiles tab to display the property page shown in figure 9.32.

Figure 9.32

The User Profiles property page.

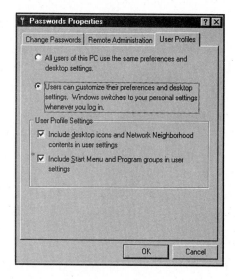

To enable user profiles, choose the second option button on the User Profiles page, labeled Users can **c**ustomize their preferences and desktop settings. This configures Windows 95 to provide a unique user profile for each user logon name.

The two check boxes in the User Profile Settings group control the way the profiles are maintained. These check boxes are explained in the following list.

◆ **Include d̲esktop icons and Network Neighborhood contents in user settings.** Enable this check box if you want the icons on the desktop and contents of the Network Neighborhood folder to be stored with each user's profile. Changes that the user makes to the desktop by adding or removing shortcuts and changing network connections in the Network Neighborhood folder are then stored in the user's profile folder. This prevents changes by one user from affecting other users' profiles.

◆ **Include S̲tart Menu and Program groups in user settings.** Enable this check box if you want changes to the Start menu and Program groups to be stored in each user's profile. If the user customizes the Start menu or adds new items to the Programs menu (usually by installing new applications), these changes are stored in the user's profile and do not affect other users.

Customizing the Start Menu and Program Groups

If you configure Windows 95 to support user profiles, and you also enable the Include §tart Menu and Program groups in user settings check box, the shortcuts for new applications that a user installs will not be added to the Programs menu for all users. Instead, the shortcuts will only appear in the Programs menu for the user who installed the program. It's relatively easy, however, to make those shortcuts available to all users of that PC.

To make the shortcuts of newly installed applications available to other users, open an Explorer window, then locate the shortcut(s) in the profile folder of the user who installed the application. If user Angie installed a program named Froboz, for example, there should be a shortcut for the program in \Windows\Profiles\angie\Start Menu\Froboz. Copy the Froboz folder to the Start Menu folder for each of the users to whom you want to make the program available.

Customizing Network Neighborhood and Desktop Settings

By default, the Network Neighborhood folder contains the Entire Network icon, icons for each computer in the user's workgroup, and icons for special services, such as HP JetDirect printers. Windows 95 automatically generates these objects in the Network Neighborhood folder. In addition, you also can place your own shortcuts in the Network Neighborhood folder. On a single-user system, these shortcuts reside in the \Windows\NetHood folder. On a multiple-profile system, however, these shortcuts reside in the \Windows\Profiles*user*\NetHood folder, where *user* is the user's logon name. To make shortcuts available in the Network Neighborhood folder of multiple users, place copies of the shortcuts in each user's \Windows\Profiles*user*\NetHood folder.

You can associate the contents of the desktop with the user profile. On a single-user system, the desktop shortcuts and objects are stored in the \Windows\Desktop folder. On multiple-profile systems, the desktop objects are stored in the \Windows\Profiles*user*\Desktop folder. To make desktop objects available to multiple users, place copies of the objects or shortcuts in each user's Desktop folder.

Tip   Each user's profile folder contains a unique User.dat file, which represents part of the user's Registry. Each profile, therefore, has a unique Registry. Even if you use a single profile, you might want to configure Windows 95 to use multiple profiles and create a second logon account for yourself that is identical to your regular working account. By creating a secondary account (called backup, for example), you effectively create a backup Registry that you can use if your regular account and Registry become corrupted or damaged.

Applying User Restrictions

Windows 95 supports a variety of Registry settings you can use to restrict access to objects and features on the desktop. These settings enable you to prevent a user from accessing any object or file other than those you make available directly on the user's desktop. For example, you can use these settings on a home computer to prevent children from opening or deleting files they shouldn't or accessing programs that should be off-limits. You also can use these settings on an office computer to prevent new users from unintentionally corrupting their desktop, applications, or other resources.

 Note The method for adding restrictions explained in the remainder of this chapter is similar to the use of user and system policies, and enables you to apply user restrictions on a stand-alone computer and on networked computers not served by a Windows NT or NetWare server. The use of policies, however, requires a Windows NT or NetWare security server. This chapter does not cover the use of system or user policies.

To apply user restrictions on a computer, first configure the computer to support user profiles, as explained previously. Next, log on to the computer as the user for whom you want to apply restrictions. Then, run the Policy Editor, which is included on the Windows 95 CD in the \Admin\Apptools\Poledit folder as the file Poledit.exe. After you start the Policy Editor, choose File, Open Registry to open the Registry of the user under which you are logged on. The Policy Editor should then look similar to the one shown in figure 9.33.

Figure 9.33

The Policy Editor.

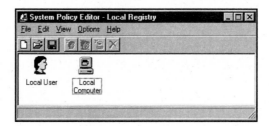

Next, double-click on the Local User icon to display the Policies property page. The Policies property page is similar to the Registry Editor in that it displays settings as a hierarchical tree. Open the \Local User\Shell\Restrictions tree to display the available restrictions, as shown in figure 9.34.

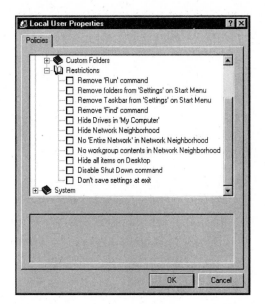

Figure 9.34

The Policies property page.

The restrictions in \Local User\Shell\Restrictions are generally self-explanatory. Enable the restrictions that you require for the current user. When you exit the Policy Editor, you'll receive a prompt asking you to verify whether you want to save the changes to the Registry. Choose <u>Y</u>es to save the changes. The next time you or someone else logs on using the current user name, the restrictions will apply. Repeat the process for any other users for whom you want to configure restrictions, first logging on as the user, then running the Policy Editor to apply the desired restrictions.

Tip   You might also want to enable restrictions in the \Local User\System\Restrictions key to further protect the computer or restrict the user from specific actions.

Using Accessibility Options

Windows 95 includes a number of features that enable people with disabilities to use Windows 95 more easily and effectively. The Windows 95 accessibility features provide special controls for using the mouse, keyboard, sound, and display. This chapter explains the following accessibility topics:

- ◆ Using the keyboard

- ◆ Controlling sound

- ◆ Using special display options

- ◆ Setting mouse options

- ◆ Setting general accessibility options

All the accessibility features in Windows 95 are enabled and controlled through the Accessibility Options object—a wheelchair icon—in the Control Panel. Double-click on this icon to display the Accessibility property sheet, which is shown in figure 10.1.

Figure 10.1

The Accessibility property sheet.

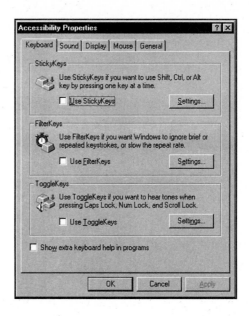

Note   The accessibility options do not install automatically. During setup, you can specifically select the accessibility options as one of the options to install. If you need to install accessibility options after installing Windows 95, open the Add/Remove Programs object in the Control Panel, then click on the Windows Setup tab. You will see the accessibility options in the list of components you can install.

The following sections explain how to set up and configure these options.

Using the Keyboard

Most people interact with the computer through the keyboard, but this tool can pose significant challenges for some users, and Windows 95 offers new features to help overcome these challenges. The accessibility options in Windows 95 include features that enable you to control the key repeat rate, how the Ctrl and Alt keys function, and other keyboard options. The following list explains the keyboard's new options:

◆ **StickyKeys.** The StickyKeys option is useful if you find it difficult to hold down the Shift, Alt, or Ctrl key while also pressing another key. With StickyKeys on, for example, you can enter the keystroke Shift+Alt+F10 by pressing and releasing Shift, pressing and releasing Alt, and pressing F10.

◆ **FilterKeys.** FilterKeys enables you to control how Windows 95 handles repeated keys in one of two ways. You can direct Windows 95 to ignore repeated keys, which eliminates repeated characters when you leave a key pressed for too long. You also can direct Windows 95 to recognize key repeats, but slow down the key repeat rate.

◆ **ToggleKeys.** Turning on ToggleKeys causes Windows 95 to issue a beep when you press the Caps Lock, Num Lock, or Scroll Lock keys. This will help you recognize when you have pressed one of these keys.

◆ **Keyboard help.** Enabling this option causes applications that are designed to do so to display additional Help information about using the keyboard.

Using StickyKeys

As explained previously, StickyKeys enables you to make the Shift, Alt, and Ctrl keys "stick down" when you press them. Rather than hold down the Shift key while you press G to get a capital G, for example, you can press and release the Shift key, then press G. Windows 95 considers the Shift key to be pressed until you press another key, which results in the equivalent of pressing Shift+G.

To turn on StickyKeys, enable the Use StickyKeys check box in the Keyboard page of the Accessibility property sheet. Then, choose the Settings button to customize the way StickyKeys works. The Settings for StickyKeys dialog box appears, as shown in figure 10.2.

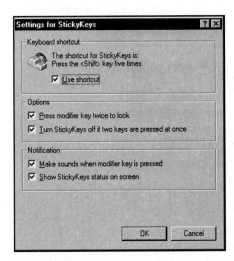

Figure 10.2

The Settings for StickyKeys dialog box.

The following list explains the options in the Settings for StickyKeys dialog box:

◆ **Use shortcut.** Enable this option if you want to be able to turn StickyKeys on and off using a keyboard shortcut. If this option is enabled, pressing Shift five times switches StickyKeys on and off. If this option is disabled, you must open the Control Panel and use the Accessibility object to turn StickyKeys on or off.

◆ **Press modifier key twice to lock.** Enable this option if you want to be able to lock the Shift, Alt, or Ctrl key down. If this option is enabled, pressing the modifier key (Shift, Alt, or Ctrl) twice causes it to remain pressed, even after you press another key. To enter the keystroke Alt+F, Alt+Q, for example, press Alt twice to lock it down, press F, press Q, then press Alt once to unlock it. This option is similar to having Alt Lock and Ctrl Lock keys to go along with the Caps Lock key. If this option is turned off, pressing the modifier key twice simply switches its state (on, then off, in this example).

◆ **Turn StickyKeys off if two keys are pressed at once.** When enabled, this option causes StickyKeys to be turned off if you press another key while pressing a modifier. If you hold down the Alt key and press Tab, for example, StickyKeys is turned off. This feature is designed primarily for situations in which more than one user works on the PC—if you press Alt+Tab, for example, Windows 95 assumes you don't need StickyKeys and turns them off.

◆ **Make sounds when modifier key is pressed.** Enable this option if you want Windows 95 to issue a beep when you press Shift, Alt, or Ctrl.

◆ **Show StickyKeys status on screen.** Enable this option if you want an indicator to appear in the tray (status area of the Taskbar) when StickyKeys is turned on.

Using FilterKeys

FilterKeys enables you to control the way Windows 95 treats repeated characters. FilterKeys is particularly useful if you have difficulty releasing the keys quickly enough to prevent characters from being repeated. You can direct Windows 95 to ignore repeated keys or ignore quick key presses and extend the key repeat interval.

To turn on FilterKeys, open the Control Panel and choose the Accessibility Options icon. From the Keyboard property page, enable the Use FilterKeys check box, then choose the Settings button to display the Settings for FilterKeys dialog box, shown in figure 10.3.

As with the shortcut key option for StickyKeys, the Use shortcut check box on the Settings for FilterKeys dialog box enables you to turn FilterKeys on and off using a

shortcut key. If the shortcut key is enabled, holding down the right shift key for eight seconds or more turns on or off the FilterKeys feature.

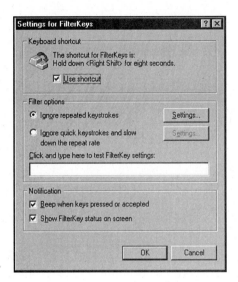

Figure 10.3

The Settings for FilterKeys dialog box.

Setting Filter Options

The controls in the Filter Options group enable you to specify how Windows 95 handles keys that are pressed for an extended period and the key repeat rate. These options are explained in the following list:

◆ **Ignore repeated keystrokes.** Choose this option to have Windows 95 treat keystrokes that are from 1/2 to 2 seconds in length as a single keystroke rather than as a repeated keystroke. Choose the Settings button beside this option to open an advanced settings dialog box (see fig. 10.4) in which you specify the time limit.

◆ **Ignore quick keystrokes and slow down the repeat rate.** Choose this option to turn off key repeat altogether or to specify specific time limits for repeat delay and repeat rate. Choose the Settings button beside this option to display an advanced settings dialog box (see fig. 10.5) that enables you to specify the following options:

　◆ **No keyboard repeat.** Choose this option to turn off keyboard repeat altogether. If this option is turned off, holding down a key does not generate multiple characters. You must release the key and press it again to repeat the character.

Figure 10.4

*The Advanced
Settings for
FilterKeys dialog
box.*

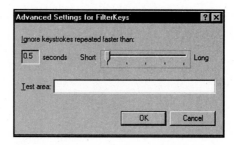

◆ **Slow down keyboard repeat rates.** Choose this option to specify
repeat delay and repeat rate values from .3 to 2 seconds. The Repeat delay
value specifies the amount of time the key can be pressed before Windows
95 treats it as a repeated keystroke. The Repeat rate value specifies how
often Windows 95 repeats a keystroke when the key is held down. If the
value is set to 2 seconds, for example, continuing to hold down the key
results in the character being repeated once every 2 seconds.

◆ **Keys must be held down for.** This setting in the SlowKeys group
specifies the amount of time a key must be held down before it is recognized as a valid keystroke. If this setting is set to 2 seconds, for example,
you can press and hold down a key for less than 2 seconds and Windows
95 ignores the keystroke altogether.

Figure 10.5

*Additional
advanced settings
for FilterKeys.*

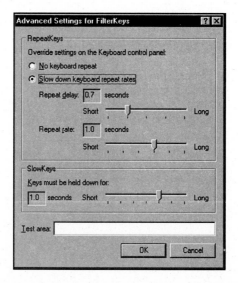

Two other controls on the main Settings for FilterKeys dialog box control sound and status information for FilterKeys:

◆ **Beep when keys pressed or accepted.** Enable this option if you want Windows 95 to beep each time a key is pressed and accepted as a repeated key.

◆ **Show FilterKey status on screen.** Enable this option to display an indicator on the tray in the Taskbar when the FilterKeys feature is enabled.

Using ToggleKeys

The ToggleKeys feature produces a beep when you press the Caps Lock, Num Lock, or Scroll Lock keys. To turn on ToggleKeys, open the Control Panel and choose the Accessibility Options icon. In the Keyboard property page, enable the check box labeled Use ToggleKeys. The Settings button on the Keyboard page displays a dialog box containing a single option that lets you turn on or off the use of a shortcut key to activate ToggleKeys. If the shortcut key is enabled, you can press and hold down the Num Lock key for 5 seconds to turn ToggleKeys on and off. If the shortcut key is disabled, you must use the Accessibility Options object in the Control Panel to turn on or off ToggleKeys.

Controlling Sound

In addition to special keyboard support, Windows 95 includes special accessibility options for sound. Windows 95 can display a visual indicator when a sound is played to help hearing-impaired users know when a sound event has occurred. You also can configure Windows 95 to display a text caption when applications generate sounds, giving the user additional visual cues that a sound event has occurred.

As with the keyboard features, accessibility options for sound are controlled through the Accessibility Options object in the Control Panel. Choose the Accessibility Options icon in the Control Panel, then click on the Sound tab on the Accessibility property sheet to display the Sound property page, shown in figure 10.6.

The Use SoundSentry check box on the Sound property page, if enabled, causes Windows 95 to display a visual indicator when a sound event occurs. Windows 95 can flash the title bar of the current application when a sound is played, for example, providing a visual cue to the user that the sound event occurred. To specify the visual cues that Windows 95 uses to indicate sound events, choose the Settings button on the Sound page to display the Settings for SoundSentry dialog box, shown in figure 10.7.

Figure 10.6

*The Sound
property page.*

Figure 10.7

*The Settings for
SoundSentry
dialog box.*

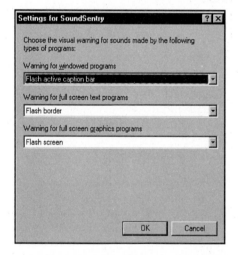

With the controls in the Settings for SoundSentry dialog box, you can specify a visual cue for windowed programs, full-screen DOS programs, and full-screen graphics programs. The available selections for each of these three program types varies from one to another. To assign a visual cue to one of the three program types, choose an option from its associated drop-down list box.

The Use ShowSounds check box on the Sound property page, if enabled, causes Windows 95 to display text captions for sounds generated by programs, effectively making the program closed-captioned. A program must be specifically written to support captioning, however, so many of your existing programs probably do not support captioning. The only setting for captioning is Use ShowSounds, which turns the feature on and off.

Using High-Contrast Desktop Schemes

Windows 95 provides a number of features designed to improve the usability of the display for users who have difficulty reading a standard Windows 95 display. These features include large menu text, high-contrast color schemes, and control over other desktop color and font settings.

Chapter 9, "Personalizing Windows 95," explains the use of desktop schemes and how you can customize colors and fonts used for various components of the Windows 95 display. Windows 95 also has some predefined high-contrast desktop schemes that are designed to help users who have limited vision read the display. These high-contrast schemes also make use of large text for menus, dialog boxes, and other interface components, as well as larger buttons and other items.

To use these high-contrast schemes, choose the Accessibility Options icon in the Control Panel, then click on the Display tab to open the Display property page shown in figure 10.8.

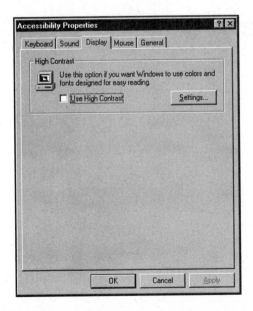

Figure 10.8

The Display property page.

The Display property page contains only one check box, labeled <u>U</u>se High Contrast. Enable this check box to use a high-contrast display, then choose the <u>S</u>ettings button to open the Settings for High Contrast dialog box (see fig. 10.9), and choose a scheme.

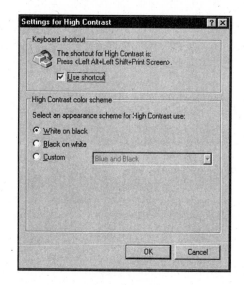

Figure 10.9

The Settings for High Contrast dialog box.

With the <u>U</u>se shortcut check box, you can enable the shortcut key for a high-contrast scheme. This means you can press the shortcut key to change from a standard scheme to a high-contrast scheme without opening the Control Panel. The shortcut key for enabling and disabling the high-contrast scheme is Left Alt+Left Shift+Print Screen.

The controls in the High Contrast color scheme group enable you to choose from predefined high-contrast schemes, or to create your own custom scheme. The name of the control group is a little misleading, however, because the high-contrast schemes not only control colors, but also use larger display fonts and other screen components. Figure 10.10 shows the black-on-white high-contrast scheme, and you can see from the illustration that the scheme includes enlarged screen fonts and control buttons.

Both the black-on-white and white-on-black high-contrast schemes use larger fonts, control buttons, and other interface objects. Choosing a scheme from the <u>C</u>ustom drop-down list selects a standard Windows 95 desktop scheme, which is no different from specifying a desktop scheme in the Display property sheet. Some of the standard desktop schemes, however, use larger fonts and display components. These large-component schemes are typically denoted by the words "large" or "extra large" in the scheme name.

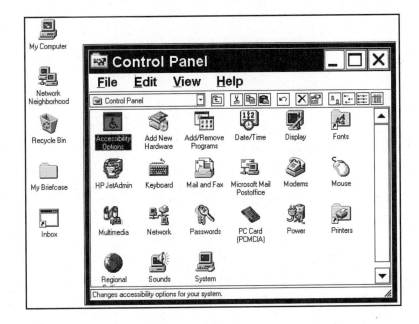

Figure 10.10

The black-on-white high-contrast scheme.

To choose a predefined high-contrast scheme other than black-on-white or white-on-black, select a scheme from the Custom drop-down list. If you want to create your own custom scheme, open the Control Panel and choose the Display icon, then create a custom scheme from the Appearance property page as explained in Chapter 9.

In addition to changing the interface components previously described, it is often advantageous to change the mouse pointer. The following section explains techniques you can use to make the mouse pointer easier to use for users with low or impaired vision, and for users who need to use the keys rather than the mouse to control the pointer.

Setting Mouse Options

The Mouse page in the Accessibility property sheet is where you can turn on and off the MouseKeys feature, which enables you to use the numeric/cursor keys on the numeric keypad to control the mouse. Enable the Use MouseKeys check box to turn on MouseKeys, then choose the Settings button to display the Settings for MouseKeys dialog box, shown in figure 10.11.

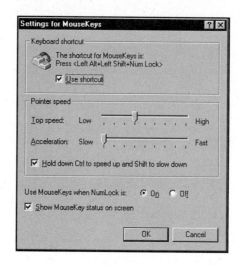

Figure 10.11

The Settings for MouseKeys dialog box.

Note MouseKeys enables you to control the pointer with the cursor keys on the numeric keypad, and does not support pointer movement with the other cursor keys.

The Use shortcut check box enables and disables the shortcut key for MouseKeys, which is Left Alt+Left Shift+Num Lock. If the Use shortcut check box is enabled, you can turn on and off MouseKeys by pressing the assigned shortcut key, which is particularly useful if you share the PC with another user.

The Pointer speed control group enables you to control the speed and acceleration options for the pointer. The Top speed slider controls the overall speed of the pointer—slide the control toward High to increase the speed of the pointer or toward Low to decrease pointer speed. The Acceleration slider controls the acceleration of the pointer. Acceleration defines how quickly the pointer begins to accelerate to top speed when you hold down a cursor key to move the pointer. In general, a slow setting is preferable for users who have difficulty controlling the pointer.

Tip MouseKeys can be a useful feature on a notebook computer if you don't have an input device such as a trackball connected to the computer, or if you don't want to use the notebook's built-in trackball.

The check box labeled Hold down Ctrl to speed up and Shift to slow down enables you to use the Ctrl and Shift keys as modifiers to speed up or slow down the pointer. If neither key is pressed and you press a cursor key to move the pointer, the pointer accelerates to the rate set by the Top speed and Acceleration keys. If you hold down the Ctrl key and press a cursor key, the pointer jumps in larger increments. Holding down the Shift key while pressing a numeric cursor key causes the pointer to jump in smaller increments.

By default, MouseKeys is on when Num Lock is on. If you need to use MouseKeys but also want to be able to use the numeric keypad to enter numbers, you also can configure MouseKeys to be on when Num Lock is off. Two option buttons on the Settings for MouseKeys dialog box, On and Off, enable you to specify which Num Lock state will turn on MouseKeys. If you want to enter numbers with the numeric keypad while MouseKeys is active, choose Off. If you want to use the cursor keys when MouseKeys is active, choose On.

The last control on the Settings for MouseKeys dialog box, Show MouseKey status on screen, enables and disables a MouseKeys indicator for the Taskbar tray.

Using Large Pointers

In some situations, the pointer can be difficult to see even for users who do not have visual limitations. On passive-matrix LCD displays, for example, locating the pointer can be very difficult.

To overcome the problem of locating the pointer, you can increase the size of all the pointers on a global basis. To do so, open the Control Panel, choose the Mouse icon, then click on the Pointers tab to display the Pointers property page shown in figure 10.12.

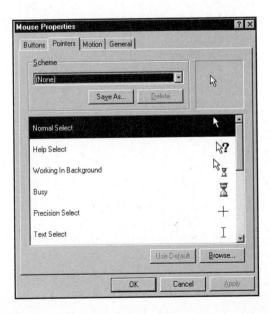

Figure 10.12

The Pointers property page.

To use larger pointers, choose the Scheme drop-down list, then select either the Windows Standard (large) or Windows Standard (extra large) options. The large pointers are approximately 50 percent larger than the standard Windows pointers, and the extra large pointers are approximately 100 percent larger than the standard pointers.

 Tip   You also might want to turn on pointer trails to make the pointer easier to locate. Pointer trails are enabled through the Motion page of the Mouse property sheet. When this feature is enabled, a set of ghost pointers follow (trail) the cursor to help you locate the cursor.

Setting General Accessibility Options

In addition to specific accessibility options, there also are general settings that affect accessibility options globally. To set these general options, open the General page (see fig. 10.13) from the Accessibility property sheet.

Figure 10.13

The General page of the Accessibility property sheet.

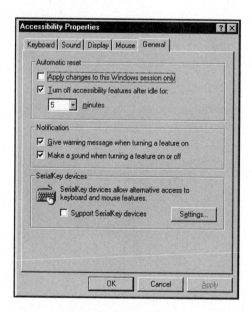

The controls in the Automatic reset group control whether changes to the accessibility options are effective only for the current Windows 95 session or for all sessions. Enable the check box labeled Apply changes to this Windows session only to have

accessibility option changes affect only your current Windows 95 session. Clear this check box if you want accessibility option changes to apply to all Windows 95 sessions, including those of other users.

The other check box in the Automatic reset group, Turn off accessibility features after idle, enables you to specify an idle time limit after which accessibility options are turned off and Windows 95 returns to its normal settings. This feature is useful if you share the computer with other users and only some use the accessibility options. Clear this check box if you want the accessibility options to be on until you specifically turn them off through their shortcut keys or through the Control Panel.

The Notification group on the General property page turns on and off visual and audio cues that inform you when accessibility options are turned on or off. By default, a dialog box appears whenever you turn on an accessibility feature through its shortcut key. To have the accessibility features turn on without Windows 95 displaying this dialog box, clear the check box labeled Give warning message when turning a feature on. Also by default, turning an accessibility feature on or off generates a tone. Turning on a feature generates an ascending tone, and turning off a feature generates a descending tone. If you do not want these audible cues, clear the check box labeled Make a sound when turning a feature on or off.

Using a SerialKey (Alternate Input) Device

A number of special input devices are now available for users who can't use a standard keyboard or mouse. Windows 95 provides support for these alternative input devices through the General page of the Accessibility property sheet. In Windows 95, these alternative input devices are referred to as SerialKey devices. To use a SerialKey device, enable the check box labeled Support SerialKey devices on the General property page. Then, choose the Settings button to display the Settings for SerialKeys dialog box, shown in figure 10.14.

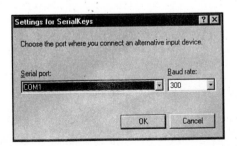

Figure 10.14

The Settings for SerialKeys dialog box.

SerialKeys devices connect to one of the PC's serial (COM) ports. The only settings you need to specify for the device are the COM port to which it is connected and its baud rate. Generally, a higher baud rate means better performance, but is limited by the capabilities of the device. Check the device's manual for more information on the correct baud rate to use. For a more detailed description of baud rate and other serial communications issues, refer to Chapter 28, "Modems and Data Communications."

Part III

Windows 95 Architecture and Optimization

Understanding the Windows 95 Architecture

Windows 95 is one of the most significant pieces of software on the market. With a projected sales rate of 20 million copies in the first year alone, Windows 95 could very well become the de facto standard desktop operating system. Although this book deals with end-user and administrator aspects of Windows 95, this chapter takes the wraps off Windows 95 and exposes its core architecture. This chapter is technical, yes, but also a useful resource if you're interested in what's under the hood in Windows 95.

Many of Windows 95's benefits are buried within the system architecture. Windows 95's design is vastly superior to Windows 3.x. This chapter familiarizes you with the improved components lurking underneath the fancy new user interface, including some of the following items:

◆ The Win32 application programming interface (API)

◆ Preemptive multitasking versus cooperative multitasking

◆ Flat memory addressing

◆ 32-bit USER and GDI heaps

◆ Virtual device drivers

◆ Virtual memory management

◆ The virtual file allocation table file system

◆ Deserialized input queues

This discussion of the Windows 95 system architecture begins with an overview of the design goals Microsoft had in mind during the development process of Windows 95.

Windows 95 Design Goals

Windows 95 is an evolutionary step from Windows 3.*x*. Rather than rewrite Windows from the ground up, Microsoft opted to update the Windows architecture by making it robust enough to handle 32-bit applications in a relatively stable environment. Consequently, Windows 95 truly is a more robust, refined, and mature operating system. At first glance, Windows 95 looks very different from Windows 3.*x*. After you start venturing around the system, however, you begin to notice remnants from Windows 3.*x*.

Windows 95 is a very ambitious step. Compromises were necessary to meet the product goals. To be a success, Windows 95 needs to do the following:

◆ Run in as little as 4 MB of RAM

◆ Support the majority of Win16 and DOS applications

◆ Offer increased stability over Windows 3.1

To reach the project team's lofty goals, Windows 95 had to keep a number of Windows 3.1 system components. To maintain Win16 compatibility, the 16-bit USER, GDI, and KERNEL modules—all Windows mainstays since its inception—continue in Windows 95. In fact, you still can find most of the window management code in the 16-bit USER module, which Win16 *and* Win32 applications call. Most of the KERNEL module now is 32-bit, but roughly half of all GDI calls are serviced by a 16-bit module.

To help understand the benefits and drawbacks of this design, the following list is a brief description of each module and the services that they offer.

◆ **USER.** USER manages I/O, primarily for input devices such as the mouse or the keyboard. The majority of USER services are window management–related—such as window displays and repaints.

◆ **GDI.** GDI stands for Graphical Device Interface. Because Windows is a graphical operating system, GDI is important because it offers functions for graphical displays—such as color management, fonts, and line drawing.

◆ **KERNEL.** The KERNEL module is the heart of Windows. KERNEL manages memory, the file system, and the task scheduler.

Note   This hybrid design should not be a problem for most purposes. 16-bit code sometimes can be as fast—or faster—than 32-bit code, depending on the code's efficiency.

In general, 32-bit code outperforms 16-bit code for operating systems, owing to the extra bandwidth that the 32-bit code enjoys. 32-bit code moves data 32 bits (4 bytes) at a time, allowing for more efficient transfer rates than on a 16-bit bus. Imagine it as like widening a freeway—the more lanes in a freeway, the more traffic it can accommodate.

Thunking in Windows 95

16-bit modules can communicate with their 32-bit counterparts—by *thunking*—and vice versa. In a nutshell, *thunks* are routines that map addresses to enable 16-bit segmented applications to seamlessly share memory with flat 32-bit applications. A Win32 application, for example, can talk to the USER32 module. USER32 goes through the thunk layer and talks to USER16. Thunking sometimes causes performance degradation, but you don't notice it for the most part, if at all. Figure 11.1 shows Windows 95's particular thunking procedure.

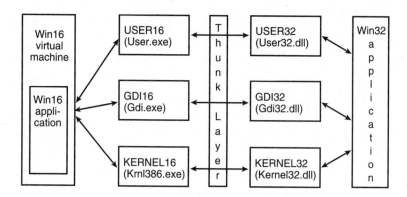

Figure 11.1

The thunk layer in Windows 95.

Understanding the Intel 32-Bit Architecture

16-bit operating systems, such as Windows 3.1 and MS-DOS, are a dying breed. A 16-bit operating system cannot keep up with today's demanding applications' workload. Although Intel released its first 32-bit processor (the 80386) 10 years ago, 32-bit operating systems have only recently gained widespread usage. Windows 95 works closely with Intel's 32-bit processors to provide a robust and stable 32-bit environment. This section overviews 32-bit processing, Intel protection rings, and Windows 95's relationship with 32-bit system architectures.

32-Bit Processing

Since the 80386 was released in 1985, Intel's "next-generation" CPUs have been able to access gigabytes of memory. Yet, the most widely used operating system on these machines is Windows 3.*x*—a 16-bit operating system that treats the CPU as a fast 16-bit 80286 processor—which puts a number of limitations on the system, especially when it comes to memory addressing.

MS-DOS divides the first megabyte of memory into segments. It reserves the first 640 KB for the operating system and applications and the remaining 384 KB for DOS system services. The rest of the physical memory is split into extended and expanded memory.

A 32-bit operating system can access a flat memory model, which enables the operating system to address up to 4 GB of linear memory, effectively eliminating the memory segmentation you find in 16-bit operating systems.

Along the same vein, data processing also benefits from a 32-bit environment. Before Intel's 80386 processor, code was handled in 16-bit quantities. Because the width of the 80286's registers was 16-bit, memory was dealt with in 64 KB blocks, which meant that applications had to break large files into smaller 64 KB segments. That same application, running on a 32-bit Intel processor, can access 4 GB of memory. The data can be referenced in a linear fashion, eliminating the extra overhead of segmentation (essentially, the amount of time that it takes to switch the processor's memory tables to point towards a different segment).

The 80386 processor also included a new feature known as *virtual 8086 mode*. Virtual 8086 mode applications that run in virtual 8086 mode actually run in protected mode, and receive all the benefits that go along with it, such as the capability to access up to 4 GB of RAM. This also saves a potentially lengthy processor mode switch from protected mode to real mode.

Without virtual 8086 mode, operating systems can run only one MS-DOS application at a time—a limitation that plagued earlier versions of Windows and hindered its chances of acceptance on desktop machines. Back when Windows 2.*x* (and OS/2 1.*x*) was released, computers mostly ran MS-DOS applications, and being able to multitask only one application posed significant operating limitations.

Virtual 8086 alleviated that problem by spawning multiple virtual machines in the processor. On the Intel 80386 processor, each MS-DOS application thinks that it has its very own 8086 machine. This provides extra security by disallowing an application to use memory reserved for another application. If one application crashes, no other applications (in separate virtual machines) are affected.

One of the most significant features of the 80386 is support for virtual memory, something covered in-depth later in this chapter in the "Virtual Memory" section.

Intel Protection Ring Architecture

System protection is important in Windows 95. If an application somehow processes certain delicate operations (such as interrupt handling or task switching), the entire system can lock up to the extent that even pressing Ctrl+Alt+Del doesn't work. Only Windows 95 system software should use these services. To ensure that only the operating system services can execute these functions, Windows 95 takes advantage of Intel's protection ring privilege levels.

All Intel processors, from the 80386 and up, maintain up to four rings. Rings are also known as *system privilege levels*. All system code or applications run at a certain ring— the lower the privilege number, the more freedom the process enjoys. Windows 95 uses only two rings: ring 0 and ring 3.

In Windows 95, all applications run at ring 3 (sometimes referred to as *user mode*), which is prevented from accessing certain memory regions. This ensures that an errant application cannot crash the entire system. The operating system components run at ring 0 (also known as *kernel mode*), the most vulnerable part of the system. Because processes that run at ring 0 have unlimited access to the system, the code has to be extremely reliable. Ring 3 processes constantly communicate with ring 0 processes. To save a file, for example, a word processor (running at ring 3) sends a message to the file system process (running at ring 0) to enable it to write the file to the disk. Figure 11.2 shows how Windows 95 takes advantage of this system feature.

Figure 11.2

The Intel protection ring architecture.

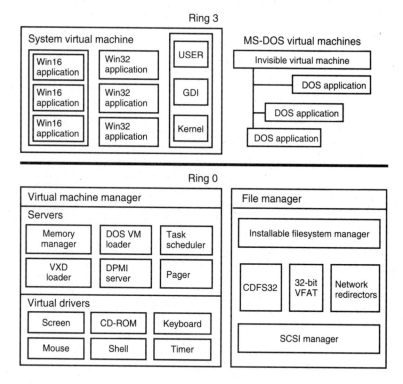

The tier design used in Intel's protection architecture offers increased system reliability because ring 0 services are isolated from ring 3 processes. When an application (running at ring 3) tries to execute a privileged instruction, the processor generates an interrupt that the operating system retrieves. After retrieving the interrupt, the operating system ends the offending process. For example, if an errant application attempts to perform a task switch (which is the job of the operating system), the processor notifies the operating system of the privilege breach, enabling the operating system to end the errant process.

Windows 95 runs the installable file systems manager, network redirectors, and virtual memory managers at ring 0. And, per the norm, all applications in Windows 95 run at the ring 3 level. As such, applications cannot step on *any* operating system service.

Understanding the Windows 95 Base Architecture

32-bit operating systems have only begun to surface in the mainstream in the past couple years, with the advent of OS/2 and Windows NT. Although Windows 95 does contain 16-bit components, it is a 32-bit operating system that fully exploits the advantages of Intel's 32-bit architecture. Windows 95 actually consists of numerous components, all closely knitted together to form a seamless environment. This chapter looks at the Windows 95 system architecture, including some of the drawbacks—such as Win16Mutex.

Understanding Win16Mutex

In a multitasking operating system, system reentrancy is a necessity. *Reentrancy* is the capability of a routine to be interrupted in the middle of processing and for the same routine to be called without loss of its local variables. Windows 3.*x* is especially susceptible to non-reentrant code. If two threads simultaneously execute non-reentrant code, certain parts of the Win16 subsystem can collapse the entire system.

Because Windows 3.*x* is a non-reentrant operating system, some of the GDI and USER calls in Windows 95's Win16 subsystems also are non-reentrant. If a routine calls these subsystems and interrupts another routine while it processes the subsystems, the interrupting routine cannot call the same routine again. The routine also is denied access to any other routine that shares common Win16 data structures with the original call.

This has serious ramifications for the Windows 95 operating system. An ill-behaved application might, can, and probably will at some time, try to call non-reentrant code while another Win16 application is already processing the same code. To prevent this from happening without completely stopping all other processes, Microsoft incorporated the *Win16Mutex* semaphore into Windows 95. *Mutex* stands for *mutual exclusion,* a technique that ensures that only one thread can access certain pieces of code at one time. If any Win16 call is being executed, this semaphore prevents other Win16 applications from executing the same code, serving as a barrier of sorts. Any Win32 API call can complete normally—the barrier affects only other Win16 calls.

Nevertheless, Win16Mutex can have a dramatic effect on Windows 95's multitasking capabilities. If a Win32 application has to access non-reentrant Win16 code, and a Win16 application sets the semaphore flag, the Win32 application also halts until the flag lowers. All other Win32 threads that do not require access to the blocked off code, however, continue to process normally.

This becomes less of a concern when you run only Win32 applications. Win32 applications can hold the semaphore, because Win32 calls often thunk down to the 16-bit USER and GDI modules. For the most part, running purely Win32 applications alleviates any possible problems with Win16Mutex.

System Stability and Resources

System resources are among Windows' most valuable commodities. Applications use resources to display windows, window items, and other objects that an application takes advantage of during normal execution. Both USER and GDI use resource heaps to service applications. A *heap* is a region of memory storage that contains different types of objects.

In Windows 3.*x,* GDI services resource requests from a single 64 KB heap. That single 64 KB heap contains regions, logical objects (such as pens, fonts, brushes), and device contexts. Most of the objects in the 64 KB heap are relatively small, except for regions. Applications use regions to draw a sequence of polygons on-screen. If you want a sufficiently complex picture, the application can use multiple regions. Because the heap is limited to 64 KB, GDI limits the number of available resources to other applications.

The USER module in Windows 3.*x* uses up to three separate 64 KB heaps. Each heap stores window handles, list box items, menu handles, and other window management code. The problem with this arrangement is that the system can access only 200 menu or window handles, which limits the number of applications you can run at one time. After the heaps fill up, Windows complains about `Out of Resources` errors and refuses to start more applications. To free up resources, you have to close applications, or in extreme cases, restart Windows.

In Windows 95, system resources have been greatly increased. By moving the larger objects, such as regions, from the 16-bit heap to a new 32-bit heap, GDI now can allocate a much larger number of resources to applications. The 16-bit version of GDI still uses a 64 KB heap, but that heap contains only smaller objects, such as the structures that define bitmap headers and brushes. Windows 95 also moves the USER window handles to a 32-bit heap. USER now can allocate up to 32,767 menu handles and 32,767 window handles per process—a substantial improvement over Windows 3.*x.*

The 32-bit heaps use Windows 95's virtual memory management, which makes them the size of your available memory. So, although the 32-bit USER and GDI heaps are not unlimited, they are large enough to remove any resource restriction that you might have encountered in Windows 3.*x*.

 Tip Windows 95 includes a resource monitor that docks on the Taskbar notification area. This resource monitor (see fig. 11.3) keeps a running tally of the free GDI and USER heaps. You can find this in the <u>P</u>rograms/Accessories/System Tools folder on the Start menu.

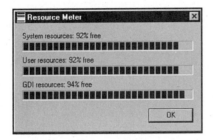

Figure 11.3

The Windows 95 Resource Monitor, showing 92 percent free resources at startup.

16-bit heaps remain in Windows 95 for compatibility purposes. Certain Win16 applications bypass the API to access the heaps directly. If you remove the 16-bit heaps, you can no longer use these applications with Windows 95.

Resource Tracking

Windows 3.1 has a reputation for being extremely unstable, typically due to *lost system resources*—allocated resources not returned to the system after an application crashes. Recovery from a *general protection fault* (what happens when an application writes over another application's memory region or over itself) is often difficult in Windows 3.*x*, because the fault handler is part of the application. If the application hangs severely, bringing up the handler might not do much good at all. As a result, system resources drop in a downward spiral, forcing you to restart Windows.

Frequently rebooting to free resources is definitely not a real solution. Because applications don't return resources, Windows 95 tracks resource usage at the system level, a rather ingenious solution: Windows 95 runs its own fault handler transparently. The fault handler does not show up in the tasklist or on the Taskbar. Each allocated resource has a thread identifier within the system. If an application crashes, the fault handler searches a table to find resources that the application was using and returns the resources to the system pool.

Unfortunately, Windows 95 cannot automatically recollect resources that Win16 applications use. Some Win16 applications leave resources behind for other programs. If Windows 95 picks up those resources, you will experience problems with applications that depend on those orphaned resources. Windows 95 intentionally leaves those resources alone until after you close all Win16 applications, then it frees all previously allocated resources. In Windows 3.1, that could lead to resource shortages. Fortunately, the expanded heaps in Windows 95 allow for a greater amount of free system resources at startup.

 Note   Because of the new 32-bit heaps, you commonly start the system with close to 98 percent free resources. On a non-networked 486DX/33 with 16 MB RAM, Windows 95 starts up with 97–98 percent free resources—a substantial improvement over Windows 3.x.

Memory Management

One of the most important parts in a computer is memory. Put a 4 MB upgrade into a 486 kitten and it transforms into a roaring tiger. This section shows how Windows 95 makes efficient use of both physical and virtual memory.

Physical Memory

Physical memory often can make a world of difference for running operating systems. A 4 MB machine generally cannot run a 32-bit operating system smoothly, but a mere 4 MB upgrade can make the system much more responsive. Windows 95 uses all of a computer's available physical memory.

Physical memory management is the process of selecting memory pages (within the system's 4 GB address space) to place into physical memory. The operating system can swap pages in and out of physical memory to virtual memory. Some pages are defined with specific roles at startup and marked nonswappable—usually a very small amount (about 1 MB).

All applications and processes compete for available physical pages. These pages can fill up quickly on memory-confined systems, causing Windows 95 to page the least recently used pages out to a virtual memory file. Windows 95 starts with 600 KB of data that it can page out if physical memory becomes sparse. Another 1.2 MB is marked as locked and unpageable.

Virtual Memory

Although Win32 processes can utilize up to 4 GB of RAM, current hardware limitations prevent most computers from containing that much memory. Thankfully, Intel took that into consideration while designing the 80386 chip. One of the most important features that the 80386 processor introduced is virtual memory management.

On the 80386, memory pages are 4 KB in size. Memory segments consist of multiple 4 KB pages. Each 4 KB page of memory is dynamic, enabling the CPU to control which page contains which piece of data for which process. The CPU can easily move these pages in the physical RAM by changing the CPU page tables. Because these pages are movable, the CPU also can store them externally—that is, outside of the physical RAM until it needs them. If an application that can address up to 4 GB tries to use more memory than is physically available, the operating system works with the CPU's virtual memory manager to swap some of the least recently used memory pages to a specified swap file on a hard disk. The freed memory pages are now available to any process that needs them.

Windows 3.*x* and Windows 95 both take advantage of virtual memory. (Windows 3.*x* only uses virtual memory when it runs in 386 Enhanced Mode.) The swap file in Windows 3.1 is limited to 30 MB, which can limit the number of applications open at one time. Windows 95 has no swap-file size limitation.

When you launch an application, Windows 95 creates a swap area equivalent to the size of the application executable to ensure that the hard disk has enough free space to swap code out.

Static Swap Files versus Dynamic Swap Files

Windows 3.1's swap file is *static*—that is, it stays at one fixed size. So if you set the swap file at 8 MB, and an application asks for another 12 MB, the swap file does not grow to accommodate the application, which causes an out of memory error.

Windows 95 uses a dynamic swap file that adjusts its size on demand. When an application requests more memory on an already overloaded 8 MB machine, Windows 95 enlarges and pages out to the swap file the least frequently used pages of memory. After you close the application, Windows 95 brings the swapped-out pages back into physical RAM and shrinks the swap file, which maintains a reasonable-sized swap file at all times and eliminates the need to keep a permanent swap file on the hard disk.

Tip You can change Windows 95's swap file behavior by right-clicking on My Computer and opening the Properties page. Select the Performance tab and click on the Virtual Memory button.

Dynamic swap file management is the default—and you probably don't need to change it—but if you work with a fixed amount of disk space, you can use this page to set the largest swap file size.

Although this scheme provides applications with more memory than physically available, you need to take into account the speed of the hard disk. As a rule, all hard disks are slower than RAM, so data retrieval from swapped-out memory pages is much slower than retrieval from physical RAM.

Windows 95 Virtual Drivers Model

Windows 95 makes heavy use of virtual drivers. Everywhere you look, you see the word *virtual* preceding a function name. This section explains the benefits—and drawbacks—of virtual drivers in Windows 95.

Virtual Device Drivers

As with Windows for Workgroups 3.11, Windows 95 supports virtual device drivers, also known as *VxDs*. Because the original Windows 3.*x* system services and drivers are not reentrant, only one application can call a certain service at a time, ultimately leading to problems, especially hardware problems. A common example is screen displays. In Windows 3.1, only one DOS window can access the physical screen, because the screen driver is non-reentrant. To address this problem, Microsoft implemented a large number of VxDs in Windows 95. *VxDs* are user-installable, 32-bit, reentrant, protected-mode drivers that run at ring 0. Using VxDs eliminates blocking by applications. VxDs also are much faster than real-mode drivers because they execute in protected mode. Because the VxD design is so efficient, Microsoft uses them liberally in Windows 95. The Virtual Memory Manager, for example, is a VxD. However, VxDs are not compatible with OS/2 or Windows NT. You cannot use any application that uses a VxD on OS/2 or Windows NT—including Win32 applications.

Note VxDs actually stands for "Virtual Anything Drivers." Each VxD manages a single resource, and VxDs are always 32-bit protected-mode code.

VxDs can cause problems. Because VxDs are ring 0 code, an errant VxD can bring the entire system down. The VxDs you find in Windows 95, however, are extremely polished, minimizing the chance of a system crash. Microsoft also discourages software vendors from implementing VxDs unless absolutely necessary.

Virtual Communications Driver

Windows 3.*x* uses a 16-bit real-mode communications driver, which causes the system to switch extremely frequently from protected mode to real mode. The lack of preemptive multitasking in the system compounds this effect. As a result, characters often get dropped during high-speed file transfer over a modem.

Windows 95 implements a 32-bit virtual communications driver (VCOMM) that services both Win16 and Win32 applications. Figure 11.4 shows how Win16 and Win32 applications take advantage of the new 32-bit communications driver.

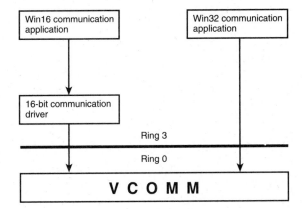

Figure 11.4

VCOMM services both Win16 and Win32 applications.

The Virtual FAT File System

One of the major performance bottlenecks in Windows 3.1 (and alleviated in Windows for Workgroups 3.11) is the file allocation table (FAT) file system. Because FAT is a 16-bit file system, Windows 3.1 makes a costly switch from protected mode to real mode every time the system accesses the file system.

Windows 95's virtual FAT file system is a full 32-bit VxD that resides under the IFS manager at ring 0. Windows 95 uses VFAT as an interface between applications and the physical file system, and it offers the following distinct benefits:

◆ Services file system requests in protected mode, eliminating the need for a processor mode switch

◆ Works hand in hand with VCACHE to provide swift I/O performance

◆ Implements long file names without requiring a reformat

Because VFAT is a protected-mode 32-bit file system, the operating system does not have to switch processor modes from protected mode to real mode every time the system accesses a file, which translates to an enormous performance gain in Windows 95.

Note Windows for Workgroups 3.11 also includes VFAT support, but not long file names. You could say that Microsoft used Windows for Workgroups 3.11 as a beta test for VFAT.

Although the VFAT implementation in Windows for Workgroups 3.11 is a subset of the Windows 95 version, it still offers incredible speed gains over the 16-bit FAT in Windows 3.x.

Because VFAT still relies on the 16-bit FAT for physical file storage, it still suffers from the problems inherent to FAT. Compared to OS/2's HPFS and Windows NT's NTFS, VFAT is extremely fragile and prone to data loss when you shut down the system improperly. Fortunately, VFAT-aware disk tools minimize this potential problem. VFAT is based on FAT, so volumes are limited to 2 GB, which often is inadequate for server use. Larger volumes (over 512 MB) also use large cluster sizes, reducing the storage capacity on the hard disk.

Long File Name Support

One of the most compelling VFAT features is the capability to use long file names without reformatting the volume. Traditionally, long file names have been available only to file systems that have specific long file name support. In OS/2, you have to reformat a drive to its High Performance File System (HPFS) before you can utilize long file names. Windows NT also supports long file names with its New Technology File System (NTFS), but Windows NT offers a file system conversion tool that enables FAT volumes to be converted to NTFS while retaining all data on the volume.

Windows 95's VFAT file system supports long file names *without* requiring a reformat or conversion. Windows 95 does this by using multiple directory entries to store long file names. Using reserved entries enables the file system to find out and retrieve the files that have long file names attached to them.

Stop Running 16-bit DOS or Windows disk utilities, such as The Norton Utilities or PC-Tools, can damage Windows 95's long file names. Use the disk tools included with Windows 95 until your existing disk tools are available for Windows 95.

However, Windows 95 includes a utility that backs up all long file names, allowing you to run your existing disk utilities. Chapter 15, "Optimizing Data Storage," explains how to use this utility.

The size of the root directory does not change after you format the disk—potentially a significant problem because of the way long file names are implemented in Windows 95.

The size of the root directory is still static after the disk is formatted. This is a potentially significant problem due to the way long file names are implemented in Windows 95. Because FAT volumes have a limitation on the number of files in the root directory, VFAT's long file name implementation could potentially meet or exceed that limit. Fortunately, this limit is fairly high, so you probably won't see a problem.

Aliases

To stay compatible with older applications that recognize short file names, Windows 95 generates a short file name alias that conforms to the 8.3 naming standard. If you generate a long file name, VFAT automatically creates an 8.3 file name that goes along with it.

The algorithm to create short file names is actually very simple. VFAT takes the first six characters of the long file name and removes all illegal characters and blank spaces, retaining the file extension. It then adds a tilde character and a number to the end of the file name to ensure that the file name is unique. If it is not a unique file name, the number after the tilde will go up by one. After the number reaches 9, VFAT removes another letter from the name that precedes the numbers and increases the number by one. As figure 11.5 shows, MS-DOS windows in Windows 95 can see both long file names and short file names.

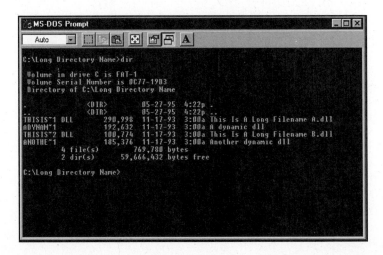

Figure 11.5

A simple DIR command shows both long file names and short file names.

The Virtual Cache

Windows 95 includes a 32-bit virtual cache (known as VCACHE) that works in conjunction with VFAT. VCACHE improves on and replaces the SmartDrive cache in MS-DOS and Windows 3.*x*. Unlike SmartDrive, the VCACHE cache size is dynamic—it grows and shrinks as needed.

The CD-ROM File System

For CD-ROM access, Windows 95 also includes a 32-bit protected-mode file system driver, known as CDFS. CDFS improves on and replaces MS-DOS and Windows 3.*x*'s MSCDEX (the Microsoft CD Extensions). As with VFAT, the 32-bit CDFS enables the CD-ROM drive to be read in protected mode, instead of forcing a switch to real mode.

Windows Applications Support

One of Windows 95's biggest selling points is the number of applications it supports. Staying compatible with existing DOS and 16-bit Windows applications and running the latest 32-bit Windows applications makes Windows 95 a robust applications environment.

This section summarizes the Win32 API capabilities, crash protection for Win32 applications, Win16 application compatibility, and MS-DOS compatibility.

Understanding the Win32 API

All operating systems provide developers an application programming interface (API). APIs enables software developers to write applications that run on a certain operating system. Win16 has been the only available Windows API for the past five years. Thus, most mainstream Windows applications are written to the Win16 API.

Windows 95 uses a subset of Windows NT's Win32 API. Win32 enables you to run 32-bit applications that are preemptively multitasked within the system. Windows 95's Win32 implementation differs slightly from the set of functions found in Windows NT. Whereas Windows 95 introduces new common dialog boxes (such as the new File Open dialog box) and device-independent color matching, Windows NT offers high-end functions, such as Unicode, security, multiple console sessions, event logging, and OpenGL. Most, if not all, of the new calls introduced in Windows 95 will end up on a future release of Windows NT. The exclusive calls found on Windows NT will not be moving to Windows 95, however. (Windows 95 is not designed to be a secure platform, hence the lack of security APIs.) For the administrator, what this means is that certain applications that call exclusive API functions might not be binary

compatible between Windows 95 and Windows NT. For the most part, the majority of the upcoming wave of Windows 95 applications will run—unmodified—on both Windows 95 and Windows NT.

Stop Although binary compatibility with Windows NT is one requirement for the "Designed for Windows 95" logo, not all applications are required to run on both Windows 95 and Windows NT. Certain disk utility packages intended for use on Windows 95, for example, often use VxDs, causing them to fail on Windows NT. As a rule of thumb, always check with the vendor before you buy if you need Windows NT compatibility.

Win32 applications are 32-bit, so each application can access 4 GB of addressable memory—a technique known as *flat model addressing*. Rather than break up a 1 MB file into multiple 64 KB chunks, a Win32 application can reference the data in a linear fashion, which translates to better performance.

Crash Protection

Each MS-DOS application receives a virtual machine from the operating system to provide memory protection. Win32 applications, by virtue of their design, are isolated from each other within the system. Whereas Win16 applications run in a common virtual machine, Win32 applications run in separate virtual machines. Each virtual machine is protected, which makes it impossible for one Win32 application to accidentally write over another Win32 application's memory.

Note One of the most common problems in Windows 3.x is susceptibility to general protection faults. Most general protection faults stem from an errant Win16 application overwriting memory allocated to another application.

Because Windows 3.x (and Windows 95) runs all Win16 applications in a single virtual machine, nothing stops a poorly coded application from trying to access memory that doesn't belong to it. For most purposes, the single virtual machine design is not a problem. If it does cause problems, you should evaluate Windows NT or OS/2—both of which can run Win16 applications in separate virtual machines (providing crash protection).

Going back to the Intel Protection Rings design, all processes running at ring 3 (usually applications) are isolated from the operating system services at ring 0. If an application running at ring 3 crashes, services sitting at ring 0 (including VxDs) are unaffected.

If an application hangs, however, killing the offending process is much easier in Windows 95. To end applications that stop responding to system requests, Windows

95 uses a technique known as local reboot. *Local reboot* is an improved version of the old Ctrl+Alt+Del sequence in Windows 3.*x*. In Windows 95, Ctrl+Alt+Del brings up a dialog box (the local reboot user interface) that lists all loaded and active applications (see fig. 11.6). If an application is stopped, the local reboot dialog box will display a `not responding` message after the offending application's name. After you choose <u>E</u>nd Task, Windows 95 attempts to let the application know that it is about to be shut down. The application can respond to the system request by yielding and prompting the user to save any unfinished work, then terminating normally. If there is no response from the application, Windows 95 automatically terminates it.

Figure 11.6

Pressing Ctrl+Atl+Del displays Windows 95's Local Reboot user interface.

Understanding Multithreading

One of the most significant additions to the Windows 95 API (Win32) is support for multithreading. *Threads* are small units of executable code. Typically, a well-written multithreaded application can house multiple threads within the main program. The system can execute every thread within the application concurrently. A multithreaded word processor, for example, can run a spelling and grammar checker while printing the document as you edit the document, all at the same time. These tasks all are executed independently of each other. Threading, properly utilized, can provide a significant productivity boon. Figure 11.7 shows an example of a multithreaded application simultaneously running four threads.

Note   Windows 95's user interface is extremely multithreaded. You can open a folder and work with the menus, for example, while waiting for the icons to populate. Multithreading gives the user interface a more polished feel.

For a hands-on example, open up WordPad. Notice that while opening a document, you can continue to work with the WordPad user interface.

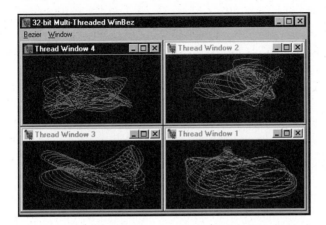

Figure 11.7

A 32-bit application that draws multiple Bézier curves with separate threads.

Understanding Multitasking Models

One of the leading reasons to use Windows as a day-to-day operating environment is multitasking capability. A computer multitasks by switching between multiple programs, allowing each program to execute for a short period of time. The computer switches between processes very rapidly, so to the user, the computer appears to be running multiple applications simultaneously. Multitasking can provide significant productivity advances. You can spell check a document while reading e-mail while a spreadsheet does a recalculation.

Multitasking takes two forms—the cooperative multitasking model and the preemptive multitasking model. This section overviews both models, and explains the differences between them.

Cooperative Multitasking

Windows 3.*x* uses a cooperative multitasking model. *Cooperative multitasking* means that each application decides when to give up processor time to other active processes. In Windows 3.*x*, all Win16 applications exist in one virtual machine, enabling the applications to be cooperatively multitasked within that virtual machine.

When the system uses a cooperative multitasking model, it is at the mercy of the applications, because the applications decide when to yield CPU time to other processes. If one application decides to do a 10-minute recalculation, the operating system can't do a thing about it—you can't use the system until the given application finishes its calculation.

Preemptive Multitasking

Preemptive multitasking is much more sophisticated than cooperative multitasking. When the system uses a preemptive multitasking model, its scheduler decides when the next process runs and sets the duration for the next process activity. The scheduler allocates time to processes for execution. Returning to the recalculation example, the scheduler can take time away from the recalculation process and give it to another application with a higher priority level. When the scheduler detects an event that has a higher priority level than the current task, it preempts the current task and gives the CPU time to the higher-priority process. You get a more responsive and productive system. In Windows 95, each Win32 application is preemptively multitasked in the system.

To keep the working set low, Windows 95 runs all Win16 applications in the same virtual machine, cooperatively multitasking the processes. Because Win16 applications are cooperatively multitasked, running them under Windows 95 feels the same as in Windows 3.1—multitasking gets quite choppy at times.

System Input Queues

In the Windows environment, applications depend on the arrival of messages that are sent out by the operating system, drivers, or applications. Typically, these messages can be events from input devices, such as the keyboard or the mouse. The system also receives regular messages from devices such as modems or printers: switching windows on the desktop, for example. When the system detects a mouse click on a background window, it places the message into the *raw input queue,* the system structure that initially houses all input events. The raw input queue passes the message to the application message queue. The applications then check the application queue for messages.

Windows 3.1 has a single input queue for the entire system. If one application fails to retrieve messages, the system most likely is unusable, because the other applications also are blocked from receiving their messages. Because message passing cannot be interrupted, the system locks up until you reboot it. Figure 11.8 shows an illustration of the single input queue design.

Windows 95 retains the single input queue for all Win16 applications for maximum compatibility. All Win16 applications behave the same way under Windows 95 as they do under Windows 3.1. However, each Win32 application has its own private message queue, a technique known as *deserialization*. The multiple message queue environment increases system stability. When you run Win32 applications, you can always switch out of hung applications. If Word 7.0 fails to retrieve its messages, Excel 7.0 remains healthy because its messages are waiting in its own private input queue. Killing the errant Word process is as easy as pressing Ctrl+Alt+Del and removing the Word task from the task list. Figure 11.9 shows the multiple message queue design.

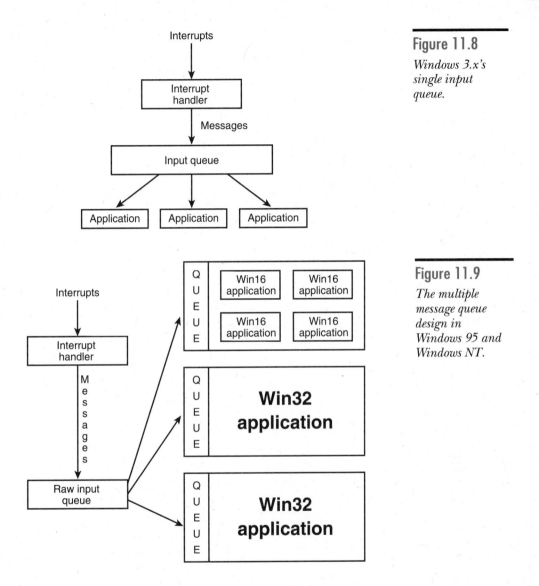

Figure 11.8

Windows 3.x's single input queue.

Figure 11.9

The multiple message queue design in Windows 95 and Windows NT.

Additionally, each thread receives the benefits of multiple input queues. When you first execute a Win32 application, Windows 95 creates an input queue for the primary application thread. As the application spawns more threads, Windows 95 generates input queues for each thread on demand. As soon as a thread makes a message queue call, Windows 95 assigns a message queue to the thread. This saves resources because the system doesn't have to assign message queues to threads that don't call queue functions.

A side benefit of the addition of input deserialization is increased responsiveness. Instead of being locked out of your system when you launch an application, Windows 95 loads the application on a separate primary thread, equipped with its own input queue, which frees up the rest of the system so that you can work with already loaded applications or to start more processes.

Understanding Virtual Machines

The heart of Windows 95 is the virtual machine manager. The virtual machine manager controls MS-DOS applications, Windows applications, virtual drivers (VxDs), and major components of the base Windows operating system. Virtual machines are always either system virtual machines or MS-DOS virtual machines. MS-DOS virtual machines house single DOS sessions, whereas system virtual machines provide the context for execution of an application. Figure 11.10 shows how Windows 95 utilizes virtual machines.

Figure 11.10

Windows 95's virtual machine usage.

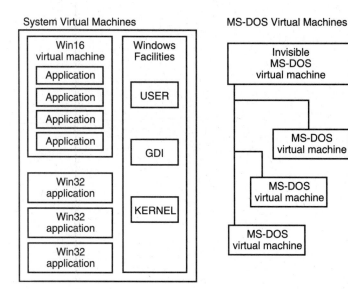

The system virtual machine houses all windowing facilities (such as USER and GDI), as well as all Windows applications. Within this system virtual machine, all Win32 applications are provided with their own virtual machines—each with protected memory.

MS-DOS Compatibility via Virtual Machines

Although MS-DOS applications are rarely upgraded—and barely stir up a blip on the sales radar—they still are widely used. Quite often, an application becomes so familiar

to a user that it becomes second nature. Bearing that in mind, Microsoft designed Windows 95 to offer maximum MS-DOS application compatibility. Windows 95 also runs MS-DOS applications in virtual machines. As with Win32 applications, MS-DOS virtual machines are isolated from each other and preemptively multitasked within the system.

MS-DOS applications run via emulation. Windows 95 re-creates an 8086 machine within the processor and allocates 1 MB of memory to the virtual machine. Applications running within this virtual machine think that they are running as a single task on a separate computer.

You set up the MS-DOS environment by running an invisible virtual machine at startup. This preloaded virtual machine contains all global elements specified in Config.sys and Autoexec.bat, such as drivers and TSRs. If a CD-ROM driver is loaded in Config.sys, the invisible virtual machine catches it and makes the driver available to all MS-DOS virtual machines. Because the driver is always loaded (rather than dynamically loaded when necessary), it always uses memory.

Win16 Support

Win16 applications probably will remain in widespread use even after Win32 applications start appearing on shelves. Win16 applications are familiar to most users, and they work fine. Windows 95 preserves your investment in software by offering full Win16 application compatibility.

Windows 95 uses familiar Win16 components to provide support for Win16 applications. As such, Win16 applications actually run natively on Windows 95. Win16 applications also run in the system virtual machine. The system virtual machine spawns a separate virtual machine in which all Win16 applications reside. All Win16 applications are cooperatively multitasked within that virtual machine.

Running Win16 applications in a single virtual machine, however, can cause problems. Win16 applications lack crash protection in Windows 95. If one application crashes, other applications might go down, too, and you can end up losing data. Fortunately, most recent Win16 applications are well behaved and less prone to crashing.

Note Windows NT and OS/2 both allow Win16 applications to run in separate, isolated virtual machines. This does provide additional stability, but it also uses more memory than the single virtual machine design that Windows 95 uses.

Comparing Windows 95 with Other 32-Bit Operating Systems

Windows 95 is in the enviable position of being a natural upgrade from Windows 3.1, and can be of benefit to users of both low-end and high-end machines. However, Windows 95 does face competition. The two most popular 32-bit operating systems currently available are Windows NT and OS/2. Both obviously influence Windows 95's design. Table 11.1 compares Windows 95 to these more mature—and arguably stronger—32-bit operating systems.

TABLE 11.1

Feature Set Comparison between Windows 95, Windows NT, and OS/2

Feature	Windows 95	Windows NT	OS/2
Preemptive multitasking	Yes	Yes	Yes
Multithreading	Yes	Yes	Yes
Symmetric multiprocessing	No	Yes	Yes*
Virtual memory	Yes	Yes	Yes
Object-oriented user interface	Yes	No**	Yes
File systems supported	VFAT, NTFS	VFAT, HPFS	FAT, HPFS
Networking out of the box	Yes	Yes	Yes*
Portable	No	Yes	No
Runs DOS applications	Yes	Yes	Yes
Runs Win16 applications	Yes	Yes	Yes
Runs Win32 applications	Yes	Yes	No***
Runs 16-bit OS/2 applications	No	Yes****	Yes

Feature	Windows 95	Windows NT	OS/2
Runs 32-bit OS/2 applications	No	No	Yes

* OS/2 comes in different versions, each targeted at a different segment of the market. OS/2 for SMP supports symmetric multiprocessing, whereas OS/2 Warp Connect includes peer-to-peer connectivity.

** The Windows 95 user interface will be available on Windows NT when version 4.0 is released. As of the current version (3.51), Windows NT only runs the Program Manager interface.

*** OS/2 Warp only supports the Win32s subset.

**** By default, Windows NT only supports 16-bit character mode OS/2 applications. An add-on subsystem that runs 16-bit graphical applications is available at a premium.

Windows 95 versus Windows 3.x

Although Windows 3.x relies on a substantial amount of 16-bit code, it really is a protected-mode operating system. This section looks at some of the major differences between Windows 95 and Windows 3.x.

Hardware Compatibility

One of the main project goals for Windows 95 is to be compatible with as much hardware as possible. At the very least, Windows 95 needs to support the same types of hardware Windows 3.x runs on. Windows 95 supports a wide range of hardware—everything from clone 486s to high-end brand-name Pentium systems.

Memory Requirements

Both Windows 3.x and Windows 95 technically can run on 4 MB 386DX systems, but 8 MB is a truer minimum, especially since some applications require up to 8 MB just to load.

User Interface

The user interfaces in Windows 95 and Windows 3.x differ vastly. Microsoft deemed the Windows 3.1 user interface (the split Program Manager/File Manager combination) too difficult for new users to learn, and embarked on a lengthy usability study. The results of that study are implemented as the Windows 95 user interface.

The most welcome new addition in the Windows 95 user interface is the capability to put programs and document objects directly on the desktop. Windows 3.*x* requires you to place all icons in groups within the main Program Manager window.

Windows 95 also includes *property sheets*—tabbed dialog boxes that enable easy customization of object properties. Although really just a glorified version of Windows 3.*x*'s PIFs (program information files), directly accessing properties is much easier than using a PIF editor to load them.

Multitasking

Because Windows 95 supports preemptive multitasking, it is a superior multitasker to Windows 3.*x*. However, because most applications used on Windows 95 are Win16, you might still find yourself multitasking cooperatively more often than not.

Win16Mutex also bottlenecks multitasking. Because all Win32 threads that call non-reentrant code are blocked on Win16Mutex, some Win32 applications might stop while waiting for the Win16Mutex semaphore flag to be raised.

Windows 95 versus Windows NT

Amazingly enough, Windows 95's biggest challenge might come from its high-end counterpart, Windows NT. Windows NT has slimmed down with each release, and now is considered one of the finest network operating systems available. This section shows how Windows 95 compares to Windows NT.

Hardware Compatibility

Although Windows 95 runs happily on clone and older hardware, Windows NT is not so gracious. Most installation problems in Windows NT stem from low-quality hardware. Windows NT always benefits from running on quality equipment.

Memory Requirements

The bare minimum for Windows 95 is 4 MB (8 MB recommended), whereas Windows NT needs 12 MB to start up (16 MB recommended). Windows NT's higher memory requirements owe primarily to the services that it provides—such as integrated networking, OS/2 support, and a client/server design.

User Interface

Windows NT uses a minimally enhanced version of the Program Manager interface from Windows 3.1. Although version 3.51 includes the Windows 95 controls (for items such as toolbar buttons and tabbed dialog boxes), Windows NT lacks object technologies on the desktop. Icons still must reside in program groups.

Multitasking

Windows NT probably offers the strongest multitasking platform today. Although Windows NT places all Win16 applications into a single virtual machine (similar to Windows 95) by default, it enables Win16 applications to run in separate virtual machines, thereby providing crash protection and preemptive multitasking. Because Windows NT does not use Win16 code (it emulates a Win16 environment using a technique dubbed WOW—Win32 on Windows) you don't have to worry about the Win16Mutex semaphore. As with Windows 95, Windows NT also preemptively multitasks MS-DOS and Win32 applications.

Backward Compatibility

Windows NT is the least compatible operating system of the bunch. Because it is a secure operating system, it does not allow applications to access hardware directly, which causes certain MS-DOS and Win16 applications to fail.

Windows NT does not include Win16 code to run Win16 applications—it uses the WOW environment. If an ill-behaved application tries to access a Windows 3.x data structure (such as USER or GDI), it fails, because those structures do not exist in Windows NT. Windows NT also does not support applications that use VxDs.

One significant benefit of the WOW environment is resource handling. WOW effectively removes all arbitrary limits on resources, making Windows NT a very strong platform for Win16 applications.

Windows 95 versus OS/2

IBM's OS/2 operating system is an extremely strong contender in the operating systems market. IBM is not shy about comparing OS/2 and Windows 95. OS/2 and Windows 95 share similar capabilities, but under the hood you can find subtle differences.

Hardware Compatibility

OS/2, like Windows NT, benefits from quality hardware. Unfortunately, OS/2 sometimes lacks hardware drivers for more obscure equipment. Windows 95 runs on a wider variety of hardware than does OS/2.

Memory Requirements

Both OS/2 and Windows 95 technically can fit in a 4 MB environment. After you start applications, however, the system becomes less comfortable. Both IBM and Microsoft recommend 8 MB as more practical—the extra 4 MB allows more memory pages to reside in physical memory, so they don't have to be paged out to the swap file.

User Interface

OS/2's user interface is known as the Workplace Shell. The Workplace Shell is completely object-oriented, supporting features such as subclassing objects and *inheritance* (the capability for a child folder to inherit settings from its parent folder).

The Workplace Shell supports file tracking for shadows (the equivalent of Windows 95's shortcuts). If you create a shadow that points to c:\os2\bonus.exe, renaming the physical file does not cause the shadow to break. Rather, the shadow automatically points to the new file name or location.

In contrast, Windows 95's shortcuts are much more fragile. When you rename a file, Windows 95 can search for the new file name when you execute the shortcut. However, if you moved the file to another drive, the shortcut can no longer find it.

The Windows 95 user interface looks much more appealing than the default Workplace Shell. The Windows 95 user interface also includes small tips within the system that help new users become more familiar with the shell. OS/2 does not provide that comfort. OS/2 expects new users to complete a short tutorial that helps them migrate from Windows 3.*x* to OS/2.

Multitasking

As with Windows NT, OS/2 can run Win16 applications cooperatively in a common virtual machine or preemptively in separate virtual machines. Like the other operating systems mentioned herein, OS/2 preemptively multitasks MS-DOS and native OS/2 applications. For multitasking Win16 applications, OS/2 comes out ahead, because it doesn't have a Win16Mutex hindering smooth multitasking.

Backward Compatibility

As with Windows 95, OS/2 has excellent support for MS-DOS and Win16 applications. Rather than use Win16 data structures (like Windows 95) or emulate the Win16 environment (like Windows NT), OS/2 uses actual Windows code to support Win16 applications. To load a Win16 application, OS/2 loads a virtual DOS machine, and Windows 3.1 inside that virtual machine, to ensure relatively clean backward compatibility, because applications then actually run on Windows 3.1. OS/2, however, does not support VxDs.

Because OS/2 uses Windows 3.1 to support Win16 applications, the resource limits are still in the system. Windows 95 comes out ahead with its expanded resource heaps.

Overview of Comparison

Windows 95 gives you the best of the old intermingled with advanced new features. Although Windows 95 has some weaknesses (especially compared to Windows NT), it does provide an excellent mix of compatibility and stability, especially well-suited to desktop computers.

Selecting and Upgrading Hardware

A major issue for new and prospective Windows 95 users alike is whether to update current systems to optimize those systems for Windows 95. Although Windows 95 provides performance improvements over Windows 3.*x*, Windows 95 still can require more of your hardware to get the best possible performance. Or, you might want to upgrade your hardware now as long as you're updating your operating system.

This chapter explains some of the hardware issues related to choosing a new system or upgrading an existing system to make the most of Windows 95. Rather than provide tips on specific manufacturers and models, however, the chapter focuses on more generic topics to help you decide whether to upgrade or replace the system or some of its components, add memory, and so on based on the strengths and peculiarities of Windows 95. The chapter covers the following topics:

◆ Choosing a new system for Windows 95

◆ Upgrading your system

◆ Adding more memory

◆ Adding more disk space

◆ Adding and replacing peripherals

Although buying a new system based on the latest technology is one of the easiest options for giving yourself more computing horsepower, upgrading also is a good alternative. If you do decide to buy a new system for Windows 95, you need to consider a number of factors. The following section offers some tips on buying a new system to use with Windows 95.

Choosing a New System for Windows 95

Choosing a new system for Windows 95 generally amounts to simply choosing the best system you can afford, but you should keep in mind a few special points. Instead of just buying the latest, fastest system you can afford with lots of RAM and hard disk space, you need to consider some of the overall considerations as well as individual components. First, should you buy a desktop or a notebook computer?

Desktop versus Portable Computers

Your first consideration should be whether you need a desktop computer or a portable computer. Until only recently, the answer to that question was more likely to be desktop rather than notebook, simply because of the limitations inherent in the available notebooks. Today, however, notebook computers offer all the power and speed of desktop systems and most of the expandability. And in many ways, notebook computers' portability makes them more versatile.

Pentium notebooks have been available for some time, complete with local bus video, large hard disks, and even high-resolution, 800×600 active-matrix displays. Many notebooks now include built-in 16-bit sound, and some include built-in CD-ROM drives or printers. As a result of greatly increased availability of PCMCIA devices, you can add SCSI adapters, special-purpose video, and other types of devices previously available only on desktop systems. Nearly all notebook computers support external video and keyboards, enabling you to use them much like desktop systems.

 Tip   Many people who have never used a notebook computer before expect the keyboard to be smaller and more difficult to use than a typical desktop keyboard. The keyboard actually is the same size, and as a frequent notebook user, I prefer the notebook keyboard over a desktop keyboard because of the reduced key travel and force required to enter a keystroke.

The same considerations apply to notebooks for CPU, RAM, disk speed, and some other components as to desktop systems. And, only you can decide whether the advantages a notebook system offers for portability outweighs its higher cost. If you do decide a notebook is for you, keep the following issues in mind when you evaluate your options:

◆ **Cash flow.** If you decide to borrow the money to buy your computer, remember that adding quite a bit more in overall cost to have an adequate system might only affect your monthly payment by $10 or $20. This is important for a notebook, which costs much more to upgrade after the purchase than if you had purchased the upgraded components with the system originally. Windows 95 is very demanding of your PC's hardware, so spending a little more up front generally is worthwhile to ensure the computer has the resources to run Windows 95 well.

◆ **CPU.** Unlike a desktop system, replacing the CPU if you decide to upgrade often proves inconvenient. Some manufacturers require that you send the computer to a registered repair facility to have the upgrade performed (you pay). Others offer an upgrade of the base unit, which essentially means that you use the display, hard disk, RAM, and battery pack (and possibly a few other removable components) from your system in a new, CPU/keyboard unit. You keep the old unit, which, unless you can find a buyer, will serve little purpose other than as a very expensive doorstop or paperweight. If a 486 notebook will serve you well for the next few years, buy one. If you think you'll need Pentium performance in six months, by the Pentium notebook now rather than hope to upgrade the CPU later.

◆ **Disk space.** Buying a replacement hard disk for a notebook computer generally is much more expensive than buying a hard disk for a desktop computer. An add-on 340 MB disk drive for a notebook, for example, can cost as much as a 1 GB drive for a desktop system. Spend as much as you can up front for an adequate hard disk. See the section "Adding More Disk Space" later in this chapter for a recommendation of disk size.

◆ **Disk compression.** Remember that Windows 95 supports DriveSpace, which enables you to compress the hard disk to get more usable space from it. You can compress a 340 MB drive to get roughly 700 MB of disk space and still leave 100 MB available uncompressed to accommodate Windows 95.

◆ **RAM.** Adding RAM to a notebook is more expensive than adding RAM to a desktop system, although installing the memory typically is much easier. Consider 8 MB to be the minimum for Windows 95 on any type of system. If you can afford the additional expense, buy a system with 16 MB of RAM.

◆ **PCMCIA slots.** Verify that Windows 95 directly supports the PCMCIA controller in the notebook. That way, you can use Windows 95's 32-bit protected-mode PCMCIA drivers for complete Plug and Play capability and best performance.

◆ **Video performance.** To provide the best video performance of Windows 95, the notebook should include local bus video.

If you need more than about 800 MB of disk space, or have special video requirements, such as very high resolution or fastest possible speed, your best option might be a desktop computer. If you need a general-purpose computer, however, and you are willing to spend the extra money for the added benefit and flexibility of having a portable system, a notebook is very good option.

Deciding on a CPU

Because Windows 95 runs only on Intel's x86/Pentium family of processors, your choices for systems are somewhat limited. Even so, you still have many different processors and speeds from which to choose.

Although Microsoft advertises that you can run Windows 95 on 386-based systems, performance is only adequate at best for general-purpose computing. Even if you want to buy a 386, however, you'll discover it difficult to find 386 systems still for sale. The entry-level system today is generally a system that contains a 486DX2 running at 50 MHz or 66 MHz.

Choosing a CPU can be difficult and confusing, however, because of the wide variety of processor speeds. Figure 12.1 provides a benchmark comparison of various processors at various speeds to offer a comparison of CPUs at different clock speeds.

Figure 12.1

A CPU benchmark comparison.

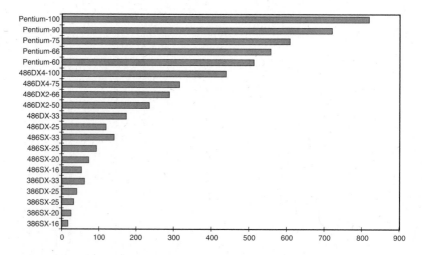

As you can see in figure 12.1, processor type is only part of the performance question. The CPU clock speed that you choose also is important. Consider a 486DX2-50 the practical minimum for Windows 95. Consider a 75 MHz Pentium to be the minimum system for high-performance workstations.

RAM

The minimum amount of RAM you need to run Windows 95 effectively depends on your system's processor speed, swap file size, and the applications you run. Although Windows 95 can run on systems with 4 MB of RAM, you should consider 8 MB to be the minimum for any new system. For high-performance workstations, 16 MB or more should be the minimum.

For more information on swap files and optimizing physical memory, refer to Chapter 14, "Optimizing Physical and Virtual Memory."

Disk Space

Windows 95 requires a considerable amount of disk space, both for the Windows 95 files and for the swap file. As well, today's applications suffer from file bloat, so you should plan for as large a disk as you can reasonably afford. If you use only a few applications, 300 MB or so of disk space is adequate. The cost per megabyte drops significantly as disk drive capacity increases, so you should consider spending the extra money to have a 1 GB drive to provide plenty of room for Windows 95, applications, and documents, and still leave room for growth. For more information on getting the most out of your system's hard disk, refer to Chapter 15, "Optimizing Data Storage."

CD-ROM

Even if you choose not to install a sound card in your new system and don't plan to run any multimedia applications, you should strongly consider a CD-ROM drive for your new system. CDs are rapidly becoming the media of choice for application distribution, and very often the CD version of an application includes additional files and features not offered with the disk-based product. The CD version of Windows 95, for example, includes a number of additional utilities, applications, and administration tools not available with the disk version.

When you shop for a CD-ROM drive, opt for a triple-speed or quad-speed drive. Also, make sure that the drive supports multisession photo-CD, which enables you to work with photo-CDs on the system. For tips on buying and using audio and CD-ROM components, refer to Chapter 23, "Working with Multimedia Audio and CD-ROM."

Sound

If you plan to run multimedia applications, you need a sound card. If you use your system for general applications that don't require sound, however, a sound card is more of a luxury. But, for a minimal cost, adding a sound card offers the capability to play audio CDs (assuming the system includes a CD-ROM drive) and to play and edit various types of audio files.

Upgrading Your System

If your computer is only a few years old, or you have made a sizable investment in peripherals, additional RAM, and other components, buying a new system to run Windows 95 probably does not appeal much to you. Buying a new system is just one option; the other option is to upgrade your existing system. Sometimes upgrading might mean simply adding more RAM, or it might mean replacing the motherboard and other components.

Upgrading the CPU

One of the easiest ways to upgrade your system is to replace the CPU. How you accomplish the upgrade depends on the type of system you have. Reasonably inexpensive CPU replacements are available to convert 386-based systems to 486-based CPUs. These CPU upgrade modules replace the existing 386 in its original socket.

Many 486-based systems include OverDrive sockets on the motherboard that accommodate a new CPU. Depending on your system, you can replace your 486 CPU with a faster 486 CPU, such as replacing a 33 MHz CPU with a 66 MHz CPU, or you can replace the 486 CPU with a Pentium CPU. Upgrading the CPU always means removing the existing CPU. The process is really very simple, and even the average user with no experience working inside a PC can accomplish the task. The only real drawback to replacing your CPU is that you get no trade-in program—you just have a CPU that you can't use.

 Tip For tips and complete instructions on upgrading and repairing your PC, read *Keeping Your PC Alive, Special Edition*, from New Riders Publishing.

If you do upgrade the CPU in your computer, consider adding a CPU cooling fan to the CPU. This cooling fan mounts on top of the CPU and draws heat away from it, potentially increasing the life of the chip and improving the performance of the PC. Before you buy the cooling fan, however, make sure it fits on and works with the upgrade CPU you buy.

Changing Motherboards

If your hard disk still has an adequate amount of free space on it and most of your other system components are adequate for Windows 95, you should consider replacing your motherboard. This is a good option for upgrading a 386 system to a fast 486 or Pentium system. Although replacing a motherboard is not by any means as simple as replacing a CPU, it nevertheless is a job that most users can perform with little effort, frustration, and danger.

When you shop for a motherboard, you should understand that two motherboards from different manufacturers with the same type and speed of CPU can perform very differently. The quality of the support components on the motherboard and the design of the board itself have a major impact on its performance. One of the best lines of motherboards available is the Intel line, but unfortunately, Intel sells them only to VARs (value-added resellers)—you can't buy one on your own. Price is often an indication of quality, but just because a motherboard is more expensive than the next isn't a sure indication of quality or performance.

If you do replace your system's motherboard, remember that you might want to use the memory from your current motherboard on the new one. Check the form factor (number of pins and package type) and speed of the memory to determine if you can use it on the new motherboard.

Adding More Memory

Consider 8 MB to be the minimum amount of RAM for Windows 95. When you plan to add memory to the system, consider how the existing RAM will be affected. Will you have to replace some of your PC's memory with greater-capacity modules? Or can you add new modules to empty slots? Also make sure that the new memory is the same speed as the original memory.

Adding More Disk Space

Windows 95 itself can consume as much as 80 MB of disk space if you install all the optional components, so you might need to add more disk space to your PC. Although replacing a hard disk is an option, it's usually a good option only if your existing drive is an old MFM drive. If your PC contains an IDE, ESDI, or SCSI drive, you can simply add another drive of the same type—you don't need to replace the existing drive unless your PC's case simply has no room for another drive. But, your case might have an available bay even if you don't think it does. If your PC uses a tower-style case, it might contain an available drive bay near the top of the case above the floppy drives. Or, if the system contains 3.5 and 5.25 floppy drives, you can replace the two drives with a single dual-drive unit, creating a bay for a new hard disk.

If you add a second IDE drive to the system, be aware that you have to configure one drive as the master drive and the other as the slave drive. You do this by changing jumpers on the drive. Check the documentation for both drives to determine how to set the jumpers on each drive.

When you add a second SCSI drive to the system, be aware that each SCSI device has a unique drive ID, which you configure by setting jumpers on the device. If your unit contains a SCSI disk only, it will be device 0. Set the new hard disk to device 1. If your system contains a SCSI CD-ROM drive and a SCSI hard disk, leave the existing drive at device 0, set the new disk drive to device 1, and set the CD-ROM drive to device 2 (or higher).

Tip You can install a SCSI drive in a system with an existing IDE controller without any problems. If you boot the system from the existing IDE drive, set the ID of the SCSI hard disk to 1. To boot from the SCSI drive, set the ID to 0. Because the SCSI drive's BIOS loads before the system initializes the IDE drive, the system boots from the SCSI drive. The IDE drive then receives the next available drive letter (probably D).

For more information on installing new hard disks, refer to *Keeping Your PC Alive, Special Edition* from New Riders Publishing.

Upgrading Video

If your system is older than three or four years, or contains a standard VGA video adapter, strongly consider replacing the video adapter with a new accelerated video adapter. Many vendors offer devices that use special video coprocessor chips to handle graphics operations and dramatically improve video performance. With many types of applications, improving video performance improves application performance. A CAD application, such as AutoCAD for Windows, for example, can actually realize a tenfold performance gain if you add an accelerated video adapter to the system. Most important, Windows 95 shows a significant performance improvement if you use a high-speed graphics adapter.

The type of video adapter you ultimately choose depends on the type of bus your system contains. If you have a standard ISA bus, many graphics adapters based on the S3, Weitek, and other graphics chips can dramatically improve video performance. If your system contains a VESA or PCI local bus, buy a VESA or PCI local bus video card that contains a graphics coprocessor.

Working with the Registry and Ini Files

The Registry is the central information storage for all the data Windows 95 and Windows 95 applications need. It contains all hardware, software, and operating system configuration information, including all information about any Plug and Play devices ever attached to the computer, OLE information for the system and all applications that support embedding and drag-and-drop, network configuration and bindings, and individual user profiles.

This chapter describes the Windows 95 Registry, and how Windows 95 uses Ini files, by covering the following topics:

- ◆ A history of the Registry

- ◆ Registry features

- ◆ Differences between the Windows 95 Registry and those of Windows 3.1 and Windows NT

- ◆ Ini files in Windows 95

- ◆ Registry keys and contents

◆ Accessing a remote Registry

◆ Corrupted or unusable Registry files

The Windows 95 Registry is designed to take the place of Windows 3.1 Ini files as well as the Windows 3.1 registry. To support older 3.1 applications, however, Windows 95 must read information placed in Ini files and maintain some information in those files. The Registry exists across a number of files (User.dat, System.dat, and possibly Config.pol), but can be viewed as a single entity using the Registry Editor (Regedit.exe).

You can use software applications, such as Control Panel applets, to modify the Registry. You also can use the Windows 95 Registry Editor to manually modify the Registry. You shouldn't attempt the latter, however, unless you know exactly what you're doing.

 Stop   The Registry contains dynamic information that the hardware, the operating system, and applications that run in Windows 95 all use. Incorrectly modifying this information can cause hardware, applications, and Windows 95 to run improperly or fail to run at all. Don't modify the Registry unless absolutely necessary, and always make a backup before you make any changes.

PC software and the people who use it have become more sophisticated over the years. Applications interact with each other in ways they never did before, and the Windows operating system keeps increasing the features it provides to applications. The Windows 95 Registry grew over time in response to the increasing interaction between applications and between applications and the operating system.

History of the Registry

Before Windows 3.1, there was no system registry. System.ini stored system configuration information and Win.ini stored application configuration information. This led to the following major problems:

◆ Difficulty finding and changing application configuration information in Win.ini. Information in the Ini files is not hierarchical and is arranged arbitrarily. Editing Win.ini manually can be difficult, dangerous, and necessary much too frequently.

◆ Ini files are limited in size to 64 KB, far too small for the Win.ini file, which can contain information for any number of applications. Further confounding matters, information in the Win.ini rarely is removed because most applications currently don't come with a deinstallation utility.

Windows 3.0 solved these problems to some extent by providing applications the capability to create and maintain their own Ini files, which unfortunately created new problems:

◆ Most applications create one or more Ini files when you install them, and these are not deleted automatically after the application is removed. Determining which Ini files go with which application often proves quite difficult. Obsolete Ini code unnecessarily clutters the Windows directory and usurps disk space.

◆ Applications that rely on their own Ini files to maintain configuration information cannot share information. Applications that use DDE (Dynamic Data Exchange) or OLE (Object Linking and Embedding) must place information such as the location of OLE servers in a globally accessible area (an OLE server is an Exe or Dll file that supports the OLE functions for a particular application).

Windows 3.1

The Windows 3.1 Registry was created to solve these problems, and its basic structure is similar to the Windows NT and Windows 95 registries. It's a hierarchy similar to the file system: registry keys are analogous to directories, registry values are analogous to files, and registry data is analogous to the information inside a file. Each key can contain other keys and a single value.

Registry keys are identified much like file directories are. For instance, there is a Network key inside the Enum key which is inside the HKEY_LOCAL_MACHINE root key which is in the registry of My Computer. The path to the Network key is "My Computer\HKEY_LOCAL_MACHINE\Enum\Network".

Windows 3.1's registry's main function was to provide a single place in which the system and applications could find shared information, such as DDE commands and OLE server locations.

Windows NT

Windows NT expanded the idea of the registry, going a long way toward cleaning up the morass of Ini, Config.sys, and Autoexec.bat files. NT's Registry contains all the information that used to be in the Ini, Config, and Autoexec files. The NT Registry also contains Program Manager information that Windows 3.1 stored in Grp files. The NT Registry's hierarchical structure is more complex and robust than the Windows 3.1 registry, and provides backward compatibility via the HKEY_CLASSES_ROOT tree, described later in this chapter in the section "Registry Keys and Contents."

Windows 95

Windows 95's Registry is both more and less than the NT Registry. In fact, Microsoft says it is a completely different implementation that supports the same functions—if not all the same keys and features. Here are the two primary differences:

◆ The Windows 95 Registry supports Plug and Play, whereas the NT Registry does not.

◆ The NT Registry supports security features (NT has robust security built-in to the operating system), whereas the Windows 95 Registry does not.

Examining the Different Registries

Figure 13.1 shows a view of the Windows 95 Registry using the Registry Editor (located in the directory in which Windows 95 is installed). It shows the six root keys and the values in the HKEY_LOCAL_MACHINE key. The values displayed show the three data types that the Registry can hold: a string, a binary value (value #1), and a DWORD (value #2).

Figure 13.1

The Windows 95 Registry.

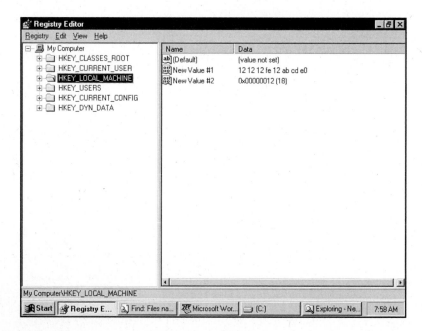

The Windows 95 Registry has a number of features that make it easy to locate, change, and track information used by applications and the system. It also provides a place for the new features in the operating system to access the information they need. One of the ways applications take advantage of those new features is by accessing information in the Registry. Those features are

◆ A hierarchy of keys (not unlike directories in the file system) that makes viewing and manipulating Registry information easier and safer than modifying information in Ini files

◆ Single storage location for DDE and OLE information

◆ Storage for Plug and Play information; information about every device ever plugged into the PC

◆ Storage for all system and application configuration information

◆ Support for multiple and roving users

◆ Registry examination and configuration over a network

◆ Registry information recoverable after system failures

◆ Multiple values and data types for each key

◆ Registry Editor, an application for viewing and modifying registry entries

◆ Autoexec.bat, Config.sys, and Ini files no longer necessary (although still supported for backward compatibility)

◆ Compatibility with Ini files for older 16-bit applications

Note Windows 95 uses the Registry, Io.sys, and other mechanisms to load drivers and set defaults, but still needs Autoexec.bat and Config.sys to load TSRs and real-mode drivers.

Some of these features are available in the Windows 3.1 or Windows NT Registry files, and some are unique to the Windows 95 Registry. The following is a look at what distinguishes the Windows 95 Registry from the other registries.

Windows 95 Registry versus Windows 3.1 Registry

Although different implementations, the Windows 3.1 registry is a subset of the Windows 95 Registry. The Windows 3.1 registry has only one root key, HKEY_CLASSES_ROOT. You can associate a single string data value with each subkey.

The Windows 3.1 registry is not intended to replace Ini files. Windows 3.1 expects to find information in the Win.ini and System.ini files, and nothing prevents applications from placing information in the Win.ini and other Ini files.

Whereas Windows 3.1 has only the one root key, the Windows 95 Registry has six root keys: HKEY_CLASSES_ROOT, HKEY_CURRENT_USER, HKEY_LOCAL_MACHINE, HKEY_USERS, HKEY_CURRENT_CONFIG, and HKEY_DYN_DATA. The HKEY_CLASSES_ROOT hierarchy in Windows 95 is a superset of the entire Windows 3.1 registry for backward compatibility.

Registry keys work the same in Windows 3.1 as in Windows 95. A key is identified as a string of characters. Windows 3.1 keys can have only one value associated with them.

Windows 95 allows each key to have many data values of string, binary, or DWORD types (or all three). Registry keys in Windows 3.1 have only one unnamed value. To maintain compatibility with the Windows 3.1 registry, each key in the Windows 95 registry contains a single unnamed string value called "(Default)," which can, but doesn't have to, have a value. The value for this key matches the single value of the corresponding key in the Windows 3.1 registry.

The entire Windows 3.1 registry is contained in the Reg.dat file, in the Windows directory. You can use the Windows 3.1 Regedit.exe application to view and modify the Windows 3.1 registry. The Windows 95 Registry is contained in the System.dat and User.dat files, and you use the Windows 95 Registry Editor to view and modify it.

Windows 3.1 requires Ini files for configuration information. Windows 95 uses Ini files for old 16-bit applications that do not use the Registry, as well as for 32-bit applications that want to go that route, although using the Registry is always preferable.

Windows 95 Registry versus Windows NT Registry

The Windows 95 Registry and the Windows NT Registry also are different implementations that provide overlapping functionality in the areas of OLE, DDE, and system files (taking over the functions of Autoexec.bat, Config.sys, and Ini files). The NT Registry provides keys for security in HKEY_LOCAL_MACHINE\Security and HKEY_LOCAL_MACHINE\SAM. The Windows 95 Registry has no integrated support for security, but unlike the NT Registry it does support Plug and Play in the HKEY_LOCAL_MACHINE\ENUM branch.

The NT Registry supports more data types than does the Windows 95 Registry. The Windows 95 Registry can only contain DWORD, binary, and string values. These data types are described later in the chapter in the section "Registry Data." The data types NT supports are summarized in the following list:

◆ **REG_BINARY.** Binary data (also supported in Windows 95).

◆ **REG_DWORD.** 32-bit number (also supported in Windows 95).

◆ **REG_DWORD_LITTLE_ENDIAN.** Little-endian format DWORD that ensures the most significant byte of a word is in the high-order byte.

◆ **REG_DWORD_BIG_ENDIAN.** Big-endian format DWORD that ensures the most significant byte of a word is in the low-order byte.

◆ **REG_EXPAND_SZ.** Unicode or ANSI string that contains unexpanded references to environment variables (such as "%PATH%").

◆ **REG_LINK.** Unicode symbolic link.

◆ **REG_MULTI_SZ.** Array of null-terminated strings, terminated by two null characters.

◆ **REG_NONE.** Indication that the value is not defined.

◆ **REG_RESOURCE_LIST.** List of device driver resources.

◆ **REG_SZ.** A null-terminated string (also supported in Windows 95).

Note The Windows NT Registry internally stores all strings as Unicode strings, even if ANSI functions are used to set and retrieve the text.

The NT Registry also maintains the HKEY_CLASSES_ROOT root key in which DDE and OLE information is kept, which provides compatibility with the Windows 3.1 and Windows 95 registries. The NT Registry does not support Windows 95's HKEY_CURRENT_CONFIG and HKEY_DYN_DATA root keys.

Registry and Ini Files in Windows 95

One of the necessarily unfortunate outcomes of creating Windows 95 is the awkward way in which Registry and Ini files work together. Windows 95 represents a transition away from old-style initialization files and their problems to a better, more robust way of maintaining system configuration information. This section describes how the old and new methods work together.

The Purpose of Ini and Startup Files in Windows 95

If the Registry contains all configuration, initialization, and startup information, Ini and startup (Autoexec.bat and Config.sys) files are no longer necessary, right? Well, true, technically—Windows 95 doesn't *need* those files, although it can use them if they're present. If you never install DOS, for instance, Windows 95 never needs startup files. It can access the Registry for all the information it needs about device drivers, the last network drive, and so on. The same goes for the Ini files. If they don't exist, Windows 95 doesn't mind just searching the Registry for whatever information the Ini files otherwise would contain, such as VxDs, mouse preferences, and so on.

Practically speaking, however, Ini and startup files are going to be around for awhile. Older 16-bit applications (many of which many people will use for many years yet) require Win.ini, Winfile.ini, and System.ini. Many 16-bit applications create their own Ini files, which Windows 95 cannot directly translate into registry entries. Most users also probably will continue to want DOS installed on their Windows 95 systems, which requires Autoexec.bat and Config.sys files.

If you install Windows 95 over an existing Windows 3.1 system, the installation program copies information from Control.ini, Progman.ini, System.ini, Win.ini, and other Ini files to the Registry (the section "Ini Information in the Registry" later in this chapter describes the actual Ini file entries that are copied to the Registry).

Some entries are not copied to the Registry so that the Ini files can remain backward compatible with older 16-bit applications. In this case Windows 95 needs the Ini files so that those older applications can run properly. To manipulate all these entries, you can use graphical tools in Windows 95, such as Control Panel applets, to change the entries in the Ini files without resorting to manual editing.

Some Ini settings also are not copied to the Registry by the Windows 95 installation procedure and cannot be modified using graphical tools (except for the Registry Editor). Windows 95 needs these entries to run some applications properly, but you should never need to modify the entries directly.

Ideally, all applications are 32-bit applications, no one runs DOS because all Windows applications run perfectly, every Windows 95 installation is a clean installation rather than an upgrade, and you need never worry about any Ini or startup files. Until that utopian day, however, anyone who maintains configuration information needs to keep the old configuration files in mind.

Files that Make Up the Registry

The Registry is a single data store existing across a number of files that the system and applications can access and use to modify configuration information. The three file types that store all Registry information are System.dat, User.dat, and policy (Pol)

files. System.dat is the only file of that name on each machine. User.dat occurs at least once on each machine and possibly more. A given machine can have zero, one, or more policy files.

Each time Windows 95 shuts down, it makes a copy of System.dat and User.dat in the Windows directory, and all other User.dat files in other directories. These files are named System.da0 and User.da0. You can rename and reuse them if the Registry becomes corrupted. The next three sections describe these files.

System.dat

When you boot Windows 95, it locates and accesses System.dat before any other part of the Registry. System.dat belongs in the main Windows 95 directory (C:\Windows on most systems) and contains all hardware-specific configuration information for the machine on which it resides.

User.dat

You generally find User.dat files in the main Windows 95 directory. Windows 95 reads User.dat right after it reads System.dat. Other User.dat files can reside in the individual profile directories for each user who can log on to a machine. John Doe's User.dat, for example, might be in directory C:\Windows\Profiles\Jdoe. These Dat files contain user-specific information, such as passwords and individual application preferences.

The User.dat files in the profile directories load after the User.dat in the Windows directory. If there are conflicts between these two files, the conflicting information in User.dat from the profile directives takes precedence.

The main User.dat file in the Windows directory contains system configuration information, such as Control Panel settings, application settings, Start menu (Program Manager) groups, desktop files, and locations of postoffice files (such as the personal address book and personal information storage files). The User.dat in the profile directories contains much the same information and takes precedence over information in the User.dat from the Windows directory. Hence, entirely different configurations can exist for multiple people on a single machine, including e-mail, Control Panel settings, and desktop file locations.

Stop The Registry remembers the location on the screen of desktop files for each user, but keeps only one list of the files (or link files) on the desktop. If one user has a copy of Myfile.lnk in the upper right corner of the desktop and another user has the same file in the middle of the screen, deleting the file from either account removes it from both. This is a limitation of Windows 95 security. If anybody deletes a file, it's gone (into the Recycle Bin, at least). Windows 95 doesn't distinguish between who owns the file and who deletes it.

Config.pol

Config.pol files are system policy files that override some information in the Registry. These files are used to force machines on a network to have the same configuration, or to enable roving users to keep their same configuration when they log on to different machines on the network.

Config.pol files are created and modified using the System Policy Editor, which comes with the Windows 95 Resource Kit. Use of the System Policy Editor and how to maintain policy files is described in the Resource Kit documentation.

Registry Data

The Registry contains three types of objects: keys, values, and data. The Registry hierarchy that uses this information resembles the file system with which most people are familiar. Keys are analogous to directories, values are analogous to files, and data is analogous to the information within a file.

Keys

Keys can contain one or more other keys and values. Each key and value must have a unique name within a key or subkey. As with the Windows 95 file system, keys are case-aware but not case-sensitive. A key name can contain any visible characters, including spaces and symbols, except for the backslash (\), because it delimits hierarchy paths in the Registry, such as paths in the file system.

Keys and subkeys contain at least one value with the special name "(Default)," for backward compatibility with the Windows 3.1 registry and old 16-bit applications. The (Default) value might not contain any data, in which case the data field reads (value not set).

Figure 13.2 uses the Registry Editor to display nested registry keys in the left pane, the written registry path in the status bar at the bottom of the window, and the default, unused value for the key in the right pane.

The root key HKEY_CLASSES_ROOT and the subkey HKEY LOCAL MACHINE\ SOFTWARE\Classes contain a superset of the information in the Windows 3.1 registry (they actually point to the same registry data). Because the Windows 3.1 registry can have only one value per key, the Windows 95 default value is the value that would be in the Windows 3.1 registry for that key, so 16-bit applications look to the default value to find DDE and OLE information. Default values are rarely used in other root keys.

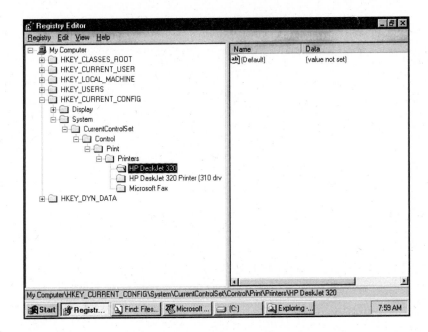

Figure 13.2
*The Windows 95
Registry with a
path displayed.*

Stop Don't modify the default value under these keys unless you know exactly what you're doing. These values are placed there by software applications and the operating system, usually when they are first installed. If this information becomes corrupted, the only way to fix it is to reinstall the application or operating system, or recover old registry files.

Values

The Registry can represent three types of data: strings, binary information, and DWORD values. The default value is always a string, although it appears as "(value not set)" until it contains data. If data is removed from the default value (by using the Registry Editor, for instance), the data appears as a null string ("") rather than "(value not set)." In other words, "(value not set)" only appears in the registry for values that have never had data entered into them.

Viewing and editing registry values is explained in the section "Registry Editor" later in this chapter.

Data

Registry data is always contained in a value. A piece of data cannot be larger than 64 KB.

◆ **String.** A *string* is a variable length null-terminated set of characters—words, phrases, path names, or any other text. The value of a string appears under the data heading of the Registry Editor surrounded by double quotes.

◆ **Binary.** A *binary* value is a variable-length set of hexadecimal digits (0–9 and A–F). Hexadecimal information appears under the data heading of the Registry Editor. Each byte is represented by two hexadecimal digits.

◆ **DWORD.** A *DWORD,* or double word, is a single 32-bit value (8 hexadecimal digits). DWORDs appear under the data heading of the Registry as an 8-digit hexadecimal number. For instance, the hexadecimal number 13 (decimal 19) is represented as 0x00000013(18).

Ini Information in the Registry

If you install Windows 95 over a previous version of Windows, selected information in System.ini and Win.ini moves to the Registry. The following tables describe the sections and entries that migrate from the Ini files to the Registry, where the information resides in the Registry, and which Ini entries are still reflected in the Windows 95 user interface. Windows 95 allows applications to access and modify information in Ini files, but it does not necessarily use that information.

Note The locations of these entries are based on the locations in a prerelease version of Windows 95, but Microsoft might have changed some locations prior to the official release and after this book has been published.

Table 13.1 lists the sections and entries of the Win.ini file that migrate to the Registry during installation. All subkeys are located in the Registry's HKEY_CURRENT_USER root key.

TABLE 13.1
Win.ini Entries Migrated to the Windows 95 Registry

Section	Entry	Subkey of HKEY_CURRENT_USER
[desktop]	GridGranularity	\Control Panel\Desktop
	Pattern	\Control Panel\Desktop
	TileWallpaper	\Control Panel\Desktop

Section	Entry	Subkey of HKEY_CURRENT_USER
[Windows]	ScreenSaveActive	\Control Panel\Desktop
	ScreenSaveTimeout	\Control Panel\Desktop
[sounds]	*sound event name*	\AppEvents\Schemes\Apps\ .Default*sound event name*\current
[hearts]	name	\Software\Microsoft\Windows\ CurrentVersion\Applets\Hearts

Table 13.2 lists the sections and entries of the System.ini file that migrate to the Registry during installation. All subkeys are located in the HKEY_LOCAL_MACHINE root key. Some of these entries might not appear on some systems, depending on the PC's network configuration. Check the subkey using the Registry Editor to see if they exist on your local machine.

TABLE 13.2
System.ini Files Migrated to the Windows 95 Registry

Section	Entry	Subkey of HKEY_LOCAL_MACHINE
[network]	Comment	System\CurrentControlSet\Services\ Vxd\VNETSUP
	ComputerName	System\CurrentControlSet\Control\ ComputerName\ComputerName
	EnableSharing	No registry entry
	LMAnnounce	System\CurrentControlSet\Services\ Vxd\VNETSUP
	LogonDomain	No registry entry
	LogonValidated	No registry entry
	MaintainServerList	System\CurrentControlSet\Services\ Vxd\VNETSUP
	Reconnect	No registry entry
	Reshare	No registry entry
	Username	Network\Logon
	WorkGroup	System\CurrentControlSet\Services\ Vxd\VNETSUP
[386Enh]	Network	No registry entry
	Transport	Software\Microsoft\Windows\ CurrentVersion\Network\Real Mode Net

Table 13.3 lists the entries that remain in the Ini files for compatibility with older 16-bit applications written to run under Windows 3.1. The UI Support column indicates whether the Windows 95 user interface supports the entry. If not, Windows 95 ignores it.

TABLE 13.3
Ini File Entries Not Migrated to the Windows 95 Registry

File Name	Section	Entry	UI Support
System.ini	[386Enh]	*Device=filename*	N
		AllEMSLocked	**Y**
		AllXMSLocked	**Y**
		AltKeyDelay	**Y**
		AltPasteDelay	**Y**
		DMABufferSize	**Y**
		Display	**Y**
		DOSPromptExitInstructions	**Y**
		KeybdPasswd	N
		Keyboard	**Y**
		KeyPasteCRSkipCount	**Y**
		KeyPasteDelay	**Y**
		KeyPasteSkipCount	**Y**
		KeyPasteTimeout	**Y**
		Local	N
		Local Reboot	N
		MaxDMAPGAddress	**Y**
		MaxPagingFileSize	**Y**
		MinUserDiskSpace	**Y**
		Mouse	**Y**
		MessageBackColor	N
		MessageTextColor	N
		NetAsyncTimeout	N
		NetAsynchFallback	N
		NetDMASize	N

File Name	Section	Entry	UI Support
		Paging	**Y**
		PagingDrive	**Y**
		ScrollFrequency	**Y**
	[boot]	386grabber=*filename*	N
		comm.drv=*filename*	N
		DISPLAY.DRV	**Y**
		drivers=*filename*	N
		fixedfon.fon=*filename*	N
		fonts.fon=*filename*	N
		KEYBOARD.DRV	**Y**
		language.dll=*library-name*	N
		MOUSE.DRV	**Y**
		NETWORK.DRV	**Y**
		oemfonts.font=*filename*	N
		shell=*filename*	N
		SOUND.DRV	**Y**
		system.drv=*filename*	N
		TaskMan.Exe=*filename*	N
	[drivers]	*alias=driver-filename*	N
	[mci]	*Entries written by apps*	N
	[NonWindowsApps]	CommandEnvSize	**Y**
Win.ini	[embedding]	*object*	N
	[fonts]	*font-name*	**Y**
	[FontSubstitute]	*font-name=font-name*	N
	[Intl]	iCountry	**Y**
		iCurrDigits	**Y**
		iCurrency	**Y**
		iDate	**Y**
		iDigits	**Y**
		iLZero	**Y**

continues

TABLE 13.3, CONTINUED
Ini File Entries Not Migrated to the Windows 95 Registry

File Name	Section	Entry	UI Support
		iMeasure	Y
		iNetCurr	Y
		iTime	Y
		iTLZero	Y
		s1159	Y
		s2359	Y
		sCountry	Y
		sCurrency	Y
		sLanguage	Y
		sDecimal	Y
		sList	Y
		sShortDate	Y
		sLongDate	Y
		sThousand	Y
		sTime	Y
	[Mail]	MAPI	N
	[mci extensions]	*extension*	N
	[ports]	*portname*	Y
	[PrinterPorts]	*device*	Y
	[Windows]	CursorBlinkRate	Y
		Device	Y
		DoubleClickHeight	Y
		DoubleClickWidth	Y
		DoubleClickSpeed	Y
		KeyboardDelay	Y
		KeyboardSpeed	Y
		Load and Run	N
		MouseSpeed	Y
		MouseTrails	Y
		SwapMouseButtons	Y

Registry Keys and Contents

This section describes a number of the important keys in the Registry. The Registry contains thousands of keys whose values can change at any time. Applications also can add and change keys and values whenever and wherever they want, but Microsoft has delineated standards for when and how applications should modify the Registry. As a result, a complete list of keys and their possible values isn't possible. This section describes all the root keys, some important subkeys, and some keys that serve as examples of Registry usage. Discussion stays with how keys are set up and affect the registry, and does not describe how to set key values for system or application functions, such as DDE and shell extensions. The best way to view this information is through the Registry Editor.

HKEY_CLASSES_ROOT

The HKEY_CLASSES_ROOT provides backward compatibility with Windows 3.1 for OLE and DDE support. It also contains OLE and DDE information specific to Windows 95, such as shell extension keys and values. In reality, this key acts as a pointer to HKEY_LOCAL_MACHINE\SOFTWARE\Classes. The information underneath these keys is the same. Microsoft made HKEY_CLASSES_ROOT a pointer to HKEY_LOCAL_MACHINE\SOFTWARE\Classes because it makes this common information easier for applications and the operating system to access, and it makes compatibility with Windows 3.1 easier.

Registered Document Types

All the subkeys under HKEY_CLASSES_ROOT refer to document types associated with the applications installed on the system (except for the "*" subkey, which is associated with all application document types). The file extension subkeys point to document description subkeys, which in turn point to class ID subkeys. These trails of keys contain DDE, OLE, shell, and shell extension information, as well as the file locations of the OLE servers that support the document type.

Note This section uses font files for a simple example of registering document types. Other document types vary in complexity, depending on the supporting application.

To locate the DDE, OLE, and shell information about a document, first find the document extension subkey under HKEY_CLASSES_ROOT, ".fon" for instance. The default value for this key is "fonfile". Locate the fonfile subkey under HKEY_CLASSES_ROOT. The default value of this key, "Font file", is the description of the document type. In the case of this document type, there is only one OLE function, which is also a shell extension. Under the "shellex" subkey is the "IconHandler" subkey. The default value shows the OLE class ID (CLSID). Under the HKEY_CLASSES_ROOT\CLSID subkey, locate the subkey with the same number as the font file icon handler subkey. The default value describes which type of OLE handler the subkey is. The InProcServer32 subkey has a default value, which is the location of the file that contains the icon handler.

Wild-Card Keys

The first subkey of HKEY_CLASSES_ROOT, "*", is a wild-card key. The Windows 95 shell extensions use a special key. *Shell extensions* are OLE servers (usually in DLL files) that provide extra user interface functionality to Windows 95. The wild-card key specifies shell extensions that apply to all applications, not just a single application. This means, for instance, that you can add information to the context menus of all icons, or you can add property pages to all property sheets shown in the shell.

File Extension Subkeys

Windows 95 begins searching for information associated with a document type by looking for the key name that matches the file extension. The main purpose of these keys is to indicate another key in HKEY_CLASSES_ROOT that describes the document type in greater detail. The default value of the key is the name of the document definition subkey.

Document Definition Subkeys

The subkeys of the document definition subkey provide most of the OLE, DDE, and shell extension attributes of the document type. The default value is a text string that gives a one-line description of the document type.

Some document definition subkeys point to a CLSID subkey, for which the default value is a long string of numbers. These are OLE class identifiers, which match the class ID subkeys under the HKEY_CLASSES_ROOT\CLSID key.

CLSID

All subkeys underneath HKEY_CLASSES_ROOT\CLSID are OLE class identifiers. The class identifier for a particular document type is guaranteed unique across all PCs in the world. The default value of the key is a description of the OLE class. The location of the file that contains the OLE implementation for that class is usually located in the InProcServer32 subkey (for a Dll) or LocalServer32 (for an Exe). If the document is supported by older 16-bit OLE applications the location may also be in InProcServer or LocalServer subkeys.

HKEY_CURRENT_USER

HKEY_CURRENT_USER is another registry key that points to another key; to the subkey of HKEY_USERS for the user currently logged on to the PC. This user profile information assures that Windows 95, the individual application setup, and the user interface all operate identically on whichever machine the user works, as long as the user's profile is available on every PC on which that user works.

Figure 13.3 shows the Registry Editor with the HKEY_CURRENT_USER and HKEY_USERS\jruehlin keys open. HKEY_CURRENT_USER is the same as HKEY_USERS\jruehlin (it's actually a pointer to KEY_USERS\jruehlin), because "jruehlin" is the logon name of the current user.

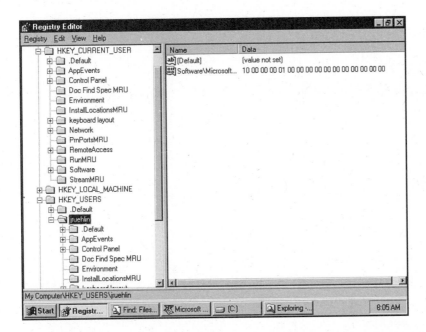

Figure 13.3

Image of HKEY_CURRENT_USER and HKEY_USERS\username.

Most applications should place registry information for this key under the HKEY_CURRENT_USER\Software and HKEY_CURRENT_USER\.Default\Software subkeys. The intent is for these keys to contain information formerly placed in the Ini files of specific applications.

When identical information exists between HKEY_CURRENT_USER and HKEY_LOCAL_MACHINE, the information in HKEY_CURRENT_USER takes precedence.

Table 13.4 explains the subkeys for HKEY_CURRENT_USER.

TABLE 13.4
Subkeys for HKEY_CURRENT_USER

Subkey	Contents
AppEvents	Subkeys that contain paths to current and past sound files that play when a system event occurs (such as a system beep).
Control Panel	Subkeys that contain information set using the Control Panel. Much of this information was stored in Win.ini and Control.ini under Windows 3.1.
Keyboard layouts	Current keyboard layout set using the Keyboard icon in the Control Panel.
Network	Subkeys that define the current state of the network.
RunMRU	A list of the most-recently run applications.
Software	A pointer to HKEY_LOCAL_MACHINE\Software. The subkeys describe settings and options for the current user's installed software. This application-specific information was previously stored in Win.ini or application-generated Ini files under Windows 3.1.
StreamMRU	Values pointing to recently used documents.

Applications will add more subkeys when installed to keep track of information specific to those applications.

HKEY_LOCAL_MACHINE

HKEY_LOCAL_MACHINE stores non-user-specific hardware and software configuration information for the local PC, which applies regardless of who logs on to the system.

◆ **Config subkey.** A PC can be set up for multiple configurations. This is useful in a few circumstances, such as when a portable PC has one configuration in a docking station and another configuration undocked.

A new hardware configuration is created from the System control panel applet under the Hardware Profiles tab. Subkeys for those configurations are listed under the Config subkey as "0001", "0002", and so on. The user defined name for a new configuration is placed by the applet under the HEKY_LOCAL_MACHINE\System\CurrentControlSet\Control\IDConfigDB subkey. The user defined name for Config\0001, for instance, is the data string in the FriendlyName001 subkey.

New Riders Publishing
INSIDE SERIES

Figure 13.4 shows the key for hardware configuration 0001 and the location of the user-defined name for that key. The name "Original Configuration" is in the value "FriendlyName0001", so the system knows it's the name of configuration 0001.

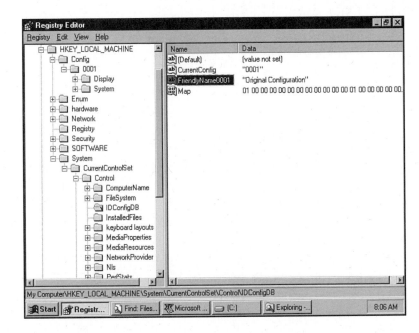

Figure 13.4

Picture of 0001 subkey and IDConfigDB subkey.

◆ **Enum subkey.** A *bus enumerator,* which is a new type of software device in Windows 95 designed to build the hardware tree, assigns a unique ID code to each device on the bus, then retrieves configuration information for that device from the Registry or from the device itself. Enum's subkeys list classes of devices and their configuration information.

Note The Network subkey enumerates network bindings, protocols, and services. It does not enumerate network adapters.

◆ **Hardware subkey.** The Hardware subkey contains information about the hardware attached to the system, such as serial ports, modems, floating-point processors, and so on. Information in this branch can originate from hardware that uses the Windows 95 Plug and Play functions, or from software that uses the standard registry API functions.

◆ **Network subkey.** The Network subkey contains network information created when a user logs on to a network, including logon name, logon validation status, primary network provider, logon domain, and other network-specific information.

◆ **Registry subkey.** This subkey contains a "DefaultUser" value, which contains the binary equivalent of a string of ASCII numbers.

◆ **Security subkey.** Windows 95 does not maintain a security subkey. This subkey holds network security information.

◆ **Software subkey.** This key contains software configuration information for the local computer. Application vendors should create a subkey under this key to store configuration information for all their products that can run on the local system. The Microsoft subkey is an example of this.

Figure 13.5 shows how Microsoft places information in the SOFTWARE subkey.

Figure 13.5

*Image of HKEY_
LOCAL_MACHINE\
Software\Microsoft
subkey.*

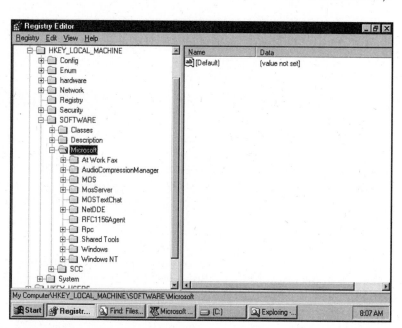

◆ **Classes subkey.** This is identical to the HKEY_CLASSES_ROOT key. See the section "HKEY_CLASSES_ROOT" earlier in this chapter for more information.

◆ **Microsoft subkey.** This subkey contains information about software that directly supports Windows 95 services.

◆ **System subkey.** The System subkey contains startup-related information that must be stored (rather than created on the fly during startup). In other words, much of the information in CONFIG.SYS and AUTOEXEC.BAT from Windows 3.1 is now stored here. Real-mode drivers and TSRs must still be kept in Config.sys and Autoexec.bat.

HKEY_USERS

The HKEY_USERS root key contains all user profiles. As described earlier, the HKEY_CURRENT_USER root key points to the HKEY_USER subkey that holds the profile information for the current user. Information in individual user profile subkeys is described under HKEY_CURRENT_USER.

HKEY_USERS always contain at least the .Default subkey. .Default is used to create a user profile for a user who logs on to the system without one. This might be someone who the system administrator adds to the system, or who signs on to the PC via a domain controller.

HKEY_CURRENT_CONFIG

This key points to the HKEY_LOCAL_MACHINE\Config subkey. It makes accessing information within that key easier for applications.

HKEY_DYN_DATA

This key holds information that must be stored in RAM at all times. Normally, information in the registry is flushed at regular intervals or by applications that write information to the registry. During a registry flush the information is written to the System.dat and User.dat files. However, some information must always be available immediately. This is the information pointed to by HKEY_DYN_DATA.

Config Manager Subkey

The Config Manager subkey is also referred to as the *hardware tree*. It is a record in RAM of the current hardware configuration. This information can be updated and changed at any time so that Plug and Play devices can be supported. This information is created during system startup and is updated whenever the system configuration changes.

PerStats Subkey

This subkey maintains performance information for network components. Performance statistics can be viewed through the SYSMON application, which will probably be either an optionally installed component of Windows 95 or part of the Windows 95 Resource Kit.

Registry Editor

The Windows 95 Registry Editor (Regedit.exe), located in the Windows directory, provides a fairly straightforward means for directly editing the Registry, although using a software tool or application, such as a Control Panel applet, offers a safer, and often more convenient, means. Using indirect editing tools greatly reduces the chances of inadvertently corrupting the Registry.

The Registry Editor displays a single, two-paned window. The left pane is a hierarchical list of keys and subkeys, and the right pane is a list of value names and the data for the values.

To expand a key, click on the plus sign (+) to the left of the folder. If you don't see a +, you can't expand the key because it doesn't have any subkeys. You can expand or shrink both frames by choosing View, Split or by using the mouse to move the splitter bar in the middle.

Table 13.5 lists the Registry Editor's shortcut keys for navigation and viewing.

TABLE 13.5
Registry Editor Navigation and Viewing Shortcut Keys

Key	Action
+	Expand the selected key one level if it has subkeys.
-	Collapse the selected key one level.
Up arrow	Move up to the next key.
Down arrow	Move down to the next key.
Left arrow	Collapse the selected key if it's open, else move up to the next key.
Right arrow	Expand the selected key if it has subkeys, else move down to the next key.
Tab	Move to the other pane.

 Tip Clicking on a key or value with the right mouse button opens a context menu that contains all its allowable operations, including renaming, deleting, modifying, and creating new objects.

New Riders Publishing
INSIDE
SERIES

Modifying Registry Information

To delete a key or value, click on the key or value and press Del or choose Edit, Delete. To modify a key or value, choose Edit, Rename or click on the text of the name, then edit the text. To create a new key or value, choose Edit, New. Select the appropriate key or data value type to insert it at or under the selected key.

To modify data (as opposed to keys or values), double-click on the value name or icon to open a window that enables you to edit the data.

Note   Windows 95 writes, or "flushes," the Registry to disk within just a few seconds after you modify data, or when an application intentionally flushes Registry data to the hard disk. Any changes you make to the Registry take effect within a few seconds. The exception to this is information in HKEY_DYN_DATA, which resides in RAM and is updated immediately.

Finding Information in the Registry

To locate information in the Registry Editor, choose Edit, Find (Ctrl+F) or Edit, Find Next (F3). You can search for keys, values, data in values, or any combination of these. Search values can be text or numbers.

When registry information is located, the item that matches the search criteria is highlighted. Any nested subkeys are opened in the left pane so that the information can be properly displayed.

Unfortunately, when a value or data item is located, it's often difficult to tell which key it belongs to. The Find operation displays an open folder in the left pane for the key associated with the value or data in the right pane, but there can be many folders showing, and it's difficult to pick out the one that looks "open."

When value or data items are located, the open folder is usually at the bottom of the left pane, as shown in figure 13.6.

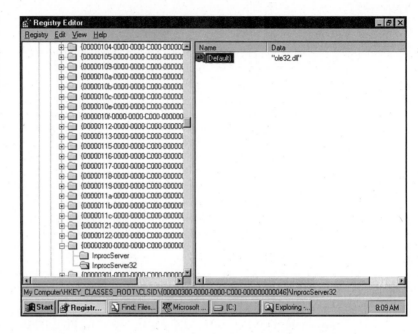

Figure 13.6

Image of value located and open folder at the bottom.

Importing and Exporting from the Registry

You use the Import and Export options to store and retrieve Registry information. This is a good way to back up registry keys and subkeys before making significant changes to them. It's also a convenient way to send information from a registry on one machine to another.

Registry information is imported and exported to and from Reg files, which are editable text files. To export a key and all its subkeys, values, and data, select the key and choose Registry, Export Registry File. To import registry information choose Registry, Import Registry File, then select the Reg file to import from the File Open dialog box.

 Tip   You can easily import the information in a REG file into the Registry by double-clicking on the file icon.

Selecting a Remote Registry

You can access the Registry on a remote machine over the network. To do so, the remote machine must have the Microsoft Remote Registry service enabled. Enable the service in the Network Control Panel applet.

To remotely access another Windows 95 registry, choose <u>R</u>egistry, <u>C</u>onnect Network Registry. You will be asked for the name of the computer of the user's Registry you want to access. If the connection is successful the Registry Editor will display the remote machine's registry information.

Printing Registry Information

To print Registry information, select the key you want to print and choose <u>R</u>egistry, <u>P</u>rint. The Printer Options dialog box appears, from which you can choose to print all information contained within the selected key or all information in the Registry, or you can type a different key name and print all information contained in it.

 Tip   A quick way to access many of the features of the Registry Editor is to select a key or value with the right mouse button. A context menu appears that offers features available for the selected item.

Other Registry Maintenance Techniques

This section describes some techniques to help you maintain and enhance your Registry.

Copying Configuration Information to Multiple Machines

You can maintain identical configuration information for numerous users across multiple machines. This enables those users to share the machines while keeping their familiar configuration settings such as desktop appearance and passwords.

To copy John Doe's configuration information from an old PC to a new one, perform the following steps:

1. On the NEW PC, create a new subdirectory in the C:\Window\Profiles directory with the same name as John Doe's logon name, JDOE (the Profiles subdirectory is in the directory Windows 95 was installed into, which is usually C:\Windows).

2. Locate the directory C:\Windows\Profiles\JDOE on the OLD PC. Copy the User.dat file from this directory to the C:\Windows\Profiles\JDOE directory you just created on the NEW PC.

Supporting Roving Users

You can allow a single user to roam to different machines and keep the same configuration information without manually copying the User.dat file if User Profiles are enabled for machines on a network. When a user logs on to a machine, Windows 95 looks at the "HKEY_LOCAL_MACHINE\SOFTWARE\Microsoft\Windows\Current Version\Profile List" key to find out where the user's profiles information is kept. Windows 95 checks the server, then the local machine, and uses the latest User.dat file to load profile information into the local Registry. The local and network copies of the profile are updated when the user logs off.

To enable user profiles for a single machine, select the Passwords option in the Control Panel. Choose the option Users can customize their preferences and desktop settings, then select the customizable profile features for that machine.

To enable user profiles centrally so they can be accessed by all machines on the network, use the Profile Editor in the Resource Kit to create a system policy file (Config.pol) with user profiles enabled. Make sure user profiles are enbled for each machine as described in the previous paragraph. If the network is a Windows NT network, place the file in the server directory "\\primary domain controller\user's home directory". If the network is a NetWare network, place the file in the server directory "\\preferred server\sys\mail\user_id" (each user must have an established Mail directory).

 Note   You will probably use only one of the previous two methods for customizing user profiles. Which one you choose depends on the size and complexity of your network and the ways your users access their PCs.

Recovering from Corrupted or Unusable Registry Files

You can run the Registry Editor (Regedit.exe) from real mode if Windows 95 doesn't start. If the system is too corrupted to run, you also can run Regedit.exe from a Windows 95 startup disk to diagnose the problem.

Table 13.6 contains command-line parameters for the Registry Editor.

TABLE 13.6
Registry Editor Command-Line Parameters

Command	Description
regedit /e export.reg	Exports entire registry to Export.reg
HKEY_USERS\Default	Exports subkey HKEY_USERS\Default and all its subkeys to Export.reg
regedit /i export.reg	Imports the file Export.reg into the Registry
regedit /c export.reg	Replaces entire Registry with Export.reg

Whenever Windows 95 boots successfully, System.dat and User.dat files copy during bootup to System.da0 and User.da0, which are always the last known good files, and consequently, which you can use to restore Registries that become terminally corrupted.

## 14

Optimizing Physical and Virtual Memory

Understanding computer memory often proves less than easy, even for experienced computer users. This chapter helps sort out conventional memory, memory addressing, virtual memory, and Windows 95's new memory model. The chapter emphasizes virtual memory, owing to its significance in Windows 95 memory management. Finally, the chapter shows you how to organize Windows 95 memory for optimum performance.

Many of Windows 95's memory management features are automatic; Windows 95 constantly searches for ways to refine and "groom" itself for performance advantages. After initial setup, therefore, you might not need to concern yourself with memory issues very often. If memory does become an issue, however, you'll find familiarity with the concepts this chapter discusses quite useful.

In this chapter, you examine the following memory concepts:

◆ Basic memory concepts

◆ Measuring memory

◆ Different types of memory

◆ Windows 95's 32-bit memory model

◆ Virtual memory

◆ Physical memory

◆ Memory pages

◆ Optimizing memory

◆ Virtual memory swap files

With a basic understanding of these memory concepts, you should be able to handle most of the memory-related issues that might arise during your use of the Windows 95 operating system. At the very least, you will be able to recognize memory-related problems and have a good start toward solving those problems.

Understanding Memory Concepts

Random-access memory (RAM) refers to the volatile storage area in which your applications, data from those applications, and the operating system are stored during use. All computer programs must load into RAM memory before you can run them. Any active data in applications on which you work, such as text in a word processor document, also resides in RAM.

RAM memory qualifies as volatile because you lose the data in RAM if the power to the computer is interrupted in any way, shape, or form: you turn it off, a terrible storm causes a blackout in your area, a cagey dog steps on the plug, or any of many other unplanned disruptions. You can see why you should know what portions of your data and programs you lose if you don't save them to disk before you turn off your computer or experience an unexpected calamity.

The opposite of volatile memory is permanent memory, commonly referred to as storage. *Storage* refers to areas to which data is written and saved, even when the computer is off—usually a floppy disk or hard drive. Chapter 15, "Optimizing Data Storage," discusses storage issues.

Measuring Memory

As the atom constitutes the primary unit of all matter, the bit constitutes the primary unit of all computer information and memory. A *bit* actually is an electronic register that is either on or off. (As discussed later, in computer programming lingo—*binary code*—the register is a 1 or 0.)

Bits are grouped together into bytes (eight bits per byte). A byte represents one character of information, such as a letter character on-screen. Bits are organized in a system called binary language. *Binary language* organizes eight bits (on or off—1 or 0) into a system that represents characters. The 8-bit code 01000001, for example, represents the character *A*.

Understanding Memory Size Terms

Before you can fully appreciate memory concepts, you need to understand the basic memory size terms:

◆ **Kilobyte.** 1,024 bytes of memory, commonly abbreviated *KB* or *K;* for example, 640 kilobytes (640 KB) = 655,360 bytes (640 × 1,024).

◆ **Megabyte.** 1,024 kilobytes of memory, commonly abbreviated *MB* or *M*, and commonly referred to as *megs;* for example, 20 megabytes (20 MB) = 20,480 KB (20 × 1,024).

◆ **Gigabyte.** 1,024 megabytes of memory, commonly abbreviated *GB* or *G*, and commonly referred to as *gigs;* for example, 9 gigabytes (9 GB) = 9,216 MB (9 × 1,024 = 9,216).

Examining the Different Types of Memory

All memory is not equal. Computers use different portions of memory in different ways and certain software applications use different areas of memory for different operations. The four main types of memory are conventional memory, extended memory, expanded memory, and virtual memory.

The following four sections cover these types of memory in turn. Understanding these types of memory will help you understand software manufacturer's requirements for memory use. For example, if a program requires a certain amount of free conventional memory, after reading these sections, you will understand how to be sure you have sufficient memory to run the program.

Conventional Memory

Conventional memory is the first 1,024 KB of memory available on your computer system, divided into two regions: system memory (the first 640 KB) and high memory (between 640 KB and 1,024 KB). MS-DOS programs use conventional memory more often than any other type of program. In fact, many MS-DOS programs require a significant amount of the system memory area (as much as 610 KB) to be free—that is, not used by any other programs—before you can load and run them.

Tip   Many programs require certain amounts of conventional memory, so you might get an out of memory error message from a program that purports to require only 500 KB of memory, even though you have 8 MB of RAM in your system. For example, if you have a CD-ROM driver program, a mouse driver, and a sound card driver loaded into memory, then you attempt to run an MS-DOS program (such as Falcon 3.0 or Aces over Europe) that requires a large amount of conventional memory, you may get an out of memory error, even though you have free memory in other memory areas.

Therefore, when you examine new programs, you should consider the total amount of *conventional* memory the program requires.

MS-DOS programs must also share conventional memory with other programs, however, such as *device drivers,* which are small programs that control certain of your system's components (like your sound card or video monitor). Because this region of memory is so small (compared to the total memory in your system), many MS-DOS programs have problems loading all the necessary information into conventional memory.

Extended Memory

Extended memory is all memory beyond 1,024 KB. (The amount of extended memory you can have on a Windows 95–configured computer is 4 GB.) Extended memory is accessed linearly, which makes it faster to use than expanded memory. It is not accessed via paging.

Expanded Memory

Expanded memory refers to memory mapped in the high memory area (HMA) by certain software, called *expanded memory manager* (EMM) software. Only applications designed to work with an EMM can use this type of memory. Expanded memory is mapped via the EMM pager. The memory pager tracks every page of memory in HMA, so it has a large overhead.

Note   Expanded memory's popularity has diminished today owing to the performance penalty you suffer from paging all expanded memory out of the HMA. EMM also gives applications limited amounts of expanded memory at a time, further impeding application performance.

Virtual Memory

Virtual memory actually involves writing pages of information that normally go into volatile memory onto a hard disk drive, thus emulating RAM memory. Mainframe operating systems have done this for years, but only recently has it become popular on PC operating systems. Virtual memory is limited only by the amount of available hard disk space.

Note   Windows 95 uses virtual memory extensively. Virtual memory is used by an application via a pager. This pager tracks the amount of RAM used by the computer, and when the need for more memory arises, the pager swaps memory pages onto disk, thus emulating memory. The application is unaware of the type of memory that is being used because the pager handles all the memory operations.

Examining the New 32-Bit Memory Model in Windows 95

Perhaps one of Windows 95's most exciting new features is its memory model—the same model Windows NT uses—called *demand-paged virtual memory*. It uses 32-bit addresses to access a flat linear address space. Each application, including the Windows 95 operating system, uses *pages*, which are pieces of this virtual address space.

Demand paging refers to the method by which information (data) moves in units (pages) from physical memory to a disk file called a *paging file*. As a given process needs its paging file's information, its information pages back into physical memory, a page at a time. Windows 95's memory pager handles paging.

The memory pager tracks in physical memory all the pages in the virtual address space and maps them to their respective processes. The memory pager acts as a buffer between the application and the computer's memory. Besides increasing speed, the memory pager prevents applications from overwriting each other in memory space. The pager also keeps the different machine processes separate and hides the actual layout of the memory pages in physical memory from the application or process using the memory.

Enhancements over Windows 3.x

Windows 3.x, a 16-bit operating system, uses a memory structure based on memory segments. Segments, 64 KB in size, reference memory using 16-bit segment addresses and 16-bit offset addresses within the segment. The small size of segments constricts the performance when applications need to access data across many segments.

Using the 32-bit capabilities of 80386 and faster processors, Windows 95 supports a flat, 32-bit, linear memory model. This model supports a 32-bit operating system and 32-bit applications (Win32 apps). Linear addressing greatly increases operating system and application performance by doing away with the segmented memory model.

Linear memory addressing is the process whereby the memory manager creates a seemingly endless stack of memory and renders it available to the applications and operating system. The stack of memory is actually made up of chunks of physical memory (or RAM) and virtual memory (or disk space). It is considered linear because the VMM handles the memory issues and determines whether to use physical or virtual memory and hide this process from the application, so all the application sees is a stack (line) of memory that is available on the system.

Linear addressing enables Windows 95 to use up to 4 GB of addressable memory space for the entire 32-bit operating system and component combined. Each 32-bit application can access up to 2 GB of addressable memory space!

Examining Virtual Memory

Virtual memory acts as the heart of the Windows 95 memory management system. *Virtual memory* is the label for the process of moving information that applications need into and out of physical memory (RAM chips) and the disk cache area, or swap file, to form logical memory. Virtual memory entails using the usually large amount of hard disk space available to handle memory-related functions, thereby enabling more information to be processed, and more complicated processes.

In Windows 95, memory is accessed using a 32-bit linear addressing scheme. A 32-bit addressing system can access up to 4 GB of memory. Thus, in Windows 95 when an application attempts to access memory, it simply specifies a 32-bit memory address. (The minimum allocation of virtual memory is a one 4 KB page.)

Virtual memory can include a physical structure or a logical structure, discussed in the following sections.

Physical Memory

Physical memory—your RAM chips or memory modules—is organized as a series of one-byte storage units that make up the machine's physical address space of the machine. Only the amount of RAM on the motherboard limits the number of physical addresses on a machine.

 Note Physical memory (RAM) resides on your system's memory modules, which consist of one or more computer chips, usually of the single in-line memory module (SIMM) standard. When you purchase extra "memory" for your system, you purchase such modules.

Logical Memory

Logical memory, the key to the virtual memory process, includes both physical memory and the swap file, or disk-cached memory. In essence, logical memory simply labels the way in which applications actually use memory. Using logical memory and the virtual memory process, some of the contents of physical memory can be moved onto the hard disk in a paging file when memory becomes scarce—when a process tries, for example, to access more memory than physically available on your computer system. In other words, when an application tries to use more RAM than the computer can offer, virtual memory mediates the gap.

As a practical matter, the virtual memory capacity available on a computer equals the space that the Virtual Memory Manager can use to store data swapped out to the hard disk. If you have a 1.2 GB hard drive with 200 MB of free hard drive space, you have only 200 MB of possible virtual memory space.

Virtual Memory Manager

Windows 95's *Virtual Memory Manager* (VMM) controls allocating physical and logical memory. When you launch a new application, the Virtual Memory Manager initializes the virtual address space.

Programmers historically have designed applications to use as little memory as possible, given most systems' limited physical memory. Windows 95's VMM can address up to 4 GB, including space on your system's hard drives, however, so now programmers can write programs to exploit large amounts of memory without worrying about the type of memory or the amount of memory available.

Windows 95's Virtual Memory Manager provides this large, virtual memory space to applications via two memory management processes: *paging*, or moving data between physical RAM and the hard disk, and translating physical memory addresses to virtual memory addresses or mapped file I/O.

Paging and Page Faults

When a set of information, for example a file, exceeds in size available RAM, the Virtual Memory Manager uses paging to move data between RAM and the hard disk by dividing all physical memory and virtual memory (the memory applications use) into equal-sized blocks or *pages* (4 KB each). When a request is made to access data not in RAM, the Virtual Memory Manager swaps a page from RAM with the desired page from the *paging file* (a file on the hard disk used solely by the Virtual Memory Manager for extra data storage).

Page states are registered in the virtual page table. A page in physical RAM and immediately available to its application is marked as valid. Pages currently already in the paging file are marked as invalid. When an application tries to access an invalid page, the CPU generates a page fault. The Virtual Memory Manager intercepts page faults, retrieves pages from the paging file, and places them into RAM. If RAM doesn't have enough room to store a new page, the VMM moves a valid page out of RAM into the paging file.

When an application accesses a virtual address in a page marked invalid, the processor uses a system trap called a *page fault.* The virtual memory system locates the required page on disk and loads it into a free page frame in physical memory. When the amount of available page frames runs short, the virtual memory system selects page frames to free and pages their contents out to disk. Paging occurs transparently for the user and the program or application.

Paging Policies

Three policies dictate how the Virtual Memory Manager determines how and when to page:

◆ **Fetch.** A demand-based paging algorithm is used to retrieve (or *fetch*) memory pages. The Virtual Memory Manager waits until a process thread attempts to access an invalid page before it loads the page into RAM. Because page faults and disk access are both somewhat slow, additional pages load along with the desired page in a process called *clustering.* VMM chooses the additional pages according to their proximity to the desired page, which reduces the number of page faults generated and the amount of disk operations, the theory being that the process might need information that spans several consecutive pages.

◆ **Placement.** *Placement* refers to the location of a page stored in RAM. The Virtual Memory Manager places a page in the first free page in RAM it finds.

◆ **Replacement.** If the placement policy fails because RAM contains no free pages, VMM uses the replacement policy to determine which page to move from RAM to the paging file. Each process has a group of valid pages in RAM, called the *working set.* For simplicity, VMM uses a first-in, first-out (FIFO) algorithm. When a page replacement is required, VMM moves the oldest page in the working set to the paging file to make room for the new page. Because the replacement scheme applies only to the working set of the current process, other processes are guaranteed that their pages will not be replaced by other processes.

Virtual Address Translation

Windows 95 transfers data in 32-bit addresses. Windows 95 divides each 32-bit address into three groups: two groups of 10 bits each and one group of 12 bits. It uses each group as an offset into a specific page of memory: the first 10 bit groups as an offset into the page directory; the second 10 bits as an offset into the page table; and the third 12 bits to address a specific byte in the page frame.

Every page of memory falls into one of three categories: *page directory, page table,* or *page frame.*

◆ **Page directories.** Each process has a single, unique page directory in the Win32 system. The directory is a 4-KB page segmented into 1,024 values of 4 bytes each, called *page directory entries.* This is the first 10 bits of the address.

◆ **Page tables.** The second 10 bits of the 32-bit segment address reference a 4-byte *page table entry* in the same way as the page directory. This table points to actual pages in memory called *page frames.*

◆ **Page frames.** The final 12 bits of the 32-bit virtual address reference a specific byte of memory in the page frame identified by the page table.

Locking Pages

For time-sensitive applications and those with other special memory performance requirements, the VMM enables a user subsystem or process with special privileges to lock selected virtual pages into its working set to ensure that a critical page is not be paged out of memory during the application.

Reserved versus Committed Memory

The VMM uses a two-level process for memory allocation: it first reserves the pages and then commits them. *Reserved memory* is a set of virtual addresses that the VMM reserves for future use. Reserving memory (virtual addresses) is fast in Windows 95.

No memory actually is used, but another application asking for a memory allocation cannot use the reserved virtual addresses.

A committed page has physical storage (RAM memory or virtual memory on disk) allocated for its use. When the VMM allocates memory for use by an application, it can reserve and commit memory simultaneously, or it can simply reserve the memory, committing it later when the application needs the memory.

When a particular range of addresses is not being used, the VMM can *decommit* them, thus freeing space in the paging file.

Mapped File I/O

If an application attempts to load a file larger than both the system RAM and the paging file (swap file) combined, Virtual Memory Manager's mapped file I/O services are used. *Mapped file I/O* enables the Virtual Memory Manager to map virtual memory addresses to a large file, inform the application that the file is available, and then load only the pieces of the file that the application actually intends to use. Because only portions of the large file are loaded into memory (RAM or page file), this greatly decreases file load time and system resource drainage. It's a very useful service for database applications that often require access to huge files.

Protection

The Windows 95 memory management system provides a new, enhanced level of protection for applications running on the system. In Windows 3.*x*, for example, a 16-bit application gone bad can easily bring down the entire system, and with it all other applications running on the system, potentially causing serious data loss. Likewise, if under Windows 3.*x* you ran a 16-bit application, then launched an MS-DOS application, the MS-DOS application could actually seek to use the 16-bit application's memory area, thereby bringing about system failure.

In Windows 95, each type of application—16-bit, 32-bit, or MS-DOS—is protected from the other. Although 32-bit based applications benefit the most from system memory protection, the improvements present in Windows 95 result in a more stable and reliable operating environment than in Windows 3.*x* for all applications.

16-bit-based applications run within a unified address space, and cooperatively multitask as they do under Windows 3.*x*. The improvements in overall system-wide robustness, owing to better system memory management support underneath the application, greatly enhance the system's capability to recover from a hung application and reduce the likelihood for application errors.

The Windows 95 memory system also helps segregate applications from other applications and from their own memory segments. General protection faults (GPFs) in Windows 3.x usually result from applications attempting to write over their own memory segments, instead of from applications overwriting memory belonging to another application. Windows 3.x does not recover gracefully when an application crashes or hangs. When a GPF halts an application in 3.x, the user must restart the system by rebooting the computer, and loses any unsaved work prior to the GPF.

Due to improved protection in Windows 95, a rebellious 16-bit-based application cannot easily bring down the system as a whole, nor can it bring down other MS-DOS applications or 32-bit applications. However, crashing 16-bit applications still can affect other running 16-bit based applications. Each type of application—16-bit, 32-bit, or DOS—has a corresponding Virtual Machine Manager. If a 16-bit application locks up for some reason, it can stop the whole 16-bit process; all 16-bit applications are stopped from working because the 16-bit Virtual Machine Manager is locked up.

Protection improvements also include the use of separate message queues for each running 32-bit application. The use of a separate message queue for the 16-bit address space and for each running 32-bit application provides for better recovery of the system as a whole and doesn't halt the system should a 16-bit application hang.

Understanding Virtual Memory and the Swap File

In implementing the virtual memory process, Windows 95 creates a hard disk swap file to which it writes information that will not fit into physical (RAM) memory. Windows 95 contains several improvements to the virtual memory swap file implementation provided in Windows 3.x. These improvements have corrected some problems and removed some limitations present in the previous systems.

In the earlier versions of Windows, you face many complex choices and configuration options when arranging a swap file. You must decide whether to use a temporary swap file or a permanent swap file, how big to make the swap file, whether to use 32-bit disk access, and with version 3.11, whether to use 32-bit file access. Users benefit from a temporary swap file in that the swap file does not need to be contiguous, and Windows allocates space on the hard disk during bootup and frees up the space when you close out Windows—but this also makes starting Windows slower. A permanent swap file provides the best performance, but it demands a large amount of disk space that will not be freed up when you exit Windows.

Windows 95's swap file simplifies configuration by combining the best features of the Windows 3.*x* temporary and permanent swap files in improved virtual memory algorithms and access methods. Windows 95's swap file is dynamic, and can shrink or grow based on the operations performed on the system. (The Windows 95 swap file still has to be "created" during system startup, slowing startup time.)

You still can adjust the parameters for defining the swap file in Windows 95. The intelligent use of system defaults, however, reduces your need to do so. Generally configuring Windows so that you prevent it from automatically managing the size of the swap file provides no benefits.

Figure 14.1 shows the new, simplified swap-file configuration options, which enable the user to specify the minimum and maximum swap file size to use.

Figure 14.1

The new swap file configuration window.

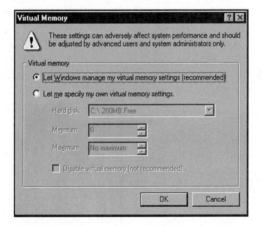

> **Stop** Disabling virtual memory completely is not recommended. Doing so can cause the system to lock and also can prevent the computer from rebooting properly. In addition, overall system performance decreases dramatically.

If you have multiple hard drives, you might want to change the location of the swap file to the fastest hard drive, or, if all drives are the same speed, you probably want to use the drive that contains the most free space. Be careful not to change the location of the swap file to a network drive. Access to network drives can be very slow, and using one for the host of your virtual memory file can adversely affect system performance.

Examining System Resources

You probably have seen `Out of Memory` error messages while running multiple Windows-based applications under Windows 3.*x,* even though the system still reported several megabytes of available free memory when you consulted the Help About dialog box. What you encountered, although you probably didn't know it, was a condition in which the system could not allocate an internal memory resource in a Windows API function call because it didn't have enough space available in the memory heap.

Windows 3.*x* maintains heaps for system components called GDI and USER. Each heap is 64 KB in size and is used for storing GDI or memory object information allocated when an application calls a Windows API. The amount of space available in the combination of these two heaps is identified as a percentage of system resources that are free, and are shown in the Windows 3.*x* Help About dialog box.

The percentage of free system resources reported in the Help About dialog box actually is the aggregate percentage of free memory in the GDI and USER heaps. When the free system resources percentage drops to a low number, it normally produces an out of memory error message, even though the amount of free memory shown in the Help About dialog box still is quite high. This error results from low memory in the GDI heap or the USER heap.

To help reduce this system resource limitation, a number of the data structures stored in the 16-bit GDI and USER heaps in Windows 3.*x* have been moved out and stored in 32-bit heaps in Windows 95, leaving more room for the remaining data elements to be created. You will notice this mostly from the fact that you do not encounter such a rapid decrease in system resources as you did with Windows 3.*x.*

Windows 95 improves the system capacity for the USER heap by moving menu and window handles to the 32-bit USER heap and raising the total limit of these data structures from 200 in Windows 3.*x* to a total limit now of 32,767 menu handles and an additional 32,767 window handles per memory process (rather than system-wide).

The improvements in Windows 95 that facilitate cleaning up the system of unfreed resources also help the system resource limitation problem. Windows 95 cleans up and deallocates leftover data structures after it determines that the other processes no longer need the resources in memory.

Performance Tuning

Even though Windows 95 handles memory much more efficiently than its predecessor systems, you might still need to enhance your system's performance. If so, you can use some of the following performance suggestions.

Tip   Enhancing the performance of the Windows 95 operating system is easier than in Windows 3.x. Many of the following performance suggestions are more effectual because of Windows 95's "self-tuning" nature.

◆ **Adding more RAM.** Always the knee-jerk reaction to poor system performance under Windows 3.1; after adding a certain amount of memory the performance "payoff" begins to drop significantly. The theory is the more memory you add, the faster the system works, and this is true to a point. But with problems such as a low GDI heap, the amount of memory you add doesn't matter because the heap eventually still runs low and drags down system performance.

In Windows 95, adding more RAM to your system does more good. The caching system performs better as you add more memory to your system.

◆ **Faster hard drive.** Hard drives have two performance features you should consider when you shop for drives: access time, measured in milliseconds, and buffer size, measured in kilobytes. The lower the access time, the faster a hard drive finds data. The larger the buffer size, the better the overall performance. Because your hard drive is a critical component of Windows 95 virtual memory system, a better hard drive not only enhances pure data exchanges, but increases memory performance as well.

◆ **Higher generation of CPU.** Because Windows 95 relies heavily on 32-bit code, it performs much better if you run it on systems that use a 486 or Pentium processor. Running Windows 95 on a 386-based computer is possible, but 486 or Pentium processors greatly increase the system performance benefits you can derive from the extensive use of 32-bit code in Windows 95.

◆ **Bus type selection.** Windows 95 can make full use of faster bus speeds. PCI type bus motherboards and peripheral cards have a much greater data throughput speed than ISA-based motherboards and peripheral cards. The video performance of a PCI system makes the largest contribution to the overall performance boost of Windows 95.

Examining Windows 95 Self-Tuning Features

Windows 95 is designed to monitor itself and perform certain actions to fine-tune itself. Windows 95 does several things automatically to enhance system performance, including the following three more noticeable ones:

◆ **Dynamic caching.** As you add more memory, Windows 95 automatically uses it in caching. This new dynamic caching feature (VCACHE) eliminates manually reconfiguring the swap file settings.

◆ **32-bit disk and file access.** The 32-bit file and disk access system enables Windows 95 to access the hard disk without going through the system's BIOS.

◆ **Background print rendering.** If memory allows, Windows 95 can print in the background while the system returns to the application faster after you issue the print request. Windows 95 actually creates an *Enhanced Metafile Format* (EMF) file on the hard disk and then feeds this file to the printer, which enables you to return to the application more quickly.

In addition to these features, Windows 95 includes a handy utility called the *Memory Troubleshooter* (see fig. 14.2), actually a Windows 95 wizard you can find in the Help system. As do most Windows 95 wizards, the Memory Troubleshooter guides you through a series of steps—in this case, steps that help you diagnose a variety of memory problems. (Some of these steps include shortcuts to other Windows 95 utilities, such as Scandisk.)

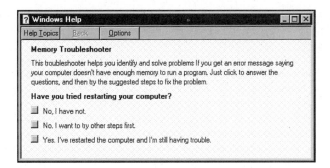

Figure 14.2

The Memory Troubleshooter.

Understanding the Zero Conventional Memory Components of Windows 95

Windows 95 helps provide the maximum conventional memory available for running your existing MS-DOS-based applications. Some MS-DOS-based applications will not run under Windows 3.*x* because after all the MS-DOS device drivers, TSRs, MS-DOS-based networking components, and the Windows 3.*x* operating system were loaded, not enough conventional memory was available to load and run the software. To help alleviate these problems, Windows 95 provides 32-bit protected-mode components that replace many of the 16-bit real-mode counterparts. These 32-bit protected-mode components, called *virtual device drivers,* provide the same functionality while improving overall system performance by using no conventional memory.

Table 14.1 provides a partial list of 16-bit real-mode device drivers that are replaced by 32-bit virtual device drivers in Windows 95, including the approximate file sizes.

TABLE 14.1
16-Bit Real-Mode Drivers Eliminated in Windows 95

Description	File(s)	Memory Saved
Microsoft Network client software	NET.EXE	95 KB
Novell NetWare client software	Various	155 KB
MS-DOS extended file sharing	SHARE.EXE	17 KB
Adaptec SCSI driver	ASPI4DOS.SYS	5 KB
Adaptec CD-ROM driver	ASPICD.SYS	11 KB
Microsoft CD-ROM Extensions	MSCDEX.EXE	39 KB
SmartDrive disk caching software	SMARTDRV.EXE	28 KB
Microsoft Mouse driver	MOUSE.COM	17 KB

As table 14.1 shows, you can save a significant amount of memory by using 32-bit protected-mode components.

Conventional Memory Compatibility

Some MS-DOS-based applications don't run properly under Windows 3.*x.* Some MS-DOS applications, for example, require lots of available free conventional memory, and thus won't run in a DOS virtual machine (VM), owing to large real-mode components such as network drivers or device drivers. Other MS-DOS-based applications will not run under Windows 3.*x* because they require direct access to the computer hardware and conflict with Windows' own device drivers.

One goal in Windows 95 is to provide better support for MS-DOS-based applications. In doing so, the designers have attempted to provide support for not only "clean" MS-DOS-based applications (those that run well under Windows 3.*x*) but also those "bad" MS-DOS-based applications that try to take over the hardware or require machine resources unavailable under Windows 3.*x.*

Many graphics-oriented MS-DOS-based games assume that they are the only application running in the system, and, therefore, they attempt to directly access and manipulate the underlying hardware. As a result, they do not run well, if at all, in an

MS-DOS VM under Windows 3.x. In fact, games are the most notorious class of MS-DOS-based applications that do not get along well with Windows 3.x. Some of these applications write to video memory directly, manipulate the hardware support resources, such as clock timers, and take over hardware resources, such as sound cards.

Windows 95 provides better support for running MS-DOS-based applications that interact with the hardware, including better virtualization of computer resources, such as timers and sound device support. In addition, 32-bit protected-mode device drivers benefit MS-DOS-based applications by providing more free conventional memory than is available under Windows 3.x, enabling a class of memory-intensive applications to run properly.

Different MS-DOS-based applications require varying levels of support from both the computer hardware and from the operating system. Some MS-DOS-based games require close to 100 percent use of the CPU to perform properly, for example, and other MS-DOS-based applications modify interrupt addresses and other low-level hardware settings. Windows 95 provides several different levels of support for running these MS-DOS-based applications. These levels of support take into account that different applications interact with the hardware in different ways.

By default, MS-DOS-based applications are preemptively multitasked with other tasks running on the system, and can run full-screen or in a window.

Single MS-DOS Application Mode

To provide support for the most intrusive set of MS-DOS-based applications that work only under MS-DOS and require 100 percent access to the system components and system resources, Windows 95 provides a mechanism equivalent to running an MS-DOS-based application from real-mode MS-DOS, called *single MS-DOS application mode*. Although fewer MS-DOS-based applications need to run in this mode because of improved compatibility support, this mode provides an escape-hatch mechanism for running applications that run only under MS-DOS.

To run an MS-DOS-based application in this mode, you can set the Single MS-DOS Application Mode property from the Program page on the MS-DOS property sheet for the application. In this mode, Windows 95 removes itself from memory (except for a small stub) and provides the MS-DOS-based application with full access to all the resources in the computer. Before you run an MS-DOS-based application in this mode, Windows 95 prompts you to tell it whether it can end other running tasks. Upon your approval, Windows 95 ends all running tasks, loads a real-mode copy of MS-DOS, and launches the specified application—kind of like exiting Windows 3.x and running the specified MS-DOS-based application under MS-DOS. After you exit the MS-DOS-based application, Windows 95 restarts and returns the screen to the Windows 95 desktop.

Improved Memory Protection

To support a higher level of memory protection for running MS-DOS-based applications, Windows 95 also includes a global memory protection attribute on the Program property page that protects the MS-DOS system area from "rogue" MS-DOS-based applications. When the global memory protection attribute is set, the MS-DOS system area sections are write-protected so that applications can't write data into this memory area and corrupt MS-DOS support and MS-DOS-based device drivers.

In addition to the system area protection, Windows 95 performs enhanced parameter validation for file I/O requests issued through the MS-DOS INT 21h function, providing a higher degree of safety.

This option is not enabled by default for all MS-DOS-based applications due to the additional overhead associated with providing improved parameter and memory address checking. You need to set this flag manually if you constantly encounter difficulty running a specific MS-DOS-based application.

32-Bit Applications versus 16-Bit Applications

A 32-bit Windows application generally requires more virtual memory than the original 16-bit Windows application. However, the 32-bit version of the application can have a smaller working set. (Recall from the section on virtual memory paging that the *working set* is the certain number of pages that the Virtual Memory Manager must keep in memory for a process to execute efficiently.) The lower the working set of an application, the fewer pages of virtual memory are needed and the less RAM is used.

Sometimes it might seem that the 32-bit version of an application running on Windows 95 requires more RAM than the 16-bit version of the same application running on the same computer system. This is because segments of a 16-bit application are loaded only as they are referenced or needed, whereas the address space is reserved for the 32-bit application and all its dynamic link libraries when the program is initially loaded.

This is why the memory count that appears in the Help About dialog box can be misleading. The free memory reported for 16-bit applications is reduced only by the number of segments actually loaded in memory, not the total number of segments. On the other hand, the free memory reported for 32-bit applications is reduced by the total address space required for the application—that is, the total amount that the

VMM reserves for the application upon initial program load. However, this free memory represents only the virtual address space that all applications share, not the amount of RAM actually used.

Understanding Hexadecimal Addressing

Serious computer users and programmers might have an occasion to address computer memory directly. Therefore, no discussion of computer memory is complete without a discussion of the numbering system used to address computer memory.

Memory addressing on the computer is done via a base-16 numbering system called *hexadecimal*. This memory addressing system enables the computer to reference each location in memory. However, because it is based on the base-16 numbering system, the addresses at first might seem a little confusing.

The decimal numbering system that we are all used to is a base-10 numbering system. So the number 655,360 seems more understandable to us than the number A0000. Table 14.2 depicts the direct relationship between these two different numbering systems.

TABLE 14.2
Hexadecimal Numbers

Hexadecimal Number	Decimal Equivalent
1	1
2	2
3	3
4	4
5	5
6	6
7	7
8	8
9	9
A	10
B	11

continues

TABLE 14.2, CONTINUED
Hexadecimal Numbers

Hexadecimal Number	Decimal Equivalent
C	12
D	13
E	14
F	15

Because the decimal numbering system is base-10, every digit is equal to its value times the base (10) to the power of its position in relation to the decimal point. For example, in the following table the number 9,999 is broken down to show you the math behind each of the digits.

TABLE 14.3
Base-10 Numbering System

9×10^3	9,000
9×10^2	900
9×10^1	90
9×10^0	9
Total:	9,999

Now, in the hexadecimal numbering system, instead of 10 being raised to the power of the digits in relation to their position to the decimal point, 16 is the number used. Rather than 1×10^4, you have 1×16^4. Table 16.4 takes the same number (9,999) and shows you the value it represents in the hexadecimal numbering system.

TABLE 14.4
Base-16 Numbering System

9×16^3	36,864
9×16^2	2,304
9×16^1	144
9×16^0	9
Total	39,321 (decimal value)

Here is one more example of a hexadecimal number, again taking the hexadecimal number and converting it to its decimal equivalent: The hexadecimal memory address for the upper limit for conventional memory (640 KB) is *A0000*. Table 14.5 converts this value to decimal. (Note the value *A* is equal to the decimal value 10 refereed to table 14.3.)

TABLE 14.5
A0000 Converted to Decimal Value

$A \times 16^4$ (10×16^4)	655,360
0×16^3	0
0×16^2	0
0×16^1	0
0×16^0	0
Total	655,360 (decimal value)

A deep knowledge of hexadecimal math usually isn't required to understand memory addressing. However an understanding of the base-16 numbering system does take some of the mystery out of those memory addresses such as *AFFF* or *FFFF*.

CHAPTER

15

Optimizing Data Storage

As operating systems and applications have become larger and the number of applications you use has become greater, disk space has become increasingly more important. Ten years ago, 40 MB hard disks were common on the average PC; today's PCs often contain hard disks that have capacities equal to 10 or 20 times that amount. A complete installation of Windows 95, *without* the optional administration tools, requires more than 80 MB of disk space, and Windows 95 accesses your disk often. Therefore, optimal hard disk performance is essential if you want optimum Windows 95 performance.

This chapter examines the FAT file system that Windows 95 uses and explains the utilities included in Windows 95 that enable you to compress and manage your disks. The chapter covers the following topics:

◆ Understanding disk and file system structure

◆ Optimizing partition and cluster size

◆ Analyzing and repairing disks using ScanDisk

◆ Defragmenting a disk

◆ Increasing disk capacity using DriveSpace

◆ Improving CD-ROM performance

◆ Preserving long file names

◆ Using troubleshooting options

Although you don't have to understand how your disks and the Windows 95 file system work before you can use the Windows 95 disk and file utilities, possessing such an understanding can help you use your disks and the disk tools more effectively. The following section explains disk and file system structure to help you maximize your computer's disks and file system.

Understanding Disk and File System Structure

In the past, understanding how your disks and file system worked wasn't very important, because you just couldn't do much about your disk's performance. The increase in drive capacities and the proliferation of disk compression has changed that—now, understanding the computer's disks and file system potentially can save wasted disk space and help you get the most out of your computer.

 Note   For the most part, Windows 95 uses the same disk and file structure as DOS. Therefore, most of the material that describes disk and file structure applies to DOS as well as Windows 95.

The first thing you should understand is the physical structure of the disk and how data is partitioned on the disk. Instead of containing a single disk like a floppy disk, a hard disk contains multiple rigid platters (disks), all spinning together on a common spindle. These platters most often are made of aluminum or glass, and are coated with a magnetically sensitive material. Above the surface of each platter rides a read-write head that reads data from and writes data to the disk.

The disk needs some form of map to enable the disk controller to position the heads to locate any given piece of data on the disk. Therefore, each of the platters is magnetically formatted in circular rings, called *tracks*. Tracks are further divided into segments, called *sectors*. A sector is the smallest unit of storage on a disk. The corresponding tracks on the disk's platters form a *cylinder*. Figure 15.1 illustrates cylinders, tracks, and sectors. Essentially, tracks and sectors break the data space on the disk into manageable, logical chunks.

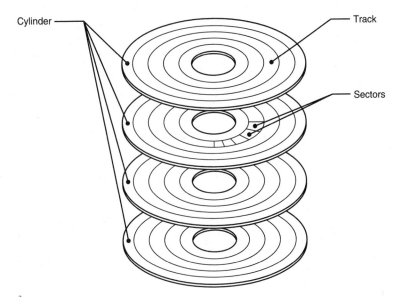

Figure 15.1

Cylinders, tracks, and sectors on a disk.

 Note The number of sectors in a track depend on the type of disk. With IDE drives, the number of tracks per sector is stored in your computer's CMOS settings. SCSI drives, however, maintain their configuration information in their own BIOS chips.

Just dividing a disk into cylinders, tracks, and sectors doesn't provide a way to locate information on the disk. Therefore, each sector is referenced by a unique number. In addition, every platter in the disk contains two surfaces, each of which is serviced by a read-write head. The cylinder number references the track, the head number identifies the surface read from or written to, and the sector number defines the exact location of the data.

For example, "cylinder 0, head 1, sector 14" represents a unique and specific sector on the disk. This three-dimensional location data defines the disk's absolute sectors. Windows 95 then allocates a relative sector number to each absolute sector. Relative sector 0, which corresponds to cylinder 0, head 1, sector 1, defines the disk's boot record location. The boot record contains information about the partitions on the disk and other information that enables Windows 95 to boot the system. Relative sector 1, the first data sector, corresponds to the absolute sector at cylinder 0, head 1, sector 2. Other data sectors are numbered sequentially as relative sectors 3, 4, 5, and so on.

Clusters

Windows 95, as with DOS before it, allocates disk space in clusters. A *cluster* is a group of sectors on a disk. The number of sectors in a cluster varies according to the drive type and partition size, as shown in table 15.1, which lists cluster and sector relationships for common PC drive types. When Windows 95 stores a file on disk, it doesn't store the file on a sector-by-sector basis. Rather, Windows 95 allocates enough clusters to contain the file. As you learn later in this chapter, in the section "Optimizing Partition and Cluster Size," Windows 95's method for storing a file can lead to a considerable waste of disk space.

TABLE 15.1
Clusters and Sectors Relationships

Type of Disk	Cluster Size (in bytes)	Sectors per Cluster
3 1/2-inch floppy	1,024	2
1.2 MB floppy	512	1
0–15 MB partition*	4,096	8
16–127 MB partition*	2,048	4
128–255 MB partition*	4,096	8
256–511 MB partition*	8,192	16
512 MB–<1 GB partition*	16,384	32
1 GB or more*	32,768	64

*Also applies to similarly sized disks consisting of a single partition and to logical drives in an extended partition.

Tip
A little division in Table 15.1 shows you that the size of one sector is 512 bytes, regardless of disk type. Each sector also contains a 59-byte sector ID header that includes head, cylinder, and sector numbers; an address mark to indicate where the sector begins; and cyclical redundancy check (CRC) information to enable error detection in the sector ID header. The 59 bytes that comprise each sector are part of the reason that a formatted disk contains less storage space than its theoretical unformatted capacity.

Primary Partitions

A hard disk is partitioned in logical storage areas. A *partition* is a series of clusters on the disk that provides a way to group clusters into logical, collective units so that the clusters can be recognized as a logical drive represented by a drive letter, such as C, D, and so on. A partition has a starting sector and an ending sector, and the number of sectors in between defines the capacity of the partition.

You can use the UNFORMAT command from the Windows 95 command line to display the partition tables for each disk in your computer. You also can use the FDISK command to display partition information, but UNFORMAT is safer because, unlike FDISK, UNFORMAT does not have the capability to remove your disk partitions. To use UNFORMAT to view your partition information, enter the command **UNFORMAT /PARTN /L** at the Windows 95 command prompt. You should see output similar to the following:

```
Hard Disk Partition Table display.
Drive # 80h has 1010 cylinders, 60 heads, 34 sectors (from BIOS).
The following table is from drive 80h, cylinder 0, head 0, sector 1:
```

Type	Total_size Bytes	Sectors	Start_partition Cyl	Head	Sector	End_partition Cyl	Head	Sector	Rel#
HUGE Boot	1006M	2060366	0	1	1	1009	59	34	34

```
Drive # 81h has 998 cylinders, 38 heads, 17 sectors (from BIOS).

The following table is from drive 81h, cylinder 0, head 0, sector 1:
```

Type	Total_size Bytes	Sectors	Start_partition Cyl	Head	Sector	End_partition Cyl	Head	Sector	Rel#
HUGE	315M	644691	0	1	1	997	37	17	17

Note UNFORMAT is a DOS command, and is not included with Windows 95. If your system does not include a set of files from your previous version of DOS, you will not have the UNFORMAT command on your computer.

The preceding sample output comes from a computer that has two physical disks, each of which contains only one partition. The first disk, which indicates "Boot" in its Type listing, is drive C. The other disk is drive D. The listing for both drives includes the starting and ending sectors specified by the cylinder (track), head, and sector number.

Note A primary partition can contain only one logical drive, such as C or D. Extended partitions, explained in the next section, can contain multiple logical drives.

Extended Partitions

A PC's disk also can contain extended partitions. The disk must contain a primary partition, but that primary partition can contain extended partitions. Unlike a primary partition, an extended partition can contain multiple logical drives. You use the FDISK command to create primary and secondary partitions.

The FAT

With so many clusters on a disk, Windows 95 needs some way to keep track of where each file and directory resides. Essentially, Windows 95 needs to know the starting and ending cluster for each file. The file allocation table, or FAT, provides that information. The FAT contains an entry for every cluster on the disk, and Windows 95 uses the FAT to keep track of which clusters are allocated to which files and directories. The FAT is the key that enables Windows 95 to locate, read, and write files on the disk.

A FAT cluster entry can contain any one of the entries listed in table 15.2.

TABLE 15.2
Possible FAT Cluster Entries

Entry	Meaning
0	Cluster is available
BAD	Cluster contains bad sector and can't be used
Reserved	Cluster has been set aside for use only by Windows 95
EOF	Marks the last cluster of a file
### (numbers)	Number identifying the next cluster in the file

The FAT isn't very useful by itself. Windows 95 uses the root directory table in conjunction with the FAT to locate a file. The root directory table contains the name of the files in the root directory (including subdirectory entries) and the starting cluster number of each file.

To understand how the two tables work together, take the following example: Assume you open Notepad and then open a text file located in the root directory. To read the file, Windows 95 first looks in the root directory table and finds that the file (for the sake of the example) starts in cluster 200. Windows 95 reads the data from cluster 200. Then, Windows 95 reads the FAT entry for clusters 200 and finds the value 201, which indicates that the next data cluster is 201. Windows 95 reads the data from

cluster 201. Windows 95 then returns to the FAT to read the entry for cluster 201 so it knows where to go next. The FAT entry for cluster 201 reads 340, indicating that the next data cluster for the file is cluster 340, so Windows 95 reads the data from cluster 340. Next, Windows 95 goes back to the FAT to read the entry for cluster 340 and finds the value to be EOF, indicating that cluster 340 represents the end of the file. The file read operation is complete.

The root directory table also contains entries for any subdirectories directly under the root directory. Subdirectory entries in the root directory reference the starting cluster of the subdirectory's file list. The subdirectory file list indicates the starting cluster for each of the files in the directory. Windows 95 then uses the information in the FAT to locate the file according to its starting cluster.

VFAT, CDFS, and VCACHE

DOS and Windows 3.*x* interact with the disk's FAT in real mode. Windows for Workgroups introduced *VFAT*, a virtual installable file system driver that provided a 32-bit interface between applications and the file system. An expanded and improved version of VFAT is an integral part of Windows 95. VFAT operates in protected mode, enabling Windows 95 and applications, 16-bit or 32-bit, to access the file system without switching the processor from protected mode to real mode, which significantly improves performance.

 Note   VFAT simply serves as an interface between applications and the FAT on the disk. There is no difference between the disk's FAT under Windows 95 or DOS.

Working in conjunction with VFAT is a virtual cache called *VCACHE,* a 32-bit protected-mode disk cache. A disk cache improves file I/O performance by caching recently used data and reading it from memory rather than disk on subsequent requests for the data. A cache also postpones disk writes until the system is inactive, which improves system performance. VCACHE replaces SmartDrive, the 16-bit disk cache used with Windows 3.*x*. Unlike SmartDrive, VCACHE provides a dynamically resizable cache to improve memory utilization. Windows 95 automatically sizes the cache at any given time according to the demands on the system.

In addition to VFAT and VCACHE, Windows 95 includes a 32-bit protected-mode CD-ROM file system driver, called CDFS. Like VFAT, CDFS improves file I/O by enabling applications to read from the CD-ROM drive in protected mode rather than requiring the system to switch to real mode to read the CD. CDFS replaces the 16-bit MSCDEX program included with DOS and Windows 3.*x*.

For more information on CDFS, refer to the section "Improving CD-ROM Performance" later in this chapter.

Optimizing Partition and Cluster Size

Now that you have some background in disk and file system structures, you're ready to begin optimizing your disk in Windows 95. One very important consideration if your computer contains a large hard disk is the size of the partition(s) you create on the disk.

At face value, the information in table 15.1 might mean very little to you in practical terms. The relationship between clusters, sectors, and disk size, however, is extremely important when you go to determine how efficiently your computer's disks store data. By simply changing your disk partition method, you can recoup a huge amount of disk space that you might otherwise waste.

You might wonder where to find that wasted space, and then, how to recover it. First, you need to understand that Windows 95, like DOS before it, allocates disk space by clusters. When a file needs to be written to the disk, Windows 95 allocates just enough clusters to contain the file. Assume that you want to store a 60 KB file (61,440 bytes). If you store the file on a 3 1/2-inch disk, which uses a cluster size of 1,024 bytes, Windows 95 allocates 60 clusters for the file. All the sectors contain data, and there are no leftover empty sectors, nor any wasted space (60 clusters × 1,024 bytes per cluster = 61,440 bytes).

Now, assume that you store that same 60 KB file on a 1 GB hard disk that has a single partition, which uses a cluster size of 32,768 bytes, 64 sectors per cluster (refer to table 15.1). One cluster doesn't provide enough space to accommodate the file. Therefore, Windows 95 allocates two clusters, totaling 65,536 bytes—4,096 bytes more than the file requires, leaving 8 empty sectors in the second cluster (4,096 bytes / 512 bytes per sector = 8 sectors). Unfortunately, Windows 95 can allocate space only by clusters, not by sectors, so those 8 sectors can't be reassigned, and so are wasted. In this example, almost 7 percent of the space the 60 KB file uses is wasted.

Note "Sector slack," or wasted sectors, is not unique to Windows 95. DOS, which relies on essentially the same FAT-based file structure as Windows 95, suffers from the same problem. Many other operating systems also suffer from sector slack, although NetWare 4.x and Windows NT are exceptions, allocating space much more efficiently.

The actual amount of wasted space on a disk as a result of unfilled sectors in a cluster depends on the number of files on the disk, the size of the files, and the disk type (which defines the sector and cluster sizes). When you consider the large number of files probably stored on your hard disk and the potential for wasted space each one offers, you can see that your disk could contain plenty of empty sectors. Using the 7 percent waste in the previous example, you would lose roughly 73 MB of space on a 1 GB disk. If your files used as much as 20 percent wasted space, it would amount to

nearly 200 MB of wasted space. Even larger percentages of wasted space are possible, so cluster size is a very important issue if you want to optimize your hard disk's space.

The solution is to reduce the cluster size so that Windows 95 allocates disk space in smaller chunks, which reduces wasted space. Wasting half of a 4,096-byte cluster is much better than wasting half of a 32,768-byte cluster. Unfortunately, the only way to change cluster size is to change the size of the partition. The only way to change the size of the partition is to delete the partition and re-create it. When you delete a partition, you lose all data in the partition. If you back up your entire disk, deleting and re-creating the partition is not a problem, because you can simply restore the files after you re-create the partition. Backing up an entire disk, particularly a high-capacity disk, can be time-consuming, however, if you don't have a high-capacity (and generally expensive) tape backup system.

If you are willing to back up your entire system, deleting the partition and re-creating it is a good way to recover a significant amount of free space from your disk. The following sections offer advice on how to go about it.

Tip   Before you begin to repartition your disks, you should understand that an alternative exists—DriveSpace, the compressed disk structure Windows 95 supports. DriveSpace allocates space in a compressed volume on a sector-by-sector basis, rather than by clusters, effectively eliminating cluster slack space. This makes DriveSpace volumes the most efficient mechanism in Windows 95 for optimizing the use of your hard disk's space. DriveSpace volumes are limited to a compressed size of no more than 512 MB. If a maximum size of 512 MB is adequate for your needs, however, creating DriveSpace volumes is considerably easier and quicker than repartitioning the disk. Refer to the section "Increasing Disk Capacity with DriveSpace" later in this chapter for a complete discussion of the advantages, disadvantages, and use of DriveSpace in Windows 95. Also, note that the DriveSpace3 utility included with Microsoft Plus! for Windows 95 supports compressed volumes larger than 512 MB. For more informatoin on Plus!, refer to Chapter 16.

Choosing a Partition Size

Reducing the size of your current partition reduces the partition's capacity. To get full use of the disk, therefore, you need to create multiple partitions. If you have a 1 GB disk, for example, the cluster size for a single partition is 32,768 bytes. If you create four partitions of 256 MB each, the cluster size in each partition is one-fourth that size, or 8,192 bytes. Reducing the partition size by 1 megabyte to 255 MB results in a cluster size of 4,096. You can see that reducing the partition size results in a reduction in cluster size and a potential savings in disk space that you otherwise would lose to unfilled clusters.

A PC's disk is limited to no more than four partitions. If you want to reduce the cluster size on a large disk, an alternative to creating multiple partitions is to create an extended partition, then create logical drives in the extended partition. You could, for example, create a primary partition of 255 MB, then create an extended partition that uses the rest of your hard disk's available clusters. Then, you would create multiple logical drives in the extended partition.

The size and configuration of drives you ultimately choose depends on the size of your drive and the cluster size you want to achieve. Whether you configure a new system or repartition your existing system, look at the applications you plan to install on the disk. Try to group the applications together so they fit on a disk without much wasted space.

Creating Partitions

The FDISK program enables you to view, create, and delete partitions and logical drives. Before you use FDISK, however, you *must* back up your existing data on the disk, because repartitioning destroys all data on the disk.

Stop Backing up your existing data is an extremely important step. Refer to Chapter 22, "Using Backup," for a discussion of backing up your computer. Also, remember that repartitioning the disk deletes your backup program from the disk. If you use a Windows 3.x-based backup program, you need to reinstall Windows 3.x and the backup program before you can restore your files after you reformat the disk. If you use a DOS-based backup program, you have to reinstall the backup program after you reformat the disk. And, if you use the Backup utility in Windows 95 to back up the system, you have to reinstall Windows 95 before you can restore the data. Plan the entire process carefully to make sure you can restore your data with the least amount of effort, and verify that you have the source files for the backup utility on disk or CD so you *can* reinstall it.

If you currently have Windows 95 on the system and want to repartition the disk to use its space more effectively, back up the entire system, including all logical disks. Then, back up to disk a copy of your Registry files, System.dat and User.dat, so you can restore them later from a new Windows 95 installation and recover all your previous Windows 95 settings. Although the Backup utility does back up the Registry files, you still should make a copy on disk. The section "Completing the Process" later in this chapter explains how to restore your Windows 95 files after you repartition a disk.

Partitioning a New Disk

If you have purchased a new computer or hard disk and Windows 95 is not installed on the disk, you must have a bootable Windows 95 disk or a bootable DOS disk that contains the FDISK and FORMAT programs. To partition the disk, insert the boot disk in drive A and turn on the computer. When the system boots, enter **FDISK** at the command prompt to start the FDISK program.

After you start FDISK, you should see a menu similar to the following:

```
1. Create DOS partition or Logical DOS Drive
2. Set active partition
3. Delete partition or logical DOS drive
4. Display partition information
5. Change current fixed disk drive
```

Select menu item 1, then on the next menu select item 1 again to create a primary DOS partition. FDISK displays a prompt similar to the following:

```
Current fixed disk drive: 1

Do you wish to use the maximum available size for a Primary DOS
➡Partition and make the partition active? (Y/N)
```

If you have a large disk, you probably do not want to use the maximum available space for the partition, because that would give you a large cluster size. Instead, answer **N** to create a primary partition of a size that results in the cluster size you want. You use the remaining space on the disk to create an extended partition and logical drives.

After you answer **N**, FDISK presents a message similar to the following:

```
Total disk space is nnn Mbytes (1 Mbyte = 1048576 bytes)
Maximum space available for partition is nnn Mbytes
Enter partition size in Mbytes or percent of disk space (%) to
➡rate a Primary DOS Partition
```

In this example, *nnn* represents a value that FDISK displays, based on the disk capacity. Enter the size, in megabytes, for the primary DOS partition. Specify a size that results in the cluster size you want (use the information in table 15.1).

 Note If you intend to install Windows NT on your computer in the future, you might want to leave partition space available for an NTFS partition. Note, however, that neither Windows 95 nor DOS can read NTFS partitions. NT, however, can read the Windows 95 (DOS) partitions.

After you create the primary DOS partition, FDISK restarts. Because the disk has not yet been formatted, you still need a bootable disk in drive A. After the system boots, run FDISK again. Then select menu item 2 to create an extended DOS partition. If you don't want to add a NTFS or HPFS partition in the future, use all remaining space on the disk for the extended partition.

After you create the extended partition, you must create logical drives in it. Follow the FDISK's prompts to create an appropriate number of logical drives in the extended partition. Remember that the size of each logical drive determines its cluster size, so choose a drive size that will give you the cluster size you want.

Repartitioning an Existing Disk

If you want to repartition an existing drive to change the partition size or divide the disk into smaller logical drives, you first must back up the entire disk. If the disk contains multiple logical drives or multiple partitions, you must back up all drives and partitions. After you back up the disk, make sure you have a copy of the backup program you used so you can reinstall the backup program after you re-create the partition(s).

 Stop   Before you run FDISK, be sure to back up all your hard disks, because FDISK will destroy all files on the disk.

After you back up the disk and ensure that you have an installable copy of the backup program, you're ready to delete the existing partition(s) and create new ones. First, make sure that you have a bootable Windows 95 or DOS disk that contains the FDISK and FORMAT programs. Then, run FDISK (you can run FDISK from the command prompt without booting from the floppy—you use the bootable disk after you remove the existing partition).

At the FDISK menu, select menu item 3, "Delete partition or Logical DOS Drive." FDISK then displays a new menu similar to the following:

```
1. Delete Primary DOS Partition
2. Delete Extended DOS Partition
3. Delete Logical DOS Drive(s) in the Extended DOS Partition
4. Delete Non-DOS Partition
```

If your disk currently contains an extended partition, select option 2 to delete the extended partition and all its logical drives. If your hard disk already has a small enough primary DOS partition to give you the cluster size you want, leave the primary DOS partition in place and simply create a new extended partition, then re-create smaller logical drives in the extended partition. If the existing primary DOS partition is larger than you want, delete the primary DOS partition.

After you delete the existing partitions, you need to create a new primary DOS partition, an extended DOS partition, and new logical drives in the extended partition. Use the procedure explained in the previous section, "Partitioning a New Disk," to create the primary DOS partition. Size the partition to achieve the cluster size you want. For a cluster size of 4,096, for example, create a primary partition of 255 MB or less. Then, use the remaining available space to create an extended partition. In the extended partition, create logical drives of whatever size results in the cluster size you want for each drive.

Formatting the Disk

After you create the partitions, exit FDISK to reboot the computer using the boot floppy. After the computer boots, use the FORMAT command to format the boot drive, which should be drive C. To do so, enter **FORMAT C: /S** at the command prompt. FORMAT formats the disk and transfers the system files to the disk. Then, use FORMAT to format each of the logical drives you created in the extended partition. You need to use the /S switch only for drive C—you don't need to format the other logical disks as system disks.

Completing the Process

After you format the disks, you can install an operating system on the disk. How you proceed here depends on whether you want to set up a new system or upgrade an existing system. For a new system, simply begin the Windows 95 Setup process and install Windows 95 as explained in Chapter 2, "Setting Up and Booting Windows 95." Then you can install your applications.

If you need to upgrade an existing system from DOS or Windows 3.x to Windows 95, however, you need to decide whether to reinstall DOS and Windows 3.x, or install Windows 95. Unfortunately, you can't just install Windows 95 and then restore your applications. You have to install Windows 95 over an existing copy of Windows 3.x or reinstall all your applications before they can function properly in Windows 95.

Tip You don't have to reinstall DOS applications before they can function in Windows 95. You also generally do not need to reinstall Windows applications that do not require settings in System.ini or Win.ini—you can restore them from the backup set. You need to reinstall only Windows 95 applications that modify the System.ini and Win.ini files, or that use OLE, to work under Windows 95. Therefore, you might not need to reinstall all your applications. You can restore some from the backup set.

If you have a number of applications that you think you need to reinstall to work under Windows 95, restore your previous copies of DOS and Windows 3.x to the disks, and rearrange them on the new disks as you want (you should, however, restore DOS and Windows 3.*x* to drive C). Reboot the system to verify that it works properly. Then, run the Windows 95 Setup program to upgrade your existing copy of Windows 3.*x* to Windows 95 (see Chapter 2).

If you have already installed Windows 95 on the system, have backed up the system using Windows 95 Backup, and have repartitioned the disk to make more efficient use of space, reinstall a minimal copy of Windows 95, including the Backup utility. Next, use Backup to restore all files to the disk, then reboot the system to the command prompt. Copy your Registry files from the disk copies you made previously to the hard disk to restore all your Registry settings from the previous Windows 95 installation. Then, reboot the system to start Windows 95.

Adding a Disk

If you add a new disk to a computer that contains an existing hard disk, you don't have to back up your existing disk, although doing so regularly is a good idea. When you install a second disk, you can retain the existing disk as the boot disk or install the new disk as a boot disk. You also need to consider a few items when you install a second disk, to ensure that it doesn't conflict with the existing disk.

If you install a second IDE drive, check the documentation for the disks to determine how to set the drive to be a slave or a master drive. Set the boot disk as the master and the second as the slave. If you install a new SCSI disk, be sure to set the SCSI ID of the new disk so that it does not conflict with the SCSI ID of the existing disk or any other SCSI devices, such as CD-ROM drives, tape drives, scanners, and so forth.

 Tip   For instructions and tips on installing a second hard disk, read *Keeping Your PC Alive, Special Edition*, from New Riders Publishing.

If you decide to install the new disk as a secondary disk (not the boot disk), just install the drive and boot the system. Run FDISK to create the necessary partitions on the disk, then use FORMAT to format the disk(s). Then you can begin using the new disk.

 Stop   When you use FDISK to partition the new hard disk, make sure you do not select the original hard disk by mistake.

If you decide to install the new disk as the boot disk, first install the drive as a secondary disk. Use FDISK to partition the disk, then use **FORMAT /S** to format the new disk as a bootable disk. Then, use **XCOPY** *source destination* **/E /H /K** to copy all files from the old disk to the new disk. To copy all files from drive C to drive F, for example, use the command **XCOPY C:*.* F: /E /H /K**. Then, shut down the system,

swap the drives (resetting their master/slave or SCSI ID status), and restart the system. You can use Explorer or File Manager to complete the file transfer process if you need to copy additional disks.

Note Some IDE drives cannot be configured as slave drives, so you might be unable to install the new drive as a second drive. Instead, you will have to use the new drive as the master drive and the existing drive as the slave (assuming the existing drive can be configured as a slave drive).

Analyzing and Repairing Disks with ScanDisk

MS-DOS 6.*x* includes a utility called ScanDisk that you can use to scan a disk for defects and repair many of those defects. Windows 95 includes a new version called ScanDisk for Windows that runs as a Windows 95 application. Windows 95 also includes a command-line version (DOS version) of ScanDisk.

Using the Windows 95 versions of ScanDisk rather than any previous version of ScanDisk you might have on your system is extremely important. Not only do the Windows 95 versions of ScanDisk ensure the security of long file names, but ScanDisk for Windows offers the capability to scan and repair disks as a background task while you work with other applications. Using a previous version of ScanDisk will destroy your system's long file names if you allow ScanDisk to repair any disk errors it finds.

ScanDisk can detect and repair a number of types of problems with your computer's file system, including the following:

◆ FAT (file allocation table) errors

◆ Invalid long file names

◆ File system structure problems, such as lost clusters and cross-linked files

◆ Directory tree errors

◆ Bad tracks (physical surface errors)

◆ DriveSpace and DoubleSpace header, file structure, compression structure, and signatures

Tip ScanDisk performs the functions of the DOS CHKDSK utility, eliminating the need to use CHKDSK.

The GUI version, ScanDisk for Windows, is contained in the file Scandskw.exe. The DOS version is contained in the file Scandisk.exe. If you open a DOS session in Windows 95 and enter **SCANDISK.EXE** at the command prompt, Windows 95 starts the GUI version, Scandskw.exe, instead. The two are functionally equivalent, but they support different command-line switches that modify the way ScanDisk runs. These command-line switches are explained later in this chapter, in the section "Using ScanDisk Switches."

Running ScanDisk

All Windows 95 disk utilities are located in the Start/Programs/Accessories/System Tools menu. To start the GUI version of ScanDisk, click on the Start button, then choose <u>P</u>rograms, Accessories, System Tools, and ScanDisk. The ScanDisk dialog box appears, as shown in figure 15.2.

Figure 15.2

The ScanDisk dialog box.

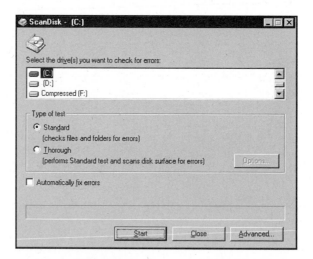

 Tip You also can start ScanDisk for a specific disk by opening the disk's property sheet and selecting the Tools page. The Tools page indicates the number of days since you last ran ScanDisk to analyze the disk.

ScanDisk offers two modes for disk detection and repair—Stan<u>d</u>ard and <u>T</u>horough. The Stan<u>d</u>ard option causes ScanDisk to check the file system structure, including the FAT, directory entries, long file names, and other file system parameters. The

Thorough option causes ScanDisk to perform a surface analysis of the disk in addition to the standard detection and repair.

To check a disk, select it from the drive list, then choose Standard or Thorough. If you choose Thorough, you can choose the Options button to specify options for the additional surface scan. Choosing Options displays the Surface Scan Options dialog box, shown in figure 15.3.

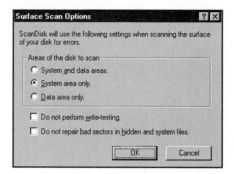

Figure 15.3

The Surface Scan Options dialog box.

The options in the Surface Scan Options dialog box are explained in the following list:

◆ **Areas of the disk to scan.** Use this group of options to specify which areas of the disk to scan for defects. You can direct ScanDisk to scan the system area, data area, or both.

◆ **Do not perform write-testing.** If you clear this check box, ScanDisk reads and writes each sector of the disk to check its integrity. If you enable this check box, ScanDisk reads the sector data only, and does not rewrite the data.

◆ **Do not repair bad sectors in hidden and system files.** By default, ScanDisk repairs bad sectors in hidden and system files by writing these sectors to a new location. A few older applications require the sectors of their hidden and system files to be in a specific sector to run the program (as a copy-protection scheme). Enabling this check box prevents ScanDisk from relocating the sectors of hidden and system files to new locations, even if their sectors are bad.

By default, ScanDisk prompts you with various dialog boxes when it encounters a disk error. Figure 15.4 shows an example of such a dialog box.

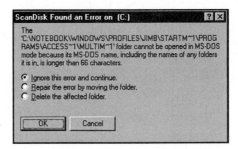

Figure 15.4

A dialog box generated by ScanDisk to report an error.

If you prefer that ScanDisk automatically repair all errors without input from you, enable the Automatically fix errors check box and choose Start in the ScanDisk dialog box.

Setting Advanced ScanDisk Options

ScanDisk includes a number of advanced options you can set to control the way ScanDisk runs, detects errors, and repairs those errors. To set these advanced options, choose the Advanced button to display the ScanDisk Advanced Options dialog box, shown in figure 15.5.

Figure 15.5

The ScanDisk Advanced Options dialog box.

Display Summary

The three options in the Display summary group control whether ScanDisk displays a summary dialog box after it finishes the detection and repair phase. Choose Always if you want ScanDisk to always display a summary report regardless of whether it detects and fixes any errors. Choose Never if you don't want ScanDisk to display a summary report. Choose the Only if errors found option if you want ScanDisk to generate a summary report only if it detects errors during its scan.

Log File

The three options in the Log file group control the way ScanDisk logs detection and repair information. If ScanDisk is configured to create a log, ScanDisk creates the file Scandisk.log in the root directory of the disk it checks. This log file contains a report of the errors ScanDisk finds and the actions ScanDisk takes regarding those errors.

Choose Replace log if you want ScanDisk to create a new log each time it runs, replacing any existing copy of Scandisk.log. Choose Append to log if you want ScanDisk to append new log entries to the end of the existing log. Choose the No log option if you don't want ScanDisk to create a log.

Cross-Linked Files

A *cross-link* occurs when two or more files use the same cluster. Typically, the cluster really belongs to only one of the files. Sometimes, the cross-linked cluster might really belong to neither file. Therefore, repairing cross-linked files usually results in only one file remaining usable.

The options in the Cross-linked files group control the way ScanDisk handles any cross-linked files it finds during detection. If you choose the Delete option, ScanDisk deletes any files that have cross-linked clusters. Choose the Make copies option if you want ScanDisk to retain the files. ScanDisk creates a separate copy of the cluster for each file. Although this removes the link between the files, it does not ensure that either file ends up usable. Choose the Ignore option if you want ScanDisk to ignore cross-linked files.

Tip   If you decide to let ScanDisk correct the cross-linked files, your best option usually would be the Make copies option. By making separate copies of the cross-linked cluster for each file and retaining the files, you make it possible to recover at least one of the files.

Lost File Fragments

Clusters can become "lost," which means that the clusters are not marked in the FAT as being available even though they are not in use. ScanDisk can recover lost clusters and convert those cluster chains into files or simply allocate the clusters as free, availing them for use. Converting the lost cluster chains to files enables you to recover files accidentally lost through disk errors. Most often, however, the lost clusters are simply improperly allocated and can be returned to the pool of available clusters.

The options in the Lost file fragments group enable you to specify how ScanDisk treats lost cluster chains. Choose the Free option if you want ScanDisk to mark the clusters in the lost chains as available for use. Choose the Convert to files option if you want ScanDisk to convert those lost cluster chains to files. If you use the Convert to files option, ScanDisk reads the cluster chains and writes them to the root folder (root directory) of the drive using the file name format FILE*nnnn*, where *nnnn* is a number.

Check Files For

The check boxes in the Check files for group enable you to specify the types of errors for which ScanDisk scans. If you enable the Invalid file names option, ScanDisk detects invalid file names and attempts to repair them. Invalid file names can prevent you from opening the associated file.

The Invalid dates and times option, if enabled, causes ScanDisk to check the creation and modification dates and times of each file. An invalid date or time can cause a file to sort incorrectly, and can cause problems with file backup and restore operations.

Check Host Drive First

The option Check host drive first, if enabled, causes ScanDisk to always check the host drive of a DriveSpace or DoubleSpace compressed volume before checking the integrity of the compressed volume. If compressed drive F is stored on drive C, for example, and you enable this option, running ScanDisk against drive F causes ScanDisk to first check drive C for errors. Generally, leaving this option enabled is a good idea, because errors on the host disk can cause errors in the compressed disk. Usually, the only reason to disable this option is if you have just finished checking and repairing the host disk, and now want to check the compressed disk.

Checking a Compressed Drive

In addition to checking standard disks, ScanDisk also can scan and repair problems with DriveSpace- and DoubleSpace-compressed volumes. DoubleSpace volumes are supported by MS-DOS 6.0, and DriveSpace volumes are supported by MS-DOS 6.2*x*. Windows 95 also enables you to create and use DriveSpace volumes, explained later in the section "Increasing Disk Capacity with DriveSpace."

A DriveSpace (and DoubleSpace) volume is a hidden file that resides on a host drive. If your PC contains a single hard disk that has a single partition (containing logical drive C), you can compress some of the free space on drive C to create a new drive D. The compressed drive D actually resides in the hidden file Drvspace.001. When the system boots, Windows 95 mounts the hidden file as drive D, enabling you to work with it as if it were a regular, physical disk.

Tip   You also can use DriveSpace to compress floppy disks, and use those disks in any PC. Compressed disks created by using DoubleSpace in MS-DOS 6.0 also are supported directly by Windows 95. The information in this section refers to DoubleSpace volumes as well as DriveSpace volumes.

As with physical disks, compressed volumes can become corrupted or contain invalid file and directory entries. Therefore, checking your PC's compressed disks is as important as checking the physical disks.

Before checking the compressed volume, you should direct ScanDisk to check the host drive. If the Check host drive first check box is enabled in the ScanDisk Advanced Options dialog box (refer to figure 15.5), ScanDisk automatically checks the host disk of the DriveSpace volume before it checks the DriveSpace volume. Or, you can manually direct ScanDisk to check the host disk, then direct it to check the compressed volume. Either way, it treats compressed volumes like any other disk. Simply open ScanDisk, select the compressed volume's logical disk ID from the list of mounted disks, then choose Start.

Running ScanDisk Automatically at Startup

Many DOS users run CHKDSK or an equivalent utility each time their PCs start, resulting in a regular check of their computer's hard disk. You might want to run ScanDisk for Windows on a regular basis on a Windows 95 system for the same reason—ensuring that your disks always perform at their best.

To automate ScanDisk so that it runs automatically each time you start Windows 95, you can add ScanDisk to your Startup folder. All applications and documents in the Startup folder open automatically when Windows 95 starts.

The process for automating ScanDisk requires two steps. The first step is to place a shortcut to ScanDisk in the Startup folder. To do so, use the following procedure:

1. Right-click on the Taskbar to display its context menu, choose Properties to display the Taskbar property sheet, then click on the Start Menu Programs tab to display the Start Menu Programs property page (see fig. 15.6).

2. Choose Add to display the Create Shortcut wizard (see fig. 15.7).

3. Choose Browse, locate and select the file Scandskw.exe in your Windows folder, and choose Open. Or, enter **C:\Windows\Scandskw.exe** in the Command line text box in the Create Shortcut dialog box.

Figure 15.6

The Start Menu Programs property page.

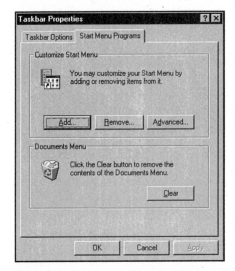

Figure 15.7

The Create Shortcut wizard.

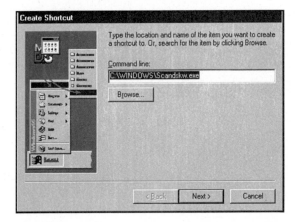

4. In the Create Shortcut dialog box, click on Next to display the Select Program Folder dialog box (fig. 15.8).

5. In the Select Program Folder dialog box, select the Startup folder, then click on Next. The wizard prompts you for a name for the shortcut. You can leave the existing name and choose Finish to create the shortcut.

Tip   If your PC is not configured for multiple user profiles, your Startup folder is located in \Windows\Start Menu\Programs\Startup. If your PC is configured for multiple user profiles, your Startup folder is located in \Windows\Profiles*your user name*\Start Menu\Programs\Startup.

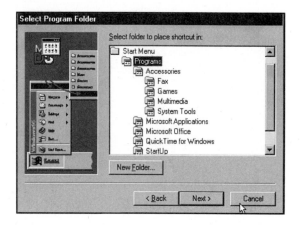

Figure 15.8

*The Select
Program Folder
dialog box.*

The second step in running ScanDisk automatically at startup is to add a couple of switches to the command line in the ScanDisk shortcut you just created in the Startup folder. All the ScanDisk command-line switches are explained in the following section. Right now, however, just understand that you need to add the /N switch to the ScanDisk command line to cause ScanDisk to start and end automatically.

To add a switch to ScanDisk's command line, open the Startup folder and right-click on the ScanDisk shortcut to display its context menu, then choose Properties. Click on the Shortcut tab to display the Shortcut property page shown in figure 15.9. Click in the Target text box, move the cursor to the end of the command line, and add the switches so that the command line reads as follows:

```
C:\WINDOWS\SCANDSKW.EXE /A /N
```

The preceding command line causes ScanDisk to scan all nonremovable hard disks and to do so non-interactively (automatically). You might want to restrict ScanDisk to analyzing only one or two disks. The following command line would cause ScanDisk to scan drives C and D automatically:

```
C:\WINDOWS\SCANDSK.EXE C: D: /N
```

After you set the command line according to your preferences, choose OK to apply the changes to the shortcut. If you want to use other command-line switches with ScanDisk, read the following section, "Using ScanDisk Switches," to learn about the additional switches ScanDisk supports.

Figure 15.9

*The Shortcut
property page.*

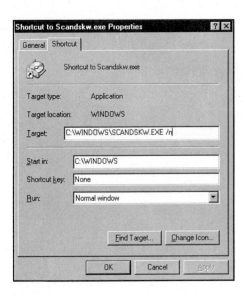

Tip   ScanDisk for Windows uses the settings stored in the Registry to determine which options to use when you run the program non-interactively. Therefore, you can run ScanDisk for Windows interactively, set options as you want, then close ScanDisk. When you run ScanDisk for Windows from the command line, the same settings are used. For example, if you want ScanDisk to automatically check for invalid file dates and times when you run the program non-interactively, enable the Invalid dates and times check box in the ScanDisk Advanced Options dialog box, then close ScanDisk. The next time you run the program, ScanDisk checks for invalid dates and times.

Using ScanDisk Switches

ScanDisk for Windows supports a number of program switches that modify the way the program works or automates its operation. The format for the ScanDisk for Windows command line is as follows:

```
SCANDSKW [drive1 drive2 drive3...] /A /N /P
```

You can add command switches to the command line if you start ScanDisk from a command prompt, or you can create a shortcut to Scandskw.exe and add the switches in the **C**ommand line text box on the shortcut's property sheet.

The ScanDisk for Windows switches are summarized in the following list:

◆ **drive.** Specify the drive ID for the disk(s) you want ScanDisk to check. You can specify multiple disks. Example to check disks C and D: **SCANDSKW C: D:**.

◆ **/A.** This switch directs ScanDisk to scan all nonremovable disks, such as C, D, E, and so on. The /A switch does not cause ScanDisk to scan CD-ROM drives, floppy disks, or other removable media. Example to scan all disks: **SCANDSKW /A**.

◆ **/N.** This switch causes ScanDisk to operate non-interactively. When you include this switch, ScanDisk opens and starts detection automatically, and closes automatically after it checks the last disk. Example to scan all disks non-interactively: **SCANDSKW /A /N**.

◆ **/P.** This switch causes ScanDisk to run in Preview mode, which means that ScanDisk appears to fix errors but does not. Instead, ScanDisk simply reports the errors but does not write changes to the disk.

Using ScanDisk for Windows at the Command Prompt

You can run ScanDisk for Windows when your computer is running the full Windows 95 operating system and GUI, from the GUI, or at a command prompt. You can run Scandisk.exe, however, only from the command prompt, and only if the GUI is not running (when you boot the system to the command prompt).

Tip If you open a command-line session from the GUI and run Scandisk.exe, located in the \Windows\Command folder, the GUI version of ScanDisk, Scandskw.exe, starts. The command-line version runs only if you boot the system to the command prompt.

You also can run ScanDisk for Windows from a batch file that you run in a DOS session under Windows 95. The following section offers some tips on running ScanDisk for Windows in batch files. Read the section "Using Scandisk.exe" later in this chapter for information on using the DOS version of ScanDisk in batch files.

Stop If you use a version of ScanDisk from DOS 6.x, you lose your long file names and also might damage your file system. Use only the Windows 95 versions of ScanDisk on a system that contains Windows 95.

Using ScanDisk for Windows in Batch Files

You can include ScanDisk for Windows in batch files to automate disk scanning and repair. To use ScanDisk in a batch file, simply add the command in the batch file. The following example batch file uses the START command to start ScanDisk and check drive C non-interactively, and returns a message based on ScanDisk's completion code:

```
echo off
start /w scandskw.exe c: /n
If errorlevel 255 goto termerror
If errorlevel 254 goto cancelled
If errorlevel 253 goto onedrive
If errorlevel 252 goto notfixed
If errorlevel 251 goto memory
If errorlevel 250 goto diskmaint
If errorlevel 1 goto allfixed
If errorlevel 0 goto noerrors
:termerror
echo Check was terminated because of an error
goto end
:cancelled
echo Check was cancelled
goto end
:onedrive
echo At least one drive could not be checked
goto end
:notfixed
echo Errors found, but at least some were not fixed
goto end
:memory
echo Could not start - insufficient memory
goto end
:diskmaint
echo Could not start - cannot load or find diskmaint.dll
goto end
:allfixed
echo Errors found, all fixed
goto end
:noerrors
echo Drive checked, no errors found
goto end
:end
```

Note Notice in the batch file that the START command is used to issue the ScanDisk command. You can use START to start a Windows or DOS application from the command line. The /W switch, used with the START command, causes the batch file to wait until the called application (in this case, ScanDisk) finishes before it proceeds with the rest of the batch file.

Checking ScanDisk Exit Codes

ScanDisk for Windows generates a result code when it finishes its work. You can base your batch file's conditional operation on the result code ScanDisk generates by testing for *errorlevel*, as indicated in the batch file in the previous section. The result codes for ScanDisk for Windows are given in table 15.3.

TABLE 15.3
ScanDisk for Windows Result Codes

Result Code	Meaning
0	Drive checked, no errors found
1	Errors found, all fixed
250	Check could not start—cannot load or find Dskmaint.dll
251	Check could not start—insufficient memory
252	Errors found, but at least some were not fixed
253	At least one drive could not be checked
254	Check was canceled
255	Check was terminated because of an error

Using Scandisk.exe

The Windows 95 DOS version of ScanDisk, Scandisk.exe, is useful for checking the disks when you boot the computer to a previous version of DOS or to the Windows 95 command prompt. Using the DOS version of ScanDisk included with Windows 95 rather than the older version of ScanDisk included with DOS ensures that you retain your long file names. You also can use Scandisk.exe in batch files that you run in a previous version of DOS or from the Windows 95 command prompt. The DOS version of ScanDisk included with Windows 95 also supports a number of switches. The format of the Scandisk.exe command is as follows:

```
SCANDISK [drive: ¦ /ALL] [/CHECKONLY ¦ /AUTOFIX [/NOSAVE]] [/SURFACE]
```

The switches supported by Scandisk.exe are described in the following list:

- ◆ **/ALL.** ScanDisk checks and repairs all local drives.

- ◆ **/AUTOFIX.** ScanDisk repairs disk errors without prompting.

- ◆ **/CHECKONLY.** ScanDisk checks a drive but does not repair any damage.

- ◆ **/CUSTOM.** ScanDisk runs based on the settings stored in Scandisk.ini.

- ◆ **/NOSAVE.** Used with the /AUTOFIX switch, ScanDisk deletes lost clusters, instead of saving the clusters as files.

- ◆ **/NOSUMMARY.** Used with the /CHECKONLY or /AUTOFIX switches, ScanDisk doesn't stop at summary screens.

- ◆ **/SURFACE.** ScanDisk does a surface scan after completing other checks.

- ◆ **/MONO.** This switch configures ScanDisk for use on a monochrome display.

You also can use Scandisk.exe to scan an unmounted DriveSpace volume, something for which you cannot use ScanDisk for Windows. The format for the ScanDisk command to check an unmounted DriveSpace volume is as follows:

```
SCANDISK drive:\DRVSPACE.nnn [/CHECKONLY ¦ /AUTOFIX[/NOSAVE]]
```

The *drive:* parameter specifies the location of the unmounted volume's file, and the DRVSPACE.*nnn* parameter specifies the actual name of the file. For example, the following command would check the first DriveSpace volume file stored on drive C:

```
SCANDISK C:\DRVSPACE.001
```

You also can use ScanDisk to examine a DriveSpace volume file for fragmentation. To do so, use the following syntax:

```
SCANDISK /FRAGMENT [drive:][path]filename
```

Include the drive, path, and file name for the DriveSpace volume file on the command line, as in the following example:

```
SCANDISK /FRAGMENT C:\DRVSPACE.001
```

Undoing ScanDisk Repairs

When ScanDisk detects an error, it displays a prompt and gives you the opportunity to write a record of the changes to a disk. You can use this record later to undo the changes ScanDisk makes.

To undo repairs ScanDisk makes, use the following syntax:

```
SCANDISK /UNDO [drive:]
```

Replace the *drive:* parameter with the drive ID on which the undo information is located.

Defragmenting a Disk

Because of the way DOS and Windows 95 allocate space for files on the disk, a file can get *fragmented,* or scattered around the disk. Instead of residing in contiguous (side-by-side) clusters, the file is spread out to noncontiguous clusters. Fragmentation doesn't pose a problem for DOS or Windows 95, because both are equally capable of following the FAT entries to locate the fragments of the file. The disadvantage of a fragmented disk is that locating and reading an entire file can take considerably longer because Windows 95 must jump around the disk, requiring multiple spins of the disk to locate the file's data—it can't read the entire file in a single pass. Fragmentation, therefore, can greatly impact Windows 95's performance, particularly for applications that extensively access the hard disk.

MS-DOS 6.*x* includes a utility called DEFRAG that defragments the disk, writing all the files in contiguous clusters and thereby improving disk performance. Windows 95 also includes a utility, appropriately called Disk Defragmenter, to defragment the disk. Disk Defragmenter is a Windows 95 application, which means you can defragment the disk as a background task while you continue to work with other applications. Your ability to continue working while Disk Defragmenter works, however, depends highly on your system's speed. On slower 486 and all 386 systems, continuing to work while Disk Defragmenter works on the disk is unlikely to prove practical.

 Stop When Setup installs Windows 95, Setup deletes the old DOS DEFRAG program and replaces it with a batch file named DEFRAG.BAT (if you install Windows 95 in your existing Windows 3.*x* directory). DEFRAG.BAT simply contains instructions on how to run the Windows 95 Disk Defragmenter. Setup deletes DEFRAG from your DOS directory to ensure the security of your long file names. Therefore, you should never run an old DOS version of DEFRAG on a disk that contains long file names.

The Disk Defragmenter can defragment local floppy disks and hard disks, including any compressed volumes Windows 95 supports. Disk Defragmenter cannot defragment CDs, remote network disks, other removable or nonwritable media, locked disks, or disks created using ASSIGN, SUBST, or JOIN.

Note Defragmenting a disk is not a once-only task. File fragmentation is an ever-present problem, and you should periodically defragment the disk to optimize its performance.

Using Disk Defragmenter

To start Disk Defragmenter, choose Start, Programs, Accessories, System Tools, then Disk Defragmenter. The Select Drive dialog box appears, as shown in figure 15.10. You also can start Disk Defragmenter from a command prompt by entering **START DEFRAG**.

Figure 15.10

Disk Defragmenter's Select Drive dialog box.

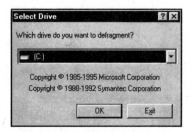

The Select Drive dialog box lists all the disks that Disk Defragmenter can defragment. Select the disk you want to defragment, then choose OK. Disk Defragmenter then displays the main Disk Defragmenter dialog box (see fig. 15.11), which contains information about the selected disk's fragmentation status and controls you can use to modify the way Disk Defragmenter works.

Figure 15.11

The Disk Defragmenter main dialog box.

Tip To defragment all your computer's hard disks, choose All Hard Drives from the Select Drive dialog box.

If fragmentation of the disk remains below a certain percentage, Disk Defragmenter indicates in its prompt that you do not need to defragment the disk. Even so, you still can defragment the disk if you want. Doing so might not improve disk performance

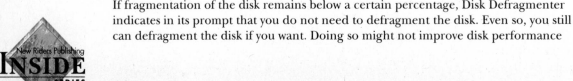

significantly, but it improves it at least slightly. The most noticeable improvement from defragmenting a disk comes when you defragment a heavily fragmented disk.

If you want to defragment the selected disk, choose the **S**tart button. Disk Defragmenter displays a status dialog of its progress, as shown in figure 15.12. If you prefer a more detailed report, choose Show **D**etails to display an expanded disk window similar to the one shown in figure 15.13.

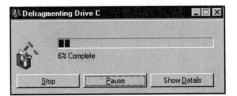

Figure 15.12

The Disk Defragmenter status dialog box.

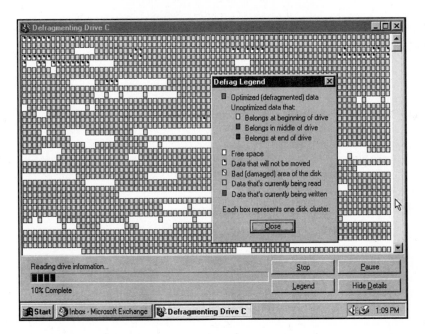

Figure 15.13

The expanded disk status window.

Setting Disk Defragmenter Options

You can specify various options that control the way Disk Defragmenter functions. To set these options, choose the **A**dvanced button in the Disk Defragmenter dialog box to display the Advanced Options dialog box (see fig. 15.14).

Figure 15.14

The Advanced Options dialog box for Disk Defragmenter.

The Defragmentation method group enables you to specify how Disk Defragmenter defragments the disk. The options in the Defragmentation method group are explained in the following list:

◆ **Full defragmentation (both files and free space).** This option (the default) causes Disk Defragmenter to rewrite all files on the disk in contiguous clusters and to consolidate all free space on the disk in a single contiguous block of clusters. Defragmenting the disk with this option takes the longest, but the time is offset by two advantages. First, all files on the disk get defragmented, which provides quicker access to those files. Second, because all free space is allocated in one block, new files are written in contiguous free clusters until your system no longer has enough free, unfragmented space to do so.

◆ **Defragment files only.** This option causes Disk Defragmenter to rewrite all files in contiguous clusters, but does not consolidate all available free space in one block of space.

◆ **Consolidate free space only.** This option causes Disk Defragmenter to consolidate free space in contiguous clusters, but not to defragment files.

The best option is the default, **F**ull defragmentation. If you don't want to spend the time to perform a complete defragmentation, however, the **D**efragment files only option is a good alternative. The last option, **C**onsolidate free space only, typically is useful if your files are not very heavily fragmented, but the free space is fragmented. Such would be the case if you have recently used the **D**efragment files only option to defragment the disk.

The Check drive for **e**rrors check box determines whether Disk Defragmenter runs ScanDisk to check the disk before defragmenting. If you enable this check box, Disk Defragmenter checks the disk using ScanDisk before it defragments the disk.

The two option buttons, **T**his time only and **S**ave these options, determine whether to save the Defragmentation method option and the state of the Check drive for **e**rrors check box for future Disk Defragmenter sessions.

Using Switches with Disk Defragmenter

Like ScanDisk and other Windows 95 utilities, Disk Defragmenter supports a number of command-line switches you can use to modify and automate the way Disk Defragmenter runs. You can create a shortcut to Disk Defragmenter and add these switches to the shortcut's <u>C</u>ommand line property. Or, you can start Disk Defragmenter from the command line and add the switches at the end of the command you use to start Disk Defragmenter.

The syntax of the Disk Defragmenter command line follows:

```
defrag [drive: ¦ /all] [/F ¦ /U ¦ /Q] [/noprompt] [/concise ¦ /detailed]
```

The command-line parameters and switches that Disk Defragmenter supports are described in the following list:

- ◆ **drive.** Specifies the disk to defragment.

- ◆ **/all.** Defragments all local disks (except those not supported by Disk Defragmenter, as explained previously).

- ◆ **/F.** Defragments both files and free space.

- ◆ **/U.** Defragments files.

- ◆ **/Q.** Defragments free space.

- ◆ **/concise.** Displays the Hide Details view (the default display mode).

- ◆ **/detailed.** Displays the Show Details view.

- ◆ **/noprompt.** Runs in unattended mode, which prevents stopping to display confirmation messages.

You can include the Disk Defragmenter command-line switches in the <u>C</u>ommand line text box of a shortcut to Disk Defragmenter. Using the shortcut to start Disk Defragmenter uses the switches in the <u>C</u>ommand line property. You can create multiple shortcuts to Disk Defragmenter, each using different command-line switches, which makes possible running Disk Defragmenter in different ways simply by choosing a particular icon.

You also can use command-line switches when you start Disk Defragmenter from the command line, explained in the next section.

Running Disk Defragmenter from the Command Prompt

As you can other Windows 95 utilities, you can start Disk Defragmenter from the Windows 95 command prompt (DOS session started under Windows 95). To start Disk Defragmenter, open a DOS session and enter **START DEFRAG**, followed by any optional switches. The following example starts Disk Defragmenter to defragment, in unattended mode, only files on drive C:

```
start defrag c: /u /concise /noprompt
```

You also can use the DEFRAG command in batch files. If you want the Disk Defragmenter program to complete operation before execution continues in the batch file, use the /W switch with the START command to cause the batch file to wait until Disk Defragmenter completes operation. The following example starts Disk Defragmenter to defragment, in unattended mode, files and free space on drive D, and waits for completion of the operation before continuing execution of the batch file:

```
start /w 95 defrag d: /f /concise /noprompt
```

Using Defrag Exit Codes

Like ScanDisk, Disk Defragmenter returns an error code after it's done. You can use the If errorlevel statement to test the value of the return code and conditionally branch in a batch file based on the code. The codes Defrag returns are listed in table 15.4.

TABLE 15.4
Disk Defragmenter Return Codes

Result Code	Meaning
0	No errors reported
2	No free clusters, no clusters large enough (16 sectors)
4	General error, run ScanDisk
5	Error reading cluster, run ScanDisk
6	Error writing cluster, run ScanDisk
10	Invalid disk type
15	Write protected

New Riders Publishing
INSIDE
SERIES

Result Code	Meaning
26	Cannot access the drive
103	Locking problem
105	Defrag could not get a lock on a drive
109	Protect mode compression driver is required

Refer to the section "Using ScanDisk for Windows in Batch Files" earlier in this chapter for an example of a batch file that tests error level and conditionally branches according to the value of the return code. You can use a similar batch file for Disk Defragmenter.

Defragmenting Compressed Volumes

Because DriveSpace allocates space sector by sector, a DriveSpace volume can contain relatively small fragments. Because only very small files can fit in these small fragments, DriveSpace volumes suffer performance degradation to a higher degree than do uncompressed disks. For that reason, you need to periodically defragment your DriveSpace volumes to ensure the best possible performance when accessing those volumes.

You don't have to do anything special to defragment a compressed volume. Disk Defragmenter treats the volume just like any other disk, at least in terms of the program interface. Simply select the compressed volume you want to defragment, choose OK, then choose Start.

Note Unlike ScanDisk, Disk Defragmenter only defragments mounted compressed volumes. You can't defragment an unmounted compressed volume. If you need to defragment the volume, first use DriveSpace to mount the volume.

Increasing Disk Capacity with DriveSpace

MS-DOS 6.0 introduced disk compression integrated with the DOS operating system, and MS-DOS 6.22 introduced DriveSpace, a functional equivalent to DoubleSpace. These disk compression tools enable DOS to compress existing data or create a new compressed disk using some or all empty space on a hard disk.

Windows 95 includes support for DoubleSpace- and DriveSpace-compressed volumes. If you install Windows 95 on a system that contains these types of compressed volumes, Windows 95 automatically recognizes and supports the compressed volumes. If your disk(s) does not yet contain compressed volumes, you can use the DriveSpace utility in Windows 95 to compress the disk. Compressing a disk can increase its capacity by a factor of as much as 3:1 or more, depending on the types of files you store on the disk. This section of the chapter explains disk compression and DriveSpace in Windows 95.

 Note   Windows 95 supports other disk compression utilities, such as Stacker (Stac Electronics), through real-mode drivers. If you use a disk compression product other than DoubleSpace or DriveSpace, contact the manufacturer to find out whether new Windows 95 versions of the product or new Windows 95 drivers are available to support the compressed disks without using a real-mode driver.

Understanding Disk Compression in Windows 95

Although disk compression might seem mysterious, a compressed volume is really nothing more than a hidden file located on a host disk (explained shortly). DriveSpace provides two methods for creating these compressed volumes: you can compress an existing disk, or create a new compressed disk.

If you compress an existing disk, DriveSpace first changes the drive letter of the drive being compressed. Assume that your computer contains one logical hard disk, C. DriveSpace changes the drive letter of the existing drive from C to H. Drive H becomes the host drive for the compressed volume, which DriveSpace creates as a hidden file on the disk. DriveSpace then compresses the uncompressed files on drive H, the original hard disk (C), and writes them in this hidden file. The operating system (Windows 95) then treats this hidden file as a logical disk, assigning to it the drive letter C. Windows 95 and your applications then treat the hidden volume as a regular disk.

You also can use the available space on a disk for creating a new compressed volume. Consider the previous example in which your PC contains a single, uncompressed disk recognized as C. Assume that drive C is a 340 MB disk, and about half of the space on the disk, or about 170 MB, is available. You can use DriveSpace to compress that available space on the disk, which has an average capacity of double its uncompressed size. The result is a new, empty drive D that has a capacity of 340 MB, and an existing drive C that has a capacity of 170 MB (with only a small amount of available disk space). You have increased your PC's total disk capacity from 340 MB to 510 MB. If you have more available space on the disk with which to work, the capacity will be greater.

Using a compression product such as DriveSpace offers relatively few drawbacks. Although you do derive a slight performance penalty from the necessity for the system to decompress and compress data on the fly, the performance degradation your system experiences using DriveSpace is so minimal you won't notice it— therefore, inconsequential. Some users, however, worry about the security of the data on a compressed volume. Although, yes, something can go wrong while the data is being written, and, yes, you can lose the data, this possibility is no greater than it is when you use an uncompressed disk. Because DriveSpace includes various built-in safeguards to prevent data loss, the risk is very minimal and you should not consider it a valid reason to not use disk compression.

Tip   If you still are concerned about data security on compressed volumes, here is a compromise: Place Windows 95 and your documents on the uncompressed disk, and place all your applications on the compressed volume. After you place the applications on the compressed volume, back up the volume to tape, a network disk, or writable CD, if possible. If you do experience a problem with the compressed volume, you can easily restore its files from the backup or reinstall the applications.

Stop   Although your compressed volumes are relatively safe, you still can destroy the volume. If you erase the hidden file that contains the compressed volume, you lose all the files. DriveSpace volumes have a file name of Drvspace.*nnn*, where *nnn* is a number, such as 001. DoubleSpace volumes have similar file names, such as Dblspace.001. Do not delete these types of files unless you want to delete the entire compressed volume and all its files.

Using DriveSpace and Compressing Disks

As with other Windows 95 disk utilities, you can run DriveSpace from the Windows 95 command prompt or within the Windows 95 GUI. To start DriveSpace in Windows 95, choose Start, Programs, Accessories, System Tools, then DriveSpace. DriveSpace displays the initial window shown in figure 15.15.

To start DriveSpace from a Windows 95 command prompt, enter the DRVSPACE command at the command prompt, followed by any optional switches or other parameters. The switches supported by DriveSpace are explained later in this chapter, in the section "Using DriveSpace Switches."

You can compress an existing disk, or create a new compressed disk using most or all available space on the existing disk. Although you can perform either function from the command prompt, starting and using DriveSpace in the Windows 95 GUI is easier.

Figure 15.15

The DriveSpace main program window.

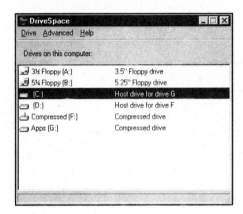

Compressing an Existing Disk

To compress an existing disk, start DriveSpace, select the disk you want to compress, then choose **D**rive, **C**ompress. DriveSpace displays a dialog box similar to the one shown in figure 15.16, which gives you information about the drive and its parameters for after it is compressed.

Figure 15.16

The Compress a Drive dialog box.

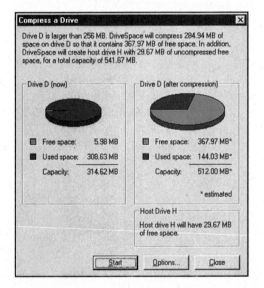

The Compress a Drive dialog box displays information about your disk as it is now, and estimates the amount of free space to be available on the disk following compression. The dialog box also indicates the drive letter to be assigned to the new disk. To specify options or change the drive letter, choose the **O**ptions button, which displays the Compression Options dialog box (see fig. 15.17).

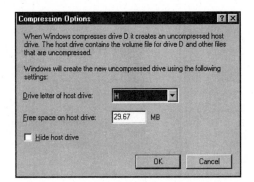

Figure 15.17

*The Compression
Options dialog
box.*

Use the Drive letter of host drive drop-down list to specify the drive letter to be assigned to the compressed volume's host drive. If you are compressing drive C, for example, and use H as the host drive's ID, your existing drive C is assigned drive letter H. The new compressed volume then is recognized as drive C. You can assign any unused drive letter to the host drive.

You also can adjust the amount of free space that will remain on the host drive. You might prefer to have more uncompressed space available on the host drive to enable you to store other files on the drive. Or, you might want to leave less uncompressed space on the host drive, to make more space available in the compressed volume. Reducing the free space on the host drive by 10 MB, for example, results in roughly 20 MB more available space on the compressed volume.

The Hide host drive check box controls whether the host drive still shows up in the My Computer and Network Neighborhood folders and File Open and Save dialog boxes. If you compress an existing disk and leave only a minimal amount of free space on the host disk (2 MB, for example), you don't need to hide the host drive because you can't store additional files on the host drive. Instead, the new files go into the compressed volume. If you leave a more sizable amount of free space on the host disk, you probably want the drive to be visible so that you can store files on it. Set the Hide host drive check box accordingly.

Stop   Do not hide the host drive if you want to continue to use the host drive to read or write files other than in the compressed volume. If you hide the host drive, its logical drive letter will no longer be visible and you will be unable to reference the drive to access it.

After you set options for the compressed volume, choose OK, then choose Start in the Compress a Drive dialog box. DriveSpace begins to compress the drive, which might take a number of hours if you have a very large drive.

Note   DriveSpace can't compress a full drive. If the drive is the boot hard disk drive, the drive must contain at least 2 MB of free space. Other disk drives must contain at least 512 KB of free space (including hard disks and floppy disks). Therefore, DriveSpace can't compress 360 KB floppy disks.

Creating a New Compressed Volume

You also can create a new, empty compressed volume by compressing some of the available space on a disk. To create an empty compressed volume, open DriveSpace and select the drive that contains the available space you want to use for the compressed volume. Then, choose Advanced, Create Empty to display the Create New Compressed Drive dialog box (see fig. 15.18).

Figure 15.18

The Create New Compressed Drive dialog box.

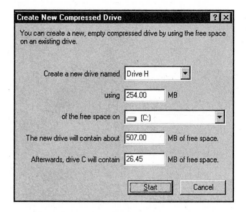

Use the controls in the Create New Compressed Drive dialog box to specify the parameters for the new disk, including its drive ID. The three size controls on the dialog box work together—if you specify a different amount in the using text box, the other two text boxes change accordingly. Specify the amount of free space you want to use for the new compressed volume, or specify the compressed capacity of the new volume.

Tip   When you specify values to create the compressed volume, remember that DriveSpace can use no more than 256 MB of space to create the volume. Specifying a compressed volume size of 800 MB, for example, does not cause DriveSpace to use 400 MB of free space for the compressed volume. Instead, DriveSpace defaults to the maximum 256 MB.

After you specify options for the new compressed volume, choose **S**tart. DriveSpace begins to create the new, empty compressed volume. The length of time varies according to the size you select for the compressed volume, but is much shorter than that required to compress an existing disk and all its data. After DriveSpace creates the volume, it prompts you to restart the system so that the new drive can be properly recognized.

Formatting a Compressed Volume

Unlike with standard uncompressed disks, you do not have to format a compressed volume before you can use it. As soon as DriveSpace creates the new disk and restarts the system, you can begin using the new volume. DriveSpace does, however, have an option you can use to format a compressed volume. As with an uncompressed disk, formatting a compressed volume removes all files from the volume and makes all space on the disk available in a contiguous block.

If you want to format a compressed volume, select the compressed volume from the DriveSpace window, then choose **D**rive, **F**ormat. DriveSpace displays a warning message that formatting the volume will delete all files. Answer **Y**es to format the volume, or **N**o to abort the format operation.

Note DriveSpace cannot format an uncompressed disk. If you try it, an error message dialog appears. Formatting a compressed volume does not affect or format its host drive, but rather, affects only the hidden file that contains the compressed volume.

Viewing and Setting Volume Properties

You can view the properties of a compressed volume to learn how much available space it contains, the estimated compression ratio for the volume, and other information. To view a compressed volume's properties, select the compressed volume from the DriveSpace main window, then choose **D**rive, **P**roperties. DriveSpace shows you a dialog box similar to the one shown in figure 15.19.

You can change only a handful of properties of a compressed volume, but these properties have a major impact on the volume's capacity and other parameters. The following sections explain the ways in which you can modify an existing compressed volume.

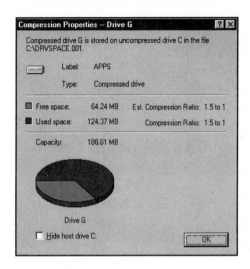

Adjusting a Volume's Size

After it is created, a compressed volume does not have to remain at a fixed capacity. Depending on the amount of available space on the host disk and in the compressed volume, you can adjust the size of the compressed volume. If the host disk contains more available space, you can increase the size of the compressed volume. Or, you might want to reduce the size of the compressed volume to make more uncompressed space available on the host disk.

To adjust a compressed volume's size, start DriveSpace and select the volume you want to change. Then, choose Drive, Adjust Free Space to display the Adjust Free Space dialog box (see fig. 15.20).

Figure 15.20

The Adjust Free Space dialog box.

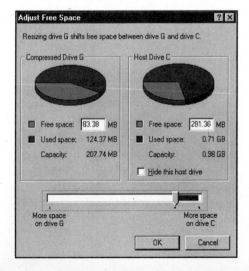

You can specify the amount of space to make available on the host disk, or the amount of compressed space for the compressed volume. You can enter the sizes directly in the two Free space text boxes or use the slider control to change the free space values. After you have the settings the way you want them, choose OK.

Changing a Volume's Compression Ratio

The amount of data that can fit in a compressed volume depends heavily on the types of files you place in the volume. Some types of files can be compressed very much, but other files can be compressed very little.

The compression ratio of a compressed volume is just a factor that DriveSpace uses to report the amount of potential free space left in the compressed volume. Adjusting the compression ratio does not make the files compress any more or less, but it does change the amount of free space DriveSpace reports as being available in the volume.

Tip Increasing the compression ratio is helpful if you are confident that an application you are attempting to install on the volume will fit, but the setup program is reporting the disk doesn't contain sufficient free space.

To adjust a volume's compression ratio, select the drive in the DriveSpace main window, then choose Advanced, Change Ratio. DriveSpace displays a Compression Ratio dialog box that shows the actual compression ratio of the data on the drive as well as the estimated compression ratio. Use the slider control to adjust the estimated compression ratio to suit your needs, then choose OK.

Tip If the actual compression ratio DriveSpace reports falls very close to the estimated compression ratio, you might want to reconsider changing the compression ratio. Unless you place highly compressible files in the volume, you have no reason to think that the files you place in the volume in the future will compress any further than the files already in the volume.

Changing a Volume's Drive Letter

Another property of a compressed volume you can change is the volume's drive letter. You might want to change the drive letter to make that letter available for a different compressed drive or new physical drive you intend to add to the system. Or, you might simply want to swap the letters assigned to two different compressed volumes.

To change a compressed volume's drive ID, open DriveSpace and select the drive whose letter you want to change. Then, choose Advanced, Change Letter to display the Select Drive dialog box (see fig. 15.21). From the drop-down list, select the drive letter you want to assign to the compressed volume, then choose OK. DriveSpace changes the drive's volume, then prompts you to restart the computer so that the change can be properly recognized.

Figure 15.21

Use the Select Drive dialog box to change volume letters.

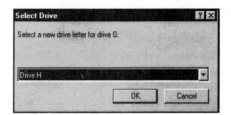

Tip

If you want to swap the drive letters for two compressed drives, you actually have to change drive letters three times. Assume that one compressed volume is drive H, and another is drive I; you would need to change drive H to J, change I to H, then change J to I. Although DriveSpace prompts you to restart the computer after each change, you can wait until the last change is complete before you restart the computer.

Mounting and Unmounting Volumes

Before you can use a compressed volume, you have to mount it. *Mounting* establishes a logical link between the volume's disk letter and the volume file. Generally, DriveSpace automatically mounts compressed volumes, so the only time you need to manually mount a volume is if you have unmounted the volume.

Only a few reasons exist for unmounting a compressed volume. You might want to move the volume to a different host disk, or you might be experiencing problems with the compressed volume and want to run ScanDisk on the volume file from the Windows 95 command prompt (outside of the GUI) to check the volume.

You cannot unmount a volume that contains open files. The first step in unmounting a disk, therefore, is to close all applications and files that reside on the disk. Then, open DriveSpace and select the drive you want to unmount. Choose Advanced, Unmount. If the volume contains no open files, DriveSpace unmounts the volume. You do not have to restart the system after you unmount a compressed volume.

To mount a volume so that you can use it again, open DriveSpace and select the volume's host disk. If the compressed volume is stored on C, for example, choose drive C. Then, choose Advanced, Mount. If the selected drive contains any DriveSpace- or DoubleSpace-compressed volume files in its root directory, DriveSpace

opens the Mount Drive dialog box (see fig. 15.22). Choose the volume file you want to mount, specify the drive letter you want to assign the volume, and then choose OK. You don't need to restart the system after you mount a compressed volume.

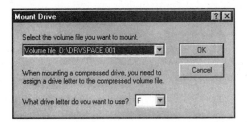

Figure 15.22

The Mount Drive dialog box.

 Tip If you use the Change Letter command in DriveSpace's **A**dvanced menu to change the drive letter of a compressed volume, Windows 95 has to restart. One method for changing drive letters that does not require a system restart is to unmount the volume, then mount it again using a different drive letter.

Uncompressing a Volume

Unlike DoubleSpace, the first disk-compression utility in DOS, DriveSpace in Windows 95 enables you to uncompress a volume. Naturally, you can uncompress a volume only if your disk contains enough available uncompressed space to contain the files in the compressed volume. Also, DriveSpace does not uncompress a compressed volume if any file names conflict between the host disk and the compressed volume. If you have files that have the same name in the root directory of the host disk and the compressed volume, for example, DriveSpace generates an error message and refuses to uncompress the volume.

To uncompress a disk, select the compressed volume you want to uncompress, then choose **D**rive, **U**ncompress. DriveSpace first checks the volume for conflicting file names and the host disk for available space. If DriveSpace does not detect any errors, it displays a dialog box that reports the state of the disk before and after compression (see fig. 15.23). Choose **S**tart to begin uncompressing the disk.

Using Compressed Floppy Disks

You can compress a floppy disk, increasing its capacity. Any system on which you use the compressed floppy disk must have DriveSpace or DoubleSpace installed, but this means you should be able to use the compressed floppy disk on any system that uses MS-DOS 6.0 or later, or Windows 95.

Figure 15.23

The status dialog box for uncompressing a disk.

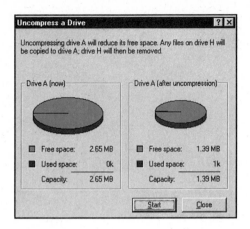

Note

You cannot create an empty compressed volume on a floppy disk. Instead, you must compress the floppy disk. Unlike when you compress a hard disk, you can't hide the floppy disk's host drive.

To compress a floppy disk, insert the disk in one of your PC's drives, then open DriveSpace. In DriveSpace, select the floppy disk you want to compress, then choose Drive, Compress. DriveSpace displays a dialog box that gives information about the disk in its uncompressed and compressed states (see fig. 15.24). The reported compressed capacity of the disk might not be accurate, however, but DriveSpace displays another more accurate report after it's done.

During compression, DriveSpace places a file named Readthis.txt on the floppy disk outside the compressed volume (essentially, on the floppy disk's host drive). This file contains instructions on how to mount the floppy disk. By default, Windows 95 automatically mounts all removable compressed volumes, which means you can insert the disk and begin using it without first manually mounting the disk. You can use DriveSpace to turn on or off automatic mounting of compressed volumes. To change this setting, open DriveSpace and choose Advanced, Settings to display the Disk Compression Settings dialog box (see fig. 15.25).

The Disk Compression Settings dialog box shows the current compression driver and includes a check box you can use to turn on or off automatic mounting of compressed volumes. Enable the check box if you want Windows 95 to automatically mount new compressed volumes after you create or insert them.

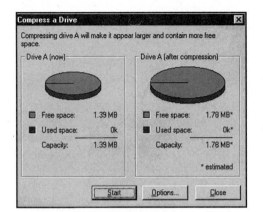

Figure 15.24

DriveSpace displays information about a floppy disk before and after compression.

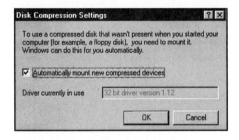

Figure 15.25

The Disk Compression Settings dialog box.

Using DriveSpace Switches

As with the other Windows 95 disk utilities, DriveSpace supports a number of command-line switches you can use to control the way the program runs. You can add these switches to the Command line text box of a shortcut to DriveSpace, or enter the DRVSPACE command at the command prompt. The syntax of the DRVSPACE command is as follows:

```
drvspace /compress d: [/size=n¦ /reserve=n] [/new=e:]
drvspace /create d: [/size=n ¦ /reserve=n] [/new=e:] [/cvf=nnn]
drvspace /delete d:\d??space.nnn
drvspace /format d:\d??space.nnn
drvspace /host=e: d:
drvspace [/info] d:
drvspace /mount {[=nnn] d: ¦ d:\d??space.nnn} [/new=e:]
drvspace /move d: /new=e:
drvspace /ratio[=n] d:
drvspace /settings
drvspace /size[=n¦ /reserve=n] d:
drvspace /uncompress d:
drvspace /unmount d:
```

In these syntax examples, *d:* and *e:* represent drive IDs, *n* represents an integer value, and *nnn* represents the numeric file extension on a compressed volume file (such as 001). D??space.*nnn* represents the volume file name, such as DBLSPACE.001, DRVSPACE.001, and so on.

The switches supported by DriveSpace are explained in the following list (syntax for each described in the previous syntax examples):

♦ **/compress.** This switch directs DriveSpace to compress a hard disk or floppy disk. You must specify the drive to compress. You also can specify the size of the compressed volume, the amount of free space to leave on the disk, and the drive letter to assign the new compressed volume.

♦ **/create.** This switch directs DriveSpace to use space on another disk to create a new compressed volume. You must specify the host drive. You also can specify the size of the new compressed disk, the amount of space to reserve on the host disk, the drive letter to assign the compressed volume, and the file extension of the CVF (Compressed Volume File).

♦ **/delete.** This switch directs DriveSpace to delete a compressed volume. You must specify the drive and file name of the CVF. DriveSpace does not delete CVFs that contain open files.

♦ **/format.** This switch directs DriveSpace to format a compressed volume. You must specify the drive and file name of the CVF.

♦ **/host.** This switch directs DriveSpace to change the drive letter of a compressed volume's host drive. To change drive H to J, for example, enter **DRVSPACE /host=J: H:**.

♦ **/info.** This switch directs DriveSpace to display information about a compressed volume. If you omit the drive ID, DriveSpace displays information about the current drive.

♦ **/mount.** This switch directs DriveSpace to mount a CVF. You can specify just the extension of a CVF located on the current drive, as in **DRVSPACE / MOUNT 001**. Or, specify the path to the CVF. You also can specify the drive letter to assign the volume by using the /new switch.

♦ **/ratio.** This switch directs DriveSpace to change the estimated compression ratio for a volume.

♦ **/size.** This switch directs DriveSpace to change the size of a compressed volume.

♦ **/uncompress.** This switch directs DriveSpace to uncompress a volume.

♦ **/unmount.** This switch directs DriveSpace to unmount a volume.

Improving CD-ROM Performance

Access to CD-ROM drives in MS-DOS is supported by a DOS extension named MSCDEX, which enables the system to read the CD-ROM drive. Like all DOS components, MSCDEX is a 16-bit, real-mode driver. Windows 95 improves CD-ROM performance by providing a 32-bit CD-ROM file system, called CDFS. CDFS eliminates the need to use MSCDEX, increasing CD-ROM performance by reducing access time and increasing throughput.

CDFS is a dynamically loadable driver. If Windows 95 detects a CD-ROM drive in the system, Windows 95 automatically loads CDFS to enable the operating system to read the CD-ROM drive. Like the other disk drivers in Windows 95, CDFS supports long file names and use of VCACHE to further improve CD-ROM performance by caching oft-used data. The cache CDFS uses is separate from the hard disk cache, however, which enables Windows 95 to page the CDFS cache to disk when the CD-ROM is idle and thus conserve memory. Using a separate cache also prevents the hard disk cache from being flushed when a large data stream is read from the CD.

Note   To further improve performance, CDFS reads ahead of the application that uses the CD, typically resulting in smoother playback and fewer pauses during playback.

Windows 95 enables you to specify the cache size for CDFS and optimize the cache for the type of CD-ROM drive in the system. To set these parameters, open the Control Panel and choose the System object. In the System property sheet, click on the Performance tab to display the Performance page. Then, choose the File System button to display the File System Properties dialog box, shown in figure 15.26.

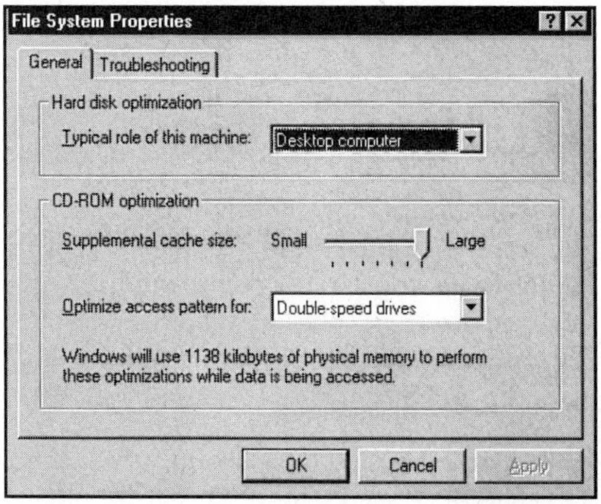

Figure 15.26

The File System Properties dialog box.

The CD-ROM Optimization group of controls enables you to specify the cache size and optimize it for your CD-ROM drive. Use the Optimize access pattern drop-down list to specify whether the CD-ROM drive in your system is a single-, double-, triple-, or quad-speed drive. Then, use the Supplemental cache size slider control to change the size of the cache based on the amount of RAM in your system. Use table 15.5 as a guide to set the cache size.

TABLE 15.5
CDFS Cache Size versus RAM

Installed RAM	Cache Size
8 MB or less	64 KB
8–12 MB	626 KB
12 MB or more	1,238 KB

The minimum and maximum cache sizes you can set using the Supplemental cache size slider change depending on the selection in the Optimize access pattern drop-down list. Choosing a slower CD-ROM speed from this drop-down list results in smaller minimum and maximum cache sizes. Choosing a faster speed results in larger minimum and maximum cache sizes. Therefore, you should specify the CD-ROM drive type first, then specify the cache size.

Although you can set the cache size to the maximum for your type of CD-ROM drive, doing so might not provide significant performance improvements over a smaller cache. If your system contains plenty of RAM, you can set the cache to its maximum. Otherwise, set the cache size to a low or medium setting. When you have the settings the way you want, choose OK, then choose OK again to close the dialog box and property sheet.

Using Troubleshooting Options

Windows 95 includes a selection of settings that you can turn on and off to trouble-shoot file system problems. Because some file system problems could prevent you from starting and running Windows 95, you can use command-line switches to enable some of these troubleshooting options when you start Windows 95. These WIN command-line switches are explained in the section "Using Startup Switches" in Chapter 3, "Troubleshooting Setup and Startup."

You also can turn on or off the troubleshooting options within Windows 95. To do so, open the Control Panel and choose the System object. On the System property sheet, click on the Performance tab to display the Performance page. Choose the File System button to display the File System property sheet, then choose the Trouble-shooting tab to display the Troubleshooting page (see fig. 15.27).

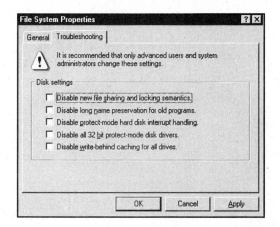

Figure 15.27

The Troubleshooting property page.

The following list explains the options on the Troubleshooting property page:

◆ **Disable new file sharing and locking semantics.** This option disables the exclusive locking and file-sharing components in Windows 95. Using this option might overcome file-sharing and locking conflicts.

◆ **Disable long name preservation for old programs.** This option turns off *tunneling,* the mechanism Windows 95 uses to retain long file names when standard applications (word processors and others) write to a file. You must turn off tunneling before you can use the LFNBK utility (described in the next section).

◆ **Disable protect-mode hard disk interrupt handling.** This option causes the hard disk controller to handle hard disk interrupts, instead of Windows 95 using its protected-mode drivers to handle them. This setting is equivalent to the WIN /D:V command used to start Windows 95, and to the setting VirtualHDIRQ=False in the [386Enh] section of System.ini.

◆ **Disable all 32 fit protect-mode disk drivers.** This option causes Windows 95 to use real-mode disk access rather than the VFAT, CDFS, IFSHLP, and other 32-bit disk driver components. This setting is equivalent to the WIN /D:F command used to start Windows 95, and to the setting 32BitDiskAccess=False in the [386Enh] section of System.ini.

◆ **Disable write-behind caching for all drives.** This option disables write-behind caching, which means that rather than wait for idle time to write disk changes, Windows 95 immediately writes disk changes as they occur.

For additional help in troubleshooting problems in Windows 95, refer to Chapter 3, "Troubleshooting Setup and Startup."

Preserving Long File Names

All the disk utilities included in Windows 95 support long file names. Older utilities, such as the DEFRAG utility in MS-DOS 6.*x,* pre-Windows 95 versions of Norton Utilities and PC Tools, and other pre-Windows 95 disk repair and backup utilities are not compatible with Windows 95's long file names and destroy those long file names if you use any of them on a Windows 95 system.

Sometimes, however, you might need to use one of these disk repair or backup utilities on a Windows 95 system. With that possibility in mind, Microsoft developed a utility that enables you to back up and restore long file names—LFNBK, included on the Windows 95 CD in the \Other\Lfnback folder. LFNBK also is available on CompuServe, on the Microsoft Network, and on the Windows 95 supplemental DOS utilities disk.

Understanding How LFNBK Works

LFNBK renames each file that has a long file name to a short file name alias. LFNBK records each file's short name and long file name in the file Lfnbk.dat, stored in the root directory of the drive being processed. This data file enables LFNBK to later rename the files using their previous long file names.

LFNBK does have some limitations. The following list explains these limitations and some of the issues to remember when you use LFNBK:

◆ You can't use LFNBK to repair problems with long file names. That calls for ScanDisk.

◆ LFNBK might not be able to rename files in which the first seven characters of the long file name aliases are identical. Consequently, you can lose these long file names.

◆ After you run LFNBK and then restart Windows 95, the default Windows 95 Start menu appears, rather than your custom Start menu. After you run LFNBK again and restore long file names, your custom Start menu appears.

◆ You can't change the directory structure disk after you run LFNBK and still restore the long file names. Do not remove directories or change directory structure, or allow disk utilities to do so, before you restore the long file names.

◆ Do not delete the file Lfnbk.dat from the root directory of the disk. After LFNBK finishes restoring long file names, it deletes the DAT file itself.

◆ After restoring the old long file names, some of the short file names might be different, because Windows 95, not LFNBK, assigns these file names.

◆ Run the restore process immediately after you run your disk repair or backup utility so that no file or directory changes occur before you restore the long file names.

◆ If your disk repair or backup utility displays a message that indicates that it cannot run in a multitasking environment, boot Windows 95 (or DOS) without any of Windows 95's protected-mode drivers, such as Ifshlp.sys.

Using LFNBK

To protect long file names with LFNBK, you first run LFNBK to back up the long file names on the disk. Then, you run the incompatible disk utility, which results in the long file names being lost. You then run LFNBK again to restore the long file names.

To run LFNBK, first copy the Lfnbk.exe program file from the source disk to the Windows directory. Then, you must turn off long file name tunneling, which causes Windows 95 to preserve long file name entries when standard applications read and write to the files. To turn off tunneling, open the Control Panel and choose the System object. In the System property sheet, click on the Performance tab, then choose the File System button. On the File System property sheet, click on the Troubleshooting tab to display the Troubleshooting property page shown in figure 15.27. Then, place a check in the Disable long name preservation for old programs check box, choose OK, and choose OK again. The system will prompt you to reboot, and you should allow it to reboot before continuing.

After you turn off tunneling, close all running programs. Open an MS-DOS session and enter an LFNBK command based on the following syntax:

```
LFNBK [/v] [/b ¦ /r ¦ /pe] [/p] [drive:]
```

The switches and parameters you can specify with LFNBK are explained in the following list:

◆ **/v.** This switch directs LFNBK to use verbose mode, reporting all actions to the display.

◆ **/b.** This switch directs LFNBK to back up and remove long file names.

◆ **/pe.** This switch directs LFNBK to extract errors from backup database, Lfnbk.dat, created in the root directory of the drive processed by LFNBK.

◆ **/r.** This switch directs LFNBK to restore backed-up long file names.

◆ **/nt.** This switch directs LFNBK to not restore backed-up file dates and times.

◆ **/p.** This switch directs LFNBK to find long file names but not convert them to short file names.

◆ **/force.** This switch forces LFNBK to run even if LFNBK detects that it is not safe to run.

## 16

Using Microsoft Plus! for Windows 95

Although Windows 95 can run on low-end 386 systems, faster machines (such as the new wave of Pentium processors) are prevalent on desktops. To take advantage of the increased speed in these processors, Microsoft introduced a companion product to Windows 95 called Microsoft Plus! for Windows 95. Microsoft Plus! is best described as a smorgasbord of additional bonus utilities and features for Windows 95. These utilities and cosmetic features require an 80486 or higher processor to run.

By default, Windows 95 can often seem bland, especially when it comes to the desktop. This is primarily due to concerns that dressing up the desktop will have an adverse effect on performance. Because Pentium processors are quickly becoming the standard for entry-level machines, however, such machines can easily take advantage of the features Plus offers.

Some say Plus "polishes" Windows 95, and they're right—Plus is well named. Plus includes a set of desktop enhancements that put the finishing touches on Windows 95, making it more aesthetically appealing. Plus also includes a rich set of System Agent tools that help you monitor system activity and maintain the system, an improved version of Microsoft's DriveSpace disk compression utility, Internet connectivity, and a simplified connection setup.

This chapter examines Microsoft Plus and explains how to use these utilities efficiently. This chapter covers the following topics:

◆ Using System Agents to automate Windows 95 maintenance

◆ Using DriveSpace 3 to increase disk capacity

◆ Exploring the Internet with Internet Explorer

◆ Applying themes to improve the look of the desktop

◆ Utilizing full window drag and font smoothing

◆ Playing Multimedia Pinball

Using the System Agent

Disk maintenance tools are essential to the health of any PC. Unfortunately, running a disk tool (such as a disk defragmentation program) often is time-consuming and CPU-intensive, and causes system downtime during its execution. To help users schedule system maintenance programs during system idle time, Plus introduces the System Agent, an application that sits in the background and triggers prespecified events.

The System Agent can be extremely useful for users who leave their PC on all the time. You can use it to set your system to activate time-consuming disk maintenance tasks overnight, which frees up your system for peak usage times during the day. You can set the System Agent to back up key data files to a tape drive at midnight on weekdays, for example. If you need to use your system during the time you've preappointed for backup, you can utilize a single keystroke to freeze the process until you return the system to idle. To save space on the Taskbar, the System agent docks on the notification area.

By default, Windows 95 places its system tools, including ScanDisk, Defrag, and the DriveSpace 3 Compression Agent, in the System Agent. This section explains how to schedule events for the default disk tools, as well as add your own programs to System Agent.

Configuring the System Agent

The System Agent can schedule system maintenance events, such as defragmenting drives or checking disk integrity (see fig. 16.1).

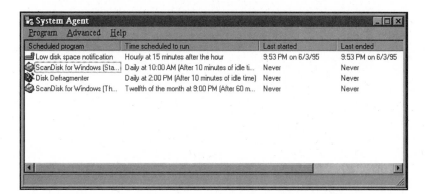

Figure 16.1

The System Agent monitors events and triggers scheduled tasks at a prespecified time.

You can modify the schedule by double-clicking on the event you want to change and then choosing the Change Schedule button. The Change Schedule dialog box (see fig. 16.2) enables you to modify all aspects of the scheduled program.

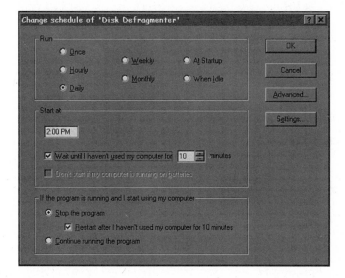

Figure 16.2

Use the Change Schedule dialog box to determine when and how often a program should be run.

You would mainly want to add time-consuming tasks to the System Agent, but you can add almost any application. Figure 16.3 shows a customized task—opening the CD player and playing the CD every day during a coffee break at 10:00 a.m. Setting it up is as easy as choosing Program, Schedule a New Program and filling in the name of task, the path to the executable file, and the time and frequency for running the task.

Figure 16.3

System Agent enables you to create your own tasks and run them from the scheduler.

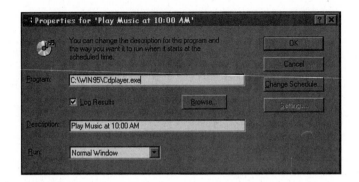

The Advanced Options box offers yet more control over the task scheduling process. The following list explains its options:

◆ **Deadline.** This area enables you to specify a deadline time. If Windows 95 can't start a task at the prespecified time, the System Agent continues to try to launch the task until the time you specify.

◆ **If the program is still running, stop at this time.** Some tasks, such as the CD Player, run until you or the system specifically tell them to stop. If you enable this check box, the system stops the running program at the deadline time.

◆ **Notify me if the program never started.** This function acts as a watchdog for the System Agent. If a program fails to start at the time you specify, the System Agent opens up a dialog box to let you know.

The Run repeatedly between the start time and the deadline group contains another set of advanced options:

◆ **Run the program every X minutes.** Checking this box enables you to access a spin box that enables you to specify how many minutes to wait before starting the task again. If you set a program to start at 10:00 a.m. and specify a deadline of 11:00 a.m., setting this spin box to five minutes runs the program every five minutes from 10:00 a.m. to 11:00 a.m.

◆ **Stop running the program if it is still running after X minutes.** Checking this box gives you access to a spin box that enables you to specify how long a program can run. Applications that are not SAGE aware do not close after they are completed. If you run a Word macro via the System Agent, for example, Word remains active after the macro is completed. If you want to

make sure that non-SAGE aware applications are closed when completed, check this box. This will enable the System Agent to reopen the application when it is run again.

Keeping the System Agent running at all times generally is a good idea, but if you want to disable or suspend it, you can do so by choosing Advanced, then Suspend System Agent or Stop System Agent.

The System Agent keeps a comprehensive log of all programs. You can view this log, stored as \Plus!\Sagelog.txt, by choosing Advanced, View Log.

The Program menu contains items that enable you to change program behavior. You might want to run a program manually, for example, rather than wait for the preset event time. You can do so by clicking on the program that you want to run and choosing Program, Run Now.

Running Third-Party Applications with System Agent

Although the System Agent supports all MS-DOS and Windows-based applications, running applications that recognize and work with the System Agent (known as *SAGE Aware* applications) provides distinct advantages (see the following list). Such applications are aptly named because SAGE refers to the underlying System Agent engine that schedules all programs.

SAGE Aware applications take advantage of key System Agent features, such as the following:

◆ All SAGE Aware applications automatically appear in the Schedule a New Program dialog box.

◆ SAGE Aware applications run without requiring input from the user.

◆ They take advantage of the System Agent's exit codes and strings to display the results of the task.

◆ They provide a Settings menu in System Agent. This enables users to modify the program settings directly from the System Agent.

Understanding DriveSpace 3

Disk capacity always has been a top concern of PC users. Today's applications and operating systems consume greater quantities of disk space—disk space that isn't always physically available. Although you can get hard disks for a relatively low price these days, adding a hard disk is not always feasible—especially one that has the older IDE standards. Disk compression's popularity stems from those limitations. When Stac first introduced PC disk compression, hard disks were expensive, and most machines couldn't handle a large number of hard disks in the same machine.

Although hard disks are available for relatively low prices, adding a hard disk is not always feasible—especially with the older IDE standards. Older IDE disk controllers can only support a maximum of two physical hard disks, and the hard disk size is limited to 540 MB. Disk compression has become popular because of those limitations.

 Note Although older IDE drives are limited to 540 MB, you can use special software for MS-DOS to access the rest of the disk space if you have an IDE drive that is larger than 540 MB. The new Enhanced IDE (EIDE) systems work with the computer's BIOS to eliminate the 540 MB barrier.

Although many vendors offer disk compression utilities, Microsoft's DoubleSpace (and later, DriveSpace) became the compression standard overnight in 1993 when they included it in MS-DOS 6.0. VertiSoft licensed the compression code, but DoubleSpace's immaturity—compounded by the "lazy-write" default option in the SmartDrive cache—occasionally caused systems to lose data. The problem really was that the cache didn't always get all data written to disk before the system was shut down, but DoubleSpace drew the blame and quickly gained a reputation for being both unstable and extremely prone to data loss.

Microsoft quickly issued an update to MS-DOS (version 6.2) that modified SmartDrive to flush all cache buffers immediately, thereby minimizing the chance of data loss. DoubleSpace became relatively stable in this version.

Microsoft changed the name from DoubleSpace because Stac (which has its own disk compression utility—Stacker) filed a lawsuit, insisting that Microsoft infringed on their patent. Microsoft revised DoubleSpace, removed the infringing code, and released it as DriveSpace in MS-DOS 6.22. Since then, DriveSpace has become the standard disk compression engine for MS-DOS. In fact, Windows 95 includes DriveSpace.

Plus includes an updated and enhanced version of DriveSpace—DriveSpace 3. DriveSpace 3 improves upon the Windows 95 and MS-DOS versions of DriveSpace by implementing the following features:

◆ Support for larger volumes (up to 2 GB)

◆ Two new compression formats (HiPack and UltraPack)

◆ Capability to customize compression levels on a file-by-file basis

This section examines the new features of DriveSpace 3 and explains the differences between the Windows 95 implementation of DriveSpace and DriveSpace 3.

Understanding Volume Sizes

Most compression utilities compress at the volume level rather than at the file or directory level (Windows NT 3.51 being the exception). A volume essentially is a *partition*—a group of clusters on the disk. A typical PC has one or more hard disks, each disk partitioned into multiple volumes.

Note Chapter 15, "Optimizing Data Storage," provides a more in-depth look at partitions and volumes.

A severe limitation in Windows 95's DriveSpace is that compressed volumes are limited to 512 MB. This limitation wasn't a problem a few years ago when 200 MB drives were the norm, but with the proliferation of large Enhanced IDE drives (and recent cost reductions), it can severely burden a system. DriveSpace 3 supports compressed volume sizes of up to 2 GB, which makes disk compression feasible for users who have large partitions.

On large partitions (1 GB and greater), DriveSpace 3 uses 32-KB clusters to fully maximize disk space in Windows 95, as well as to increase speed, since data isn't compressed in little 8 KB pieces. Unfortunately, using large clusters on the FAT file system often wastes disk space. FAT assigns at least one cluster to a file, no matter how small the file, so a single 4-byte text file uses 32,763 bytes on the disk.

DriveSpace 3 alleviates disk space waste by storing files in sectors, a smaller unit of space on the disk. A 32-KB cluster consists of 64 sectors, each sector 512 bytes in size; therefore, the same 4-byte text file wastes only 508 bytes on the disk. This can save a significant amount of disk space on larger drives that use the FAT file system. The smaller cluster size on smaller drives saves less space.

Understanding DriveSpace Compression Formats

One significant new feature in DriveSpace 3 is the capability to select the level of compression that you want. Earlier releases of DriveSpace only let you compress at a preset level. If you wanted to optimize compression to provide the most speed or the smallest file sizes, you were out of luck.

DriveSpace 3 improves upon Windows 95 DriveSpace by utilizing three levels of compression, each level using its own compression algorithm. These levels are

◆ Standard compression

◆ HiPack compression

◆ UltraPack compression

The capability to use various levels of compression makes DriveSpace 3 an ideal compression utility if you find compression too slow or that it returns insufficient disk space. This section examines the compression formats in DriveSpace 3.

Standard Compression

Standard compression uses the same compression format that the Windows 95 version of DriveSpace offers. Data is compressed in 8-KB pieces, which is optimal on partitions that have 8-KB clusters because the compressed data can be read in one cluster. Data compresses at an average of 1.8:1, depending on the type of data. Standard compression results in a slight performance penalty when you access compressed volumes.

HiPack Compression

HiPack compresses data so that it is 10–20 percent smaller than standard DriveSpace compression, by compressing data in 32-KB pieces—ideal for partitions that have 32-KB clusters. Compressing data with HiPack is slightly slower than standard compression, because reading and writing 32 KB of data takes longer. After compression, however, reading and decompressing data often equals the speed of standard compression. HiPack averages between 2.0–2.3:1.

Note Both standard compression and HiPack use the same basic compression algorithm. You can think of HiPack as an optimized version of standard compression.

UltraPack Compression

UltraPack was originally intended for use on floppy disks, but because today's high-end processors are significantly faster at disk I/O, UltraPack is now feasible for everyday compression of infrequently used data on hard disks. Because the compression and decompression of files is extremely CPU intensive, UltraPack is recommended for use on Pentium processors only. It is possible to use UltraPack on 486 systems, but file access becomes excruciatingly slow. UltraPack provides the greatest level of compression in DriveSpace 3, ranging from 2.2:1 to 2.6:1.

Compressing a Disk

DriveSpace 3 is available only as a Win32 application, which you can start from the Start Menu/Programs/Accessories/System Tools folder. DriveSpace 3 replaces the older version of DriveSpace from that folder. Figure 16.4 shows the slightly modified DriveSpace 3 interface, reflecting the change in version number.

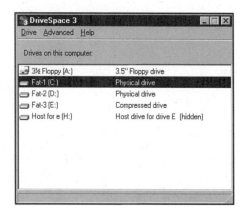

Figure 16.4

The DriveSpace 3 window.

To compress a drive with DriveSpace 3, select the drive that you want to compress, then choose Drive, Compress. DriveSpace 3 displays a dialog box that shows you how much extra space you could gain by compressing the drive. Choosing Options brings you to the Compression Options dialog box, which enables you to assign a drive letter to the host drive and set its size, as figure 16.5 shows. (For a more detailed explanation of host drives, refer to Chapter 15, "Optimizing Data Storage.")

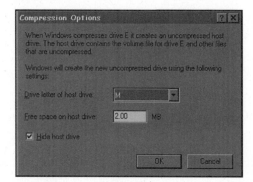

Figure 16.5

The Compression Options dialog box.

To begin compressing the drive, choose <u>S</u>tart in DriveSpace's Compress a Drive dialog box (see fig. 16.6). Compression might take a while if the drive is large or contains a substantial amount of data. After DriveSpace compresses the drive, the Compress a Drive dialog box shows before and after data, giving the old and new sizes of the compressed volume.

Figure 16.6

The Compress a Drive dialog box shows the uncompressed and compressed sizes of the volume.

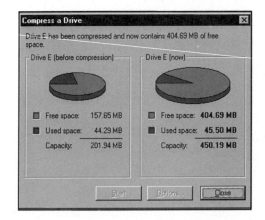

After DriveSpace finishes compressing the drive, it displays a status dialog box, which shows a before and after view of the drive size. When the status dialog box is closed, DriveSpace presents you with an enhanced compression menu, shown in figure 16.7. This dialog box enables you to optimize the compression level for the volume. You can select the compression that you want by clicking on one of the three buttons.

Figure 16.7

DriveSpace 3 enables you to select varying levels of compression.

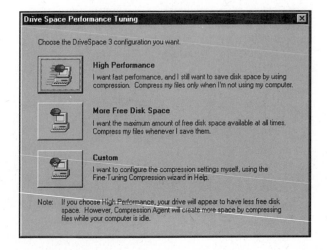

Note High Performance is actually HiPack, whereas More Free Disk Space is UltraPack.

The High Performance and More Free Disk Space compression options both offer advantages, depending on your needs. If you're willing to sacrifice some speed to obtain more free space, the More Free Disk Space automatically recompresses files whenever you save them. On the other hand, if you prefer speed over maximum free space, High Performance recompresses files only during system idle.

 Tip The compression level you set after DriveSpace 3 compresses data is not permanent. If you want to change the level of compression later on, you can use the Compression Agent to recompress or change compression levels.

Upgrading to DriveSpace 3

Although you can use the older version of DriveSpace in Windows 95, you lose certain benefits if you do. To get up to speed easily, DriveSpace 3 can convert a DriveSpace compressed volume to a DriveSpace 3 compressed volume that reaps all the benefits of DriveSpace 3. To upgrade to DriveSpace 3, open DriveSpace 3, select the compressed drive you want to upgrade, then choose Drive, Upgrade. DriveSpace 3 prompts you to back up your files before you start (see fig. 16.8). After the backup, DriveSpace 3 checks your drive for errors. If it finds no errors, it begins the upgrade, which can take a considerable amount of time if the volume contains much data.

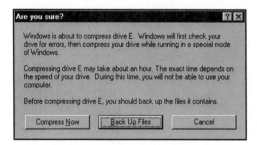

Figure 16.8

The DriveSpace 3 confirmation box. You should back up your files before upgrading to the new DriveSpace 3 compression format.

Changing Settings with the Compression Agent

The Compression Agent is a new tool in DriveSpace 3 that enables you to recompress previously compressed volumes. The Compression Agent automatically chooses the most appropriate compression level file by file. The Compression Agent works with the System Agent, so you can maximize your compression without taking a performance hit by allowing the Compression Agent to recompress files during times your PC is idle. The Compression Agent includes a number of comprehensive options, explained in the following section.

Running the Compression Agent

As with all other disk tools, you access the Compression Agent from the Start/ Programs/Accessories/System Tools menu. To start the Compression Agent, click on the Start button, then choose Programs, Accessories, System Tools, and Compression Agent to open the initial Compression Agent window, which prompts you to select a drive.

Note   You cannot start the Compression Agent unless you have at least one volume compressed with DriveSpace.

At this point, you can choose the Settings button to open the Compression Agent Settings dialog box (see fig. 16.9). Here, you set compression levels on the compressed volume that you want to optimize. The following list explains each option:

◆ **Do not UltraPack any files (maximum performance).** Choose this radio button to disable UltraPack, which makes file sizes slightly larger and file access a bit faster.

◆ **UltraPack all files (maximum disk space, not recommended for 486-based computers).** Choose this radio button to compress all files with UltraPack, giving you more free disk space, although you pay a penalty in performance. Ideal for Pentium systems.

◆ **UltraPack only files not used within the last xx days.** This setting is ideal for users who have archived files that are not accessed frequently. If this setting is used, the Compression Agent UltraPacks all files that have not been accessed within a user-specified amount of time. This ensures that your files are always at your finger tips and compressed to their full extent without penalizing you too much in performance.

The Compression Agent also enables you to HiPack the non-UltraPacked files. If you're low on disk space, HiPacking the rest of the files can help you regain some extra disk space while offering decent performance.

Figure 16.9

The Compression Agent Settings dialog box.

The Compression Agent lets you use HiPack and UltraPack on the same volume. The Compression Agent can UltraPack a set of files that fit your criteria, and HiPack the rest of the files.

You also can have the Compression Agent compress only when the drive contains a certain amount of data. To do so, just load DriveSpace 3 and choose Advanced, Settings. Select the option No compression unless the drive is xx% full, and choose the percentage you want. To save the settings, choose OK and close DriveSpace 3.

Using the System Agent to Recompress Drives

The Compression Agent is a SAGE Aware application, and you can schedule it to run unattended at a specific time. To set the Compression Agent properties from the System Agent, double-click on the Compression Agent in the System Agent window. Choose the Settings button in the Compression Agent Properties dialog box to change its settings. Now you can recompress files automatically at a predetermined time.

Microsoft Plus and the Internet

One of Microsoft Plus's most compelling features is the Internet connectivity tools it includes. Plus includes a World Wide Web browser that takes full advantage of Windows 95's system features, such as multithreading, drag-and-drop, and shortcuts.

This section examines the various Internet features included in Plus, such as the Internet Wizard, the Internet Explorer, and the Internet mail driver for Microsoft Exchange.

Getting Connected

Finding a way onto the Internet is simple these days. Everywhere you look, service providers are offering low-cost accounts on the Internet. Even the large online services (such as America Online and CompuServe) offer full Internet access through their systems. Microsoft, with its own online service (the Microsoft Network), also is jumping into the Internet provider game.

Most service providers do include a set of utilities that get your PC "Internet-ready"— utilities usually designed to use under Windows 3.11. Windows 95, however, includes its own 32-bit Winsock (Windows socket interface) and TCP/IP protocol, as well as a Dial-Up Networking utility that can connect you to the Internet. Unfortunately, setting up Windows 95 to connect to a service provider often turns out to be rather difficult.

Plus includes an Internet Wizard that helps you connect to the Microsoft Network or a third-party service provider (see fig. 16.10). When you first install Plus, the Internet wizard appears at the end of the installation. With the Internet wizard, you can easily set up an Internet dial-up account on your machine to access your service provider. All information is entered in a wizard, shielding users from complex information such as scripts, post-connect logons, and so on. If you choose not to run the Internet Explorer, you can access it later from the Start/Programs/Accessories/Internet Tools menu after you install Plus.

Figure 16.10

The Internet wizard enables you to easily set up Windows 95 to connect to the Internet.

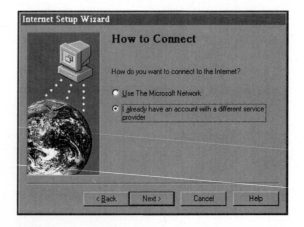

Tip   You must have a modem installed and Exchange configured before using the Internet and before Exchange can handle your mail.

If you have multiple Internet accounts with different service providers for each account, you can run the Internet wizard to set up each account. All account dial-up objects appear in the Dial-up Networking folder.

To connect to another service provider, choose the option titled I a̲lready have an account with a different service provider, then click on Next. The next page asks you for the name of your service provider. After you enter your provider name, click on Next again and enter the phone number and country code of your provider. If your provider requires a special sequence to log on, enable the Bring up t̲erminal window after dialing check box so that the Internet Dialer opens a terminal window after it connects with your provider. Here, you can enter the special logon sequence.

Enter your user name and password (generated by your provider) on the next page. This enables the Internet Dialer to automatically log on for you.

Tip   If others have access to your machine, you might want to leave the password field blank, enabling you to enter your password every time you connect to your provider, as a rudimentary form of security against unauthorized use of your account.

The next screen of the Internet Setup wizard sets up your IP address. An *IP address* is a unique number that consists of four parts, each part separated by a period, such as 192.168.124.215. Data is sent in packets on the Internet. Each packet contains bytes of information. Every system on the Internet has an IP address used in communication with other systems to identify where the packets come from. Essentially, an IP address serves as a telephone number.

Many providers use dynamic IP addressing; an IP address is generated for you every time you connect to your provider. If that is the case with your provider, choose the M̲y Internet Service Provider automatically assigns me one radio button. If you have a static (permanent) IP address, choose the A̲lways use the following radio button and enter your IP address in the I̲P Address entry field. There is also an entry field for a subnet mask, but unless told otherwise by your provider, you generally don't need to use it.

Clicking on Next brings you to the DNS Server Address page, which sets up the Domain Name Service (DNS) server address. A *domain name* is a unique name that identifies an Internet site. Although most domain names are connected to the

Internet, you can have an entry in the DNS not directly connected to the Internet. You would do so for various reasons, one being to enable transfer of e-mail to sites not directly on the Internet by forwarding the mail to another computer on the Internet that can then forward it to the nonconnected site.

When you sign up for an Internet account, your provider gives you the IP address of their DNS server. Your system uses the server at this address to translate host names to and from IP addresses. If incorrect, you might notice problems, such as being able to connect to a remote system using an IP address but not to a domain name. Domain names are combinations of characters—normally letters and numbers—separated by periods. An example of a domain name would be inhouse.mail.jon.com.

Note   Although most Internet addresses include an at sign (@), they are not domain names. The letters that precede the @ are a user name, whereas the letters or words following the @ are the location of the user.

For example, 76711.1205@compuserve.com signifies that the user name is 76711,1205 on the CompuServe system.

After entering the DNS server IP address, you will have the opportunity to set up Internet Mail access via Exchange on the Internet Mail page, accessible by clicking on Next on the DNS Server Address page. If you want to be able to send and receive Internet mail, enable the Use Internet Mail check box. You can then enter your e-mail address and the domain name of the Internet mail server that you want to use.

After you complete the Internet Setup wizard, Windows 95 generates a profile in the Start/Programs/Accessories/Dial-Up Networking folder. To start your Internet connection, open the profile and you are connected within seconds.

Exploring the Internet

Now that Windows 95 is ready to become part of the Internet, you can use the Internet Explorer to utilize the vast resources of the World Wide Web. The World Wide Web is the most popular and visible part of the Internet. Imagine a global information network capable of displaying text, graphics, and even multimedia. Now imagine it all available on your desktop PC—everything from your favorite television shows to software information at your fingertips. You can even order a pizza on the World Wide Web. (Seriously; see figure 16.11, which shows the Pizza Hut web server.)

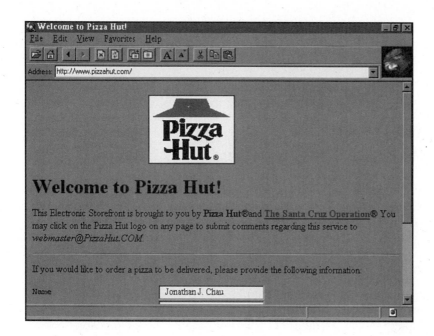

Figure 16.11

Phone line tied up? Order a pizza through Pizza Hut's World Wide Web server!

Understanding Web Browsers

A web browser is one of the most important tools for accessing the Internet because it incorporates the following features, reducing the need for multiple Internet utilities:

◆ **Web browsing.** Web browsers first and foremost are designed to retrieve information from the World Wide Web in pages. These pages are stored in HTML (Hypertext Markup Language) format—a format that supports hyperlinks and graphical images embedded within text. Each page opens on the server side and downloads to the client. Web browsers enable you to visit various sites by clicking on links, usually underlined words. Links are set apart from other non-hyperlinked text by a different color.

◆ **File downloads.** File transfers on the Internet usually depend on the FTP protocol. FTP stands for File Transfer Protocol and is the standard file transferring mechanism on the Internet. Rather than require you to use a separate FTP client, most web browsers support FTP retrieval (downloading) directly.

◆ **Mail sending.** Rather than force you to copy the contents of an HTML page to your e-mail client, some browsers let you send e-mail directly from your browser application.

◆ **News reading.** One of the most popular features on the Internet is USENET, a world-wide bulletin board that covers just about every topic available. People from around the world can discuss favorite issues by posting news or a message. You can use some browsers as a news reader, eliminating the need for a separate news reader client.

Using the Internet Explorer

The Internet Explorer is a modified version of Spry Mosaic, one of the most popular web browsers available for Windows. Microsoft licensed Spry's code and revamped it, turning it into a full-fledged Windows 95 application. This section shows how you can use Internet Explorer to tap into the Internet's overwhelming power.

The Internet wizard automatically puts a shortcut to the Internet Explorer (with the name "The Internet") on the desktop after it successfully creates an Internet profile. Alternatively, you can open the Internet Explorer from Start/Programs/Accessories/ Internet Tools. When Internet Explorer is first opened, you are automatically connected to your Internet provider, and an introductory page is opened. This page, seen in figure 16.12, is stored on Microsoft's web server (in this case, http:// www.msn.net) and contains three links that serve as an introduction to the Internet. These links are represented by buttons. The blue Info button brings you to another page on Microsoft's server that familiarizes you with the Internet. The red Explore button loads up a page with a number of links that serve as a database of popular web sites. The green Search button enables you to quickly find information you are interested in and to jump to the corresponding site. If you are new to the Internet, you will probably want to start by clicking on Info. This loads up another local HTML page that contains a brief description of the Internet, as well as a short tutorial.

Tip   If you're new to the Internet, Yahoo is a great starting point to the World Wide Web. Yahoo is a collection of links sorted into categories. You might click on Entertainment, for example, from the top menu, which brings up another page with more subcategories, such as Movies, Television, or Magazines.

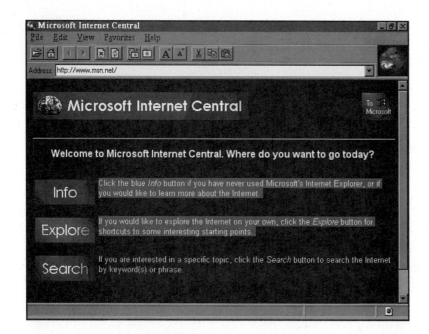

Figure 16.12

The Internet Explorer enables you to drag pages out to the desktop and view them with QuickView.

Navigating the Internet Explorer

The user interface for the Internet Explorer is designed to be simple enough for the novice Internet user to use. As with most other Windows 95 applications, the Internet Explorer includes a toolbar for easy, one-click access to commonly used features. The following is a list of the toolbar navigation button functions in the order that they appear.

- ◆ **Open.** Enables you to open a local HTML page or a page on a remote site. This button looks like an open file folder.

- ◆ **Go Home.** Returns you to your home page, the page on which Internet Explorer starts up. This button looks like a small house.

- ◆ **Go Back.** Jumps back to the previous loaded page. This is represented by a back arrow.

- ◆ **Go Forward.** Proceeds to the next page. This button is represented by a forward arrow.

Typically, you click on links to move around on the World Wide Web. To open a specified web page, click on the Open button and type the following in the dialog box:

```
http://your.sitename.here
```

HTTP stands for Hypertext Transfer Protocol, and lets the server know that you want to venture to a web page. If you want to access an FTP site, type the following in the Open dialog box:

```
ftp://your.sitename.here
```

 Tip   To find out the address of your currently loaded page, look at the Address entry field in the Internet Explorer, located under the toolbar. Figure 16.13 shows the address for Microsoft's web server.

Figure 16.13

Microsoft's web server (http://www.microsoft.com).

At the right side of the Internet Explorer, you will see a visual representation of a globe. The globe is a status indicator—when a document is being loaded or downloaded, the globe rotates. When the Internet Explorer is idle, the globe stops rotating.

A simpler method for visiting web sites is the Favorite Places feature of Internet Explorer. Favorite Places is a list of your favorite web sites. By choosing the Favorites

menu, you easily can jump to a prespecified site without typing the address of the site or weeding through links to find it. To add a site to your Favorite Places menu, choose Favorites, Add to Favorites after you load the page you want to add. Because you keep the list of favorite sites in the \windows\favorites directory, you can easily drag shortcuts to your favorite web sites to the desktop. If you want to remove a site from the Internet Explorer's Favorite Places menu, you can delete the site from the \windows\favorites directory.

Alternatively, you can drag a URL (Uniform Resource Locator, commonly seen as links) to the desktop to create a shortcut to that site. Launching that shortcut opens the Internet Explorer, connects you to your provider, and loads the requested page. Figure 16.14 shows the URL properties of a shortcut that points to Microsoft's web server.

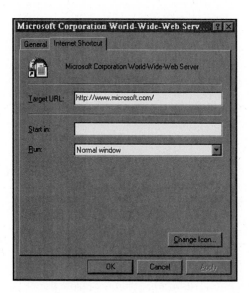

Figure 16.14

A shortcut to Microsoft's web server.

Advanced Internet Explorer Configuration

One of the Internet Explorer's key elements is its vast customization features. You can configure most external and internal aspects of the Internet Explorer by choosing View, Options from the main Internet Explorer menu, which brings up a tabbed dialog box containing four pages. These pages are explained in the following sections.

Appearance

The Appearance page is separated into three sections: Page, Shortcuts, and Addresses. The Page section includes two options: Show Pictures and Custom Colors.

For slower dial-up connections (9,600 Kbps and lower), downloading pages often takes a substantial amount of time. Although this is offset by the Internet Explorer retrieving the document text before the graphics, it can still be a bottleneck, especially if you pay by the hour for your Internet access. To tell the Internet Explorer not to download pictures (but rather, just download the text), disable the Show Pictures check box.

The Use Custom Colors check box enables you to specify colors to use for the text and background of an HTML document. The default colors are black text on a gray background.

Start Page

The Start page also is known as a Home page, and is the first document the Internet Explorer loads. Typically, this would be a links archive, such as Yahoo. The two buttons on this page both change your Start Page. If you're at Microsoft's home page and would like to use it as your Start page, click on the Use Current button. When you click on the House icon on the Internet Explorer's toolbar, you automatically are transferred to Microsoft's home page.

To use the default Start page, click on the Use Default button.

Advanced Page

The Advanced page is separated into two sections: History and Cache. The History section lets you specify the number of pages you want the Internet Explorer to remember. These History pages are stored in \Plus!\Microsoft Internet\History, and you can drag them to your desktop as shortcuts. Launching an Internet shortcut causes the Internet Explorer to connect you to your service provider and automatically load the page to which the shortcut corresponds.

The *cache*, on the other hand, is a dedicated directory on your hard disk (usually on the partition that houses Plus) that stores downloaded HTML pages and graphics. When the Internet Explorer retrieves a page from a remote server, it automatically stores a copy in the cache directory, speeding up browsing between pages. This provides a significant speed boost if you browse between multiple pages, because the Internet Explorer doesn't have to retrieve the page again. The cached pages and graphics are stored in \Plus!\Microsoft Internet\Cache by default.

The default size for the cache is 10 percent of your disk space. You can easily shrink or enlarge the cache size by moving the slider bar. Additionally, both History and Cache can be emptied to free up more disk space. To empty the cache (or the history archives), choose the Empty button.

Sending and Receiving Internet E-Mail

Internet mail is one of the most compelling reasons to use the Internet. Using the Internet enables you to send mail to corporations, universities, government agencies, and anyone who has access to an Internet account, an online service (such as America Online, CompuServe or the Microsoft Network), or a BBS that supports UUCP (Unix to Unix Copy Program, a way of transporting Usenet news and Internet mail without a direct Internet connection).

Microsoft Plus includes an Internet mail driver that works in conjunction with its Dial-Up Networking support to deliver and receive mail from your Internet provider. Figure 16.15 shows Exchange sending a message to an Internet address.

Figure 16.15

Plus includes an Internet driver for the Microsoft Exchange in-box.

Note Even though the message in figure 16.15 is addressed to a CompuServe account, it still must travel via the Internet to go from your desktop to your recipient's.

Chapter 30, "Using Microsoft Exchange," contains a comprehensive overview of Microsoft Exchange and the Internet.

Desktop Enhancements

Plus offers a handful of desktop enhancements intended for high-end machines, such as 486s and Pentiums. They aren't crucial enhancements, but they make navigating through the Windows 95 desktop much more pleasing by offering cosmetic improvements to the desktop. This section looks at the following desktop enhancements:

◆ Desktop themes

◆ Full window drag

◆ Font smoothing

◆ Stretching bitmaps

Using Desktop Themes

One of the most welcome additions to Windows 95 is the set of desktop themes included with Plus. These themes, ranging from various sports items to a tour inside your computer, turn the otherwise mundane Windows 95 desktop into a more pleasing environment. *Themes* are a collection of desktop bitmaps, icons, mouse pointers, fonts, and sound files. Put together, they transform your desktop into a virtual art gallery. Plus includes the following themes:

◆ **Dangerous Creatures.** Dangerous Creatures spotlights a number of rare creatures that are, well, dangerous. Dangerous Creatures includes tigers, blowfish, hornets, and many other animals.

◆ **Inside your Computer.** A tour inside your computer, highlighted by chips and silicon galore.

◆ **Leonardo da Vinci.** Based on the artist and his work. Features diagrams from his famous notebook.

◆ **Mystery.** Spend a night inside the chilling confines of your PC. This theme turns your desktop into a Clue-esque study, complete with flying bats and fingerprints.

◆ **Nature.** Butterflies, bees, leaves, birds, caterpillars and trees. A complete tour of the woods without having to leave your PC.

◆ **Science.** This theme turns your Windows 95 desktop into a laboratory by using atoms, beakers, and chemicals as icons and wallpaper.

◆ **Sports.** From skiing to football to tennis—this theme covers it all.

◆ **The '60s USA.** Peace, love, tie-dye, and lava lamps.

◆ **The Golden Era.** The '40s—industrial and on your desktop.

◆ **Travel.** This theme gives you a vintage tour by car, train or plane.

◆ **Windows 95.** The official desktop of Windows 95. This theme splashes the colors and sights of Windows 95 on your Windows 95 desktop.

Stop Although most themes can run in 256 colors, some require 16-bit high-color (65,000 colors). For optimal clarity, high-color themes should not be run on a 256-color desktop. High-color themes try to use more colors than the 256-color palette supports, so when a high-color image is displayed, the Windows palette manager has to shift the system colors around to accommodate the high-color graphic.

Applying and Changing Desktop Themes

You can change themes easily from the Control Panel's Desktop Themes object, which appears during installation of Plus. The Desktop Themes dialog box (see fig. 16.16) enables you to customize nearly every aspect of a theme.

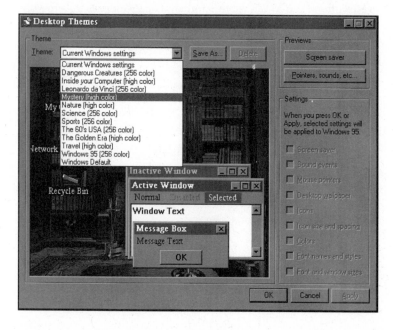

Figure 16.16

The Desktop Themes dialog box.

To apply a theme to the desktop, click on the Theme drop-down box for a list of the available themes on your system. To select a theme, simply click on the theme name from the list.

After you select a theme, the preview area of the Desktop Themes dialog box updates to reflect the changes to your desktop configuration. The right side of the dialog box contains more options for customizing themes. The Settings group enables you to select the components you want to update. If you want to apply the Sports scheme, for example, but retain your own custom icons, disable the Icons check box to apply all theme components except for the theme icons.

You also preview certain components not shown in the Previews area, including mouse pointers, system sounds, and screen savers. To view these pieces before you apply the theme, click on the appropriate button—Screen Saver or Pointers, sounds, and so forth—to open a tabbed dialog box in which you can view and modify icons and sounds. After you decide on a theme, choose OK or Apply to close the Desktop Themes dialog box.

Using Full Window Drag and Font Smoothing

To polish off the Windows 95 desktop, Plus offers full window drag as well as font smoothing. Both features give the desktop a more professional look and feel. To access these features, right-click on the desktop and choose Properties to bring up the Display property sheet.

Full Window Drag

Full window drag is a relatively minor feature that's had a tumultuous history. It first appeared in a beta version of Windows 3.1, but the video cards at that time were not fast enough to handle smooth full window dragging, so Microsoft removed it. It reappeared in an earlier version of Windows 95, but again, Microsoft removed it. Finally, Microsoft added it to Microsoft Plus, and now it's here to stay.

Full window drag is the capability to drag or resize the entire window. In most graphical operating systems, you only see the frame of the window when you drag (or move) it. With full window drag, the window moves as one solid image, rather than just a frame outline. This makes resizing windows a bit more precise and gives a more polished look to the Windows 95 desktop.

 Note   Full window drag also has been available in Windows NT since the release of version 3.5.

Full window drag is on by default after you install Plus. Plus utilizes Windows 95's user interface properties and adds a special Plus page to the display properties, shown in figure 16.17. If full window drag is too slow, you can disable it by disabling the Show window contents while dragging check box.

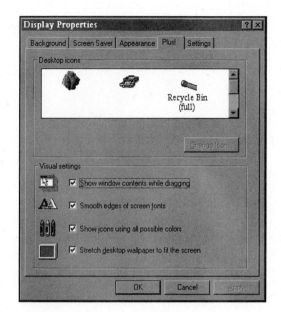

Figure 16.17

The desktop enhancements page in Plus.

Font Smoothing

Font smoothing is a new feature that gives Windows 95 a more professional look by smoothing the jagged edges of fonts. When you enable font smoothing, Windows 95 automatically fills the jagged edges with complementary colors, creating a smoother look. It takes up a bit more memory and requires a color depth of at least 256 colors. If you want to conserve memory, you can disable font smoothing by clearing the Smooth edges of screen fonts check box on the Plus properties page.

Desktop Bitmap Stretching

Many bitmaps used as desktop wallpaper typically are created and saved at 640×480. If your resolution is set at 800×600 or 1,024×768, therefore, you have a wide border around any bitmap you have centered.

Plus stretches bitmaps out to the full resolution without diminishing visual quality. You can enable or disable bitmap stretching by checking or unchecking the Stretch desktop wallpaper to fit the screen check box in the Plus properties page. Figure 16.18 shows a 800×600 bitmap running in a 1,024×768 screen area with bitmap stretching disabled. Figure 16.19 shows the same bitmap with stretching enabled.

Figure 16.18

A 800×600 bitmap running in a 1,024×768 screen area with bitmap stretching disabled.

Figure 16.19

The same bitmap, but stretched out to fill the entire screen. Notice that there is no noticeable loss of quality.

Stop Bitmap stretching doesn't work if you have the wallpaper tiled; you have to have it centered if you want it to stretch. You can change the behavior from tiled to centered from the Background page of the Display property sheet.

Playing 3D Pinball

A full-featured multimedia game rounds off the list of features in Plus. 3D Pinball is not a stripped-down version either—it's a fully functioning pinball game designed for Windows 95. 3D Pinball takes advantage of key Windows 95 features such as direct video access. You might notice that 3D Pinball's performance running in a window equals many DOS pinball games! Figure 16.20 shows a sample 3D Pinball game.

Figure 16.20

The 3D Pinball game.

3D Pinball is extremely simple to play. The Z and ? keys activate the left and right flippers, respectively. Pressing X tilts the table to the left, while pressing > tilts the table to the right. The spacebar launches the ball—and just like on a real pinball table, the longer you hold the spacebar, the more powerful the launch. To remap the keys, choose Options, Player Controls.

Part IV

Putting Windows 95 to Work

New Riders Publishing
INSIDE SERIES

C H A P T E R

17

Installing and Uninstalling Applications

One of the fundamental ways you will put Windows to work is installing and uninstalling new applications. You can install three types of applications in the new version of Windows: Windows 95 applications, Windows 3.*x* applications (also known as Win16-based applications), and DOS-based applications. Because of the number of options presented during installation, the process of installing new applications in Windows 95 is slightly more complicated than in previous versions of Windows. Although the installation of new applications in any version of Windows is an easy task, uninstalling applications can be frustrating and time-consuming. Identifying all the files an application has installed can be troublesome, which makes removing all traces of an unwanted application difficult. To ease the uninstallation pain, Windows 95 applications must include a facility to uninstall applications easily.

This chapter looks at how the user installs and removes applications in Windows 95, including using the Add/Remove Programs wizard. The chapter covers the following topics:

◆ Managing and organizing installed applications on your system

◆ Using the Add/Remove Programs wizard

◆ Installing Windows 95, Win16-based, and DOS-based applications into Windows 95

◆ Uninstalling applications

Managing Application Installation

A natural instinct of PC users is to install new software as soon as they receive it. Software developers accommodate this instinct—a great majority of Windows applications ship with an automated installation process that saves the user from manually copying files. Without an understanding of how an installation program affects your system, however, and without a solid plan for organizing the file and directory system on your PC, blindly installing applications can lead to disaster. Installation programs often modify important files, and this process can sometimes—though rarely—leave your system unbootable. To avoid disasters related to application installation, you should follow these three rules:

◆ Have some understanding of what an installation program will do to your system by reading the supplied documentation or talking to other people who have installed the same application.

◆ Be prepared to halt the installation if it seems as if the installation program will make undesirable changes to your system.

◆ Have a strategy to efficiently organize the programs and data on your system.

Stop   A potential area for trouble during installation of a new application is with the installation program itself. The installation program is usually the last component of a new application to be developed, and the quality and dependability of the installation program is often at a level significantly lower than that of the application. Installation programs are not always forgiving if they encounter unexpected conditions. The programs sometimes halt prematurely, leaving the application in a half-installed state. Sometimes it is easy to reinitiate the installation without issue; sometimes it is impossible to restart installation without erasing all of the files the program loaded before it crashed. An even worse—but not unheard of—situation is when a failed installation program leaves a PC unbootable.

This section of the chapter helps you develop a strategy for monitoring the installation of new software applications and for organizing applications as they are installed.

Modifying Important Files

One of the most compelling reasons for monitoring the installation program of a new application is the modifications the program might make to your system, which includes modifying important system files. Although the installation of Windows 95 applications usually affects only the system registry files (see the section "Changes to the Registry during Installation" later in this chapter for more information), the installation of Windows 3.*x* and DOS-based applications usually affects important system files, such as Config.sys, Autoexec.bat, System.ini, and Win.ini, sometimes adversely.

 Note Although Windows 95 does not specifically use system files from DOS and Windows 3.*x*, such as Config.sys, Autoexec.bat, System.ini, and Win.ini, these files are maintained for compatibility with non-Windows 95 applications. Windows 3.*x* and DOS applications that must read and write to those files can do so under Windows 95.

Many Windows 3.1 applications modify the Win.ini and System.ini files—key system files in Windows 3.*x*—during installation. These applications write and store information about themselves in Win.ini and System.ini, instead of installing proprietary Ini files to store application-specific information. If you have installed more than six Windows applications, your Win.ini and System.ini files probably have become extremely difficult to manage because of their size and number of sections.

This problem of applications modifying Windows Ini files is compounded if you want to remove an application from your system. Typically, if you are forced to remove an application from your system, you will do a marvelous job of deleting the files and directory structure for the application, but you might fall short in removing all the relevant sections from the Ini files. Your Windows system might not be able to load properly because of invalidated sections in Win.ini and System.ini that direct the system to access files that cannot be found.

Although installation of Windows 95 applications affects fewer components of the Windows system during installation than Windows 3.*x* or DOS-based applications, it's still a good idea to monitor installation, even if you plan to install only Windows 95 applications. During installation, these applications write to the system registry, which is arguably the most critical part of the Windows 95 system. An errant application that adversely affects the registry could render your system unusable.

Surviving a New Application Installation

Now that you have seen the problems an installation can cause with your system, it is obvious you should take steps to protect your system from disaster. This section presents a series of short advisory topics to help you survive the installation of a new application.

Make Changes to Important Files Yourself

Usually an installation program informs you if it is about to modify an important system file, such as Win.ini, System.ini, Config.sys, or Autoexec.bat. The program probably will ask you for permission to do so or will let you complete the modification to the file(s) yourself. If given the choice, always choose to modify the file yourself. This way, you are in a position to evaluate the changes before they are made and, perhaps, make alternative modifications or not modify the file(s) at all. Although the installation program for a Windows 95 application will not be interested in any of these four system files, Windows 3.*x* and DOS-based applications usually expect to see these files during installation, write to them during installation, and read them during operation.

 Tip   The easiest way to edit a system file is to open the folder where the file is located and then click on the file's name or icon (depending upon the view you are using for the folder). Next, right-click on the object to display its context menu, and then choose Open. The file will then be opened, ready for editing, in the Notepad application.

An example of an application that gives the user the option to make changes to important files is called Brief, from Borland. A programmer's text editor, Brief clearly informs the user of the changes it proposes to make to the Autoexec.bat file and asks the user if he would like to make the changes instead. If the user chooses to make the changes manually, the proposed edits to Autoexec.bat are written to a file that the user can examine and incorporate into Autoexec.bat as he sees fit. Figure 17.1 shows Brief in mid-installation, querying the user as to how to proceed with proposed changes to Autoexec.bat.

Have a Boot Disk Ready

Before beginning installation of a new application, be sure you have a boot disk ready. This way, if the installation fails and leaves your system in an unbootable state, you can always start your system from the disk and get it running again. You should re-create your boot disk every time you change your Windows 95 configuration.

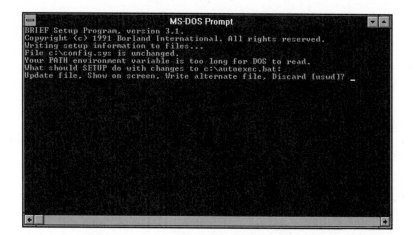

Figure 17.1

Brief gives the user control over modifications to important files.

Windows 95 gives you the option to create a startup disk during its installation process. (A *startup disk* is another name for a boot disk.) If you did not create a startup disk during the Windows 95 installation, you can still create one now. Start the Add/Remove Programs wizard in the Control Panel and then choose the Startup Disk page. Read the instructions that appear on the page and then choose Create Disk.

Back Up Important Files Regularly

Make it a habit to back up important files. Copy the files to a floppy disk and squirrel away the disk for safe keeping. Be sure to do this just prior to installing a new application. A list of important files that you should back up includes the following: Config.sys (for Win16- and DOS-based apps), Autoexec.bat (for Win16- and DOS-based apps), System.ini (for Win16- and DOS-based apps), Win.ini (for Win16- and DOS-based apps), User.dat (for the Windows 95 system), and System.dat (for the Windows 95 system).

Catalog Your System Regularly

Another good habit is to catalog your entire system regularly, especially just before and after installing a new application. By redirecting the DIR /S command to a file, you can create a snapshot of your system, showing every file and directory (including timestamp) on the drive from which you executed the DIR statement. By comparing catalogs of your system made just before and after certain operations, such as installation of a new application, it's easy to see how your system and important files have changed. Following is sample output from the DIR /S command:

```
FINAL91   T92       15,118  03-21-93  4:39p  FINAL91.T92
FINAL91   T91       11,665  04-12-92 11:20a  FINAL91.T91
TEST91    T91       13,481  03-29-92  7:14a  TEST91.T91
TC93      CFG           94  03-07-95  1:35a  TC93.CFG
          51 file(s)      7,389,361 bytes


Directory of C:\WIN95

.              <DIR>        02-22-95 10:25p .
..             <DIR>        02-22-95 10:25p ..
COMMAND        <DIR>        02-22-95 11:01p COMMAND
SYSTEM         <DIR>        02-22-95 11:01p SYSTEM
NETDET    Ini    3,821     02-15-95  3:00p NETDET.Ini
README    TXT   31,434     02-22-95 10:12p README.TXT
SMARTDRV  EXE   45,145     02-22-95 10:12p SMARTDRV.EXE
REGEDIT   EXE  119,296     02-15-95  3:00p REGEDIT.EXE
RIVETS    BMP      630     02-15-95  3:00p Rivets.bmp
SQUARES   BMP      630     02-15-95  3:00p Squares.bmp
ZIGZAG    BMP      630     02-15-95  3:00p Zig Zag.bmp
HELP           <DIR>        02-22-95 11:03p HELP
CALC      EXE   62,976     02-15-95  3:00p CALC.EXE
NOTEPAD   EXE   32,768     02-15-95  3:00p NOTEPAD.EXE
PACKAGER  EXE   65,824     02-15-95  3:00p PACKAGER.EXE
PBRUSH    EXE    5,632     02-15-95  3:00p PBRUSH.EXE
WRITE     EXE    5,632     02-15-95  3:00p WRITE.EXE
DIALER    EXE   63,128     02-15-95  3:00p DIALER.EXE
WIN       COM   22,311     02-15-95  3:00p WIN.COM
IOS       Ini    7,933     02-15-95  3:00p IOS.Ini
ASPI2HLP  SYS    1,105     02-15-95  3:00p ASPI2HLP.SYS
HIMEM     SYS   32,935     02-15-95  3:00p HIMEM.SYS
CARS      BMP      630     02-15-95  3:00p Cars.bmp
HONEYC~1  BMP      854     02-15-95  3:00p Honeycomb.bmp
EFORMS         <DIR>        02-23-95 12:50a EFORMS
DOSPRMPT  PIF      545     02-15-95  3:00p DOSPRMPT.PIF
WINBUG    DAT   35,654     02-16-95  2:37p WINBUG.DAT
WINBUG10  DLL    5,907     02-15-95  3:00p WINBUG10.DLL
WINBUG    EXE  113,152     02-16-95  2:37p WINBUG.EXE
DEFRAG    EXE  212,512     02-15-95  3:00p DEFRAG.EXE
WINHELP   EXE  297,984     02-15-95  3:00p WINHELP.EXE
```

Choose the Custom Installation Option

Many Windows applications, especially from Microsoft, enable you to choose the mode of installation the application will use. You can choose the Typical option, in which the installation program chooses the most likely options you will use in the application and installs just those; the Minimum/Laptop option, in which the installation program installs just the minimum files required to run the application; or the Complete/Custom option, in which you choose the options to be installed. The safest choice to make is the Complete/Custom option. Although it involves more work to manually choose each component of the application to install, you have the comfort of knowing which components will be installed, to which directories they will be installed, and how much disk space they will occupy.

Install Windows 95 Applications

One of the requirements for an application to be officially classified as a Windows 95 application (by Microsoft) is that the application support the Windows 95 uninstall specification. This means that the application must contain support for Windows 95 to uninstall the application if the user chooses to do so. Considering how difficult it is to remove an application from your system (see the section "Uninstalling Windows 95 Applications" later in this chapter), it makes sense to install a Windows 95 application rather than a Windows 3.*x* application if given the choice.

Organizing the File and Directory System

Users today often take advantage of more than one application to complete a specific task. For a single project, for example, an engineering manager might use a word processor for memos and other documents, project planning software, a spreadsheet to help with calculations, and a drawing application for creating technical illustrations. It would be helpful, therefore, to find all the files related to that task.

An organized system of applications and data will make it easy for you to locate all the data associated with a particular project or a task. Other advantages to organizing your system by project include the following:

◆ **Ease in finding files.** If all the files associated with a project are in one location, it is easy to find all of the documents, pictures, spreadsheets, figures, and other components associated with the project. Otherwise, to find all the files associated with a particular project or task, you will have to search as many directories as applications you used to complete the project.

◆ **Ease in backing up.** If all the data in your system is located in a central location, it is easy to back up all your data. If your data is scattered around your hard drive, it can be difficult to locate and identify all the files you want to back up.

Figure 17.2 suggests a possible hard disk layout for efficiently organizing files and directories.

Figure 17.2

Organizing your applications and data by project.

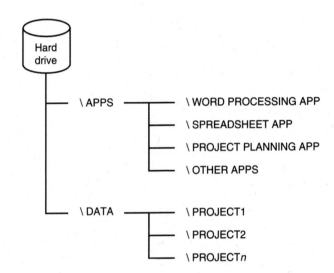

Installing Applications in Windows 95

You can install three types of applications in Windows 95:

◆ Windows 95 applications

◆ Windows 3.*x* applications

◆ DOS-based applications

Installation of each type of application is handled differently in Windows 95. This section of the chapter explains the differences in installing each type of application and what effect installation will have on your system. This section also covers the procedure for installing an application using the Add/Remove Programs wizard, discussed next.

Using the Add/Remove Programs Wizard

Windows 95 uses a dedicated utility for installing and uninstalling applications. This utility, called the Add/Remove Programs wizard, is used to install and uninstall all types of applications, including Windows 3.*x* applications, DOS-based applications, and Windows 95 applications. Like the other wizards in Windows 95, the Add/Remove Programs wizard walks you through each step of the task you are performing.

 Note   Although you can install an application simply by running its Setup program independent from the Add/Remove Programs wizard, the installation might not run properly. Running the wizard alerts Windows 95 that an installation is occurring, thus enabling the system to monitor the installation. By monitoring the installation, Windows can optimize itself for running the application, set up the registry for the time when the application might be uninstalled (for Windows 95 applications), and better recover from a failed or aborted installation.

In addition to installing applications, the Add/Remove Programs wizard is responsible for two other tasks:

◆ **Installing and uninstalling Windows components.** Windows 95 ships with a number of additional components and accessories that are not installed when you set up Windows 95. The Add/Remove Programs wizard helps you install these additional components.

◆ **Create a boot disk.** The Add/Remove Programs wizard helps you create a special disk that you use to boot your system should it become unbootable for some reason. See Chapter 2, "Setting Up and Booting Windows 95," for more information about the use of a boot disk and the process for creating one.

The Add/Remove Programs wizard is found in the Control Panel folder. By double-clicking on its icon, you start the wizard and display its initial dialog box, shown in figure 17.3. Select the Install/Uninstall page and then choose Install. The Install Program From Floppy Disk or CD-ROM dialog box appears (see fig. 17.4), enabling you to insert the installation disk into the appropriate drive. Check the application's supplied documentation if the application contains more than one disk and you are not sure which one contains the setup program.

After you have inserted the installation disk, choose the Next button. Windows 95 next searches your floppy drives for installation programs, looking for files with typical installation program names, such as Setup.exe, Setup.bat, Install.exe, and Install.bat. Windows 95 searches alphabetically through all your available drives and displays the first installation program it finds in the Command line for installation program text box in the Run Installation Program dialog box (see fig. 17.5).

Figure 17.3

The initial dialog box of the Add/ Remove Programs wizard.

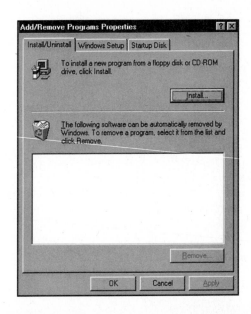

Figure 17.4

The Add/Remove Programs wizard prompts you to insert the installation disk or CD.

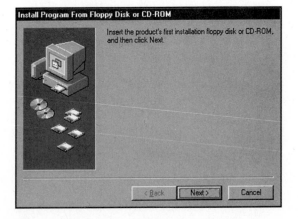

If Windows 95 cannot find a file that it believes to be an installation program, it leaves the Command line for installation program text box blank. In this case, you will have to supply the file name of the program and the path to it that installs your application. You can type the file name directly in the edit box or you can use the Browse button to help specify the name of the installation program. Again, if you are unsure of which file on your application's distribution media is the installation program, consult the application's documentation. After you have specified the file, click on the Finish button, and Windows 95 runs the installation program for your application. After completion, the Add/Remove Programs wizard shuts down, and you return to the Control Panel folder.

Figure 17.5

If Windows 95 cannot find a setup program on its own, it prompts you to supply the name and path of the setup program for the application you are installing.

Installing Windows 95 Applications

Of the three different types of applications you can install into Windows 95, official Windows 95 applications are the easiest. These applications require very little information from you during installation, and the installation process for most Windows 95 applications is similar.

All Windows 95 applications use a standard setup program. This means that all Windows 95 applications use the same set of installation services provided by the Windows 95 system, and that all Windows 95 applications behave similarly during installation. In addition, because Windows 95 handles most of the installation chores for the application, there is very little user interaction required during installation. Windows 95 requires specific information from the application during the installation (which Windows 95 then stores in the Registry database), so there usually is little additional information required from the installer.

The next two sections take a closer look at the standard Windows 95 setup program and how installation works with the Registry.

The Standard Windows 95 Setup Program

One of the primary reasons for the success of Windows is the similarity between Windows applications—if a user is able to master one Windows application, he is generally able to master others. The user interface across most Windows 3.*x* applications is consistent, and most Windows applications handle common tasks in the same manner, such as Print, Preview, and Save As.

Another component of Windows that is standard across most Windows 3.*x* applications is the setup program. Developers who used Microsoft's tools for developing the Setup program for their applications produced the same style and appearance in their installation process. These similarities have not changed with Windows 95—developers can still use a set of tools distributed by Microsoft to develop a setup program. These tools enable the developer to build an installation program that both fulfills the setup requirements and is stylistically and functionally similar to other installation programs built with the same tools and specifications. The following sections detail the standard Windows 95 setup program.

Install and Uninstall Requirements for Windows 95 Applications

Microsoft has established strict criteria in order for applications to be officially classified as Windows 95 applications. This set of criteria is known as *logo requirements,* because only applications that meet the criteria are allowed to use the official Windows 95 logo on their packaging. Windows 95 applications must register themselves properly with Windows 95 when they are installed. This means that applications must load information into the system registry so that Windows 95 can recognize the application. Applications being installed must provide full uninstall capability, which is partially a product of being loaded into the registry, and they cannot write to or read from System.ini or Win.ini, critical system files used in previous versions of Windows.

 Note It is impossible for a Win16-based application to qualify as a Windows 95 application without modification. Win16-based applications cannot possibly know about the system registry in Windows 95, so these applications are not able to register themselves properly in the system. Therefore, all native Win16-based applications fail the Windows 95 logo qualification.

Changes to the Registry during Installation

The Registry database in Windows 95 stores hardware and software configuration information. The intent of this feature is to replace many of the text files used in DOS and previous versions of Windows to manage the PC's hardware and software with a central repository of data. This section looks at what happens to the Registry database during installation. For detailed information about the Registry database, refer to Chapter 13, "Working with the Registry and Ini Files."

When a Windows 95 application is installed, it enters information into the Registry database. This information is the data that the application will maintain in the database and use when it runs, such as color information, content of the context menu, file extensions the application uses, version information, location of the installed files, and more. This information can be specific to the machine the software is installed on or specific to the application itself. By loading this information during installation, you spend less time configuring Windows and the application both during installation and the first time you run the application, and more time using the software. This aspect of installation is also critical to uninstallation. By registering itself with Windows 95 during installation, Windows 95 can efficiently remove an application when you choose to uninstall it. Uninstallation is covered later in this chapter.

Note System administrators at organizations that are deploying Windows 95 on a large scale have the option of installing Windows 95 via automated scripts. These scripts also can be used to install applications into Windows 95. For more information about the custom setup scripts, see Chapter 3, "Troubleshooting Setup and Startup."

Installing Windows 3.x Applications

At the time of the release of Windows 95, only a small percentage of the applications developed for Windows 3.x were available in Windows 95 versions. Therefore, it is likely you will install Windows 3.x applications into Windows 95. Fortunately, Microsoft promises that there will be no compatibility issues for Windows 3.x applications running under Windows 95, and Microsoft even makes the claim that all Windows 3.x applications run as well or better in Windows 95 on systems with at least 4 MB of RAM. The same promise of compatibility between Windows 3.x applications and Windows 95 extends to the installation of Windows 3.x applications.

Although Windows 95 provides a dedicated utility for launching the installation of all applications and Windows 3.x does not, there is little difference in installing a Windows 3.x application into Windows 95 compared to installing the same application into Windows 3.x. Because Windows 3.x applications know nothing of Windows 95, these applications will expect the same environment in Windows 95 as they would in Windows 3.x. It is up to Windows 95, therefore, to anticipate that the installation program for Windows 3.x applications will function as they would as if they were being installed into Windows 3.x.

Windows 3.x applications interact with Windows in three primary areas during installation. These are the areas that Windows 95 must be concerned with when a Windows 3.x application is installed. These areas are the following:

◆ **The SYSTEM directory.** Windows 3.x applications often install files into a directory named SYSTEM located one level below the main Windows directory.

◆ **System.ini and Win.ini.** Windows applications often interact with these two Windows system files.

◆ **Common DLLs.** Windows 3.x applications often uses common dynamic link libraries (DLLs), and sometimes applications install their own versions of these files.

The next three sections describe how Windows 95 handles these areas of interaction with a Windows 3.*x* installation program.

System Directory

As with Windows 3.*x*, Windows 95 uses a directory named SYSTEM for storing critical system files and maintains the SYSTEM directory one level below the main Windows directory. As such, the installation program for Windows 3.*x* applications will be able to copy and read files to and from the same location under Windows 95.

Win.ini and System.ini

One of the most important components of Windows 3.*x* and Windows 3.*x* applications is Ini files. These files, with the extension Ini, store important information about applications that run under Windows (and about Windows itself). Although the Windows system stores much of its critical system information in two files, Win.ini and System.ini, many applications also store information in those files. Though Microsoft prefers applications to use their own Ini files, many applications, nonetheless, use these files. Examples of applications that use their own Ini files are Excel 5.0 from Microsoft (Excel5.ini) and Quicken from Intuit (Quicken.ini).

Although Windows 95 does not explicitly use Win.ini, System.ini, or any other Ini files, these files are maintained for compatibility with Windows 3.*x* applications. Information that Windows 3.*x* stored in Win.ini and System.ini now is stored in the registry in Windows 95, as well as information from some of the other less-critical system Ini files, such as Control.ini (Control Panel). Windows 95 also will not interfere if an installation program for a Windows 3.*x* application attempts to create its own Ini file. As an experienced Windows 3.*x* user, therefore, you might be surprised to see System.ini and Win.ini in the Windows 95 directory—their only purpose is to support Windows 3.*x* applications running under Windows 95.

Replace System DLLs

Many Windows 3.*x* applications redistribute important system DLLs, such as CTRL3D.DLL (3D-style controls library) and COMMDLG.DLL (common dialog box library). This means that during the installation of such applications, these files, which were originally installed with Windows, are replaced with versions that ship with the application. In Windows 95, the functionality for many of these system DLLs has been merged into a single large file to enhance performance of system initialization. Windows 95 intercepts and processes calls made to these files created by Windows 3.*x* applications; during installation of Windows 3.*x* applications, Windows 95 ignores attempts to install these new files. If an application is critically dependent upon the existence of these files, they should be copied to the Windows SYSTEM\VMM32 directory.

Note If you already have installed Windows 95, you might have unwittingly chosen to become an application installation expert. If you choose to install Windows 95 into a new directory rather than over your existing Windows system, you will have to reinstall each of your Windows 3.x applications into Windows 95 in order to run them in Windows 95. Creating a shortcut that points to the Windows 3.x application will not be sufficient—you will have to run the Add/Remove Programs wizard for just about every application you installed in Windows 3.1.

Specify a Working Directory

Windows 3.x enables the user to specify a working directory for an application. The working directory is the default directory used for the work you perform with an application. This directory might be different from the directory in which the application's executable file and other program files are stored. Excel 5.0 can be launched by executing the Excel.exe file in the Excel5 directory, for example, but you might have specified \BUDGETS as the working directory. This way, Excel saves files to the \BUDGETS directory and always defaults to that directory in the Open and Save As dialog boxes. Specifying the working directory for an application in Windows 3.x is an easy task. The user creates a program item (icon) and specifies the working directory in the Working Directory text box in the Program Item Properties dialog box.

Unfortunately, it is slightly more difficult to specify a working directory for a Win16-based application running in Windows 95. To specify the working directory for a Windows 3.x application running in Windows 95, you must create a shortcut to the application. Most applications appear on the Programs menu in Windows 95 after they have been installed. The Programs menu launches the executable file for the application, which is stored in the directory where it was installed. Your first instinct, therefore, might be to examine the property sheet for the application's executable file in order to change the working directory there. Unfortunately, the working directory might not be changed on the property sheet because the application is counting on constant path information. Instead, a shortcut must be created with information about the working directory.

To specify a working directory for a Win16-based application, right-click at the location where you plan to create a shortcut to the application. After you specify the executable file for the shortcut, as well as its label, click on Finish. After the shortcut appears on your screen, right-click on it to display the shortcut's property sheet. (Figure 17.6 shows the property sheet for the shortcut to a Windows 3.x application.) Specify the working directory for the application in the Start In text box. This way, whenever the shortcut is executed, the application associated with it will be opened with the directory you specified in the Start in text box as the default directory.

Figure 17.6

The property sheet for a shortcut to a Windows 3.x application enables you to specify a working directory, as you could in prior versions of Windows.

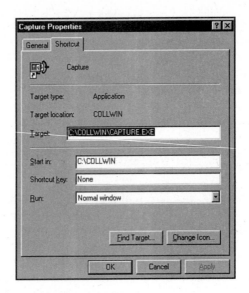

Installing DOS Applications

Because DOS-based applications have no true interaction with Windows, it's difficult for Windows 95 to monitor and control the installation of DOS applications. In fact, installation of a DOS application is simply a matter of letting the Add/Remove Programs wizard run the application's setup program, and that setup program might be a simple batch file that copies files, a batch file that extracts files from an archive file, or an executable installation file. Regardless of which form the installation program takes, you should use the Add/Remove Programs wizard to run this installation. Doing so enables Windows 95 to monitor the installation and recover from a failed installation.

Running the Installation Wizard for DOS Applications

To install a DOS-based application, start the Add/Remove Programs wizard from the Control Panel. Select the Install/Uninstall property sheet and then choose Install. When the next dialog box appears, insert the CD or disk containing the installation program into the appropriate drive. Check the application's supplied documentation if the application contains more than one disk and you are not sure which disk contains the setup program. Click on the Next button.

In the Run Installation Program dialog box that appears, if Windows 95 is able to automatically detect the installation program (typically looking for files named Setup.exe or Install.bat on disks in any disk drives), the file—including its path—already will be displayed in the text box. If this is the case, be sure the file name and

path are correct. If Windows 95 is unable to find what it believes to be an installation program, Windows 95 leaves the box blank. If this is the case, enter the installation program file name, including the path to it, into the text box. You can use the Browse button to help specify the name of the installation program. Again, if you are unsure of which file on your application's distribution media is the installation program, consult the DOS application's documentation. After you specify the file, click on the Finish button. Windows 95 will now run the installation program for your application.

Preparing DOS-Based Applications to Run

After using the Add/Remove Programs wizard for installing a DOS-based application, there is still one more step to take before you can run the application. This is different from the installation of Windows 3.x and Windows 95 applications, which you can run immediately after using the wizard.

In the case of a Windows application installation, after the files are installed on your system and the appropriate system files are modified, a menu item might be added to the Programs menu. In addition, a choice associated with your application might also be added to that menu. This is analogous to adding a program group and program item in Windows 3.x. For a great majority of DOS-based applications, no facility for running the application from Windows is established, so the user must do this.

Preparing a DOS-based application to run in Windows 95 is actually a simple task. All you have to do is create a shortcut at the location from which you plan to launch the application. If you plan to launch the application from the desktop, for example, create a shortcut to the application on the desktop. To create a shortcut, right-click at the location and then choose New, Shortcut from the menu. Then, follow the instructions that appear for specifying the executable file for the application and for specifying the label that will appear for the application's shortcut icon. After Windows 95 has created the shortcut, you can start the application by selecting the icon.

You should always create a shortcut for starting a DOS-based application, instead of starting it by choosing Run on the Start menu. The shortcut contains all of the special information Windows 95 needs in order to run the DOS application. Without that information, Windows 95 will run the application using default settings, which might not be compatible with the application, and might not even allow the application to run.

Note   Windows 3.x used program information files (PIF files) to specify how DOS applications ran in Windows 3.x. Windows 95 also stores information about DOS applications in PIF files, and the settings in these files can be viewed and modified by displaying the property sheets for the shortcut to a DOS application. For more information about running and configuring DOS applications, refer to Chapter 21, "Integrating Windows and DOS."

To set up a DOS application to run in Windows 95, perform the following steps:

1. Select a DOS-based application that you would like to install in Windows 95. Collect all the distribution media for the application.

2. Open the Control Panel folder and select the Add/Remove Programs wizard.

3. Select the Install/Uninstall property page and then choose Install.

4. Insert the disk with the Setup program into the appropriate disk drive.

5. Choose Next.

6. From the Run Installation Program dialog box, examine the contents of the Command line for installation program text box to see if Windows 95 was able to find the installation program. If the proper installation program is displayed in the text box, click on the Finish button. Otherwise, specify the fully qualified file name for the installation program and click on Finish.

7. Complete the installation of the DOS-based application. After installation is complete, close the Control Panel folder.

8. Create a shortcut to the file that launches the application you just installed.

9. Run the application to verify that it installed properly. If required, modify the settings for the DOS application by right-clicking on the shortcut and choosing Properties from the menu to display the application's DOS-mode property sheets.

Uninstalling Applications in Windows 95

Removing an application from your system can be a challenging task. It is sometimes difficult to identify all the files that were installed by an application, and care must be taken not to remove a critical file that might be used by another application. This task is made easier in Windows 95 only if you are removing a Windows 95 application. Uninstalling a DOS- or Win16-based application still is difficult. The next three sections look at the easiest and safest method for removing applications from Windows 95.

Uninstalling Windows 95 Applications

Of the three different types of applications discussed in this chapter, the uninstallation of Windows 95 applications from Windows 95 is the safest and easiest. Even compared to the few DOS- and Win16-based applications that provide their own uninstallation routines, Windows 95 applications present the fewest potential problems because of the built-in support for Windows 95 applications present in the Windows 95 system.

Instead of the application doing the work, Windows 95 manages the uninstallation of Windows 95 applications. The uninstallation of Windows 95 applications is integrated into the Windows 95 system, so removing a Windows 95 application is both easy to do from the user perspective and generally protected from failure or unexpected events. This is achieved by the requirement that Windows 95 applications provide uninstall information to the Registry database during installation. This way, when you start to uninstall a Windows 95 application, Windows 95 knows how which files to uninstall, where they are located, and if another application uses one of the files. Furthermore, Windows 95 provides an easy-to-use interface that enables you to uninstall a Windows 95 application with just a few mouse clicks. Figure 17.7 shows the Add/Remove Programs property sheet, which is where you uninstall Windows 95 applications.

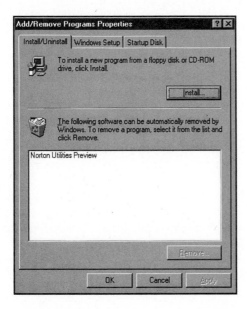

Figure 17.7

The Add/Remove Programs property sheet is where you uninstall (and install) Windows 95 applications.

Perform the following steps to uninstall a Windows 95 application:

1. Open the Control Panel folder and start the Add/Remove Programs wizard.

2. Click on the Install/Uninstall tab to display the Install/Uninstall property page.

3. From the list box that appears at the bottom of the Install/Uninstall property page, select the Windows 95 application to uninstall. The **R**emove button becomes active.

4. Choose the **R**emove button, and then answer Yes to the prompt to confirm the uninstallation.

Uninstalling Windows 3.x Applications

Windows 3.x applications play a sinister role during installation by distributing files to different directories and modifying Windows system files such as Win.ini and System.ini. This poor situation is made worse if the user chooses to uninstall Win16-based applications. Only a small percentage of Win16-based applications ship with a dedicated uninstall program, so the user is left with a manual effort to remove a Win16-based application from Windows 95, as well as from prior versions of Windows.

Although the strategies for surviving an installation described earlier in this chapter can help you identify changed files and other modifications made to your system, there is no single bulletproof method for uninstalling Windows 3.x applications from Windows 95. Probably the best approach is to employ some of the strategies described in the "Surviving a New Application Installation" section of this chapter. That section describes how to make logs of your system before and after installation of new applications. With this information, it will be easy to identify parts of your system that the installation affected, and then either remove files that were added or restore modified files.

Stop   A few commercially available products help the user uninstall applications from Windows 3.x, as well as other Windows components you identify, such as fonts, Ini files, unused DLLs, icons, and program groups. It is not recommended that you use an uninstall product unless it has been built for Windows 95. There are significant differences between Windows 95 and earlier versions of Windows, especially in terms of file use and location, so it is impossible for such an uninstall application to reliably remove an application or other component from Windows 95 without harming the rest of the system.

Uninstalling DOS Applications

There is no simple method for uninstalling DOS applications from Windows 95 systems. DOS-based applications do not have the required uninstall program that Windows 95 applications do; therefore, unless the application contains its own uninstall program, you are left to manual work. The best strategy for uninstalling a DOS application is to have a good installation strategy. Read the section "Managing Application Installation" earlier in this chapter for more information.

CHAPTER 18

Running Applications

Windows 95 serves first and foremost as a PC operating system, but it does ship with a set of tools, a few games, some accessories, and components that enable network resource access. Windows 95 is not designed to be a stand-alone product; it's built to run applications, including word processors, e-mail systems, online services, databases, compilers, games, and more—and these applications need not be native Windows 95 applications. Windows 95 supports DOS-based applications, old Windows 3.*x* applications, and, of course, Windows 95 applications. This chapter looks at how Windows 95 runs these three types of applications, covering the technical details as well the issues that directly affect the user.

This chapter covers the following topics:

- ◆ Launching applications

- ◆ Running Win16 applications

- ◆ Ini Files, Config.sys, and Autoexec.bat

- ◆ Running Win32 applications

- ◆ Running DOS applications

Windows 95 divides all applications into four groups:

◆ **Windows 3 applications.** Applications built for Windows 3.0, Windows 3.1, or Windows for Workgroups. Because these applications are written to work with the Win16 API (application programming interface), these applications are known as Win16-based, or simply, Win16 apps.

◆ **DOS applications.** Applications built to run under DOS versions 6.22 or earlier but not Windows applications.

◆ **Windows 95 applications.** Applications built with the new Win32 API with specific Windows 95 extensions. The applications also are known as Win32-based, or simply, Win32 apps.

◆ **Applications Windows 95 cannot run.** (Such as OS/2 and Unix applications.) This chapter looks only at the first three types of applications.

Launching Your Applications in Windows 95

You can install Windows 95 over an existing Windows 3 application or to a new directory, leaving Windows 3 unchanged. If you install Windows 95 to a new directory, you must install into Windows 95 any applications you ran in Windows 3. If you choose to overwrite your Windows setup, the Start menu in Windows 95 will reflect the organization of program groups in items you had in place in Windows 3.

 Note   Chapter 17, "Installing and Uninstalling Applications," covers installing Win16 applications.

You can set up applications to launch from Windows 95 in the following four ways:

◆ Set up a shortcut at the point where you intend to launch the application

◆ Modify the Start menu to display the application

◆ Use the **R**un command on the Start menu

◆ Select the application and then choose Open from the context menu

Creating a Shortcut

You can use a *shortcut,* a sort of pointer to an application or a document, as a means to launch an application. To create a shortcut, perform the following steps:

1. Open the folder in which you intend to create the shortcut to the application. If you plan to create the shortcut on the desktop, minimize any applications currently running so that you can see part of the desktop.

2. Right-click at the location at which you want the shortcut to appear and choose New, Shortcut from the menu to display the Create Shortcut dialog box (see fig. 18.1).

3. In the Command line text box, enter the file name and path that starts the application. Click on the Browse button if you need help specifying the file.

4. Next, click on the Next button to display the Select a Title for the Program dialog box. Enter the text you want to appear as the caption for the shortcut icon. Click on Finish to complete creating the shortcut.

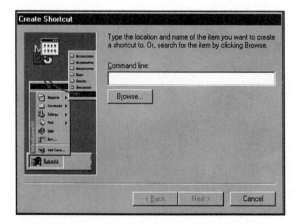

Figure 18.1

The Create Shortcut dialog box.

Customizing the Start Menu

You can modify the Start menu to display as many submenus and menu choices as you like (see fig. 18.2). You can customize the Start menu to include new applications by using either the wizard or Explorer. Using the wizard guides you through each of the steps in adding your application to some point in the Start menu hierarchy, whereas using Explorer is a more manual chore. Either method results in the same outcome, however. Because the Start menu actually is no more than a set of special folders that contain shortcuts or other folders, both methods accomplish simple chores: adding a folder to a folder, or adding a shortcut to a folder.

Figure 18.2

An example of customizing the Start menu, the MCS MusicRack folder has been added to the Programs menu.

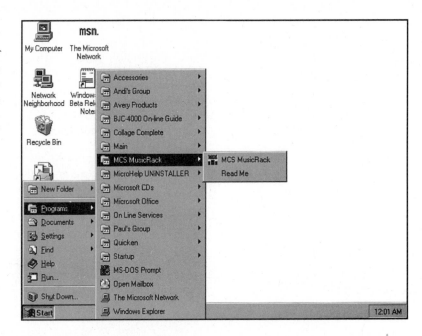

Whichever method you choose to customize the Start menu, you begin by displaying the Taskbar property sheet. To do so, right-click anywhere on the Taskbar and choose Properties. Then, click on the Start Menu Programs tab to display the properties page for the Start menu (see fig. 18.3).

Figure 18.3

The Start Menu Programs property page.

The next two sections show you the steps necessary to customize the Start menu, first using the wizard and next using the Explorer.

Using the Wizard to Customize the Start Menu

The wizard is a good choice for customizing the Start menu because it shows you each of the steps you must complete. If you are relatively new to Windows 95 or if you are unfamiliar with the Windows 95 folder system, you probably will want to use the wizard to help customize the Start menu. The following instructions show you how to use the wizard to customize the Start menu:

1. The first step is to create a shortcut to the application you add. Choose the Add button on the Start Menu Programs property page to open the Create Shortcut dialog box (refer to figure 18.1).

2. In the Command line text box, enter the file name with path that starts the application you want to add to the Start menu. For example, to launch the Lotus Organize application located on your D drive with this shortcut, you might specify D:\Apps\Organize\Organize.exe. Choose Browse if you need help specifying the file.

3. After you specify the file name, click on the Next button to display the Select Program Folder dialog box, shown in figure 18.4.

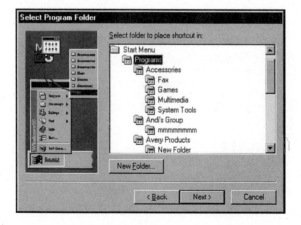

Figure 18.4

The Select Program Folder dialog box is where you add applications and submenus to the Start menu.

4. Select the location on the Start menu for the menu choice that starts your application. In effect, you are choosing the folder in which to store the shortcut. You can choose any of the folders that already exist in the Start menu hierarchy, or you can add a new folder, which actually becomes a new submenu. To add a submenu, select the menu choice for opening your new submenu and then choose the New Folder button. A new menu choice appears in the hierarchy, and

you can enter a name for it in its label. Simply type the name of the menu choice, and then click on the Next button. If you want to add your application to an existing menu choice, just click on the menu and then click on the Next button.

5. In the Select a Title from the Program dialog box, enter the text that you want to appear on the menu in the text box. This text will also appear as the caption for the shortcut, which you can see when you open the folder where the shortcut is located. After you have entered the text, click on the Finish button to return to the Taskbar property sheet. Choose OK to add your new choice to the Start menu.

6. Choose OK to include your shortcut in the menu.

Using Explorer to Customize the Start menu

Because the Start menu is simply a set of special folders and shortcuts, you can manage the Start menu the same as you manage any other set of files and folders. Explorer offers a convenient way to work with the Start menu system, because it presents files and folders in a hierarchical view.

To use Explorer to customize the Start menu, perform the following steps:

1. Choose the Advanced button on the Start Menu Programs property page. The Explorer window appears with the Start menu folder opened, as shown in figure 18.5.

Figure 18.5

You use Windows Explorer to modify the Start menu.

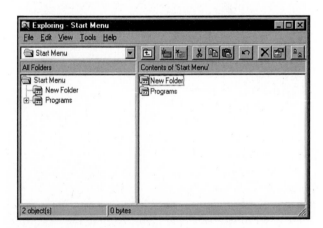

2. To add folders or shortcuts to the Start menu folder, navigate through the list of folders in the All Folders pane and select the folder you want to modify.

3. Right-click in the Contents pane to display the context menu, and then choose New to add a new folder or shortcut to the folder you selected in the Contents pane.

4. If you select Folder from the New menu, Windows 95 lets you supply a name for the folder immediately. Enter the folder name in the edit field that appears next to the open folder. After you enter the folder's name, you can double-click on the new folder to add a shortcut or another folder to your new folder.

5. After you modify the Start menu folder and its contents to your satisfaction, close the Explorer window. Next, choose OK from the Taskbar property sheet to cause these changes to take effect and to return to the desktop.

Note   When you open Explorer from the Start Menu Programs property page, you can change only the contents of the Start menu folder and its subfolders.

Using the Run Command to Launch an Application

You can choose Run from the Start menu to start any application. If you want to use the Run command to start an application, you must manually select the application you want to run. Windows 95 assists you in tracking down the executable file for the application you want to run by enabling you to browse the system. Choosing Start, Run displays the Run dialog box, shown in figure 18.6.

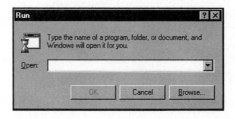

Figure 18.6

The Run dialog box.

Windows 95 stores special information about how Win16 and DOS applications should run in a special file, Apps.inf. You also can find much of this information in the property sheets for the shortcut to a DOS application. If your application is not listed in Apps.inf, and you haven't set up a shortcut to tell Windows 95 how to run the application, then Windows 95 uses default settings that might not be compatible with the application. For more information on Apps.inf and how Windows 95 runs Win16 and DOS applications, see the sections "Running Win16 Applications" and "Running DOS Applications under Windows 95" later in this chapter.

Using Open from the Context Menu

Windows 95 prefers to look at your system as a group of objects and tasks rather than as a set of applications that use files. As such, you can select any file or device in your system and work with it outside of the context of the application that controls it. You probably have noticed that you can right-click on any file or object in your system to display the context menu. You also might have noticed that the first choice on that menu is usually <u>O</u>pen or Op<u>e</u>n With. This menu choice enables you to open a file without specifically launching the application associated with it first. If Windows 95 recognizes the type of file you try to open, it automatically calls that application to launch the file you select. If Windows 95 does not recognize the file you select, it replaces the <u>O</u>pen choice on the context menu with Op<u>e</u>n With, in which case you must specify the application that launches the file you select. If you select an application, Windows 95 automatically runs that application.

Running Win16 Applications

Windows 95 includes full support for Win16-based applications. Windows 95 provides all the support that Windows 3.*x* provided Win16-based applications. This section looks at how Windows 95 runs Win16-based applications, from both a user's point of view and internally, and how Windows 95 provides the same support as Windows 3.*x* for these applications. This section also explains how to change various settings to run Win16-based applications.

New User Interface Components

All Win16-based applications appear almost exactly the same in Windows 95 as in Windows 3.*x*. Also, interactive user interface elements, such as buttons, list boxes, and menu accelerators, perform the same in Windows 95 as in Windows 3.*x*. The only differences occur with common user interface elements, such as check boxes, radio buttons, and minimize and maximize buttons. Windows 95 sports a new style for some of these elements, and all Windows applications use them. Figure 18.7 shows the new look for many of the interface elements with a Win16-based application.

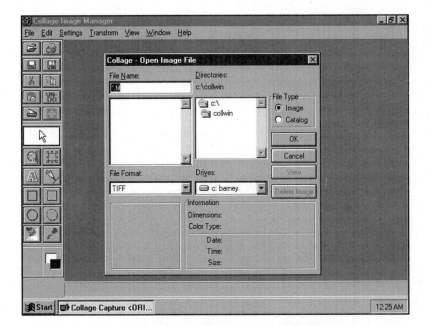

Figure 18.7

A Win16-based application with new Windows 95 user interface elements.

Critical Files: Ini, Config.sys, Autoexec.bat

As much as Windows 95 represents significant improvements over Windows 3.*x* in many areas, it does not help free Win16-based and DOS-based applications from their dependence on the myriad of pre-Windows 95 system files. The file list on which a Win16 or DOS application might rely includes Config.sys, Win.ini, System.ini, and Autoexec.bat, as well as any proprietary Ini file in Windows. Although native Windows 95 applications have no use for these files, Windows 95 includes these files for compatibility purposes.

When Windows 95 boots, it scans Win.ini and System.ini (if they are present) for the appropriate device drivers or settings that it might need to load if you launch a Win16 application. The same generally holds true for Config.sys and Autoexec.bat. Although Windows 95 uses the settings in these files to set the global environment, such as the appearance of the cursor on the DOS command line, only Win16 and DOS applications use the other settings in these files. Windows 95 loads any appropriate drivers specified in Config.sys or Autoexec.bat only for use with Win16 and DOS applications.

Specifying a Working Directory

In Windows 3.*x*, you can specify a *working directory* for an application—the default directory from which an application will open files and to which the application will save files. This directory usually differs from the directory from which you launch the application; you can launch Excel 5.0 by executing the Excel.exe file in the Excel5 directory, for example, but you might have specified \BUDGETS as the working directory. Specifying the working directory for an application in Windows 3.*x* is easy: with the application's icon highlighted in Program Manager, choose <u>F</u>ile, <u>P</u>roperties, then type the working directory in the <u>W</u>orking Directory text box. Specifying a working directory for a Win16 application running in Windows 95 is more difficult.

To specify the working directory for a Windows 3.*x* application running in Windows 95, you must specify information in the shortcut to the Win16 application. Unless you use a shortcut to start an application, you can't specify a working directory. If your application appears on the Start menu, then a shortcut for the application already exists. If the application does not appear on the Start menu, you must create a shortcut for it.

With the shortcut created, open the property sheet for the application's shortcut. To locate the shortcut for an application that already appears on the Start menu, refer to the section "Customizing the Start Menu" earlier in this chapter. Right-click on the shortcut to display its property sheet and then select the Shortcut tab; figure 18.8 shows the property sheet for shortcut to a Windows 3.*x* application. Specify the working directory for the application in the <u>S</u>tart in text box. This way, whenever you execute the shortcut, the application associated with it opens with the directory you specify in the <u>S</u>tart in edit box as the default directory for file opens and saves.

Figure 18.8

The property sheet for a shortcut to a Windows 3.x application enables you to specify a working directory as you would in prior versions of Windows.

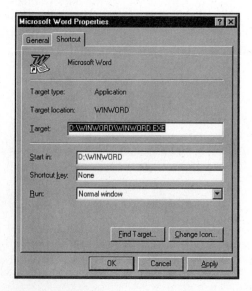

Under the Hood

This section takes a look at the way Windows 95 internally manages Win16 applications. Windows 95's challenge is to somehow run Win16 applications unmodified in a 32-bit environment without destabilizing the rest of the system, and still take advantage of some of the 32-bit subsystems, such as printing.

All Win16 applications run in a single, shared, cooperative multitasking address space—that is, Win16-based applications run in the same memory address space. Microsoft designed Windows 95 up this way to preserve the system requirements originally established for Windows 3.1—specifically, an Intel-based 386DX chip with at least 4 MB of RAM.

For more information on multitasking and other Windows 95 architectural issues, refer to Chapter 11, "Understanding the Windows 95 Architecture."

Crash Protection

One of the most annoying, but certainly not uncommon, occurrences in Windows 3.1 is the general protection fault (GPF) or, more familiarly, the crash. For any number of reasons, Win16 applications will collapse, often taking other applications—and sometimes even the entire Windows system—down with them.

Because Windows 95 runs all Win16-based applications in a single memory space, errant applications are less likely to crash the entire system than in Windows 3.1. In a separate memory space, Win16 applications do not have access to the memory space Win32-based applications or MS-DOS applications use. Keep in mind, however, that a Win16 application running in Windows 95 is just as likely to crash another Win16 application as in Windows 3.1; Windows 95 cannot prevent a Win16 application from writing to the memory space of another Win16 application or from corrupting a segment of memory that it uses.

Another method Windows 95 uses to protect Win16 applications from crashing is parameter validation. An application communicates with the application programming interface (API) by using function calls. The application passes information to the API and receives data back, or passes data to the API and expects an action to occur, such as painting a region of the screen. All too often, however, applications pass bad data to the API. An application might, in a function call for example, pass the API the address of a particular segment of memory—known as passing a Null pointer. In Windows 3.*x*, this causes an unknown application error. In Windows 3.1, it causes a GPF. In Windows 95, parameter validation traps these errors in advance and prevents an application from crashing.

Windows 95 monitors calls to the API and watches for invalid parameters. Rather than let the API process a function call with bad data passed in from the application, Windows 95 traps the errant call and returns an error code to the application. Although the application still has to respond to the error notification, the likelihood of application crashes is greatly diminished in Windows 95.

 Note All Win16 applications talk to the Windows API. In fact, Win32 applications talk to the Win32 API in Windows 95. The API provides an interface between the application and the operating system in terms of Windows 95, and the environment in terms of Windows 3.1. The API provides most of the services an application needs, such as painting the application on-screen, managing memory, providing access to devices and to files, and other services.

Running Win32 Applications in Windows 95

Windows 95 is mostly a 32-bit system, so 32-bit applications naturally run smoothly in Windows 95. Of the three different types of applications that can run in Windows 95, Win16- and DOS-based applications are the exception to the most of the application support rules in Windows 95. In fact, the bulk of this chapter describes the special support Windows 95 provides for those two types of applications. Not much information exists on running Win32-based applications under Windows 95. Most of the functionality for running Win32-based applications in Windows 95 is built-in and shielded from the user.

This section looks at the few user issues for running Win32-based applications. Specifically, this section presents information about the Registry, as well as the Microsoft-decreed requirements for an application to use the official Win95 logo in packaging, advertisements, and promotions. (*Hint:* One of the requirements is that the application be Win32-based.) Also, this section presents a brief technical overview about Win32 applications.

Win95 Logo Requirements

Banking on the assumption that many users will soon be running Windows 95, and therefore will want to buy applications designed for it, software developers will want their applications closely associated with Windows 95. Understanding this, Microsoft has developed a set of criteria an application should meet before it can display the Windows 95 logo (see fig. 18.9) on its packaging.

Figure 18.9

The official logo for Windows 95 applications.

The following list reviews these Windows 95 logo requirements:

◆ **Use the Win32 API.** Applications must be built using the Win32 API, the layer that exists between an application and the Windows 95 internals. By using the Win32 API, applications benefit from preemptive multitasking, linear memory address referencing, running in a private memory space, and more.

◆ **Follow the Windows UI style guidelines.** Applications must have a user interface consistent with the guidelines established and published in *Windows User Interface Style Guidelines 4.0,* which describes how Windows 95 applications must appear and interact with the user. The product of this requirement is that most, if not all, Windows 95 applications appear and behave very similarly to one another, which makes learning new applications easy for users to as they acquire them.

◆ **Support long file names.** Windows 95 applications must provide support for long file names. File names can be up to 255 characters in length, although Windows 95 does maintain an 8.3 version of the file name for compatibility purposes with Win16 and DOS applications.

◆ **Provide OLE support.** OLE (Object Linking and Embedding) helps different applications work together by enabling them to function in the context of a single document rather than in the context of all the programs and applications used to complete a task. An example of OLE would be to create a chart in Microsoft Excel and embed it in a Microsoft Word for Windows document. OLE support in both applications enables the Microsoft Excel menu structure to replace the Microsoft Word structure when you click on the chart in the Word document. For more information on OLE, see Chapter 25 "Understanding and Using OLE."

◆ **Automate installation and uninstallation.** Windows 95 applications must make installation and uninstallation an automatic and safe task for users. This means that applications must use the support provided in the Win32 API for installing and uninstalling. You derive three significant benefits from standard installation and uninstallation:

　　◆ Tighter control of an application during installation, reducing chance for critical files to be adversely affected during installation.

◆ Similar installation process for all applications into Windows 95, which means you need learn this task only once.

◆ Significantly easier and safer uninstallation, because Windows 95 tracks the changes made to the system by a Windows 95 application as it is being installed. This way, Windows 95 knows exactly which files should be removed when you choose to uninstall an application, as well as where they are located and if another application is using one of them. This saves you from doing this work, which you typically would be forced to do with Windows 3.*x*.

See Chapter 17, "Installing and Uninstalling Applications," for more information about these processes.

Registry Information

Besides the application, the only area of the system in which a user can view and modify settings for Win32-based applications is the Registry. The *Registry* is a database that stores all information about your Windows 95 system, including its hardware and software. More than a replacement for the Ini files used in prior versions of Windows, the Registry allows multiple user configurations for the same computer, provides remote management of the system configuration (across an enterprise network), provides support for Plug and Play, and more. Figure 18.10 shows a sample of information the Registry stores. For more information about the Registry, see Chapter 13, "Working with the Registry and Ini Files."

Figure 18.10

The Registry stores information about Windows 95 hardware and software configuration.

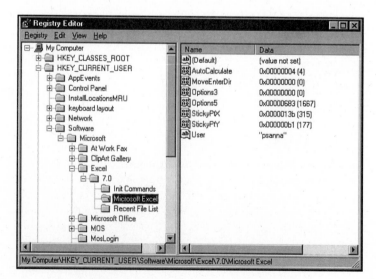

Under the Hood

Win32 applications take advantage of preemptive multitasking under Windows 95. The system kernel decides when Win32 applications can access the CPU. This represents an improvement over previous versions of Windows. In Windows 3.*x*, the application checks the message queue and gets access to the CPU in a cooperative multitasking system. If a poorly built application ignores the message queue for a certain amount of time, or even crashes while doing so, other applications are blocked from CPU access.

All Win32-based applications run in their own memory space, which means that Win32-based applications do not share system resources directly with other applications. All applications technically use the same set of resources in a computer, but a Win32-based application does not actually share resources at the system level with any other application. A Win32 application, then, is far less likely to crash other applications when it misbehaves.

Memory management for Win32-based applications is different overall than for other types of applications in Windows 95. Windows 3.*x*, as a 16-bit operating system, forces applications to work within the boundaries of 16-bit segments, which figures to 64 KB of memory. When applications must reference memory in another segment, a stiff performance price must be paid. Although Intel's 386 chip did support 32-bit instructions, Windows 95, as a 32-bit operating system, finally lets Windows applications take advantage. Win32-based applications are not constrained by the 16-bit segment boundary. Applications can reference all memory, which is laid out in linear address space. Applications can take advantage of up to 4 GB of virtual memory.

As with Win16-based applications running in Windows 95, Win32 applications provide an added measure of stability via parameter validation. For more information on Win32 stability, see the section "Crash Protection" earlier in the chapter. For more information on using the API and function calls in Windows 95, see the section "Running Win16 Applications" earlier in this chapter.

Running DOS Applications under Windows 95

DOS applications are among the most finicky applications on any PC. They have very specific operating system requirements, and the slightest change in a computer's configuration can mean that a DOS application that ran flawlessly before the modification no longer can run. Some DOS applications have extremely demanding memory requirements, while others take over the entire computer and modify hardware settings such as video and interrupt addresses.

Windows 95 uses a number of different techniques to provide different levels of support for DOS applications. Depending on a given DOS application's requirements, configuring the application to run in Windows 95 might be a simple matter of modifying settings, or it might mean configuring Windows 95 so that the DOS application believes it is the only application running.

Because of the complexity of running DOS applications in Windows 95, *Inside Windows 95* devotes an entire chapter of this book to the topic (see Chapter 21, "Integrating Windows and DOS"). This section overviews the support Windows 95 provides for DOS applications.

Preparing DOS-Based Applications to Run

When you install a Windows application (Win16 or Win32, Windows 95 or otherwise), after you load all the files and modify the appropriate system files, you can add a submenu to the Start menu and a choice associated with the application to that menu. This is analogous to adding a program group and program item in Windows 3.*x*. For a great majority of DOS-based applications, however, no facility for running the application from Windows is established, so you must do this.

Preparing a DOS-based application to run in Windows 95 actually is simple: all you have to do is create a shortcut at the location from which you plan to launch the application. If you plan to launch the application from the desktop, for example, create a shortcut to the application on the desktop. To create a shortcut, right-click at the location from which you plan to launch the application, choose New, Shortcut, then follow the instructions that appear for specifying the executable file for the application and for specifying the label that will appear for the application's shortcut icon. After Windows 95 has created the shortcut, you can start the application by selecting the icon.

You should always create a shortcut to launch a DOS application rather than start it using the Run choice on the Start menu. The shortcut always contains the special information Windows 95 needs to run the DOS application. Without that information, Windows 95 runs the application using default settings that are not necessarily compatible with the application, and which might not even allow the application to run.

Apps.inf and PIF Files

Users have attempted with varying amounts of success to run thousands of DOS applications in Windows since Windows 3.*x* became available. Through the experience of supporting millions of Windows users, Microsoft has identified the settings Windows needs to properly run the most popular DOS applications, including games. Rather than force those millions of users to relearn how to run those applications in a new version of Windows, Microsoft has built those settings into Windows 95 so that Windows 95 automatically uses them.

You can find the settings for these applications in the [PIF95] section of Apps.inf. For each application listed, settings are shown that correspond directly to the settings Windows 95 uses to run the DOS application. When you run a DOS application for the first time, Windows 95 checks for the application in Apps.inf. If Windows 95 finds the application, it copies the settings out of the file and to the PIF (program information file) for the application. Windows 95 stores all settings for DOS applications in PIFs, which you can view and modify on the property sheet for the shortcut to the DOS application. Chapter 21, "Integrating Windows and DOS," covers the structure of the Apps.inf file. The next section describes the settings Windows 95 maintains for a DOS application.

Settings for DOS Applications

When you create a shortcut for a DOS application in Windows 95, Windows 95 recognizes the application and assigns the appropriate property sheet for the shortcut. Every DOS application has six property pages, and each page enables you to view and modify the settings Windows 95 uses to run the application. Figure 18.11 shows a typical property sheet for a DOS application, open to the General page. Most of what appears on the General page is purely informational, providing details about the shortcut and the DOS application.

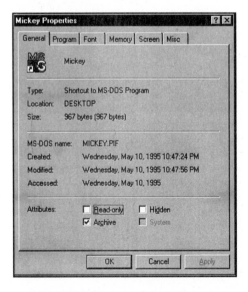

Figure 18.11

The General property page for a shortcut to a DOS application.

The settings on the Program page (see fig. 18.12) control the way the DOS application launches, including command-line arguments, a batch file that might run during launching, and whether the application appears full-screen or in a window. You can choose the Advanced button to specify Config.sys and Autoexec.bat information for the application, or to specify that the application run in MS-DOS mode, in which the application believes it is the only program running the PC.

Figure 18.12

The Program property page for a shortcut to a DOS application.

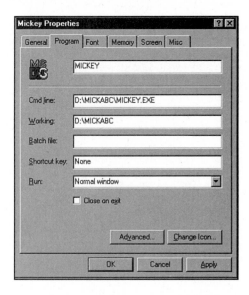

You use the Font page (see fig. 18.13) to specify font settings for text that appears in the application. This page also provides two viewers for previewing how the font selections will appear.

Figure 18.13

The Font property page for a shortcut to a DOS application.

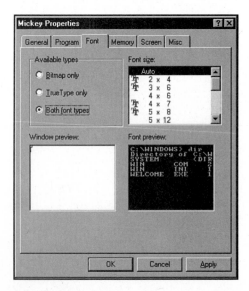

The Memory page (see fig. 18.14) enables you to specify the memory configuration for the application, including extended, expanded, conventional, and protected-mode memory.

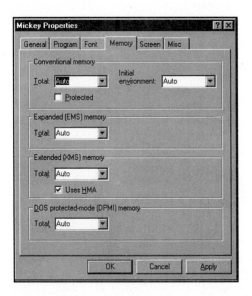

Figure 18.14

The Memory property page for a shortcut to a DOS application.

The Screen page (see fig. 18.15) enables you to specify the appearance of the screen when you run the application, including toolbar placement, size, and video performance.

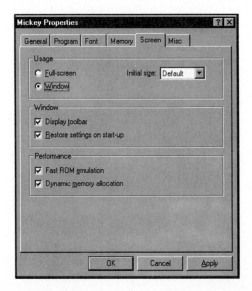

Figure 18.15

The Screen property page for a shortcut to a DOS application.

Figure 18.16 shows the Misc property sheet, a catchall location for all the settings that don't fit in any of the other five property sheets. Use the Misc property sheet to control screen saver activation for when you run the DOS application, the effect of shortcut keys on the application, and more.

Figure 18.16

The Misc property page for a shortcut to a DOS application.

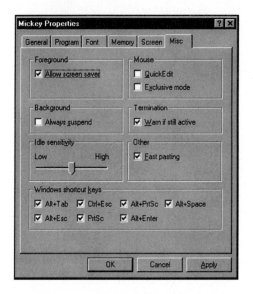

For more information on running DOS applications in Windows 95, read the entire chapter devoted to the topic: Chapter 21, "Integrating Windows and DOS."

C H A P T E R

19

Creating and Using a Briefcase

The explosion of the PC market since the mid-'80s has fundamentally changed how both corporations and their employees work. Procedures that used to be manual now are automated, information is dramatically more accessible than ever before, and in one of the most striking trends, corporate PC users are completing much of their PC work outside of the office. This later trend is facilitated by yet another trend in the corporate PC business: the significant drop in the cost of hardware. Companies now cost-effectively generate more productivity by purchasing PCs for their employees to use at home or by outfitting employees with portable computers. This new routine of mobile computing means more man-hours for business and convenience for workers.

Unfortunately, like many other new initiates in computing, innovation arrives with a cost. One of the main costs of mobile computing is the hassle of trying to keep copies of files on different computers in sync. Windows 95 attempts to solve that problem with the Briefcase utility. The Briefcase utility helps you manage different versions of the same file, including identifying different versions and merging them.

The chapter covers the following topics:

◆ Overview of the Briefcase utility

◆ Installing Briefcase

◆ Working in Briefcase

◆ Synchronizing files on a disk

◆ Synchronizing files over the network

◆ Separating Briefcase documents from the original

◆ Overview of Briefcase reconcilers

Understanding and Installing Briefcase

Briefcase is a new utility in Windows 95 that tries to solve the remote computing conundrum of keeping track of different versions of the same file as users modify these files at remote locations. Although the intended purpose of this utility is somewhat easy to understand, the process for using it might not be. This section overviews Briefcase, including a typical scenario for using Briefcase.

What Is Briefcase?

Briefcase is a Windows 95 applet (mini-application) that helps you manage different versions of the same document. Specifically, Briefcase helps you solve the problem of working on the same document on different computers, such as bringing work home at the end of the day, or planning to work with a document but having to leave a copy of the document at your main office.

One of the toughest tasks a software developer endeavors is associating a new feature or function with a concept the user can understand. The briefcase metaphor employed with the Briefcase utility really works. In Windows 95, you actually store and work on documents remotely in a Briefcase. Briefcase also happens to be a special type of Windows 95 folder, so viewing and working with the documents in the Briefcase is easy, especially if you are adept at working in the Windows 95 user interface.

Briefcase's capabilities include the following:

◆ View information about any file in the Briefcase, including whether the file differs from its original

◆ Split a file in the Briefcase from its original so that the two versions are no longer synchronized

◆ Locate the original version of a file in the Briefcase

◆ Select one, all, or some files in the Briefcase for updating

◆ Update the original version of a file(s) in the Briefcase

◆ Update a file(s) in the Briefcase if the original version of the file has changed

In addition, because Briefcase is a special type of folder, you can use all the capabilities built into Windows 95 folders with Briefcase, such as viewing the contents of Briefcase as a list, small icons, or large icons.

How to Work with Briefcase

More so than with many of the other applets shipped with Windows 95, Briefcase forces you to follow a specific process. Briefcase makes a few assumptions about how you work at a remote location, so understanding how to use Briefcase as intended is important for taking maximum advantage of its capabilities. Here is a quick overview of how to work with Briefcase.

1. You complete PC work at a central location, such as a main office, and sometimes work at a separate remote location, such as at home or traveling on business. You work at that remote location using one of two methods: 1) you transport your work (files) on a floppy disk and then load the files on the remote computer you plan to use; or 2) the computer on which you plan to work at the remote location is accessible at your central location, so you directly update the computer with your work files before you leave that location.

2. Before leaving the central location and knowing that you plan to work on a specific document(s), you create a Briefcase. You copy the files you plan to work on to the Briefcase, and then copy the Briefcase to a floppy disk or to the computer you will use at the remote location.

3. At the remote location, you start the application you will use with the documents in your Briefcase. You open the documents from the Briefcase. When work is complete on those documents, you save them to the Briefcase as you normally would to another folder.

4. You return to the location where the original version of the file(s) in the Briefcase is located, presumably your main office or computer. If the Briefcase is on a floppy disk, you insert the floppy disk into a PC that can see (directly or via a network) the original versions of the files in the Briefcase.

If the Briefcase is on a PC, you reconnect the PC to the network where it can see the original versions of files in the Briefcase. These original versions can be on another PC or on a network drive. You also might use a null-modem cable to directly connect the remote computer to the PC on which the original files are located.

5. Open the Briefcase and select the file(s) you want to update and then issue the update command. Briefcase compares the versions of the files in the Briefcase to the original versions. If it finds differences, it reconciles the differences and merges the files.

A much simpler version of this workflow description appears the first time you open a Briefcase. Figure 19.1 shows the first dialog box that appears when you open a new Briefcase for the first time. For more information on creating a Briefcase, see the section "Creating and Naming a Briefcase" later in this chapter.

Figure 19.1

The dialog box that appears the first time you open a new Briefcase briefly explains how Briefcase works.

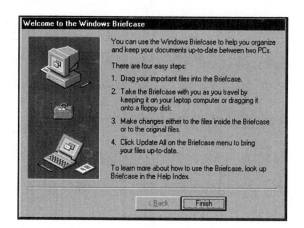

Installing Briefcase

The Briefcase utility is installed automatically only if you choose the Portable option in the main Windows 95 setup wizard. If you did not specify the Portable option during setup, then you must complete the installation process for Briefcase. If you're not sure, you can determine whether Briefcase has been set up on your system by looking at the desktop. If you see a Briefcase icon like the one pictured in figure 19.2, then Briefcase probably has been installed, though a Briefcase may have been created and then moved off of the desktop. Another way to determine if Briefcase has been installed is to right-click on the desktop to display the context menu and then choose New. If Briefcase appears on the New menu, you know Briefcase has been installed.

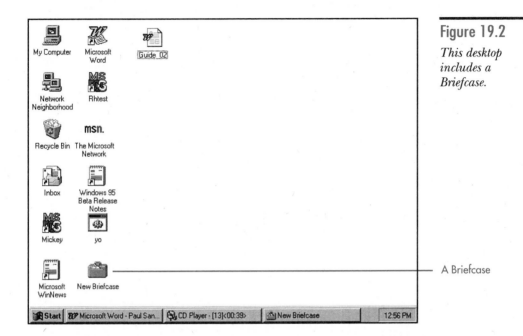

Figure 19.2

This desktop includes a Briefcase.

A Briefcase

To install Briefcase, you must use the Add/Remove Programs wizard, located in the Control Panel folder. Choose the Control Panel from the Settings menu on the Start menu. Start the wizard and then click on the Windows Setup tab. On this property sheet, you install and uninstall the mini-applications and utilities that ship with Windows 95, Briefcase being one of them. From the Components list box, choose Accessories, and then choose the Details button to open the Accessories dialog box. Next, choose Briefcase from the list box and then choose OK. Choose OK again for the wizard to install Briefcase.

Working in a Briefcase

In the "How to Work with Briefcase" section earlier in this chapter, you learned how Briefcase would be used in a typical working scenario. In this section you will learn how to put Briefcase's functions and features to work in that scenario.

This section covers the following topics:

◆ Creating and naming a Briefcase

◆ Adding files to a Briefcase

◆ Changing what you see in a Briefcase

◆ Checking the status of a Briefcase document

◆ Separating documents from the original

◆ Removing files from a Briefcase

Creating and Naming a Briefcase

Even after you install Briefcase in Windows 95, you still need a Briefcase with which to work. You can create as many Briefcases as you choose, but just one will probably suffice. After you install Briefcase, Windows 95 creates, by default, a new Briefcase on the desktop. To create a new Briefcase, right-click at the location where you want to store the Briefcase. The context menu appears when you right-click. Choose New, Briefcase.

Location of Your Briefcase

You can create the Briefcase at the location where you plan to work on the files in it, or you can create the Briefcase at the source location of the files and then move the Briefcase with the files in it to the working location. If you must use a disk to transport your Briefcase, for example, you can create the Briefcase on the disk and add files directly to the Briefcase on the disk. You might also create the Briefcase on the desktop, add files to it, and then use the context menu of the Briefcase to send the Briefcase to a floppy disk.

Note   Because you move the Briefcase from location to location, the location at which you create a Briefcase really doesn't matter. A Briefcase actually is a special type of folder, so whenever you create a Briefcase, you create a folder. If you create a Briefcase on the desktop, the effect is adding a folder to the desktop folder.

Briefcase Naming

The first Briefcase you create is named My Briefcase. If you already have a Briefcase, the new Briefcase that appears is named New Briefcase. Subsequent Briefcases you create have numbers to distinguish them from the other briefcases. You can change the name of the Briefcase by right-clicking on the Briefcase to display the context menu and then choosing Rename.

Adding Files to a Briefcase

After you create a Briefcase, you need to add files to it. Only files in your Briefcase can take advantage of the utility's capability to reconcile differences with other versions and merge changes, so you must add any files you plan to work with remotely.

You add those files to the Briefcase that you plan to work with at a location different from where the main versions of the files are stored. If you maintain a schedule document at your office and you plan to make changes to the document at home, for example, you would add that document to your Briefcase. You also can add a file to your Briefcase that you know other individuals might work with at the original location while you work with it at home.

Although this is a simple drag-and-drop or menu procedure, adding a file to a Briefcase is significant. When you add a file to a Briefcase, you create a *copy* of that file—technically, you never *move* files to the Briefcase. Even if you attempt to cut and paste a file to the Briefcase, you complete a copy and paste operation. Briefcase remembers and stores the original location of any file you copy to the Briefcase, and compares versions of the file in the Briefcase to that original to determine if the original should be updated.

Because Briefcase behaves generally like a folder, to add a file to a Briefcase, you can employ any of the techniques you use to copy files to folders, such as the following:

◆ Select the file you want to add to the Briefcase and then right-click to display its context menu. Next, choose Copy, or press Ctrl+C. Then, open the Briefcase, and choose Edit, Paste or Context, Paste, or press Ctrl+V.

◆ Click-and-drag the file to the Briefcase.

Changing What You See in a Briefcase

The user interface in a Briefcase is no different from the user interface in any folder. In the Briefcase folder you can display or hide the toolbar, see other resources on your computer and network by selecting from the Object drop-down list on the toolbar, arrange icons, cut, copy, and paste, and more. Figure 19.3 shows a Briefcase window containing a folder, a shortcut, and a few documents.

The most significant difference between the Briefcase folder and other folders in Windows 95 is the details shown when View is in Details mode. You can see the greatest amount of detail about the files in your Briefcase and their status by changing View to Detail. You change how contents appear in any folder from the View menu. You also can choose how to display the contents of a briefcase from the context menu. Figure 19.4 shows a Briefcase in Details mode.

Figure 19.3

The Briefcase folder looks very similar to other folders in Windows 95.

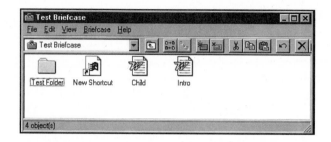

Figure 19.4

You can see information about files in your Briefcase by displaying the details about the folder.

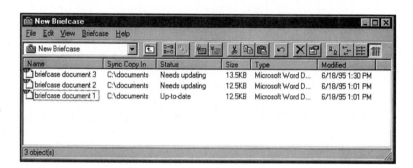

The Briefcase folder contains a Briefcase menu, which provides choices for updating the files in your Briefcase, the original versions, or both. You can choose whether to update all the files in your Briefcase or just those you select. You can use toolbar buttons to start these two processes, which are pointed out in figure 19.5. You also can separate a file in a Briefcase from its original with the Split From Original choice on the Briefcase menu and via the file's property sheet in the Briefcase. This topic is covered in more detail in the "Separating Documents from the Original" section, which appears later in this chapter.

Figure 19.5

The Briefcase Toolbar includes Update All and Update Selection buttons.

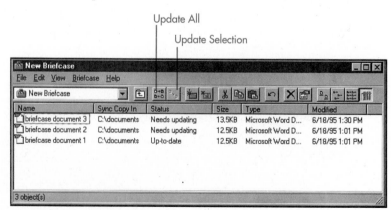

Checking the Status of a Briefcase Document

If the Briefcase folder view is in Details mode, you can see immediately whether you need to update any files, original or in the Briefcase. The Status column shows whether an update operation should occur for every file in the Briefcase. This status is updated immediately when you open the Briefcase. If the Briefcase has been open for some time, you can update the status for all files by choosing View, Refresh.

If the Briefcase folder view is not in Details mode, you still can see the status of files in the Briefcase (although you must do so one file at a time). To view the status of any file in the Briefcase, choose the file, right-click to display the object's context menu, and then choose Properties. Next, display the Update Status page of the Briefcase document property sheet (see fig. 19.6).

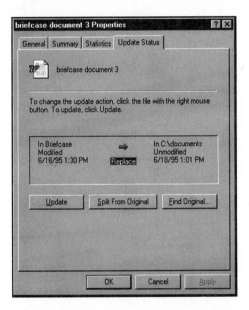

Figure 19.6

The Update Status property page for a Briefcase file.

Tip   Although the Briefcase folder shows you whether any files need to be updated when the folder is in View Details mode, the only way to see which file—original or Briefcase—has changed is to view the file's property sheet. Displaying the property sheet to examine which file has changed before blindly starting an update operation that could overwrite important information in the file makes perfect sense.

The critical pieces of the Update Status page are the status information shown in the frame. The frame shows the file in the Briefcase you selected and the original version of the file. The graphic element between the two files shows the status of their relationship. If either file has changed, the status graphic suggests which file should replace the other (see fig. 19.7). If both files have changed, the status graphic suggests that you skip an update of either file (see fig. 19.8). The status graphic also might report that neither file has changed (see fig. 19.9).

Figure 19.7

The arrow in the middle of the Update Status page shows that the original version of the file should be updated.

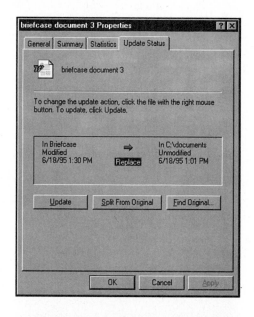

Figure 19.8

The graphic shows that both the original version of the file and the version in the Briefcase have changed.

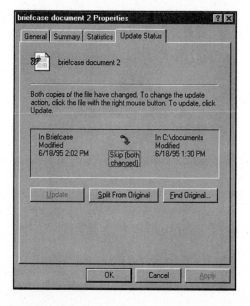

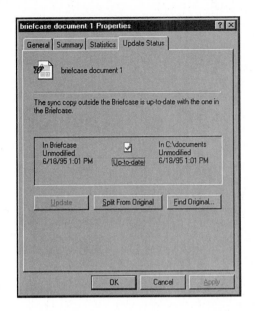

Figure 19.9

The graphic shows that the original version of the file and the version in the Briefcase are up-to-date

Separating Documents from the Original

You might want to cease synchronizing a file in your Briefcase with its original version but still keep the file in your Briefcase. Briefcase enables you to split a file in your Briefcase from its original, either by using a menu choice or a button click on the file's property sheet. After you split a file from its original, its status changes to Orphan (see fig. 19.10). To split a file from the original, select the file in the Briefcase and then choose **B**riefcase, **S**plit From Original. Alternatively, you can click on the **S**plit From Original button on the file's Update Status property page.

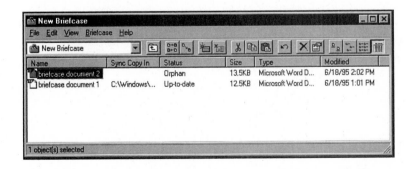

Figure 19.10

A file with a status of Orphan has been split from the original version of the file.

Removing Files from a Briefcase

If you no longer want to keep a Briefcase file synchronized with another version and you no longer want to keep the file in your Briefcase, you can completely remove the file from the Briefcase. This is different from a file being split from its original in that the file no longer exists in the Briefcase.

You can use a couple methods to remove a file from a Briefcase, each with slightly different consequences. In either case, when you remove a file from a Briefcase, you permanently lose its link to the original file, so you should approach removing a file from a Briefcase with caution.

One method for removing a file from the Briefcase is to select the file and then choose File, Delete. Because a Briefcase actually is a folder, and a file that resides in a Briefcase actually resides in the Briefcase folder, when you delete a file from Brief-case, you actually remove the file from the disk where the Briefcase pointer is located. Before you delete a file from the Briefcase, you should ensure that no changes are pending to the original version of the file.

Another method for removing a file from a Briefcase is to move the file to another location. You can cut and paste the file elsewhere, or drag it out of the Briefcase and drop it into another folder or on the desktop. As with the method described earlier, you must be careful when you move a file out of a Briefcase. You should ensure that no changes are pending to the original version of the file.

Synchronizing Files in Your Briefcase

After you complete work on the files in your Briefcase and return to the location of the original versions of the files, you can update your Briefcase. The first step after you return is to check the status of all files in the Briefcase. You might find that all files are already up-to-date, in which case you need not do any updating. You also might find that the original version of a file has changed, which means you must update the version of the file in your Briefcase.

After you establish the update requirements for each of your files in your Briefcase, you synchronize your files. Based on how your Briefcase is set up, you synchronize your Briefcase from a floppy disk or from a network connection.

Maintaining a Briefcase on a Floppy Disk

Maintaining your Briefcase on a floppy disk is one of the scenarios described in one of the first sections of this chapter. You would use a disk to store your Briefcase, most likely, if your off-site computer were not portable.

To synchronize a Briefcase on a disk, insert the disk storing the Briefcase in a floppy drive on a PC that can see the original versions. The disk should be loaded on a PC on which the original versions might also be stored on a fixed drive, or the disk should be loaded on a PC that is properly connected and mapped to the network drive where the original versions are located. To speed performance, after you load the disk, you can then move the Briefcase to a fixed drive on the PC from the disk, such as moving the Briefcase to the desktop. Next, follow the steps in the section "Completing the Update," later in this chapter.

Maintaining a Briefcase on a Portable Computer

Maintaining a briefcase on a portable computer can be a convenient option. You can store the original versions of files in your Briefcase on a network drive, on a fixed drive that might be attached to a docking station that you plug your portable PC into, or on another PC connected to the network. To synchronize a Briefcase on a portable computer, just reattach the PC to the network, docking station, or other PC and map drives in the same manner as when the Briefcase was created and files added to it. This ensures that your Briefcase can locate the original versions of the files it contains when you start updating.

Completing the Update

After you load your Briefcase or connect it to the point where it can find the original versions of the files it contains, you are ready to set up the update operation. The first step is to select the file(s) you need to update. To select more than one file, hold the Shift or Ctrl keys as you select files.

Next, choose Briefcase, Update Selection. If you want to update all files that have a status of "Needs updating," you can choose Update All. Next, Briefcase asks you for confirmation in the Update Briefcase dialog box (see fig. 19.11). You can launch the update immediately by clicking on the Update button, or you can change the update for any of the items in the dialog box. To change the Update action, right-click on the status graphic that appears between each pair of files. A menu appears that enables you to change the update action (see fig. 19.12). Choose appropriately from the menu and then click on Update to start the synchronization.

Figure 19.11

The Update Briefcase dialog box.

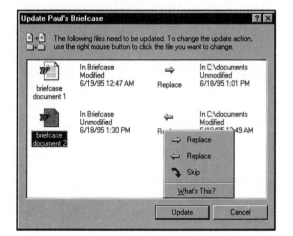

Figure 19.12

The Update Briefcase dialog box enables you to change the update action.

After the update is complete, the status of files you selected for the update changes to "Up-to-date."

Briefcase Reconcilers

The key to Briefcase's capability to merge different versions of the same file is built into the application associated with the file. Every file type is associated with a specific application; by default, a Doc file is associated with Microsoft Word, an Xls file is associated with Microsoft Excel, and a Dbf file is associated with dBASE. Of course, you can associate a file type with any application you choose. Windows 95 stores the application associated with every file type in the Registry. Briefcase will look to the application associated with a file type for help in reconciling different versions of the same file. This occurs when you issue the Update command in the Briefcase.

Applications that support Briefcase include a reconciler, which manages the update of different versions of the same file for Briefcase. A *reconciler* is a set of internal functions that examines two versions of the same document and merges them. A reconciler also can determine which, if any, parts of the files can be discarded based on work done to the other version. Applications might have reconcilers built in, or they can be included separately in a dynamic link library. This enables developers to deliver Windows 95 applications close to the release of the operating system without being slowed by development of the reconciler.

Future versions of Briefcase might prompt the user for help in reconciling different versions of files as they are updated. Other possible enhancements to Briefcase include the provision of a residue file to the user, which would contain data from the files being updated that the reconciler suggests should be discarded.

It is likely not all Windows 95 application will support Briefcase updates. Obviously, Microsoft products, such as Word for Windows and Excel, support Briefcase. Be sure to check with the supplied documentation to check if your application supports Briefcase reconciliation.

Using and Building Windows Help

Windows 95 provides a standard interface for getting help about any application whose developer provides a Help utility, including Windows 95 itself. The given developer dictates the form Help takes in a given application. Help might contain detailed steps for completing common tasks in one application, or additional technical details that supplement the information in a printed reference, such as a manual, for another application. This chapter shows you how to use Windows 95 Help. Because developing a custom Help file is fairly easy with little programming or development experience, this chapter also overviews creating a Help file to use with Windows 95.

The chapter covers the following topics:

- ◆ Understanding Help

- ◆ Finding and getting help

- ◆ Understanding the Help Topics dialog box

◆ Understanding the Help Window

◆ Building and compiling Help files

The following section takes a look at Help both in Windows 95 and in previous versions of Windows, and at the types of materials that make up the different Help in the applications you use today.

What Is Help?

Windows 95 provides a standard interface for accessing Help for any Windows 95 application, including Windows 95 itself. The process and user interface for finding and then viewing Help remains consistent for all Windows 95 applications. Figures 20.1 and 20.2 show Help from Windows 95 and Help from Norton Utilities for Windows 95, respectively. Note that although the two Help topics are for two different applications and created by two different software developers, they appear very similar. The standard Help application that ships with Windows and runs a standard format Help file makes this possible.

Figure 20.1

Help about Windows 95.

Figure 20.2

*Help about
Norton Utilities
for Windows 95.*

Developers who want to include Help with their application prepare a special Help file in accordance with standards and procedures prescribed by Microsoft. The Help file can contain different graphical elements, jump to other parts of their application or to other parts of Help, and more. Besides creating a Help file, the developer also must install the proper hooks into the software to launch the Help application. The developer must prepare the application so that it at least launches Help from a main menu selection. The developer might (but does not have to) prepare the application to provide *context-sensitive Help,* which enables a user to get Help specifically related to whatever task they happen to be performing or whatever control they happen to be on, by pressing a specific key (usually the F1 function key). If you're in the Print dialog box and press the Help key, for example, Help appears, displaying the Help topics pertaining specifically to printing for that application.

The content of the Help file rides solely on the shoulders of the developer. Developers frequently simply convert the information from certain printed documentation into a Help file, which offers you no additional value other than that you don't have to go get your user manual. Sometimes Help includes context-sensitive Help so that you can get help about a specific task or a certain control, window, or dialog box on the fly. Still other Help might offer you information you couldn't find in the other materials that ship with the application, such as technical information or processes for getting more information.

After the Help developer decides on content for the Help file, Windows 95 offers a range of options for presenting the information. The following list shows some of the user interface elements a Help developer can incorporate into the Help file:

◆ Various font types, styles, sizes, and colors

◆ Graphics in up to 16 colors

◆ Cross-reference jumps that link two similar explanations or discussions in the same Help file

◆ Keywords that help you search the Help file

◆ Special pop-up windows to display additional information

◆ Special graphics with hot spots that initiate jumps when the hot spots are clicked

Now that you are familiar with some of the items that make up a Help application, it is time to learn how to use Help. The next section looks at how Help can be accessed from almost anywhere in Windows.

How to Find and Get Help

Windows 95 provides a number of methods for accessing Help. Different forms of Help are available, depending on the context of your work or your location in Windows 95. This section looks at the different types of Help you can use for Windows 95 and Windows 95 applications.

General Windows 95 Help

In addition to the help you can get in Windows 95 about the various applications you run, such as Word for Windows, Paint, Briefcase, and Norton System Doctor, you naturally can get help about Windows 95 itself. Windows 95 Help covers topics ranging from creating a new folder to configuring your modem. There are different ways you can get Help about Windows 95: you can press F1 from anywhere in Windows 95 as long as you are not in an application (in which case you would see Help pertaining to the application), or you can choose Help from the Start menu. Figure 20.3 shows a portion of the table of contents from the Windows 95 Help.

Figure 20.3

The table of contents from the main Windows Help file.

Application Help

You activate Help the same way in most Windows 95 applets applications for which Help is available. You can press F1 if the application is the active window. If a menu is open in the application and Help appears on that menu, the first choice on the Help menu usually activates Help for that application. The Help Topics choice might appear at the top of the Help menu, or perhaps something else. In the Norton System Doctor for Windows 95 program from Symantec, for example, you start Help by choosing Info Desk from the Help menu. For most Windows 95 applications, the choice Help Topics executes the main Help for the application. Developers can use any text on the Help menu, so they might use something similar but not quite the same as Help Topics.

Help About Dialog Box Controls

Most dialog boxes in Windows 95 show a number of controls, such as list boxes and check boxes, but few dialog boxes include menus from which you can get help. Windows 95 provides help in dialog boxes that enable you to see information about every control in the dialog box. This help is known as *What's This* Help.

Dialog boxes that provide What's This Help have a question mark button near the Close button. To display What's This Help for any control in a dialog box, click on the question mark button. The mouse pointer changes to a question mark; position the mouse pointer over the control for which you want help and then click. A pop-up box appears, displaying help about the control you selected (see fig. 20.4).

Figure 20.4

Help in a dialog box gives you What's This information about any control.

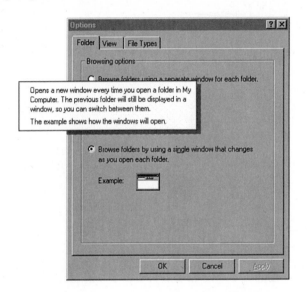

Another way to display What's This Help is to right-click on the control for which you want help. You will see a What's This button appear; click on this button to display Help about the control.

You can print or copy the contents of What's This Help. Right-click on the pop-up window to display a menu. To copy the entire contents of the pop-up window, choose Copy from the menu. To print the entire contents of the pop-up window, choose Print from the menu.

Using the Help Topics Dialog Box

The Help Topics dialog box is your primary source point for Help information. Just as Windows 3.*x* users became accustomed to the standard Windows Help window (see fig. 20.5), Windows 95 users will become accustomed to the standard Help Topics dialog box, shown in figure 20.6.

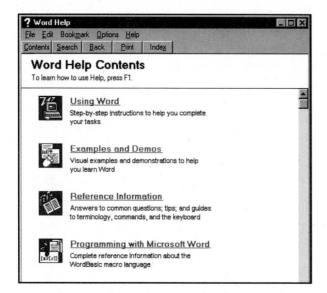

Figure 20.5

The Help window from Windows 3.1.

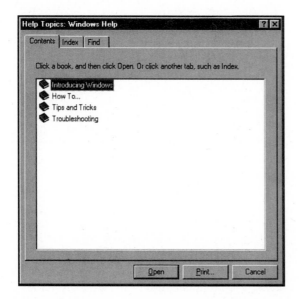

Figure 20.6

The Help Topics dialog box from Windows 95.

The Help Topics dialog box displays three pages for most applications: Contents, Index, and Find. Each page provides a different method for accessing Help information. This section reviews the functionality behind these three pages.

Contents

The Contents page in the Help Topics dialog box presents a table of contents for the Help file in a hierarchical format (see fig. 20.7). A book icon accompanies section headings to their left. A question mark page icon appears to the left of actual *topic pages*. A particular section's list of topics appears only if it's open. You open a section by double-clicking on its label or icon, or by selecting it and choosing <u>O</u>pen. After you open a section, the book icon becomes an open book icon. To view a topic in a section, double-click on its label or icon, or click on it and choose <u>D</u>isplay.

Figure 20.7

The table of contents view of Help.

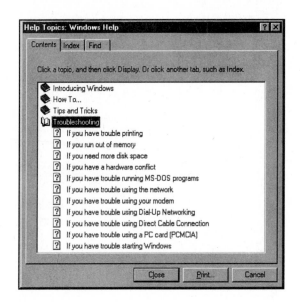

Index

The Index page (see fig. 20.8) enables you to access Help based on a keyword list the developer supplies. You can enter a keyword on which to base a search in the <u>T</u>ype the first few letters text box, or you can select an index entry from the <u>C</u>lick the index entry you want list box. If the application offers more than one Help file, you can view the combined index list for all its Help files by enabling <u>U</u>se the combined index for Windows Help topics check box. If you disable the check box, a drop-down menu appears, from which you can select the index you want to use.

Find

The Find page (see fig. 20.9) enables you to locate Help based on any word that appears in the topic title or in the topic text. You can enter words in the text box at

the top of the dialog box on which to search directly, or you can select from all words that appear in the Help file from a list in the middle of the dialog box. Before you use the Find option for the first time with a particular Help file, Windows 95 prompts you to build the word list. To build a word list, you just follow a series of simple prompts.

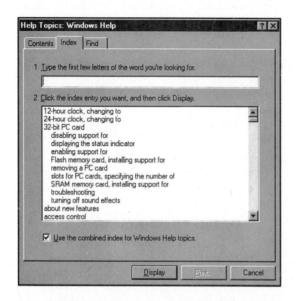

Figure 20.8

The Index page of Help.

Figure 20.9

The Find page in the Help Topics dialog box.

You can specify that Help search immediately for matching Help topics when you enter characters into the text box or select words from the list; doing so deactivates the Find Now button. Alternatively, you can specify that Help search only when you click on the Find Now button. These options are specified in the Find Options dialog box (see fig. 20.10), which you open by choosing the Options button. If you choose the Begin searching immediately option, as you specify words to search for by entering directly or selecting from a list, Windows 95 updates a list of Help topics in which the word appears. At the same time, the topics found panel at the bottom of the Find page updates to inform you of the number of topics that include the word(s) you specify. To open any of the topics shown in the topic list box, double-click on the topic name, or select the topic name and choose the Display button.

Figure 20.10

The Find Options dialog box from the Windows 95 Help.

To specify a phrase in your search, enter a space between words in the text box on the Find page. To expand your search to include more topics, you can specify multiple words to search for in the list box. Windows 95 will select all topics that include one or more of the words you specify. To select multiple words in the list box, press Ctrl while selecting subsequent words after the first one. When you specify more than one word in your find criteria, you can use the Show words that drop-down list in the Find Options dialog box to specify whether each of the words appear in the topic, at least one of the words appear in the topic, or all of the words appear in the topic in the exact order you specify.

The Help Window

The Help window is where the actual Help topics are displayed. A Help window can contain a few different components in addition to the text that makes up the bulk of

the topic. In addition, there are a few tasks you can run from the Help window, such as annotating a topic. This section discusses those additional Help elements and tasks, such as the Related Topics button, shortcut buttons, and printing from Help.

Related Topics Button

Windows 95 provides a Related Topics button that brings you to any Help topic(s) related to the topic you are viewing (see fig. 20.11). If more than one Help topic is related to the one you are viewing, you can choose which topic to jump to. For example, in the Help topic that explains how to customize the Start menu, you can click on the Related Topics button to jump to Help topics for adding a program to the Start menu and removing a program from the Start menu.

Figure 20.11

The Related Topics button enables you to jump immediately to related Help topics.

Shortcut Button

A key element of Windows 95 is the liberal use of *wizards,* special utilities that step you through potentially complicated tasks, such as setting up hardware devices. Rather than duplicate in Help the instructions that a wizard might provide, Help simply provides shortcuts to these wizards when applicable. Most Help topics that contain a reference to a task for which a Wizard already exists also provide a shortcut button you can use to launch the appropriate wizard. The Help topic for creating a briefcase on the desktop (see Chapter 19, "Creating and Using a Briefcase"), for example, includes as the first step a shortcut to the Add/Remove Programs wizard (see fig. 20.12), in which you install the Briefcase application.

Figure 20.12

The Help topic for the Briefcase utility includes a shortcut to the wizard that installs the utility.

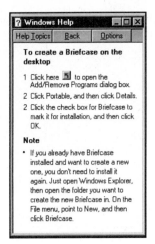

Printing a Help Topic

Printing information in Help can be useful. Windows 95 provides an interface to standard Windows 95 print services when you use Help. To print the current Help topic, choose Options, Print Topic, which opens the standard Print dialog box from which you control printing as usual.

Bookmarks in Help

For long Help topics, you can specify a bookmark so that you can easily return to a useful or significant point in the Help file. A *bookmark* is a special placeholder to particular location in the Help file. As you build a list of bookmarks for a Help file, you can move quickly to points in the Help file to which you often refer.

To add a bookmark to the Help topic, choose Bookmark, Define from the menu (any bookmarks already specified for the Help file also appear on the Bookmark menu) to display the Bookmark Define dialog box (see fig. 20.13). Type the text you want to use as a bookmark in the Bookmark name text box, then choose OK. You also can use the title of the Help topic as the bookmark; Windows 95 provides this as the default bookmark. To delete an existing bookmark, open the Bookmark Define dialog box, select the bookmark you want to delete, and then choose Delete. To move to a bookmark you have previously set up, choose it from the Bookmark menu.

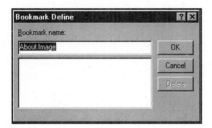

Figure 20.13

You define bookmarks in the Bookmark Define dialog box.

Annotating a Help Topic

You can add your own information to Help topics and then refer to that information later, which is helpful if you want to add context to the information that appears in Help, such as describing how the help applies to how you use a feature. To annotate a Help topic, choose Options, Annotate from the menu to open the Annotate dialog box (see fig. 20.14). Enter the annotation in the Current annotation text box, then choose Save. You can use the Copy and Paste options to copy text from the text box to the Clipboard, or you can paste data from the Clipboard into the text box so it becomes part of the annotation.

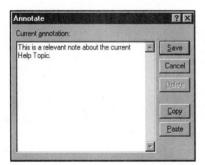

Figure 20.14

The Annotate dialog box.

Copying Help Information

You can copy information out of any Windows 95 Help topic to the Clipboard, which is useful if you need to create a special document that contains information from a Help topic. You also can copy text from Help into any document, such as a spreadsheet or a graphic. To copy text in a Help topic, open the Help topic window that contains the text and highlight the text you want to copy. Next, choose Options, Copy. The highlighted data is now on the Clipboard, and you can use the Paste command in another application to move the data to that application.

Controlling the Appearance of Help

You can change the size of the text that appears in a Help topic. Choose <u>O</u>ptions, <u>F</u>ont. You can choose from three sizes: small, medium, and large. You also can specify how the Help topic window is positioned when other windows are open. You can specify that the Help topic window always appear on top of or behind all other windows. Because the Help developer can specify the way the Help window appears, you also can specify to use this default setting. To set the position of the Help topic window, choose <u>O</u>ptions, <u>K</u>eep Help on Top.

Building Windows Help

You don't need years of programming experience to be able to create Help files. A documentation or support team frequently handles this chore at many software development companies. At the same time, online Help appears in almost every Windows application, so any software developer, be it one person in a home office or an entire Help team, can provide online Help. This section reviews the reasons to build online Help and overviews actually doing it.

Why Build Custom Help?

The architecture behind Windows Help, including Windows 3.x and Windows 95, makes creating Help files possible for almost any PC power user. Not only does Microsoft make available many tools for creating Help files, but a few third-party vendors sell special software that eases the pain of creating Help. The Help you create is no less powerful or functional than the Help many of today's top applications provide. The only requirements for building a Help file is a plan, some creativity, a Help compiler, and the files that contain the information, text, and graphics.

There are a number of reasons for building Help. For the corporate support specialist, there might be an enterprise need for supplementing the Help supplied by the software vendor whose application is used at the company. For any application in use at a corporation, additional Help can be provided. This custom help could include information about corporate standards for using the application, such as, in the case of a word processing program, how to format specific types of documents or where to find and how to use the corporate dictionary file for spell checking. The Help file in use at a corporate location might also provide information on how to take advantage of any customization applied to the application, such as custom menus or macros.

Online Help is very much within reach for the software developer or corporation that already has printed documentation for a software application. Leveraging the effort that has gone into a printed document into an online Help system is easy. A number

of utilities are available on the market that convert word processing documents into online Help for Windows 3.*x*. These vendors are sure to come out with versions for Windows 95.

Overview of Building Help

All the work you complete to build online Help can be considered your Help application, which consists of the topic file, supplemental files, the Help compiler, and the Help project file.

Note Depending upon the Help compiler you use, you might not need a Help project file. Certain Help compilers use different systems for managing the different components of a Help application.

The following sections take a look at some of the common components of a Help project.

Topic File

The *topic file* contains text and special information about the text that constitutes the heart of your Help application. The special information includes the jumps that move the user from one topic to another, the Related Topics information, and more.

To write the Help topic file, you need to work in a word processor that can save documents in Rich Text Format (RTF). A file saved in RTF contains all the information for displaying the text on the screen or printer—namely, the special codes that tell the application using the RTF file how to display the data in the file. The Help compiler you use provides specific information about how to format the RTF file. The RTF format enables users of different operating systems, such as Macintosh or OS/2, to share files.

Supplemental Files

Supplemental files include any extra material you plan to include in your help, such as graphics. If you plan to include graphics in your Help, then you need software to develop these graphics. Windows 95 comes with an application that makes developing graphics for Help files possible. The Paint application can save files in the Bitmap (BMW) format, which is compatible with the Windows Help compiler. In addition, you can create graphics in WMF (placeable Windows metafile), MRB (multiple-resolution bitmap), or SHG (segmented-graphics bitmap) formats. You need to save each of these graphics to a separate file. Any other special files that supplement your main topic file fall in this group, including special animation or other multimedia pieces.

Help Compiler

The *Help compiler* builds the topic file and any supplemental files into the Help file you ship. The compiler does so based on the special information you provide in the Help project file. Microsoft provides a Help compiler in its software development kit (SDK) for Win32 applications. A number of other vendors have Help compilers available for Win16-applications, and it's only a matter of time before these vendors offer versions for building Help files for Win32 applications. All the compilers achieve the same goal; some take different routes. If you use the Microsoft compiler, you can be sure your Help file is built to the most up-to-date standards and with the least amount of problems. Some of the third-party compilers, however, feature time-savers and conveniences that the Microsoft compiler certainly lacks.

Help Project File

You also need a Help project file for creating Help. The Project file tells the Help compiler how the build the Help file. It includes all special information about your Help application, including the following:

◆ The list of files that make up your Help application

◆ Version tagging information

◆ Context-sensitive Help information (linking Help to specific controls in your application)

◆ Special elements of Help, including custom buttons and menus

◆ Secondary Help window information

The requirements for the Help project file vary based on the Help compiler you use. The Windows SDK for Win32 application has special requirements for the Help project file, so you should check with its Help or printed documentation for exact file format. Some non-Microsoft Help compilers do not require a specific Help project file, so you can save yourself some work if you use one of their products.

C H A P T E R

21

Integrating Windows and DOS

Windows 95 does not retain the concept of the Windows environment running on top of the DOS operating system. Despite the intensity with which many Windows 3.*x* users have tried to distinguish and distance Windows from DOS—and often themselves from DOS users—until the advent of Windows 95, you couldn't have Windows if you didn't have DOS. Windows was basically DOS wearing a nicer, more colorful interface—DOS was the necessary operating system, no two ways about it.

Now, you get Windows and DOS in Windows 95: the pretty, graphical shell that users became comfortable with using Windows 3.*x*, and the powerful, character-based, operating system that users learned to live with. Windows 95 is an operating system, separate and distinct, in its own right, and does not need DOS. DOS is alive and well, however, in Windows 95. Windows 95 provides better support for DOS applications than in any previous Windows versions, and adds greater functionality to the DOS command line, which remains part of Windows 95. This chapter explores DOS issues related to Windows 95, including running applications and the DOS command line.

The chapter covers the following topics:

◆ Windows 95 support for DOS applications

◆ Elements of the DOS application PIF file

◆ Working in the DOS application window

◆ Using the DOS command line in Windows 95

Windows 95 Support for DOS Applications

Considering the large number of popular DOS-based applications, any operating system, including a new operating system, must support running DOS applications smoothly. Windows 95 has a questionable legacy to overcome, because users of previous versions of Windows have to carefully manage their Windows configuration if they want to run DOS applications under Windows. In Windows defense, however, some DOS applications seldom ran smoothly, even in real-mode DOS. In any case, Windows 95 does a good job of providing support for DOS applications. This section looks at two parts of the DOS/Windows 95 support strategy. The first part involves the way Windows 95 provides more conventional memory for DOS applications; the second area involves the special settings you can specify for each DOS application you run in Windows 95.

Virtual Device Drivers for Common Services

Perhaps the greatest challenge you faced if you wanted to run a DOS application in Windows 3.*x* or in real-mode DOS was finding enough conventional memory to meet the application's requirements. Unfortunately, many applications required that you load specific device drivers before you could run them, such as drivers for a mouse, CD player, network card, sound card, and so on, frequently leaving your system with insufficient memory to run the application. Windows 95 solves this problem by virtualizing many of the common services a DOS application requires. Many of the 16-bit real-mode drivers you find in the pre-Windows 95 world have been replaced with 32-bit virtual device drivers, also known as VxDs. The following list shows the services appropriate to DOS applications that Windows 95 VxDs provide:

Microsoft Network client

Novell NetWare client

DOS file-sharing support

Adaptec SCSI driver

Adaptec CD-ROM driver

Microsoft CD-ROM extensions

SmartDrive disk-caching software

Microsoft Mouse driver

Microsoft DriveSpace disk compression driver

Depending on the configuration you use, you can save close to 250 KB on some systems.

PIF Files and Property Pages

Many DOS applications require very specific, complicated configurations before they can run properly. Some applications have very specific memory requirements, whereas others need to think they're the only application running on your PC. Windows 95 enables you to specify a number of different settings to customize the configuration and the environment in which DOS applications run. These settings are stored in program information files (PIFs). PIF gets its name from Windows 3.x, in which a file name that had the extension PIF also stored information about DOS applications.

 Note   This chapter presents technical information about the way Windows 95 interrelates with DOS applications, as well as about the DOS command line. Chapter 18, "Running Applications," covers specific information about how to run a DOS application.

You don't modify the PIF files directly in Windows 95; rather, you modify the settings in the file by working with the property pages for the DOS application. The property pages are not assigned directly to the DOS application, though. You must set up a shortcut to launch each DOS application you plan to run in Windows 95. Because Windows 95 recognizes the application behind the shortcut as a DOS application, the property page for the shortcut includes the settings specific to DOS applications. You can use the Run command on the Start menu to launch a DOS application, but if you use this method, Windows 95 uses default DOS settings that might not be compatible with your application.

Now that you have seen how PIF files relate to property sheets for DOS applications, the next section examines the settings that Windows 95 stores in the files and that you find on the property pages.

DOS Application PIF File Settings

Windows 95 supports DOS applications by providing numerous options for running the application and configuring the application's run-time environment. Among the options you can specify for your application is the name of a batch file that runs just before your application, which might set up some environment variables. You also can specify the amount of extended, expanded, conventional, and protected-mode memory to allocate to the application, and more. You can use the property sheet for the shortcut to the application to view and change the options. The settings are stored in the application's PIF file. This section presents each of the options on the six property pages.

The General Property Page

The General property page (see fig. 21.1) provides information about the shortcut to the DOS application and the PIF file the shortcut references.

Figure 21.1

The General property page for a shortcut to a DOS application.

Mickey Properties	? X

General | Program | Font | Memory | Screen | Misc

Mickey

Type: Shortcut to MS-DOS Program
Location: DESKTOP
Size: 1.31KB (1,348 bytes)

MS-DOS name: MICKEY.PIF
Created: Wednesday, May 10, 1995 10:47:24 PM
Modified: Monday, May 29, 1995 5:25:12 PM
Accessed: Monday, May 29, 1995

Attributes: ☐ Read-only ☐ Hidden
☑ Archive ☐ System

[OK] [Cancel] [Apply]

New Riders Publishing
INSIDE
SERIES

The information and options presented in the General property page are explained in the following list:

◆ **Icon.** You can see the icon you click to activate the shortcut near the top of the General property page below the horizontal row of menu buttons. The caption for the icon appears beside it. You can change both from the Program property page.

◆ **Type.** Tells you the type of object you selected. (Of course, in the case of a DOS application, the type is a Shortcut to MS-DOS Program.)

◆ **Location.** Shows the name of the folder in which the object you selected resides.

◆ **Size.** Shows the size of the file the icon represents. In the case of a shortcut to a DOS application, the size of the PIF file storing information about the DOS application is displayed, not the size of the shortcut file.

◆ **MS-DOS name.** Shows the MS-DOS version of the PIF file.

◆ **Created.** Shows the time and date at which the PIF file for the DOS application was created.

◆ **Modified.** Shows the most recent time and date at which the PIF file for the DOS application was modified. As such, this field indicates the last time any of the properties for the DOS application were modified.

◆ **Accessed.** Shows the last time any of the property pages for the DOS application were opened.

◆ **Attributes.** The four check boxes in the Attributes section enable you to set the file attributes for the PIF file for the DOS application. The Read-only option determines whether users can change the file. The Hidden option determines whether users can see the file while viewing the contents of the directory in which the file resides. The System option determines whether you consider the file a system file. The Archive option determines whether the archive bit for the file is set.

The Program Property Page

The Program property page (see fig. 21.2) enables you to specify the basic information for the DOS application, such as the name of the file that starts the application. You can choose the Advanced button if you want to customize the environment in which the DOS application runs, and you can choose Change Icon if you want to specify an icon for the shortcut that launches the application. These options are covered individually in the section "Advanced DOS Application Options."

Figure 21.2

The Program property page for a shortcut to a DOS application.

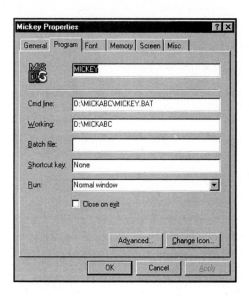

The following list explains the settings in the Program property page:

◆ **Icon caption.** In the text box next to the icon, you can enter the label (up to 29 characters) you want to appear under the icon for the shortcut to the DOS application.

◆ **Cmd line.** Specify the full path, file name, and any switches necessary to launch the DOS application in this text box.

◆ **Working.** Some DOS applications enable you to specify a directory—other than the directory from which you launch the application—in which to store run-time information for the application. If so, you can specify that directory in the Working text box.

◆ **Batch file.** If you want a batch file to execute just before the system launches the DOS application (this batch file might load device drivers, or it might set environment variables), specify the path name for the file in the Batch file text box.

Note The Batch file text box enables you to specify a batch file that executes just before the system launches the DOS application. If you run a DOS application in MS-DOS mode, however, you can specify Config.sys and Autoexec.bat settings for the DOS application to use. For information about MS-DOS mode, see the following section, "Advanced DOS Application Options."

◆ **Shortcut key.** To specify a *shortcut key* (a key or key combination that switches you to the DOS application when you press it), you select this text box and press the key(s) you want to use. You can specify a single key, such as F6, or a combination of keys, such as Alt+F2. The key(s) you press will appear in the text box.

◆ **Run.** To specify the appearance of the window that houses the DOS application, you use this drop-down list to select Normal, Minimized, or Maximized.

◆ **Close on exit.** If you enable this check box, the window in which the DOS application runs closes after the application completes.

Advanced DOS Application Options

DOS applications are among the most sensitive to their run-time environment, so running a DOS application in Windows 3.*x* is not always easy. In fact, you have no guarantee that a DOS application can run smoothly on a PC if Windows isn't running. In Windows 95, in addition to the settings on the six property pages described in this section, you can use a set of options designed to help you run the most finicky DOS applications. You access these options by choosing the Advanced button on the Program property page, which displays the Advanced Program Settings dialog box shown in figure 21.3.

Figure 21.3

The Advanced Program Settings dialog box enables you to set run-time options for sensitive DOS applications.

Many DOS applications run normally in Windows 95 as long as you choose the correct options from the six property pages. When you have more sensitive DOS applications, the options in the Advanced Program Settings enable you to specify more stringent run-time options, further isolating the DOS application from Windows 95. One such option is the detect Windows setting. To prevent possible problems related to running their application under Windows, some DOS applications developers code their applications to detect Windows at run-time. If the application detects Windows, it doesn't run. Windows 95 overcomes this problem by providing a switch that prevents DOS applications from detecting Windows at run-time. If you choose the Prevent MS-DOS-based programs from detecting Windows option, MS-DOS-based applications cannot detect Windows.

The most sensitive DOS applications necessitate use of Windows 95's MS-DOS mode. If you run an application in MS-DOS mode, Windows 95 disappears from memory, except for a small anchor point that enables Windows 95 to return after the DOS application closes. You can specify for Windows 95 to let you know if it thinks MS-DOS mode would benefit the DOS application. Unfortunately, this setting exists per application; you must enable the Suggest MS-DOS mode as necessary option for each DOS application for which you want Windows 95 to make its recommendation concerning MS-DOS mode. The following section discusses the different options you can specify for MS-DOS mode.

MS-DOS Mode

To run an application in MS-DOS mode, you must enable the MS-DOS mode check box in the Advanced Program Settings dialog box. Checking this box activates the other MS-DOS mode options in the dialog box, and deactivates the options to detect Windows and suggest MS-DOS mode. The reverse happens when you clear the MS-DOS mode check box. You can customize the DOS environment for the application with the options in the MS-DOS mode group. Keep in mind that the settings you specify here override any other comparable settings in the system. The following are the MS-DOS mode options you can specify:

◆ **Warn before entering MS-DOS mode.** Enabling this check box displays a dialog box when you run the application that warns you that all other applications will close if you run this DOS application (see fig. 21.4). It gives you the opportunity to shut down any open applications yourself. If you do not check this option, no warning occurs.

◆ **Use current MS-DOS configuration.** Use this option to have the DOS application use the configuration specified in the Config.sys and Autoexec.bat files as they were when you booted Windows 95.

◆ **Specify a new MS-DOS configuration.** This option enables you to specify Config.sys and Autoexec.bat settings for the DOS application. Choosing this option activates the scrollable text boxes for Config.sys and Autoexec.bat. You can edit or remove existing settings, and you can add new lines.

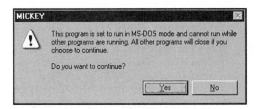

Figure 21.4

You can specify that Windows 95 warn you before it enters MS-DOS mode.

More MS-DOS mode options become available when you choose the Configuration button, which activates the Select MS-DOS Mode Configuration Options dialog box (see fig. 21.5). These options use the virtual device drivers described in the section "Virtual Device Drivers for Common Services" earlier in this chapter.

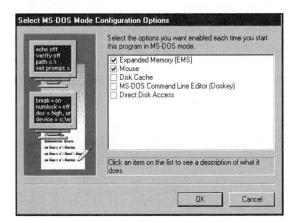

Figure 21.5

The Select MS-DOS Mode Configuration Options dialog box.

The following list describes the options you can specify in the Select MS-DOS Mode Configuration Options dialog box.

◆ **Expanded Memory (EMS).** Loads the EMM386 driver to provide simulated expanded memory to the application.

◆ **Mouse.** Enables you to use the mouse with the DOS application.

◆ **Disk Cache.** Loads Microsoft's SmartDrive disk cache software, making it available to the DOS application.

◆ **MS-DOS Command Line Editor (Doskey).** Loads the DOS command-line editor, making recalling and editing past command-line directives easy.

◆ **Direct Disk Access.** Gives the DOS application direct access to the disk, enabling it to view and modify data structures on the disk.

Selecting an Icon for the DOS Application

You can specify the icon that appears for the shortcut to the DOS application. You select the icon from the Change Icon dialog box (see fig. 21.6), which appears after you choose the Change Icon button on the Program property page.

Figure 21.6

You can use the Change Icon dialog box to specify an icon for the shortcut to the DOS application.

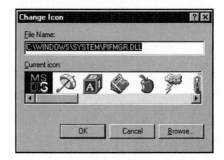

The icons that appear in the Current icon list box are those available from the Pifmgr.dll file, which controls all the property pages. You can select one of the icons that appear in the list box, or you can choose an icon from another file. To choose an icon from another file, type the name of the file in the File Name text box and choose OK. Icons typically are stored in DLL, EXE, and ICO files. If you need help selecting a file, choose Browse to display the standard file selection dialog box in Windows 95. After you select a file and choose Open, any icons stored in that file appear in the Change Icon dialog box. Windows 95 informs you if the file you select stores no icons.

The Font Property Page

The Font property page (see fig. 21.7) enables you to specify font settings for the DOS application and to preview how the fonts appear. The options are valid only when the application is running in a window; they have no effect when the application runs in full-screen mode. You can specify a Bitmap or TrueType font, or both, depending on the size you select. You also can select the size of the font from the property page. Two windows on the property page (Window preview and Font preview) preview for you the font type and size selections you make. If you select Auto in the Font size list box, Windows 95 automatically resizes the contents to display the entire window based on how you size the screen.

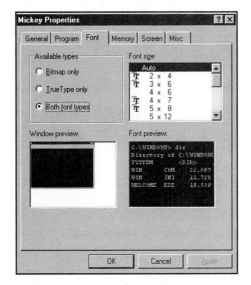

Figure 21.7

The Font property page for a shortcut to a DOS application.

The Memory Property Page

The Memory property page (see fig. 21.8) provides you with numerous options to configure the memory environment for the DOS application. You can specify the amount of conventional, expanded, extended, and protected-mode memory available to the DOS application when it runs.

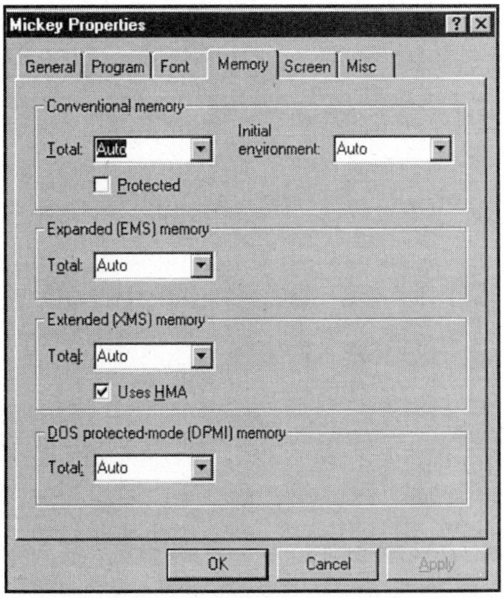

Figure 21.8

The Memory property page for a shortcut to a DOS application.

The following list explains the options in the Memory property page:

◆ **Total conventional memory.** This setting specifies the amount of conventional memory (in kilobytes) allocated to the DOS application. Conventional memory is the first 640 KB of memory on your system. If you set this option to Auto, Windows 95 determines the amount of memory to allocate based on the application's needs.

◆ **Initial environment.** You specify the amount of memory allocated to the MS-DOS command interpreter (in kilobytes) in this list box. This value also applies to any batch file application. This setting is comparable to the SHELL= statement in the Config.sys file.

◆ **Protected.** Use this check box in the Conventional memory area to have the system protect the MS-DOS system area, which includes support for DOS applications as well as DOS drivers. This switch essentially makes those areas read-only. Although this option does provide increased stability for DOS applications, the additional overhead degrades performance.

◆ **Expanded memory.** The Total list box enables you to specify the amount of expanded memory to allocate to the DOS application. Expanded memory is either found on an expanded memory board on your system, or is simulated with existing memory.

◆ **Extended memory.** This Total list box enables you to specify the amount of extended memory to allocate the DOS application. Extended memory starts at the 1,024 KB address space and extends upward.

◆ **Uses HMA.** This check box in the Extended (XMS) memory area enables you to specify whether Windows 95 makes the high memory area available to your application. The high memory area represents a portion of the memory address space that exists between conventional memory at 640 KB and the start of extended memory at about 1 MB.

◆ **DOS protected-mode memory.** This drop-down list enables you to specify the amount of protected-mode memory to allocate to the DOS application.

The Screen Property Page

The Screen property page (see fig. 21.9) enables you to specify how the screen and video behave during a DOS application. You can specify options such as whether the toolbar appears in the DOS application's windows and whether Windows uses its own video ROM services with the application.

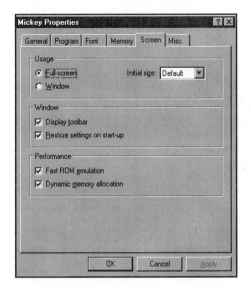

Figure 21.9

The Screen property page for a shortcut to a DOS application.

The following list explains the options in the Screen property page:

◆ **Usage.** You can use the Full-screen and Window options in the Usage group to specify how the DOS application window appears. You can pass data between DOS-based and Window-based applications only when the DOS application window is in Window mode, so if you want to share data with other applications often, you probably want to use the default Window option.

◆ **Initial size.** You use this list box in the Usage group to specify the number of lines that appear in the DOS application window during full-screen mode. Setting the size to more lines displays more information, but the text size is smaller and significantly more difficult to read.

◆ **Display toolbar.** You use this check box in the Window area to specify whether the toolbar appears in the DOS application window. If you enable this option, however, the toolbar appears only in Window mode. For more information on the DOS window, refer to the section "The DOS Application Window" later in this chapter.

◆ **Restore settings on start-up.** Enable this check box in the Window area if you want Windows 95 to restore certain screen settings to their last value the next time you run the DOS application. These settings include the Display toolbar option setting, and the font type and font size on the Font property page. If you do not check this option, these settings return to their default value the next time you run the DOS application.

◆ **Fast ROM emulation.** Enable this check box in the Performance area if you want to improve the DOS application's performance. When you enable this option, Windows 95 uses its own virtual device drivers to simulate video ROM services for the DOS application. Choosing this option does improve performance, but if the DOS application or the video hardware bypasses standard procedures in accessing ROM, you might experience technical difficulties.

◆ **Dynamic memory allocation.** Enabling this check box in the Performance area makes memory dynamically available to the rest of the system if the DOS application uses both text and graphic modes. If you choose this option, Windows 95 dynamically supplements or reclaims memory available to other applications as the DOS application switches between video modes.

The Misc Property Page

The Misc property page (see fig. 21.10) contains eight options that enable you to apply the finishing touches to your customized DOS application and environment for running in Windows 95. The options in this property page range from dictating Windows 95's sensitivity to inactivity in the DOS application, to reserving special shortcut key combinations for Windows 95.

Figure 21.10

The Misc property page for a shortcut to a DOS application.

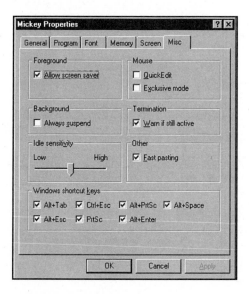

The following list explains the options in the Misc property page:

◆ **Allow screen saver.** Clear this check box in the Foreground area to specify that no screen saver is activated during the DOS application; enable it if you do want a screen saver to be activated during the application. Among the occasions when you might want to disable the screen saver is when the screen saver interferes with the DOS application's graphics processing. Also, if you are using a screen capture program, you might want to disable the screen saver to ensure the screen saver does not activate at the time when you capture a screen.

◆ **QuickEdit.** Enable this check box in the Mouse area if you want to use the mouse to mark data to copy elsewhere in the DOS application window. If you don't enable this option, you can't use the mouse to copy data; you have to use the Mark option on the toolbar.

◆ **Exclusive mode.** Enable this check box in the Mouse area to specify that the mouse work only with the DOS application; as long as the DOS application runs, other applications cannot use the mouse pointer.

◆ **Always suspend.** Enable this check box in the Background area to specify for the DOS application to free up its use of system resources when it is not running in the foreground.

◆ **Warn if still active.** Enable this check box in the Termination area if you want Windows 95 to always warn you when you try to close the DOS application window in which the application is running.

◆ **Fast pasting.** Use this check box option in the Other area to tell Windows 95 to use a different set of algorithms to paste data into the DOS application.

◆ **Idle sensitivity.** Use this slider to specify Windows 95's degree of sensitivity to inactivity in the DOS application. Keyboard input signals activity to Windows 95. The closer you specify to High, the less time Windows 95 waits before it decides that the DOS application is idle and reallocates resources to other applications. The closer you specify to Low, the more patiently Windows 95 behaves.

◆ **Windows shortcut keys.** Each shortcut key combination shown in this area represents specific functionality in Windows 95. Ctrl+Esc, for example, displays the Start menu. If the DOS application uses any of these key combinations, you can disable their activation from Windows 95 by clearing the corresponding check box. Table 21.1 shows the use for each shortcut key combination.

TABLE 21.1
Windows Shortcut Keys

Shortcut Key Combination	Function
Alt+Tab	Displays list of running applications
Alt+Esc	Switches in order through each running application
Ctrl+Esc	Displays the Start menu
PrtScr	Copies the entire screen image to the Clipboard
Alt+PrtScr	Copies the current window or dialog box to the Clipboard
Alt+Enter	Switches an application between full-screen and window mode
Alt+Space	Activates an application's Control menu

The DOS Application Window

Windows 95 provides the DOS application window, a useful and somewhat-customizable window for running DOS applications when the DOS application window is not in full-screen mode. The DOS application window features TrueType fonts that scale as you resize the window and a toolbar that gives you access to some useful features, such as changing the font size and displaying the DOS application's property sheet. This section examines the toolbar options and copying and pasting data to and from the DOS application window.

DOS Application Toolbar

Figure 21.11 shows the DOS application window with labels for each of the buttons on the toolbar. To display the toolbar, you must enable the Display toolbar option on the Screen property page.

The toolbar buttons are explained in the following list:

◆ **Font size.** This drop-down list contains the same choices as the Font Size list box in the Font property page. The list enables you to specify the size of the text that appears in the window.

◆ **Mark.** Enables you to select text in the DOS application window.

◆ **Copy.** Copies the data selected in the window to the Clipboard.

◆ **Paste.** Inserts the contents of the Clipboard to the cursor location in the window.

◆ **Full screen.** Switches the DOS application window to full-screen mode.

◆ **Properties.** Displays the property pages for the DOS application.

◆ **Background.** Moves the application to the background.

◆ **Font properties.** Displays the Font property page for the DOS application (you can use this button to access the other four property pages, too).

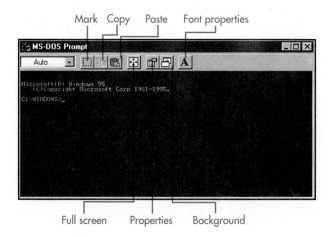

Figure 21.11

Toolbar buttons on a DOS application window.

Copying and Pasting Data in the DOS Application Window

When the DOS application window is in window mode, you can copy and paste data to and from the window the same as you can with a Windows application. To select and copy text that appears in the DOS application window, click on the Mark button on the toolbar, then use the mouse to click and drag over the text you want to copy. Alternatively, you can use the keyboard to select text. To do so, move the cursor to the beginning of the text that you want to copy. Then, press and hold Shift as you use the cursor keys to select the text you want. After you select the text, click on the Copy button on the toolbar to copy the data you selected to the Clipboard.

To paste data into the DOS application window, position the cursor at the point to which you want to copy the data, then click on the Paste button on the toolbar.

Tip
If you enable QuickEdit mode on the Misc property page for the DOS application, you can use the mouse to highlight and copy text. Click and drag over the text you want to copy. After you highlight all the text, right-click to copy the text to the Clipboard.

The DOS Command Line

Although much of Windows 95's user functionality is built into its new graphical design, users who prefer to use DOS command-line functionality can still do so in Windows 95. The MS-DOS prompt is a standard choice in the Program group of the Start menu, so the DOS command line is just a menu choice away. The DOS command-line functionality Windows 95 provides has been modified to include new commands and tools, and is streamlined by the removal of inappropriate, obsolete commands.

DOS Commands

Table 21.2 shows the commands you can issue at the DOS command line. The table includes those commands that you can use to configure Windows 95 in Config.sys and Autoexec.bat, as well as batch file utilities. To get help with any of these commands, type the command, followed by /? at the DOS prompt, and then press Enter. Table 21.3 shows those commands you no longer can use in Windows 95.

Not included in these tables are those commands you use to configure TCP/IP. For information on command-line TCP/IP utilities, see Chapter 36, "TCP/IP and the Internet Connection."

TABLE 21.2
Windows 95 DOS Commands

ATTRIB	BREAK	BUFFERS	CALL
CD	CHCP	CHDIR	CHKDSK
CHOICE	CLS	COMMAND	COPY
COUNTRY	CTTY	DATE	DEBUG
DEFRAG	DEL (erase)	DELTREE	DEVICE
DEVICEHIGH	DIR	DISKCOPY	DOS
DOSKEY	DRVPARM	DRVSPACE	ECHO
EDIT	EMM386	ERASE	EXIT

New Riders Publishing
INSIDE SERIES

EXPAND	FC	FCBS	FDISK
FILES	FIND	FOR	FORMAT
GOTO	IF	INCLUDE	INSTALL
KEYB	LABEL	LASTDRIVE	LH
LOADFIX	LOADHIGH (lh)	MD	MEM
MENUCOLOR	MENUDEFAULT	MENUITEM	MKDIR
MODE	MORE	MOVE	MSD
NET CONFIG	NET DIAG	NET INIT	NET LOGOFF
NET LOGON	NET PASSWORD	NET PRINT	NET START
NET STOP	NET TIME	NET USE	NET VER
NET VIEW	NLSFUNC	NUMLOCK	PATH
PAUSE	PROMPT	RD	REM
REN	RENAME	RMDIR	SCANDISK
SET	SETVER	SHELL	SHIFT
SMARTDRV	SORT	STACKS	START
SUBMENU	SUBST	SWITCHES	SYS
TIME	TYPE	VER	VERIFY
VOL	XCOPY		

TABLE 21.3
Obsolete DOS Commands

APPEND	ASSIGN	BACKUP	COMP
DOSSHELL	EDLIN	EGA.SYS	FASTHELP
FASTOPEN	GRAFTABL	GRAPHICS	HELP
INTERLINK	INTERSVR	JOIN	MEMCARD
MEMMAKER	MIRROR	MSAV	MSBACKUP
POWER	PRINT	PRINTER.SYS	QBASIC
RAMDRIVE.SYS	RECOVER	REPLACE	RESTORE
ROMDRIVE.SYS	SHARE	SMARTMON	TREE
UNDELETE	UNFORMAT	VSAFE	

Starting Applications from the Command Line

The DOS command line has been extended in Windows 95 to provide support for starting applications. You can start a Windows-based or a DOS-based application from the command line, using the START command.

To start an application, type the following:

START *<application name>*

Typing **START WINWORD.EXE**, for example, launches Microsoft Word for Windows. You also can launch an application and open a file at the same time from the DOS command line. Windows 95 launches the application that it associates with the file name. To do so, type the following:

START *<document name>*

Typing **START EXPENSES.XLS**, for example, launches Microsoft Excel for Windows because Windows 95 associates the Xls extension with Excel. You can launch a DOS application the same way. To launch the DOS editor, type the following:

START EDIT

To get help with the START command, or to see any of the options for the command, type **START** /? at the command line.

CHAPTER

22

Using Backup

The most important computer-related possessions for most PC users are the data created by using the PC. You can replace hardware and software, but not the ideas and effort that take form in the data files, documents, spreadsheets, databases, and graphics on your PC. Despite the confidence with which software and hardware developers try to assure you that your data is protected from unexpected hardware failure or software crashes, you *can* lose critical data in a number of ways. You might carelessly overwrite critical files, for example, or you might encounter power supply problems during a save operation and corrupt an important file.

It's obvious, then, that one of your most critical tasks—but one users often overlook—is backing up important data. Before Windows 95, you had to obtain backup software from a large number of third-party providers. Windows 95, however, includes a Backup applet (mini-application). This chapter shows you how to use the Backup utility by covering the following topics:

- ◆ How to install and run Backup

- ◆ Selecting files to back up

- ◆ Backing up files

- ◆ Restoring files from Backup

The following section looks at how to install Backup into Windows 95, how to start Backup, and the actual backup process.

Installing Backup

Backup will not be installed unless you choose the Custom option during setup of Windows 95. You use the Custom option if you want to explicitly choose which Windows applets to install, and Backup is one of many applets you can choose to install. If you did not specify that Backup be installed during Windows 95 setup, you can still install Backup after Windows 95 is installed. If you don't know whether Backup is installed in your Windows 95 system, open the Start menu, then choose Programs, Accessories, System Tools. If Backup is installed, it appears on the menu along with other system tools.

Perform the following steps to install Backup:

1. Open the Control Panel folder either by choosing Control Panel from the Settings menu, which appears on the Start menu, or by double-clicking on the Control Panel folder in My Computer.

2. Start the Add/Remove Programs wizard. The Add/Remove Programs property sheet appears.

3. Click on the Windows Setup tab.

4. Choose Disk Tools from the Components list box and then choose the Details button. The Disk Tools dialog box appears.

5. Click on the check box next to the word Backup in the Components list box.

6. Choose OK. You are returned to the Add/Remove Programs property sheet.

7. Choose OK. Backup will now be installed into your Windows 95 system.

Starting Backup

After you install the Backup utility, it appears on a menu. To start it, from the Start menu, choose Programs, Accessories, System Tools, and then Backup. Of course, you can customize the menus in your Windows 95 applications so that Backup (and any other application) appears anywhere you choose. Chapter 18, "Running Applications," provides good instructions if you're interested in customizing the menus in Windows 95.

Tip   A good way to help prod you to run Backup often is to place a shortcut to the utility on the desktop. The shortcut's constant presence turns your desktop into a reminder to back up every time you see it. Create a shortcut that points to the Backup shortcut in the Windows\Start Menu\Programs\Accessories\System Tools folder.

Backup displays certain messages when you start it up, shown in the dialog box in figure 22.1. Depending on your actions in this dialog box, you might not see them again. The messages give you very general definition of the Backup utility, and provides three basic steps for backing up files. You can tell Backup not to bother you with this message dialog box again by enabling the **D**on't show this again check box.

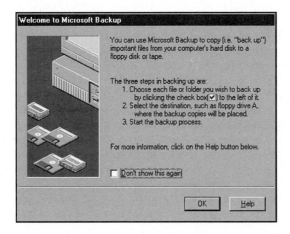

Figure 22.1

Backup displays general information about backing up important data when you start the utility.

In case you checked the **D**on't show this again check box in the dialog box that explains the three basic steps to Backup, here is a review of the steps:

1. Choose the files or folders you would like to back up by checking the box that appears next to the name of the files or folders.

2. Specify the target destination for the backup.

3. Start the backup.

After you clear the introductory dialog box, Backup might tell you that it has created a *full backup file set*—a list of all the files on your hard drive—if you haven't completed a full backup of your system (see fig. 22.2). The first time you use Backup, you use this full backup file set to specify which files to back up. Unless you use the full backup file set to create a backup of your system, or enable the **D**on't show this again check box, this message appears every time you start Backup.

Figure 22.2

Backup warns you at startup if you have not completed a full backup of your hard drive.

Special Backup Options

You can specify options that control Backup's general behavior, regardless of whether you are backing up data, restoring data, or comparing backed-up data to files on your hard disk. The options (audible prompt, status log preservation, file filtering, and drag-and-drop backup) are covered in the next four short sections.

Audible Prompts

When you use audible prompts, Backup warns you that certain steps in the backup process are complete by beeping, including when you should insert another floppy disk. Otherwise, Backup uses only on-screen messages to alert you. If you want to activate audible prompts, choose Settings, Options from the Backup menu, which opens the Settings - Options dialog box (see fig. 22.3). From the General page, enable the Turn on audible prompts check box.

Figure 22.3

The Settings - Options dialog box enables you to specify options for the Backup utility.

Overwrite Status Logs

The status logs in Backup provide summary data about any Backup and Restore jobs you run. The logs include information such as the time the tasks were started and stopped and whether they completed successfully. The status log in Windows 95 is found in the file Error.log. If you choose to overwrite the status log, then Error.log is deleted just before a Backup, Restore, or Compare is started. If not, Backup appends logs of backup operations, including backup or restore, to the end of the existing log. You also use the General page in the Settings - Options dialog box to arrange for Backup to overwrite status logs: just enable the Overwrite old status log files check box, or clear it if you want Backup to append logs to Error.log.

Drag-and-Drop Options

You should place a shortcut to Backup on your desktop as a reminder to back up regularly, as mentioned earlier in this chapter. Windows 95 makes backing up easy by letting you drag backup file sets to a Backup shortcut to launch a backup operation. All you have to do is open the folder that contains the backup file set and position the folder so you can see the shortcut to Backup. Next, drag the icon for the backup file set to the shortcut to Backup, which launches a backup operation of the files specified in the backup file set.

Backup provides a few options you can use to control this drag-and-drop behavior. Choose Settings, Drag and Drop to open the Settings - Drag and Drop dialog box, shown in figure 22.4. The following list explains the check-box options:

◆ **Run Backup minimized.** If you enable this check box, Backup runs minimized when you drag a file set to its icon. Otherwise, the Backup window remains on-screen during the drag-and-drop-initiated backup.

◆ **Confirm operation before beginning.** If you enable this check box, Backup confirms that you want to start a backup operation when you drag a backup file set to its icon. Otherwise, Backup starts immediately after you drop the backup file set.

◆ **Quit Backup after operation is finished.** If you don't enable this check box, Backup continues to run after it finishes the drag-and-drop-initiated backup.

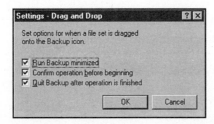

Figure 22.4

Use this dialog box to control Backup's behavior when you drag and drop a backup file set on the Backup icon.

File Filtering

Backup enables you to explicitly choose which files to back up and restore. You might decide you want to back up only certain types of files. Or, you might decide you want to always exclude a few types of files. Either way, you might not want to see every type of file listed in the Backup window from which you select files to back up and restore. The Backup utility enables you to specify which file types you want to appear here. To access this filtering functionality, choose Settings, File Filtering to open the File Filtering dialog box (see fig. 22.5).

Figure 22.5

The File Filtering dialog box enables you to select which file types to back up.

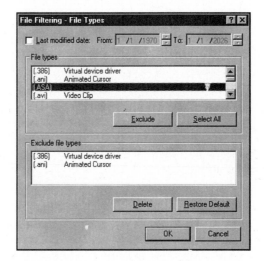

The File types list box shows the file types that appear in the Backup window. To specify that a file type not appear in the window, select the file type (.ASA, for example), then choose Exclude. You can select multiple file types by holding the Ctrl key as you select file types after the first one. You also can select a contiguous range of files by holding the Shift key while you click on the last file in the range. To select all file types in the list box, choose Select All.

Any file types you exclude appear in the Exclude file types list box. To restore a certain file type to appear in the Backup window (that is, to "de-exclude" a file type), select the file type, then choose the Delete button. To completely restore the original list of file types to appear in the Backup window, choose the Restore Default button.

You also can specify which files appear in the list of those you select for backup and restore based on the date the file was modified. To activate this option, enable the Last modified date check box near the upper left corner of the dialog box. Doing so activates the From and To date controls in the dialog box. You can enter the dates directly into the controls or you can use the spin controls to increment or decrement the dates by day.

Preparing to Back Up

Before you actually back up your data, you need to take care of a few chores. You must specify which files and/or folders to back up by explicitly choosing the files and/or folders or opening a backup file set. You also have a number of options you can use to control the backup operation. This section presents information to help you prepare to back up your data.

Specifying Files for Backup

The first step in preparing to back up data is to select the files and/or folders you intend to back up. You specify the files and/or folders in the Backup window, which appears when you start Backup and after you clear any of the introductory dialog boxes and prompts discussed in the "Starting Backup" section.

The Backup window contains three pages: Backup, Restore, and Compare. You do all the work that goes into backing up data from the Backup page (see fig. 22.6), so click on the Backup tab if you plan to back up data. The Backup page contains two primary areas: the Tree pane, which shows all objects in your system, and the Contents pane, which shows all objects selected for backup. In addition, two buttons that help you start the backup appear above the Contents pane.

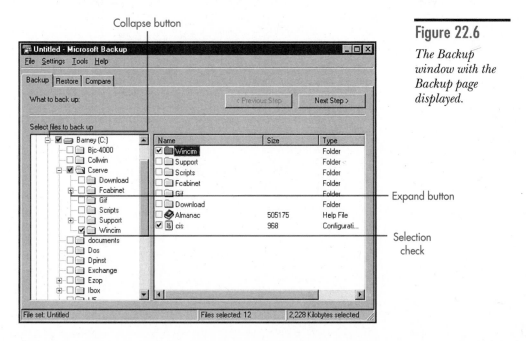

Figure 22.6

The Backup window with the Backup page displayed.

An *expand button* (a plus sign in a box) appears to the left of all objects in the Tree pane that you can open, such as folders. To use the plus button to display the contents of an object, click once on it. After you open an object, a *collapse button* (a minus sign in a box) replaces the expand button. To hide the contents of an object, click once on the collapse button. You also can open and close objects by double-clicking on their names.

A check box appears next to all objects in both panels. You use this check box to specify objects for backup, as explained in the next section.

Selecting files and/or folders you want to back up is one of the easiest things you can do in Backup. You can select any object in the left and right panes of the Backup window simply by enabling the check box next to the object's name. Or, you can use the object's context menu to select/deselect it for backup: just click on a folder or file and then right-click to open its context menu, then choose Tag/Untag as a toggle to select or deselect the object.

 Tip　Here's a simple rule to follow when you select files and/or folders for backup: choose entire folders and drives from the Tree pane and individual files and or folders from the Contents pane.

Windows 95 Backup does a good job of graphically presenting the file set you select for backup; for example:

◆ An object with a check in its box has been selected for backup.

◆ A folder with a check in its box has been selected for backup, as have all its contents.

◆ A folder with a check in its box, but with the box appearing with a gray background rather than white, has been selected for backup, but not all of its contents have been selected for backup.

◆ If you select a folder in the Tree pane for backup, all of its contents appear in the Contents pane also selected for backup.

◆ If you click on a folder or file already selected for backup, the check disappears from the box.

File Sets

A *backup file set* in Windows 95 is a group of files and/or folders that you back up regularly. You can create as many file sets as you like, or you might be content to use just one. You might have a file set for each day of the week, or you might have one file set of all the data on your system. To work with a particular backup file set, choose File, Open File set to activate the Open dialog box, then select a file set. Before you can open a file set, you need to create at least one file set. To create a backup file set, perform the following steps:

1. Select the files and/or folders you want to include in your file set.

2. Choose the Next Step button. The Tree pane switches to display the same organization of files and folders as displayed previously, but without the selecting check boxes.

3. Select the location where the backup file set will reside from the directory tree in the Tree pane.

4. Choose File, Save As to display the Save As dialog box. Type the name of the backup file set and then choose OK.

For more information on selecting a location for the backup files, see the section "Running Backup" later in this chapter.

Backup Options

Several options are available for specifically setting Backup's general behavior, such as the type of backup it performs, and whether it closes after executing, uses data compression, erases on tape backups, and so forth. To access these settings, choose Settings, Options to open the Settings - Options dialog box, then click on the Backup tab to display the Backup page (see fig. 22.7).

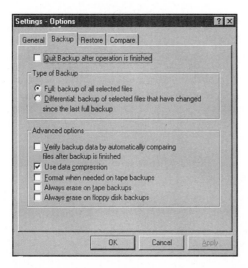

Figure 22.7

A number of options on the Backup property sheet enable you to control how Backup behaves during a backup operation.

Backup Type

In the Type of Backup area, choose the F**u**ll backup button option if you want Backup to back up every file in backup file set, or choose the **D**ifferential option button if you want it to back up only files that have changed since the last time you backed up.

You can use the options in the Advanced options group for settings that include ensuring that Backup functions to its full capacity by erasing backup media before usage; protecting against errors that might occur during backup, such as a momentary power loss, by comparing the backup to the original file set; and saving time by automatically formatting backup media before backing up if necessary. The following list reviews the check box options available in this area:

◆ **Verify backup data by automatically comparing files after backup is finished.** Use this check box option to specify that Backup compare the backed up version of the files to the original files in the file set immediately after it finishes the backup. This is a good way to ensure that files are properly backed up to the backup media.

◆ **Use data compression.** This option enables you to specify that any data compression software found on your system that Windows 95 recognizes be used to replace the compression algorithms that Backup uses by default.

◆ **Format when needed on tape backups.** Enable this check box to specify that Backup format any unformatted tapes you use as backup media. If you don't enable this setting, you must manually format tapes before you can start a backup.

◆ **Always erase on tape backups.** Enable this check box to specify for Backup to always erase a backup tape before the backup.

◆ **Always erase on floppy disk backups.** Enable this check box to specify that Backup always erase floppy disks before the backup.

The Backup Media

Another preparation for backing up is getting your backup media ready. If you use floppy disks, you need to have enough disks to accommodate all the data to be backed up. You might need a box of 10–20 disks if you perform a full backup of the full backup set. If you use tape (QIC-compatible only), you also need to have a tape that has enough memory to accommodate the data you plan to back up. If you plan to back up to a network drive, you should free up enough room for your data to fit. Backup informs you how much room you need to accommodate the data on the status bar, which updates as you select files and folders for backup.

Running Backup

At this point, you know how to specify files and/or folders for backup, and you understand the special options you can use. Following are the steps for backing up your data:

1. Prepare the target media; specify any options for backup, such as the type of backup (Full or Differential); and specify the files and folder to back up. You might need to make selections in the Backup window or open an existing backup file set.

2. In the Backup page, click on the Next Step button. The Contents pane changes to display a field in which the target location for the backup appears. The Tree pane still contains all the objects in your system, but the expand/collapse buttons and the selection check boxes disappear. If Backup detects a tape drive, it also appears in the Tree pane (see fig. 22.8). If you want to change the files and/or folders you select, click on the Previous Step button.

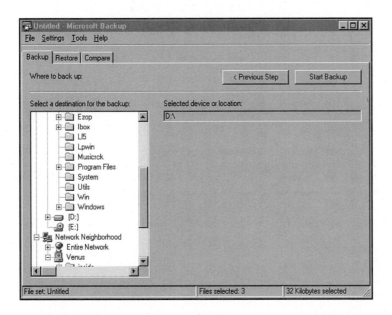

Figure 22.8

The Backup property sheet changes when you click on the Next Step button so that you can choose the target location for the backup files.

3. Select the target location for the backup in the Tree pane. As you select a folder in the Tree pane, its name appears in the Contents pane. You can select any object you see in the Tree pane, including a disk drive, a tape drive, a location on your hard drive, or a location on the network.

4. Click on the Start Backup button. Backup prompts you for the name of the backup set if you are not already using a predefined backup file set. Enter any name you like for the backup set. You also can protect against anyone viewing or updating data in the set by supplying a password.

Next, Backup starts the backup operation. On-screen graphics help you track the progress of the backup. After Backup finishes the job, a message in the Backup status box tells you that the backup operation is complete (see fig. 22.9). Choose OK to return to the Backup window. At this point, Backup has backed up the selected files and/or folders, and has updated (if you used an existing set) or created a backup file.

Figure 22.9

A message appears in the Backup status box when a backup operation has been completed.

Restoring Files from Backup

If disaster strikes and you must restore lost data, Windows 95 Backup soothes your pain. The restore process is relatively simple to use, and you have enough options to make Restore act the way you want. This section tells you how to restore data from backup media and how to use Restore's different features.

Working in the Restore Page

The Restore page (see fig. 22.10), in which you do all your work when restoring data, resembles the Backup property sheet (not to mention the Compare property sheet). The Tree pane presents all the objects in your system, and the Contents pane shows the contents of objects you select in the Tree pane.

You use the Restore page to specify the files and/or folders in a backup set that you want to restore. Just move through the objects in the Tree pane to select the location of backed up data, be it a floppy disk, tape drive, hard drive, or network location. Because you are on the Restore page, only Windows 95 backup file sets appear in the Contents pane. Select the backup file set you want to restore, then click on the Next Step button. The Tree and Contents panes change to give you a detailed view of the

contents of the backup file set you selected (see fig. 22.11). The Tree pane shows you the name of the backup file set, from where in your system the backup was created, and the directories that stored files that were backed up. The Contents pane shows the list of files in the backup file set. Now you can select the specific files you want to restore in the Contents pane.

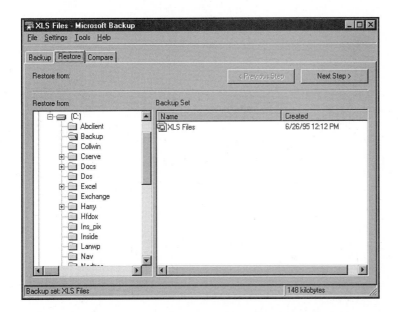

Figure 22.10

The Backup window with Restore page active.

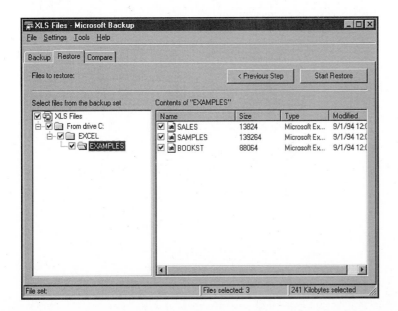

Figure 22.11

The Restore page displays all the files and folders contained in a backup file set.

Selecting Files to Restore

Selecting files to restore is similar to selecting files to back up. You can expand and collapse folders by clicking the plus or minus buttons, and you can select and deselect objects by enabling or disabling the selection check boxes to the left of the object names.

 Note You also can select and deselect any object by displaying its context menu and then choosing Tag/Untag.

The following visual cues can help you determine whether a file or folder has been selected for restoration:

◆ If an object has a check in its box, it has been selected for restoration.

◆ If a folder has a check in its box, it and all of its contents have been selected for restoration.

◆ If a folder has a check in its box but the box is grayed, then some but not all of its contents have been selected for restoration.

Restore Options

Several Restore options enable you to customize Restore's behavior. You can find them on the Restore page of the Settings - Options dialog box (see fig. 22.12), accessed by choosing Settings, Options and clicking on the Restore tab.

Figure 22.12

Restore options from the Settings - Options dialog box.

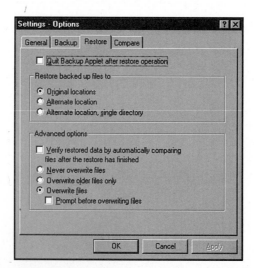

The following list explains the options in the Restore page:

◆ **Restored backed up files to.** This group provides three options you can use to specify where to restore the files. Choose the Original locations option to restore the files to the same location from which they were backed up. Using the Alternate location option, you also can specify to restore files to a new location for which Restore prompts you after the operation begins. If you choose a new location, you also can specify to restore all files to the root of a directory you specify, by using the Alternate location, single directory option.

◆ **Advanced options.** The options in this area enable you to control treatment of existing files during a restore. You can use the overwrite option buttons to specify that files by the same name as those you're about to restore are never overwritten (choose Never overwrite files), overwritten if their last modified date is older than the date of the file being restored (choose Overwrite older files only), or overwritten only with your permission (choose Overwrite files and enable the Prompt before overwriting files check box). The Advanced options group also contains the following check box:

   ◆ **Verify restored data by automatically comparing files after the restore has finished.** Enable this check box in the Advanced options group to specify that Backup compare files as they restore to the hard disk to the backed up version retained in the backup file sets. Backup alerts you if the files differ. Using this option lends a measure of verification to the restore process.

◆ **Quit Backup Applet after restore operation.** Use this check box at the top of the Restore page to specify that Backup shut down after completing a restore.

Restoring Data

After you select the files and folders you want to restore, and after you specify any special restore options, starting the restore operation is simple: click on the Start Restore button in the Backup window. If you choose the Never overwrite files option button in the Settings - Options dialog box, Restore prompts you for the location of the restored files. After Backup finishes the restore, it displays a message that informs you of whether the restore was a success. Choose OK to clear the message box and return to the Backup window.

Comparing Backup Sets to Files

Considering the increasing capacity and decreasing price of hard disks, you probably have more data on your hard disk than ever. If you've been diligent, you probably have backed up much or all of that data. The problem with backing up a large amount of data, however, is keeping the backup sets up-to-date. Somewhere along the line, you might need to check whether your backup sets contain all the files and/or folders you think they do, as well as whether you need to update any of the data on your hard disk because it has changed. The Compare feature in Windows 95 Backup helps compare backup file sets to the original files. This section shows you how to use Compare.

You compare backed-up data to original data from the Compare page, so if you want to compare backup data, click on the Compare tab in the Backup window. The Compare page (see fig. 22.13) resembles the Backup and Restore pages. The Tree pane shows all the objects in your system, and the Contents pane shows the contents of objects you select in the Tree pane.

Figure 22.13

*The Compare
page in the
Backup window.*

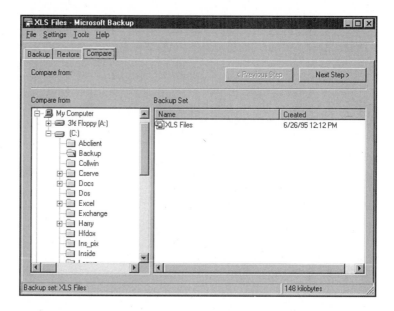

Compare Options

Backup supplies you with a few options for controlling Compare's behavior, and you can find them on the Compare page of the Settings - Options dialog box (see fig. 22.14).

Figure 22.14

Compare options from the Settings - Options dialog box.

The following list summarizes the Compare options:

◆ **Location of Compare.** The options in this frame enable you to specify the location of the files you want to compare to the files in the backup file set.

  ◆ **Original locations.** The files are in the same location as when the backup file set was created.

  ◆ **Alternate location.** The files are in a different location from when the backup file set was created. Windows 95 prompts you for the location with this option selected when you launch the Compare.

  ◆ **Alternate location, Single directory.** The files are in a different location from when the backup file set was created, and all the files are in a single directory regardless of the directory structure that was in place when the backup file set was created. Windows 95 prompts you for the location with this option selected when you launch the Compare.

◆ **Quit Backup Applet after compare operation.** Enable this check box if you want Backup to close out after completing the compare operation.

How to Compare Backup Sets

Comparing files to backup file sets is easy, especially if you already know how to use the Backup and/or Restore features. Here are the steps necessary to launch a compare:

1. From the Backup window, move through the list of objects on your system in the Tree pane to select the directory that contains the backup file set you want to use in the compare.

2. Select the backup file set in the Contents pane and click on the Next Step button.

3. Click in the appropriate selection check boxes to select the files and/or folders you want to compare to other files.

4. Click on the Start Compare button. Depending upon the Location of Compare option you specify, you might need to specify to what location to compare the file set.

Backup compares the files in the backup set to files by the same name in the location you specify. Backup alerts you of any mismatched files, including those it finds in the backup set but not in the target location.

Working with Multimedia Audio and CD-ROM

The term *multimedia* is becoming a household word, which is perhaps one of the primary reasons for the increase in the use of computers in the home. All the new power of modern computers and their capability to talk, listen, and play movies and music while you work has stimulated a tremendous growth spurt in applications geared to this new multimedia-aware market.

Of course, before you can take advantage of these new multimedia features, you need a sound board. Installing and configuring sound boards and other multimedia accessories has not always been easy, but Windows 95 does simplify this process. This chapter shows you how Windows 95 works with multimedia accessories by covering the following topics:

◆ Installing and configuring a sound card

◆ Working with the Media Player

◆ Playing audio CDs with the CD Player

The first section of this chapter shows you how to install and configure the software necessary to run your sound board. If you have not already installed the sound board in your machine, refer to the manufacturer's instructions for installing and connecting the various cables.

Installing and Configuring a Sound Card

To install the software for your sound board, open the Control Panel folder (choose Start, Settings, Control Panel) and choose the Add New Hardware wizard program. When you open the Add New Hardware wizard, you see the introductory dialog box. Click on the Next button to continue the installation of your sound card.

Next, the Add New Hardware Wizard dialog box appears (see fig. 23.1), in which you define the type of hardware you want to install into your system. If you choose the Automatically detect installed hardware option, Windows 95 tries to auto-detect your hardware, which can save you from needing to know much about the configuration details of your peripherals. To install just the sound card, though, choose the Install specific hardware radio button and select Sound, video and game controllers, as shown in figure 23.1. Click on the Next button to continue the installation.

Figure 23.1

The Add New Hardware Wizard dialog box.

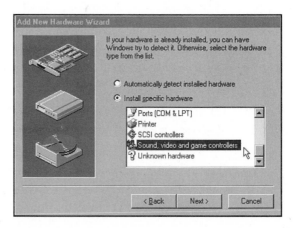

The next screen of the Add New Hardware wizard includes a Manufacturers list box and a corresponding Models list box (see fig. 23.2), which combine to indicate the hardware that Windows 95 can support without additional drivers or programs. Select the manufacturer of your sound board from the Manufacturers list box, and any supported sound cards they make appear in the Models list box. Figure 23.2 shows the Creative Labs Soundblaster family of products. If you don't find your sound board listed, you need to supply the drivers for the card. Choose the Have Disk button and follow the directions from your manufacturer to ensure proper installation of the drivers.

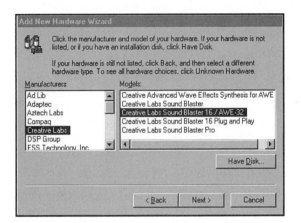

Figure 23.2

Choosing your sound board.

After you select your sound board or install the necessary drivers for a card that Windows doesn't natively support, click on the Next button to continue. Windows 95 tries to locate the sound card you chose, and shows you the Direct Memory Access (DMA) settings for 8- and 16-bit operation, the address of the card, and the Interrupt Request (IRQ) level it will use for the card (see fig. 23.3). This enables you to keep a reference of your components and identify potential conflicts in resources.

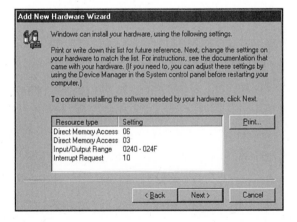

Figure 23.3

The settings for a Soundblaster 16 Pro.

Tip

It is always a good idea to write down the settings of the different cards installed in your system. This can make the identification of potential conflicts easy when installing new cards or devices. Always keep the list up to date. The list will serve no purpose if it is not updated each time you modify your system or settings.

Click on the Next button for Windows 95 to install the software necessary to support your new sound card. After Windows 95 finishes, it displays a dialog box that informs you it is done. Click on the Finish button to continue. You now must reboot your computer before the new configuration changes can take effect.

After rebooting your system, you should test it to make sure that it works properly. If you get errors on startup, chances are that Windows 95 is attempting to communicate through the wrong IRQ, a bad address, or to the wrong type of sound card. Windows 95's advanced configuration capabilities makes addressing all these problems rather simple. The following section on troubleshooting installations will illustrate the ease with which Windows 95 can help you identify these problems.

If you experience bootup problems, the following section on troubleshooting might offer some help for solving your problems. If Windows 95 installed your card properly, see section "Configuring the Volume Control" to test that the installation works as expected.

Troubleshooting Installations

If you don't get any sound from your sound card, several problems are possible. Your sound card might not be properly installed in your system. Check with your sound card user manuals to make sure that you have installed all cables correctly. If you're sure the card is installed properly, you might have a configuration conflict, which arises from more than one peripheral trying to use the same address, IRQ setting, or DMA channels.

Windows 95 installs your sound card with the factory defaults for the card. If you change the settings on your card, you must manually configure your sound card. You can do so by choosing the System icon in the Control Panel folder. Click on the Device Manager tab and highlight your sound card in the list of installed devices (see fig. 23.4).

You can double-click on the device in the list or highlight the choice and choose **P**roperties to open the property sheet for your sound card. The property sheet has three pages, each of which represents the different properties available for your sound card. The General page tells you if your card functions properly (see fig. 23.5). The Driver page (see fig. 23.6) lists the files required for proper operation of your sound card. You might need to choose a different driver, for example, if you change sound cards or choose the wrong driver when you initially install the card.

If you want to install a new driver, choose the **C**hange Driver button in the Driver page, which enables you to choose another type of sound board or use a driver disk supplied by a card manufacturer.

New Riders Publishing
INSIDE
SERIES

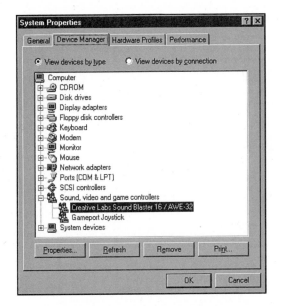

Figure 23.4

The Device Manager, showing the Soundblaster 16 Pro Driver highlighted.

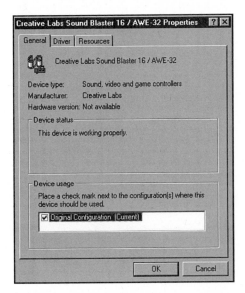

Figure 23.5

The General property page for a Soundblaster 16 Pro.

Note   Choosing the wrong card is easy enough when the same manufacturer makes many different models. This can sometimes make it seem like the installation went right, because Windows 95 recognizes the card as being from the correct manufacturer and doesn't protest, but you find out later that the driver and card combination just doesn't work right.

Figure 23.6

The Driver properties page for a Soundblaster 16 Pro.

Figure 23.6

The Driver properties page for a Soundblaster 16 Pro.

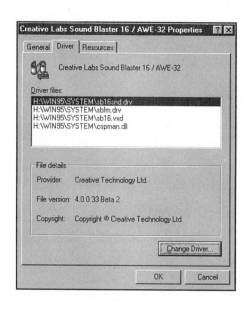

Unless you suspect that you have damaged drivers or have chosen the wrong drivers, you shouldn't need to reinstall the drivers. The most likely place to discover why your sound card isn't working is on the Resources property page (see fig. 23.7).

Figure 23.7

The Resources property page for a Soundblaster 16 Pro.

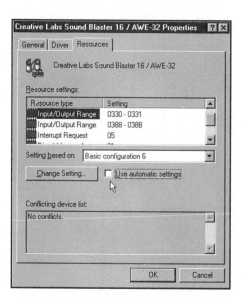

If you install your sound card with the default settings, the <u>U</u>se automatic settings check box is enabled and the <u>C</u>hange Setting button is disabled.

You can step through each item in the <u>R</u>esource settings list box and use the interactive Conflicting device list at the bottom of the page to see which setting is causing problems. After you uncover the conflicting setting, you can choose the <u>C</u>hange Settings button to manually set the values. Figure 23.8 shows a conflict with the network card.

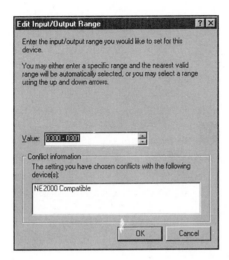

Figure 23.8

Conflicting addresses between sound and network cards.

You can use the <u>V</u>alue list's spin button to make another selection for your address, then save your choice by choosing OK.

Tip   When you change drivers or resource settings for any sound card, you should always check your documentation to see whether you need to update the card as well. Some cards auto-detect their settings from the drivers, others must be set using software, and still others must be changed on the card itself using jumpers or DIP switches.

Configuring the Volume Control

After you install your sound card and everything appears to run normally, you should test it to make sure that everything works as expected. This section explains how to configure the volume control and test your sound card.

Windows 95 has two built-in volume controls, both of which you can activate from the speaker icon that appears on the Taskbar. Clicking on the speaker icon enables you to access the master volume control (see fig. 23.9). This is probably the control that you will use most often, unless you plan to do a lot of multimedia recording and mixing.

Figure 23.9

The master volume control.

The master volume control handles the overall system volume. The second volume control resembles a stereo mixer, and is an application called Volume Control (see fig. 23.10). You can access the Volume Control application by double-clicking on the speaker icon. Both the master volume control and the Volume Control application can be used to control the volume in your system. The Volume Control application provides the capability to control the volume of individual devices as well as the overall system volume. As shown in figure 23.10, a Volume Control section appears on the left side of the application. This Volume Control and the master system volume control perform the same functions.

Figure 23.10

The Volume Control application.

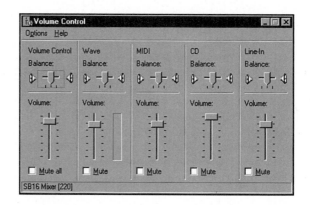

To see how both of the volume controls work, display the Sounds property sheet (see fig. 23.11) by choosing the Sounds icon in Control Panel, and experiment with a few of the WAV files in Windows 95. The Events list shows the different Windows 95 events to which you can attach sounds. Events denoted by a speaker have a sound attached to them. To find out the sound attached to an event, highlight the event and the sound name appears in the Sound area. Asterisk, highlighted in figure 23.11, for example, has the Chord WAV associated to it, shown in the Name list box in the Sound area. By clicking on the play button in the preview section of the Sounds property sheet, you can hear the sound associated with that event. Try playing a sound at different volume levels to get a feel for the range of your sound card. Many different sound schemes are available, and you can even create your own. The following section, "Using Sound Schemes," covers creating your own sound schemes.

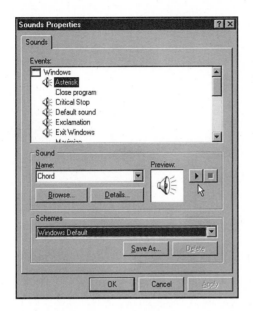

Figure 23.11

The Sounds property sheet.

To experiment in this dialog box, highlight an event to which a sound is associated and click on the play button (the arrow) in the Preview area. If you can't hear the sound, bring up the volume control by right-clicking on the speaker icon in the Taskbar and adjusting the volume.

Using Sound Schemes

Windows 95 has certain system events to which sounds can be attached. The events available can be viewed in the Sounds property sheet, shown earlier in figure 23.11. A *sound scheme* is a certain combination of events and the sounds associated with them. If you are familiar or comfortable with the sounds that were the default in Windows 3.1 you might want to use the Windows Default sound scheme. The following section shows you how you can customize an existing sound scheme or create your own.

Using an Existing Scheme

Windows 95 includes five predefined sound schemes that you can select to help you customize your system: Musica, Windows Default, Nature, Robotz, and Utopia. (There also is a No Sounds setting, which disables system sounds.) To test the different schemes, select the scheme you want to try from the Schemes list box in the Sounds property sheet (refer to figure 23.11), and choose the Apply button. You now can try out the scheme simply by opening a minimized application or performing any other task to which a sound is associated.

You can choose any of the predefined sound schemes if you like one of them; if not, you can create your own.

Creating a Custom Scheme

If you want to create your own personal sound scheme in Windows 95, all you have to do is to associate the events you want with the sounds you choose. The easiest way to do this is to choose the No Sounds scheme, and save it to a new name, which gives you a blank template with which to create your own sound scheme.

To associate an event and a sound, in the Sounds property sheet, select an event from the Events list box and a sound from the Sound area's Name list box. When you select the sound, a speaker icon appears next to the event to which you just associated the sound. You can mix and match any of the system sounds that come with Windows 95, or you can choose your own sounds.

 Note   Before you can use your own WAV files, you must have them on your hard drive. Windows 95 needs to be able to find them every time you boot. Choosing a WAV file located on a CD can cause problems. If the CD isn't always in the player, Windows 95 can't always use it.

If you want to use sounds other than the ones that come with Windows 95, you must first choose the event to which you want to associate the sound. Next, choose the Browse button to display the Browse dialog box shown in figure 23.12.

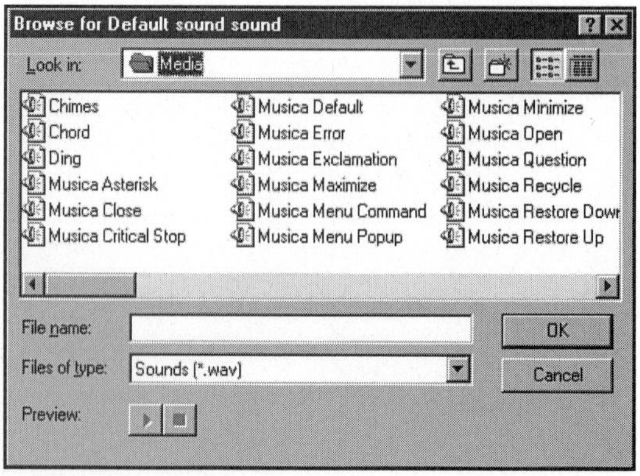

Figure 23.12

Finding other sounds to use in sound schemes.

Using no sound scheme in Windows 95 is very easy. Simply select the No Sounds scheme from the Schemes list, just like choosing any other sound scheme, and choose OK. Your system now makes no interesting sounds—period.

Using the Media Player

The Media Player that comes with Windows 95 is a very versatile application that enables you to play different types of multimedia files. These files can be video files that have an Avi extension, audio files that have a Wav extension, or MIDI files, which have an Mid extension.

You start the Media Player by choosing Start, Programs, Accessories, Multimedia, and then Media Player. Before the Media player can know the type of file you want to play, you must select the device you want the player to use. The Device menu, shown in figure 23.13, provides the choices of devices supported by the Media Player.

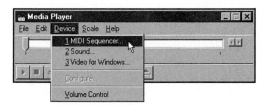

Figure 23.13

Devices supported by the Media Player.

The MIDI Sequencer

To use the Media Player to play MID files, choose MIDI Sequencer, the first item in the Device menu. You can use this personality of the Media Player to play any musical files that have the extension MID. When you choose MIDI Sequencer, a File Open dialog box appears. The Media Player needs to know which file you want to play. Windows 95 comes with two sample MIDI files: Canyon and Passport. You can choose either file to test the MIDI sequencer.

Playing MIDI Files

After you choose a file, you can use the play button to play back the file. The Media Player's button controls emulate typical stereo controls. If you are unsure of what function a button performs, position the cursor over the button to display a ToolTip that tells you what the control does (see fig. 23.14).

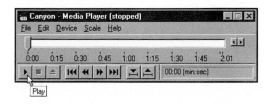

Figure 23.14

The MIDI Sequencer and a ToolTip.

Click on the play button to hear the MIDI file play. You have complete control over playback. If you want to pause, stop, or close this file, you need only click on the appropriate button.

Setting MIDI Properties

You do have some control over the different properties of the MIDI Sequencer, by choosing **D**evice, **C**onfigure. With the options available, you can choose to add schemes for new instruments, or you can customize the existing scheme. Unless you use MIDI instruments, you really don't need to change these defaults. The default settings will enable you to play all MIDI files; all others require a MIDI instrument.

Playing Sound (WAV) Files

You can use the Media Player to play any file that has the extension of WAV. Choosing **D**evice, **2** Sound opens a File Open dialog box, in which you need to choose a WAV file. After you choose a file, you can use the Media Player to play and manipulate the sound files.

To use the Media Player to play sound files, choose Sound from the Media Players **D**evice menu, which gives you list of files similar to those shown in figure 23.15.

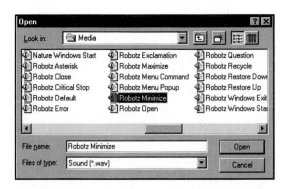

After you choose a file, you can use the Media Player controls just as you to play a MIDI file (see the preceding section).

MCI Waveform Driver Setup

Windows 95 and its support for multimedia uses the Media Control Interface (MCI). This interface uses a driver to buffer the audio and video so that the Media Player is never waiting for the next segment to be played. The default value for this buffer is four seconds. This means that when you are playing a file that is longer than four

seconds, the MCI Waveform Driver will always read in four seconds of data at a time and keep this amount buffered for playback.

For most users, the default of four seconds is just fine. But if you find yourself needing or wanting to have a larger buffer for playback, you can adjust this value between two and nine seconds. Keep in mind that the larger the buffer, the more memory will be required for the buffer.

With the Sound device chosen, choose <u>D</u>evice, <u>C</u>onfigure to open a dialog box similar to the one shown in figure 23.16. You can change the amount of data the MCI driver buffers by adjusting the slider shown in figure 23.16.

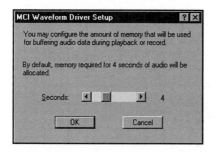

Figure 23.16

The MCI Waveform Driver Setup.

Although you can use the Media Player to play audio CD's, the CD Player that comes with the Multimedia extensions of Windows 95 is much more powerful and easy to use.

Playing Audio CDs with the CD Player

In Windows 3.1, there is no CD Player. The Media Player is what you need to use to play your CDs if you do not have another program to use. Most sound cards and CD drives usually come bundled with software that will enable you to play your CDs. With Windows 95, these programs are not necessary because of the built-in CD Player. In this section you will see how to use the basic features of the CD Player.

One of the easiest ways to launch the CD Player is to insert an audio CD into your CD-ROM drive. Windows 95's AutoPlay feature automatically detects the audio CD and launches the CD Player, shown in figure 23.17.

The CD Player in Windows 95 resembles the one you might already have in your home. When you stop or pause the CD, clicking on the Play button begins, or resumes, play. When the CD is playing, the Play button is disabled. The Pause button, to the right of the Play button, suspends play. You can restart play by clicking on the Play button.

Figure 23.17

The Windows 95 CD Player.

Changing Tracks

You can change tracks several different ways with the CD Player, the easiest being to use the Previous and Next Track buttons. Choosing these buttons enables you to skip forward or backward through your CD until you find the song you want.

You also can select a particular track from the playlist of available tracks in the Track drop-down list (see fig. 23.18). You might prefer this method to surfing through all the tracks until you find the one you want.

Figure 23.18

The track list of the CD Player.

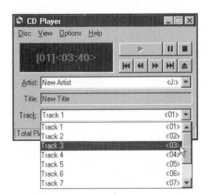

Setting the Play Order

Another feature of the CD Player is that it allows you to select the order in which you hear your songs. Much like the shuffle play of commercial home CD Players, the Windows 95 CD Player supports random play. Choosing the Random Play option will shuffle the songs on the CD and then play them. To enable Random Play, choose Options, Random Order. This will not change the song that you are currently listening to, but the remainder of the songs on the CD will be played in a random order.

Changing the Look of Your CD Player

You can customize the look of your CD Player to suit your own particular tastes by using the options in the View menu. The menu is divided into several groupings. The first grouping represents different items that you can turn on or off: Toolbar (off by default), Disc/Track Info, and Status Bar. Figure 23.19 shows the CD Player with all options chosen, and figure 23.20 shows the CD Player with all options turned off.

Figure 23.19

The CD Player with all options on.

Figure 23.20

The CD Player with all options off.

Storing CD Titles, Tracks, and Artists

One of the nicest features of computer-based CD players is the capability to maintain a database of your CDs. You can edit the playlist of any CD, and Windows 95 stores this information in a database. Then, when you next play the CD, Windows 95 knows to use your edited playlist.

To edit a CD's information, choose Disc, Edit Play List to display the Disc Settings dialog box (see fig. 23.21). Setting CD information is easy and straightforward. Each CD contains a unique number embedded into the CD that distinguishes it from any other CD. First, type the artist's name in the Artist text box, then type the title in the Title text box. Choose OK to save the artist and title. The next time you want to play the CD, this information automatically appears.

To set a playlist for a CD, choose the track number from the Available Tracks list. This is done by clicking on the desired track in the Available Track list to highlight it. The name assigned to this track will appear in the Entry field marked TrackXX, where the XX stands for the track number that you have chosen. Simply type in the track name and choose the Set Name button.

Figure 23.21

The Disc Settings dialog box of the CD Player.

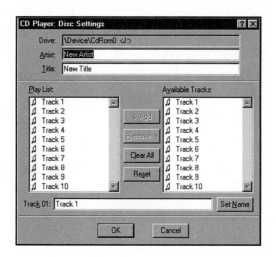

Part V

Integration and Automation

C H A P T E R

24

Exchanging Data between Applications

One of the advantages of the Windows 95 environment (and Windows 3.*x* before it) is the capability to share data among documents, even documents created using different applications. Windows 95 makes copying data from one document to another as simple as pressing a few keys.

This chapter begins with a look at *scraps,* a new mechanism in Windows 95 that enables you to copy data between OLE-aware applications using drag-and-drop. This chapter also explores static data exchange in Windows 95 through the Clipboard. Although it isn't necessary to understand how the Clipboard works in order to use it, understanding how it works will help you realize some of its limitations and behavior. To help you understand data exchange, this chapter covers the following topics:

◆ Exchanging data through document scraps

◆ Understanding the Clipboard

◆ Using Clipboard data formats

◆ Exchanging data between Windows applications

◆ Tips for using the Clipboard Viewer

◆ Exchanging data across the network

The Clipboard is an extremely useful tool for sharing data among applications. Other methods, such as OLE and DDE, offer better alternatives in some situations. For more information on OLE and DDE, refer to Chapter 25, "Understanding and Using OLE," and Chapter 26, "Understanding and Using DDE."

Understanding and Using Document Scraps

Although you can use the Clipboard to copy data from one document or application to another, Windows 95 adds a new method for transferring data, called *document scraps*. A document scrap is exactly what its name implies—a scrap, or portion, of a document.

Document scraps enable you to use the OLE and drag-and-drop capability built into Windows 95 and OLE-aware applications to copy data from document to document simply by dragging the data with the cursor. In addition, you also can copy data to the desktop or to a folder, creating a new file that contains the data.

Copying between Document and Application Windows

Using scraps to copy data between documents and applications is simple, but it does require that the application or applications involved in the data transfer support OLE. Most of the common applications for word processing, spreadsheets, and other productivity applications support OLE, as do many of the more specialized applications. Even applications written for Windows 3.*x*, such as Word 6.0 for example, can support data exchange through scraps.

To copy data between two open document windows within an application or between two applications, use the following procedure:

1. In the source document, select the data you want to copy.

2. Click on the data and drag the data to the other document or application window.

3. Release the mouse button, and the data will be copied to the destination document.

Note As you are dragging the data, you probably will notice that the pointer changes to show a small rectangle attached to the standard mouse pointer. This pointer indicates that you are dragging data with the cursor. When the cursor moves outside of the source application's window, the cursor changes again to include a small plus sign (+), indicating that you are copying the data.

Copying to the Taskbar

If you are working from an application that is maximized, you won't be able to see the application window of the document to which you want to copy data. The application's tile will appear in the Taskbar, however, which enables you to copy the data to the application.

After you select the data you want to copy from the source application, drag the data onto the destination application's tile on the Taskbar. Instead of releasing the mouse button, hold the pointer over the tile. After a second, the application will open, and you can drag the data into the application's document window.

Note You can't drop the data on the application's tile in the Taskbar. You must hold the pointer over the tile, then release the data in the destination window after it opens.

Creating Documents on the Desktop and in Folders

Windows 95 enables you to quickly create a new document from a scrap. If you drag data from an application and release it on the desktop, Windows 95 creates a new document file on the desktop that contains the copied data. You also can drag a scrap into a folder window, onto a folder icon, or onto a disk or folder shortcut.

Understanding the Clipboard

Many Windows users think of the Clipboard as an application—namely, the Clipboard Viewer. The Clipboard actually is a class of API (application programming interface) functions located in the USER library that manages data exchange between applications. The Clipboard Viewer is simply an application that enables you to view the content of the Clipboard, which resides in your PC's memory. You don't need to use the Clipboard Viewer to exchange data between applications, but it can help you understand how the Clipboard works by giving you a peek inside it.

To open the Clipboard Viewer in Windows 95, choose the Start button, then choose
Programs, Accessories, and Clipboard Viewer. Or, run the program Clipbrd.exe in
the Windows directory. Figure 24.1 shows the Clipboard Viewer with some text on the
Clipboard.

Figure 24.1

*The Clipboard
Viewer with text
on the Clipboard.*

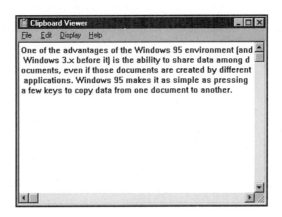

 Note   Depending on the options you selected when you installed Windows 95, the
Clipboard Viewer application might not be installed on your system. If you try to
run Clipbrd.exe and receive an error message, use the Add/Remove Programs
object in the Control Panel to add the Clipboard Viewer.

Later in this chapter, you can read about data formats and how you can use the
Clipboard Viewer to view data in different formats. First, though, the following
sections explain how easily you can move data between Windows applications by
using the Clipboard.

Using the Clipboard

You don't have to open the Clipboard Viewer to copy data between documents or
applications. Most applications include an Edit menu that contains the commands for
using the Clipboard. The following common commands appear in an application's
Edit menu if the application supports the Clipboard:

◆ **Cut.** Removes the selection from the active window and places it in the
Clipboard.

◆ **Copy.** Copies the selection from the active window to the Clipboard.

◆ **Paste.** Inserts the contents of the Clipboard to the active widow at the cursor's
position.

Each Clipboard command uses a standard shortcut key combination, which means you can cut, copy, and paste information without even opening the Edit menu. Each command actually has two shortcut combinations, as shown in table 24.1. The second set of shortcut keys are holdovers from Windows 3.0.

TABLE 24.1
Cut, Copy, and Paste Shortcut Keys

Command	New Shortcut	Old Shortcut
Cut	Ctrl+X	Shift+Del
Copy	Ctrl+C	Ctrl+Ins
Paste	Ctrl+V	Shift+Ins

Any standard Windows application, whether written for Windows 3.*x* or Windows 95, should support the new shortcut keys listed in table 24.1. Many applications also support the older shortcut keys, but some do not.

Copying Data

What can you do with the Clipboard? The Clipboard enables static data exchanges between applications. In a *static exchange,* the data does not update automatically once the exchange takes place. If you copy a drawing from a graphics program to a report, for example, then change the drawing in the graphics program, it does not automatically update in the report. Often, however, these types of static exchange are adequate.

Note　Object Linking and Embedding (OLE) and Dynamic Data Exchange (DDE) enable automated and dynamic exchange of data in which documents update automatically when the source data changes. For more information on OLE and DDE, refer to Chapters 25 and 26.

The Clipboard enables you to copy text, graphics, and other types of data from one place to another in a document, between two documents, or even between applications. You can copy an illustration from a drawing program to a report you created using a word processor, for example, and also copy charts and numeric data from a spreadsheet to the report (see fig. 24.2). The Clipboard, therefore, enables you to reuse data without having to re-create the data each time you need it in a new document. This not only saves time, but also eliminates errors that might creep into the data each time you re-create it.

Figure 24.2

Spreadsheet data copied to a report.

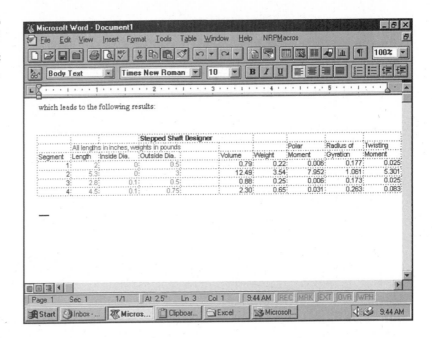

Figure 24.2

Spreadsheet data copied to a report.

Tip

The Clipboard is not limited to copying just text, graphics, and spreadsheet data. You can use the Clipboard to copy nearly any type of data—including sounds, files, and other objects—from one document to another.

Using the Clipboard to copy data is so easy that it generally requires very little explanation. You simply select the data you want to copy to the Clipboard, then choose **E**dit, **C**opy, or choose **E**dit, Cu**t**, depending on whether you want to copy the data from the source document or remove the data. Either choice places the data on the Clipboard. Then, you place the cursor in the location in the destination document in which you want to insert the data, and choose **E**dit, **P**aste. Windows 95 copies the data from the Clipboard to the document.

Note

If you place data on the Clipboard, then open the **E**dit menu and find the **P**aste command dimmed, the destination application doesn't support the data type stored in the Clipboard. This means you can't copy the data to the document. If you copy text to the Clipboard, for example, then try to paste the text into a graphics program that accepts only bitmap data, the graphics program's **P**aste command appears dimmed and you can't paste the text into the graphics program.

A little experimentation will show you that you can use the Clipboard to copy some very complex types of data between applications. One relatively simple example is the

capability to copy text from one word processor to another without losing character and paragraph formatting. How does the Clipboard "know" how to retain those special data formats? The answer lies in the way applications place data on the Clipboard, explained in the following section.

Using Clipboard Data Formats

If you've ever tried to use one application to open a document from another application, such as using WordPerfect to open a Word for Windows file, you've probably found that the data was garbled because the applications' data formats are different. How can you copy data from one application to another at all, and even retain special formatting, if those data formats are different? The answer is multiple common data formats.

When you copy data from an application to the Clipboard, the application typically places the data in the Clipboard in multiple formats. If you copy some text from WordPad to the Clipboard, for example, WordPad places the data in the Clipboard in 14 different formats. These formats include plain text, formatted text, graphics, and other special formats to enable WordPad to support OLE (explained in Chapter 25, "Understanding and Using OLE"). You can see an example of these multiple formats using WordPad and the Clipboard Viewer:

1. Open WordPad and type a few lines of text.

2. Select the text in WordPad, then choose Edit, Copy or press Ctrl+C to copy the text to the Clipboard.

3. Open the Clipboard Viewer by choosing Start, Programs, Accessories, and Clipboard Viewer.

4. In the Clipboard Viewer, choose the Display menu and note the different formats listed in the menu.

5. From the Display menu, choose the OEM Text item to display the contents of the Clipboard using the OEM character set.

Many of the data types listed in the Display menu appear dimmed because they are not displayable. However, the data formats really are contained in the Clipboard, and an application that supports these data types can retrieve the data from the Clipboard and use the necessary format.

Many different standard Clipboard data formats exist, and applications can create and support their own data types. Table 24.2 lists some of the most common Clipboard data formats. Many other data formats also exist—table 24.2 lists only the most common types.

TABLE 24.2
Common Clipboard Data Formats

Data Type	Format	Description
(varies)	Owner	Identifies data stored in a format that requires the source application to be running. If the source application is closed, you cannot display the data in Owner format.
	Native	Identifies data stored in a source application's internal, native data format.
Text	Text	Identifies unformatted text using the ANSI character set.
	OEM Text	Identifies unformatted text using the Original Equipment Manufacturer (OEM) character set.
	RTF Text	Identifies formatted text (including typeface and font style specifications) in Microsoft's Rich Text Format (RTF).
Spreadsheet/ Database	SYLK	Identifies tabular data in Microsoft's Symbolic Link format (used by older Microsoft applications, such as early versions of Excel).
	DIF	Identifies data stored in Software Arts' Data Interchange Format (DIF). Originally used to transfer VisiCalc data, but now used for transferring Lotus 1-2-3 data.
	BIFF	Identifies data in Microsoft Binary File Format (BIFF). BIFF is used for transferring Excel data.
	WK1	Identifies spreadsheet data stored in Lotus 1-2-3 version 2 format.
	CSV	Identifies data stored in Comma-Separated Variable (CSV) format. Each line consists of comma-delimited spreadsheet cells or database fields, and is terminated with a carriage return and line feed.
Graphics	Bitmap	Identifies graphical data stored as a bitmap image. A *bitmap* consists of a series of small dots, or *pixels*.
	DIB	Identifies a Device-Independent Bitmap (DIB). Unlike a normal bitmap, a DIB image is independent of the device on which it is displayed.

Data Type	Format	Description
	Picture	Identifies graphical data stored as a metafile. In contrast with a bitmap, a *picture* consists of a series of drawing commands from the Windows 95 Graphical Device Interface (GDI). These commands are stored and generate an image each time you view or use the graphic.
	Palette	Identifies a Windows color palette. A palette can be stored in the Clipboard with a graphic image.
	TIFF	Identifies information stored in Tag Image File Format.
Sound	WAVE	Identifies waveform data, the standard Windows 95 sound format.
Link	Link	Identifies data that can be linked using OLE and DDE.
	OwnerLink	Identifies a data object that can be embedded through OLE in a compound document. OwnerLink contains an object's class, document name, and object name.
	ObjectLink	Identifies a data object that can be linked through OLE into a compound document. ObjectLink format contains an object's class, document name, and object name.

Typical Windows applications most often use the Owner, Text, and Graphics formats. The following sections explain these formats. The section "Pasting Data with a Specific Format" later in this chapter explains how you can choose a specific format to paste in a document.

Owner Format

You can use the Owner format for text and graphical data. If you select the Owner item from the Display menu, a source application that copies Owner format data to the Clipboard is responsible for displaying that data in the Clipboard Viewer. The Clipboard depends on the source application to display the data, so if you close the source application, you lose the Owner format. You can see an example of this by copying data from WordPad to the Clipboard, then closing WordPad. You have 14 data formats in the Clipboard when WordPad is open, but only 5 when WordPad is closed.

Text Formats

Word processing applications typically send text to the Clipboard in numerous formats, including the three most common, described in the following list:

◆ **Text format.** Consists of unformatted ASCII characters. Each line of text ends with a carriage return and linefeed character. The Clipboard Viewer uses the system font to display text format. Applications that support only unformatted ASCII characters, such as Notepad, can use the text format to exchange data. In addition, you can use the text format to exchange data between other word processors that do not support any other common format.

◆ **OEM Text format.** Consists of unformatted characters in the OEM character set, which is based on the U.S. code page 437. In the OEM character format, each line ends with a carriage return and linefeed character.

Note   You can't display all the characters from the OEM character set if you use an ANSI font. Although the ANSI and OEM character sets use the same characters in positions 32–127 for most of the code pages, OEM characters 0–31 and 128–255 do not have ANSI equivalents, or the equivalents are in a different position from the corresponding ANSI characters. As a result, if you want to display nonmatching characters, you must use OEM Text format.

◆ **Rich Text Format (RTF).** Retains formatting characteristics, such as typeface, point size, and font style (bold, italic, underline, and so on). If both the source and destination applications support RTF, you can cut, copy, and paste between the applications without losing text formatting.

Graphics Formats

Many graphics applications place data in the Clipboard in Owner format, but most of them also include common formats, such as Bitmap and Metafile, as well as a palette. The following list includes explanations of the bitmap, metafile, and palette types:

◆ **Bitmap.** A *bitmap* image consists of a series of dots, or picture elements (pixels). A *pixel* is the smallest picture element the computer can recognize. A bitmap is stored as a table of numeric values and other data that defines the location and color of each pixel in the image—this table is referred to as a *map*, and each element in the table is defined by one or more *bits*; thus the term bitmap. Figure 24.3 shows a bitmap image.

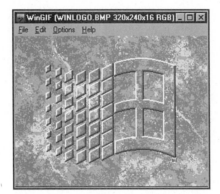

Figure 24.3

A simple bitmap image.

The file size of a bitmap depends on the size of the bitmap and its color depth. An image that uses 64,000 colors, for example, has a larger file size than the same image in 16 colors. In addition, you can't scale or stretch a bitmap without decreasing its original resolution and quality. Figures 24.4 and 24.5 illustrate what happens when you resize a bitmap.

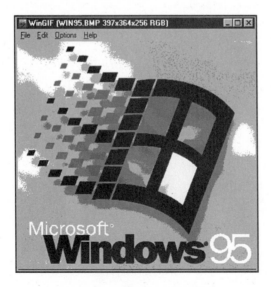

Figure 24.4

A bitmap before you resize it.

Tip

You can scale a bitmap with a minimum loss of image quality and resolution, but you have to use a special image editing program to do it. One such program, Smooth Scaling from WexTech Systems (800-WEX-TECH or 212-949-9595), enables you to reduce a bitmap as much as 90 percent without a loss of clarity.

Figure 24.5

A bitmap after you resize it.

◆ **Metafile.** A *metafile* image consists of GDI drawing commands that produce various graphical objects, such as lines, circles, curves, and filled areas. When you place a metafile in a document or view a metafile in the Clipboard Viewer, the Windows 95 GDI renders the image by "replaying" the GDI commands contained in the metafile. Because you render an image from drawing commands, you can scale and resize a metafile image without losing any clarity or resolution. And because the GDI commands are an integral part of the Windows 95 core, the source application isn't required before you can display the metafile. Figures 24.6 and 24.7 illustrate what happens when you resize a metafile.

◆ **Palette.** A palette is stored in the Clipboard each time you copy an image to the Clipboard. Windows 95 and the Clipboard Viewer use the palette to render the image. 16-color images all use the same standard 16-color VGA palette. Images that use more than 16 colors, however, use a different palette from one image to the next.

Figure 24.6

A metafile before resizing.

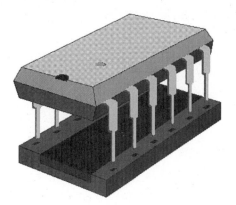

Figure 24.7

A metafile after resizing.

Pasting Data with a Specific Format

You might wonder, what with so many potential data formats in the Clipboard, how the receiving application determines which format to use. Typically, each application has a default data type that it uses automatically if you do not specify otherwise. Notepad, for example, supports only plain text, so Notepad always uses the Text format during pastes. Therefore, when you choose Edit, Paste, the application pastes the data from the Clipboard to the current document in the receiving application's default format, which is integral to the application and not something you can change.

You often can paste data from the Clipboard to a document in a format other than the application's default format, however. To do so, choose Edit, Paste Special. A dialog box appears, similar to the one shown in figure 24.8, in which you choose the format you want to use to paste the data into the document. If the application has no Paste Special command in its Edit menu, the application pastes using only its default format.

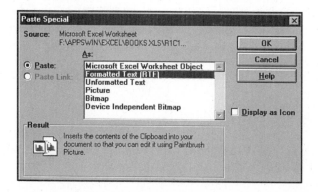

Figure 24.8

A typical Paste Special dialog box.

Tips for Using the Clipboard

Earlier in this chapter you learned how to open the Clipboard Viewer and use it to view the contents of the Clipboard in various formats. This section of the chapter offers a few tips for using the Clipboard Viewer to control the contents of the Clipboard and save those contents to disk.

Clearing the Clipboard

Normally when you copy data to the Clipboard, that data remains in the Clipboard until you place something else in it. The data usually remains in the Clipboard even after you close the source application. Depending on the application and data formats it places in the Clipboard, you might lose some formats after the application closes, but the data typically remains in the Clipboard in at least a few formats.

Some applications place very complex and numerous data formats in the Clipboard, and you also can place a very large amount of data in the Clipboard. The more formats used and the more data in the Clipboard, the more memory required to maintain that data, even after the application closes. Because of this, being able to clear the contents of the Clipboard and free up the memory for other applications sometimes proves helpful.

To clear the contents of the Clipboard, open the Clipboard Viewer and choose <u>E</u>dit, <u>D</u>elete, or simply open the Clipboard and press the Del key. The Clipboard Viewer displays a dialog box that asks you if you want to clear the contents of the Clipboard. Choose <u>Y</u>es to clear the Clipboard, or <u>N</u>o to cancel the operation.

Tip If you have an application open and want to clear the contents of the Clipboard without opening the Clipboard Viewer, simply select a small amount of data in the application and press Ctrl+C to copy the data to the Clipboard. The new data replaces any other data previously stored in the Clipboard. If you want to be able to open the Clipboard Viewer quickly, create a shortcut to the Clipboard Viewer on your desktop and assign a shortcut key to the shortcut. Press the shortcut key whenever you want to open the Clipboard Viewer.

Saving the Clipboard to Disk

You might encounter situations in which you need to save the data in the Clipboard to use later. You might have some data in the Clipboard, for example, but need to place some additional data in the Clipboard without losing the current data. For

these situations, the Clipboard Viewer enables you to save the contents of the Clipboard to disk. To save the contents of the Clipboard to disk, open the Clipboard Viewer and choose <u>F</u>ile, Save <u>A</u>s. The Clipboard Viewer then displays a standard Save As dialog box you can use to specify a file name for the Clipboard data. Enter a file name, then choose OK.

Tip Unlike other Windows 95 applets, the Clipboard Viewer does not support long file names—you must enter a file name using standard short file-name format. The Clipboard Viewer automatically appends a file extension of CLP onto the file.

Clipboard files are somewhat limited. A CLP file is relatively device-dependent. If you capture a 24-bit image to the Clipboard, then save the contents of the Clipboard to a CLP file, the image's palette also is saved. If you try to paste the same image from the CLP file while using a 256-color display, however, the image remaps to 256 colors and consequently loses considerable image quality. If you attempt to view the image in the Clipboard Viewer, you can view the image in Palette and DIB formats, but not in Bitmap format. In addition, the DIB format displays the image using a 256-color palette.

Text stored in the Clipboard and saved to a CLP generally does not have any limitations, however. Text formatting is saved in the CLP file, enabling you to retain the text formatting even if the source application is no longer open.

Capturing the Display with the Clipboard

If you need to capture the display, but don't have a screen capture program (or for some reason your screen capture program won't work), you can use the Clipboard to capture the display. Capturing the display to the Clipboard stores the image in the Clipboard in bitmap formats (Bitmap, DIB, and Palette). After you capture the display to the Clipboard, you can paste the image into Paint or another graphics application, then use that application to save the image to disk in a specific file format (such as BMP, PCX, GIF, and so on).

To capture the entire display to the Clipboard, press the Prnt Scrn key. To capture the current window or a dialog box rather than the entire display, press Alt+Print Scrn.

Tip You can't capture a single child window in a MDI (multiple document interface) application, such as Word, Excel, or any other MDI application. Instead of capturing the current child window, pressing Alt+Print Scrn captures the active parent window.

Copying Files with the Clipboard

Windows 95 adds a new capability to the Clipboard that enables you to copy files and folders without using the Explorer or File Manager applications. If you have a folder or Explorer window open, you can select multiple objects, including folders and files, then press Ctrl+C to copy the list of selected objects to the Clipboard. Then, you can open a different folder or Explorer window and press Ctrl+V to copy the objects to the current folder.

Exchanging Data across the Network

Besides being able to copy data from one document or application to another on your own PC, you can share data between multiple PCs on a LAN by using an optional Windows 95 program called the ClipBook Viewer. The ClipBook Viewer application and the ClipBook Server application (Clipsrv.exe) are located on the Windows 95 CD in the \Other\Clipbook folder.

Tip   The ClipBook Viewer in Windows 95 is functionally identical to the ClipBook Viewer application in Windows for Workgroups.

The ClipBook Viewer program combines the Clipboard Viewer with a new feature called ClipBooks. ClipBooks are similar to a multipage Clipboard, but you can do more with them than just maintain multiple items and quickly place them in the Clipboard for local use. ClipBooks enable you to share data with other users on remote nodes. Figure 24.9 shows the ClipBook Viewer.

Figure 24.9

The ClipBook Viewer enables you to share data with other computers.

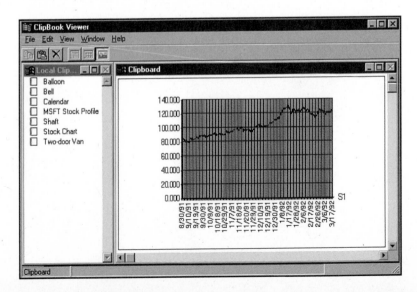

Understanding ClipBooks

Each node running Windows 95 can have its own ClipBook. A *ClipBook* is a logical entity that the ClipBook Viewer program and a program called Clipsrv.exe combine efforts to maintain. Clipsrv.exe is a NetDDE server application that handles the sharing of ClipBook items between nodes.

ClipBook items store as Clipboard files. The Local ClipBook window in the ClipBook Viewer serves much the same function as the Clipboard window—it enables you to view and manage Clipboard items. The difference is that you don't have to store the item in the Clipboard in a Clipboard file, but an item in the ClipBook must exist as a CLP file.

When you want to share information with another user on the network, you place the data in your local Clipboard, then copy it to a ClipBook page. The ClipBook Viewer automatically creates the necessary Clipboard file and adds entries for the new page in your System.ini file and in the Registry. The ClipBook Viewer also adds a password entry to the appropriate password file if you add a password to protect the ClipBook page. You then can direct the ClipBook Viewer to share the new page.

When a ClipBook page has been shared, a user at a remote node can use the ClipBook Viewer to connect to your system and view the shared items in your local ClipBook. Your local ClipBook appears in a window in the other user's ClipBook Viewer. The other user then can copy a ClipBook page from your ClipBook to his or her local ClipBook. The other user then can copy or link the data in his or her Clipboard into documents on the remote node.

Working with ClipBook Windows

By default, the ClipBook Viewer displays the Clipboard window and the Local ClipBook window. The Clipboard window operates identically to the Clipboard Viewer application. The Local ClipBook window resembles the Clipboard window, except it supports multiple items, or pages.

You can view ClipBook pages in three ways: as a list, as thumbnails, and in native format. When displayed as a list, the ClipBook pages appear as icons that indicate whether the page is currently shared. Beside the icon is the name of the ClipBook page. In a local ClipBook window you can see shared pages and nonshared pages. In a remote ClipBook window, only pages shared by the remote node appear in the list—you do not see pages listed if they are not being shared, even if they exist in the remote ClipBook.

Figure 24.10 shows a Local ClipBook window display of a list of ClipBook pages.

Figure 24.10

*ClipBook pages
displayed as a list
in the Local
ClipBook.*

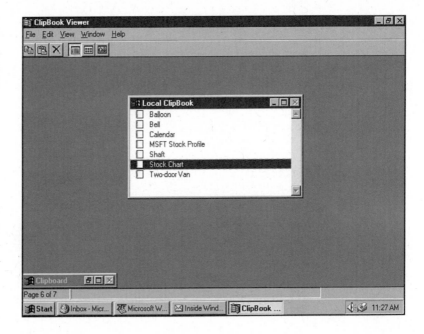

In addition to displaying the ClipBook pages as a list, you can display them as thumbnails. A *thumbnail* is a small image that represents the data in the ClipBook page. The contents of the page determine the accuracy of the thumbnail sketch. More often than not, the thumbnails look like ink blots or a maniacal scrawl, and are not very useful as a visual indicator of the page's contents. Figure 24.11 shows pages displayed in a ClipBook window as thumbnails.

The third method of viewing pages in a ClipBook window is in native format. You can display a page in the same way you display the contents of the Clipboard. In fact, in native format, the ClipBook window is virtually identical to the Clipboard window. Only one page can be displayed in the window at a time when you use this display method. Figure 24.12 shows a ClipBook page and the contents of the Clipboard displayed in the same format.

When you create a ClipBook page from the contents of the Clipboard, the ClipBook page contains the same data formats that were available in the Clipboard. When you view a page in full-page mode, you often can view it in different formats, just as you can in the Clipboard. Figure 24.13 shows a page that contains Excel data and multiple formats available for the page in the View menu.

You can switch between different page-display methods by using the View command. The Table of Contents command displays the pages as a list. The Thumbnails command displays the pages as thumbnails. The Full Page command displays the contents of the page in native format. You also can use the three buttons at the rightmost end of the ClipBook Viewer's toolbar to switch between page display modes.

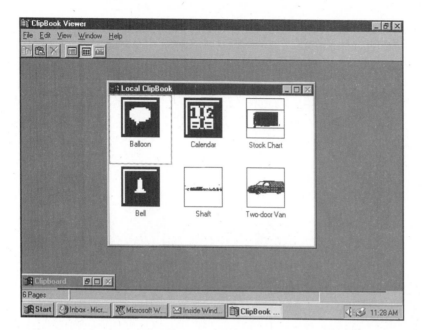

Figure 24.11

ClipBook pages displayed as thumbnails.

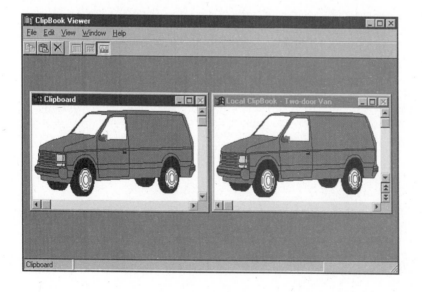

Figure 24.12

The Clipboard and ClipBook windows displayed using the same format.

Figure 24.13

Multiple formats for a ClipBook page.

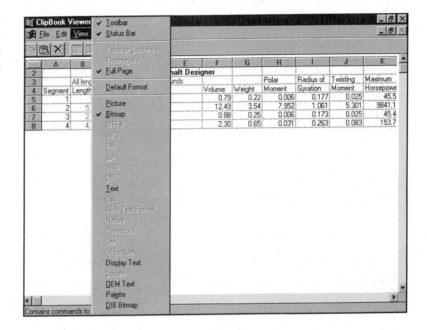

Tip

A quick way to display the entire image of a ClipBook page is to double-click either on its page description in a list or on its thumbnail. Double-click in the same full-page display to change the display to its previous mode (list or thumbnail).

The ClipBook Viewer automatically updates the display or remote ClipBook windows. Updates might not occur immediately after a change occurs to a ClipBook at a remote node because the update speed depends on the tasks running on your local computer and network traffic. You can generate an update immediately by choosing the **R**efresh command in the **W**indow menu.

Sharing Data through the ClipBook

You can use the ClipBook Viewer to share local data with remote users and to access remote data that other users are sharing. The process for sharing your local data is simple: place it in your local Clipboard, create a ClipBook page, and share the page. After you perform these steps, other users can connect to your ClipBook and access the contents of the page.

Sharing Local Data

You learned how to place data in the Clipboard earlier in this chapter. When the data is in the Clipboard, choose the **P**aste command from the ClipBook Viewer's **E**dit

New Riders Publishing
INSIDE
SERIES

menu or click on the Paste button on the toolbar (the button shows a document on a clipboard), either of which initiate the Paste dialog box (see fig. 24.14).

Figure 24.14

The Paste dialog box in the ClipBook Viewer.

Enter a name for the page in the Page name text box. This name represents the page in the ClipBook window, and is the name by which other users access the page. The page's description can contain spaces; therefore, be as descriptive as you like.

If you want to share the page immediately, check the Share item now check box. When you choose OK with this item enabled, the ClipBook Viewer displays the Share ClipBook Page dialog box, shown in figure 24.15.

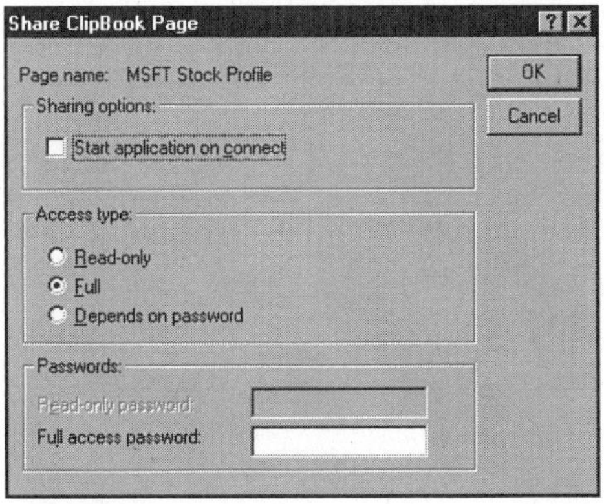

Figure 24.15

The Share ClipBook Page dialog box.

The Share ClipBook Page dialog box shows the name of the ClipBook page at the top of the dialog box. The Start application on connect check box, if enabled, causes the page's source application to start whenever a user accesses the page and links it into a document. If you want other users to be able to establish a dynamic link to the data contained in the page, you must enable this item. If other users are only going to copy the information in the page to the destination document but not link it, you don't need to enable this check box.

The next step in sharing a ClipBook page is to specify the level of access other users have to the page. You can set password protection to Read-only, Full, or both (Depends on password). If protection is set to Full, users who have the proper password can edit the contents of a ClipBook page.

Tip   Very few applications support the capability for a user to change a ClipBook page on a remote node. The less-than-stellar success of ClipBooks on Windows for Workgroups, and the fact that the ClipBook Viewer and Clipsrv.exe applications are included with Windows 95 as optional applications, leaves it open as to whether major developers will support the capability to modify ClipBooks directly in their applications. You can consider it unlikely, however, that very many applications will support the capability.

The Read-only setting prevents other users from changing the contents of the ClipBook page. The Depends on password setting grants either type of access, depending on the password the user provides. For nearly all applications, the settings Read-only and Full have the same effect, because most applications do not enable the user to modify the ClipBook anyway. To specify access level and passwords, choose the appropriate Access type option button, then enter a password in the Passwords group box.

After you complete the entries in the dialog box and choose OK, the new page appears in your Local ClipBook window accompanied alongside it by a shared page icon. The new shared page also appears in the ClipBook window for your computer on any remote nodes connected to your ClipBook.

If you want to share a page not currently being shared, select it in your Local ClipBook and choose File, Share or click on the Share button on the toolbar. Then complete the information in the Share dialog box to share the page.

Removing an Item from Sharing

After you share an item, you can stop sharing it so that other users cannot access the page. Times you might want to stop sharing a ClipBook page include when it is no longer valid, when you need to update it, or when you want to prevent other users from accessing it.

To stop sharing an item, first select it from your Local ClipBook window. Then choose the Stop Sharing command from the ClipBook Viewer's File menu or click on the Stop Sharing button on the toolbar. The icon beside the page list or thumbnail changes to indicate that the page is no longer shared.

Accessing a Remote ClipBook Page

Copying remote data to your Clipboard is simple. If the data you need is shared as a ClipBook page on a remote computer, open your ClipBook Viewer and connect to the remote node's ClipBook. Select the shared page you need to copy, then choose Copy from the ClipBook Viewer's Edit menu. You also can click on the Copy button on the toolbar (which shows two document pages together).

If the page requires a password not yet stored in your password list file, a dialog box appears, prompting you for the password. This is the standard Enter Network Password dialog box (see fig. 24.16) that appears whenever a remote resource requires a password not yet stored in your password list file.

Figure 24.16

The Enter Network Password dialog box.

Enter the password in the **P**assword text box. If you want to save the password in your password list file, enable the **S**ave this password in your password list check box. After you specify the options you want, choose OK. If you supply the correct password, the data copies to your local Clipboard. If the Clipboard window is open, the data appears in the Clipboard window. When the data has been placed in your local Clipboard, you can paste it into a local document.

Disconnecting a Remote ClipBook

After you finish using a remote ClipBook, you can disconnect it from your system, which terminates the conversation between your local copy of ClipBook Viewer and the remote node's Clipsrv.exe application. To disconnect a remote ClipBook from your local node and remove its window from your ClipBook Viewer, choose the **C**lose command from the Control menu in the remote ClipBook's window. If you prefer to use the ClipBook Viewer's menu, choose **F**ile, **D**isconnect.

If you later want to access a page contained in a remote ClipBook, you have to reconnect to it. Choose **F**ile, **C**onnect or click on the Connect button in the toolbar to reconnect to the remote ClipBook.

C H A P T E R

25

Understanding and Using OLE

Object Linking and Embedding (OLE), inherent in Windows 95, enables you to move information (such as an Excel chart or Word document) from one application to another quickly and easily.

As with most Windows 95 features, you don't have to fully understand OLE technology before you can take advantage of its powerful data exchange capabilities. In fact, OLE operates invisibly as you move information from application to application. However, understanding OLE concepts can help you use your Windows 95 applications more efficiently.

This chapter introduces the main concepts and features of OLE 2.0, covering the following topics:

◆ Examining the benefits of OLE

◆ Understanding OLE objects

◆ Linking and embedding objects

◆ Creating OLE compound objects

◆ Examining new OLE 2.0 features

◆ Examining in-place, or visual, editing

◆ Understanding OLE automation

Object Linking and Embedding enables you to work more productively. You can use OLE container applications to create and manage *compound documents,* containers that holds objects created using another application. A compound document can be any container of objects, such as a spreadsheet that contains a word processing document or a presentation that contains a sales forecasts from a spreadsheet. These containers are documents that can seamlessly incorporate objects of different formats. Sound clips, spreadsheets, text, and bitmaps are objects commonly used in compound documents. Each object is created and maintained by its object application, but OLE allows the integration of services of different object applications.

When you use compound documents, your computer acts just like when you use a single application, with all the functionality of each of the object applications.

 Note   Previous versions of Windows (and older Windows applications) use OLE 1.0; since Windows 3.11, however, OLE 2.0 has become the standard. The material in this chapter, unless otherwise noted, refers to OLE 2.0.

If you want to get the most out of this chapter, you should familiarize yourself with the OLE-related terms that table 25.1 defines.

TABLE 25.1
OLE Terms

Term	Meaning
Objects	Information created by OLE-compatible applications
Native data	All of an object's information needed to display, control, and edit the data
Presentation data	That portion of an object's information necessary to display the object
Compound document	An OLE document made up of objects created with more than one application and linked with OLE
Drag and drop	Moving objects from one application or document to another using the mouse (or keyboard) to grab the object and drag it to the new location

Term	Meaning
Container	The application that is used to hold the various objects that make up a compound document
DDE	Dynamic Data Exchange (see Chapter 26)
Visual editing	(Also called *in-place editing*) The capability to edit an object embedded in another application without having to switch between applications
Scrap objects	Special OLE objects that can be placed directly on the Windows 95 desktop

Understanding OLE Basics

An enhancement to Dynamic Data Exchange (DDE) protocol (see Chapter 26, "Understanding and Using DDE"), OLE enables you to embed, or link, data (called objects) you create within one application with data created by another application. You then can edit the data from the object application in the original application without leaving the compound document. An object can be almost anything, such as a bitmap, sound file, a video clip, or a spreadsheet.

 Note The term *compound document* refers to the container of objects. It does not necessarily refer to a word processing document. An Excel spreadsheet in which a bitmap image is embedded, for example, is a compound document: it serves as a container for the picture object.

OLE 2.0 technology enables software developers to use the object concept to create sophisticated applications, which provides for a new level of application interoperability: different applications can work with each other better, even applications developed by separate software vendors. OLE facilitates application integration by creating and defining a set of standard interfaces through which one application accesses the services of another. This standard is based on the Component Object Model, which specifies how data objects interact. A component object, created by any developer, conforms to this model by implementing and using the interfaces that support object interaction. The Component Object Model defines a standard for object implementation independent of programming language, and provides the basis for OLE 2.0 functionality.

Understanding Container and Object Applications

A *container application* stores and maintains OLE objects. (The application need not be associated with the object application.) The part of the container application that holds the embedded objects is called the container document.

Note   Previous versions of OLE referred to container applications as "client applications."

Container applications can communicate with the object application through interfaces available through the OLE library file's process intercommunication. An *object application* acts as a server that provides the data object. (In previous versions of OLE, these applications were sometimes referred to as *server applications*.) Object applications also can use OLE interfaces to communicate with container applications.

Mini and Full OLE Servers

An OLE server, also referred to as source application, must provide and manipulate the data component of an OLE object. Servers can be miniservers or full servers. Miniservers and full servers support embedded components, but only full servers can embed *and* link.

Miniservers resemble a dialog box, and usually are applications you can launch only from a host application. Miniservers support only embedded components (not linked components) because they can't save files to disk. Microsoft WordArt, Microsoft Note-It, and Microsoft Draw are examples of 16-bit miniservers—small applications; more or less add-ins to the Windows 3.*x* operating system.

Full servers are stand-alone applications that contain a full complement of menus and functions. Although they support OLE functions, they don't need a host application to run. Full servers can be single document interface (SDI) applications, which allow only one open document at a time, such as Paintbrush, or multiple document interface applications (MDI), which enable you to edit multiple documents simultaneously, such as Microsoft Excel and Microsoft Word for Windows.

Understanding OLE Objects

An *OLE object* is a discrete unit of information created by using an OLE-compatible application. Examples include bitmaps, text, line art, charts, and spreadsheets. Objects consist of two components: presentation data and native data. *Presentation*

data enables the data to appear on-screen and print to a printer. The *native data* is all the information (such as the object application's toolbar and controls) required to edit or maintain the object.

Windows 95 enables you to create special objects, called *scrap objects* (see fig 25.1), which are sections of text from the word processor that you can place directly on the desktop. In this situation, the desktop functions much like a "visible clipboard."

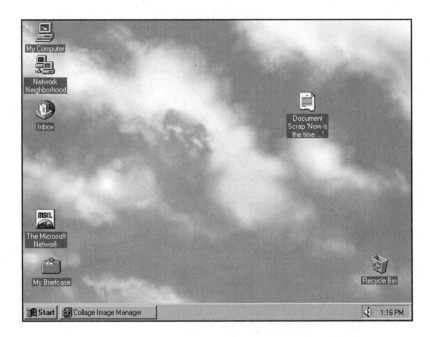

Figure 25.1

A scrap object.

To create a scrap object, follow these steps:

1. While in a document (such as a Word document), select the text or graphic that you want to copy.

2. Use the left mouse button to drag the selected area onto the Windows 95 desktop.

   Notice that the scrap object on the desktop has the same properties as any other item on the desktop. Figure 25.2 shows the context menu of a scrap object after it has been right-clicked.

Figure 25.2

*The context menu
of a scrap object.*

Linking and Embedding Objects

You can use OLE to link or embed an object into a document. *Linking* is the process by which you place only the object's presentation data and a pointer to its native data in a document. The native data for this object exists in some other location, such as a file on the disk. Because the native data for an object resides separately on disk, linking limits the object from traveling outside the local file system. The lack of system overhead required, however, makes linking more efficient than embedding.

An example of this concept is an Excel worksheet linked to a Word document. If the worksheet is moved onto a disk and taken off the local computer system, the link between the worksheet and the document is broken. Because the worksheet and document are linked, however, the Word document does not contain the native data of the worksheet—just the presentation data—so the file size is smaller, providing greater efficiency.

To link an object to another document, follow these steps:

1. Open a document from which you want to establish a link; for example, a Word text document.

2. Place the mouse pointer at the position in the document at which you want to establish the link.

3. Open the application for the object you want to link—for example, an Access database.

4. Select the data you want to link.

5. Open the Edit menu and choose Copy.

6. Switch back to Word.

7. Choose Edit, Paste Special, which pastes the selected data into the Word document.

Your application might open a dialog box after you select Paste Special, such as the one shown in figure 25.3. If so, choose the Paste or Paste Link option.

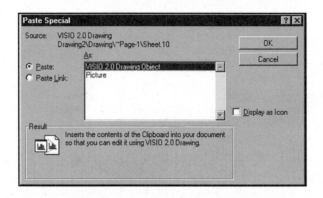

Figure 25.3

Word for Windows' Paste Special dialog box.

When you link an object, the linked object remains part of the original (or source) document and simply is tied to the compound document via the OLE link. Thus, whenever you update the source document, it automatically updates the compound document. Consider the steps described previously, for example. Following those steps creates a link from the Word document to the Access data. If you now open the Access application and change the data, the next time you open the linked Word document, the changes automatically appear in that document as well.

Stop If you link an object to another document, then use the object's original application to delete that object, you effectively delete the object from the container document, too.

Links can be constructed in different relationships. The following section explains these two types of relationships.

One-Way Links

A *one-way link* consists of a source document that shares its data (an object) with the container document. Because of that link, changes to the source document automatically affect the container document accordingly.

One object can have several one-way links to multiple destinations. A logo created in Microsoft Paint, for example, might be linked into an Excel spreadsheet and to a letterhead document in Word, as well as to a PowerPoint presentation. Anytime you modify the logo in Paint, all the one-way links are recognized and updated automatically and the new logo appears when you open the linked document, spreadsheet, or presentation. Figure 25.4 illustrates this preceding linking structure.

Figure 25.4

A typical one-way link.

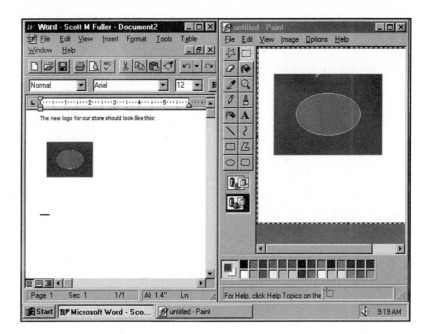

Two-Way Links

Two-way links consist of the source document sharing its data (the object) with the destination document, and the destination document sharing its own data back to the object source document (see fig. 25.5).

Consider data that originates in a Word document, for example, such as sales forecasting information. This data links to an Excel spreadsheet, and from this data a chart is created in the spreadsheet. Next, a two-way link forms when the Excel chart links back into the Word document. This two-way link means that if the source data (in Word) changes, the Excel spreadsheet is updated as well. Because the Excel chart is based on this data, Excel in turn updates the information in the chart. Finally, the two-way link updates the OLE object (the chart) in the Word document.

This particular two-way link exploits the strengths of the two applications: Excel's capacity to create charts and Word's capacity to present narrative and data in a readable format. Owing to the linked information, the chart in the Word document (the end product) responds to any changes you make to the text data in the same document.

After you establish the two-way link, the changes to the chart in the source document *appear* to occur directly; that is, you might not see Excel's intervention as changes in the Word data cause changes in the chart. (Also, note that in this scenario, the source document also acts simultaneously as a container document.)

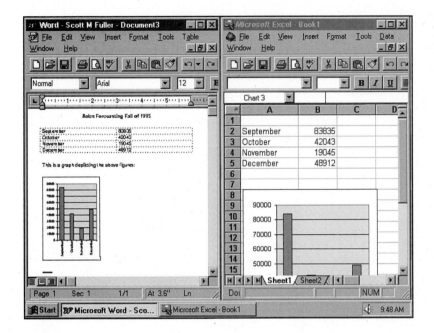

Figure 25.5

A two-way link.

Tip All this talk of source documents and container documents, although useful for understanding OLE principles, is not essential (indeed, not even necessary) for productive OLE usage.

OLE's power is its capability that enables you to manipulate data between applications, without even thinking about which applications you are using. Future applications might in fact eliminate visible distinctions between applications such as word processors, spreadsheets, database applications, and so on.

Embedding Objects

Embedding an object involves placing the object's presentation data and native data in the container document. All information necessary for editing the object now resides in the container document. If the document travels to another file system, all the object's application services travel with it.

Note Embedding the object does make the container document file much larger than if you simply link the object, because you place the native data in the container document along with the presentation data.

To embed an object into another document, follow these steps:

1. Open a document, such as a Word text document.

2. Place the mouse pointer at the place in the Word document where you want to embed the new object.

3. Choose Insert, Object, which opens the Object dialog box (see fig. 25.6).

Figure 25.6

The Object dialog box.

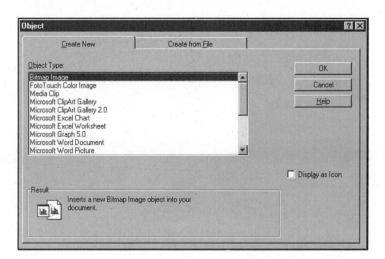

Note Depending on the application you are using, you might need a command other than Insert, Object to access this dialog box. In some applications you embed objects from the Edit menu.

4. In the Object dialog box, you can create the type of data that you want (such as an Excel chart) or use the Create from File panel to embed a previously created object (see fig. 25.7).

When you embed an object, the object effectively becomes part of the new, or container, document. Thus, you should make changes to the embedded objects by double-clicking on the embedded objects within the container document.

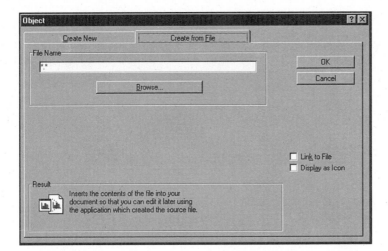

Figure 25.7

The Object dialog box's Create from File panel.

Creating Compound Documents

Compound documents are documents that seamlessly incorporate objects of different data types. You can integrate sound clips, spreadsheets, bitmaps, and text all into a single compound document. You create and edit these objects using their respective object applications; however, you can use OLE to integrate each of these services into the compound document. Using such a document enables you to concentrate on the compound document without the distractions of switching between applications.

You might have needed in the past to learn to create different types of information by using different applications and then manually integrating the information. You might have created a spreadsheet showing sales figures, for example, then manually attached a hard copy of that sheet to a word processed narrative of your sales program.

In Windows 95, you can use OLE technology to seamlessly integrate the two objects. Simply open the spreadsheet and select the information you want, then drag that information into an open word processing document. From this compound document, you can edit any of the information without changing applications.

Using Drag-and-Drop to Create Compound Documents

Figures 25.8 and 25.9 show the ease with which you can use the drag-and-drop method to create OLE compound documents. When you select the Excel chart on the right, then drag and drop it into the Word document on the left, you get a compound document: you now have embedded the chart into the document.

Figure 25.8

To prepare for the drag-and-drop operation, you should have both applications running and positioned side by side.

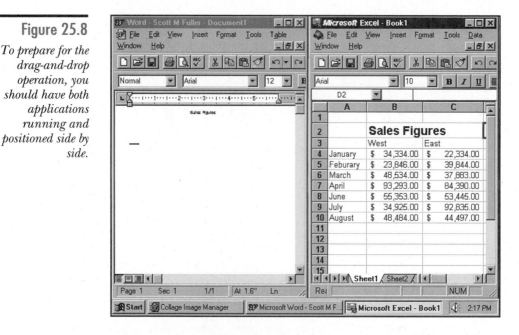

Figure 25.9

After the cells have been selected and dropped into the Word document, the spreadsheet is embedded into the document.

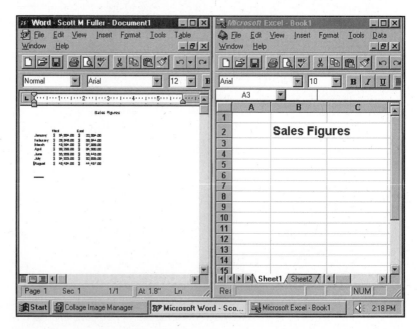

OLE Menu Commands

Windows applications that support OLE links and objects have the following commands (located in the Edit menu) to support placing and editing embedded objects:

◆ **Copy.** Copies selected data from a source document to the Clipboard, which an object application then can use to create an embedded object or link it to the source document.

◆ **Cut.** Removes data from a source document and places it on the Clipboard, which an application then can use to create an embedded object.

◆ **Paste.** Places data from the Clipboard into the destination document.

◆ **Paste Link.** Inserts a DDE link between a document and the file that contains the object. The object appears in the destination document, but the original data that defines the object is stored in the source document.

◆ **Paste Special.** Opens a dialog box in which you can choose the format of the data for the object on the Clipboard and choose to paste a link or paste the data without making it an object (that is, create a "static" entry).

◆ **Insert Object.** Opens a dialog box so that you can choose which server application to start, then embeds the object the server produces into the destination document. (This is the same as running the object application, copying the data to the Clipboard, then pasting it into the destination document.) Some applications also have a second panel that enables you to use this option to embed an object already created in another application.

Note that you don't always find all of these commands in all Windows OLE applications.

Understanding OLE Interfaces

An interface provides the means for OLE applications to access object services, such as saving or visual editing. Interfaces are defined by OLE, but can be implemented by OLE, the object application, or the container application, depending on which service the interface is providing.

The services that are standard for all applications are implemented in interfaces provided with OLE 2.0. Applications use these standard interfaces to make calls to the member functions. Application-, document-, or object-specific services (such as pasting from the Clipboard) are supported by interfaces implemented by the respective application. Implementation involves providing code for each of the member functions defined for the interface.

The container application and the object application both implement interfaces that enable you to use their services or functions. If you are using the container application and want to edit an embedded object, for example, the container application makes a function call to the appropriate interface implemented by the object application. Likewise, after the object application completes an operation, such as resizing an object, it calls functions that the container application implements to change the layout of the object. The communications between the container and object applications are maintained through the OLE library (see fig. 25.10). The library intercepts calls and provides a variety of services through its interfaces. Services provided by OLE library interfaces include the packaging and sending of parameters between the different process spaces, and providing storage for objects.

Figure 25.10

How container and object server applications communicate.

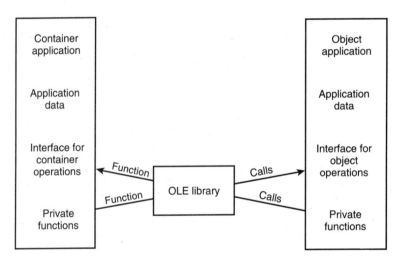

The services that interfaces provide fall into one of the following four general areas:

◆ Communication between objects

◆ Infrastructure support

◆ Basic linking and embedding

◆ Advanced features

An application developer need only implement a few interfaces from those in the first two areas to achieve basic OLE functionality. The specific interfaces required differ

somewhat, depending on whether the application acts as a container, an object, or both. As more features are required, a developer can implement the appropriate additional interfaces.

Looking At the Structured Storage System for Objects

OLE includes a hierarchical storage system for embedded objects—actually a miniature file system within a file—that it implements in every compound document. The purpose of this storage system is to keep track of all the information necessary to maintain the embedded object, such as file type, native data location, presentation data location, and certain directory information.

There are two levels of storage in the OLE object storage system, explained in the following list:

◆ **Storage objects.** You can view storage objects at the directory level in a typical file system. A storage object can contain streams and/or other storage objects. Each OLE object is assigned its own storage object.

◆ **Stream objects.** You can view stream objects at the file level. A *stream object* is the part of this mini-file system that contains the data. The data can be a bitmap, text, worksheet cells, or any other OLE data.

Access to objects and data within the OLE storage system is through a set of the interfaces provided by OLE.

Although OLE applications do not have to use compound files, compound file usage is common because the OLE object storage system provides efficient access to object data. The storage system interfaces enable objects to be read from disk to memory without loading an entire file, which is very handy when you load a compound document that contains large numbers of objects or compound documents that contain a single large object such as a video clip. Loading only the data the application currently needs is more efficient because applications don't have to wait for unnecessary data to load before they can make the needed data available.

Figure 25.11 shows an sample storage model of a compound document that consists of text, an embedded worksheet object, and a nested embedded chart object.

Figure 25.11

An OLE object storage model.

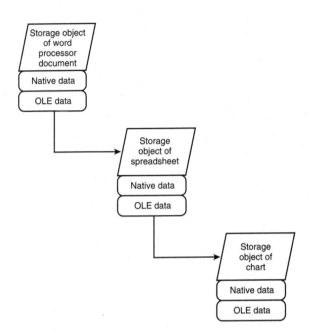

For those applications that require the capability to undo changes you make to a document during editing, the storage system includes a two-phase commit operation. An application that saves in transacted mode keeps both the old and new copies of the document available until you decide to save or undo the changes. Applications that do not need this feature can save in a direct mode where changes to the document and its objects are incorporated as you make the changes.

Examining Features New in OLE 2.0

OLE 2.0 functionality has been expanded far beyond the limitations of OLE 1.0. Communication between applications in the new OLE technology, for example, is considerably improved. The concepts of client application and server application have been replaced by container application and object application. Additionally, the Registry in Windows 95 uses an identification tag for the objects along with a program identifier to keep an entry for each OLE object.

Following are of some of the new features found in OLE 2.0:

◆ Adaptable links

◆ Drag-and-drop

◆ Storage-independent links

◆ Nested object support

◆ Logical object pagination

◆ Searching and spell checking

◆ Version management

◆ Object conversion

◆ Programmability

◆ Inplace activation or visual editing

◆ Optimized storage of objects

Adaptable Links

You could not maintain a link in OLE 1.0 if you moved both the linked object and the source object from their original file locations. OLE 2.0, however, maintains links even if you move or copy both the linked object and the source object; these adaptable links simply point to the new locations of the objects.

As an example, consider two files that reside in the DATA directory and share a link. Now if you move both files to the NEWDATA directory, the link is maintained. In the previous version of OLE, the link could not have been maintained if both files were moved to the new directory.

Drag-and-Drop

Following the natural impulse of Windows users to "pick up and move" objects, OLE drag-and-drop provides a simpler, more powerful way to move objects from application to application. You now can click on an object and then drag it into a container document. Releasing the mouse button places the object into the container document. Moving OLE objects in this way effectively eliminates the barriers between different applications and facilitates information sharing.

The OLE 2.0 drag-and-drop model supports the following capabilities:

◆ **Interwindow dragging.** You can drag objects from one application window and drop them into another application window. You can drag a bitmap from a graphics application window, for example, and drop it into a word processing document.

◆ **Interobject dragging.** You can drag objects nested within other objects out of their containing objects to another window or to another container object. As well, you can drag objects to other objects and drop them inside them; this is called *nesting objects.*

◆ **Dropping over icons.** You can drag objects over the desktop to system resource icons, such as printers and mailboxes. The Recycle Bin in Windows 95, for example, is a *fundamental resource* that supports OLE drag-and-drop functionality. If you drag an object to the Recycle Bin and drop it, Windows 95 marks the object for deletion according the parameters of your Recycle Bin.

Storage-Independent Links

You can update links between objects within the same or different documents without the objects existing on disk. Previously, you could establish a link only to an object stored within the computer's file system. Now, you can establish and maintain links across a network file system. If the accounting department has some information in a spreadsheet that would be useful to you in the marketing department, for example, you now can create a link to that spreadsheet file even if it exists on a disk other than your workstation, such as a network drive.

Nested Object Support

You can link objects to or embed them in another object in the same compound document. You can embed a chart in an Excel spreadsheet, for example, that in turn is embedded in a Word document. Nested object linking enables greater consistency in the OLE model, because you can directly manipulate the nested objects. You don't have to launch several applications to arrive at the object's application to edit a given object. Nesting objects enables you to use unlimited combinations on the OLE model throughout your applications and the Windows 95 operating system.

Logical Object Pagination

The OLE 1.0 object model did not allow an object to span a page break—you had to contain objects on a single page. OLE 2.0 introduces a more sophisticated object model that enables objects to span page boundaries. Logical object pagination also enables objects to break at logical points. If an Excel spreadsheet is larger than one page, for example, it can break along cell boundaries, thereby allowing the data to remain readable.

Searching and Spell Checking

Although compound documents can consist of objects created from two, three, four, or more applications, users want to be able to treat these compound documents as a single entity, instead of as a group of objects from different sources gathered in one place. OLE now offers two operations that possess the capability to act on entire documents, regardless of the application used to create them: searches and spell checks.

OLE defines a group of functions that let string searches and spell checks travel inside embedded objects—even within nested objects. This new capability means that you don't have to run several applications when you need to search or spell check the entire compound document. All objects whose applications understand OLE's search and spell check functions can invoke those functions to perform the specified operation.

Figure 25.12 illustrates how the spell check operation works through a compound document that contains nested, embedded objects. Spell checking begins with the Word text, then moves hierarchically through the embedded objects, first checking the top-level object, the Excel spreadsheet, and then the pie chart object contained within the spreadsheet. After the operation finishes with the spreadsheet and the pie chart, it continues with the Word text that immediately follows these objects.

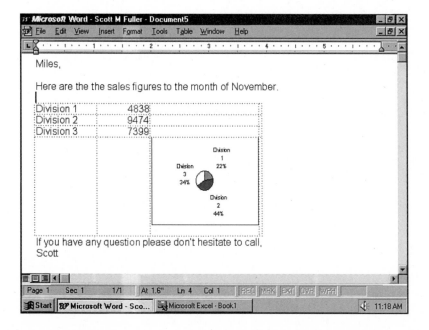

Figure 25.12

The spell check operation starts with the text on the top of this Word document and then move down through the embedded Excel worksheet, through the embedded chart, and then through the remainder of the Word text.

Version Management

Objects in OLE 2.0 contain information about the application that created them, including the name and version. This gives applications more information about the objects they host, enabling them to handle objects according to the specific applications (and versions of) used to create them.

Assume you used Excel for Windows version 5 to create a worksheet object, which you then embedded into a Word document. Then you upgraded the version of Excel on your system to Excel for Windows 95 version 7. Now if you double-click on the worksheet object in the Word document, Excel version 7 (because of OLE 2.0) recognizes that the object is from version 5 and prompts you to upgrade the worksheet object to the new version.

Object Conversion

OLE 2.0 provides a method for converting an object from one application to another. Suppose you insert an Excel-created object into a Word document, then give the document to a co-worker who doesn't have Excel, but does have another spreadsheet application, say, Lotus 1-2-3. The OLE object conversion feature enables the co-worker to whom you gave the Word document to convert the Excel spreadsheet object to work with Lotus 1-2-3, thereby enabling your co-worker to edit it. The conversion can be temporary or permanent.

Programmability

OLE 2.0 offers much greater integration and interoperability between applications than does OLE 1.0. In previous versions of OLE, you performed this integration interactively. OLE 2.0 programmability now enables application developers to define a set of commands and make them accessible to other applications. These commands can even have argument lists, much like a function call in a programming language. This capability enables applications to interact with one another minus user intervention. In other words, programmability enables you to create command sets that operate across applications. You can invoke a command from the word processing program that sorts a range of cells in an Excel spreadsheet.

Inplace Activation or Visual Editing

Double-clicking on an object in OLE 1.0 started up the object application. The application would appear on-screen and after you edited the object and closed the application, the screen would switch back to the original document. *Visual editing* greatly improves this process of interacting with the object application.

Visual editing enables you to double-click on an object in a compound document and interact with it without switching to a different application or window. The menus, toolbars, palettes, and other controls necessary to maintain the object temporarily replace the existing menus and controls of the active window. The application that you need before you can interact with the object partially takes over the document window. When you return the focus to the container application, the original container menus and controls are restored.

You quickly apprehend the advantage of visual editing when you have compound documents that consist of large numbers of objects created in different applications. Rather than switch between different windows (that contain different applications) to update objects, a single document window remains open in which you can do most editing and other interactions.

Note   Visual editing represents a fundamental change in the way users interact with personal computers. It offers a more document-centric approach, putting the primary focus on creating and manipulating information rather than on operating the environment and its applications. This approach enables users to work within the document.

Optimized Storage of Objects

As compound documents grow in size and complexity, the objects within these documents consume a lot of memory and take considerable time to load from disk. With OLE 1.0, you didn't need to load all objects into memory, but those that you did need to load, you had to load in their entirety. This doesn't present a problem for smaller compound documents, but can be inefficient when you have documents that consist of large objects.

OLE 2.0 includes a new object storage system that gives application developers increased flexibility in the way they load objects from and store objects to disk, and in what portions. Part of this new storage system is an incremental read/write capability that enables objects to load from disk into memory as needed. If you don't need to edit the object, you don't have to load it from disk. However, if you double-click on an object to edit, the container application that can read the object directly from disk for editing is loaded. Even during editing, the application can load only the parts of the object you need to edit. The result of this process is maximally efficient memory usage, producing higher performance overall and enabling you to use the Undo command.

Object Properties

Objects have properties that are relevant to the type of object. Property inheritance is used most commonly for copying a range of cells from an Excel spreadsheet application and embedding them in a Word compound document. The spreadsheet application's italic style and type of font might be inconsistent with the word processor's bold style and font, but enabling the embedded object to inherit the characteristics of the containing document's font lets the embedded spreadsheet look as if it's native to the compound document.

An example of this would be a chart with properties such as color and line thickness, and a text object with properties such as font type, font size, and underlining. When you embed an object within a container document, its properties are not consistent with the properties of its container. To make embedded objects more closely resemble their containing documents, OLE enables containers to export properties to an embedded object. The object then inherits these properties, and its appearance transforms to match the properties on the object's container document.

Copying to the Clipboard

Any time you cut or copy data onto the Clipboard, you actually use OLE. An OLE-compatible application renders the object to the Clipboard. The OLE server must render the data in the three OLE formats: *Native, OwnerLink,* and *ObjectLink.* If the application can support other data formats, it also can render the data in those formats.

The following list presents all the possible data formats used when copying to the Clipboard.

- ◆ Application-specific data

- ◆ Native OLE format

- ◆ OwnerLink OLE format

- ◆ CF_METAFILEPICT format

- ◆ CF_DIB or CF_BITMAP format

- ◆ ObjectLink OLE format

An object application renders data in OwnerLink format only if it can provide an embedded object. It renders data in ObjectLink format only when the application has a known file name under which the object is stored and only when the user copies the

data to the Clipboard. If the object is new and it does not have a known file name, or if the user cuts the data to the Clipboard, the server does not provide the ObjectLink data format.

Pasting from the Clipboard

When you paste data into a destination document, several things can occur, based on the format of the data on the Clipboard and the capabilities of the container application:

◆ If you choose Paste in an application that does not support OLE, then the Native, OwnerLink, and ObjectLink formats are ignored by the application. The application pastes the data in the best Clipboard data format it supports.

◆ If you choose Paste in an OLE application, the application checks the Clipboard and places the data in the first acceptable format it finds. If Word for Windows finds data in RTF format, for example, it pastes the data that way rather than create an embedded object.

◆ If you choose Paste Special in an OLE application, the dialog box lists the formats you can choose to paste the data as an embedded or linked object.

◆ If you choose Paste Link in an OLE client application, the application looks for ObjectLink information and makes an OLE link to the source document. If ObjectLink format isn't available, the application looks for the Link format and creates a DDE link.

When you copy a linked object to the Clipboard, the information associated with the linked object remains with it. So when you paste the object into another destination document, that other document can take advantage of the original link to the source document.

Understanding OLE Theory, Automation, and the Windows 95 Operating System

OLE 2.0 provides a new level of sophistication for applications in the Windows 95 environment. As software developers implement the new features of OLE 2.0 in their applications, you will begin to notice and appreciate the added simplicity and power of OLE.

However, OLE 2.0 is more than a set of new features to implement within applications. It is the foundation of a new model of computing used throughout the Windows 95 operating system. OLE 2.0 enables Windows 95 to offer a more intuitive user interface and a distributed object computing model that extends the power of objects to networks while hiding the sometimes complex nature of network environments. For example, a shortcut on the desktop is simply an object that can point to a data file across the network.

The extension of object technology across networks means that users can access almost unlimited information, regardless of type of information or application used to create it. Users gain increased functionality and can achieve more work with less effort by manipulating objects on their local desktop system and across large networks.

OLE Automation

The *OLE automation* feature of OLE 2.0 provides a way to create and access applications by programming simple routines. OLE 2.0 includes all the documentation, dynamic link libraries (DLLs), and samples that you need to start using OLE automation. OLE automation enables your custom application to borrow functions from other applications by sending them commands. This functionality acts much like an application "remote control."

OLE automation provides a standard for components to expose functionality through object methods and properties, as well as a standard to access and control that functionality using OLE automation controllers. Word can contain code, for example, that Excel can initiate and drive. Excel (through OLE automation) can invoke a command that automatically creates a report in Word.

Object-oriented programmers are probably familiar with the utility of custom controls. *Custom controls* are the objects or building blocks used in building object-oriented applications. Implementing OLE automation in your application can turn it into a collection of custom controls. The application still looks the same, but now you can use each part (object) of the application individually or in conjunction with other objects in Visual Basic or C/C++ applications.

Programmable Objects

A *programmable object* is an instance of a class within an application that is manipulated. New classes' sole purpose can be to collect data and functions in a way that makes sense to you, the user of the application. Each object has member functions that apply solely to that object. The object becomes programmable when you expose those member functions.

OLE automation defines two types of members that you can expose for an object. *Methods* are member functions that perform an action on an object, such as resizing. *Properties* are member function pairs that set or return information about the object's current state—for example, whether it's visible.

One key advantage of the Windows 95 interface in relation to object-oriented programming is the uniformity of elements it provides users. Programmable objects and the methods and properties they expose provide a language equivalent to the visual interface. A window itself is an object, for example. It's methods are the actions you can perform from a window's Control menu: Activate, Restore, Minimize, and Close. The window object's properties describe the appearance of a window: Height, Width, and WindowState.

To provide access to more than one instance of an object, OLE automation provides collections. A *collection* is a grouping of objects that you can refer to all at once. The window object, for example, addresses all the "Windows" collection, enabling you to act on all the windows in an application at once. In Visual Basic, a code statement such as "Windows.Minimize" would minimize all of an application's windows.

The New Component Object Model

For years, when software vendors wanted to increase their applications' functionality, they simply created the necessary code and added it to the application's EXE file. Besides making the EXE file quite large, it forced inclusion of several other support files.

If a developer created a word processing program for just simple word processing, and wanted to add features, such as a graphing feature to create charts within the application, the software developer had to add this functionality to the base word processor by generating additional code to the original EXE file, making the executable file quite large. Another software developer, wanting to add graphing capability to a spreadsheet application, would add the same functionality to that application by building onto its executable file as well.

With the use of OLE 2.0, application developers are implementing additional features in their software without adding additional code to the original Exe file. If a word processor application and a spreadsheet application both need graphing capabilities, a mini-OLE server can be created that contains all the graphing capabilities that both applications can share.

Component object modeling enables developers to reduce the amount of redundant code that is used in their applications. It also enables more interoperability between applications—the different functions, such as graphing, work the same way because they are the same mini-application.

Figure 25.13 shows a sample Component Object Model similar to what several popular software suites currently use. The added functionality that software developers want to add to their applications is divided into separate objects. This example contains the functions of equations, spreadsheet capabilities, drawing, voice annotation, AVI video clips, and ORG charts in addition to graphing.

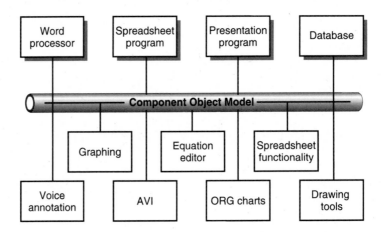

Figure 25.13

The top row of objects are the base applications. The objects that are below the line labeled Component Object Model are mini-OLE servers that each perform a particular function.

The Component Object Model offers several advantages. First, if you need to add graphs into a container document, the applications use the same graphing OLE miniserver and apply the same user interface, reducing the need to learn two separate graphing features.

Second, each base executable file is smaller and the separate objects (OLE miniservers) are not duplicated on the hard disk, which saves drive space.

 Note The separate objects are installed in a common directory so that they can be easily called from each base application. This prevents the base application from having to hunt through several directories to find the needed object.

Third, the base applications initially load faster because of the reduced EXE file size. The application does not need to load the graphing or drawing functionality until you call for it, which enables faster overall system performance.

Finally, this method facilitates better interoperability between applications. Because they share the same subcomponents, applications that participate in this technology appear seamless.

An example of a group of applications built on this model is the Microsoft Office package. MS Office contains a word processor, spreadsheet application, presentation graphics application, and database application that all use the same group of mini-OLE servers. If you create a voice annotation in Excel (the spreadsheet application), you will use the same object as you will use if you were to create the voice annotation in Word (the word processor). Because the mini-OLE server is the same, the interface that you use and the steps taken are identical for these two different applications.

Understanding and Using DDE

The Windows Dynamic Data Exchange (DDE) system is actually a protocol (or set of guidelines) that enables DDE-compatible Windows applications to easily share data with other compatible applications. You can use DDE to perform one-time data transfers or ongoing *conversations,* in which applications send updates to one another as new data becomes available.

This chapter introduces you to Windows 95 DDE concepts, primarily through examples and sample code, and by examining the following topics:

- ◆ DDE terminology

- ◆ Practical uses for DDE

- ◆ DDE and Windows 95 communications

- ◆ DDE function codes

- ◆ DDE conversations

- ◆ DDE servers and clients

Understanding DDE Terminology

To better understand DDE concepts (and the examples later in this chapter), you should first familiarize yourself with the following basic DDE terms.

◆ **Conversation.** A DDE *conversation* simply refers to two Windows applications using DDE to exchange data.

◆ **Channel.** DDE conversations are conducted through *channels*, which are the computer links between the applications.

◆ **Client application.** The DDE *client* is the application that initiates a conversation.

◆ **Server application.** The DDE *server* is the application that responds to the DDE client.

◆ **Application names.** Each Windows-based application that supports DDE has a unique DDE *application name,* usually the name of the executable file for that application minus the EXE extension. Application names are used when referencing the application in a DDE command. If you aren't sure about an application's DDE application name, check its property sheet for its the file name. Also, don't forget that application names are not case-sensitive.

The following list provides application names for some popular Microsoft applications:

Application	DDE Application Name
Microsoft Access	MSAccess
Microsoft Excel	Excel
Microsoft FoxPro	FoxPro
Microsoft Project	Project
Microsoft Word for Windows	WinWord

◆ **Task identification number.** A *task identification number* (also known as a *task ID)* is a unique number that identifies one particular copy of an application when several copies of that application run at the same time. The task ID is appended to the application name to identify the application (for example, Word5661).

◆ **Item.** A DDE *item* refers to a piece of data (such as a range of cells in a worksheet, a chart, or a bitmap) that two applications engaged in a DDE conversation can pass between them.

New Riders Publishing
INSIDE
SERIES

◆ **Topic.** A DDE *topic* is information that defines the subject matter of the DDE conversation and represents some unit of data that is meaningful to the DDE server conversation. For applications that can save and retrieve files, a topic is the file name (for example, Sales.xls).

◆ **System.** *System* is a special DDE topic that many applications recognize. Unlike some other topics, which might or might not be available, depending on whether a file is open, the System topic always remains available and provides a list of the other topics currently available, as well as other information about the application.

Examining Practical Uses for Dynamic Data Exchange

Before you can appreciate the practical uses of DDE, consider the following example. Assume you have a spreadsheet that contains all the prices, item numbers, and descriptions for your company's inventory. In addition, you also have a word processing document that essentially serves as the price catalog you distribute to your customers. If the price of a particular item changes, and you don't have DDE, you must launch both the spreadsheet application and the word processor and separately go in and change the data to reflect the price change. DDE provides a better way to update your prices.

DDE enables you to set up a conversation between the spreadsheet application and the word processor that enables the spreadsheet to inform the word processing document of any changes in the price of the items. If you don't have DDE, you can, of course, use the Clipboard to update this word processing document by manually copying numbers from the spreadsheet application into the word processing document, but this method requires switching between applications and a great deal of effort. In addition, after you update the spreadsheet, you must remember to perform the manual copy and paste function.

DDE automates the process, providing the word processing document with the current prices for multiple items without any manual intervention on your part. After you establish this DDE connection, the value of each item in the word processing document always reflects the most current data available from the spreadsheet.

Here are some other examples of uses for DDE:

◆ Using a database program from within your word processor to access customer address information

◆ Creating a simple inventory management system, similar to the previously described process

◆ Extracting stock or futures prices from a quote-retrieving package and automatically placing them in an Excel spreadsheet chart

You might notice that many DDE features are similar to OLE (Object Linking and Embedding) functions, as discussed in Chapter 25, "Understanding and Using OLE." In fact, OLE essentially enhances the DDE protocol and effectively automates many DDE functions discussed in this chapter. You could use OLE's link function, for instance, to establish a DDE-like conversation in the preceding example.

You might find customizing the conversations between your applications necessary from time to time, however, in which case possessing a basic understanding of DDE concepts can prove helpful.

Now that you understand the basic DDE concepts and terms, here is how a typical DDE conversation takes place:

1. The client application initiates the conversation and the server application responds.

2. The applications exchange data by any or all of the following methods:

   ◆ The server application sends data to the client at the client's request.

   ◆ The client application sends unsolicited data to the server application.

   ◆ The client application requests the server application to send data whenever the data changes.

   ◆ The client application requests the server application to notify the client whenever a data item changes.

   ◆ The server application carries out a command at the client's request.

3. Either the client or server application ends the conversation.

An example of this conversation between server and client applications can be found in a typical DDE link between Excel and Word. If you have a DDE link established between Word and Excel for which Excel is the server application and Word is the client application, the conversation would happen as follows:

1. Upon retrieving the document that contains the DDE link, Word initiates a DDE conversation with Excel and waits for Excel to respond.

2. Excel sends the updated data to Word (assuming that the data has been updated).

3. After all the updated data has been received, Excel ends the DDE conversation.

Understanding DDE Communications

Windows 95 allows for very flexible communication between applications. The primary means of communication is a process of messaging between the involved applications. Windows applications receive all input as messages. The characters you type at the keyboard, the clicks of a mouse, and all menu selections are sent to applications through messages.

In Windows 95, applications can define special messages that have a unique meaning throughout the system. The DDE system provides new messages for communication between the applications that use DDE. The DDE protocol uses shared memory to transfer data from application to application. DDE also defines *structures* to use for the contents of the shared memory objects.

The two basic types of DDE linking processes are interactive links and macro conversations. *Interactive links* are essentially the same as OLE paste-link operations, whereas *macro links* are created by a series of instructions written by the user.

Because OLE paste-link operations are discussed at length in Chapter 25, "Understanding and Using OLE," this chapter focuses on the macro type DDE conversations. A comparison of OLE and DDE occurs later in this chapter.

Examining DDE Protocol

The DDE protocol enables applications to exchange data on a *real-time* basis—as data is updated in a server application, the client application is updated simultaneously. To perform this exchange, the two participating applications must first engage in a DDE conversation. As noted earlier, the application that initiates the conversation is known as the *client application,* and the application responding to the client's request is known as the *server application.*

Applications can engage in several DDE conversations at the same time, as well as act as the client application in some conversations and as the server application in other conversations. Information transferred between applications using DDE can be formatted in a number of ways. Client applications might not support all available formats or might prefer certain formats.

Tip As a DDE user, you need not worry too much about the different formats the DDE protocol uses. The client and server applications automatically determine an appropriate format and then use the selected format to transfer the information.

A DDE conversation between two applications actually takes place between windows, where each of the participating applications opens a window. In addition, an application opens a window for each conversation in which it engages. (You typically don't see these windows.)

The DDE protocol identifies each unit of data in a DDE conversation by using an addressing system. This addressing system uses a three-level hierarchy to identify these units of data:

◆ **Application.** The name of the DDE server.

◆ **Topic.** The logical data context. For applications that operate on file-based documents, topics usually are file names; for other applications, they are other application-specific names.

◆ **Item.** The data object that is passed in the DDE data exchange.

Looking At DDE Transactions

After a conversation is initiated, the client application interacts with the server by issuing transactions. When issuing a transaction, the client asks the server to perform a given action.

There are six basic types of DDE transactions:

◆ Request

◆ Advise

◆ Unadvise

◆ Poke

◆ Execute

◆ Terminate

The client application always issues these transactions. If the server application must issue a transaction to the client application, the server has to initiate a new

conversation just for that purpose—in other words, the server becomes the client. These transactions are discussed in the following section.

Understanding DDE Functions

All DDE communications between applications occur in a channel. The DDE functions Initiate and Terminate serve to open and close the channel. The client application controls the channel and requests services from the server.

In the following discussion, Word for Windows serves as the sample application from which transactions are issued. However, most other DDE compatible applications function similarly. In addition, examples from other applications follow later in the chapter.

Initiate

The Initiate function opens a DDE channel from the client application to the server application. This function has two parameters: the server application name and the topic. The application name is the server program name minus the EXE extension; for example, Excel. (If the server application is not running, the Initiate function launches the application.)

In addition to opening the channel, Initiate returns a channel number to the client application. The *channel number* is used as a parameter in all other DDE functions thereafter to identify the channel.

You can have more than one channel open by calling the Initiate function several times. Each channel is numbered after the Initiate function is called. You get an error message if the server application is not running and cannot be started, or if the topic is not valid.

Other DDE Functions

Other DDE functions include Terminate, Request, Poke, and Execute, summarized in the following list:

◆ **Terminate.** Closes a DDE channel. The parameter for this function is the channel number of the DDE channel to close. You get an error if the channel number is not valid.

◆ **Request.** Retrieves data from the server application. The parameters this function uses are the channel number and the item. The channel number is the value the Initiate function returns. The item identifies the actual data to be returned. The server application returns the desired data. You receive an error message if the channel number is not valid, the item is not valid, or if the server cannot find the desired data.

◆ **Poke.** Sends data to the server application. The parameters are the channel number, the item, and the data. The item identifies the type of data being sent. The data is the actual data to be sent to the server.

An error is returned if the channel number is not valid, the item is not valid, or the server is not able to accept the data.

◆ **Execute.** Sends commands to the server application. The parameters are the channel number and the execute string. The channel number is the value returned by Initiate. The execute string contains the command to be executed by the server. Several commands can be sent to the server.

Different server applications support different commands. The commands that can be sent to an application are the commands in that application's menus. An error is returned if the channel number is not valid, or if any errors occur when the server executes the commands in the execute string.

Initiating a DDE Conversation

Before a DDE conversation can occur, both the client and server applications must be running. Therefore, a macro to initiate a DDE conversation usually should include instructions that carry out the following three steps:

1. Determine whether the server application it is calling is running.

2. Start the application if it is not running.

3. Initiate the DDE conversation.

You can use the AppIsRunning() function to determine whether an application is running, using the following syntax:

```
AppIsRunning(WindowName$)
```

WindowName$ is the name of the application as it appears in the title bar of the application window. For example, you would use the following syntax to determine whether Microsoft Excel is running:

```
status = AppIsRunning("Microsoft Excel")
```

Stop The *WindowName$* for an application is not the same as the DDE application name.

If the server application is not running, you can use the Shell statement to start it. The Shell function requires the actual application file name with the extension; for example, Excel.exe. (If the application you want to start is not in the current directory or path, you must specify the path as well as the file name.) For example:

```
Shell "C:\Excel\Excel.exe"
```

To open a document at the same time you start the application, you can add a parameter that specifies a document file name with the application file name or just the document file name, assuming the file-name extension has been associated with the application you want to start:

```
Shell "C:\Excel\Examples\Budget.xls"
```

Here is another example of how you might use AppIsRunning() and Shell together:

```
If AppIsRunning("Microsoft Excel") = 0 Then Shell "Excel.exe"
```

After you establish that the application you want to use as the server is running, you can use DDEInitiate() to initiate the DDE conversation, as follows:

```
DDEInitiate(Application$, Topic$)
```

Application$* is the DDE application name of the application with which you want to initiate a conversation. *Topic$ is the name of a topic the application currently supports. For example, the following instruction initiates a conversation with Microsoft Excel on the System topic:

```
chan = DDEInitiate("Excel", "System")
```

If DDEInitiate() successfully initiates a conversation with the specified server application and topic, it returns a channel number. You then can use this channel number as an argument in other DDE statements and functions to refer to this particular DDE conversation.

An error occurs if the application is not running or if the application does not recognize the topic. If you specify Microsoft Excel as the application name and "Budget.xls" as the topic, but Budget.xls is not open, for example, Windows 95 generates an error.

Requesting Information

Now that you have initiated a DDE conversation with another application, you can use the DDERequest$() function to obtain information from an item within the specified topic, using the following syntax:

```
DDERequest$(ChanNum, Item$)
```

ChanNum is the number of a channel the DDEInitiate() function returns. *Item$* is an item the DDE conversation's topic supports.

The following is an example of a DDERequest$() to query the System topic in Microsoft Excel to produce a list of the currently supported topics:

```
If AppIsRunning("Microsoft Excel") = 0 Then Shell "Excel.exe", 1
chan = DDEInitiate("Excel", "System")
topics$ = DDERequest$(chan, "Topics")
```

"Topics" is an item in the System topic that lists all the topics currently available. You can add a MsgBox instruction if you want to display the list of topics in a message box.

Topic names are separated by tab marks, which appear as spaces in the message box. For example, C:\ Excel\ Examples\ Amortize.xls, C:\ Excel\ Examples\ Budget.xls, and Sheet2 are the names of open Microsoft Excel documents that can be accessed as topics in DDE conversations.

If the specified channel number does not refer to an active DDE conversation, DDERequest$() generates an error. You also get an error if the other application does not recognize the specified item.

Note that because DDERequest$() is a string function, it always returns information to the Word macro in the form of a string.

Sending Information

Although the client in a DDE conversation usually obtains information from the server, the client also can send information to the server, using the DDEPoke statement with the following syntax:

```
DDEPoke ChanNum, Item$, Data$
```

ChanNum is the channel number returned by the DDEInitiate() instruction that began the DDE conversation. *Item$* is the name of an item supported by the DDE

conversation's topic. *Data$* is the information, in the form of a string, that you want to insert into the item. (All numbers must be first converted to strings using the Str$() function.)

The following example "pokes" the numeric value 100 into the first cell of the Microsoft Excel worksheet that is the topic of the DDE conversation. The Str$() function converts the value into a string:

```
DDEPoke chan1, "R1C1", Str$(100)
```

Sending Commands

You use the DDEExecute statement to send a command recognized by the server application:

```
DDEExecute ChanNum, Command$
```

ChanNum is the channel number DDEInitiate() returns.

In Microsoft Excel and many other applications that support DDE, *Command$* is a statement or function in the application's macro language. For example, in Microsoft Excel the XLM macro statement that creates a new worksheet is NEW(1).

To send the same command through a DDE channel, use the following:

```
DDEExecute chan1, "[NEW(1)]"
```

Most DDE applications, such as Microsoft Excel, require that each command received through a DDE channel be enclosed in brackets. You can send more than one command through a single DDEExecute instruction by enclosing each command in brackets. For example, the following instruction instructs Microsoft Excel to open and close a worksheet:

```
DDEExecute chan1, "[NEW(1)][FILE.CLOSE(0)]"
```

Sending multiple commands can speed up the DDE macro a great deal. The preceding instruction is equivalent to the following two instructions:

```
DDEExecute chan1, "[NEW(1)]"
DDEExecute chan1, "[FILE.CLOSE(0)]"
```

Some commands require arguments in the form of strings enclosed in quotation marks. Because the quotation mark indicates the beginning and end of a string in WordBasic, you must use Chr$(34) to include that quotation mark in a command string. In order to send the Microsoft Excel macro instruction OPEN("Sales.xls"), you would use the following instruction:

```
DDEExecute chan1, "[OPEN(" + Chr$(34) + "Sales.xls" + Chr$(34) + ")]"
```

Terminating DDE Conversations

DDE channels do not close automatically until you exit the client application. If you do not close a channel, it remains open, even after the macro ends. Because each channel uses system resources, you should always close channels after you no longer need them to improve overall system performance.

You use DDETerminate to terminate a DDE conversation, as follows:

```
DDETerminate ChanNum
```

ChanNum is the channel number DDEInitiate() returns.

After you close Word, it automatically terminates all active DDE conversations. However, you might want to terminate all conversations without closing Word. WordBasic includes the DDETerminateAll function as a shortcut to close channels one by one. DDETerminateAll terminates all active DDE conversations that Word initiates. However, it does not terminate DDE conversations that another application might have initiated with Word as the server.

Using Microsoft Excel as a Server

The previous sections focused primarily on Word for Windows. You should keep a few points in mind when you use Excel as the DDE server application:

◆ The DDE application name is *Excel*.

◆ Microsoft Excel supports the standard System topic, which supports the items shown in table 26.1.

TABLE 26.1
Items Supported in MS Excel

SysItems	Provides a list of the items in the System topic
Topics	Provides a list of the currently valid topics

Status	Indicates whether Microsoft Excel is ready to receive DDE messages
Formats	Provides the list of formats supported
Selection	Indicates the currently selected cell or range of cells

◆ Any open document is a valid DDE topic in Microsoft Excel

◆ A cell or range of cells is an item within a worksheet. To specify a cell or range of cells as an item, you can use a name defined in Microsoft Excel that identifies them, or you can indicate the cells themselves. You must use the "R1C1" (row number, column number) convention to refer to cells rather than the "A1" convention. In other words, to refer to a cell in the second column of the fourth row, you specify "R4C5" *not* "D5".

◆ Using the DDEExecute statement, you can send Excel Xlm macro commands enclosed in brackets. You can send more than one command with a single DDEExecute statement, but each macro command must be enclosed in brackets. You also can send a macro command that runs a Microsoft Excel macro. For example, the following instruction runs the an Excel macro called FormatCells:

```
DDEExecute chan, "[run(" + Chr$(34) + "Macros.xlm!FormatCells"
➥+ \  Chr$(34) + ")]"
```

◆ Excel includes an option to prevent other applications from initiating DDE conversations with it. To check the setting of this option, choose <u>T</u>ools, <u>O</u>ptions, and the General tab. If the <u>I</u>gnore Other Applications check box is selected, you cannot initiate a DDE conversation with Excel.

Using Microsoft Word as a Server

Earlier examples of DDE conversations show Word for Windows used as the client application; however, you also can use Word as a DDE server application. Here are some things to keep in mind when you use Word as a server:

◆ The DDE application name is WinWord.

◆ Word supports the standard System topic, which supports the following items:

SysItems	Provides a list of the items in the System topic
Topics	Provides a list of the currently valid topics, including all open documents
Formats	Not applicable

◆ Word supports all open documents and templates as topics. A template is considered to be open under the following conditions: if it is attached to an open document, loaded as a global template, or is open in a document window. It is best to include the complete path when specifying a document or template as a topic. This assures Word can find the document.

◆ In both documents and templates, Word supports bookmarks as items. Three of the predefined bookmarks are supported as items: "\StartOfDoc", "\EndOfDoc", and "\Doc". An error will occur if an application requests a bookmark that marks a location in a document but not any text. For example, if the predefined bookmark "\StartOfDoc" does not mark any text, an error will occur if an application requests it. However, you can poke information into a bookmark that does not mark any text. You could use the "\StartOfDoc" bookmark to poke information into the beginning of an empty document.

◆ You do not have to write any WordBasic code to use Word as a server. If you want to use Microsoft Access as the client and Word as the server, for example, you write a procedure in Access Basic.

◆ The client application uses its equivalent of the DDEExecute statement to send WordBasic instructions to Word.

You can use Word as a DDE server when the client application that you are using doesn't have word processing capabilities. An example of this is Microsoft Excel. If you have a lengthy report to create that is 95 percent spreadsheet and 5 percent text, it is more efficient to create a DDE link from Excel to Word, instead of creating the report in Word with numerous links to Excel. This way you can have elaborate word processing capabilities in your spreadsheet.

Understanding System Access Time and DDE

When an application receives DDE messages, the messages are posted on the application's message queue along with all the other Windows messages. Before the application processes DDE messages, the messages are taken from the application's queue and stored in a DDE queue. The maximum number of messages that can be queued at the same time is eight.

On a priority basis, the DDE messages are then processed with Windows messages. This accounts for the speed problems that can occur when DDE messages are passed to an application.

Comparing DDE and OLE

DDE actually is the foundation on which OLE technology is built. You can perform many DDE functions more easily by using OLE. For example, you can use the "paste-link" process described in the chapter on OLE to establish a link between a word processing document and a spreadsheet, instead of including a macro (such as the one described earlier in this chapter) in your document. You might find this more convenient most often.

However, situations might arise, particularly if you engage in even basic application programming, in which you need to exercise more control over the link between applications. Then you might find DDE better suited to the task. In addition, OLE can tie up substantial amounts of your system's resources in establishing links. Using DDE, you can exercise more control over the data exchanges and, in the process, determine appropriate levels of data exchange.

Data Exchange with DOS Applications

Data exchange has come a long way from the limited exchange capabilities in DOS and DOS programs. Not only do DOS applications typically require that you learn a completely new interface and command structure, but most DOS applications provide little, if any, support for exchanging data with other applications. You typically cannot transfer data in a DOS program except by using common file formats (such as ASCII files).

Even though DOS programs themselves often do not support data exchange, you still can use the Clipboard to exchange data between DOS programs and Windows programs. This chapter explains how to perform data exchange with DOS applications, covering the following topics:

◆ Exchanging data through common file formats

◆ Understanding DOS data exchange

◆ Exchanging DOS data through the Clipboard

◆ Embedding DOS applications in Windows documents

Often copying DOS data through the Clipboard wipes out formatting or other data attributes. In such situations, using a common file format is more effective for transferring the data, as explained in the following section.

Exchanging Data through Common File Formats

Although no mechanism in DOS serves the same function as the Windows Clipboard, many DOS applications do support a selection of common file formats. These common file formats enable you to transfer data between DOS applications, and between DOS and Windows applications. The following list explains some of these common file formats.

◆ **ASCII.** Many DOS applications (and Windows applications) support the ASCII file format, and can read and write ASCII files. ASCII files contain only printable alphanumeric characters, without special formatting characters. Some applications create variations of simple ASCII files, such as Comma-Delimited-Format (CDF) files. These ASCII files store the alphanumeric data in data fields separated from one another by commas, creating a simple ASCII database. Some applications use a variation of the CDF format in which the data fields are separated by spaces or other characters rather than commas.

◆ **RTF.** The Rich Text Format is a common file format for storing text with character and paragraph formatting. Most word processors support RTF, enabling you to read and write a formatted text file with different applications. You can create a file in WordPad, for example, store it as an RTF file, then open the file in Word or another word processing application.

◆ **Graphics formats.** Many common graphics file formats exist that enable DOS and Windows applications to share graphics. The most common file formats are PCX, BMP, TIF, JPG, and GIF. A number of graphics translation programs exist that can convert a graphics file from one format to another, enabling you to transfer graphics from one application to another.

◆ **Special formats.** In addition to general-purpose file formats, a few common special-purpose file formats exist. The DXF file format, for example, is a special ASCII file format that many computer-aided design (CAD) and 3D modeling programs support. The DXF format enables these applications to share two-dimensional drawings and three-dimensional models.

Your ability to exchange data through common file formats depends almost exclusively on the capabilities of the applications you use. If you try to move data from a

DOS application to the Windows 95 environment, however, knowing a few certain tips can help make the transfer easier.

To transfer text documents from a DOS application to a Windows 95 application, use the RTF file format if the DOS application supports it. RTF enables you to transfer the documents, complete with most or all formatting, to Windows 95. If your Windows 95 application doesn't directly support the RTF format, but the DOS program does support RTF, store the file in RTF format. Then, open the document in WordPad, copy the entire document to the Clipboard, and paste the document into your other Windows 95 application. If the DOS program doesn't support RTF or any other common file format your Windows 95 application supports, you probably need to use an ASCII file to transfer the data and, unfortunately, lose the document's formatting.

The best method for transferring graphics between DOS and Windows 95 is to use a BMP (bitmap) file. The BMP file format is supported by Paint and almost every other Windows 95 application that supports graphics files, including word processing, spreadsheet, and other applications not designed specifically for editing graphics files. If your DOS application doesn't support the BMP file format but does use one of the other common graphics formats to store a file, save the file, then use one of the many available graphics file converters to convert it to a BMP file.

 Tip A search on the Internet and commercial online services will turn up a number of different graphics conversion programs. One commercial application that supports many different formats, including photo-CD, is Image Manager, from Inner Media (603-465-3216).

Understanding DOS Data Exchange

If your DOS applications do not support common file formats that enable you to copy data to other DOS applications or to the Windows 95 environment, you can use the Windows 95 Clipboard to transfer the data. When you begin trying to move data from DOS to Windows 95, keep in mind the following general rules:

◆ You can copy text from DOS to Windows 95, from Windows 95 applications to DOS, and between DOS applications using the Windows 95 Clipboard (see fig. 27.1).

◆ You can use the Clipboard to transfer graphics from DOS to Windows 95 applications (see fig 27.2). You can capture a DOS application's screen as a Windows bitmap and use the bitmap in Windows 95 applications. But, you can't paste a bitmap from the Clipboard into a DOS application. You might, however, be able to paste the data from the Clipboard into a Windows-based graphics translator such as Image Manager, then save the image in a file format that the DOS application supports.

Figure 27.1

Text transfer between DOS and Windows applications.

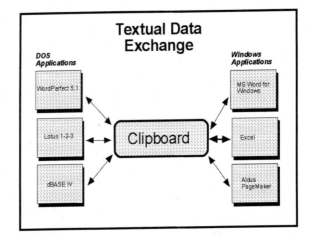

Figure 27.2

Graphics transfer between DOS and Windows applications.

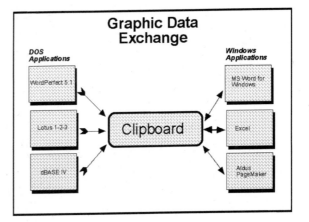

◆ You can use the Object Packager to embed DOS applications and documents as OLE objects in Windows documents (see fig. 27.3).

◆ DOS applications do not support Dynamic Data Exchange (DDE) or Object Linking and Embedding (OLE) as do Windows applications (see fig. 27.4).

Although the Clipboard doesn't offer the ideal data exchange solution for DOS programs, it nevertheless makes exchanging data possible in at least some situations. Even though you might spend some time reformatting the data, you still eliminate most of the time you would have to spend reentering data, and thereby gain significant time savings.

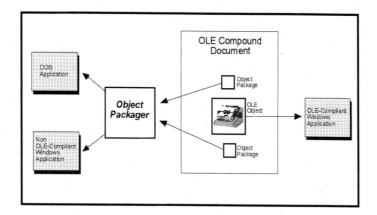

Figure 27.3

Using DOS appli-cations with OLE.

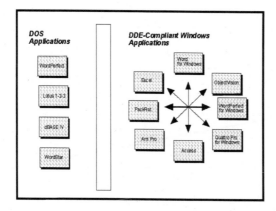

Figure 27.4

DOS applications do not support DDE or OLE.

The remainder of this chapter explains the mechanics of moving data between DOS and Windows 95, and also explains how you can use OLE to embed DOS data in Windows 95 documents.

Exchanging DOS Data through the Clipboard

Most DOS applications do not provide much data transfer capability, other than through common file formats as explained earlier in this chapter. DOS doesn't offer an equivalent of the Clipboard, which makes transferring data out of a DOS applica-tion difficult, if not impossible. When you run a DOS program under Windows 95, however, you open up the possibility of using the Clipboard with those DOS applications, providing a capability for data exchange previously nonexistent for those DOS applications. You can move text from DOS to Windows 95, and from Windows 95 to DOS. You also can move graphics from DOS to Windows 95.

Tip Text that you transfer between DOS and Windows 95 through the Clipboard loses all character formatting because no mechanism in the DOS application enables it to accept the data in any other way. This is because the Clipboard moves text into the DOS application through the keyboard buffer, essentially typing the text from the Clipboard to the DOS application's keyboard input buffer. You lose character enhancements such as bold, italic, and underline during Clipboard transfer, and tabs are converted to five spaces.

Moving DOS Text to Windows 95

Most Windows 95 applications include in their Edit menus Cut, Copy, and Paste commands that enable you to move data between the application and the Clipboard. DOS applications that you run under Windows 95 also have special data-exchange commands, but these commands are in the DOS application window's control menu, which is located in the upper left corner of the DOS window. To be able to access these commands, you must run the DOS application in a window. To switch a DOS application from full-screen to a window, press Alt+Enter. Or, simply press Alt+Spacebar, which switches from the full-screen DOS application to Windows 95 and opens the DOS application's control menu.

From the DOS program's control menu, choose Edit, which opens a cascading menu. The cascading menu includes the following commands:

◆ **Mark.** Use this command to mark (highlight) the text in the DOS program that you want to copy to the Clipboard.

◆ **Copy.** Use this command to copy selected text from the DOS program to the Clipboard. The shortcut key for the Copy command is Enter, so you can use the Mark command to highlight the text, then simply press Enter to copy it to the Clipboard. You seldom need to use the Copy command to copy the text to the Clipboard.

◆ **Paste.** Use this command to paste text from the Clipboard to the DOS program. The text is pasted as if it were typed from the keyboard.

◆ **Scroll.** This command enables you to scroll the DOS program window when the window does not display the entire DOS program screen. This command doesn't actually support data exchange in any way.

Rather than simply describe the process you use to copy text from DOS to Windows 95, the following steps take you through the process using the DOS Edit program and Notepad:

1. Choose Start, Programs, and MS-DOS Prompt to open a DOS session. If the DOS session starts up in full-screen mode, press Alt+Enter to switch the DOS session to window mode.

2. At the DOS prompt, enter **EDIT WINNEWS.TXT** to open Edit and load the file Winnews.txt (see fig. 27.5).

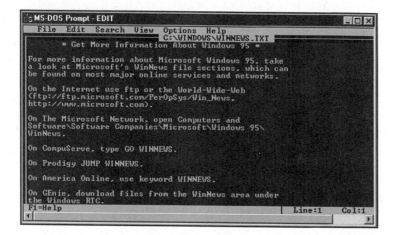

Figure 27.5

The Edit program with Winnews.txt opened.

3. From the DOS program's control menu, choose Edit, then choose Mark. Note the flashing block cursor in the upper left corner of the DOS program's window, but below the toolbar (if displayed) and title bar.

4. You can hold down the Shift key and use the arrow key to expand the flashing cursor to highlight a rectangular area of the DOS program's display, or you can use the mouse pointer to highlight an area. Highlight the first few paragraphs of the document (see fig. 27.6), then press Enter to copy the text to the Clipboard.

5. Choose Start, Programs, Accessories, then Notepad to open Notepad.

6. Press Ctrl+V to paste the contents of the Clipboard to the Notepad window (see fig. 27.7).

After you copy the text from the DOS application to the Clipboard, you can copy the text into any Windows 95 application. In addition, you can paste the data into most DOS applications.

Figure 27.6

A selection of a DOS program window highlighted.

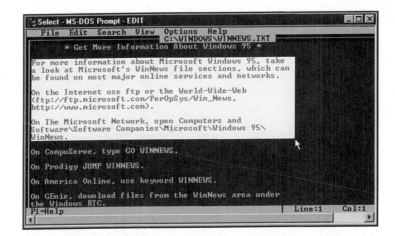

Figure 27.7

Text copied from a DOS program to Notepad.

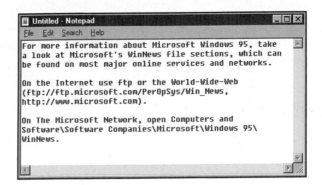

Tip You don't have to run a DOS program in a window to be able to copy text from the DOS program to the Clipboard. If the program is running in full-screen mode, press the Print Scrn key (or Alt+Print Scrn), which copies the entire DOS program window to the Clipboard as text. Then, you can switch to Windows 95 or to another DOS program to paste the text from the Clipboard. If the DOS application is running in graphics mode, however, pressing Print Scrn will copy a graphic image to the Clipboard, and you can paste the graphic only into an application that can accept a bitmap.

Copying Text from Windows 95 to DOS

After you place text on the Windows 95 Clipboard, you can paste that text into a DOS program. To paste text to a DOS program, the DOS program must be running in a

window or minimized on the Taskbar before you can open the DOS program's control menu. After you copy the text to the Clipboard from another DOS program or from a Windows 95 program, open the DOS program's control menu and choose Edit, Paste. Windows 95 pastes the text from the Clipboard to the DOS application.

Tip
To switch a full-screen DOS application from full-screen to minimized, press Alt+Esc. If this doesn't switch to Windows 95 and minimize the DOS application, check the DOS application's properties to verify that the Alt+Esc key sequence has not been disabled for the application. Shortcut keys are located on the Misc property page for the DOS application. To check the shortcut key assignments, right-click on the DOS application's icon and choose Properties. Then, click on the Misc tab. If a shortcut key's check box is enabled (contains a check), the shortcut key should work in the DOS program.

If you have trouble pasting text to a DOS program, open the Misc properties page for the DOS application and disable the Fast pasting check box, then choose OK and restart the DOS application. This should enable the DOS application to accept data from the Clipboard.

Transferring Text from DOS to DOS

The process for transferring text from one DOS application to another is just a combination of the two processes described in the previous two sections. First, open the source DOS program and copy the text to the Clipboard. Then, open the second DOS program and copy the text from the Clipboard to the DOS program.

Tip
When you copy between DOS programs, remember that you can copy text to the Clipboard from a full-screen DOS program, but you must run the destination program in a window or minimized before you can copy text from the Clipboard to the program.

Transferring Graphics from DOS to Windows 95

In addition to exchanging text between DOS and Windows 95 applications, you also can transfer graphics from a DOS application to the Clipboard. This capability enables you to import graphics you create in DOS to the Windows 95 environment when no common file format or conversion method will suffice. The ability to capture a DOS application's display also enables you to use those captured images in presentations or documents.

Tip

Your ability to run a DOS graphics application in a window depends on the application's video resolution, your PC's video card, and the Windows 95 video driver you use. Usually, you can run low-resolution DOS graphics programs in a window, but you must run high-resolution programs full-screen. To specify the default display state for a DOS program, open the DOS program's property sheet and choose either the **F**ull-screen or **W**indow check box on the Screen property page.

You can copy graphics from a DOS application to the Windows 95 Clipboard with the DOS program running in window or full-screen mode. With the application running full-screen, display the graphics you want to capture, then press Print+Scrn to copy the DOS application's entire screen to the Clipboard as a bitmap. If the program is running in a window (see fig. 27.8), first make the DOS program the foreground application (click on its title bar, for example), then press Alt+Print Scrn to copy the current window to the Clipboard. After you copy the image to the Clipboard, you can open a Windows 95 application and paste the image into the document.

Figure 27.8

A DOS program running in a window.

Tip

If you want to save the DOS image to a file, open Paint and paste the image into Paint. Then, save the image as a bitmap file.

Embedding DOS Applications and Data

DOS applications do not support OLE, but you can use the Object Packager (a utility program included with Windows 95) to link DOS applications to compound Windows 95 documents. You can, for example, embed a document from a DOS application in a compound document. The Object Packager (see fig. 27.9) enables you to encapsulate non-OLE data in an object package that you can embed into a compound document. The object appears in the compound object as an icon, and you can access the data in the package by double-clicking on the object's icon. Double-clicking on an object that contains embedded DOS data causes the DOS program to open and load the data.

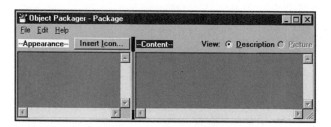

Figure 27.9

The Object Packager.

Tip   If you embed DOS data in an object, the DOS parent application for the data must support a document command-line parameter. Many applications, for example, enable you to enter the name of a document on the command line when you start the program, which loads the document file when the program starts.

In addition to embedding DOS data in a package, you also can embed DOS commands and batch files. Double-clicking on the object's icon executes the embedded DOS command or batch file.

To create an object package that contains DOS data, follow these steps:

1. Choose Start, <u>R</u>un, enter **PACKAGER** in the <u>O</u>pen text box, then choose OK to start the Object Packager.

2. In the Object Packager, choose <u>E</u>dit, Co<u>m</u>mand Line to open the Command Line dialog box (see fig. 27.10).

Figure 27.10

The Command Line dialog box.

3. In the Command text box, type the DOS command required to start the DOS program, including any optional parameters to open a specific file, set the program operating mode, and so on. Then choose OK.

◆Tip   To run a DOS command or batch file, enter the name of the DOS command or batch file, with any necessary parameters, in the Command text box.

4. Choose the Insert Icon button to open the Change Icon dialog box (see fig. 27.11). Select an icon to represent the object package. By default, the Change Icon dialog box shows the icons contained in the Shell32.dll file, but you can choose the Browse button to locate and choose an icon in an ICO, EXE, or DLL file. After you choose an icon, choose OK.

Figure 27.11

The Change Icon dialog box.

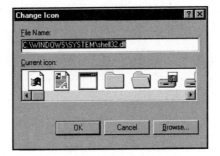

5. After you specify the command and icon for the object, the object is complete. Choose Edit, Copy Package to copy the object to the Clipboard.

6. Open the application and document in which you want to use the object package, then paste the object package into the document.

The graphic that you associate with the object package does not have to be an icon—you can use any graphic for object. For example, you can open Paint, create or open a bitmap, then copy that bitmap to the Clipboard. In the Object Packager, click in the Appearance window to make the window active, then choose Edit, Paste to paste the bitmap from the Clipboard to the Appearance window. Then, choose Edit, Copy Package to copy the package to the Clipboard, making it available for pasting into your document.

Part VI

Messaging and Communications

## 28

Modems and Data Communications

The personal computer industry has seen rapid growth in data communications in the mid-'90s, fueled partly by the growth in the number of personal computers and partly by the expansion of commercial information services and the Internet. Although the communications capabilities in Windows 3.*x* are adequate for most users, they sometimes fall short for users who demand higher-speed access and cooperative use by multiple applications of a single COM port and modem.

Windows 95 changes the way you and your applications configure and use modems, and improves on the communications capabilities in Windows 3.*x*. Many of the new data communications features in Windows 95 require 32-bit communication programs, but even your existing 16-bit programs can take advantage of some of the improvements in Windows 95. This chapter explains the features in Windows 95 that support data communications, including the following topics:

- ◆ Understanding data communications and COM ports

- ◆ Installing and configuring a modem

- ◆ Configuring and using telephony services

◆ Using communications programs

◆ Tips for optimizing data communications

You certainly don't have to understand how your computer's COM ports or modem work before you can use a communications program, but understanding how they work can help you optimize communications on your PC. The following section provides a basic primer on data communications and modems that will help you more effectively configure and use your modem.

Understanding COM Ports and Data Communications

Data communications capabilities have come a long way in the last decade. You can transfer data between computers at much higher speeds over a standard phone line than you could before, and communications programs typically are much easier to use, thanks partly to the graphical interface in Windows 3.*x* and Windows 95. Unfortunately, however, connecting to an online service or connecting to another user's computer still is not simple. Therefore, the more you understand the processes involved, the easier configuring and using your communications software more effectively becomes.

A very critical component in any data communications link is your computer's modem. Modems aren't mysterious, but they certainly can pose challenges to the uninitiated. The following section explains in general how modems work and how you control them in Windows 95.

Understanding Modems

Computers are not designed to simply "talk" to one another. Unless computers are connected on a local area network (LAN) or wide area network (WAN) and communicate using a typical network protocol, they require a modem to communicate. A modem *modulates*—that is, converts digital data coming from the PC into analog signals that can be transmitted over a standard telephone connection. The modem also *demodulates,* or converts analog signals coming through the phone line into digital signals that the computer can understand. The word *modem,* therefore, is an acronym of MOdulator/DEModulator.

Numerous types and brands of modems are available today for the average PC user, from relatively slow models operating at 2,400 bps (bits per second) to higher-speed modems capable of operating at 28,800 bps. Modems typically come in one of the four form factors described in the following list:

◆ **Internal.** Internal modems install inside the computer in one of the computer's bus slots. The disadvantages of an internal modem are that they are not easily portable between computers, and have no status lights you can use to troubleshoot communication problems. An internal modem replaces one of the computer's COM ports.

Tip
When you use a communications program designed for Windows 95, a modem status indicator appears in the tray. These modem lights provide a visual indicator of the status of the SD (Send Data) and RD (Receive Data) lines in the modem. Double-click on the status lights to view a dialog box that provides additional modem status information.

◆ **External.** External modems connect externally to one of the computer's COM ports (internal modems configure as one of the computers COM ports). The primary advantages of an external modem are easy portability between computers and a bank of status lights on the modem you can use for monitoring and troubleshooting.

◆ **Pocket.** These miniature external modems also connect externally to one of the computer's COM ports. Their smaller size makes them ideal for notebook computers.

◆ **PCMCIA.** These credit card-sized modems insert in one of the computer's PCMCIA slots (most often found in notebook computers, but also available for desktop systems).

Tip
Modems that support speeds higher than 28.8 Kbps are available, but these special-purpose modems typically are used for dedicated connections between networks, forming a wide area network (WAN). Depending on the modem's design and the connection media it uses (wire, fiber, and so on), these types of modems operate at 56 Kbps and higher.

Most modems today do more than support data communication. They also support faxing, enabling you to send and receive faxes through the modem. For more information on faxing in Windows 95, refer to Chapter 31, "Using Microsoft Fax."

Understanding Modem Standards

Numerous standards define the way modems function and communicate with one another. These standards define methods the modems use for establishing a reliable connection, data compression, error correction, and other operating parameters. The United Nations standards organization ITU-TSS, formerly known as the Comité

Consultatif International de Telegraphie et Telephonie (CCITT), sets many of these standards. These standards include some that have become very common in today's modems: V.32 and V.42 for error correction, and V.42bis for data compression. Other common standards include those defined by Microcom (a modem manufacturer), which are prefixed by MNP, which stands for Microcom Network Protocol.

Most modems also support the Hayes AT command set, a set of standard modem commands that applications (and you) can use to control the modem. Hayes Micro-computer Products, Inc., a long-standing and popular modem manufacturer, developed the AT command set, and it has become an ad hoc industry standard.

 Tip If Windows 95 does not specifically support your modem, but it is Hayes-compatible, choose one of the Standard modem types Windows 95 provides in the Add New Modem wizard. Base your selection on the maximum speed of your modem—if your modem is a 14.4 Kbps modem, for example, choose the 14400 model from the Standard group.

Error Correction Standards

The two most common standards for error correction are ITU-TSS V.42 and MNP-4 (which also includes the standards MNP-2 and MNP-3). These standards define the protocol the modems use to verify that the data transmitted is received correctly. If a received data packet turns out to be incorrect, the receiving system prompts the sender to resend the packet.

ITU-TSS V.42 comprises two error control methods: a primary method, known as LAP-M (Link Access Procedure for Modems), and a secondary method, MNP-4. This means that a V.42-compliant modem can establish a reliable link with other V.42 modems, or with modems that support any level of MNP error correction from MNP-2 through MNP-4. Some modems also support proprietary error-correction methods. These proprietary methods have the disadvantage of requiring that both the sending and receiving systems use the same type of modem.

Compression Standards

The most common compression standards today are ITU-TSS V.42bis and MNP-5, and some modems use proprietary compression protocols. As with error correction, using a proprietary compression protocol generally requires that you have similar types of modems at the ends of the connection. Therefore, the V.42bis standard is the most likely for the majority of modems to support, followed by MNP-5.

Note Additional Microcom compression standards, notably MNP-10, are generally supported only on Microcom modems and are not common on modems from other vendors. MNP-10 incorporates MNP-5, however, so an MNP-10-compliant modem can connect to a MNP-5-compliant modem and use the MNP-5 compression protocol.

The MNP-5 protocol provides compression of up to about 2:1. V.42bis supports compression up to about 4:1, making V.42bis a better option for compression than MNP-5. A V.42bis modem, therefore, theoretically enables you to achieve a throughput of 57.6 Kbps on a 14.4 Kbps modem. Unfortunately, compression typically is effective only for transmitting text. Compression is less effective on binary data (such as file downloads or uploads). When you transmit compressed files, such as Zip and Arc files and self-extracting archives, using modem compression actually increases transfer time. If you transfer compressed files, you should disable modem compression as explained in the upcoming section "Installing and Configuring Modems and COM Ports."

Tip If you primarily deal with character-based data in your modem connections, such as browsing Web pages on the Internet, enable modem compression for best throughput. When you plan to download or upload one or more large files, close the connection, turn off modem compression, then reestablish the connection to transmit the file(s).

Combining Error Correction and Compression

You can use error correction without using compression; for example, you can use V.42 without using V.42bis. If you want to use compression, however, you must use error correction. V.42bis requires V.42 or MNP-4, and MNP-5 requires MNP-4. Most modems today support these protocols, however, and the modems handle establishing the proper protocols during handshaking (when the modems establish the connection).

Understanding Communications in Windows 95

Windows 95 *virtualizes* the computer's COM ports, as it does with most system devices. This means that rather than access the COM ports directly, applications communicate with a device driver that provides a virtual representation of the device. The device driver then handles actual manipulation of the port.

In Windows 3.*x*, a single monolithic device driver, Comm.drv, handled applications' access to the COM ports. Windows 95 changes that driver model for Windows 95 applications, breaking the COM port functions into three primary areas: Win32 communication APIs and TAPI, a universal modem driver, and communications port drivers, including VCOMM. VCOMM is a virtual communications driver that provides protected-mode communications services for Windows-based applications, including Win32 and Win16 applications. Win16 applications still use the same mechanism and driver, Comm.drv. DOS applications use the virtual communications drivers built into Windows 95.

Figure 28.1 shows the interaction between different application types and Windows 95 communications components. Win32 applications communicate through the Win32 TAPI and Win32 COMM API. Win16 applications communicate through the Win16 COMM API. The communication for both Win16 and Win32 applications is handled through VCOMM and various virtual device drivers. DOS applications, however, have fewer levels through which to communicate (but with fewer capabilities), communicating through a set of virtual device drivers directly to the hardware.

Figure 28.1

Data communications flow in Windows 95.

Win32 applications	Win16 applications	DOS applications

Control	Data			
Win32 Telephony API (TAPI)	Win32 COMM API	Win16 COMM API	*VCD	XVCOMM
Unimodem driver		COMM.DRV		
VCOMM				
Serial port driver		Other port drivers		

Serial port	Other devices	
Serial Modem	Modem	Other comm devices	Hardware

Communications APIs and TAPI

An *API,* or *application programming interface,* is a set of predefined system functions that applications can use to interact with Windows 95 and the PC's hardware. Major parts of the Windows 95 communications services are the communications APIs and telephony API, or TAPI. The communications APIs provide an interface for applications to communicate with modems and other devices connected to the computer's COM ports or other communications ports.

TAPI provides a set of functions that enable applications to perform telephony functions for data, voice, and fax calls. These telephony functions provided by TAPI include basic functions such as dialing, answering a call, and hanging up a call, as well

as advanced functions, such as hold, transfer, conferencing, and other special-purpose functions. In addition to supporting POTS (Plain Old Telephone System), TAPI supports functions on PBX, ISDN, and other types of telephone systems. Through TAPI, application developers can create Windows 95 applications that enable voice messaging, call routing, desktop conferencing, and other special-purpose telephony applications.

Windows 3.*x* provides very little in terms of device arbitration for the computer's COM ports. If a fax program is monitoring the phone line for incoming calls, for example, no other applications can access the line. A communications program that attempts to connect to an online service will find the port busy, and the connection will fail, even if there is no fax activity on the line and the line is available. TAPI overcomes this limitation by arbitrating requests for access to the COM ports. Win32-based applications can use TAPI to gain access to a COM port, even if another Win32 application (such as Exchange) is monitoring the port for incoming calls. Win16 applications, however, still will find the port busy. To give a Win16 application access to the port, you must take offline the application that is monitoring the port, making the port available to the Win16 application.

For more information on TAPI, consult the Windows 95 Resource Kit, contained in the \Admin\Reskit\Helpfile folder on the Windows 95 CD-ROM.

The Universal Modem Driver

Microsoft has incorporated the same design structure into the modem support components in Windows 95 as it has for printers. A single, unified modem driver (unimodem) provides basic modem services for applications. Unimodem uses mini-drivers provided by modem manufacturers to control specific modems. By providing a universal modem driver, Windows 95 simplifies writing modem drivers and also provides a uniform interface for configuring modems, eliminating the need to configure a modem separately in each application that uses the modem.

Port Drivers

To further modularize its communications components, Windows 95 uses individual port drivers that provide base-level access to the system's communications ports. These port drivers interact with VCOMM to control the ports and provide I/O services through the ports. Windows 95 includes a serial port driver, and other manufacturers can provide drivers for special-purpose devices such as ISDN adapters, multiport adapters, and other I/O devices.

In addition to understanding how the Windows 95 communications components control your PC's hardware and I/O devices, you also need to have a basic under-standing of how your computer's COM ports work so that you can configure them correctly. The following section offers an overview of COM ports and how they function.

Understanding COM Ports

Windows 95 provides numerous settings you can use to control your computer's COM ports, and these settings are important for ensuring that your COM ports work properly. To understand these settings, you need a basic understanding of how your computer's COM ports work.

You probably have heard COM ports referred to as *serial*, or *RS-232 ports*. RS-232C is an EIA-defined standard (EIA stands for Electronic Industry Association) that defines the way asynchronous communication ports function.

Asynchronous, in port terms, means that the data flowing between the computer and the peripheral (such as a printer, modem, or plotter) is not synchronized; that is, the computer and peripheral are not necessarily in step with each other. To ensure that data flows between them without getting lost in translation, the data must include some sort of marker so that the two communicating devices can intercept and interpret the signals properly.

The first step in that process is to break up the data into packets of information, each consisting of a set number of bits. A *bit* is the smallest unit of information a computer can use; a bit can be set to be off (0) or on (1). Eight bits make a byte, 1,024 bytes form a kilobyte, and 1,048,576 bytes make a megabyte. Each letter, punctuation mark, or other character takes up 1 byte, so you can see that a bit is a small amount of data—just one-eighth of a character.

When data is passed down a serial line, it is sent as a *word* from four to eight bits long (some systems use more). The word is not one you can read; it is just a collection of bits. The number of bits in the word is called the *word length*, and seven or eight bits is the most common word length used in the United States.

 Tip   Many online information services use eight bits, no parity, and one stop bit, often referred to as *8-N-1*.

Understanding Start and Stop Bits

The first parameters to consider are the start bits and stop bits. When you use a serial line, the computer can send only one data bit at a time. The problem is that the receiving device needs a way to know where a received bit fits within the word. To keep communication from breaking down, a start bit, a stop bit, a pair of stop bits, or some combination of start and stop bits can be added to the ends of the word. These bits frame the word, enabling the receiving unit to identify the meaningful part of the signal (see fig 28.2).

To fully understand stop bits, you have to realize that you are not actually sending anything down the line when you use a serial port. You are pulsing the line from its

normal positive state to a negative one. If you send a 0, you do not pulse the line. If you send a 1, you do pulse the line. Each negative pulse is interpreted at the other end of the line as a 1 (a bit that is turned on).

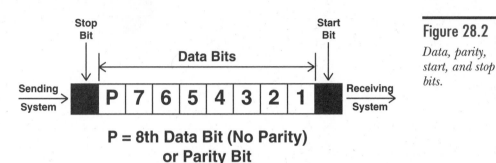

Figure 28.2

Data, parity, start, and stop bits.

Asynchronous serial communication shares an important aspect of comedy—timing is of the essence. Stop bits really are just timing values that define the amount of time between one data packet and the next. If you pulse the line for the same amount of time as a single data bit, you have 1 stop bit. If you hold the pulse for the equivalent of 1 1/2 bits, you have 1.5 stop bits. If the pulse lasts the equivalent of 2 data bits, you have 2 stop bits.

Without some form of timing, the receiving system can't know that it has received a NUL (eight no pulses). Because the start and stop bits mark the ends of the word, a receiver, sensing no pulses between them, recognizes that it has "received" a NUL.

Understanding Parity

Although stop and start bits are very important for serial communication, the most common way to check whether the proper information is being received is to use a parity bit. The *parity bit* provides a way for the sent data to be checked against the received data to make sure that everything came through properly. Parity checking comes in four types: odd, even, mark, and space.

If *odd parity* checking is used, the sending system adjusts (turns on or off) the parity bit to make the total number of on bits in the packet always odd. If the word contains an even number of on bits, the parity bit is turned on to make the total number of on bits odd. If the word total starts out odd, the parity bit is left turned off. The receiving system checks to make sure that it has received an odd number of bits. If the system has not received an odd number, it generates an error; otherwise, processing continues. This process enables the system to check the contents of the word as well as its length. *Even parity* uses the same concept, but sets the parity bit so there is always an even number of on bits. Figure 28.3 illustrates even and odd parity checking.

Figure 28.3

The two most common error-detecting methods.

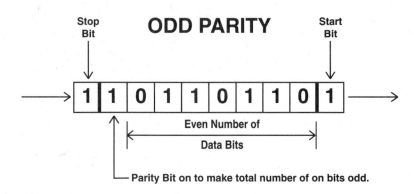

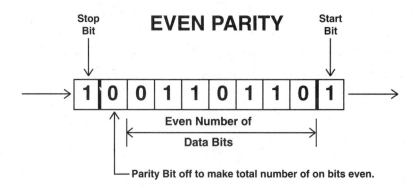

In *mark parity,* the parity bit is always turned on, regardless of whether the total number of bits is odd or even. This is similar to the function of a start or stop bit; mark parity enables the receiver to check for a pattern that marks the data. In the case of a seven-bit word with a final marked parity bit, every eighth bit is on, regardless of the word being sent. In *space parity,* the parity bit is always off. Again, this provides a pattern for the system to recognize, but it does not confirm that the correct bits have been received. With *no parity,* a parity bit is not included in the data at all.

The way in which you set the number of data bits, stop bits, and parity depends on what you connect to the port and how you use the device. If you connect a modem to the port, your settings depend on the settings expected by the remote site or online service to which you connect.

Understanding Flow Control

The computer and modem need some way to control the flow of data through the modem. In effect, flow control enables the modem to direct the CPU to halt transmission until it is ready to receive more data. Flow control also enables the CPU to do the same to the modem, providing a two-way means of preventing data overrun.

The three common types of flow control are none, Xon/Xoff, and hardware (RTS/CTS). Xon/Xoff is a software method of flow control, in which you use the Xon character (11 hex, DC3, or Ctrl+Q) and Xoff character (13 hex, DC1, or Ctrl+S) to tell the sending device when to start and stop data transmission. Hardware flow control uses a dedicated wire in the cable (or connection on the bus, in the case of an internal modem). Hardware flow control is the preferred option because it offers better speed and less software overhead than Xon/Xoff, but sometimes is required if the device doesn't support hardware flow control. In the case of most modems, hardware flow control works.

Understanding Modulation

Modulation refers to the method the modem uses to convert the digital data coming from the computer to analog data that can be transmitted over the phone line, and modulation protocols also define the data transfer speed and encoding method the modem uses. Numerous modulation protocols exist, but most modems support recognized standards. Windows 95 provides support for most common protocols.

Using the 16550 UART

Each serial port contains a Universal Asynchronous Receiver/Transmitter, or UART. The UART converts the parallel signals from the CPU to serial signals that can be transmitted over a serial interface. The UART also controls other aspects of serial communications management. Unfortunately, the UART is often the weak link in the entire serial port chain. Many older systems use the 8250 or 16450 UARTs, which are designed to buffer only a single byte of data. When a byte arrives at the UART, the serial port generates an interrupt request to inform the CPU that the byte is waiting in the buffer for retrieval. If the CPU is busy with other tasks, often the case in Windows 95, another byte probably will arrive at the UART before the CPU can process the original byte, which causes an *overrun,* in which the incoming byte overwrites the waiting byte. The lost byte then must be retransmitted, slowing down performance.

Newer systems use an upgraded version, called the 16550. The 16550 UART contains a 16-byte FIFO (first in/first out) buffer that improves data communications by providing a much larger buffer in which data can be held until the CPU can process the next byte. The 16550 includes a level-sensitive trigger that you can configure to generate an interrupt request when one of the buffers reaches a certain number of bytes.

Tip If your system's I/O adapter uses a socketed 8250 or 16450 UART, you can remove the UART and replace it with a 16550 UART and gain the benefits of the 16550's FIFO buffer. If your UART is soldered to your I/O adapter or is integrated

continues

into a VLSI (Very Large Scale Integration) device on the I/O adapter or on your computer's motherboard, you need to get a new I/O adapter that contains 16550-equipped serial ports. If your PC contains a 8250 or 16450 UART, you probably will be unable to use a fast modem (14.4 Kbps or higher speed) at its fastest transfer speed.

If you configure the UART to generate an interrupt request at eight bytes, for example, the 16550 receives eight bytes of data and then prompts the serial port to generate an interrupt request. While the port is waiting for the CPU to service the interrupt and process the waiting eight bytes, the UART can receive another eight bytes and store those incoming bytes in the FIFO buffer.

The default receive trigger in Windows 3.x was set to 14 bytes, which left only 2 bytes in the buffer when the serial port generated an interrupt requesting the CPU to service the port. In Windows 95, the default transmit trigger is set to 16, and the default receive trigger is 8, which improves COM performance over Windows 3.x. You can set the transmit trigger value to 1, 6, 11, or 16, and the receive trigger value to 1, 4, 8, or 14. For relatively slow transfer speeds and with few applications running, a higher receive trigger can improve performance somewhat by reducing interrupts. As transfer speed and the number of applications running increases, you should reduce the receive trigger value if you begin experiencing buffer overruns. You can set the trigger values in the Modem property sheet and in Device Manager's port property sheet.

To set the trigger values, open the Control Panel and choose the Modems object. Select the modem connected to the port whose values you want to change, then choose the Properties button. Click on the Connection tab, then choose the Port Settings button to display the Advanced Port Settings dialog box shown in figure 28.4. Enable the Use FIFO buffers check box, then use the two slider controls to set the transmit and receive triggers. Choose OK when the settings are as you require.

Figure 28.4

Set trigger values in the Advanced Port Settings dialog box.

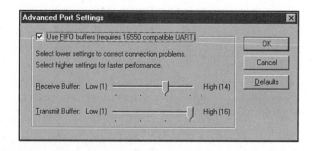

A second method to set the trigger values is to open the System object in Control Panel, then click on the Device Manager tab. Open the Ports tree, then select the port whose settings you want to change. Choose Properties, then the Port Settings

tab, then the **A**dvanced button to display the Advanced Port Settings dialog
box shown in figure 28.4.

By default, Windows 95 enables 16550 support for all applications, including Win32,
Win16, and DOS applications.

Managing Multiple COM Ports

Each COM port, as well as many other devices in the PC, require an interrupt request
(IRQ) line to enable the device to communicate with the CPU. Most of today's PCs do
not enable devices to share an interrupt—the exception being EISA- and MCA-bus
PCs. Even so, the COM ports in a majority of ISA systems, which do not support
interrupt sharing, are configured to share interrupts.

Typically, IRQ4 is assigned to COM1 and COM3, and IRQ3 is assigned to COM2 and
COM4. Assigning the same interrupt to two COM ports works fine, as long as you
don't try to use both ports at the same time. Attempting to do so causes a conflict
between the two ports, and you must ultimately disable one of them.

Today's PCs support only 16 interrupt lines, and with so many other devices in the PC
requiring IRQs, assigning a unique IRQ to each COM port isn't practical. In addition
to the COM ports, some of the other devices in the system that require IRQ lines are
the hard disk host adapter, floppy controller, parallel port(s), keyboard, system timer,
network adapters, sound card, and other devices.

If you have a mouse on COM1 and a modem or other device on COM2, and then try
to use COM3, the mouse becomes inoperative because COM1 and COM3 probably
share an interrupt. Rather then use COM3, therefore, consider using COM4 for the
other serial device. But, remember that you can't use the devices on COM2 and
COM4 simultaneously.

Another point to remember is that some video adapters conflict with COM4. These
adapters include the 8514A, ATI Mach8, and S3-based adapters. If your system
contains one of these video adapters, you can't use COM4 unless you assign different
settings to the COM port.

Tip

If you install a new internal or PCMCIA modem in Windows 95 and all your COM
ports are already assigned, Windows 95 assigns COM5 to the modem, or a higher
COM port number if COM5 is already in use. Some applications can't access the
modem at a higher port number than COM4, so you might have to adjust ports to
free a base address for the new modem, which enables Windows 95 to configure
the modem with a lower port number. To adjust the COM port values, use the

continues

Device Manager from the System object in Control Panel. Windows 95 uses the following default base addresses for the COM ports:

COM1 at 3F8
COM2 at 2F8
COM3 at 3E8
COM4 at 2E8

Now that you have some background knowledge about COM ports, modems, and communications in Windows 95, you can begin to install and configure a modem. The next section explains how to configure ports and modems in Windows 95.

Installing and Configuring Modems and COM Ports

Your modem and COM port work hand-in-hand. Therefore, you must set both properly for your modem to work at its best. Your COM ports probably were configured properly when you installed Windows 95. But, you might want to modify some of the COM port settings, such as changing IRQ or other values. The following section explains how to use the Device Manager to configure the COM ports.

Configuring COM Ports

To configure your system's COM ports, open the Control Panel and choose the System object. Then, open the Device Manager property page and expand the Ports branch. Select the port you want to configure, then choose Properties to display the Port property sheet shown in figure 28.5.

The General property page, shown in figure 28.5, provides information about the port and enables you to specify with which hardware profiles the port will be used (refer to Chapter 4, "Adding and Configuring New Hardware," for more information on hardware profiles). To specify settings for the port, click on the Port Settings tab to display the Port Settings page, shown in figure 28.6.

The settings on the Port Settings page control parameters such as bits per second, stop bits, parity method, and number of data bits, explained earlier in the section "Understanding COM Ports." You also can specify the flow control method for the port, explained later in the section "Setting Advanced Options." In the case of a modem, you really don't have to configure the port settings to match the modem's requirements, because the modem settings override the port settings. If you occasionally use other devices on the same COM port, however, you need to configure the port according to those other devices' requirements.

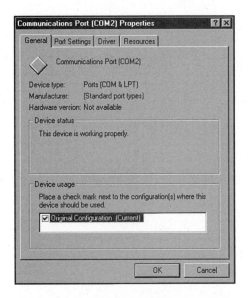

Figure 28.5

A typical COM port property sheet.

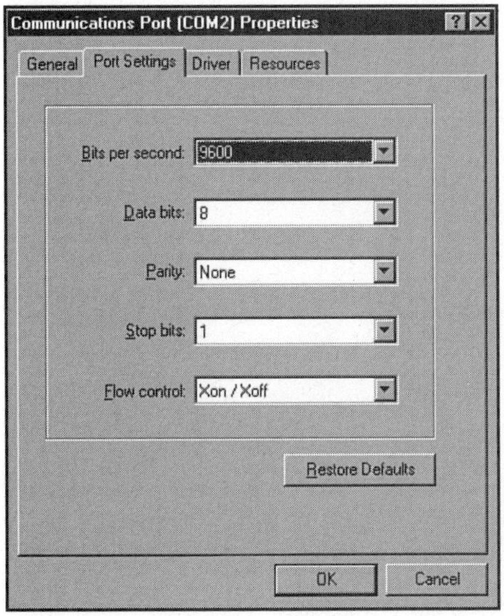

Figure 28.6

The Port Settings property page.

To change the IRQ or I/O base address of the port, click on the Resources tab to display the Resources page, then specify the new I/O address and IRQ values. If you are unsure how to accomplish the change, refer to Chapter 4, "Adding and Configuring New Hardware," which explains how use the Device Manager to set resources. Table 28.1 provides a list of common IRQ assignments for your reference in configuring your computer's COM ports.

Note Even though some of the IRQ lines listed in table 28.1 indicate that they are available, these interrupts might not be available on your system. If your PC contains a network adapter, sound card, or other devices, these IRQs might already be assigned to these devices. For an explanation of how to scan the system for IRQ assignments, refer to Chapter 4, "Adding and Configuring New Hardware."

TABLE 28.1
Common IRQ Assignments

IRQ Number	Typical Assignment
NMI	Non-Maskable Interrupt, reports parity errors
0	System timer
1	Keyboard
2	EGA/VGA and cascaded interrupt for second IRQ controller (IRQ9-15)
3	COM2, COM4
4	COM1, COM3
5	LPT2 (printer port 2)
6	Floppy disk
7	LPT1 (printer port 1)
8	Real-time clock
9	Software redirected to IRQ2
10	Available
11	Available
12	Available
13	Math coprocessor
14	Hard disk controller or host adapter
15	Available, or hard disk controller

Installing a Modem

If you have a modem connected or installed in your PC when you install Windows 95, with the modem on, Setup probably can automatically recognize and install support for the modem. If you change modems or add a new modem, you can use the

Modems object in the Control Panel to install support for the modem yourself. To install a new modem, open the Control Panel and choose the Modems object. From the General page of the modem property sheet, choose the <u>A</u>dd button. Windows 95 starts a modem installation wizard, and the dialog box shown in figure 28.7 appears. You have two options for installing the modem. By default, the wizard automatically scans your PC's COM ports for a new modem. Or, you can place a check in the check box labeled <u>D</u>on't detect my modem, which enables you to choose a modem from a device list.

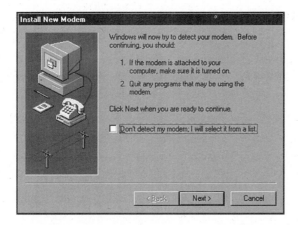

Figure 28.7

The Install New Modem wizard.

If your modem is installed and turned on (if, for example, you have an external modem), leave the check box cleared, which enables the wizard to search for the modem. If you have not yet installed the modem, place a check in the check box, which bypasses the detection phase and enables you to select your modem from a list (see fig. 28.8). If you direct the wizard to detect the modem and the wizard doesn't find a new modem, the wizard tells you it can't find a new modem and displays this same dialog box, enabling you to select the modem manually.

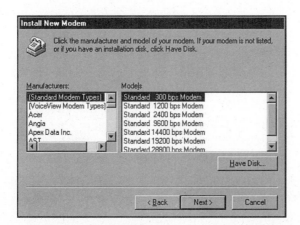

Figure 28.8

A modem selection dialog box.

Search through the **M**anufacturers list to select your modem's manufacturer, then select the model from the Mode**l**s list. If the list doesn't include your modem, select Standard Modem Types from the **M**anufacturers list, then select the model from the Mode**l**s list that matches the maximum speed of your modem. If yours is a 14.4 Kbps modem, for example, choose the 14,400 model from the Mode**l**s list.

 Tip   If your modem isn't listed, it might be compatible with a model from another manufacturer, or with a different model from the same manufacturer, because the command sets for the modems might be the same. Choosing a compatible modem rather than one of the standard types could make additional features available that the standard models don't support. If you can't find a compatible model, however, the standard types should provide adequate support in most situations. Or, you can check with the your modem's manufacturer to determine if the manufacturer has a Windows 95 driver available for your model or can suggest a compatible selection. Check the modem's manual to determine if it is compatible with a specific type of modem.

After you specify the modem model and click on Next, the wizard prompts you to specify the port to which the modem is connected. Choose the appropriate port, then click on Next. The wizard then copies any required files and installs support for the modem.

 Note   You can install multiple modems for a single COM port. When you configure a Win32 application that uses the Windows 95 communications APIs and TAPI, you select which modem to associate with the application. Installing two or more instances of the same modem driver enables you to use different sets of settings for various applications. You might configure one set of settings to use compression, for example, but configure another to disable compression.

Configuring a Modem

When you install a new modem, the modem installation wizard uses an appropriate set of default parameters for that modem. You might need to change those settings to optimize the modem's performance or tailor it for specific applications.

To configure a modem, open the Control Panel and choose the Modems object. From the General modem property page, select the modem you want to configure, then choose P**r**operties. Windows 95 displays a property sheet for the modem, as shown in figure 28.9.

The General property page enables you to specify the port to which the modem is connected, the volume level for the modem's speaker, and the connection speed you

want to use for the modem. To specify the port, just select the appropriate port from the Port drop-down list. To set the modem's volume, move the Speaker volume slider control. Most modems support four volume levels: off, low, medium, and high. Set yours according to your preferences.

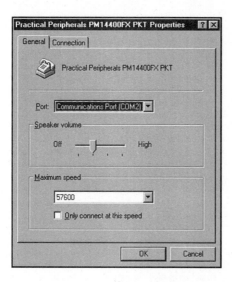

Figure 28.9

A typical modem property sheet.

When you set the Maximum speed for the modem in the General property page, you need to take your modem's capabilities into account. If you set the speed too high, you could experience problems with the modem. To determine the optimum setting, run the diagnostics on the modem as explained in the section "Testing a Modem" later in this chapter. One value the diagnostics reports is the maximum speed for the modem—in general, you shouldn't go any higher than the diagnostics-specified maximum.

 Tip

If you want the modem to connect only at the highest possible speed and not renegotiate the connection to a lower speed, enable the check box labeled Only connect at this speed. If you want to connect to your pay-per-use online service only at the highest possible speed, for example, enabling this option will prevent a connection from taking place at a lower speed.

Specifying Connection Settings

The Connection property page (see fig. 28.10) enables you to specify a variety of settings that control the port and other connection options. Some of these settings—Data bits, Parity, and Stop bits—override similar settings in the Port Settings property page for the selected COM port.

Figure 28.10

The Connection property page.

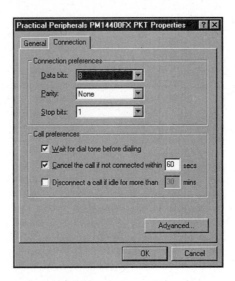

The following list details the other settings on the Connection property, located in the Call preferences group:

◆ **Wait for dial tone before dialing.** If your modem supports dial tone recognition (most do), enable this check box to prevent the modem from dialing if it can't detect a dial tone. If you have trouble with the modem detecting a dial tone that should be present, or you manually dial the phone, clear this check box.

◆ **Cancel the call if not connected within *n* secs.** Use this check box to control whether Windows 95 cancels the call if a connection is not established within the specified amount of time.

◆ **Disconnect a call if idle for more than *n* mins.** Use this control to enable Windows 95 to hang up the modem if no activity occurs on the modem for a specified amount of time. If you perform a lengthy unattended download, for example, enable this check box and specify an appropriate time limit to cause Windows 95 to hang up the connection after the specified amount of time expires.

Note Some online services and remote dial-up connections disconnect you automatically after no activity occurs on the connection for a specified amount of time. CompuServe, for example, disconnects after four minutes of no activity.

Setting Advanced Options

In addition to the standard settings in the Connection property page, you can use a few advanced settings to control other parameters for the modem. To set these advanced settings, choose the Advanced button from the Connection property page to display the Advanced Connection Settings dialog box (see fig. 28.11).

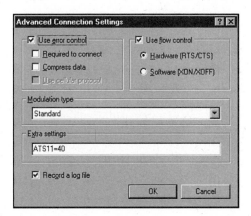

Figure 28.11

The Advanced Connection Settings dialog box.

The following list explains the settings in the Advanced Connection Settings dialog box:

◆ **Use error control.** Enable this check box if you want the connection to use the modem's error-correction capabilities (V.42 or MNP-4, for example). You almost always benefit from using error correction.

 ◆ **Required to connect.** This option, if enabled, requires that the connection be established using error correction. If the modem cannot establish a reliable connection, the connection is refused. If you want to ensure that the connection uses error correction, enable this check box.

 ◆ **Compress data.** This option, if enabled, causes the connection to use the modem's error compression protocol, such as V.42bis or MNP-5. You should enable this selection for text transfers and binary transfers, but disable it when you transfer compressed files.

 ◆ **Use cellular protocol.** This option, if enabled, causes the connection to use the modem's cellular error-correction protocol. Cellular error correction is becoming increasingly common in faster PCMCIA modems, enabling you to use your cellular phone to establish data connections. This option is dimmed if the selected modem does not support cellular protocols.

◆ **Use flow control.** This control specifies whether the connection uses flow control. If enabled, the connection uses the flow control method specified by the accompanying Modulation type setting (explained next). For best performance, use hardware flow control (RTS/CTS) whenever possible. To specify a flow control method, choose the Hardware (RTS/CTS) or the Software (XON/XOFF) option button.

◆ **Modulation type.** This setting specifies the type of modulation the modem uses to establish the connection. The available settings depend on the modem type, but most often are Standard and Non-Standard. The Standard setting uses the ITU-TSS standards (V.32bis, V.32, and so forth) and the Non-Standard uses the Bell and HST protocols. The Standard setting usually should work, but if you have trouble connecting, try the Non-Standard option.

◆ **Extra settings.** Use this text box to specify additional modem setup commands, such as setting the dialing speed, modem response mode (text, numeric), and other parameters, such as disabling call waiting. For tips on these settings, refer to the section "Tips for Optimizing Communications" later in this chapter.

◆ **Record a log file.** Enable this check box if you want Windows 95 to create a log file that tracks connection status and events. Windows 95 creates the log, Modemlog.txt, in the Windows 95 folder, and it can be very useful for troubleshooting and fixing connection problems.

After you specify the necessary advanced settings, choose OK to exit the Advanced Connection Settings dialog box.

Testing a Modem

In addition to providing controls that enable you to configure the modem and its COM port, Windows 95 enables you to perform troubleshooting on the modem. If you click on the Diagnostics tab on the Modems property sheet, the Diagnostics page appears, as shown in figure 28.12.

To test a modem, select the modem from the list by clicking on its assigned port, then choose More Info. Windows 95 attempts to communicate with the modem, and if successful, displays a More Info dialog box similar to the one shown in figure 28.13. The More Info dialog box contains information about the COM port and modem, including the interrupt, I/O base address, UART type, and recommended maximum speed, as well as modem commands that the diagnostic utility sent to the modem and the responses it received.

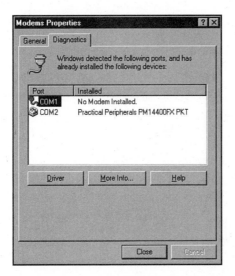

Figure 28.12

The Diagnostics property page for modems.

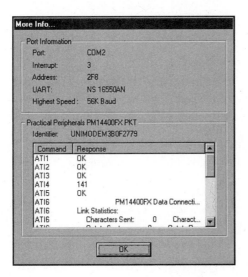

Figure 28.13

The More Info dialog box.

Note Some responses in the More Info dialog box might read ERROR, which does not necessarily indicate a modem error. The modem might not support the related command. If the diagnostic utility reported more than a few ERROR states, however, you probably have a problem with the modem or are using the wrong driver for the modem.

If Windows 95 can't communicate with the modem, an error message appears, followed by a More Info dialog box that reports the COM port information (interrupt, base address, and UART) but no other information.

Tip   The modem diagnostic utility is a 16-bit application, which means that it can't test the port if you're using the port. If Microsoft Fax is monitoring the port for incoming calls, for example, you must set the answer mode to **D**on't Answer, making the port available to the diagnostic utility. And because the diagnostic utility is a 16-bit application, it can't test for parallel-port modems.

At this point, you should have your COM ports and modem(s) configured and working properly. In addition, you might need to configure a few telephony options, which includes specifying the location from which you dial. The following section explains how to configure telephony services, and also discusses one of Windows 95 telephony-aware accessories, the Phone Dialer.

Configuring and Using Telephony Services

In addition to providing support for features such as call-routing, call waiting, conference calls, and other call functions, the telephony services in Windows 95 simplify dialing in various ways. You no longer have to use cryptic setup strings to program your modem to dial your calling card number for credit calls, for example. You now can provide Windows 95 with the calling card number and let TAPI do the rest. TAPI also simplifies using a modem from a variety of different locations, such as hotels and businesses, that require you to dial a special prefix to get an outside line. The following section explains these and other dialing parameters you can set for a connection.

Specifying Dialing Properties

Each modem definition in Windows 95 has associated with it various dialing properties. These dialing properties control the way the modem dials the number that you specify for the connection. Dialing properties are associated by dialing location, which enables you to create different sets of dialing properties for each location from which you use the modem. You might have one configuration for your office, another for your home, and a third for dialing from hotels. The office location might require you to dial a 9 for an outside line, whereas the home location would not. The hotel location might require you to dial an 8 for an outside line, and you also might want to

use a credit card to charge all calls that you make from a hotel. Dialing properties enable you to configure as many unique dialing locations you need.

Note Dialing properties affect only Win32 applications that use TAPI to access the modem. Dialing properties do not affect Win16 or DOS applications. These applications control the modem themselves, and the application must handle any special dialing functions separately.

You usually can specify dialing properties from within the Windows 95 application that uses the modem. In the Phone Dialer application, for example (choose Start, Programs, Accessories, and Phone Dialer), you can choose Tools, Dialing Properties to specify dialing properties. You also can use the Modems object in the Control Panel to set dialing properties. To do so, choose the Modems object from the Control Panel, select the modem you want to change, then choose Dialing Properties. Windows 95 displays the Dialing property sheet shown in figure 28.14. (If this is the first time you set dialing properties, Windows 95 will prompt you for your current area code before displaying this property sheet.)

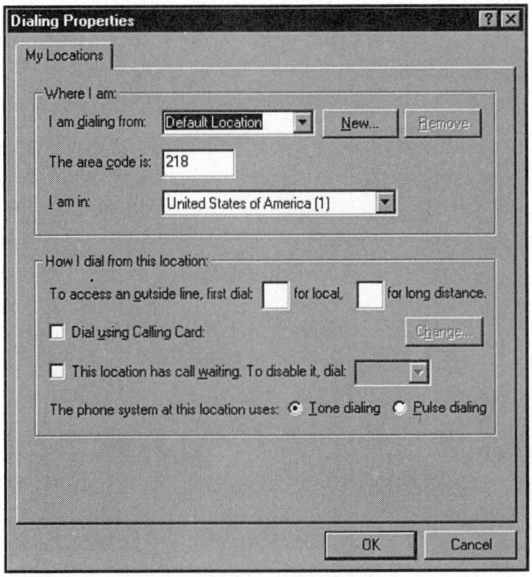

Figure 28.14

The Dialing property sheet.

Windows 95 creates a set of default dialing properties stored with the Default Location. You can modify this group of settings or create a new dialing location. To create a new location, choose the New button. Windows 95 displays a simple dialog box (see fig. 28.15) that you can use to specify a name for the dialing location.

Figure 28.15

Specify a name for the new dialing location.

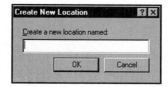

Next, set any special properties required for the dialing location. The following list describes the settings on the Dialing property sheet:

◆ **I am dialing from.** This is the name of the dialing location. To change the name, click in the text box portion of the combo box and type the new name.

◆ **The area code is.** Enter the area code of the location from which you are dialing to help Windows 95 differentiate between local and long distance calls, although you might also need to specify toll prefixes (prefixes in your area code that are long-distance calls, explained later).

◆ **I am in.** Choose the country of the location from which you are dialing. This enables Windows 95 to recognize when special codes are needed for international calls, and also helps define the modulation protocol used.

◆ **for local.** Specify the access number, if any, you must dial to get an outside local line. At many businesses, for example, you must dial a 9 for an outside local line.

◆ **for long distance.** Specify the access number, if any, you must dial to get an outside long distance line. This access number is in addition to the 1 used in 1-plus dialing, which Windows 95 adds automatically if necessary. An example is the 8 required at most hotels to place credit-card long distance calls.

◆ **Dial using Calling Card.** If you enable this check box, Windows 95 displays a dialog box you can use to specify the type of calling card you are using, the card number, and other information. Setting up a calling card is explained in the next section.

◆ **This location has call waiting.** Enable this check box if your phone line supports call waiting. Then, choose the appropriate method for disabling call waiting from the associated drop-down list. The predefined choices include *70, 70#, and 1170. If the prefix you need to enter to disable call waiting is different, click in the text box portion of the combo box and enter the necessary characters. Specifying the correct parameters enables Windows 95 to turn off call waiting, which prevents incoming calls from disrupting modem connections.

◆ **Tone dialing and Pulse dialing.** Choose the dialing method your phone system uses.

Configuring Calling Card Options

If you are making a connection from a pay-per-use phone, such as from a hotel or airport, you probably want to charge toll calls to your phone calling card. DOS and Win16 applications typically complicate using a calling card in a dialing string, and making connections often is difficult to accomplish. On the other hand, it's relatively simple with Win32 applications and TAPI.

Each dialing location can use a different calling card setup. To define the calling card parameters for a dialing location, first enable the Dial using Calling Card check box. After you click on the check box to enable it, Windows 95 displays the Change Calling Card dialog box shown in figure 28.16.

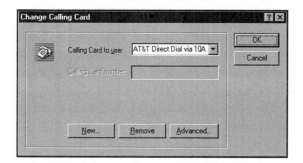

Figure 28.16

The Change Calling Card dialog box.

Tip

In addition to enabling you to use a calling card to make calls, the Change Calling Card dialog box enables you to use special dialing strings that apply to specific long-distance carriers, without using a credit card. To access an AT&T long distance network from a phone that a different carrier (such as MCI or Sprint) normally services, for example, you typically dial 10ATT1 (102881) and then the number you want to dial. The initial string connects you to the carrier, and the call is billed to the number from which you call, which is why you don't need a credit card number. These special carrier access options are identified by the string "Direct Dial" in their names, such as "AT&T Direct Dial via 10ATT1." When you select one of these calling card options, Windows 95 disables the Calling Card number text box.

To use a credit card, select from the Calling card to use drop-down list the carrier and dialing method you want to use. Unless the option you select is a direct-dial option that does not require a credit card, Windows 95 enables the Calling Card number text box. Enter your calling card number in the text box. To view the calling string Windows 95 uses, choose Advanced to display the Dialing Rules dialog box (see fig. 28.17).

Figure 28.17

*The Dialing
Rules dialog box.*

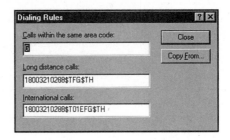

Tip   If you select one of the predefined calling card options, the controls in the Dialing
Rules dialog box are dimmed, preventing you from changing any of the dialing
strings. This is a safety feature to prevent the entries from becoming corrupted. If
you want to change dialing rules, you must create a new calling card definition,
explained later in this section.

Because you can change dialing rules only if you create a new calling card, the dialing
rule codes and their meanings are explained later in the section "Creating a New
Calling Card." For now, click on Close to close the Dialing Rules dialog box.

After you specify the calling card and card number, choose OK, then close the
Dialing Properties and Modem Properties pages. The next time your Win32 application (such as HyperTerminal or Phone Dialer) uses the calling location with which
you have associated your calling card options, the call is directed to the carrier you
have specified, and uses your calling card number to establish the call. If you wonder
how this process works, read the next section.

Creating a New Calling Card

The Change Calling Card dialog box contains many predefined calling cards and
methods used in parts of the world. You also can create your own calling card, which
enables you to customize the way the calling card connection is made. For example,
you can't change the predefined "AT&T via 1-800-321-0288" entry, but you can create
a new entry based on it, then modify the new entry.

To create a new calling card, open the Modems object in the Control Panel, select the
modem, and choose Dialing Properties. Enable the Dial using Calling Card check
box, or if it is already enabled, choose the Change button to activate the Change
Calling Card dialog box. Next, choose New. Windows 95 displays a simple dialog box
that prompts you to enter a name for the new calling card. Enter a unique name and
choose OK.

Next, you need to specify the dialing rules to be used for your new calling card entry.
Choose Advanced to activate the Dialing Rules dialog box. All the text boxes in the
Dialing Rules dialog box are blank, and you can enter your own settings or copy from

an existing calling card. To copy from an existing calling card, choose Copy From to bring up the Copy Dialing Rules dialog box. Select the calling card upon which you want to model your new card, then choose OK. Windows 95 fills in the fields in the Dialing Rules dialog box based on the selected calling card. Unlike with a predefined calling card, however, the text boxes are enabled, which lets you change their contents.

The fields in the Dialing Rules dialog box consist of dialing numbers and special codes. The codes you can use are described in table 28.2.

TABLE 28.2
Codes for Dialing Rules

Code	Description
E	Country code
F	Area code
G	Destination local number
H	Calling card number
P	Pulse dial
T	Tone dial
W	Wait for a second dial tone
@	Wait for a ringing tone followed by five seconds of silence
,	Two-second pause
$	Wait for a calling card prompt tone if your modem supports it (such as the "bong" tone used by AT&T)
?	Display an on-screen prompt to the user to continue dialing manually

Consider this scenario: You want to use your calling card from your hotel room. The hotel phone system requires that you dial 8 to get an outside long-distance line. You have an AT&T calling card, but you want to use the 1-800-CALL-ATT number (1-800-225-5288). When this number connects, you hear the AT&T chime, following by instructions to dial 1 for a credit card call. After you dial 1, you receive another chime tone and instructions to dial the number you want to call. After you dial the number, you receive another chime tone, followed by instructions to dial your card number and PIN.

You specify the 8 to get the outside line through the main Dialing Properties page so that you don't have to include it in your dialing rules string. This is the string you need in the long-distance calls field:

18002255288$1$TFG$H

The first set of numbers dials the AT&T access number. The $1 waits for the first chime tone, then dials 1 to specify a calling card call. The $TFG waits for the second chime tone, then tone-dials the area code and local number. The $H waits for the "bong" tone, then dials your calling card number.

 Tip   For an explanation of how to dial numbers manually, refer to the section "Dialing Manually" under "Using Communications Programs" later in this chapter.

Editing the Toll Prefix List

Although some of the prefixes in your area code probably are local numbers, most aren't. In many areas of the country, you must also dial your area code even when you call within your own area code. Windows 95 keeps track of which numbers in your area code must be treated as long-distance numbers (requiring the area code) and which can be treated as local calls (no area code) through a toll prefix list.

Unfortunately, the ability to edit toll prefixes directly was dropped early in the Windows 95 beta cycle. Nevertheless, a couple of methods remain that enable you to edit the toll prefix list relatively easily. If you use the Microsoft Fax provider in Exchange, open Exchange and choose Tools, Microsoft Fax Tools, Options. When the Microsoft Fax property sheet appears, click on the Dialing tab to display the Dialing property page, then choose the Toll Prefixes button to activate the Toll Prefixes dialog box shown in figure 28.18.

Figure 28.18

The Toll Prefixes dialog box.

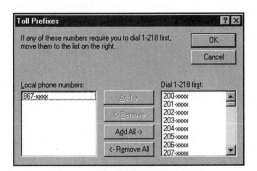

The Toll Prefixes dialog box lists all phone prefixes from 200 through 999. To specify prefixes in your area code that require you to include the area code in the dialing string, select the prefix from the Local phone numbers list, then choose Add.

 **Tip**   If all the prefixes in your area code require that you dial the area code, you can choose Add All to add all of the prefix numbers to the toll list, then locate and remove your own local prefix from the list. When you choose OK, however, you

can expect to wait for a minute or so while Windows 95 updates the toll list to reflect all the numbers you selected.

If you don't use Microsoft Fax, a couple other methods help you specify toll prefixes. The Dialing property sheet includes a Dial as a long distance call check box (located at the bottom of the page). Enable this check box to tell Windows 95 to treat the call as a long-distance call and add the prefix to the toll list.

You also can use the Phone Dialer to edit the Toll Prefix list. Open the Phone Dialer and enter a seven-digit phone number in the Number to dial combo box. Then, choose Tools, Dialing Properties to open the Dialing Properties page. Enable the Dial as a long distance call check box to add the prefix to the toll list, or disable it to remove the prefix from the toll list.

Tip

Using the Phone Dialer to edit the toll prefix list has the advantage of not requiring you to install the Microsoft Fax profile if you aren't using Microsoft Fax. If you have many numbers to add to or remove from the toll prefix list, however, you might want to install the Microsoft Fax provider, even if you don't plan to use Microsoft Fax. After you add the provider, edit the toll list. After you edit the toll list, open the Control Panel and remove the Microsoft Fax provider from your Exchange profile. Chapter 29, "Installing and Configuring Exchange," explains how to add the Microsoft Fax provider to your Exchange profile.

Using the Phone Dialer

Windows 95 includes a TAPI accessory program that you might find useful. The Phone Dialer (fig. 28.19) enables you to store often-used phone numbers and have your modem automatically dial for you. It stores only eight numbers in its speed dial list, but you still might find it useful.

Figure 28.19

The Phone Dialer.

The Phone Dialer is nearly self-explanatory. To enter a number in the speed dial list, click on an empty button. Phone Dialer displays a simple dialog box (see fig. 28.20) you can use to enter the name for the speed dial entry and the phone number. Enter the name and number, then choose <u>S</u>ave. Phone Dialer adds the name to the button. Repeat the process for any other blank speed dial buttons you want to program. When you're ready to dial the number, just click on its button.

Figure 28.20

*The Program
Speed Dial
dialog box.*

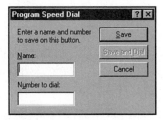

To edit an existing speed-dial button, choose <u>E</u>dit, <u>S</u>peed Dial. Click on the entry you want to change, then enter the new name and number in the appropriate text boxes.

Besides the speed dial buttons, you can use the keyboard or the key buttons on the Phone Dialer to enter a number. The Phone Dialer keeps track of the numbers it dials, and you can select previously dialed numbers from the <u>N</u>umber to dial combo box.

Using Communications Programs

No two communications programs are alike, but all share some common characteristics, settings, and features. Windows 95 includes a general-purpose communications program, called HyperTerminal, that you can use to connect to BBSs (bulletin board services), commercial online services, and other computers. This section uses HyperTerminal as an example to explain common issues for communications programs in lieu of covering HyperTerminal in detail. Whether you use HyperTerminal or some other communications program, this section should help you understand some of the configuration and communication issues involved in using you communications program.

Note To start HyperTerminal, choose Start, <u>P</u>rograms, Accessories, HyperTerminal. Windows 95 then will open the HyperTerminal folder.

Setting Connection Parameters

When you use a communications program to connect to a BBS, another computer, and some online services, you must set the appropriate terminal emulation. *Terminal emulation* defines the keyboard mapping, number of lines per screen, and other information that enables the PC to interact with the remote computer.

To configure terminal emulation in HyperTerminal, choose File, Properties. Then, click on the Settings tab to bring up the Settings property page shown in figure 28.21.

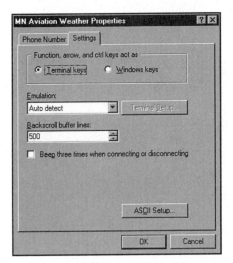

Figure 28.21

The Settings property page.

The Function, arrow, and ctrl keys act as group at the top of the Settings property page determines how HyperTerminal treats function, arrow, and control keys. Choose the Terminal keys option button if you want these keys to be transmitted to the remote computer, or choose the Windows keys option button if you would rather the keys affect the Windows 95 environment.

From the Emulation drop-down list, select the type of terminal expected by the remote computer you are calling. You can select Auto detect to enable HyperTerminal to attempt to automatically detect terminal type, or you can choose a specific terminal type. If you choose a specific terminal type, Windows 95 enables the Terminal Setup button. Choosing Terminal Setup issues the Terminal Settings dialog box, shown in figure 28.22.

The settings that appear in the Terminal Settings dialog box vary according to the terminal type you select. For information about a particular control, click on the question mark button, then click on the control to view a brief description of the control's function. The key point is to specify the settings the remote computer expects. If you are unsure what those settings should be, leave the settings at their default values.

Figure 28.22

The Terminal Settings dialog box.

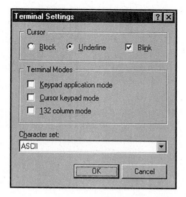

The Settings property page also contains other settings you might want to change. The **B**ackscroll buffer lines spin control enables you to specify the number of lines that HyperTerminal will buffer, enabling you to use the scroll bar and page up key to view lines that have been received. The setting is set to the maximum of 500 lines by default.

 Tip   If you enable the Bee**p** three times when connecting or disconnecting check box, Windows 95 provides an audible indicator anytime a connection is established or broken.

The AS**C**II Setup button enables you to control a variety of other terminal parameters. Clicking on the AS**C**II Setup button brings up the ASCII Setup dialog box (see fig. 28.23). For more information about these controls, click on the question mark button, then click on the control.

Figure 28.23

The ASCII Setup dialog box.

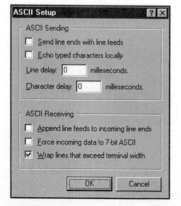

Dialing Manually

Sometimes you simply must manually dial the phone. When you use HyperTerminal, you enable manual dialing through the properties for the port. To configure manual dialing, open the HyperTerminal connection file for which you want to enable manual dialing. Choose File, Properties to display the Phone Number property sheet, then choose the Configure button to display the property sheet for the modem. Next, click on the Options tab to display the Options property page shown in figure 28.24.

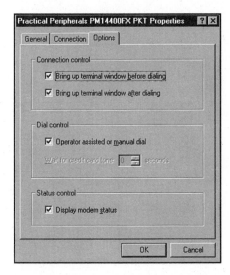

Figure 28.24

The Options property page.

Enable the Operator assisted or manual dial check box. If you need to manually enter special modem commands in addition to dialing manually, enable one or both of the check boxes in the Connection control group at the top of the dialog box. Enable the Bring up terminal window before dialing check box if you need to enter modem commands before you dial the number. Enable the Bring up terminal window after dialing check box if you need to enter modem commands after you dial the number. Enabling either check box causes a simple terminal window to open at the appropriate time, making it possible for you to type modem commands directly to the modem before or after you dial. Figure 28.25 shows a typical pre-dial terminal window.

Next, direct HyperTerminal to open the connection by clicking on the Dial button or by choosing Call, Connect, Dial. After you specify any necessary modem commands (assuming you enable the terminal window), click on Continue. HyperTerminal displays the message box shown in figure 28.26. Lift the phone receiver and dial the number. When the remote computer picks up the line, choose Connect to establish the connection.

Figure 28.25

A typical pre-dial terminal window.

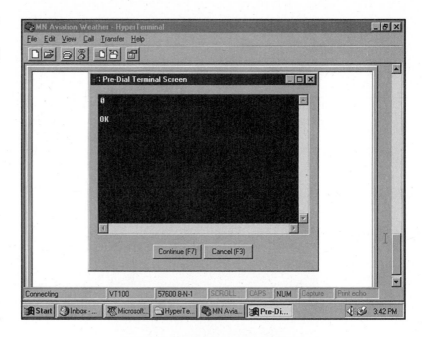

Figure 28.25

A typical pre-dial terminal window.

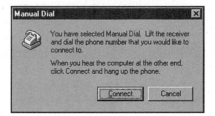

Figure 28.26

The Manual Dial message box.

Using File Transfer Protocols

When two computers transfer a file between one another, the computers must both use the same file transfer protocol. Transfer protocols define the data encoding methods, error correction methods, and other parameters that ensure an error-free transfer. Encoding enables the data to transfer without being incorrectly interpreted as terminal commands. Error correction provides a mechanism by which the receiving system can notify the sender of incorrectly received bytes, request those bytes to be resent, and acknowledge correct receipt. This guards against lost data due to overruns, line noise, time-outs, or other problems during the transfer.

There are many different file transfer protocols; one of the most popular general-purpose protocols is Zmodem, developed by Chuck Foresberg. One of Zmodem's

strengths is that it enables *streaming transfer,* in which the entire file is transferred as a series of blocks without any acknowledgment from the receiving system. Only incorrectly received blocks are acknowledged, and only so that they can be re-sent.

Zmodem also offers other advantages. You can configure most aspects of its operation, and Zmodem can restart a previously interrupted file transfer—a great feature if the connection or transfer fails or hangs for some reason during a long download. Zmodem sends only those blocks not sent in the previous attempt rather than the entire file over again.

Other common protocols include Ymodem, Xmodem, Kermit, and CompuServeB/B+, all of which are *block-oriented protocols*—they send data in a predefined block size (such as 1 KB), and the receiver must acknowledge each block. By requiring acknowledgment of each block, these protocols slow down transfer, because the sender has to wait for an acknowledgment before sending another block.

CompuServeB/B+ is a special-purpose transfer protocol used to transfer files to and from CompuServe. CompuServeB/B+ is block-oriented, but also includes an autoresume feature similar to Zmodem. Kermit was developed in the Unix community and is used primarily for transferring files to and from Unix-based minicomputers. Table 28.3 lists the most common file transfer protocols.

TABLE 28.3
Common File Transfer Protocols

Protocol	Transfer	Error Correction	Autoresume
Xmodem	Block	CRC or Checksum	No
Ymodem	Block	CRC or Checksum	No
Ymodem-G	Streaming	None	No
Zmodem	Streaming	CRC	Yes
CompuServeB/B+	Block	CRC	Yes
Kermit	Block	CRC or Checksum	No

Generally, your best choices for file transfer protocols are Zmodem and CompuServeB/B+ (for CompuServe transfers). You can choose a protocol before you begin downloading a file. Unfortunately, HyperTerminal does not enable you to change any of Zmodem's properties. Other communications programs, however, do support changing protocol properties.

Tips for Optimizing Communications

This section provides tips on using special modem settings, as well as some tips for CompuServe and America Online users. These tips help you configure your modem properly and make the most of your time online.

Using Special Settings

Sometimes you might want to include special initialization settings for the modem. You might want to include the command ATS11=50, for example, to speed up the rate at which the modem dials. To make the modem use special initialization commands, choose the Modems object from the Control Panel, select the modem, then choose the Properties button. From the Connection property page for the modem, choose the Advanced button. Enter the special modem string in the Extra settings text box, then choose OK.

 Tip Windows 95 stores your special initialization string in the Registry in the UserInit subkey for the modem.

Changing Modem Registry Keys

The Modems object in the Control Panel enables you to select which modem to use, but it doesn't enable you to directly modify the initialization string or many other settings for the modem. Instead, Windows 95 uses a group of settings defined by your modem type.

You can, however, use the Registry Editor to modify modem configuration settings directly. The modem settings are stored in \Hkey_Local_Machine\System\ CurrentControlSet\Services\Class\Modem*modemID,* where *modemID* is the identifier for your modem (such as 0001). By modifying modem settings, you can tailor the way Windows 95 uses the modem. If Windows 95 doesn't include a driver specifically for your modem, modifying the Registry settings enables you to customize the settings of a partially compatible driver to be fully compatible with your modem.

The following list describes the main subkeys for the modem:

◆ **Answer.** This subkey specifies the command the modem uses to answer an incoming call, usually ATA<cr>.

◆ **Hangup.** This subkey specifies the command the modem uses to hang up a call, usually ATH<cr>.

◆ **Init.** The first key entry in the Init subkey typically specifies the command Windows 95 uses to "wake up" the modem, generally AT<cr>. Other keys specify the initialization string(s) for the modem.

◆ **Monitor.** This subkey specifies the command Windows 95 uses to place the modem in auto-answer mode, usually ATS0=0<cr>.

◆ **Responses.** The key entries in this subkey define the response strings for the modem.

◆ **Settings.** This subkey contains key entries that define many of the modem's commands for specific functions. Table 28.4 describes these key entries.

TABLE 28.4
Modem Configuration Keys

Subkey	Description	Example
Blind_Off	Detect dial tone before dialing	X4
Blind_On	Do not detect dial tone before dialing	X3
CallSetupFailTimer time-out	Specify call setup	S7=<#>
Compression_Off	Compression disabled	S46=136
Compression_On	Compression enabled	S46=138
DialPrefix	Dial command prefix	D
DialSuffix	Dial command suffix	;
ErrorControl_Cellular	Cellular protocol enabled	\N3-K1)M1-Q1*H1
ErrorControl_Forced	Error control required to connect (reliable)	+Q5S36=4S48=7
ErrorControl_Off	Error control disabled (normal mode, not direct)	+Q6S36=3S48=128
ErrorControl_On	Error control enabled (auto reliable)	+Q5S36=7S48=7
FlowControl_Hard	Hardware flow control	&K1
FlowControl_Off	No flow control	&K0
FlowControl_Soft	Software flow control	&K2

continues

TABLE 28.4, CONTINUED
Modem Configuration Keys

Subkey	Description	Example
InactivityTimeout	Specify inactivity time-out	S30=<#>
Modulation_Bell	Use Bell modulations for 300 and 1,200 bps	B1
Modulation_CCITT	Use CCITT modulations for 300 and 1,200 bps	B0
Prefix	Configuration command prefix	AT
Pulse	Use pulse dialing	P
SpeakerMode_Dial	Speaker on during dial and negotiation	M1
SpeakerMode_Off	Speaker always off	M0
SpeakerMode_On	Speaker always on	M2
SpeakerMode_Setup	Speaker on only during negotiation	M3
SpeakerVolume_High	High speaker volume	L3
SpeakerVolume_Low	Low speaker volume	L1
SpeakerVolume_Med	Medium speaker volume	L2
SpeedNegotiation_Off	Connect only at default modem speed; do not fall back	N0
SpeedNegotiation_On	Use lower DCE speed to connect, if necessary	N1
Terminator	Configuration command suffix	<cr>
Tone	Use tone dialing	T

Note   The settings for your modem might be different from those shown in table 28.4.

CompuServe Tips for Windows 95

As of Summer '95, CompuServe does not have a version of WinCIM or CompuServe Navigator for Windows 95, although the latest versions do work under Windows 95 as

16-bit Windows applications. (CompuServe is working on Windows 95 versions of their front-end applications.) However, you can do a few neat tricks using WinCIM and CompuServe Navigator under Windows 95.

Connecting to CompuServe through the Internet

If you have dial-up or hard-wired access to the Internet, you can connect to CompuServe and enjoy all the same CompuServe services as you normally can using a regular CompuServe dial-up connection. Sometimes this might increase your access speed or reduce your costs. You might have a local 14,400 bps Internet access number, for example, but only a 9,600 bps local CompuServe access number. By connecting through the Internet, you increase your access speed. Or, if you have a local hard-wired or dial-up connection to the Internet, but no local CompuServe access number, connecting through the Internet helps you avoid long-distance charges or the 800-number communications surcharge to connect to CompuServe.

Tip

Connecting to CompuServe through the Internet can sometimes cost more than a dial-up connection to CompuServe. If you pay a service provider for Internet connectivity based on connect time, you pay your Internet connect time *and* CompuServe connect time. After you try to determine whether connecting to CompuServe through the Internet makes sense, keep in mind all your phone and connect charges.

Before you can establish a connection to CompuServe over the Internet, you need WinCIM version 1.4. First, you should verify that your Internet connection works. Use ping, Netscape, or another Internet application to connect and test your connection. When the Internet connection works properly, you can configure WinCIM for the connection.

To configure WinCIM to use your existing Internet connection to connect to CompuServe, start WinCIM and choose Special, Session Settings. WinCIM issues the Setup Sessions Settings dialog box shown in figure 28.27.

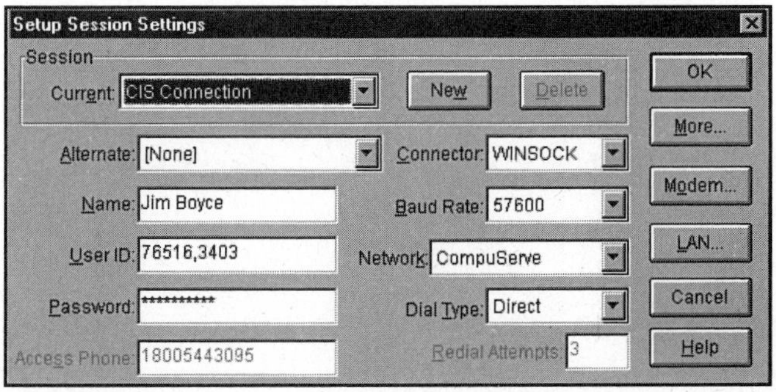

Figure 28.27

The WinCIM Setup Session Settings dialog box.

Next, open the Connector drop-down list and select WINSOCK. From the Network drop-down list, select CompuServe. From the Dial Type drop-down list, select Direct. Make sure your user name, ID, and password are correct.

Next, choose the LAN button to activate the WinSock Settings dialog box (see fig. 28.28). Enter **compuserve.com** in the Host Name text box, then choose OK. Choose OK in the Setup Session Settings dialog box. You should now be ready to connect WinCIM to CompuServe through your TCP/IP connection. Establish your Internet connection first, then open WinCIM and choose File, Connect, or click on any of the other buttons you normally use to connect to CompuServe.

Figure 28.28

The WinSock Settings dialog box.

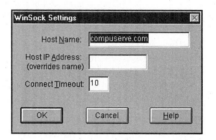

 Tip   You also can use CompuServe Navigator over an Internet connection to CompuServe.

Automating WinCIM

A little-known and unsupported switch in WinCIM enables you to turn on an undocumented feature in WinCIM and automate WinCIM's operation, potentially saving quite a bit on connect charges. CompuServe never formerly released this feature, called Auto-Pilot. Nevertheless, the code is still buried in WinCIM and you can take advantage of it.

Auto-Pilot enables you to automate your WinCIM sessions. Essentially, you can use WinCIM as an offline reader for your mail and forum messages. Using Auto-Pilot also enables you to automate file transfers.

To turn on Auto-Pilot for WinCIM, open the Wincim.ini file located in the CSERVE\WINCIM folder, then add the following setting at the end of the [General Preferences] section:

```
Auto-Pilot=On
```

Be sure to include the hyphen in the setting name. Then, save Wincim.ini and start WinCIM. You'll find a new menu item named Auto Pilot in the Special menu. For

help using Auto-Pilot, consult the Pilot.hlp file located in the \WinCIM folder on your *Inside Windows 95* CD.

Tips for America Online Users

America Online users will be interested to know that you can connect to America Online through the Internet. If you currently have a hard-wired or dial-up connection to the Internet, you can use that same connection to access America Online, including connections you make using the Windows 95 RAS client.

To configure America Online for an Internet connection, click on the Setup button in the Welcome dialog box to activate the Network & Modem Setup dialog box. Click on the Modem Setup button to display the Modem Selection and Customization dialog box (see fig. 28.29).

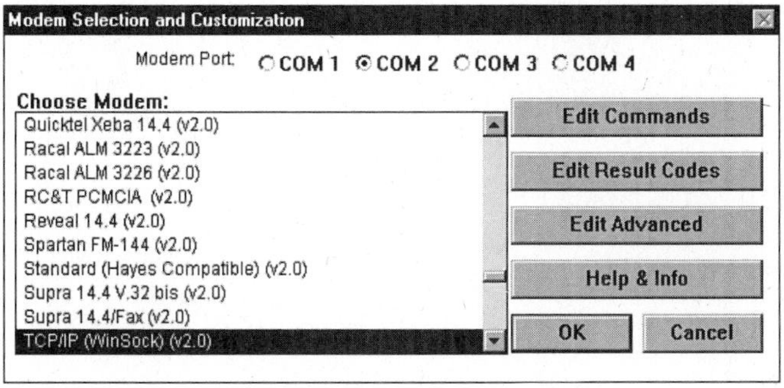

Figure 28.29

The Modem Selection and Customization dialog box.

Scroll through the modem list to locate the TCP/IP (WinSock) entry. Then, click on the Edit Advanced button to display the TCP/IP configuration dialog box shown in figure 28.30.

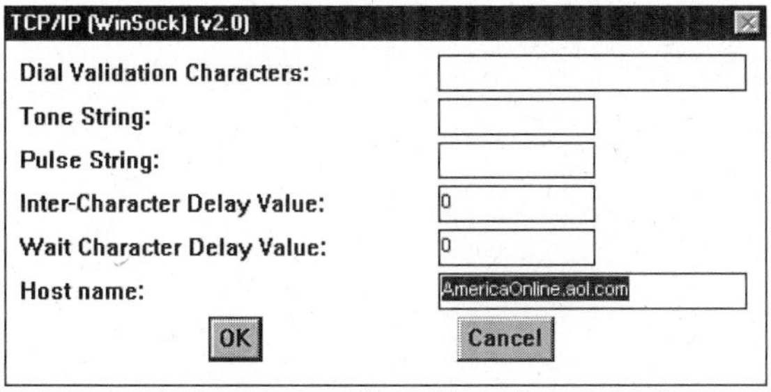

Figure 28.30

The TCP/IP configuration dialog box.

Enter **AmericaOnline.aol.com** in the Host name text box, and choose OK. Click on OK in the remaining dialog boxes to return to the Welcome dialog box. After you establish your connection to the Internet, choose Sign On to establish the connection.

## 29

Installing and Configuring Exchange

Windows 95 includes an e-mail client named Exchange that provides an integrated inbox and send/receive capability for LAN mail, remote mail, CompuServe mail, the Microsoft Network, Microsoft Fax, and Internet mail. Exchange supports all the features you expect from an e-mail client, including spell checking and message prioritization. Exchange also provides some features you might not expect, including support for rich-text messages, fax send and receive, and support for Internet mail.

Note   Exchange provides spell checking only if you install a 32-bit spelling dictionary.

This book's Exchange coverage is divided among multiple chapters. This chapter explains how to install and configure Exchange, including the following topics:

◆ Understanding Exchange

◆ Installing Exchange

◆ Creating and editing user profiles

◆ Configuring Exchange service providers

◆ Creating and managing a workgroup postoffice

◆ Expanding the mail system

Additional chapters cover other Exchange topics. Chapter 30 explains how to use Exchange to send and receive e-mail, including CompuServe mail. Chapter 31 explains how to use Microsoft Fax to send and receive faxes. Chapter 32 explains how to use Exchange to send and receive mail on the Microsoft Network. And Chapter 37 explains how to use Exchange to send and receive Internet mail.

Note   Parts of this chapter are written from the perspective of a postoffice administrator, under the assumption that you intend to set up and manage a postoffice for other users. Even so, this chapter also is geared to individual users who want to understand Exchange and need assistance creating and configuring service providers for Exchange. For information on using Exchange, refer to Chapters 30 31, 32, and 37.

The next section provides an overview of Exchange to help you understand how to best apply it to your needs.

Understanding Exchange

Windows for Workgroups includes an e-mail client compatible with Microsoft Mail. The Mail client in Windows for Workgroups does not offer the full set of features in Microsoft Mail 3.x, but the client does enable you to connect to a Microsoft Mail postoffice to send and receive e-mail.

Microsoft has redesigned its e-mail product and given it a new name—Exchange. The Exchange client in Windows 95 (see fig. 29.1) offers a considerably improved range of features over the old Microsoft Mail client, including the following:

◆ Integrated inbox for all message types, including e-mail and fax

◆ Support for rich-text (formatted) messages

◆ Capacity to embed attachments, such as binary files, in messages

◆ Remote mail and remote message preview

◆ Capability to create multiple folders to organize messages

◆ Capability to use filters and rules to sort messages

◆ A CompuServe provider that enables you to use Exchange to send and retrieve CompuServe mail

◆ Microsoft Fax, which enables you to send and receive faxes, and to share a fax modem among multiple users

◆ Support for direct binary transfer of attachments to compatible mail systems

◆ Support for Internet mail

◆ Expanded address book for contact management

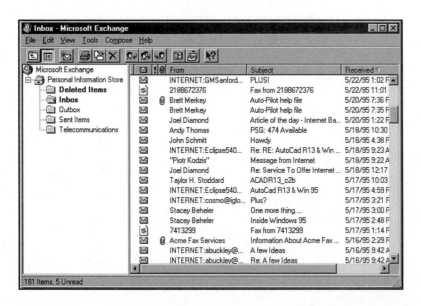

Figure 29.1

The Windows 95 Exchange client.

One of the primary advantages of the Windows 95 Exchange client is its integration—all messaging services are combined into a single inbox, making all your messages quickly accessible, regardless of their origins. A common interface also makes it easier to work with the different message types—you don't have to learn a new interface for each one.

Understanding the Exchange Infrastructure

Microsoft Exchange is a MAPI (Mail Application Programming Interface) application. *MAPI* is a set of API functions combined with an OLE interface that enable an application to interact with various MAPI service providers. *MAPI service providers* act as an intermediary between a mail client at one end of a connection and a message server at the other end of the connection. Windows 95's mail client is Exchange. The MAPI service providers are the Microsoft Mail, Microsoft Fax, Microsoft Network Mail, and CompuServe Mail providers. Figure 29.2 illustrates the concept.

Figure 29.2

The relationship between MAPI clients and MAPI service providers.

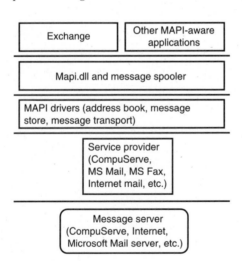

Essentially, Exchange provides a set of common features for managing, viewing, and manipulating message folders and messages. Without MAPI service providers to provide a connection to a message server—whether a workgroup postoffice on the LAN or a CompuServe mail box—Exchange is useless. This doesn't mean that Exchange is a useless application; on the contrary, when you add service providers to Exchange, you get a single application that you can use to manage messages of many types from many sources. Most important of all, Exchange is open-ended—any e-mail application vendor or service provider can write a MAPI service provider for Exchange, integrating its messaging server with the Exchange inbox. A developer can write a MAPI service provider for voice-messaging, for example, replacing your answering machine or office voice-mail system with a new message type in Exchange.

Tip   Not only *can* a developer write a MAPI provider to integrate voice-messaging in Exchange, but multiple companies are *doing* just that. You can expect to see voice-messaging providers for Exchange soon after the release of Windows 95. Naturally, using a voice-messaging service provider requires that your PC be capable of recording and playing back sounds (through a sound card, for example).

Exchange Components

When you install and configure Exchange, you must create at least one profile. A *profile* defines the service providers Exchange will use. If you want to use Exchange for your local LAN mail and CompuServe mail, for example, you would create a profile that contains the Microsoft Mail provider and the CompuServe Mail provider. Figure 29.3 shows a profile that contains a selection of providers.

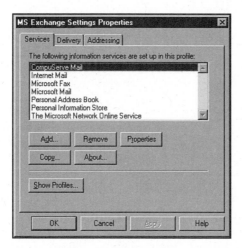

Figure 29.3

A profile containing a selection of providers.

Besides adding service providers to enable access to specific message servers, you need to add a couple of general-purpose providers to each profile. These include the Personal Information Store (PST) and Personal Address Book (PAB). Windows 95 uses the PST to store all your messages and essentially to form your personal mail box. The PST includes not only your inbox, but also the outbox, sentmail folder, and any additional mail folders that you create.

The PAB provides a unified electronic address book (see fig. 29.4) you can use to store all your message recipient addresses, including addresses for all providers. Whether you store a CompuServe address or a fax address, the entry is added to your PAB.

Figure 29.4

A typical Personal Address Book.

The Exchange Service Providers

The message providers you use with Exchange determine the message servers to which you can connect to send and receive messages. The following sections provide a brief overview of the service providers included with Windows 95, as well as a few service providers that Microsoft offers separately.

Microsoft Mail

This service provider enables you to connect to a Microsoft Mail postoffice. The postoffice can be one created with Windows 95, Windows for Workgroups, Windows NT, Microsoft Mail 3.*x*, or Microsoft Mail Server. The postoffice can be located on your LAN, or you can use a remote access services (RAS) connection to connect to the postoffice. A computer on the network can run Windows Dial-Up Networking server (included with the Plus! product), for example, and thus provide dial-in access to the postoffice, which can be located on the dial-in server or another node on the network. Users connected locally to the LAN send and receive mail across the LAN. Remote users, such as those working from home or out of town, can connect to the RAS server and gain access to the postoffice as if they are connected locally to the LAN. If you want to use Exchange for remote mail (connecting to a remote LAN), CompuServe mail, Microsoft Fax, or Internet Mail, you don't need a workgroup postoffice on your computer or on the LAN.

Tip The remote mail capability in Exchange differs from the mechanism Microsoft Mail Remote uses. Rather than rely on a proprietary dial-in connection like Mail Remote, Exchange relies on a RAS connection that third-party software or hardware, or Windows 95, can provide. This eliminates the need for users to run two separate versions of their mail client to connect when moving from the LAN to a remote site.

The Windows 95 postoffice does not offer the same level of features as the full Microsoft Mail 3.*x* or Mail Server products. The Windows 95 Exchange postoffice lacks the capability to communicate with other postoffices and does not support mail gateways. Windows 95 also includes simplified versions of the administration tools provided with the full Mail Server and Mail 3.*x* products.

 Tip You can upgrade your postoffice by acquiring the Microsoft Mail Post Office Upgrade. The features in this upgrade are explained later in the section "Extending the Mail System."

Microsoft Exchange Server

This service provider enables an Exchange client to connect to a Microsoft Exchange Server. The Exchange Server is a client-server messaging service that runs under Windows NT Server. In addition to providing features similar to the Microsoft Mail service provider, the Exchange Server provider includes Inbox Assistant, which is a set of server-based rules for filtering, forwarding, replying to, and deleting messages. The Exchange Server provider also includes Out of Office Assistant, which is a set of server-based rules for forwarding and replying to mail when you are out of the office.

CompuServe Mail

This service provider enables you to use Exchange to send and receive mail through the CompuServe Information Service (CIS). Because CompuServe's mail system supports a wide variety of message types and gateways, you can use the CompuServe service provider to send mail to many different types of recipients, including other CompuServe users, the Internet, MCI Mail, Novell MHS, fax, and many others. To use the CompuServe service provider, you must have a CompuServe account. The CIS service provider included with Windows 95 requires a dial-up connection to a standard CompuServe access point of presence (POP), such as your local CompuServe access number or one of CompuServe's 800 numbers. CompuServe offers advanced service providers that extend Exchange's capability by enabling connection through WinSock (Internet) and adding the capability to manage forum messages in Exchange.

Microsoft Fax

The Microsoft Fax service provider enables you to use Exchange to send and receive faxes without a fax machine. Like At Work Fax, which is included with Windows for Workgroups, the Microsoft Fax provider enables you to use a modem connected directly to your PC or a modem connected to another node on your LAN. Faxes that you send through a shared fax modem are treated much like print jobs placed in a network print queue. Incoming faxes are placed in a fax manager's mail box and must be forwarded manually through the e-mail system to the recipient's mail box.

The Microsoft Network

Windows 95 includes a service provider that enables you to send and receive messages on the Microsoft Network, Microsoft's online information service. For more information about the Microsoft Network, refer to Chapter 32, "Using the Microsoft Network." The front-end for the Microsoft Network is included with Windows 95.

Internet Mail

Included with Microsoft Plus! for Windows 95 is a message service provider that enables you to send and receive mail through an Internet server. The Internet Mail provider supports Simple Mail Transport Protocol (SMTP) and Post Office Protocol 3 (POP3) over a TCP/IP connection. If you have a direct or dial-up connection to the Internet or to an SMTP server, the Internet Mail service provider makes it possible for you use Exchange to send and receive your Internet mail.

Installing and Administering Exchange

Now armed with some background information about Exchange, you are ready to begin installing and configuring Exchange. This section of the chapter offers advice on planning your e-mail system, and provides specific instructions and tips on installing and configuring Exchange. First, you need to understand the postoffice.

 Note If you aren't going to use the Microsoft Mail service provider, you can skip to the section "Installing Exchange Clients" later in this chapter.

Understanding the Postoffice

Before you begin to install Exchange, you should spend some time planning the e-mail system. The first thing to understand is that you don't need a mail server

application. The Exchange client in Windows 95 can exchange mail with other Exchange users on the LAN, or other MAPI-based applications, including Microsoft Mail 3.x users. Message exchange occurs through a common workgroup postoffice (WGPO). The WGPO can be a postoffice created with a previous version of Windows for Workgroups or Mail 3.x. Or, you can use a utility included with Windows 95 to create the postoffice yourself.

You might have only one postoffice on your LAN, or you might have multiple postoffices; each workgroup, for example, might have its own postoffice. The drawback, however, is that the Windows 95 postoffice does not support transfer of messages between postoffices, which would prevent users in one workgroup from messaging users in other workgroups. The solution is to create a single postoffice for all users on the LAN or to upgrade to the Mail Server. If you create a single postoffice (rather than upgrade), every user must have an account in the WGPO.

The WGPO is really just a shared directory structure that resides on one of the workgroup's nodes. The WGPO actually serves a number of purposes. It contains information about each user's mail account, as well as information about mail in transit to a user.

When you send a message, it does not actually go out on the network looking for a mailbox into which to drop. The message goes instead into the workgroup postoffice and resides in a temporary file in one of the WGPO's directories. The message remains in the temporary file until the recipient (or recipients) logs on and starts Exchange on his workstation, or until the recipient selects **T**ools, **D**eliver Now Using, and Microsoft Mail to retrieve his messages. Windows 95 then copies the data in the temporary file to the user's own message store and deletes the temporary file.

The message store can reside on the user's workstation, on the same system as the workgroup postoffice, or on any network server. By default, Exchange creates the message store on the user's workstation, using the file extension PST for the file and whatever file name the user specifies during Exchange setup.

A single message file contains all a user's messages, regardless of message type (mail, fax, and so on). In addition, the message store contains the user's private message folders. Receiving messages increases the file's size, deleting messages decreases its size.

Unlike the Microsoft Mail Server or Exchange Server, the Windows 95 postoffice does not support shared folders. You can create and view message folders only in your own message store. Upgrading to the Mail Server or Exchange Server, however, enables you to create and view shared folders, and share messages with other users.

Planning the Mail System

Before you create the WGPO, you should plan the WGPO's location and means of access for the LAN's users. Generally, you should locate the WGPO on a network server for security and simplified backup. You can put the WGPO on any node on the network, however, as long as the node is configured to share its resources. Any Windows 95 or Windows for Workgroups node, for example, can host the postoffice, as can servers such as Novell NetWare and Windows NT servers.

You also must plan for adequate disk space to contain the WGPO. The WGPO requires approximately 360 KB for the empty postoffice and 16 KB for each user account. The size of a user message store (which is stored outside of the WGPO) depends entirely on the number and types of messages stored in the file. A message store can be as small as 100 KB or require many megabytes. If any of your users work from diskless workstations, remember that you must allow for space in each users' home directory on the server for their message stores.

Also, remember that the computer hosting the postoffice must be on and sharing its resources before users can connect to the WGPO to send and retrieve mail.

An important thing to understand is that each postoffice supports one administrative account that you use to create, modify, and delete user mail accounts, as well as to manage the mail system in other ways. After you create the postoffice, be prepared to create an administrative account for the postoffice. You at least need to specify a user account name and password. This account can be your own personal mail account, or you can create a mail account specifically for managing the postoffice. You might create an account named Postmaster, for example, to manage the postoffice.

Tip Creating an account specifically to manage the postoffice is good practice, because it enables more than one person to manage the postoffice (each using the same account name and password) without exposing personal mail messages to the other administrators. You (the account administrator) cannot remove or delete the postoffice, but you can modify it.

Creating the Workgroup Postoffice

You can create the WGPO on any Windows 95, Windows for Workgroups, Windows NT, Novell NetWare, or other server. The postoffice can be located on any computer (and platform) that presents that directory structure in the manner in which the Exchange clients expect, because it's really nothing more than a shared directory structure. The following section explains how to create the WGPO on a Windows 95 server. Following sections explain how to create the WGPO on Windows NT and Novell NetWare servers.

New Riders Publishing
INSIDE
SERIES

Creating a WGPO on a Windows 95 Server

Although you can install Exchange clients before you set up a WGPO, you can't completely configure the Exchange clients. Therefore, you should create the WGPO before you install and configure the Exchange clients. To create the WGPO, open the Control Panel and choose the Microsoft Mail Postoffice object. Windows 95 starts a wizard you use to create the WGPO. In the initial wizard dialog box, you specify whether you want to create a new postoffice or administer an existing postoffice. Choose the Create a New Workgroup Postoffice option button, then click on Next.

The postoffice wizard then prompts you to specify the location for the WGPO. You must specify an existing directory. If you specify C:\, for example, the wizard automatically uses the directory name C:\WGPO0000 for the postoffice. After you click on Next to continue, the wizard displays an administrator account dialog box similar to the one shown in figure 29.5.

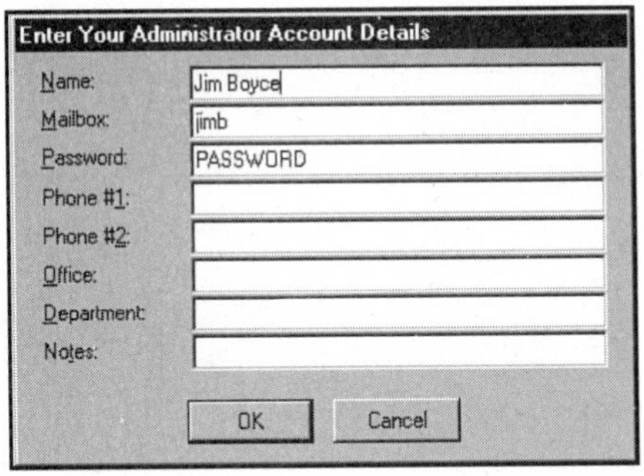

Enter Your Administrator Account Details
Name: Jim Boyce
Mailbox: jimb
Password: PASSWORD
Phone #1:
Phone #2:
Office:
Department:
Notes:
OK   Cancel

Figure 29.5

Enter the account information for the Administrator account.

Enter the administrator account name in the dialog box. If you do not want to use your own personal mail account to manage the WGPO, enter a name such as Postmaster for the account. By default, the wizard suggests a password of PASSWORD, but you should change the password.

Stop Don't forget the password for the postoffice administrative account. If you forget the password, you have to re-create the WGPO before you can regain the administrative privileges. Re-creating the WGPO will lose all existing accounts and messages.

You also should fill in the other information the account dialog box requests, including office location, phone numbers, and other data. This information will be available to other users who browse the postoffice address list. After you enter the account information, choose OK to finish creating the postoffice.

After you create the WGPO, you must share the postoffice directory. Open a folder window or Explorer and right-click on the postoffice directory, then choose Sharing. Windows 95 displays the Sharing property page shown in figure 29.6. Choose the Shared As option button, then specify a share name in the Share Name text box. By default, Windows 95 uses the directory name as the share name. To make it easy for users to recognize the postoffice, however, you might want to share it by another name, such as Postoffice.

Figure 29.6

The Sharing property page.

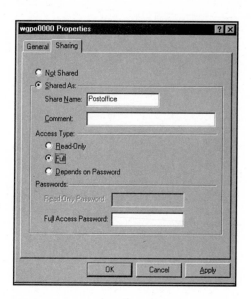

Next, you must specify full access rights for the shared directory. To do so, choose the Full option button in the Access Type group. If you want to protect the share, specify a password in the Full Access Password text box. Before users can connect to the postoffice, they must specify this password.

Note   Users must have write privileges in the WGPO before they can send mail. One disadvantage of using a Windows 95 or Windows for Workgroups server to host the postoffice is the lack of sophisticated access control for the WGPO. Because the WGPO is shared with full access, nothing can prevent a user from deleting the entire WGPO. By installing the postoffice on a Windows NT or Novell NetWare server, you can specify more selective access rights, enabling users to read and write to the WGPO, but not delete it.

After you share the WGPO, you can begin to install and configure Exchange clients on the user nodes on the network, and users can begin to access the postoffice.

Creating a Postoffice under Windows NT

The process for creating a WGPO under Windows NT 3.5 (Server or Workstation) is similar to the process you use in Windows 95, but because you are using the Mail client in Windows NT rather than Exchange, the steps are somewhat different.

First, log on to the Windows NT Server or Workstation node with administrator privileges. Then, open the Main program group in Program Manager and start Mail. If no Msmail.ini file exists when you start Mail, Mail gives you the dialog box shown in figure 29.7. Choose the Create a new Workgroup Postoffice option button, then choose OK.

Figure 29.7

The Welcome to Mail dialog box appears if no Msmail.ini file exists when you start Mail.

Note   An Msmail.ini file exists on the computer only if you have previously run Mail. If you do have an Msmail.ini file on the system for some reason, but no WGPO, you probably will receive an error message. If so delete the Msmail.ini file and restart Mail.

Mail responds by showing you a message box (see fig. 29.8) that suggests creating only one WGPO for each workgroup. If you already have a WGPO set up for your workgroup, choose No to cancel the WGPO creation process. If you still want to create a new WGPO, choose Yes.

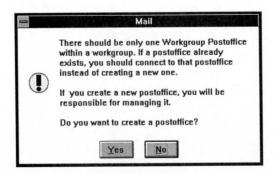

Figure 29.8

Verifying the creation of a WGPO.

If you choose <u>Y</u>es to create the WGPO, Mail displays a disk browse dialog box you can use to select the directory in which you want to create the WGPO. Find the directory in which you want to create the WGPO directory structure. If you choose C:\, for example, Mail creates a directory named C:\WGPO, then creates the WGPO structure in that directory. If the server on which you create the postoffice contains an NTFS partition, you should place the postoffice in the NTFS partition if possible to gain the added security features NTFS provides.

After you specify the directory to contain the WGPO, Mail displays an account details dialog box similar to the one shown in figure 29.9. You must fill in the <u>N</u>ame and <u>M</u>ailbox fields—the other fields, including the password, are optional. Although you can leave the password blank, you should specify a password for the account. Also, remember that you are creating the postoffice administrator account. You should create a special account for administering the postoffice, instead of using your personal account.

Figure 29.9

Specify the user account information in this dialog box.

Enter Your Administrator Account Details
<u>N</u>ame: Postmaster
<u>M</u>ailbox: Postmaster
<u>P</u>assword: PASSWORD
Phone #<u>1</u>:
Phone #<u>2</u>:
<u>O</u>ffice:
<u>D</u>epartment:
No<u>t</u>es:
OK   Cancel

After you create the postoffice administrator's account, you must share the WGPO directory. Open File Manager, select the directory, and give it a logical share name, such as Postoffice. Then, specify the access level for the directory, giving all users Change access to the directory. By using Change access rather than Full Control access, you prevent users from being able to delete the WGPO directory or take ownership of it.

Note Before you can apply Change access to the directory, WGPO has to be in an NTFS partition.

Creating a Postoffice under Novell NetWare

You can create the postoffice on a Novell NetWare server as well as on a Windows 95 or Windows NT server. To do so, log on to the directory with Administrator privileges and create a directory to contain the WGPO. Then, grant full trustee rights to the

WGPO directory. After the directory is ready, create the WGPO from a Windows 95 or Windows NT node as explained in the previous two sections.

Note Naturally, your workstation must be able to connect to the NetWare server, whether you run Windows 95 or Windows NT.

Managing the Workgroup Postoffice

To manage a postoffice, use the Microsoft Mail Postoffice object in the Control Panel. When you choose the Microsoft Mail Postoffice object, Windows 95 prompts you to specify whether you want to create a new postoffice or administer an existing postoffice. Choose the option **A**dminister an Existing Workgroup Postoffice. Windows 95 then displays a dialog box you use to specify the WGPO's location. Enter the path to the WGPO in the text box or choose the **B**rowse button to browse the network (including a remote connection) for the WGPO.

Tip You can use the Microsoft Mail Postoffice object to administer more than one postoffice simply by specifying the location of the postoffice you want to administer, followed by the appropriate postoffice administrator mailbox name and password.

Windows 95 then prompts you to specify the mailbox name and password for the administrator's account. You used this account when you created the postoffice (described previously in this chapter). Enter the mailbox name and password, enter the appropriate account name and password, and then click on the Next button. The Postoffice Manager dialog box appears (see fig. 29.10).

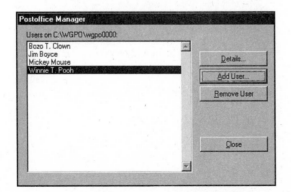

Figure 29.10

The Postoffice Manager dialog box.

Note You must create a mailbox account for a user before the user can log on to the postoffice to send and receive mail. Users can't create mail accounts on the fly the way they could with Windows for Workgroups.

You can use the Postoffice Manager dialog box to add new user accounts, view and modify existing accounts, and remove user accounts. To add a user, choose **A**dd User to open the Add User dialog box (similar to the Account Details dialog box shown in figure 29.9). To modify a user account, select the account from the list and choose the **D**etails button to open the Account Details dialog box. Modify the settings as necessary, then choose OK to save the changes.

Tip If a user forgets the mailbox password, open the user's account in the Account Details dialog box and specify a new password.

To remove a user's mail account, select the account name and choose the **R**emove User button.

Installing Exchange Clients

If you don't direct Setup to install Exchange when you install Windows 95, you can easily add Exchange later. To add Exchange, open the Control Panel and choose the Add/Remove Programs object, then click on the Windows Setup tab to display the Windows Setup property page (see fig. 29.11).

Figure 29.11

The Windows Setup property page.

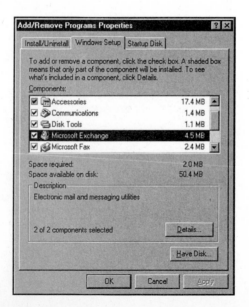

Scroll through the list of options to locate and select the Microsoft Exchange entry, then choose the Details button to specify which Exchange components you want to add. Windows 95 displays the dialog box shown in figure 29.12. Select the Exchange items you want to install. The Microsoft Mail Services include the Microsoft Mail and Microsoft Fax service providers. After you make your selection, choose OK, then choose OK again to begin installing the Exchange software. Depending on how you install Windows 95 the first time, you might be prompted to insert the Windows 95 disks or the CD.

Figure 29.12

Choose the Exchange components you want to install.

After you install Exchange, you must create at least one service provider profile, explained in the next section.

Creating, Managing, and Configuring User Profiles

Exchange is useless without any message service providers to enable it to connect to mail servers. To specify which service providers you want to use, you must create at least one Exchange profile. A *profile* defines the service providers used in an Exchange session, as well as the settings used by individual service providers in the profile.

You can create multiple Exchange profiles to suit your needs and preferences. Each profile can contain different service providers, or you can include the same service provider in more than one profile. If you include the same service provider in multiple profiles, each instance of the service provider can use different settings. For example, you might create a profile that contains an instance of the Microsoft Mail provider for your local LAN mail and a second profile that contains the Microsoft Mail provider for connection to a remote site.

Tip   Unfortunately, you can't add multiple instances of a same-service provider to a single profile. If you need to connect to a local Microsoft Mail postoffice as well as a remote Microsoft Mail postoffice, for example, you must create separate profiles.

Regardless of how many profiles you create, Exchange uses only one profile in each session. To use a different profile, you must restart Exchange. To specify which profile Exchange uses, choose the **S**how Profiles button on the Services property page. Then, from the drop-down list at the bottom of the property page, choose the profile that you want Exchange to use when it starts.

Creating and Configuring a Profile

To create a profile, open the Control Panel and choose the Mail and Fax object to display the MS Exchange Settings property sheet (see fig. 29.13). The Services property page enables you to create and manage profiles. If you do not yet have a profile, the General property page appears (see fig. 29.14).

Figure 29.13

The MS Exchange Settings property sheet, showing the Services property page.

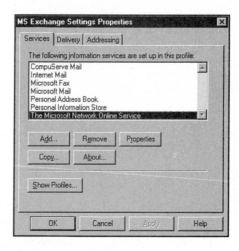

Figure 29.14

*The General
property page for
Exchange.*

To create a profile from the General property page, choose the A**d**d button. To
create a profile from the Services property page, choose the **S**how Profiles button to
display the General property page, then choose A**d**d. When you choose A**d**d, Windows 95 displays a dialog box that lists the service providers included with Windows
95 (see fig. 29.15). Choose the service provider you want to install, or choose Have
Disk if you have a service provider on disk that you want to install.

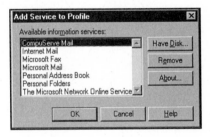

Figure 29.15

*Select the service
provider to
install.*

After you install a service provider in a profile, you must specify a variety of settings
for the service provider. The following sections explain how to configure the five
service providers included with Windows 95 and the Plus! add-on, as well as the
Personal Information Store (PST) and Personal Address Book (PAB).

Tip   The Delivery property page for a profile enables you to specify the information store
in which Exchange delivers incoming mail, as well as the order in which Exchange
cycles through the providers in a profile to deliver outgoing mail. The Addressing
property page enables you to specify which address book Exchange displays by
default, and also to specify the order in which Exchange processes your address
books to verify addresses.

Configuring Microsoft Mail

The Microsoft Mail service provider includes a number of property sheets you can use to configure the provider. After you install the Microsoft Mail service provider as explained previously, select the service provider from the Services property page, then choose Properties to display the Microsoft Mail property sheet shown in figure 29.16.

Figure 29.16

The Microsoft Mail property sheet.

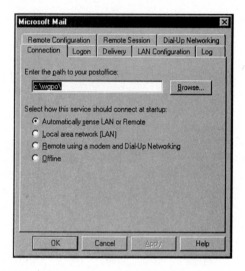

> **Note**   If you want to use the Microsoft Mail provider to send and receive mail to a remote site over a modem connection, you must install Dial-Up Networking. For an explanation of Dial-Up Networking, refer to Chapter 33, "Using Remote Access Services." For information on using Exchange to send and receive mail to and from a Microsoft Mail postoffice, refer to Chapter 30, "Using Microsoft Exchange."

The Connection page of the property sheet (refer to figure 29.16) enables you to define how Exchange connects to your postoffice. Whether you configure the provider for a LAN postoffice or a remote postoffice, you must specify the location of the postoffice in the path text box. If the postoffice is located on your computer, simply specify the drive and directory that contains the postoffice. If the postoffice is located on a server or other node on your LAN, you have two options: you can map a local drive letter to the postoffice's shared directory, or you can specify the UNC path to the shared directory.

Assume that your postoffice is located on a server named SERVER1 and the postoffice is shared on SERVER1 by the name Postoffice. (It doesn't matter in which directory on SERVER1 the postoffice is located, because you connect to it using its share name,

not its directory name.) The first option is to associate one of your local drive IDs with \\SERVER1\Postoffice. To associate your local drive M with the postoffice share, for example, you would enter **M:** in the path text box in the Connection property page.

Tip   To map a local drive ID to a remote share, right-click on the My Computer or Network Neighborhood icon to display the context menu, then choose Map **N**etwork Drive, which produces the Map Network Drive dialog box. Specify the drive letter to associate with the remote share, and the path to the share, such as \\SERVER1\Postoffice.

Although you can map a local logical drive ID to the remote postoffice, you don't have to—you can simply reference the postoffice by its UNC name. In the path text box on the Connection property page, enter the postoffice's UNC path name, such as \\SERVER1\Postoffice. Remember that the UNC name consists of the machine name, followed by the share name for the postoffice directory (the name by which you share the directory when you create the WGPO).

If you set up your MS Mail provider for a remote connection to a postoffice, specify the UNC name for the remote shared postoffice.

In the Connection property page, you also need to specify which type of connection the provider will use to connect to the postoffice. The four option buttons on the Connection property page enable you to specify a LAN connection, remote connection, or offline startup. If you want Exchange to determine automatically which type of connection to use, choose the Automatically **s**ense LAN or Remote option button. Otherwise, use the appropriate option button to specify a LAN or remote connection. If you want the MS Mail provider to start up offline (if you don't want to make a connection), choose the **O**ffline option button.

Note   If you want to connect to the postoffice using a remote connection, you also must specify the connection information for the remote server on the Dial-Up Networking page.

Specifying Logon Options

Use the Logon page of the Microsoft Mail property sheet (see fig. 29.17) to specify your postoffice mailbox name and logon password. The postoffice administrator creates the mailbox and password. Unlike the Mail client in Windows for Workgroups, the Exchange client does not let you create an account on the fly. You must have an existing mailbox in the postoffice before you can connect. Enter the mailbox name provided by the mail administrator—not the user name associated with the account—in the mailbox text box. Your user name, for example, might be Mickey Mouse, but the mailbox name might be mmouse. Therefore, you would enter **mmouse** in the mailbox text box.

Figure 29.17

The Logon property page.

If you want Exchange to enter your password for you automatically when it logs on to the postoffice, enable the password check box. If you want Exchange to prompt you for a password, clear the password check box. You also can omit the password from the password text box, which causes Exchange to prompt you for the password whenever you log on to the postoffice.

Tip   If you use different accounts (such as an administrator account and regular user account) to log on to the postoffice, and want Exchange to prompt you for the mailbox name each time, leave both the mailbox and password text boxes empty. Exchange then prompts you to specify the mailbox and password whenever you log on to the postoffice.

If you want to change your mailbox password, choose the **C**hange Mailbox Password button. Windows 95 displays a simple password dialog box. Enter your existing password, then enter your new password in the **N**ew password and **V**erify new password text boxes. The next time you connect to the postoffice, Exchange changes your mailbox password.

Tip   If you have difficulty changing your password, or you forget your password, contact the postoffice administrator. The administrator can specify a new password for you, enabling you to once again log on to your mailbox.

Configuring Delivery Options

The Delivery property page (see fig. 29.18) enables you to control how the Microsoft Mail provider delivers and receives mail.

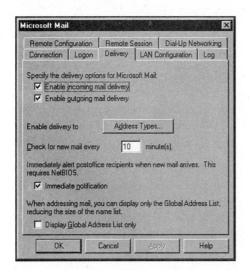

Figure 29.18

The Delivery property page.

The following list explains the controls and settings on the Delivery property page:

- ◆ **Enable incoming mail delivery.** Enable this check box if you want Exchange to transfer incoming mail from the postoffice to your inbox. If you want your mail held in the postoffice even when you connect to send mail, clear this check box.

- ◆ **Enable outgoing mail delivery.** Enable this check box if you want Exchange to transfer mail from your outbox to the postoffice. If you want outgoing mail held in your outbox (not delivered), clear this check box.

- ◆ **Address Types.** Choose the Address Types button to specify the types of addresses to which the Microsoft Mail provider can respond. This enables you to temporarily (or indefinitely) suspend mail service to specific address types.

- ◆ **Check for new mail every n minute(s).** Use this control to specify how often Exchange checks the postoffice for new mail.

- ◆ **Immediate notification.** Enable this check box if you want to be notified as soon as new mail arrives in your postoffice mailbox. Enabling this check box also causes recipients to whom you send messages to be notified when your messages arrive in their mailboxes. Using this feature requires that the sending and receiving users' machines support NetBIOS.

◆ **Display Global Address List only.** Normally, Exchange displays the Global Address List from the postoffice and your Personal Address Book. Enable this check box if you want Exchange to display only the Global Address List.

Configuring LAN Options

The LAN Configuration property page (see fig. 29.19) controls how the Microsoft Mail provider handles various features when you connect to the postoffice through a LAN connection (instead of a remote connection).

Figure 29.19

The LAN Configuration property page.

The following list explains the options on the LAN Configuration property page:

◆ **Use Remote Mail.** Enable this check box if you don't want Exchange to automatically retrieve all your mail from the postoffice. You can direct Exchange to retrieve headers for the messages, then specify which messages you want to get, based on the headers. This is useful for postponing the delivery of low-priority messages or messages that have large attachments. Use the Remote item in the Exchange Tools menu to control remote preview.

◆ **Use local copy.** If you want Exchange to create and use a local copy of the Postoffice Address List, enable this check box. If you leave this check box cleared, Exchange uses the Postoffice Address List stored in the postoffice. To update your local copy of the Postoffice Address Book, choose Tools, Microsoft Mail Tools, Download Address Lists.

◆ **Use external delivery agent.** Enable this check box if you use a slow network connection and want to minimize mail transfer time. When you enable this option, the External.exe mail transfer agent (included with a Microsoft Mail Server upgrade and run on a dedicated PC on your network) handles message delivery.

Configuring Log Options

Maintaining a log of mail sessions can help you troubleshoot mail problems. The Log property page (see fig. 29.20) enables you to determine how Exchange handles logging of mail sessions.

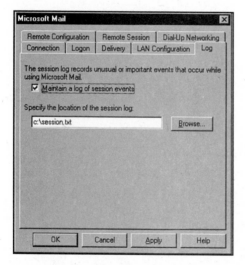

Figure 29.20

The Log property page.

Enable the Maintain a log of session events check box if you want Exchange to keep a log of your mail sessions. In the associated text box, specify the name of the mail session log file. By default, Exchange creates the file in Session.txt in your boot disk's root directory.

Configuring Remote Settings

If you use the Microsoft Mail provider to connect to a postoffice through a remote dial-up connection, you need to specify a few settings that determine how Exchange handles message transfer and the dial-up connection. Three property pages enable you to control these settings. The first of the three pages, the Remote Configuration property page (see fig. 29.21), resembles the LAN Configuration property page and controls similar features. Refer to the section "Configuring LAN Options" earlier in this chapter for information on the settings on the Remote Configuration property page. Remember, however, that the LAN Configuration property page controls how Exchange uses the Microsoft Mail provider over a LAN connection, but that the Remote Configuration page controls those settings when Exchange is connected to the postoffice through a remote connection.

Figure 29.21

The Remote Configuration property page.

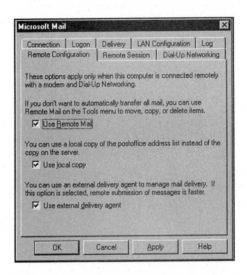

The Remote Session property page (see fig. 29.22), which appears when the dial-up network connection is started and stopped, enables you to control when and how the connection between Exchange and the remote postoffice occurs.

Figure 29.22

The Remote Session property page.

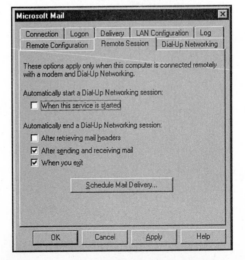

The following list explains the options on the Remote Session property page:

◆ **When this service is started.** Enable this check box if you want Exchange to connect to the remote postoffice through the dial-up connection as soon as you start Exchange. Exchange initiates the connection automatically, using the dial-up networking client. For information on how to configure the dial-up networking client, refer to Chapter 33, "Using Remote Access Services."

◆ **After retrieving mail headers.** Enable this check box if you want Exchange to terminate the dial-up networking connection after Exchange retrieves mail headers from your mailbox (when you use remote preview).

◆ **After sending and receiving mail.** Enable this check box if you want Exchange to terminate the dial-up networking connection after it sends pending messages and retrieves your mail from the postoffice.

◆ **When you exit.** Enable this check box if you want the dial-up networking connection to terminate after you exit Exchange. If you use the dial-up connection for other reasons, such as access to printers or disks, you might want to clear this check box to ensure that Windows 95 retains the connection after you exit Exchange.

In addition to using the check boxes on the Remote Session page to control connection times, you can choose the Schedule Mail Delivery button to set up specific times when you want Exchange to connect to the remote postoffice. When you choose Schedule Mail Delivery, Windows 95 displays the Remote Scheduled Sessions dialog box (see fig. 29.23).

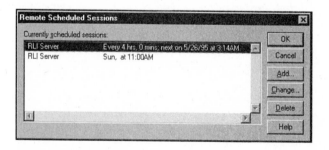

Figure 29.23

The Remote Scheduled Sessions dialog box.

You can use the Remote Scheduled Sessions dialog box to configure multiple, specific times at which Exchange connects to the postoffice. You can schedule Exchange, for example, to connect at 7:00 a.m. on Mondays, every two hours of each day, 9:30 a.m. on Tuesdays, and at 5:00 p.m. on Fridays. This capability to schedule remote connections provides a very fine degree of control and flexibility in scheduling remote mail connections.

To schedule a remote mail session, open the Remote Scheduled Sessions dialog box, then choose Add to display the Add Scheduled Session dialog box, shown in figure 29.24.

Figure 29.24

The Add Scheduled Session dialog box.

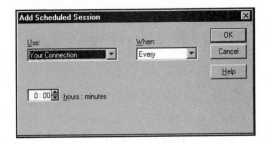

First, decide the timing method you want to use for the connection by selecting an option from the When drop-down list. You can choose from the following three options:

◆ **Every.** Select this option to specify a timespan in hours and minutes between sessions. If you want to schedule a connection for every four hours, for example, you would use the Every option, then use the hours:minutes control to specify 4:00.

◆ **Weekly on.** Select this option if you want to specify a specific time on a specific day of the week for the connection. The dialog box's appearance changes to resemble to the one in figure 29.25. The day and time you specify becomes a recurring connection. If you specify Monday, Wednesday, and Friday at 8:00 a.m., for example, Exchange establishes a connection every Monday, Wednesday, and Friday at 8:00 a.m..

◆ **Once at.** Choose this option if you want to specify a one-time-only connection on a specific date and at a specific time.

Figure 29.25

Add Scheduled Session for weekly recurring connections.

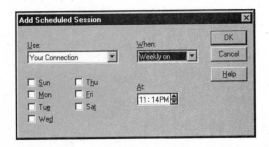

After you specify the frequency and time of the connection, select from the Use drop-down list the dial-up networking connection you want to use for the connection to the postoffice. This drop-down list shows all the dial-up networking connections in your Dial-Up Networking folder. After you arrange your session settings to your satisfaction, choose OK to add the scheduled session to the list.

You also can cause Exchange to connect to different postoffices using different dial-up connections. Assume you're a system administrator responsible for the e-mail systems at three different sites, none of which is connected by a mail transfer agent, and you want to be able to connect from your office to each of those three sites and automatically retrieve your mail from each one. You can create three different dial-up networking connections; one for each of the three sites. Then, you can use the Remote Scheduled Sessions dialog box to schedule regular connections to each one of the sites.

Note The only drawback to being able to connect to multiple remote postoffices is that you can't specify a unique postoffice location for each connection. The postoffice server name and WGPO directory location must be the same on each server, enabling you to map a local drive ID to the postoffice or specify the same UNC path for each postoffice. You then can specify that local drive ID as the path to the postoffice. Because the drive ID is associated with a remote node, it doesn't matter that the drive ID actually references three (or more) different physical servers. Windows 95 just thinks it's connecting the drive to the same share.

If you are a consultant or system administrator who must manage mail systems at different sites, consider using a consistent server and WGPO naming scheme to simplify managing the multiple sites. If you can't specify the same name or WGPO share name for each site, you must use separate profiles to connect to each site.

The final Microsoft Mail property page, the Dial-Up Networking page (see fig. 29.26), enables you to select, create, and modify dial-up networking connections for your remote mail sessions, which enables you to create and edit connections without opening the Dial-Up Networking folder. Choosing the Add Entry button starts the Add New Connection wizard, which automates creating a dial-up connection. Choosing the Edit Entry button produces a property page for the selected connection, which you can use to change its settings. For more information on creating and modifying dial-up networking connections, refer to Chapter 33, "Using Remote Access Services."

Figure 29.26

*The Dial-Up
Networking
property page.*

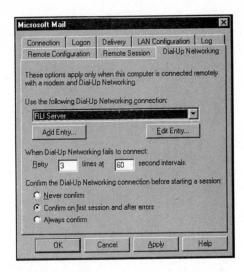

Three option buttons on the Dial-Up Networking property page enable you to control whether Exchange prompts you to verify that you want it to establish a remote connection before it does so. The following list tells about these option buttons:

◆ **Never confirm.** If you choose this option, Exchange does not prompt you to confirm a session before it establishes the session. Choose this option if you want the a completely automated process for every session.

◆ **Confirm on first session and after errors.** Choose this option if you want Exchange to prompt you to confirm the connection only on the first session and after any errors occur.

◆ **Always confirm.** Choose this option if you want Exchange to always prompt you to confirm that you want it to establish a remote connection.

Configuring Microsoft Fax

You can use the Microsoft Fax service provider to enable Exchange to send and receive faxes. The Microsoft Fax provider can use a fax modem connected to your computer, or it can use a shared fax modem connected to another computer elsewhere on your LAN. And, you can share your fax modem so that other users on the network can access your modem to send and receive faxes. Incoming faxes to a shared fax modem are placed in the fax administrator's mailbox, and that administrator must then manually forward the faxes to their recipients.

Planning for Microsoft Fax

Before you begin to install and configure Microsoft Fax, you should allot a little time to analyze your requirements and plan the installation. The following are some key points to consider when you plan to implement Microsoft Fax:

◆ **Individual or shared fax modems?** If only a few of your users need fax send and receive capability, providing each user with a fax modem and fax line makes sense, thereby eliminating the need to share a fax modem or designate a fax administrator to forward incoming faxes. If you want many users to be able to send and receive faxes, sharing a fax modem on the network might make more sense. Or, you might implement a combination of individual and shared fax modems—designating the individual fax modems to users who have the highest fax traffic.

◆ **Fax hardware requirements.** A computer that runs the Microsoft Fax service provider for a private fax modem (not shared) should contain at least 8 MB of RAM. A computer that shares a fax modem with other users should contain at least 12 MB of RAM.

◆ **Restricting access.** You can password-protect a shared fax modem to prevent unauthorized use.

◆ **Compatibility.** Microsoft Fax is compatible with most fax modems and can receive faxes sent from Class 1 and Class 2 fax modems, and from Group 3 fax machines. You must have a Class 1 modem to support Binary File Transfer (BFT) and security.

◆ **Need for advanced features.** If you need support for fax broadcast, automatic routing, or other advanced features, one of the many third-party LAN fax servers or fax applications might be a better choice than Microsoft Fax.

The following sections explain the configuration steps for the Microsoft Fax provider you must perform after you add the provider to your profile. To configure Microsoft Fax, select Microsoft Fax from the Services property page, then choose Properties.

Configuring Message Options

The Message property page for the Microsoft Fax provider (see fig. 29.27) enables you to specify a wide range of settings that control the appearance and format of faxes that you send, as well as the time at which they are sent.

Figure 29.27

The Message page in the Microsoft Fax property sheet.

The Time to send group on the Message property page enables you to specify when pending faxes are sent. The controls in the Time to send group are described in the following list:

◆ **As soon as possible.** Choose this option if you want Exchange to send pending faxes as soon as possible—that is, when the modem becomes available or when Exchange can transfer the pending faxes to the shared fax directory on the network.

◆ **Discount rates.** Use this option to specify a time when off-peak phone rates are in effect. Choose the associated **S**et button to specify the beginning and ending time for when off-peak rates are in effect.

◆ **Specific time.** Use this option to enter a specific time when Exchange should transmit pending faxes.

The controls in the Message format group specify the format for transmitting the fax, described in the following list:

◆ **Editable, if possible.** If you choose this option, Exchange transfers the fax as an editable binary document if the receiving system is Microsoft Fax–compatible (such as another user or server running the Microsoft Fax service provider). If you fax the document from Word, for example, Exchange transfers the fax as a Word document file. If the receiving system is not Microsoft Fax–compatible, the fax is transferred as a standard bitmapped fax. Windows 95, Windows for

Workgroups, and other At Work Fax devices support transfer of faxes as editable documents.

◆ **Editable only.** This option directs Exchange to transmit the fax as a binary document only if the receiving system is Microsoft Fax–compatible (determined during the connection phase). If the receiving system is not Microsoft Fax–compatible (such as a standard fax machine), the fax is not sent.

◆ **Not editable.** Choose this option if you want Exchange to send the fax as a bitmapped fax, even if the receiving system can accept the fax in binary document format. Choose the <u>P</u>aper button to open the Message Format dialog box (see fig. 29.28) and specify paper size, resolution, and paper orientation for transmitted faxes.

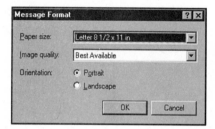

Figure 29.28

The Message Format dialog box.

The Default cover page group in the Message page enables you to specify a default cover sheet for all faxes. You also can view and edit the cover sheets supplied with Windows 95 or create your own. For an explanation of how to create and modify cover sheets, refer to Chapter 31, "Using Microsoft Fax." If you don't want to use a cover sheet for sending faxes, clear the Send co<u>v</u>er page check box.

Tip

If you want to create your own custom cover page, you might want to use one of the standard Windows 95 cover pages as a template. To do so, select the cover page that most closely fits what you want for your custom page, then choose <u>O</u>pen. After the Fax Cover Page Editor appears, choose <u>F</u>ile, Save <u>A</u>s to save the fax cover page with a new name.

The <u>L</u>et me change the subject line of new faxes I receive check box at the bottom of the Message property page enables you to control how incoming faxes appear in the inbox. If you enable this check box, incoming faxes appear in a message window as an attachment (see fig. 29.29) when you open the fax. You then can double-click on the fax icon to view the fax itself. If you clear this check box, incoming faxes are listed in the inbox by the sending system's fax number, or by the header "Unknown Fax Machine" if Exchange can't determine the sender's fax ID. By enabling this check box, you make changing the subject of a fax in the inbox possible, which can make identifying a fax by name in the inbox easier. Enabling this check box, however, adds one additional step to opening and viewing a received fax.

Figure 29.29

A fax stored as an attachment in a message.

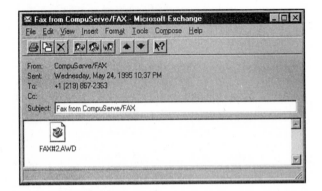

Configuring Dialing Options

The Dialing page of the Microsoft Fax property sheet (see fig. 29.30) enables you to control telephony properties for the fax connection, including dialing properties such as dialing location, and toll prefixes, which define prefixes in your area code that are long-distance calls. For information on setting telephony properties, refer to Chapter 28, "Modems and Data Communications."

Figure 29.30

The Dialing property page.

The Dialing property page also enables you to specify the number of retries the Microsoft Fax provider attempts if a connection fails. You also can specify the amount of time between attempts.

Configuring Modem Options

The Modem property page (see fig. 29.31) enables you to associate a modem with your Microsoft Fax provider, set various modem properties, add modems and shared fax servers, and share your own fax modem with other users.

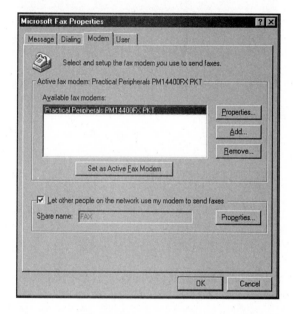

Figure 29.31

The Modem property page.

To associate a modem with the Microsoft Fax provider, select a modem from the Available fax modems list. To set the selected modem's properties, choose the Properties button to open the Fax Modem Properties dialog box (see fig. 29.32).

Tip You also can display the Fax Modem Properties dialog box when the Microsoft Fax provider is running by right-clicking on the fax icon in the tray, then choosing **M**odem Properties from the context menu. This enables you to control the way the Microsoft Fax provider monitors the fax line without opening the Control Panel or restoring the Exchange window.

Figure 29.32

The Fax Modem Properties dialog box.

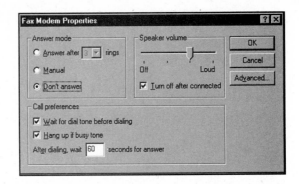

Most of the controls on the Fax Modem Properties dialog box are self-explanatory. The Answer Mode group of controls, however, deserves a little explanation:

◆ **Answer after n rings.** Choose this option to set the fax modem to auto-answer mode (monitor for incoming calls) and specify the number of rings after which the fax modem answers the call. You can set the number of rings from 2 to 10.

◆ **Manual.** Choose this option if you want the Microsoft Fax provider to notify you when the fax line is ringing and give you the option of answering the call manually or ignoring the call.

◆ **Don't answer.** Choose this option if you do not want the Microsoft Fax provider to monitor the fax line.

Tip

When the Microsoft Fax provider monitors the port for incoming calls, only Win32 applications that use TAPI to request access to the port can access the port from Microsoft Fax. Use the **D**on't answer option when you have a Win16 or DOS application that needs to use the modem.

You also can set a number of advanced fax modem properties. To do so, choose the Ad**v**anced button on the Fax Modem Properties dialog box to open the Advanced dialog box (see fig. 29.33).

The controls in the Advanced dialog box are explained in the following list:

◆ **Disable high speed transmission.** Enable this check box to prevent the fax modem from transferring at speeds higher than 9,600 bps. Enabling this option can overcome problems you might be having transmitting or receiving faxes reliably.

Figure 29.33

The Advanced dialog box for a fax modem.

◆ **Disable error correction mode.** This option controls whether the Microsoft Fax provider uses the modem's error correction capabilities when sending a noneditable (bitmapped) fax. Enable this check box if you are having trouble sending or receiving faxes.

◆ **Enable MR compression.** This option specifies whether Microsoft Fax uses compression when sending and receiving faxes. Compressing generally reduces transmission time (particularly for bitmapped faxes), but makes Microsoft Fax more sensitive to noise on the fax line.

◆ **Use Class 2 if available.** Enable this check box if you want Microsoft Fax to operate your fax modem as a Class 2 device, even if it supports Class 1. Forcing the modem to Class 2 can sometimes overcome transmission errors. Forcing the modem to Class 2, however, disables binary file transfer and security.

◆ **Reject pages received with errors.** Enable this check box if you want Microsoft Fax to reject pages received with errors. Use the Tolerance drop-down list to specify the error level that must be reached before rejecting the page. Clear this check box if you don't want pages with errors rejected (which can enable you to receive a fax that otherwise would be rejected).

Configuring Your User Information

The User property page (see fig. 29.34) enables you to specify information about yourself, including your name, fax number, phone number, and other information. Most of this information is included on the fax. The settings on this property page are self-explanatory.

Figure 29.34

The User property page.

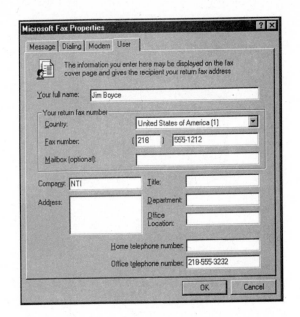

Configuring CompuServe Mail

Windows 95 includes an Exchange service provider that enables you to use Exchange to send and receive mail from your CompuServe account. Exchange automatically logs on to CompuServe, sends pending mail messages, retrieves waiting mail messages, and logs off. The following sections explain how to configure the CompuServe Mail service provider.

Setting General Options

You use the General property page of the CompuServe provider to specify your name, CompuServe account number, and account password. If you don't want the CompuServe provider to store your password (it is stored encrypted), leave the password field blank. Exchange prompts you for the password when the service provider starts.

Setting Connection Options

Use the Connection property page (see fig. 29.35) to specify the CompuServe access number you want to use for the connection. Unlike other CompuServe utilities, such as WinCIM, the CompuServe Mail provider does not support connection through WinSock, which would enable you to connect through a TCP/IP connection to

CompuServe. CompuServe might offer an enhanced CompuServe Mail provider for Exchange sometime before Spring of 1996, so you might want to check periodically with CompuServe about the availability of one that offers additional features, such as the capability to connect through WinSock.

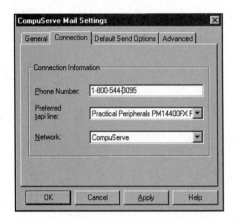

Figure 29.35

The Connection property page.

From the Preferred tapi line drop-down list, select the modem you want to use for the connection. This drop-down list includes all modems you have configured using the Modems object in the Control Panel. Then from the Network drop-down list, select the type of network connection you are using to connect to CompuServe.

Tip Although the CompuServe provider includes support for an Internet connection, you still must connect through a dial-up connection to an Internet service provider. In addition, no mechanism in the Internet connection script enables the script to log on to the Internet provider and authenticate your logon ID and password. Depending on your Internet access server's configuration, you might be able to modify the connection script to enable it to connect and authenticate your account. By default, the CompuServe connection scripts are located in the \Exchange\Scripts folder. If you can't locate the scripts, use Find to search for the file Internet.scr. These connection scripts are ASCII files, and you can use Notepad or WordPad to edit them.

Setting Default Send Options

The Default Send Options property page (see fig. 29.36) defines how and when your messages are sent, when the messages expire, and how the mail charges are handled. By default, the CompuServe provider sends CompuServe mail messages using ASCII text, even if you compose the message using rich text (with formatting, colors, and so on). If you enable the Send using Microsoft Exchange rich-text format check box, the provider includes the rich text formatting with the message. Before the recipient can read the message, the recipient must use Exchange as his CompuServe mail provider.

Figure 29.36

The Default Send Options property page.

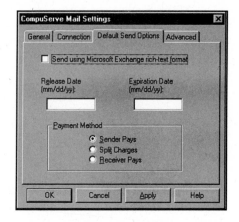

Tip
Using rich text to send mail through CompuServe results in slightly larger message sizes, which ultimately increases your mail charges.

The Release Date text box enables you to specify a date until which your messages are held in your mailbox. Upon arrival of the specified date, the messages are forwarded to the recipient(s). If you don't specify a date, messages are forwarded as soon as you send them.

The Expiration Date text box enables you to specify an expiration date for messages. The message is deleted from the recipient's mailbox on the specified date.

The Payment Method group of controls enables you to specify handling of the mail charges for sending and receiving mail. You have the following options:

◆ **Sender Pays.** This option causes the sender to pay for all mail charges, and is the default setting.

◆ **Split Charges.** This option causes the delivery charges to be split evenly between the sender and receiver.

◆ **Receiver Pays.** This option causes all delivery charges to be paid by the recipient. The delivery charges are paid only by the recipient if the message is read or retrieved.

Setting Advanced Options

Use the Advanced property page (see fig. 29.37) to specify additional settings that control how the CompuServe Mail provider functions.

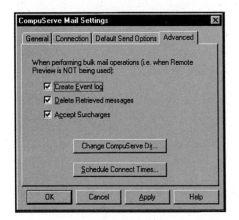

Figure 29.37

The Advanced property page.

The Advanced property page contains three check boxes, explained in the following list:

◆ **Create Event log.** Enable this check box if you want the CompuServe provider to maintain a log of your CompuServe Mail sessions. Rather than store the log in a file, the provider places a log message in your inbox. These log messages are useful for verifying mail delivery and troubleshooting connection problems.

◆ **Delete Retrieved messages.** Enable this check box if you want the CompuServe provider to delete messages from your CompuServe mailbox after Exchange retrieves the messages.

◆ **Accept Surcharges.** Enable this check box if you are willing to accept mail surcharges for incoming mail. This typically is required if you want to receive mail from the Internet or other mail services that require a transfer or handling charge.

Note You can choose the Change CompuServe Dir button to change the directory in which your CompuServe configuration data and logon scripts are stored.

Although the CompuServe Mail provider doesn't support the same remote session scheduling flexibility that the Microsoft Mail provider does, you can schedule

unattended connections. To do so, choose the <u>S</u>chedule Connect Times button on
the Advanced property page, which opens the Connection Times dialog box (see fig.
29.38).

Figure 29.38

*The Connection
Times dialog box.*

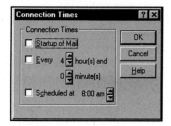

If you want the CompuServe Mail provider to connect to CompuServe each time you
start Exchange, enable the <u>S</u>tartup of Mail check box. To schedule regular sessions
throughout the day, enable the <u>E</u>very check box, then use the associated spin controls
to specify hours and minutes between sessions. And, if you want to schedule a connection at a specific time of the day, enable the <u>S</u>cheduled at check box.

Tip You can use any or all of the options in the Connection Times dialog box to specify
when the CompuServe Mail provider connects to CompuServe. The <u>E</u>very check box
and the <u>S</u>cheduled at check box, however, do not work in tandem. If you specify
8:00 a.m. with the <u>S</u>cheduled at control, for example, then schedule connections for
every four hours with the <u>E</u>very control, the CompuServe Mail provider does not
necessarily connect at 8:00, then 12:00, then 4:00, then 8:00, and so on. The
<u>E</u>very control specifies the time between sessions, regardless of how the sessions are
initiated, so if the provider automatically connects at 8:00 a.m., then you manually
connect at 9:15, the next automatic connection probably will occur at 1:15, four
hours since that last connection.

Configuring Microsoft Network Mail

If you become a member of the Microsoft Network (MSN), Microsoft's online service,
you can use Exchange to send and receive e-mail through the MSN. Windows 95
includes an Exchange service provider that is simple to configure and use. You add
the provider using the method explained in the "Creating, Managing, and Configuring User Profiles" section, earlier in this chapter. Then, select the MSN service
provider from the Services property page and choose P<u>r</u>operties. Windows 95 displays
The Microsoft Network property sheet, shown in figure 29.39.

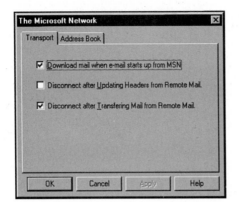

Figure 29.39

The Microsoft Network property sheet.

The Transport page determines how and when Exchange connects to the MSN to handle your mail. You have the following settings on the Transport page:

◆ **Download mail when e-mail starts up from MSN.** Enable this check box if you want Exchange to automatically download mail from the MSN to your inbox when you are connected to the MSN and start Exchange.

◆ **Disconnect after Updating Headers from Remote Mail.** This option enables you to preview your mail before you download it. If enabled, Exchange connects to MSN, downloads your mail headers, then disconnects. You can review and select messages for download while offline, thereby saving connect and phone charges.

◆ **Disconnect after Transferring Mail from Remote Mail.** This option directs Exchange to disconnect from the MSN after it retrieves your mail, enabling you to read your mail offline.

The Address Book property page contains only one control, the Connect to MSN to check names check box. If this check box is enabled, Exchange connects to the MSN to verify address names. If you want to compose messages offline, leave this option cleared.

Note For tips on using the MSN, read Chapter 32, "Using the Microsoft Network."

Configuring Internet Mail

The Internet Mail service provider for Exchange is included with the Microsoft Plus!
add-on for Windows 95. The Internet Mail provider enables you to send and receive
mail to and from an Internet mail server, such as a Unix host, and through a LAN or
dial-up connection.

 Note This section of the chapter explains how to configure the Internet Mail provider.
Chapter 37, "Using Internet Utilities," offers tips on using Exchange to send and
receive Internet mail.

When you add the Internet Mail provider to your profile, a wizard automatically starts
up and steps you through the configuration process. The settings you specify for the
wizard match settings in the configuration property sheet for the provider. Rather
than explain the wizard, the following sections explain the settings in the Internet
Mail property sheet, which help you configure the provider, not only during installation by the wizard, but also for day-to-day use.

Configuring General Options

The settings on the General property page for the Internet Mail provider specify
information about you and your mail account. The two settings in the Personal
Information group specify your user name and your e-mail address:

- **Your Full Name.** The name you specify appears in headings of messages you
  send. Generally, you should enter your full name, but you also might include a
  company name.

- **Email Address.** Enter your mail account and domain name, such as
  joeblow@nowhere.com.

The controls in the Mailbox Information group identify the location of your Internet
mail server, your mail account name, and your password for the account:

- **Internet Mail Server.** Specify the domain name of your Internet mail server,
  such as **newriders.mcp.com**.

- **Account Name.** Enter your mail account name on the Internet server, such as
  jimb. The Internet mail server's administrator must assign and configure this
  account for you.

- **Account Password.** Enter the password for your mail account on the
  Internet mail server.

Choosing the Message Format button on the General property page produces a simple dialog box you can use to specify the type of coding to use to transfer attachments. You can choose from MIME (Multipurpose Internet Mail Extensions) format or UUENCODE. The Message Format dialog box also enables you to choose the character set to use to transfer attachments.

Choosing the Advanced Options button on the General property page opens a dialog box you can use to specify the location of the Internet server that processes your outgoing mail. Normally, you can leave this setting blank. If your Internet mail server does not process outbound mail, however, you must specify the domain name of a secondary server to process your mail.

Configuring Connection Options

The Connection property page (see fig. 29.40) enables you to specify the dial-up connection to use to establish the Internet connection, or to specify a LAN connection to the Internet.

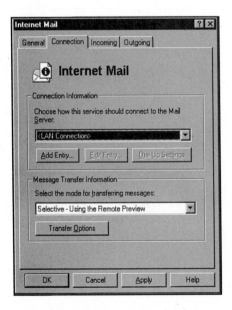

Figure 29.40

The Connection property page.

 Note You can use a SLIP connection to connect to a remote host. For instructions on setting up a SLIP connection, refer to Chapter 33, "Using Remote Access Services." Chapter 33 also explains how to set up and configure other dial-up networking connections.

From the Server drop-down list, select <LAN Connection> if your computer is connected to the Internet through your LAN. If you need to use a dial-up networking connection to connect to the Internet, select a dial-up session from the Server list. If you have not yet configured dial-up networking on your computer, you must do so before configuring the Internet Mail provider for a dial-up connection.

Next, you need to select the method the provider uses to transfer mail. From the drop-down list in the Message Transfer Information group, choose Selective or Automatic. If you choose Automatic, Exchange automatically initiates a connection to the Internet to check your mail as soon as it opens. If you choose Selective, Exchange only connects when you use Remote Preview or choose from the Exchange window Tools, Deliver Now Using, and Internet Mail to direct it to connect. To set up a session log for Internet Mail sessions, or specify the frequency at which Internet Mail polls the server for new mail, choose the Transfer Options button and specify your preferences in the resulting dialog box.

 Tip   The Incoming and Outgoing property pages enable you to specify how various types of file attachments are handled for MIME coding and decoding.

Configuring the Personal Information Store

You must have at least one Personal Information Store (PST) file in your profiles. The PST contains your standard folders (Inbox, outbox, and so forth), new folders that you create, and your messages. When you install Exchange, the configuration wizard steps you through creating a default message store, referenced as the Personal Information Store in your profile. To specify properties for the message store, select it from the Services page, then choose Properties. Windows 95 displays the Personal Folders dialog box, shown in figure 29.41.

In the Personal Folders dialog box, you can change the name by which the store appears in your profile, assign or change a password to protect the store, and compact the message store to reduce the amount of disk space it requires. When you create a PST, you can specify the name and encryption the store uses. When you modify the properties of an existing store, however, you can change only the name—you can't change the encryption method. Encryption and other options are explained in the next section.

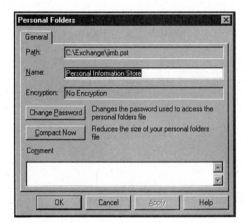

Figure 29.41

*The Personal
Folders dialog
box.*

Using Multiple Message Stores (Personal Folders)

Although you can create as many folders as you like in your default message store, you
might want to keep some types of messages completely separate from others in a
different PST. Or, you might want to create a set of message folders (a new PST),
copy messages to the new PST, then place the PST on a different computer, such as
your notebook computer.

To create a new PST or add an existing PST in your profile, open the Control Panel
and choose the Mail and Fax object. Then choose the **A**dd button on the Services
property page. After the Add Service to Profile dialog box appears, select Personal
Folders from the list of available services, then choose OK. Windows 95 then displays
a common file dialog box you can use to select an existing PST file or create a new
one. If you are importing a PST file, find it in the dialog box and choose **O**pen. To
create a new PST, enter a file name for the PST and choose **O**pen. If you specify a
new name, Windows 95 displays the Create Microsoft Personal Folders dialog box
(see fig. 29.42).

In the **N**ame text box, specify the name by which you want the PST to appear in your
profile. Then, choose one of the three option buttons in the **E**ncryption Setting
control group to specify the type of encryption the PST uses. The following list
describes your encryption choices:

Figure 29.42

Specify options for the new PST.

◆ **No Encryption.** With this option, your PST can be opened and read using another program (such as a word processing program) even if the PST is password-protected.

◆ **Compressable Encryption.** This option applies encryption to your PST file for security, and also enables you to compress the PST file to conserve disk space.

◆ **Best Encryption.** This option offers the best security, but does not enable you to compress the PST. Choose this option if you want to ensure the highest level possible of security for your PST.

 Tip
Encryption and security are particularly important if you store the PST on a network server where other users might gain access to the directory that contains the PST. You can't encrypt your existing default PST, but you can create a new encrypted PST. Then, move all your messages and folders from the default PST to the new PST, and remove the original.

Next, use the controls in the Password control group to specify an optional password for the PST. If you want to store the password in your password list so that you don't have to enter the password each time you want to use the PST, enable the associated check box.

 Note
When you add multiple message stores to a profile, Exchange displays a new branch in the tree view for each set of folders you add (see fig. 29.43). Also, each new set of folders you create contains its own Deleted Items folder.

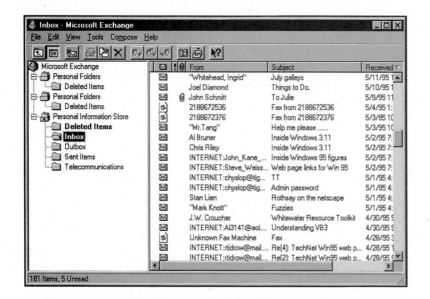

Figure 29.43

Multiple PSTs in the Exchange tree.

Converting and Importing Message Files

Although you can add a Pst file to a profile directly by using the Control Panel, you must import old message files from previous versions of Microsoft Mail (Mmf files) and Personal Address Book (Pab) files through Exchange. To import Mmf or Pab files into your Exchange profile, open Exchange and choose File, Import. Exchange displays a common file dialog box you can use to locate the file you want to import.

If you select an Mmf file to import, Exchange opens a dialog box that prompts you to enter the password for the Mmf file (see fig. 29.44). You also can use the Import Mail Data dialog box to specify whether you want to import messages, Pab entries, or both. Enter the necessary password and choose which types of data to import, then choose OK.

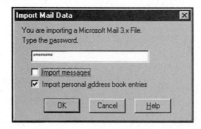

Figure 29.44

The Import Mail Data dialog box.

Exchange then displays an expanded Import Mail Data dialog box (see fig. 29.45). You can choose to place incoming folders and messages into an existing set of personal folders (a PST), or you can create a new PST to contain the incoming folders and messages. Choose an existing PST or specify a name for a new PST. If you create a new PST and want to add it to your profile and the new folders displayed in Exchange, enable the Display new Personal Folders check box. If you want to convert only the file to a PST file and don't want to add it to your profile, clear this check box.

Figure 29.45

Specify where you want the incoming data placed.

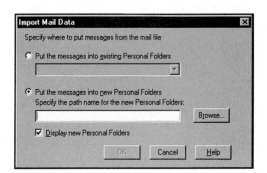

Note   When you import an Mmf file into a Pst file, Exchange does not alter the original Mmf file. Exchange simply copies the folders and messages from the Mmf file to the Pst file. Therefore, you can continue to use the Mmf file with Microsoft Mail if necessary.

Extending the Mail System

The e-mail capability offered by the Exchange client in Windows 95 is by no means a full-featured e-mail system, although the service providers included with Windows 95 and Plus! for Windows 95 offer a wide range of connectivity options. Microsoft offers a number of additional products that extend your e-mail system's capabilities. This section provides a brief overview of many of these e-mail upgrade products.

Microsoft Mail Server 3.x

The Microsoft Mail Server 3.x upgrade adds many features to your existing postoffice, including the following:

◆ Capability to connect to external postoffices and gateways

◆ Mail transfer among multiple workgroup postoffices

◆ Enhanced postoffice administration utilities, including administration from any node on the network

◆ Support for mail transfer to external postoffices through a modem connection

◆ Client software for Windows 3.*x*, DOS, and Macintosh computers

If you want to upgrade a Windows 95 postoffice to route mail between multiple workgroup postoffices, you need the Microsoft Mail Post Office Upgrade for each workgroup postoffice. You also need a dedicated DOS PC to run the External.exe mail transfer agent, or a version of External running on a Windows NT server or OS/2 server on the LAN. If the postoffices are not on the same LAN, you need a dedicated PC to run External, as well as a modem to establish the connection between the PC and the other site(s).

Tip The Academic version of the Microsoft Mail Server 3.x product includes Microsoft SMPT gateway, enabling mail clients on the network to send and receive mail through an SMTP server such as a Unix or VAX server.

Microsoft Exchange Server

The Microsoft Exchange Server, which runs on Windows NT Server 3.5*x*, provides a client/server messaging system. The Exchange Server provides e-mail, scheduling, groupware, custom forms, document sharing, and the capability to develop custom messaging applications for the client/server environment. Additional mail features provided by the Exchange Server include replicated public folders and additional sorting and filtering capabilities.

The Exchange Server also includes built-in support for SMTP and X.400, so you don't have to acquire separate X.400 or SMTP gateway software (or a dedicated PC to run the gateway software). The Exchange Server also provides support for Microsoft mail clients on Intel-based and Macintosh computers, which enables PCs and Macs on your network to share postoffices and exchange mail.

Microsoft Mail Gateways

Microsoft offers a number of gateway products to support mail exchange with a variety of mail systems. These gateways include the following:

◆ X.400

◆ SMTP

◆ MCI MAIL

◆ IBM PROFS

◆ MHS

◆ FAX

◆ SNADS

◆ AT&T Easylink

For additional information about Microsoft mail gateway products, consult the Microsoft Windows 95 Resource Kit (included on the Windows 95 CD) or contact Microsoft Sales at 1-800-426-9400.

Using Microsoft Exchange

Chapter 29, "Installing and Configuring Exchange," introduces you to Microsoft's new universal communications tool, Microsoft Exchange. In that chapter, you discover that you can use Exchange to collect e-mail from various sources (such as MS Mail, CompuServe, and the Internet), faxes, and routing forms. Chapter 29 also shows you how to set up and configure the various components that make up Exchange. This chapter shows you how to use Exchange to read, compose, and sort your e-mail. Chapter 31, "Using Microsoft Fax," shows you how to use Exchange to send and receive faxes through Windows 95.

If you have not installed or configured Exchange, see Chapter 29 now. Specifically, this chapter discusses the following:

- ◆ Receiving and composing messages in Exchange

- ◆ Viewing and printing messages in Exchange

- ◆ Using the Personal Address Book

- ◆ Using distribution lists

Starting Microsoft Exchange

When you first start Exchange, what you see might confuse you a bit. You might ask yourself, "So this is what all the hoopla and press is all about?" In reality, the Exchange interface is simple and easy to use. If you are familiar with e-mail applications, such as Microsoft Mail, cc:Mail, and others, you shouldn't have any problem getting used to Exchange.

When you start Exchange by clicking on the Start button, pointing to the Programs option, and clicking on Microsoft Exchange, a window similar to the one shown in figure 30.1 appears. This is the Exchange Viewer and it displays the items configured in the Personal Information Store(s) you set up in Chapter 29.

Figure 30.1

The MS Exchange Viewer interface.

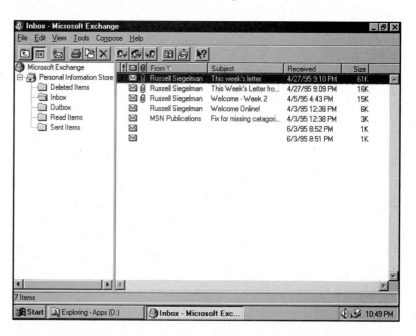

Tip   If you start Exchange by clicking on the Inbox shortcut on your desktop, Windows 95 does not display the folder list area. The folder list area appears on the left side of the Viewer in figure 30.1, and you can display it by choosing **V**iew, Fol**d**ers.

When you have new e-mail waiting for you, you see it announced by an envelope notification at the right end of the Taskbar, next to the time display. When you see this icon, you can open Exchange and read your latest e-mail message or see your latest fax, if you have the Microsoft Fax option installed.

Examining the Exchange Viewer

Because Microsoft Exchange is a new product and you might not yet be familiar with it, you should take a few minutes to familiarize yourself with each component of the Exchange Viewer interface. When you first activate the Viewer, you see two sections. The left section is the Exchange folder list area (see fig. 30.2), which shows your mailbox and personal folders. Personal folders can contain e-mail messages, files created in other applications, fax messages, and messages from other information services, such as online services.

Folder list

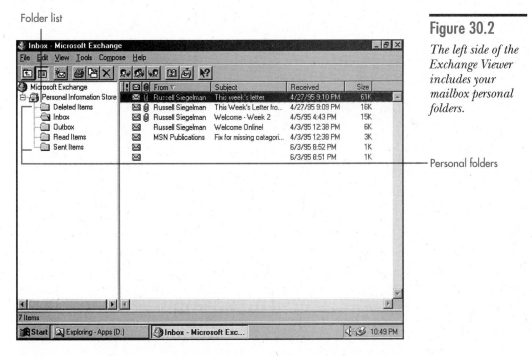

Figure 30.2

The left side of the Exchange Viewer includes your mailbox personal folders.

Personal folders

 Tip

You can use the personal folder area to store related documents. You can, for instance, store spreadsheets, word processing documents, and e-mail all in the same place. This enables you to easily keep track of these files and view them quickly when you need to.

To view a folder's contents, double-click on the folder. The contents appear on the right side of the Viewer, arranged under specific fields. The From field shows you the sender's name, the Subject field shows the subject of the message, and the Received field shows the date and time you received the message.

Other fields in the Viewer include the following:

◆ **Importance.** Each message or item you send or receive can have a priority attached to it. The Importance field, denoted by an exclamation point (!), shows you the type of priority the message has on it. A red exclamation point icon tells you the message has the highest importance. No icon indicates normal priority. A blue down-arrow says the message has low priority.

Tip   If you belong to a workgroup environment that tends to send a large amount of e-mail or faxes, you might want to devise a system that denotes high-, normal-, and low-priority messages. You might, for instance, attach a high-importance flag to messages that contain information pertaining to meeting scheduling or events that require immediate feedback. Messages of normal importance tend to indicate general information gathering or dissemination. Low-priority messages can be ignored for several days or altogether. You might find it difficult to think of your messages as anything less than urgent (why would you send them if they weren't important), but you should get in the habit of attaching priorities to your messages to help increase the productivity of your workforce.

◆ **Type of message.** Because Exchange was designed to handle a number of different types of messages and documents, you need to know the type of message that awaits you in your inbox. You can determine this by looking in the field denoted by the envelope icon. If your document is an e-mail message or fax message, an envelope appears on this line. A red arrow next to your message name indicates a returned mail notification.

◆ **Attachment.** One of the most useful parts of Exchange is its capability to handle rich-text messages, which enables you to embed OLE 2 objects, use RTF document elements, and add special characters to your messages. The attachment field, denoted by a paper clip, shows whether the message contains an attachment. Messages with attachments show a paper clip icon; those without attachments show nothing.

◆ **Size.** This column, to the right of the Received column, indicates the message's file size.

◆ **Conversation topic.** If the message belongs to a specific thread, such as to one on the Microsoft Network, you see the thread name in this column. This column does not show up if no messages are part of a thread.

Other parts of the Exchange Viewer include the menu bar and toolbar. The menu bar stores commands and options associated with Exchange. The toolbar, which you can customize or turn on or off, includes tools that help you quickly select actions you want to perform.

Tip
You can customize the toolbar by selecting Tools, Customize Toolbar. The Customize Toolbar dialog box appears (see fig. 30.3), from which you can select toolbar buttons from the Available Buttons list and add them to the Toolbar buttons list. Conversely, you can select items from the Toolbar buttons list and remove them from the toolbar. If you make a mistake or change your mind about these changes and want to return to the original toolbar, choose the Reset button.

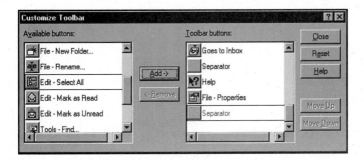

Figure 30.3

You can customize the toolbar in Exchange using the Customize Toolbar dialog box.

ToolTips pop up for each toolbar button over which you drag and stop your mouse pointer. ToolTips look like the one shown in figure 30.4 and give you a hint of the action associated with each button. When you drag and stop your mouse pointer over the button that has a document, arrow, and folder graphic, for instance, a ToolTip pops up that reads "Move Item," which tells you that you can move a message, folder, or other item by simply clicking on this button.

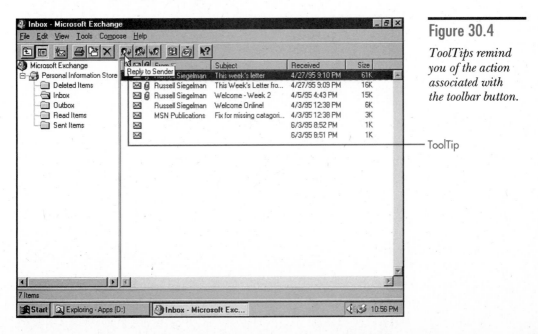

Figure 30.4

ToolTips remind you of the action associated with the toolbar button.

You can resize the viewing area in the Exchange Viewer the same way you resize columns in Microsoft Windows 3.*x*'s File Manager. You can drag the thick bar that runs vertically between the folder area and message area to the left or right to increase or decrease the viewing area. This benefit enables you to see more of the fields in the message area. Sometimes you might not be able to see the last two or three fields to the right of your Subject field without resizing the columns.

Reading Messages in Exchange

After you gain familiarity with the Exchange interface, you should become more comfortable using it. New messages or those you have not yet read are indicated by boldface in the Inbox folder in the message area. To read a message, double-click on it or click on it and choose File, Open. The message opens in a new window, such as the one shown in figure 30.5, in which you can read the message and perform other related tasks, such as printing, storing, or deleting the message.

Figure 30.5

Reading a message in Exchange.

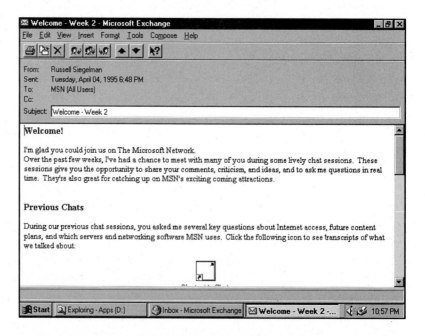

After you read your message, you can perform several tasks. The most common action is to reply. If you want to reply to the sender of the e-mail, click on the Reply to Sender toolbar button, or choose Compose, Reply to Sender, to open a new window in which you can write a response to the message (see fig. 30.6). Type your message and then choose File, Send, or click on the Send button on the toolbar.

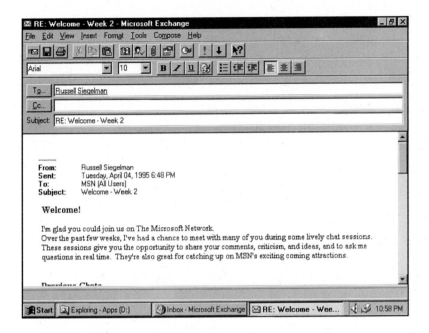

Figure 30.6

Replying to a message in Exchange.

Another option you might want to use when you reply to a message is the Reply to All option in the Compose menu. This option enables you to send a reply to all the people listed on the recipient list of the message to which you reply.

Tip
You don't have to open a message to reply to it. Click on the message to which you want to reply, choose Compose, and then select the option you want. An area appears in which you can write your new message. The only problem that might occur when you use this method is if you pick the wrong message to which to send a reply. Before you send the message, you might want to double-check that the message was sent to you or the recipient's name to ensure that you aren't going to embarrass yourself.

After some time, an e-mail exchange can get rather lengthy. Instead of simply replying to messages and retaining the original message every time, you should consider not including the original message text with your reply message. This reduces the file size of the message and, if you send the message over a commercial service provider, saves you online time and charges. To turn off the Include Original Message Text In Reply option, choose Tools, Options, and click on the Read tab (see fig. 30.7). In the Read page, click in the Include the original text when replying check box to clear it.

Figure 30.7

You can turn off the option to send the original message text with your reply.

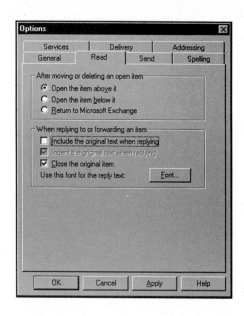

Saving Messages in Exchange

Similar to e-mail applications, such as Lotus cc:Mail or Microsoft Mail, Exchange enables you to store your messages after you create or read them. Exchange saves these files with the name, location, and file format you specify. Exchange also enables you to save messages or other files that might be attached with your message. To save a message or file in the default directory on your hard disk or network disk, click on the Disk button on the toolbar, or choose File, Save. Either method displays a Save As dialog box, as shown in figure 30.8.

Figure 30.8

Saving a file or attachment in Exchange.

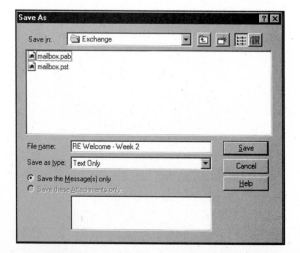

New Riders Publishing
INSIDE SERIES

Other ways to save your messages or attachments is to change the folder in which you store them, save the items in a specific format, or change the file name. Exchange offers the following options from which to select when you choose File, Save As rather than File, Save:

◆ **Save In.** Enables you to select a location in which to save your file. You might want to create a new folder in which to store all your read messages.

◆ **File Name.** Displays the name of the selected file. You can highlight this name and modify it as you choose.

◆ **Save As Type.** Saves messages and attachments in one of three formats: text only, rich text, or message.

Note Not sure what these three formats are? Text Only (*.txt) saves your message without extra formatting. As you see later, in the section "Creating a New Message," you can use RTF formatting characters in your Exchange messages. The Text Only option strips out these special characters. You should select the Text Only format only if the destination application cannot read rich text format.

The Rich Text Format (*.rtf) option enables you to save the message with all its formatting intact. During the save operation, Exchange automatically converts your message to instructions that other applications, including Microsoft-compatible applications, can read and interpret. This is handy when you want to apply special fonts, character enhancements, or other special features to your messages.

When you just have to keep a message intact exactly as it arrives, including saving the To, From, and Subject properties, select the Message Format (*.msg) option. This saves the message as a message file.

◆ **Save The Message(s) Only.** Enables you to save an open message or one (or several) selected in the Exchange Viewer. If you select more than one message, this option saves the messages in one text file, which comes in handy if you have a thread of messages you want to store together. You can append a message to an existing file by selecting the file and choosing Save. When the Save As message box appears, choose Append to.

◆ **Save These Attachments Only.** Saves selected attachments. Attachments previously selected in a message are selected in the list. You can select or clear attachments in the list before you save.

Printing Exchange Messages

Electronic documents are ideal for many of the business and personal communications needs you have. Sometimes, however, you need to file or distribute hard copies of messages or documents. Microsoft Exchange enables you to quickly and easily print one or many of your messages. With the Viewer open, select the item or items you want to print, and then choose File, Print. In the Print dialog box (see fig. 30.9), select the proper settings for your printer in the Name field, select the number of copies you want to print, and choose OK.

Figure 30.9

Printing messages from Exchange.

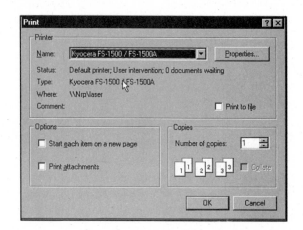

A couple options in this dialog box include Start each item on a new page and Print attachments. The Start each item option enables you to select several messages in the Viewer and print each of them on new pages. If you don't enable this option, your messages print one after another without page breaks. You use the Print attachments option when you want to print attachments to your message. You might want to check the size of the attachments before you select this option, in case the attachment is a large document that could tie up your printer for a long time. Someone might send you an attachment that is several hundred pages long, not intending for you to print it all out.

Tip   Another option you can choose from the Print dialog box is the Print to file option. You use this feature to print the document to a file rather than a printer. When you select this option, Windows 95 prompts you to insert a file name and file location.

Composing and Delivering Messages in Exchange

When you're ready to create your own message in Exchange, you'll find that the Viewer presents a friendly yet powerful interface (see fig. 30.10). In many ways, this

interface looks like a word processor, such as Microsoft WordPad. Many users create memos and general correspondence primarily through an e-mail application. Unfortunately, the appearance of standard e-mail messages often is ugly and difficult to read. When Microsoft designed Exchange, they included features that users wanted, one of which being the capability to create e-mail messages that replicate the appearance of word processing documents.

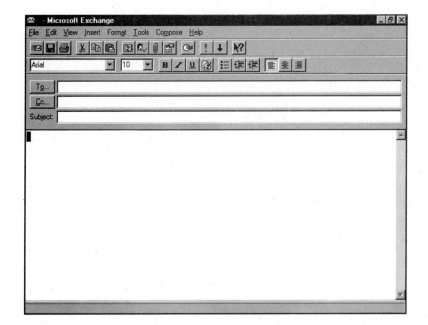

Figure 30.10

The New Message interface in Exchange.

Note Not only are standard e-mail messages (such as those cc:Mail create) formatted in ASCII text, they also sometimes come across in weird configurations. How many times have you received e-mail messages that seem to have been written in some unknown or lost language? Sporadic line breaks and unreadable character conversions (such as when you try to use something from an enhanced character set) make reading some messages difficult, if not impossible. You can eliminate many of these problems by using features that Exchange provides along with the RTF formatting feature.

Exchange addresses many of the problems associated with difficult-to-decipher e-mail messages by enabling messages to include specific fonts (including resizable TrueType fonts), colors, shortcuts, and objects. Because Exchange is an OLE-compliant application, you also can embed several types of objects into your messages, which enables you to create messages that include spreadsheet objects, graphics objects, and similar items.

Creating a New Message

To create a new message, choose Compose, New Message from the Exchange Viewer to open the New Message window (refer to figure 30.10). To help you get an idea of the type of message you can create, you can follow this set of steps, which leads you through creating a message that includes special formatting and an Excel spreadsheet object:

1. In the To: field, enter the recipient or recipients for your message. To access the universal address book, choose the To: button, which opens the Address Book dialog box (see fig. 30.11). (The Address Book is described in greater detail in a following section, "Understanding Address Books.")

Figure 30.11

Selecting a user or set of users in the Address Book dialog box.

Note As Chapters 31 through 33 explain, you also can use this address book when you create new fax messages, Microsoft Online Network messages, and Internet e-mail messages. Microsoft Exchange controls all these actions, enabling you to create one source with your contact information and use it for several different information sources. Ideally, this address book will be available for Schedule+ 2.0 and other Microsoft Office for Windows 95 applications.

2. In the Address Book dialog box, select the name and address of the recipient of your message. Select the address list that includes the names you want from the Show names from the: drop-down list.

3. In the Type Name or Select from List area, double-click on the name of the person to whom you want to send your message, or type the person's name in the field. This places the name in the To: section in the Message recipients box. If you want to send your message to the selected person as a Cc: recipient ("carbon copy"), click on the name in the Type Name or Select from List area and choose the **C**c: button. Choose OK to return to the New Message window.

4. Move your cursor to the Subject line and type a message subject. This subject name also becomes the default name of the message file if you decide to save the message. With Windows 95's long file name feature, your subject can contain as many as 256 characters—about the size of this paragraph.

5. Type your message in the message section, such as **Boss, the Fiscal '95 Sales Report is shown below. Tell me what you think.** You can use the various toolbar buttons, such as bold, italic, and underline, to format this text. You also can choose the Form**a**t menu and use the **F**ont or **P**aragraph options. For the most part, if you know how to use a Windows word processor or Windows 95's new WordPad application, you should understand the various formatting features of the New Message window.

6. To illustrate Exchange's power and OLE capabilities, insert a new Excel worksheet. To do this, choose **I**nsert, **O**bject from the New Message window menu bar to open the Insert Object dialog box (see fig. 30.12), from which you can choose the type of object you want to insert in your message. Scroll down the Object Type list and click on the Microsoft Excel Worksheet item.

Figure 30.12

The Insert Object dialog box enables you to insert specific OLE objects into your Exchange messages.

Note Does this dialog box look familiar? It should. It's the same dialog box that appears when you use OLE 2-compliant Windows applications, such as Word 6 or Excel 5, and insert embedded or linked objects into a document. Because of Microsoft's commitment to make using compound documents in your messages easier,

continues

regardless of the application that originally created the document or object, Exchange has been built from the ground up with OLE 2 functionality, which makes inserting a worksheet or graphics file into your message very easy.

One final note: For this example, you need to have Microsoft Excel 5 for Windows. If you have another OLE 2.0-compliant application, such as Word 6 for Windows, CorelDRAW! 5, or Visio 3, you can substitute that application for the following Excel example.

7. Choose OK to return to your new message, but notice the new look of the interface, including the toolbars and menus. If you are familiar at all with OLE 2 in Windows 3.1 or 3.11, you recognize what happened. The container application interface—in this case, the Exchange New Message interface—adopted the Microsoft Excel 5 interface to enable you to create and edit your new Excel object inside your new message.

In figure 30.13, for instance, notice how the interface now has many more tools on the toolbars. Also, look at the new menu choice, the Data menu. It has replaced the Compose menu, which you don't need for Excel. Although you can't see it in the illustration, the contents of the menus have changed to reflect Excel's. The Tools menu, for example, has changed from Spelling, Address Book, and so on, to Spelling, Auditing, AutoCorrect, and so on.

Figure 30.13

When you insert an OLE object, such as an Excel worksheet, your container application changes.

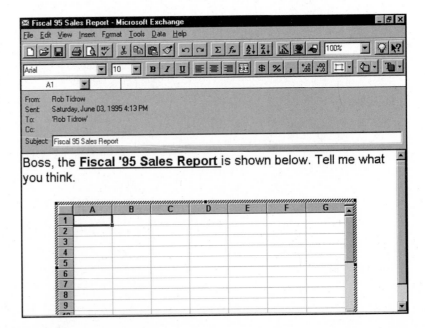

If you have never experienced this type of behavior (that is, inserting OLE objects in a document), don't worry. The New Message interface returns to normal after you create your new Excel worksheet and click outside the worksheet.

8. Fill in some data in the worksheet and format it or add formulas as needed. In fact, you can create a worksheet that is as sophisticated as you want. Exchange allows you to do this. Why? Again, because it's an OLE-compliant application. You might, for instance, want to add one of Excel's custom table formats to the worksheet. Choose F**o**rmat, **A**utoFormat and then select the type of format you want from the **T**able Format list.

Tip You also can insert a worksheet that has already been created. To do this, in step 7 before you choose OK in the Insert Object dialog box, choose the Create from **f**ile button on the left side of the dialog box, which enables you to open a file from your hard disk or server. Type the full path and file name of the document, or use the Browse feature to locate it.

To save file space when you choose this option, you should choose the **L**ink button in the Insert Object dialog box, which inserts a "picture" of the file into your message and links the picture to the file. When you want to edit the document, simply double-click on the picture, which activates the host application so that you can edit the file. Unlike embedding the object in the container application, when you link an object the New Message interface does not change when you double-click on the picture. The host application starts up and displays the file. After you edit the file, choose **F**ile, **S**ave to automatically update the picture in your message. To close the container application, choose **F**ile, E**x**it.

To shift the focus away from the worksheet or any other object you have inserted in your message, click anywhere outside the object. This returns the New Message interface to its original state. If you need to edit the object again, double-click anywhere inside the object. This changes the toolbars and menus to the Excel ones, enabling you once again to edit your worksheet.

If you want to delete this object you have embedded in your new application, click on the object and press Del or click on the Cut toolbar button. You also can choose **E**dit, **C**ut after you select the object you want to cut.

9. After you create your message, choose **F**ile, Se**n**d from the New Message window, or click on the Send button on the toolbar. Exchange sends the file to the Outbox folder in your Personal Folder.

In the next section, you learn how to deliver your new message.

Delivering New Messages

When you send a new message in Exchange, unless you currently are logged on to your e-mail system, such as Microsoft Mail, Exchange stores the message in the Outbox folder until you use one or several of the services you have configured to deliver it. These services can be Microsoft Mail, the Microsoft Network, Microsoft Fax, the Internet, CompuServe, and other supported systems.

Note   As of this writing, Microsoft had not announced all the services available to which Exchange could send messages. To get a complete list of these services, see the Windows 95 documentation that comes with your software. You also should be able to find discussions of this topic on the Microsoft Network and Microsoft-related CompuServe forums.

To deliver a message or several messages, click on the Outbox folder in Exchange Viewer to display the messages awaiting delivery. In figure 30.14, for instance, two messages are queued up for delivery. Click on the message you want to deliver, or hold down the Ctrl key and click on other messages you want to select. (To select the entire list of messages, choose Edit, Select All.)

Figure 30.14

Queuing messages for delivery in MS Exchange.

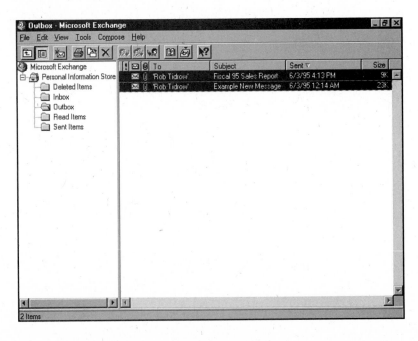

Next, choose Tools, Deliver Now Using to display the flyout menu that contains the services you have configured. To send your message(s) to all the services, select All

Services. You probably don't want to do this if you are sending an RTF formatted file to a non-Microsoft Mail or Microsoft Network recipient. If, for example, you send an RTF message to a CompuServe user, the message ends up stripped of all special characters and objects and converted to plain ASCII text. Likewise, any RTF file you send to an Internet address ends up minus any special characters or objects. In Chapter 29, "Installing and Configuring Exchange," you set many of the options associated with sending messages. See that chapter if you need to reconfigure or check these settings.

Stop If you try to send a message that contains attachments, objects, or embedded messages to an Internet address through the Microsoft Network, you receive the following message:

```
Your message did not reach some or all of the intended recipients.
Subject: Fiscal 95 Sales Report
Sent: 6/3/95 4:13:46 PM
The following recipient(s) could not be reached:
        rtidrow@iquest.net
             MSN does not support attachments, objects, or embedded
messages in Internet mail at this time.
```

Your best bet in this situation is to re-create your message and use only ASCII-supported characters. Of course, you don't have the advantage of embedding an Excel worksheet or other object in your Exchange message, but you can send that type of file as a separate binary file to your recipient.

Understanding Address Books

Microsoft Exchange uses address books, including a Personal Address Book (PAB), that you can cram full of contact information, e-mail addresses, and other interesting tidbits on a person. This contact information, in keeping with the Windows 95 theme, is called *Properties*.

Deciding Which Address Book to Use

When you create your first profile (as shown in Chapter 29), Exchange creates two address books. You maintain the Personal Address Book, and the postoffice administrator maintains the Post Office Address List. Other address books you might create can include a Microsoft Network (MSN) address book and a CompuServe address book.

If you have a Microsoft Mail postoffice set up, you can use the Post Office Address List across the network, enabling you to access the entire list of contacts your company maintains and ensuring that you have the most current address of a contact. If you want to work out of your Personal Address Book but use the Post Office Address List for names and updates, you can quickly and easily copy addresses and properties into your PAB.

To specify the address book you want to use, choose Tools, Address Book in Exchange. (When you create a new message, you also can select the address book from the Compose menu.) In the Address Book dialog box (see fig. 30.15), select the address book from the Show Names from the: drop-down list. Depending on the type of services you configured in Chapter 29, such as Microsoft Mail, Microsoft Network, or others, you see a list of address books from which to choose.

Figure 30.15

Selecting the address book to use.

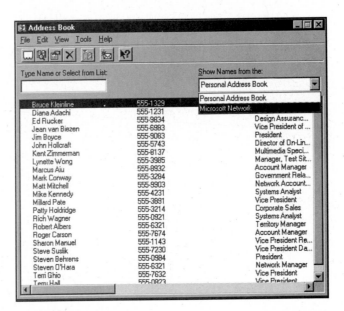

Click on the address book you want to use. The names in the address book you select appear in the resulting list box.

Finding a Name in the Address Book

To find a name in the address list, type the name in the Type Name or Select from List text box. As you type the name, Exchange starts searching for this name and, as you continue to type the name, highlights a name that matches your search criteria.

As you provide more information, Exchange continues to jump from name to name until the correct one is found. As nerve-racking as this might sound, in practice it's not that bad. In fact, Exchange usually doesn't start searching for a match until you pause for a moment as you type or when you place a space between names.

> **Tip** You can type the first or last name, or both names, of the person for whom you search. This is convenient if you don't remember the exact spelling of someone's last name, or if you commonly refer to someone by their first name. On the other hand, this feature is nice when you have several Daves or Jims or Tracys stored in your address books. You can key in their first name and just the initial of their last name.

After you find a name, you can store it in your Personal Address Book (if you haven't already) by choosing File, Add to Personal Address Book. The convenience of adding names from other address books to your PAB is greatly rewarding when you are locating names in a large list, such as on the Microsoft Network or the networked Post Office Address Book. (Chapter 32, "Using the Microsoft Network," goes into more detail on saving names from MSN to your PAB.)

Viewing Properties of Address Listings

Each name has properties associated with it. These properties include e-mail addresses, business addresses, phone numbers, and other items. You can even include notes on the contact. The following sections detail the pages you can fill in for each contact person.

> **Tip** Another way to see the properties of a person in your address book is to select the person's name and right-click. This displays a context-sensitive menu from which you can choose Properties.

Address

The New - Address page (see fig. 30.16) shows three fields: Display Name, E-mail Address, and E-mail type. You also can select a check box to always send messages to this recipient using RTF format. The Display Name field lists the name of the contact person. This field can include any name or word, so you also can use aliases or nicknames in this field. The E-mail Address field contains the full e-mail address.

The E-mail type field lists the type of service that carries the e-mail, such as MSN, the Internet, CompuServe, or others. Exchange uses the name you place in this field as the title of the tab, such as MSN - Address.

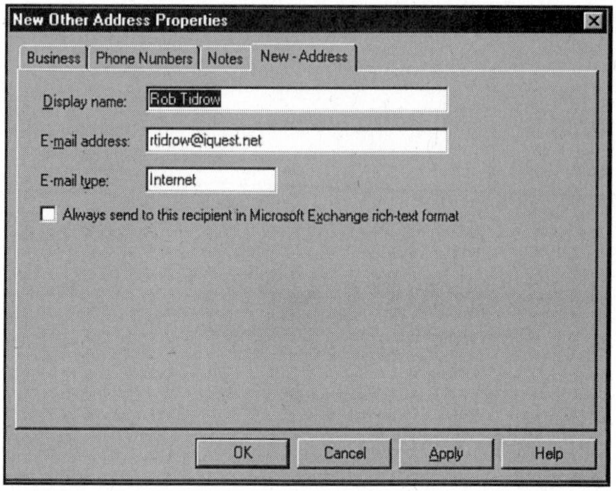

Figure 30.16

*The New -
Address page in
the Address Book
area of Exchange.*

Business

The Business page (see fig. 30.17) shows the mailing address, phone numbers, title, company names, and other address criteria. These fields are basically self-explanatory. The Phone number drop-down list at the bottom right of the page is handy when your contact has numerous phone numbers, including Business, Business 2, Fax, Assistant, Home, Home 2, Mobile, and Page.

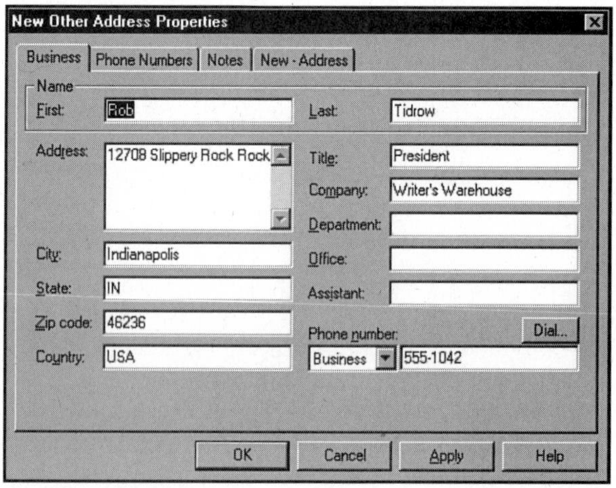

Figure 30.17

*The Business
page.*

Tip

Here's a cool option on the Business page (and the next one—Phone Numbers) that uses Windows 95's TAPI support. You can dial a phone by choosing the **D**ial button, lifting up your hand set, and talking. To be able to do this, you need to have your phone connected to your modem device directly. By having your computer make the connection, you can avoid keying in the number by hand or constantly changing your autodial numbers on your phone.

Phone Numbers

The Phone Numbers page (see fig. 30.18) simply lists all the phone numbers associated with the Phone number drop-down list in the Business properties tab. Use this page when you want to quickly change the number of one of these fields.

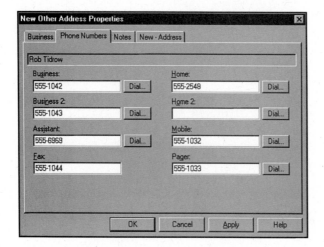

Figure 30.18

The Phone Number properties tab.

Notes

The Notes page (see fig. 30.19) is useful for jotting down simple notes about a contact. Unfortunately, you can't automatically add a date or time header to your notes, but you can use this tab to help remind you of conversations, actions, or other items specific to a contact.

Figure 30.19

*You can keep
notes on someone
in the Notes page.*

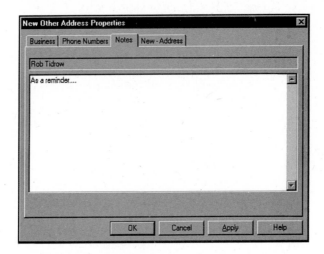

Creating New Entries in a PAB

One of these days you're going to need to create a listing in your Personal Address
Book. To do this, open the Personal Address Book and click on the New Entry icon
(looks like an index card) on the toolbar, or choose File, New Entry to open the New
Entry dialog box (see fig. 30.20), in which you select the type of entry you want to
create. You can, for example, create a Microsoft Fax entry (as you'll see in Chapter
31) or a Microsoft Network entry. If you can't find an address type that suits your
contact's e-mail address syntax, select the Other Address option.

Figure 30.20

*The New Entry
dialog box.*

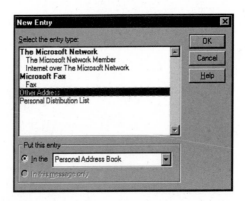

Before you choose OK in this dialog box, look at the Put this entry area. This area
gives you two main options. The In the drop-down list box lists the various address
books in which you can place your new entry. For the most part, you want to make
sure that you have the Personal Address Book option selected here. The other option

in this area is the In this message only option, handy if you create a new message and need to create a one-time address listing for your message. When you select this option, Exchange does not store the information as a permanent record.

After you select your options, choose OK to display the New Address Properties pages. Simply fill in these boxes for the contact information. For specific information on any of these pages, see the previous sections that describe each field and option.

Tip You might want to uncheck the Always send to this recipient in Microsoft Exchange rich-text format option on the New-Address page if your contact person is not using a MS Mail or Microsoft Network address. Otherwise, you might create a message that has embedded objects or enhanced characters that you can't send over most e-mail systems.

Using Personal Distribution Lists (PDLs)

Most businesses rely heavily on e-mail for daily communications. In fact, many businesses seem to shut down when the e-mail system crashes. Gone are the rapid updates, concise conversations, and information exchange associated with e-mail. As a business person, you probably send several e-mail messages to different people during the day or course of a week. You rely on this system because it is efficient. So why, when you create a new message, do you still select recipient names one at a time when you have a message that goes out to several people at the same time?

To make Exchange more efficient and work for workgroup or team environments, Microsoft includes a handy feature that enables you to build distribution lists. In the Distribution List page of the New Personal Distribution List property sheet (see fig. 30.21), you can create groups of recipients that you can quickly attach to a new message.

You can create a new PDL by selecting the Personal Distribution List option in the New Entry dialog box. The New Personal Distribution List property sheet appears, with the Distribution List tab displayed (as shown in figure 30.21). In the Name field, type a logical name of the group, such as **Windows 95 Consultants** or **Senior Management**. This name appears in the address book.

After you enter the name, choose the Add/Remove Members button to open the Edit Members of dialog box, in which you can select all the names you want to add to your new distribution list. After you select all the names you want, choose OK twice. You return to the Address Book dialog box, which displays the new distribution list in bold letters with an icon to the left of the name to denote that it is a distribution list.

Figure 30.21

The Personal Distribution List enables you to set up logical groups of recipients.

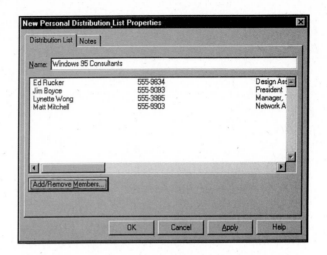

Now, when you create a new message and add recipients to the message, you can select the Personal Distribution List item and Exchange adds it to the recipient list. You can add more than one PDL to your address book and use as many as you want in your recipient list.

 Tip   Forget who belongs in which PDL? Don't worry. You can easily find out the identities of the members of your PDL by checking out its properties. Just right-click on the PDL and select Properties on the context-sensitive menu to reveal the names of the PDL's members.

CHAPTER 31

Using Microsoft Fax

Have you ever wanted to send a fax to someone straight from your PC without having to print it out and send it through a fax machine? You might even have done this several thousands of times using software (such as WinFax Pro) and a fax/modem board. But you've never had an operating system with built-in faxing capability. As an MAPI (messaging application programming interface) provider, Microsoft Fax in Windows 95 turns your PC and fax modem into a true fax machine.

With Microsoft Fax, you can create custom cover pages, send editable faxes (ones that the recipient can modify), send noneditable faxes, print a document to a fax machine, send protected faxes, and set up a fax server on a network. Another nice feature of Microsoft Fax is its capability to use the same address books you configured for Microsoft Exchange in Chapters 29 and 30.

This chapter examines how to use Microsoft Fax on your local machine as well as how to set up a shared fax modem on a LAN. Specifically, this chapter covers the following:

◆ Understanding the features and requirements of Microsoft Fax

◆ Sending and receiving faxes

◆ Using security options

◆ Using the Cover Page Editor

◆ Retrieving an on-demand fax message

Understanding Microsoft Fax

Think for a moment about how and why you currently use a fax machine or fax software. For the most part, many of your fax transmissions can be handled by e-mail messages. In fact, e-mail messages have replaced faxes for many business or communication needs. One of the problems associated with e-mail, however, is that not everyone has it. On the other hand, fax machines are as vital to business as telephones, so many, if not most, businesses today have a fax machine or fax modem board in their PCs.

Another problem with e-mail is its speed and dependability. Sometimes when you send an e-mail, you have no idea when—or whether—it reaches its destination. When you send a fax, however, you can quickly connect to your recipient's fax machine or fax modem and send your document, and feel fairly confident that the recipient got the fax clean.

Note   Granted, you can use return receipt features in many e-mail applications, but sometimes this only reports when the recipient's e-mail system receives the message, not when the recipient reads it.

Features of MS Fax

Before you start using Microsoft Fax, you might want to step back a little and get an overall view of Microsoft Fax and some of its features. This section discusses the key features of MS Fax. The next section details the requirements for using Microsoft Fax. For information on using specific parts of Microsoft Fax, see the section "Sending Microsoft Fax Documents."

Microsoft Fax is an MAPI provider and service that is part of Microsoft Exchange, which means you can create a new fax within Exchange, or create a document in an MAPI-compliant application and send it by choosing File, Send. Microsoft Word and Excel both are MAPI-compliant applications you can use to send faxes. Microsoft Fax also includes fax printer drivers so that you can print to a fax machine from within any Windows application. The Microsoft Exchange universal inbox enables you to

store and receive all your messages, whether they are fax messages, Microsoft Mail messages, CompuServe mail messages, or messages of another supported message type.

You can send a Microsoft Fax message in two ways: as a binary file or as a hard-copy fax. The latter option is the traditional way you send and receive fax messages using a fax machine, known as a Group 3 fax machine. The problem with traditional hard-copy faxes is that the recipient cannot edit the document or use it as a binary file without scanning it or keystroking it into a file. Another frustrating aspect of paper faxes is that you sometimes simply can't read them, especially if the sender has illegible handwriting or uses a small or decorative font.

When you use Microsoft Fax to send a binary file (that is, an electronic document) to another fax modem, the recipient can view and edit the fax in the application in which it was created, owing to Microsoft Fax's Binary File Transfer (BFT) capability. BFT was originally created for Microsoft's At Work program, and now Microsoft Exchange supports it so that you can create a mail message and attach a binary file to it. Windows for Workgroups 3.11 and other Microsoft At Work–enabled platforms also can receive BFT messages.

One way to take advantage of the BFT feature in Microsoft Fax is to create an Excel worksheet, attach it to an Exchange message, and send it to a fax number. Any recipient who has a fax modem and Microsoft Fax installed can open the message and click on the Excel icon embedded in the mail message to read and edit the worksheet (assuming the recipient also has Excel installed).

Stop   If the recipient doesn't have a fax modem card and Microsoft Fax but does have a Group 3 fax machine, Microsoft Fax automatically prints the Excel document as a printed fax image. One of the snags in this scenario is the transmission speed and compression feature of the recipient's fax machine. Fax machines are much slower than fax modems, so a large binary file (such as an Excel worksheet) can take a long time to transmit and print. You might want to test this feature before you send a large attached document to someone's fax machine.

One of the most discussed topics in the computer industry is security. You hear about security and the Internet. You hear about LAN security. You hear about voice mail security. Microsoft Fax enables you to securely send fax messages using public key encryption developed by one of the leaders in security, RSA Inc. Microsoft Fax also enables you to confidently password-encrypt and use digital signatures on your messages. The security features, of course, extend only to sending digital messages and files, not to printed or hard-copy faxes. These types of faxes are still subject to the eyes of anyone who happens along by the fax machine when your transmission arrives.

Note What is a digital signature? A *digital signature* is an electronic version of your John Hancock, if you will. Most business transactions, such as purchase requests and employee time sheets, require a signature for processing. Hard copies of these requests now fill up virtually millions of filing cabinets around the world.

What if you could take all this paper work and make it a digital message and store it on a server someplace? Storing, managing, and backing up electronic documents costs far less than doing the same for traditional mediums. You can use a secure digital signature to "sign" requests, time sheets, and other sensitive documents without worrying that someone might modify the message or any attachments during transmissions, and without worrying that errors might occur during transmission.

Another nice feature of Microsoft Fax is its connectivity to fax-on-demand systems via its built-in, poll-retrieve feature that enables you to receive rendered faxes or editable documents from a fax service. The proliferation of computer telephony applications being used as fax servers or fax-back services is making information easier to acquire using no more than a phone line and fax machine. Microsoft Fax enables you to retrieve this information straight to your desktop.

If you belong to a workgroup or want to share a modem on a network, Microsoft Fax enables you to share a modem much like you can share a printer on the LAN. Chapter 29, "Installing and Configuring Exchange," provides information on installing and configuring Microsoft Fax for a LAN.

Requirements of Microsoft Fax

Installing and configuring Microsoft Fax on your local machine, rather than on the network, is the easiest way to set it up. This reduces administrative tasks and document management problems, such as using e-mail to route faxes to individuals, that you encounter when you share a fax modem on a network. Before you install Microsoft Fax on a stand-alone machine, however, you should consider whether using a shared fax modem might benefit the workgroup. If you think it would, set up Microsoft Fax to handle this.

You must have the following system requirements before you can install and configure Microsoft Fax on a network to support up to 25 users:

◆ Minimally, an 80486-based computer with 8 MB of RAM

◆ For a workstation, at least 12 MB of RAM

◆ High-speed fax modem, such as a 14.4 Kbps fax modem

◆ Phone line

If you decide to install Microsoft Fax on a stand-alone workstation, you need the following:

◆ Windows 95 minimum requirements, but an 80486-based computer with 8 MB of RAM recommended

◆ High-speed fax modem, such as a 14.4 Kbps fax modem

◆ Phone line

The following sections discuss the types of modems that Microsoft Fax can or cannot use. See these sections if you have questions about a specific fax modem type. Also, see Chapter 28, "Modems and Data Communications," for information on setting up and configuring a modem on your computer.

Compatible Fax Modems and Fax Machines

Regardless of whether you set up Microsoft Fax as a stand-alone or networked fax service, you need to make sure your fax modem is compatible with Microsoft Fax. Because Microsoft At Work was introduced with Windows for Workgroups 3.11, and At Work included Microsoft Fax capabilities, many fax modem manufacturers already have ensured that their hardware meets Microsoft Fax's needs.

Table 31.1 lists and describes the compatible fax modems and fax machines that you can use with Microsoft Fax.

TABLE 31.1
MS Fax–Compatible Fax Modems and Fax Machines

Type of Modem or Fax Machine	Explanation
Class 1 and Class 2	You need Class 1 or Class 2 fax modems before you can send BFT messages with attachments. These classes of fax modems also must use security features in Microsoft Fax.
ITU T.30 Standard	This standard is for Group 3 fax machines. Microsoft Fax converts any BFT fax messages to a T.30 NSF (nonstandard facilities) transmission to enable compatibility with these types of fax machines. ITU is the International Telecommunications Union, formerly known as the CCITT.

continues

TABLE 31.1, CONTINUED
MS Fax–Compatible Fax Modems and Fax Machines

Type of Modem or Fax Machine	Explanation
ITU V.17, V.29, V.27ter standards	These types of modems serve for high-speed faxes up to 14.4 Kbps.
Microsoft At Work platforms	You need Windows 95, Windows for Workgroups 3.11, or another Microsoft At Work–compatible platform to be able to use Microsoft Fax.

Incompatible Fax Modems

Microsoft has released a list of fax modems not compatible with Microsoft Fax. Table 31.2 lists fax modems tested and known not to work during the beta cycle of Windows 95. Check with specific modem vendors or look for announcements on the Microsoft Network, CompuServe, or the Internet for a more up-to-date list of incompatible fax modems. For the most part, any modem manufactured after Spring '95 for Windows 95 and not listed in this table should be compatible with Windows 95.

 Stop If you use an internationally manufactured fax modem, you might want to double-check about compatibility with the manufacturer. Microsoft warns that it could not check all international fax modems for this list.

TABLE 31.2
Fax Modems Known Not to Work with Microsoft Fax

Manufacturer and Country	Model Name
AT&T Paradyne, U.S.	Keep in Touch Card 3761
Best Communications Inc., U.S.	14496EC
Cardinal, U.S.	14400 V.32bis, MB2296SR
Datatronics, U.S.	Discovery 2496CX
DIGICOM, U.S.	SNM28, SNM41PC
Digicom Systems, Inc., U.S.	Scout Plus
E-Tech Research, U.S.	E1414MX
Gateway, U.S.	Telepath PM144
Macronix, Inc., U.S.	Maxfax 9624s, VOMAX 2000

Manufacturer and Country	Model Name
Megahertz, U.S.	P22 Pocket Fax Modem
MulitTech Systems, U.S.	MT932ba
Practical Peripherals, U.S.	PM2400, FX96SA, V.32 Pocket
Quickcomm, U.S.	Sprint II V.32 Fax
Sysnet, U.S.	SMF44 Fax
TeleJet, U.S.	TeleJet 14400
US Robotics, U.S.	Sportster 28.8 V.F.C., Sportster 9600
Zoom Telephonics, U.S.	FC 96/24, VFX 28.8
PNB, France	TT9624
CPV Datensysteme, Germany	F-1114HV, StarLine
CTK-Systeme, Germany	CTK V.32
EEH GmbH, Germany	Elink 301
ELSA, Germany	MicroLink, MicroLine
Kortex, Germany	KX PRO 2400
LCE, Germany	MiniModem 23
National Semiconductor, Germany	TyIN 2000
Neuhaus Mikroelektronik, Germany	Fury 2400
Woerlein GmbH, Germany	M288Fax
BIT, Italy	MX-6, XM124S
Hidem, Japan	14400 Fax

Sending Microsoft Fax Documents

After you familiarize yourself with some of the features and requirements of Microsoft Fax, you can use Microsoft Fax to create and send messages.

Note If you do not have Microsoft Fax installed or configured, see Chapter 29, "Installing and Configuring Exchange," which examines adding Microsoft Fax as an Exchange profile, setting up configuration options, and adding user information. If you don't have your modem installed yet, see Chapter 28, "Modems and Data Communications."

Creating a fax message in Exchange is easy using the Fax wizard. You also can create a fax message by creating a document and using File, Send to send it in an MAPI-compliant application.

To start the Fax wizard in Exchange, choose Compose, New Fax to bring up the Compose New Fax wizard (see fig. 31.1). The I'm dialing from field shows the name of the location from which you call, such as office, home, or other settings you specify. Chapter 29 shows how to configure this field when configuring Microsoft Fax. The My Locations dialog box contains this setting.

Figure 31.1

Starting the Fax wizard to create a new fax message.

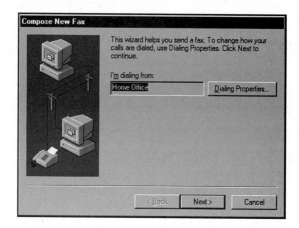

If you want to change the location setting, choose Dialing Properties and change the name in the My Locations dialog box. You might, for instance, want to set up several different locations if you are a mobile user and have to use several different phone numbers from which to call. The My Locations dialog box contains key information, such as PBX numbers that enable you to access outside phone lines from within a business setting, long-distance prefixes, and whether you want to use a calling card to make the fax call. You also should check to see if the phone line from which you call has call waiting features. If so, you can disable call waiting by adding the special key code to the To disable, dial drop-down list. See the following Tip for specific code information.

Tip Different phone services use different codes to disable call waiting. To get this code, contact your local phone company and ask them if they offer a service called Call Waiting Disable. A couple of the codes are as follows:

*70 (touch tone)
1170 (rotary dial)
70# (for GTE systems)

New Riders Publishing
INSIDE
SERIES

> If you don't disable call waiting and you send a fax (or use your modem for any
> other transmission), you lose the connection if someone calls and activates the call
> waiting feature. This can drive you nuts if you keep getting disconnected and you
> think it's a modem or software problem.

After you set the location from which to call, click on Next to advance to the second
screen of the Compose New Fax wizard (see fig. 31.2), in which you select the
recipients of your message. You can type any known recipient name(s) in the To
field. Or, to quickly select a number of recipients, choose the Address Book button
to access the address books you configured in Chapter 30. In the Show Names drop-
down list, you can select the address from which to pull the recipient names. Select
the names of the recipients just as you do when you create an Exchange mail message. Choose OK after you select the names to return to the Compose New Fax
wizard.

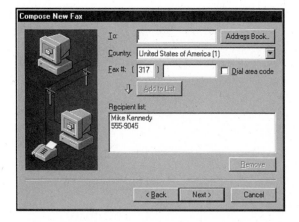

Figure 31.2

*Add recipients to
your fax message
from the Compose
New Fax wizard.*

Just like a normal fax you send with a fax machine, you can send a fax cover page with
your Microsoft Fax message. The next screen in the Compose New Fax wizard (see
fig. 31.3) enables you to choose the type of cover sheet for your fax. The default cover
pages that come with Microsoft Fax include Confidential!, For your information,
Generic, and Urgent!. In the section "Editing Cover Pages" later in this chapter, you
are shown how to modify these templates and how to create your own cover sheets.

The screen shown in figure 31.3 also enables you to set other options for the fax
message. Choose the Options button to open the Send Options for this Message
dialog box (see fig. 31.4), in which you can set the time to send the fax (ASAP, during
discount rate time, or at a specific time), the type of message format, dialing options,
and security options.

Figure 31.3

Select the type of cover page to send with your fax message.

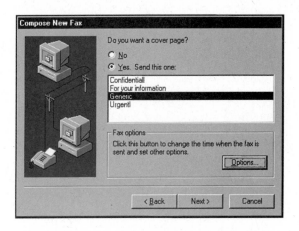

Figure 31.4

You can set fax properties for your new fax message in the Send Options for this Message dialog box.

The Message format area of the Send Options for this Message dialog box contains the following three option buttons:

◆ **Editable, if possible.** Use this option to send your fax message as a BTF message if the recipient has a fax modem that can accept this format. If not, Microsoft Fax reformats the message to a noneditable message so that the fax modem can accept it.

◆ **Editable only.** Use this option if you need to send your fax as a BTF message only. If the fax on the other end cannot accept this format, you get an error message stating that the fax transmission was unsuccessful. You should use this option when your message contains large binary files or documents that might

not reformat properly for a Group 3 fax machine. Another reason to use this option is to send secure documents, such as documents that you encrypt using public key encryption. See the section "Setting Up Key Encryption" later in this chapter for more information on this topic.

◆ **Not editable.** Use this option when you send a fax message to a fax machine. You can set the paper size, orientation, and image quality here as well.

If you've ever sent a fax by fax modem or fax machine, you know how many attempts getting through on the line sometimes takes. The fax line is busy or down, or some glitch in the phone connection messes things up. Then you stand and watch the phone number dial repeatedly until you get a connection. Microsoft Fax enables you to set the number and time between these retries by choosing the Dialing button on the Send Options for this Message dialog box. You also can set dialing properties and toll prefixes here. Choose OK after you configure these settings.

The Send Options for this Message dialog box also enables you to set the level of security for your fax message. Choose the Security button to open the Message Security Options dialog box (see fig. 31.5). You must set up public key encryption before you can use the Key-encrypted option (see the following section) or use a digital signature on your message. You can, however, secure the fax message with a password by choosing the Password-protected option. Figure 31.6 shows the Fax Security - Password Protection dialog box, which you fill out when you want to send a message with a password.

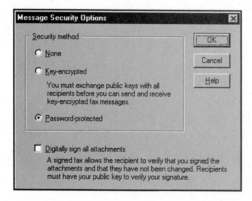

Figure 31.5

You can set the type of security for your fax message in the Message Security Options dialog box.

Tip   Make sure your recipient(s) has your password so that your document can be opened when it is received. A message is worthless if no one can read it.

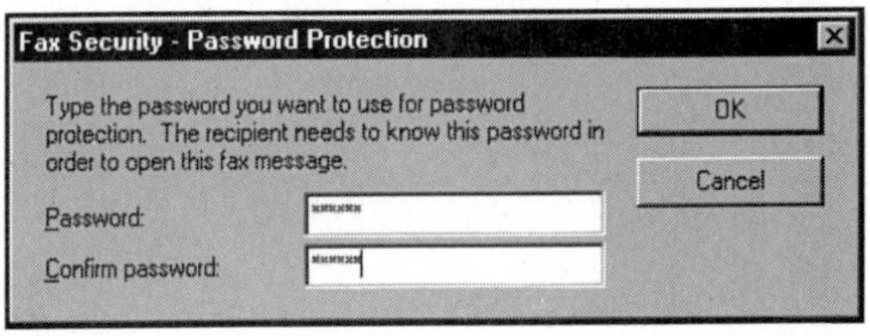

Figure 31.6

Enter a password for your password-protected fax message.

Setting Up Key Encryption

A *key-encrypted message* uses a public key to unlock the message for viewing. You make this public key available to your fax recipients so that only they can open your document.

You must create a public key in Exchange. To do this, choose **T**ools, Microsoft Fa**x** Tools, **A**dvanced Security to open the Advanced Fax Security dialog box (see fig. 31.7). The first time you create a public key, you can choose only the last option, **N**ew Key Set. This opens the Fax Security - New Key Set dialog box, shown in figure 31.8.

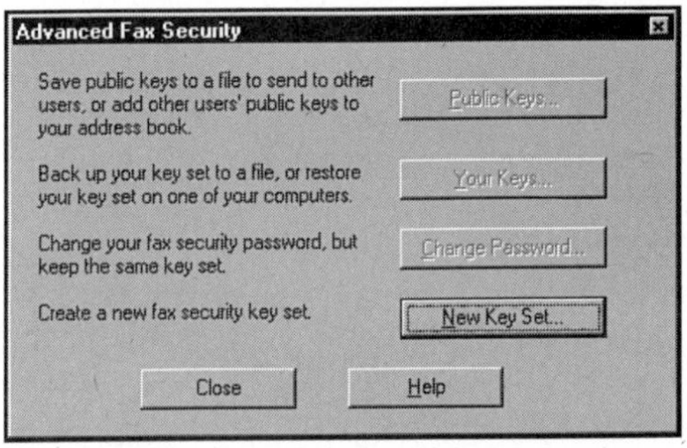

Figure 31.7

Creating a public key.

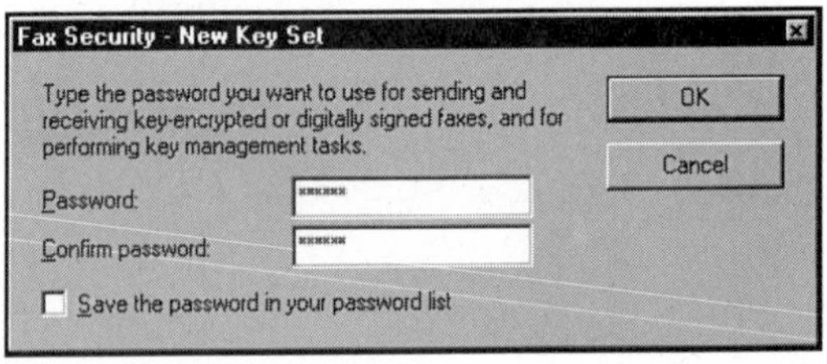

Figure 31.8

Entering a password for a new public key.

In the Fax Security - New Key Set dialog box, type a password in the **P**assword field, then retype it in the **C**onfirm password field. Not surprisingly, Exchange doesn't display the password—it displays only a string of asterisks (*****) to denote the characters of your password (refer to figure 31.8). Don't forget this password—it's

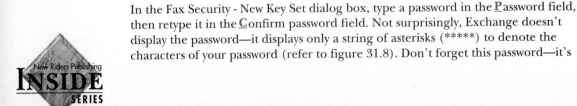

your public key. Choose OK for Exchange to create a new public key set on your system. An information box appears, telling you that creating your key set might take a few moments.

Sending a Public Key to Fax Recipients

After you create a public key set, you need to distribute it to your fax recipients so that they can read your key-encrypted messages. To do so, choose the <u>P</u>ublic Keys button in the Advanced Fax Security dialog box to open the Fax Security - Managing Public Keys dialog box, then choose <u>S</u>ave to save your public key to a file so that you can send it to other recipients.

In the Fax Security - Save Public Keys dialog box, click on the name or names of the public keys you want to share. You should click on your name here at the very least. Choose OK, then select a name and directory in which to store the keys in the resulting window. This file has an Awp extension. To finish the job, send the file to your recipients as an attachment to a Microsoft Exchange message or give it to them on a floppy disk.

Receiving a Public Key from a User

When you send your public key to a list of recipients, they need to import the Awp file into Microsoft Fax. Likewise, when you receive a public key from someone, you need to import it into your Microsoft Fax settings and add it to your address book so that you can read key-encrypted messages from those users.

After you receive an Awp file from someone, store it on your system and choose the <u>A</u>dd button in the Fax Security - Managing Public Keys dialog box. Locate the file name that contains the public keys and choose <u>O</u>pen. Select the key or keys you want to add.

Tip

If you receive a set of public keys from someone and you don't want the name of the key in your address book, you can change it. To do this, open your address book, choose the Change <u>N</u>ame button, and choose the name you want to assign to the key.

Another thing to keep in mind is that when you send a set of your public keys, the recipient might not know what to do with them. You might want to create a simple document to send along with the message to lead them through importing Awp files. In fact, the previous three paragraphs might be all you need for this purpose.

Finishing Sending a Fax Message

After you set the proper security, if any, for your fax message in the Send Options for this Message dialog box, choose OK to return to the Compose New Fax wizard. Click on Next to create the subject and message text for the message (see fig. 31.9). Enable the Start note on cover page check box if you want the message to begin on the cover page. The information you provide in the Note section appears as text in your fax. Click on Next after you finish.

Figure 31.9

Writing the subject and message text for your fax message.

The next screen enables you to attach files (such as your public key file) to your fax message. Remember, if you want to send binary files, the recipient must have a fax modem that can receive them. If not, Microsoft Fax converts them so that Group 3 fax machines can handle them. Click on Next and then Finish when you are ready to send your fax message. The Microsoft Fax Status window appears while Microsoft Fax formats your message for delivery and sends it.

Tip Maybe one of the most unique ways to send a document as a fax is to create a shortcut to the fax printer on your desktop and then drag and drop the document to the icon. Create the shortcut on your desktop and drag a document from the Windows Explorer to the fax printer. This action starts that New Fax wizard, in which you can provide the necessary information to send your new fax message.

Editing Cover Pages

You can send a cover page with your faxes or create a custom cover page to add with your faxes. This section shows you how to use the Cover Page Editor to customize and

create a cover page. Some of the features that you can add to your cover pages include graphics, logos, and rich-text characters. The Cover Page Editor also is an OLE application, so you can embed OLE-compliant objects in your cover pages, such as Excel worksheets, CorelDRAW drawings, or a Media Clip (if you intend to send the fax message as an editable document).

To start the Cover Page Editor, choose Fax from the Accessories folder. In the Fax folder, choose Cover Page Editor to open the Cover Page Editor, shown in figure 31.10.

Figure 31.10

The Cover Page Editor.

To customize an existing cover page, choose File, Open and select one of the Microsoft Fax cover pages, such as Confidential!. The first thing you might notice is that the Cover Page Editor has features that might suit a graphics or desktop publishing application. This is because the Cover Page Editor enables you to create different shapes on your pages and lay out the cover page as you desire.

 Tip   You should keep in mind a few basics as you create and modify cover pages. First, always use fonts that transfer cleanly to a fax machine. Decorative or script fonts usually do not transfer very nicely to printed faxes. Also, make sure that your typefaces are large enough (at least 11 or 12 points) to read in printed form. Many fax machines print at 177 dpi (although Microsoft Fax supports up to 300 dpi), not the greatest resolution.

Another point to keep in mind is that you should always include sender name, sender fax or phone number, recipient name, and date on the cover page. The following section discusses these information fields.

Inserting Information Fields

You might feel overwhelmed a little by the Cover Page Editor at first, but you soon get comfortable using it. One of the elements that a cover page contains is a set of information fields that Microsoft Fax fills in when you send a fax message. Some of these fields are filled in using the User tab in the Fax Setup dialog box or from your address book properties.

 Tip   As you work on your cover page, you might want to move an item out of the way temporarily. If you scroll to the extreme right side of the Cover Page Editor, you see a gray area. You can place items here until you need to use them again. If you print out your cover page, any items in the gray area do not print.

Information fields are stored in the Insert menu under the Recipient, Sender, and Message options. You can select an information field to place in your cover page from one of these menus. Table 31.3 lists the menus and available information fields.

TABLE 31.3

Fax Cover Page Information Fields

Menu	Option
Recipient	Name, Fax Number, Company, Street Address, City, State, Zip Code, Country, Title, Department, Office Location, Home Telephone Number, Office Telephone Number, To: List, and CC: List
Sender	Name, Fax Number, Company, Address, Title, Department, Office Location, Home Telephone Number, and Office Telephone Number
Message	Note, Subject, Time Sent, Number of Pages, and Number of Attachments

After you select an information field, the field appears on the cover page surrounded by sizing and moving handles. You can grab the field with your mouse and move or resize the field. Continue inserting fields as necessary. If you want to delete a field, click on the field and press Del.

Tip As you move fields around on your cover sheets, you might need to view your cover sheet as it will appear printed. To see a preview of the cover sheet, choose **F**ile, Print Pre**v**iew.

Adding Formatting to Cover Pages

Some of the special enhancements that you can add to your cover pages include shading, line fills, and text color (black, white, or shades of gray). To add these elements to a field or object, click on the object and right-click the mouse button. From the context-sensitive menu, choose the Line, **F**ill, and Color option, which opens the Line, Fill and Color dialog box (see fig. 31.11).

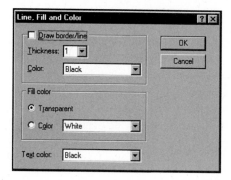

Figure 31.11

You can add borders, fill colors, and textual colors to your cover sheets.

Some of the other formatting options at your disposal include font definition, font choice, and aligning text. You can, for example, include any typeface installed on your system and add font styles, such as italic, bold, and underline, to the lettering. The Align Text feature enables you to left-, center-, or right-align text within a text frame.

Tip To help you align the text frame and objects on your cover sheets, turn on the grid lines by choosing **V**iew, **G**rid Lines. A matrix of blue lines appears on-screen to help you line up each element on the cover page. When you choose **F**ile, Print Pre**v**iew, the grid lines do not show. Turn them off by choosing **V**iew, **G**rid Lines again.

Using Cover Page Tools

The Cover Page Editor contains six drawing tools on the Drawing toolbar that enable you to add text and shapes to your cover pages. Table 31.4 shows and explains each of these tools.

TABLE 31.4
Cover Page Editor Drawing Tools

Icon	Name of Tool	Function
ab|	Text Tool	Adds text to your cover page. Click on this button and then click on the cover page document in which you want the text to begin. Drag the pointer to create a text frame and then type the text you want to appear on the cover page.
\	Line Tool	Draws straight lines on your cover page.
▭	Rectangle Tool	Draws four-sided shapes.
▢	Rounded Rectangle Tool	Draws rectangles with rounded corners.
◿	Polygon Tool	Draws multisided, closed shapes. Click anywhere in the cover page document to set your first point and then click the left mouse button. Drag the frame until you want to set your next point. Click the mouse button. Do this until you create the shape of your choice. Double-click the left mouse button to finish.
⬭	Ellipse Tool	Draws ovals and circles.

After you create and modify your cover pages, save them by choosing File, Save or File, Save As. The next time you use a cover page for a fax message, you can use your new cover page.

Receiving Fax-On-Demand Faxes

Many business and information sources provide documents on fax servers and by fax-back services. These types of services enable you to retrieve documents, software updates, drivers, and fax messages by using Microsoft Fax's poll-retrieve capability. This capability enables Microsoft Fax to request the name of a binary file on the service, which in turn sends a fax or editable file to your computer.

Retrieving fax-on-demand messages is easy. First, choose <u>T</u>ools, Tools for Microsoft Fa<u>x</u> in Microsoft Exchange. Then choose <u>R</u>equest a Fax Service, which starts the Request a Fax wizard (see fig. 31.12). The first screen gives you two choices: you can retrieve whatever is available at the fax number you specify on the next screen, or you can access a specific document or file by choosing Retrieve a <u>s</u>pecific document. If you take the second choice, you must then provide the title of the document and possibly a password.

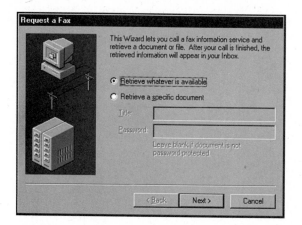

Figure 31.12

Requesting a fax-on-demand fax.

In the next screen, you need to provide the name and phone number of the service. If you plan to access this service again, you should place the name and number in your address book, which you can activate by clicking on the Address Book. Conversely, if you already have the service in your address book, you can select it by accessing your address book. Click on Next and then on Finish to start the transaction.

Using the Microsoft Network

You knew it had to happen sooner or later. With the release of Windows 95 in Fall 1995, Microsoft also is announcing their new commercial online service, the Microsoft Network (MSN). The Microsoft Network offers many of the same features that other, highly successful commercial services, such as CompuServe and America Online, offer, but with the extra advantage of the connection software built into the Windows 95 operating system. Some might see this built-in functionality as an unfair advantage. Others see it as an opportunity for their operating system, modem, and an online service to work together to make them more productive, keep them informed better, and make electronic communications easier and more powerful.

This chapter looks at the basic features of the Microsoft Network, how to become a member, how to access the service, and the types of services and forums available. Specifically, this chapter covers the following:

◆ Looking at Microsoft Network features

◆ Becoming a member of the Microsoft Network

◆ Using the Microsoft Network

◆ Becoming an information provider

Looking at Microsoft Network Features

You can use the Microsoft Network to perform many business, personal, and group functions that require a phone line, computer, and modem. In fact, you can expand the scope of your knowledge of other parts of the country or world, learn about business dealings in foreign countries, and communicate with other members from around the globe. If you've never used an online service before, you should find the Microsoft Network easy to use and well-integrated with your Windows desktop (see fig. 32.1). If, on the other hand, you're a veteran of online services or BBSs, the MSN should satisfy some of your online needs.

Figure 32.1

A look at the Microsoft Network's interface.

 Note   As of this writing, access to the Microsoft Network was limited to systems running Windows 95. If a later version of Windows NT 3.51 adopts the Windows 95 interface, look for Windows NT to support the Microsoft Network. As many online services and BBS managers know, providing access to as many operating systems as possible is a very important ingredient for the success of a service. Just ask Apple's e-World, which provides access only to users using a Macintosh. You can be sure that Microsoft will make the Microsoft Network available to the largest possible market segment that doesn't require them to downscale MSN's feature set.

To help you get an idea of the Microsoft Network's services and features, the following list names and briefly describes some of the most important ones:

◆ **E-mail.** You can send and receive e-mail to and from other MSN members. You also can send and receive e-mail to and from people who have Internet e-mail accounts.

◆ **Bulletin Boards (BBS).** If you are familiar with message forums on CompuServe, you will find the MSN Bulletin Boards a friendly spot to communicate with other members who share your interests.

◆ **Shortcuts.** Because the Microsoft Network is integrated with Windows 95, you can duplicate many features on your local desktop with the MSN resources: creating shortcuts on your desktop, for example, linked to online resources. This feature is handy when you often locate and use frequently updated resources. You also can embed these shortcuts in messages that you send to other users, enabling them to access those resources quickly without typing in paths or file names.

◆ **Chats.** Do you enjoy communicating with people in a real-time conversation? Do you feel limited by the area in which you live or the various restrictions on traveling long distances? MSN Chat rooms enable you to carry on conversations with members from all over the world. With the number of chat rooms available, you should find one of them that interests you. If not, create your own chat room. If you don't feel like talking today, you can still enter a chat room and listen to the conversation and send a comment only when you feel like it.

◆ **File libraries.** One of CompuServe's strongest features is its tremendous resource of files, utilities, device drivers, documents, and product support information. Microsoft is building a similar type of resource on the Microsoft Network that should be well stocked within 12 months after it introduces Windows 95.

◆ **Microsoft information.** This area enables you to get product information and access to customer support online. You also can get some technical support through this feature. Look for this area to increase as Microsoft continues to decrease their free technical support.

◆ **Information superhighway.** Available as part of the Microsoft Plus! package is a version of Spry's Mosaic product that enables you to access the World Wide Web's resources through the Microsoft Network. The Microsoft Network also has access to newsgroups and e-mail services.

Note You might wonder how much all this will cost. No one knows. Because the Microsoft Network was still in beta testing during the writing of this book, Microsoft had not established pricing structures for it. Some of the general press releases and information sheets distributed by Microsoft explain how each forum manager and business can set pricing for their online services. You might find, for example, a chat room in an area that charges $1.00 for admission. Or, to download a file, you might be assessed a $5.00 fee. Along with these costs, Microsoft also imposes an hourly fee or another service fee. Watch for pricing plans to be announced the fall of 1995 when the service opens to all users. One known fact, however, is that Microsoft will handle all the billing and payment receiving.

Becoming a Member of the Microsoft Network

Before you try to set up the Microsoft Network, be sure to install your modem so that it works for Windows 95. If you haven't installed Windows 95 yet, you can set up your modem and the Microsoft Network during installation: select the Microsoft Network option in the Custom setup choices to add MSN support during the installation.

Most of you probably have Windows 95 installed and just want to install the Microsoft Network software and become a member of MSN. Choose Add/Remove Programs from the Control Panel and click on the Windows Setup tab. In the Components list, be sure to enable the Microsoft Network check box. Choose OK to install the Windows 95 software. Have your setup disks or CD-ROM handy at this point.

After you install the Microsoft Network software, you need to sign up for the MSN before you can access and start using it. During sign up, specify your name, address, and payment method, then read the rules and the etiquette of MSN. Although not reading this information might be tempting, you should read through the rules to understand your rights and responsibilities as an online member. For information on the rules of joining specific chats or BBS message areas, see the sections "Entering Chats" and "Using MSN BBSs" later in this chapter.

To start sign up, click on the Signup Now shortcut on your desktop, or choose the Sign Up For the Microsoft Network icon in the Accessories menu. If you have already signed up for MSN access, neither of these icons appear on your system, which means you can skip to the section "Using the Microsoft Network."

After the Microsoft Network opening screen appears, choose OK. The next screen gives you three steps for signing on. Click on the first button to fill in your user

information, such as name, address, country, and phone number. Choose OK after you finish doing that. Click on the second button to establish the billing option. You need to provide a valid credit card and expiration date. Choose OK, then click on the last button to read the rules of being a Microsoft Network member. Choose OK when you're done.

Next, a series of dialog boxes leads you through choosing a member ID and password. You must have a member ID, but you don't have to use your name if you want to protect your identification. When you create the ID, the Microsoft Network checks your requested ID against those already set up to make sure that your ID is unique. If not, MSN prompts you to choose another ID. The ID you choose is similar to the handle in other online services. You use it only to identify yourself while you are on MSN. For billing purposes, you still are required to use your legal name.

 Stop While a member of the Microsoft Network, you must follow the MSN's established rules and maintain good a credit rating with them. If you constantly violate these rules or fail to pay your bills, the Microsoft Network can deny you access to the service. If this occurs, you appear on the MSN Client Negation list, which is referenced each time a user requests to log on to the network. If your name is on this list, you cannot log on to the MSN.

You also must have a password before you can log on to the MSN. You can and should frequently change this password to ensure that no one else uses it and your member ID to access the MSN. Together, the password and member ID authenticate and protect you as a member. Authentication identifies valid members to distinguish them from invalid members.

After you sign on to the Microsoft Network and establish member IDs and a password, you can make your first connection to the MSN.

Using the Microsoft Network

When Microsoft released Windows 3.1 in Spring '92, the press was full of stories that reported Bill Gates's "Information at Your Fingertips" vision. His vision saw everyone in the world with access to electronic information and communications by way of a world-wide electronic network and computer software. Gates wanted (and still wants) the Windows platform to help make this vision a reality by giving the average user easier-to-use software and a consistent interface with which to interact with the plethora of files, documents, messages, and databases available in the electronic world.

Although Gates and Microsoft don't say who would control such an enterprise or who would provide the backbone for the network, you can feel comfortable (or uncomfortable) knowing that Microsoft probably wants to control the various parts of the "vision." The introduction of the Microsoft Network and the mergers and agreements that Microsoft has made with communications giants, such as UUNET and AT&T, brings Gates's idea that much closer to reality.

After you establish an account for the Microsoft Network, you can navigate easily from one service to another, giving you true information at your fingertips (or at least at your mouse pointer).

MSN Central

To start your journey through the MSN, you usually start at MSN Central. If you have any experience with the World Wide Web (WWW), you are familiar with the term *home page.* On the WWW, a home page refers to the starting point of a site or resource. In essence, the home page is the front door to the Web site. On CompuServe, this initial screen is called Basic Service and gives you a starting point from which to navigate the various services available on CompuServe. Technically speaking, MSN Central on the Microsoft Network is the highest-level content tree, which is the way in which the MSN structures the information it presents to you. In real terms, this means it gives you a point from which to start, as well as a place to go when you feel lost during your online journey.

 Tip   As on CompuServe, the WWW, or other online services, you can jump to specific sites on the Microsoft Network without going through MSN Central. You can, for example, set a shortcut to one of your favorite sites and access it directly from the desktop, similar to pointing your Web browser to a specific URL, or providing a GO word in WinCIM before you connect to CompuServe. The Microsoft Network also uses GO words that help you navigate the network.

A close look at MSN Central (see fig. 32.2) reveals several services from which you can start your online navigation. To move to any one of these areas, click on the icon and MSN opens that service or tool.

The five services available to you from MSN Central include the following:

◆ **MSN TODAY.** Reports any special events, newly added services, or general MSN tips and ideas. In the left column of the screen (see fig. 32.3), you can click on Calendar of Events to see a list of events, online conferences, and other items of interest. You also can click on Member Assistance for help.

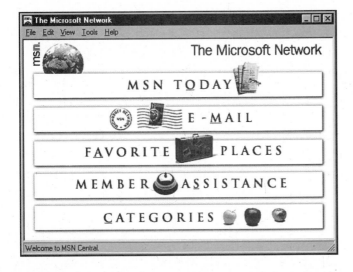

Figure 32.2

MSN Central is where you start your online experience.

Figure 32.3

The MSN Today service is a nice place to start your day online.

 Note Although the documentation does not say so, the first screen you actually see when you start MSN is the MSN Today screen, because the MSN Central screen sits behind the open MSN Today screen. Move this screen to see MSN Central.

◆ **E-MAIL.** Starts Microsoft Exchange (see fig. 32.4) and gives you access to your e-mail. You can receive this mail from other MSN members and people on the Internet. See Chapters 29 and 30 for more information on Exchange.

Figure 32.4

Microsoft Exchange provides access to your e-mail.

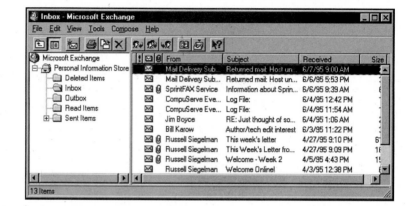

◆ **FAVORITE PLACES.** Enables you to save a directory of the services and places you like to visit on MSN. To add places to this option, drag icons from bulletin boards and chat rooms to this area (see fig. 32.5).

Figure 32.5

You can gather all your favorite online places in this area.

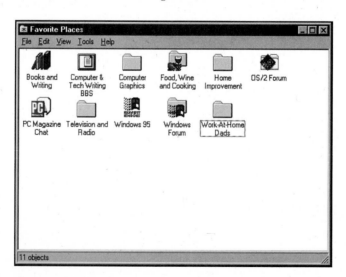

◆ **MEMBER ASSISTANCE.** Enables you to access MSN help items. Some of the assistance you find here includes the Member Assistance Kiosks, Member Guidelines, and the MSN Member Lobby (see fig. 32.6).

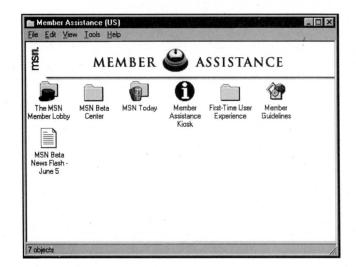

Figure 32.6

Need help? Choose the Member Assistance option at MSN Central to access MSN help items.

◆ **CATEGORIES.** Shows you all the forums available on the MSN (see fig. 32.7). A *forum* is a collection of services on the MSN, such as the Internet Center forum, Science and Technology forum, and Business and Finance forum. See the following section, "MSN Forums," for a discussion of these items.

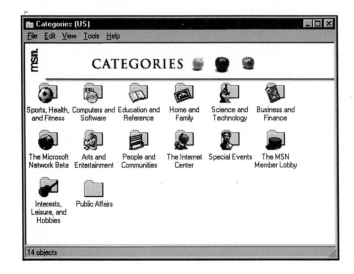

Figure 32.7

MSN forums give you access to various BBSs, files, and chat areas.

Tip   To return to MSN Central, choose **F**ile, **U**p One Level while you are in one of the services or tools.

MSN Forums

When you choose the Categories icon at MSN Central, you gain access to the dozen or so forums available online, represented by folders. When you double-click on one of these folders, you are presented with all the services that are part of that forum. Some of the items you find in a forum folder include bulletin boards, chat areas, kiosks, and file libraries. Some forum folders also contain folders in which topics are organized to help members locate similar items. One of the forums available now, for example, is the Computers & Software forum (see fig. 32.8). When you open this folder, a number of different services are available, including Desktop Publishing, Multimedia & CD-ROM, and The MIDI Forum. Many of these services are represented by folders that you can open to find other services or tools.

Figure 32.8

The Computers & Software forum in MSN.

 Note   A *kiosk* is a file (usually in Word for Windows format) that gives information about the forum. This document usually lists the forum manager, the Go word, a calendar of events, and other useful information. A *Go word* is a word that you can enter in the Edit, Go To menu option to go immediately to that forum or service. You can find Go words in the Properties of the forum, as well as in the kiosks.

In general, to navigate a forum, double-click on the icons of interest or open a folder. Depending on the forum, you might need to drill down through one or two folders to get to a service you can join and participate in. If you are interested in joining a chat or using a bulletin board system, see the next two sections of this chapter.

Another activity in which you might be interested is downloading files from a forum. To learn how to do this, see the section "Downloading Files." You should keep in mind, however, that downloading files usually costs you a charge additional to your basic online fee.

Entering Chats

A *chat room* is the online equivalent of carrying on a live conversation with someone or a group of people, the difference being that you type your comments rather than speak out loud (at least no one on the other end can hear you talk out loud). When you type something during a chat session, you see your conversation at the bottom of the chat window, and the members of the chat session see it in real time at the top of the chat window (see fig. 32.9).

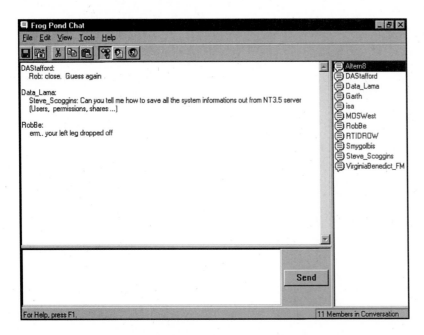

Figure 32.9

A chat room with a conversation taking place.

To join a chat room, double-click on the chat icon that interests you. One example is in the Small Office/Home Office forum in the Business and Finance category. If you open the SOHO Advisors folder, you can find the Alice Breedin Works Anywhere, Inc. service. When you double-click on this item, the New Chat Room icon appears. Double-click on this icon to enter the chat room. If other people are carrying on a conversation in the room, their names appear on the right side of the screen. If you see only your name, you're alone in the chat room. You can wait until someone else enters the room, or you can leave and find an active chat room.

When you find an active chat room, you can participate in the conversation or become a spectator. This status is determined by the chat host. (Not all chat rooms have a chat host, but all are maintained by the forum manager.) The chat host is the MSN member who moderates the chat room and determines if someone is a spectator or participant. Some chat rooms are set up to have only a few participants and several spectators, much like a television talk show. Other chat rooms are designed to be one-on-one conversations.

Tip   Are you a spectator but want to be a participant? If you want to join the conversation and have something to say, send the chat host an e-mail message asking permission to join. If the host agrees, you are granted access. Sometimes the chat host cannot create additional participants if the capacity of the chat room has been met.

If a chat room does not have a chat host, send a message to the forum manager to change your spectator status to participant. You can find the forum manager's ID in the kiosk for that forum.

The chat window has three panes: the history pane, the compose pane, and the member list pane. You can resize or hide each pane according to your needs. The chat window also has a menu bar, toolbar, and status bar. Figure 32.10 identifies each element of the chat window.

Figure 32.10

The chat window and its elements.

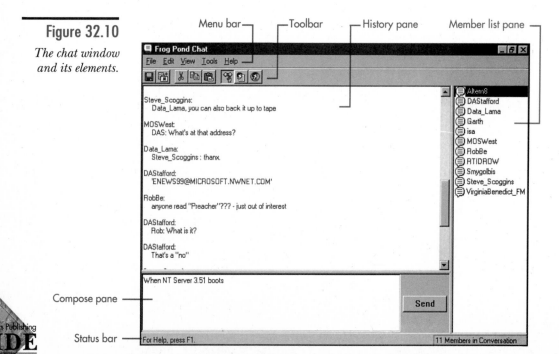

New Riders Publishing
INSIDE
SERIES

You can see the messages from the participants in the history pane. All the action takes place here. New messages appear at the end of the chat history. When a member joins or leaves a chat, messages appear in boldface, unless you turn off this option in the **T**ools, **O**ption dialog box. You type the message you want to appear in the history pane in the compose pane at the bottom left of the chat window. After you type your message in the compose window, press Enter or click on the Send button to place your message in the history pane.

The member list pane appears on the right side of the chat window and identifies the members in the chat room. Participants, spectators, and chat hosts are identified as such in this pane. You also can ignore a member by clicking on the Ignore tool on the toolbar (it looks like a face with a red circle and line through it).

When you ignore a member, you cannot see that person's messages on your screen. You might want to do this if a specific member's comments are upsetting you, but you don't want to leave the chat room. Chat members do not know if you are ignoring them, and vice versa.

Tip
One way to chat with a few people in a large conversation is to click on the members with whom you want to chat. Then choose **V**iew, **I**gnore Members. Next, choose **T**ools, **S**elect Members, **I**nvert Selection, to select all the members whom you want to ignore, which leaves only those members with whom you want to chat.

In the member list pane, you can find out more about each member by clicking on them and viewing their properties. Right-click and choose P**r**operties to open the Member property sheet (see fig. 32.11), which contains the member's information if the member filled out a member profile in Microsoft Exchange.

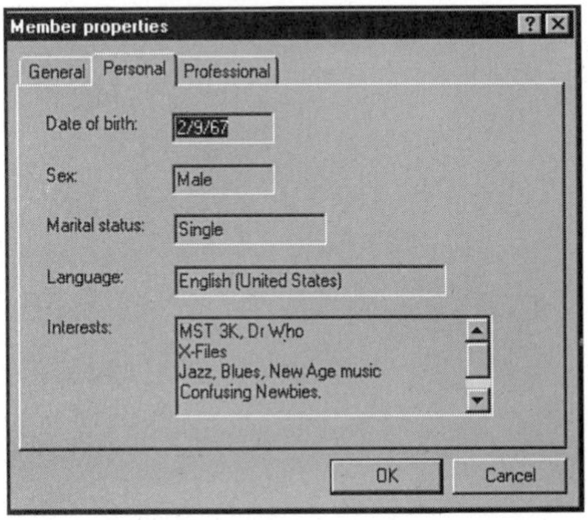

![Member properties dialog box showing the Personal tab with Date of birth: 2/9/67, Sex: Male, Marital status: Single, Language: English (United States), Interests: MST 3K, Dr Who, X-Files, Jazz, Blues, New Age music, Confusing Newbies.]

Figure 32.11

Viewing member information in the Member property sheet.

Using MSN BBSs

Another way to communicate with other MSN members is to join a Bulletin Board (BBS). An MSN Bulletin Board has a topic to help keep the message exchanges focused. Some of the BBSs available include computer graphics, multimedia, work at home dads (WAHD), and current events. As a member of a BBS, you can learn a lot about other members, get information on a specific topic, or just enjoy communicating with others who have similar interests.

An individual BBS in MSN is called a *newsgroup* and contains threads of messages organized in folders. These threads are organized hierarchically and chronologically to show the flow of a discussion from its starting point. A *message* is a posting to a BBS.

Figure 32.12 shows a BBS window. You can view a BBS window in three different views, which you can select from the View menu. The Conversation view lists messages according to a conversation thread. This view shows the original posting to a new thread, and has a plus sign next to replies. Click on this plus sign to expand the thread and read the other messages. The Conversation view probably is the most effective way to view and read messages in a BBS because of the way messages are organized around threads.

Figure 32.12

A typical BBS window.

Subject	Author	Size	Date
⇒ Go ahead—shoot!	Durant Imboden	833 bytes	5/1/95 9:21 PM
⇒ Sue Grafton Fans?	Wayne Hazle	632 bytes	5/6/95 6:40 PM
⇒ RE: Sue Grafton Fans?	Durant Imboden	1.03KB	5/7/95 12:12 PM
⇒ RE: Sue Grafton Fans?	Wayne Hazle	739 bytes	5/8/95 10:26 AM
⇒ RE: Sue Grafton Fans?	Rose Vines	768 bytes	5/24/95 7:37 PM
⇒ RE: Sue Grafton Fans?	Wayne Hazle	0.98KB	5/25/95 1:33 PM
⇒ "Everywhere That Mary Went"	Michael Hayes	568 bytes	5/14/95 8:28 AM
⇒ RE: "Everywhere That M...	Durant Imboden	673 bytes	5/14/95 2:44 PM
⇒ Parker Fans Anywhere?	FORBIN *	592 bytes	5/16/95 9:34 AM
⇒ RE: Parker Fans Anywhere?	Rose Vines	677 bytes	5/24/95 7:40 PM
⇒ John Grisham Goes Back T...	John Gilbert	511 bytes	5/27/95 11:44 AM
⇒ unspeakable crimes	Tony Markidis	655 bytes	5/31/95 11:00 PM

Mystery & Crime BBS
File Edit View Tools Compose Help

6 conversations, 6 with unread messages

The List view shows the messages in chronological order, regardless of the thread to which the message belongs. The Attachment View shows only messages with attachments. Sometimes no messages appear in this view because no one has attached a file to their message.

To reply to a message, double-click on the message to which you want to reply and choose Compose, Reply to BBS. In the window that appears, you can keep the Subject line as is or change it as necessary. Type your message in the message area. Choose File, Post Message to send your file to the BBS. It appears a few minutes after you post it.

> **Note** Some BBSs are restricted and read-only, meaning you can read posted messages but cannot reply to them. In these cases, the Reply to BBS option in the Compose menu is grayed out. This occurs often in file libraries, which an information provider maintains to enable members to download files and read messages about the files.
>
> Another thing to keep in mind when you post messages to a BBS is that you can use RTF formatting in your message text. This means that you can add special characters, color to your fonts, and other formatting to jazz up your messages. Because the MSN is an OLE-compliant application, you also can embed object and files in your messages.

If you want to start your own message thread in a BBS or send a single message, choose Compose, New Message in the BBS window. Enter a subject in the Subject line and write your message. Choose File, Post Message to send your message to the BBS.

Downloading Files

Online services, such as the MSN and CompuServe, provide a quick and efficient way to access various computer files, including graphics, software, beta software, articles, marketing information, and more. When you select a file (or group of files) to download in the MSN, you can view its size, price, and the time necessary for downloading it. The File Transfer Manager (see fig. 32.13) helps you download the files, enabling you to set the destination of the file you download and automatically decompressing files after downloading.

You can identify a file to be downloaded by the paper clip icon next to the message subject in a BBS or file library. One example of a rich file library is the Windows App Software Library in the Windows Applications forum. To start a file download, double-click on the file that you want to download. This displays a message that briefly describes the file(s) and has pictures embedded that are linked to the actual file (see fig. 32.14).

Figure 32.13

The File Transfer Manager helps you control the way in which you download an MSN file to your computer.

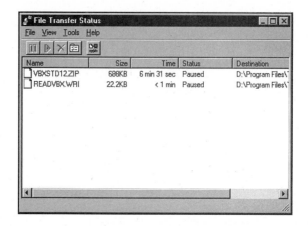

Figure 32.14

Viewing a message with a file attached.

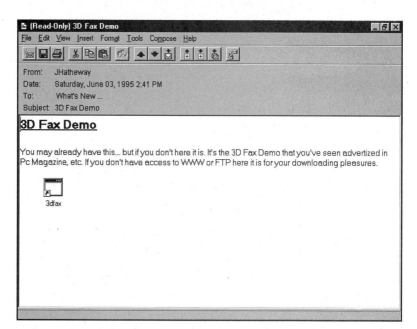

Double-click on these pictures to view the Attached File property sheet (see fig. 32.15), on which you can see the size of the file, download time, file name, upload date, and the number of times downloaded. To start the download, choose the **D**ownload File button at the bottom of the sheet.

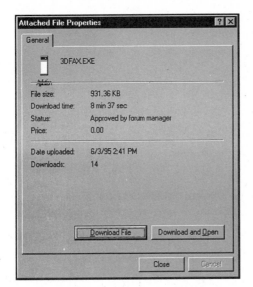

Figure 32.15

Viewing the properties of a file in the Attached File property sheet.

 Tip   You also can download files that members have attached to BBS messages. Use the same procedures as previously described to do this.

Becoming a Forum Manager

Online services need to be accessible by thousands if not millions of users to stay afloat. By making the Microsoft Network an integral part of Windows 95, Microsoft almost assures itself millions of computer users subscribing to MSN. Just because a user subscribes, however, does not mean that the user continues to visit the service consistently. Repeat visits is the second most important factor of an online service.

One way to keep users interested in online service is to keep the information fresh and provide new services weekly. To meet this need, Microsoft offers an open program that enables anyone interested in being a forum manager to submit a business proposal for acceptance. As a forum manager, you manage the forum and produce revenue for it. You generate revenue any way you want and split it with Microsoft. Forum managers set the prices of the different items that users can access.

 Note   The key objective as a forum manager is to create a sense of community in your forum, which you do by being active on BBSs, hosting chats, providing files to download, and even giving away some free stuff.

Some of the ways in which Microsoft suggests forum managers produce revenue are described in the following list:

◆ **Chat rooms with cover charges.** Forum managers can invite well-known personalities to show up in a chat room and talk to other members. The forum manager could charge a small fee for admission.

◆ **Document files.** Forum managers can provide documents, such as newsletters or information packets, related to the forum for members to download. A fee can be attached to these documents as long as the forum manger has the appropriate licensing rights to distribute the material for a fee.

◆ **Software that can be downloaded.** Forum managers can set up deals with software manufacturers and shareware authors to distribute software files in their forum. Again, appropriate licensing contracts need to be established.

◆ **Fulfillment transactions.** Forum managers can sell goods and services online by providing electronic forms for members to fill out to order items. These goods and services can be ones that the forum manager owns, or deals can be made with smaller vendors to see their goods.

For updated information on starting a forum and becoming a forum manager, look for guidelines in the Member Assistance area.

Using Remote Access Services

Windows 95 includes a feature called Dial-Up Networking that enables you to use your computer to dial into a server to connect to remote networks, including the Internet. The capability to connect to remote systems is called *remote access,* and the services in Windows 95 that enable you to do so are referred to as *remote access services,* or RAS. This chapter explains RAS and Windows 95's Dial-Up Networking, covering the following topics:

◆ Understanding Dial-Up Networking

◆ Installing and configuring Dial-Up Networking

◆ Using remote LAN resources

◆ Using a SLIP connection

◆ Using a PPP connection

◆ Creating dial-up scripts

◆ Using RAS for remote mail

◆ Setting up a Windows 95 RAS server

In addition to enabling you to connect to remote computers and LANs, a RAS server module in the Plus! product enables you to use your Windows 95 workstation as a RAS server, enabling other users to dial into the computer to gain access to your local resources or to your LAN. The section "Setting Up a Windows 95 RAS Server" later in this chapter explains using Windows 95 as a RAS server.

If you want to use Windows 95 to connect through a dial-up Internet service provider to the Internet, read the section "Using SLIP and CSLIP Connections" later in this chapter for tips on how to connect.

Understanding Dial-Up Networking

The capability to dial into a remote computer or network to use the computer's or network's resources is called *remote access*. In Windows 95 and Windows NT, the capability to dial into a remote system or act as a dial-in server is generally termed *remote access services*, or *RAS*. The computer that dials in is called the RAS client. The computer that provides access is called the RAS server. Figure 33.1 illustrates a RAS connection.

Figure 33.1

An example of a RAS connection.

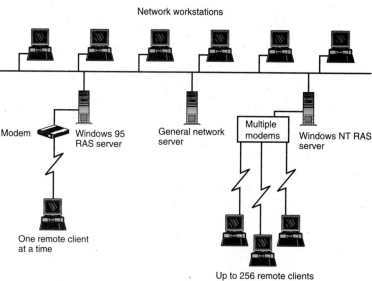

Windows 95 includes a RAS client that Microsoft has named Dial-Up Networking. You can use Dial-Up Networking to connect to a RAS server to gain access to the server's shared resources and gain access to the network to which the server is connected. If you have a RAS server connected to your office LAN, for example, you can dial into the server from your home or hotel and access the LAN as if you were sitting in your office with your computer connected directly to the LAN. You can use the dial-up connection to access directories and files, send mail, perform scheduling, and even print.

The Windows 95 RAS client also enables you to connect to the Internet through a dial-up Internet service provider. If your office LAN is connected to the Internet, you can dial into a RAS server at the office to access the Internet, provided the RAS server supports IP routing (explained in the section "Support for RAS Servers" later in this chapter).

To use the Dial-Up Networking client in Windows 95, you must have the following:

◆ A Windows 95-compatible modem

◆ Approximately 3 MB of disk space to accommodate the Dial-Up Networking software

◆ File and printer sharing service (if you want to share the Dial-Up Networking server's resources with dial-in users)

To use Windows 95 as a Dial-Up Networking server, you must have the Dial-Up Networking Server software, included with Microsoft Plus! for Windows 95.

Understanding the Dial-Up Networking Client

The Dial-Up Networking client in Windows 95 (see fig. 33.2) uses the Dial-Up Adapter driver supplied with Windows 95 to enable the computer to connect to remote servers through a modem. The Dial-Up Networking client supports the following selection of connection protocols:

◆ **Point-to-Point (PPP).** The PPP protocol is rapidly becoming a standard protocol for remote access. Windows 95, Windows NT 3.5*x*, and many other remote access clients and servers support PPP. Many Internet service providers offer PPP support for their dial-in Internet access services.

◆ **Novell NetWare Connect.** NetWare Connect is a proprietary RAS protocol that enables RAS clients to connect to a NetWare Connect server and remotely access resources on a NetWare LAN.

◆ **Windows NT 3.1 and Windows for Workgroups 3.11 RAS.** These servers use asynchronous NetBEUI, and Windows 95 supports connections to these servers. The server and client must both run NetBEUI.

◆ **Serial Line Interface Protocol (SLIP).** SLIP is a remote access protocol standard that originated in the Unix environment. Windows 95 supports SLIP connections, which enables you to connect to Unix servers through a dial-up connection. The software you need before you can establish a SLIP connection with Windows 95 is included on the Windows 95 CD. Using SLIP requires that the server and client run TCP/IP. The Windows 95 Dial-Up Networking Server does not support using Windows 95 as a SLIP server.

Figure 33.2

The Dial-Up Networking client.

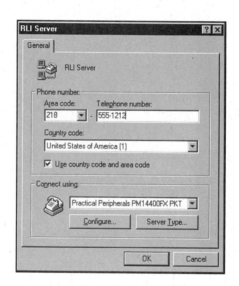

You can use the Dial-Up Networking client for a variety of purposes, including accessing remote LANs, connecting to the Internet, sending and receiving mail remotely, and sharing files and printers with other non-networked users. If you simply want to share a few files with a friend, for example, one of you can configure your Windows 95 workstation as a Dial-Up Networking server, and the other can use the Dial-Up Networking client to connect to the server to copy files between the systems. Dial-Up Networking also is the mechanism Microsoft Exchange uses to enable you to process remote mail, sending and receiving mail from a LAN-based Microsoft Mail postoffice. For more information on configuring and using remote mail, refer to Chapter 29, "Installing and Configuring Exchange," and Chapter 30, "Using Microsoft Exchange." Dial-Up Networking also makes possible dialing into a Unix mail server to send and receive Internet mail.

If you use an online service, such as America Online or CompuServe, you can use Dial-Up Networking to connect to an Internet provider or your LAN IP server, and then connect to the information service through the dial-up connection. If you don't have a local CompuServe access number, for example, but your office LAN is tied to the Internet, you can dial into your LAN's server to establish a TCP/IP connection to the Internet, then use WinCIM to establish a connection to CompuServe over that TCP/IP connection. For more information on connecting to CompuServe and America Online through a dial-up connection, refer to the section "Tips for Optimizing Communications" in Chapter 28, "Modems and Data Communications."

 Tip You must have a dial-up server that routes TCP/IP protocol before you can use the Windows 95 RAS client to establish a dial-up connection to the Internet. Windows NT and Unix dial-up servers support IP routing. The Windows 95 Dial-Up Networking server cannot route IP, which prevents a Windows 95 Dial-Up Networking server from acting as a TCP/IP gateway.

Support for RAS Servers

The Dial-Up Networking client software is included with Windows 95. You can use this RAS client to dial into one of several types of RAS servers using a variety of protocols, including NetBEUI, IPX/SPX, and TCP/IP. The following sections describe the types of RAS servers to which you can connect using Windows 95, and explores some of the advantages and limitations of each one.

Windows 95 Dial-Up Networking Server

The Dial-Up Networking server for Windows 95 is included with Microsoft Plus! for Windows 95. This Dial-Up Networking server enables you to use your Windows 95 workstation as a RAS server (see fig. 33.3), which enables other users to dial into your computer to access its resources and to access your LAN. The Windows 95 Dial-Up Networking server enables only one dial-in connection at a time. The Windows 95 Dial-Up Networking server supports NetBEUI, IPX/SPX, and TCP/IP protocols for dial-in clients, but does not support IP routing. Clients that dial in using TCP/IP, therefore, can access only the resources shared by the dial-up server, but not other resources on the LAN to which the server is connected. These clients can gain LAN access by running the NetBEUI or IPX/SPX protocols, in place of or in conjunction with TCP/IP.

 Tip The Windows 95 Dial-Up Networking server provides a limited capability to monitor and administer the server through system policies. If you use a Windows NT RAS server, you can administer the server remotely through a dial-up connection or LAN connection.

Figure 33.3

You can use Windows 95 as a RAS server.

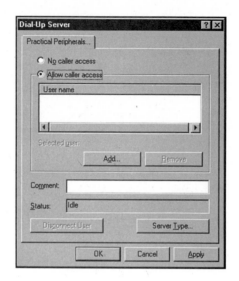

The Windows 95 Dial-Up Networking server supports the following clients:

◆ Windows 95

◆ Windows for Workgroups 3.11 and Windows NT 3.1

◆ Windows 3.1 RAS Client

◆ PPP (Windows NT 3.5 and others)

Windows NT 3.5*x* RAS Server

The Windows 95 Dial-Up Networking client supports connection to a Windows NT 3.5*x* Server or Windows NT 3.5*x* Workstation RAS server. These servers use the standard PPP protocol, enabling Windows 95 and other PPP-capable clients to connect through the RAS server. PPP is the default protocol the Windows 95 Dial-Up Networking client uses.

Tip Unlike the Windows 95 Dial-Up Networking server, a Windows NT 3.5x RAS server can support up to 256 simultaneous connections.

Windows NT 3.1 and Windows for Workgroups 3.11 RAS Server

The Dial-Up Networking client in Windows 95 can connect to a Windows NT 3.1 or Windows for Workgroups 3.11 RAS server. These servers use the RAS asynchronous NetBEUI protocol, which Windows 95 supports. In addition, clients that run Windows

for Workgroups 3.11 or Windows NT 3.1 can use their RAS clients to connect to a Windows 95 Dial-Up Networking server.

Shiva NetModem or LanRover

Shiva Corporation (617-270-8300, 800-458-3550, or sales@shiva.com) manufactures a variety of RAS products, including modems and software. Windows 95 supports Shiva's NetModem and LanRover series of RAS server modems, enabling Windows 95 clients to dial into these servers. The Shiva RAS products offer some enhancements to the Windows 95 RAS capabilities, including the following:

◆ IPX/SPX, TCP/IP, and AppleTalk routing

◆ Apple Remote Access dial-in support

◆ Integrated ISDN support

◆ Modem pooling for shared dial-out

Novell NetWare Connect

Novell NetWare Connect is a proprietary NetWare RAS server. The Windows 95 dial-up client can connect to a NetWare Connect RAS server to access NetWare servers on the remote LAN. To access NetWare servers remotely, however, you must run a NetWare client, such as Client for NetWare Networks, which is included with Windows 95. For more information on configuring network clients and NetWare support in Windows 95, refer to Chapter 34, "Network Concepts and Configuration."

SLIP

SLIP, which stands for Serial Line Interface Protocol, is the standard dial-in protocol many Unix systems use. SLIP enables you to dial into a TCP/IP-based network served by a Unix dial-up server running TCP/IP. Your client also must be running TCP/IP. The software that enables the Dial-Up Networking client in Windows 95 to connect to SLIP servers is included only on the Windows 95 CD. For information on how to connect to a SLIP server, refer to the section "Using SLIP and CSLIP Connections" later in this chapter.

Understanding Security

The Windows 95 RAS client and server support pass-through security, which enables the dial-in server or another server on the network to handle remote user authentication. If you use a Windows 95 RAS server, the server can use share-level security to authenticate dial-in access. When a user dials into the server, the user provides a password, which you have assigned in the Dial-Up Networking server's configuration.

If the passwords match, the dial-in user is connected and can begin to use the resources on the server or on the network to which the server is connected, provided the user has the necessary passwords for the resources.

The Windows 95 Dial-Up Networking server also can use pass-through, user-level security to authenticate access to the server and to the LAN. When the server is configured for user-level security, a Windows NT server authenticates user logon, just as it does for LAN clients who attempt to access user-level security-protected resources on the LAN. The user dials into the Windows 95 Dial-Up Networking server, which then transmits the authentication request to the Windows NT-based security server on the LAN. If the server responds with security authentication, the dial-in user is connected and can begin to use the Dial-Up Networking server's resources and other shared resources on the LAN for which the user has passwords or access permission. If the security server denies authentication, the dial-in connection is denied and the connection fails.

The security that other types of dial-up servers provide depends on the operating system and dial-up server software. For information on using share-level and user-level security, refer to Chapter 35, "Sharing Resources in Windows 95."

Installing and Configuring Dial-Up Networking

Now that you have some background regarding RAS in Windows 95, you're ready to install and configure the Dial-Up adapter and software. The following section explains how to configure the dial-up adapter.

Planning Your Installation

Before you install the Dial-Up Adapter, you should determine which network transport protocol(s) you want to use with the Dial-Up Adapter. If you intend to use Microsoft TCP/IP, you should read Chapter 36, "TCP/IP and the Internet Connection," to determine the necessary TCP/IP settings. If you plan to use the Dial-Up Adapter to provide remote sharing of resources, you also need to install a suitable client, such as Client for Microsoft Networks or Client for NetWare Networks. The following list provides a guideline for installing protocols, clients, and services to support a dial-up connection:

◆ **Internet only.** If you want to use the dial-up connection only to access the Internet, you need to install only the TCP/IP protocol. You do not need to install a file- or printer-sharing service or a network client.

- ◆ **Windows-based network access.** If you want to dial into a network that consists of Windows 95 and/or Windows NT computers, and want to be able to access shared resources on those computers, you must install an appropriate protocol. Generally, NetBEUI is best because it is Windows 95's default protocol. However, you must match the protocol you use to the protocol that the remote computers use. If you want your computer's resources to be available to users on the remote LAN when your computer connects, you must also install File and Printer Sharing Services for Microsoft Networks on your computer.

- ◆ **NetWare-based network access.** If you want to dial into a network that contains NetWare servers and want to access those servers, you must install the IPX/SPX protocol and the Client for NetWare Networks.

- ◆ **Internet and remote LAN access.** If you want to dial into a server to access the remote LAN's resources and also gain an Internet connection, install the Microsoft TCP/IP protocol and the protocol required to access the LAN's resources. If you connect to a Windows-based network, for example, install the Microsoft TCP/IP and NetBEUI protocols.

In addition to installing the necessary network protocols and services, you also should install the modem you will use for Dial-Up Networking before you install the Dial-Up Adapter.

Installing the Dial-Up Adapter

Before you can begin to use RAS in Windows 95, you must install the Microsoft Dial-Up Adapter. This adapter driver, which is included with Windows 95, serves as a virtual network interface card between your computer and its modem. The Dial-Up Adapter serves much the same purpose as a physical network adapter. The primary difference is that rather than connect your computer to others through a LAN cable, the Dial-Up Adapter provides the link through your computer's modem.

To install the Dial-Up Adapter, open the Control Panel and choose the Network object. From the Configuration page of the Network property sheet, choose the Add button to open the Select Network Component Type dialog box. Select Adapter from the list, then choose Add. Select Microsoft from the Manufacturers list. The only entry in the Microsoft list is Dial-Up Adapter. Select the Dial-Up Adapter from the Network Adapters list, then choose OK.

The Dial-Up Adapter provides three property pages you can use to configure the adapter after you install it. To set the adapter's properties, open the Network object in Control Panel, select the Dial-Up Adapter from the network components list, then choose Properties to open the Dial-Up Adapter property sheet (see fig. 33.4).

Figure 33.4

The Dial-Up Adapter property sheet.

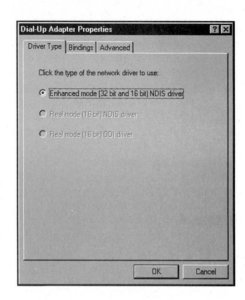

The Driver Type property page enables you to specify which network driver you want to use with the Dial-Up Adapter. You must choose a client that is a protected-mode driver.

The Bindings property page (see fig. 33.5) enables you to specify which network protocols the Dial-Up Adapter uses. Based on which protocols you decide to use (see "Planning Your Installation" earlier in this chapter), place checks in the check boxes for the protocols you want to bind to the Dial-Up Adapter. If you installed only one protocol, only that one protocol appears in the list and is selected automatically.

Figure 33.5

The Bindings property page.

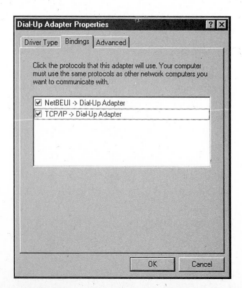

Note You must use at least one protocol with the Dial-Up Adapter, even if you do not use a network client.

The Advanced property page (see fig. 33.6) enables you to set a couple of advanced settings for the Dial-Up Adapter. The Record a log file option enables you to specify whether Windows 95 maintains a log file of your dial-up connections. If you choose Yes, Windows 95 creates a log named Ppplog.txt in the Windows folder and stores PPP session information in the log file. The Ppplog.txt file can be very useful for trouble-shooting connection problems. If you are not experiencing any problems, however, choosing No improves performance slightly.

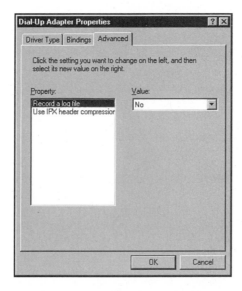

Figure 33.6

The Advanced property page.

The other setting on the Advanced property page, Use IPX header compression, specifies whether Windows 95 compresses IP packets. If you connect to a CSLIP (Compressed Serial Line Interface Protocol) server, enable this setting; otherwise, you generally can leave it disabled.

After you specify the necessary settings on the Dial-Up Adapter property sheet, choose OK to apply the changes. Windows 95 prompts you to restart the system for the changes to take effect.

Creating a Dial-Up Networking Session

After you install the Dial-Up Adapter, you can use Dial-Up Networking. You access Dial-Up Networking in Windows 95 through the Dial-Up Networking folder, located in My Computer. The Dial-Up Networking folder contains a wizard you can use to add new dial-up connections, as well as connections you have already defined (see fig. 33.7).

Figure 33.7

The Dial-Up Networking folder.

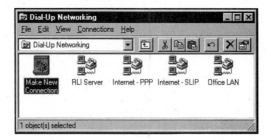

To define a new Dial-Up Networking connection, run the Make New Connection wizard by selecting it from the Dial-Up Networking folder. The wizard prompts you for a name for the connection and enables you to choose which modem you want to use for the connection. You also specify the phone number to dial, and can specify the COM port settings for the connection if you want to use settings other than the default port settings. If you're not familiar with configuring a COM port, refer to Chapter 28, "Modems and Data Communications."

After you specify the connection data, the wizard creates an icon in the Dial-Up Networking folder with the name you specified for the connection as the icon's description. To change the connection's properties, open the icon context menu and choose Properties. Windows 95 displays a property sheet similar to the one shown in figure 33.8.

Figure 33.8

Property sheet for a Dial-Up Networking connection.

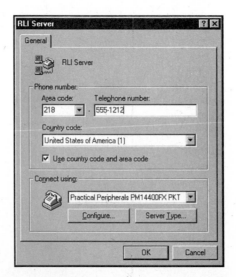

Most of the controls on the property page are self-explanatory. To configure the COM port, choose the Configure button. To specify the type of server to dial into, choose the Server Type button to open the Server Types dialog box (see fig. 33.9).

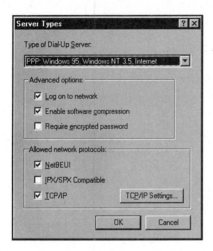

Figure 33.9

The Server Types dialog box.

From the Type of Dial-Up Server drop-down list, select the type of server protocol you want to use. By default, the list contains three choices: NRN NetWare Connect, PPP, and Windows for Workgroups and Windows NT 3.1 (RAS). If you have installed the optional SLIP driver, the list also contains options for CSLIP and SLIP. Select a server type based on the protocol the dial-up server uses. If you connect to a Windows 95, Windows NT 3.5, or other PPP server (such as an Internet service provider), select the PPP option. If you connect to a NetWare Connect RAS server, select the NRN option. For connection to a server that uses the asynchronous NetBEUI protocol, select Windows for Workgroups or Windows NT 3.1 server. For uncompressed SLIP connections to Unix servers, select SLIP. For compressed SLIP, select CSLIP.

Tip

If you choose Default, Dial-Up Networking attempts to use PPP to establish the connection. If the PPP negotiation fails, Dial-Up Networking attempts a connection using the asynchronous NetBEUI protocol. If you choose a specific protocol rather than Default, Dial-Up Networking doesn't try to switch protocols if the first protocol negotiation fails.

Some additional options in the Server Types dialog box enable you to control the way the connection is established and the protocols used for the connection. The settings in the Advanced options group are explained in the following list:

◆ **Log on to network.** Enable this check box if you want to be logged on to the network as soon as the connection is established. If you disable this check box, you are connected to the server but not logged on to the network. If you dial a Windows 95 server, for example, you have access to the resources on the server but not to resources on its network. If the server uses pass-through security, however, you must log on to the network before the server grants access to its shared resources.

◆ **Enable software compression.** Enable this check box if you want the connection to use data compression. If you transfer a number of compressed files, clear this check box to provide better transfer time (using compression when transferring compressed files actually slows down transfer speed). Both the server and the client must support compression to enable compression to function.

◆ **Require encrypted password.** If you leave this check box blank, your password is sent unencrypted. For best security, enable this check box so that Windows 95 encrypts your password before it sends it. The server must support password encryption for this feature to work.

In addition to setting advanced options, you also must choose which protocols to use during the connection. The selections include NetBEUI, IPX/SPX Compatible, and TCP/IP. Enable the check boxes for only those protocols you want the dial-up connection to use.

Using Session-Dependent TCP/IP Settings

The TCP/IP Settings button in the Server Types dialog box enables you to specify TCP/IP settings for the connection that differ from your global TCP/IP settings for the adapter. Each Dial-Up Networking connection can use a different IP address, DNS servers, and other options. Choosing the TCP/IP Settings button displays the TCP/IP Settings dialog box, shown in figure 33.10.

If you want the server to assign your IP address, using DHCP or another method, choose the Server assigned IP address option button. If you need to provide an explicit IP address, choose the Specify an IP address option button, then enter your IP address in the IP address text box. If you're not sure what IP address to use or whether you should use an explicit address or rely on a server to supply the address, read Chapter 36, "TCP/IP and the Internet Connection," for an explanation.

If you rely on DHCP to define the DNS servers, choose the Server assigned name server addresses option button. If you need to specify explicit DNS and/or WINS server IP addresses, choose the Specify name server addresses option button and enter the IP addresses of the primary and secondary DNS and WINS servers in the text boxes.

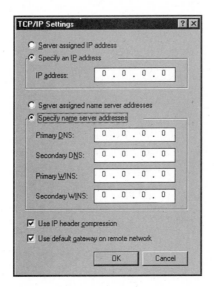

Figure 33.10

The TCP/IP Settings dialog box.

The TCP/IP Settings dialog box contains the following two additional check boxes:

◆ **Use IP header compression.** Enable this check box if you connect to a CSLIP server or other server that requires IP header compression. Leave this disabled for all other servers.

◆ **Use default gateway on remote network.** Enable this check box if you want the connection to use the default gateway on the remote network to route IP packets.

Using Remote LAN Resources

After you define a Dial-Up Networking connection, you can connect to the remote server in various ways. You can open the Dial-Up Networking folder, for example, and double-click on the icon of the connection you want to use. Windows 95 opens a dialog box similar to the one shown in figure 33.11.

Enter your user name and password in the User name and Password text boxes. If you need to modify the phone number for the connection, make the change in the Phone number text box. From the Dialing from drop-down list, select your dialing location. If you need to define dialing properties such as a calling card number, prefix dialing numbers, disable call waiting, or set other dialing options, choose Dial Properties. If you're not familiar with defining or using dialing locations or options, refer to the section "Configuring and Using Telephony Services" in Chapter 28,

"Modems and Data Communications." When you are ready to make the connection, click on the Connect button. Windows 95 dials the server and attempts to establish a connection. After the connection is established, a status dialog box appears, similar to the one shown in figure 33.12.

Figure 33.11

The Connect To dialog box.

Figure 33.12

The remote connection status dialog box.

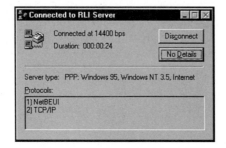

Windows 95 also can make remote connections automatically. The following list describes situations in which Windows 95 automatically starts a Dial-Up Networking connection:

◆ **No network.** If you try to access a remote resource using a shortcut or UNC name when no network is loaded, Windows 95 automatically opens a Dial-Up Networking connection for the resource.

◆ **UNC name not on the LAN.** If you specify a UNC name in an application and the name can't be identified on the LAN, Windows 95 opens a Dial-Up Networking session.

◆ **Remote OLE.** If you reconnect or activate a remote OLE object, Windows 95 opens a Dial-Up Networking connection to the OLE server or object.

Windows 95 caches remote server names and their resources for future use. If Windows 95 can't determine which Dial-Up Networking connection to use to access a resource, Windows 95 prompts you to choose a connection from the Dial-Up Networking folder or enter a server name. If the connection is successful, Windows 95 associates the server and remote resource name so that it can automatically establish the connection in the future.

Tip   Sometimes Dial-Up Networking is completely automatic from session initiation to termination. If you use remote preview in Exchange to access a remote mail server, for example, Exchange establishes the connection, downloads your mail headers, and terminates the connection, all automatically.

After a remote connection is established, you can use remote resources as if they were located on your LAN or local computer. Remote nodes with which you share a workgroup name appear in the Network Neighborhood folder. You can access other workgroups and servers on the remote LAN through the Entire Network folder. Essentially, accessing a remote resource through a Dial-Up Networking connection is exactly the same as accessing it through a LAN connection, except the Dial-Up Networking connection is slower.

For more information on how to connect to remote resources, map resources to local drive IDs and ports, and share resources, refer to Chapter 35, "Sharing Resources in Windows 95."

Using SLIP and CSLIP Connections

Although the number of networks connected directly to the Internet continues to increase, many networks do not have a direct connection to the Internet. And, the number of home-based users or users who have non-networked stand-alone workstations and want access to the Internet is also growing rapidly.

Windows 95's Dial-Up Networking supports the Microsoft TCP/IP protocol stack, which enables you to dial into various types of remote access servers and Internet service providers to gain access to the Internet. Many Internet service providers use Point-to-Point (PPP) protocol to provide dial-up Internet connections. PPP is Dial-Up Networking's default protocol in Windows 95 and is used when you connect to a Windows 95 or Windows NT 3.5 RAS server.

Many Unix servers, however, use Serial Line Interface Protocol (SLIP) or Compressed SLIP (CSLIP). Windows 95 provides a SLIP driver on the Windows 95 CD that supports SLIP and CSLIP (the SLIP/CSLIP driver is not available on the Windows 95 floppy disk set). The SLIP driver enables you to use Windows 95's Dial-Up Networking to connect to SLIP and CSLIP servers. This section explains how to install and use the SLIP driver.

Installing the SLIP Driver

To install the SLIP driver, insert the Windows 95 CD in your computer's **CD-ROM** drive. If you have enabled insert notification, the CD autoplays, displaying a window with a menu of icon choices. Select the Add/Remove Software icon to display the Windows Setup property page shown in figure 33.13. If insert notification is turned off on your computer and the CD doesn't autoplay, open the Control Panel and choose the Add/Remove Programs icon to display the Windows Setup property page.

Figure 33.13

The Windows Setup property page.

Next, choose the **H**ave Disk button to open the Install From Disk dialog box. Choose the **B**rowse button, then locate and select the file \Admin\Apptools\Slip\Rnaplus.inf. Choose OK, then OK again, to open the Have Disk dialog box (see fig. 33.14). Place a check beside the Unix Connection for Dial-Up Networking item in the **C**omponents list, then choose **I**nstall to begin installing the SLIP driver.

Figure 33.14

*Place a check
beside the SLIP
driver to select it.*

Selecting and Using SLIP and CSLIP

After you install the SLIP driver, you select it for use when you create or modify a
Dial-Up Networking connection. Use the steps specified earlier in this chapter to
create the Dial-Up Networking connection for the SLIP or CSLIP server to which you
want to connect. After you use the Make New Connection wizard to create the
connection, open the connection icon's context menu and choose Properties to
display its General property page. Choose the Server Type button to open the Server
Types dialog box (see fig. 33.15).

Figure 33.15

*The Server Types
dialog box
showing the SLIP
driver.*

From the Type of Dial-Up Server drop-down list, select CSLIP:Unix Connection with IP Header Compression if you want to connect to a CSLIP server, or select SLIP:Unix Connection if you want to connect to a SLIP server. Set the logon and TCP/IP options according to your server's requirements, then choose OK. Now you can begin to use the SLIP or CSLIP connection.

Connecting to the Server

When you connect to a SLIP or CSLIP server, the server generally prompts you for a user logon name and password. When you use Dial-Up Networking to connect to a SLIP server, Windows 95 displays a Post Dial Terminal Screen dialog box after the connection is established, which enables you to enter your user name and password to log on and receive the IP addresses of the server and your workstation. Write down the IP addresses, then choose F7. Windows 95 displays a SLIP IP Connection Address dialog box in which you must enter the IP address the SLIP connection has assigned your computer. After you enter the IP address, choose OK to begin using the SLIP connection.

You might think the method described above for connecting to a SLIP server could be easier. You're right. Fortunately, you can use a script to automate the process. The next section explains how to use scripting with Dial-Up Networking to automate connections.

Creating Dial-Up Scripts

Many RAS servers and service providers require you to respond to prompts or choose from a menu of options to establish a connection. If you have the Windows 95 CD, you can use an optional scripting component to automate connections to any type of server, regardless of the type of protocol it uses. If you connect to CompuServe through Dial-Up Networking, for example, you can use scripting to automate the CompuServe logon process.

You can find the Scripting for Dial-Up Networking component on the Windows 95 CD. To install Scripting for Dial-Up Networking if your computer's CD-ROM drive is configured for AutoPlay, insert the CD in the drive, then choose the Add/Remove Software icon from the AutoPlay window when it appears. Or, if not, open the Control Panel and choose the Add/Remove Programs icon.

From the Windows Setup property page, choose the Have Disk button, then enter the path to the dial-up scripting files, or use Browse to locate the file. Then choose OK twice to open the Have Disk dialog box. Place a check beside the SLIP and Scripting for Dial-Up Networking item in the Components list, and choose Install.

After you install the scripting component, Windows 95 places some sample Dial-Up Networking scripts in the \Program Files\Accessories folder. Windows 95 also adds a Dial-Up Scripting Tool item to the Accessories menu in the Start menu. Windows 95 uses the Dial-Up Scripting Tool to associate a script with a Dial-Up Networking connection and debug the script, which you learn later. Right now, you need to learn how to create and edit scripts.

Creating and Editing Scripts

You can use Notepad, WordPad, or any ASCII file editor to write and edit Dial-Up Networking scripts. A *script* consists of various statements that set the port properties, transmit a string to the server, wait for a string from the server, retrieve IP address information, and perform other tasks that help automate the logon and connection configuration process.

Each script includes a procedure named main, which defines the entry point (starting point) of the script. The main procedure contains statements that automate the connection or other task you use the script to accomplish.

The scripting language used in Scripting for Dial-Up Networking resembles the scripting languages that many communications programs use. If you're not familiar with scripting or writing scripts, the easiest way to begin to understand scripting is to open and view one of the sample scripts provided with Scripting for Dial-Up Networking. You can use these scripts as starting points for your own scripts, modifying them as necessary to suit your needs. The following is the CompuServe script (Cis.scp) provided with Scripting for Dial-Up Networking:

```
; This is a script file that demonstrates how
; to establish a PPP connection with Compuserve,
; which requires changing the port settings to
; log in.

; Main entry point to script
;
proc main

    ; Set the port settings so we can wait for
    ; non-gibberish text.

    set port databits 7
    set port parity even

    transmit "^M"
```

```
waitfor "Host Name:"
transmit "CIS^M"

waitfor "User ID:"
transmit $USERID
transmit "/go:pppconnect^M"

waitfor "Password: "
transmit $PASSWORD
transmit "^M"

waitfor "One moment please..."

; Set the port settings back to allow successful
; negotiation.

set port databits 8
set port parity none
```

```
endproc
```

This script is fairly simple. It sets the data bits and parity of the connection, then transmits a carriage return (Enter) to CompuServe and waits for the Host Name: prompt. After the script receives the Host Name: prompt, it transmits a command to CompuServe (/go:pppconnect^M) to establish the PPP protocol. Then, the script waits for the Password: prompt, and responds with the password when the prompt is received. After the connection is established, the script changes the port settings again. The endproc statement ends the script.

Browsing through this script shows you that the script relies on some variables for the user ID and password. Scripting for Dial-Up Networking supports a couple common variable names that define Dial-Up Networking variables, as follows:

◆ **$USERID.** This variable corresponds to the user name you enter in the Dial-Up Networking connection's dialog box when you start the connection process.

◆ **$PASSWORD.** This variable corresponds to the user password you enter in the Dial-Up Networking connection's dialog box when you start the connection process.

Later in this section is a script command reference that explains the script commands that Scripting for Dial-Up Networking supports. The next section explains how to associate a script with a Dial-Up Networking connection and debug the script.

Using the Dial-Up Scripting Tool

Installing Scripting for Dial-Up Networking adds a new item, named Dial-Up Scripting Tool, to your Accessories menu (and places it in the \Program Files\Accessories folder). The Dial-Up Scripting Tool dialog box (see fig. 33.16) enables you to select a Dial-Up Networking connection with which to associate a script, change the properties of a Dial-Up Networking connection, and control a few properties that define how the script runs.

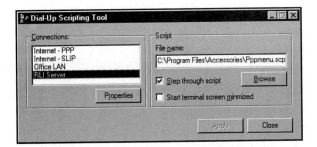

Figure 33.16

The Dial-Up Scripting Tool dialog box.

To associate a script with a Dial-Up Networking connection, choose Start, Programs, Accessories, and Dial-Up Scripting Tool to open the Dial-Up Scripting Tool dialog box. In the Dial-Up Scripting Tool dialog box, select a connection from the Connections list. Then, enter the path and file name of the script file in the File name text box or use the Browse button to browse for the file.

If you want the terminal window to appear minimized, enable the Start terminal screen minimized check box. Otherwise, the terminal window appears on the desktop so that you can monitor the progress of the connection (see fig. 33.17). To debug the script, enable the Step through script check box. The script executes one line at a time and you verify each line, which enables you to monitor the script's success (see fig. 33.18).

Script Command Reference

The following sections explain the Dial-Up Networking scripting commands supported by Windows 95. Microsoft will be adding more commands in future releases of Windows 95.

Figure 33.17

The Dial-Up Networking terminal screen dialog box.

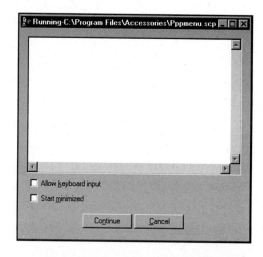

Figure 33.18

You can step through a script to debug it.

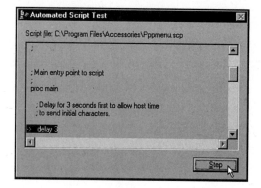

proc <*name*>

This statement begins a script procedure, where *name* is the name of the procedure. Every script must have a procedure named main that serves as the entry point of the script. Processing of the script begins with the proc main statement and ends with the main procedure's endproc statement.

Example:

```
proc main
```

endproc

This statement ends a script procedure. When the endproc statement for the main procedure is reached, Dial-Up Networking starts PPP or SLIP, depending on the server type selected for the connection.

delay *<n seconds>*

This statement causes the script to pause for the specified number of seconds.

Example to delay four seconds:

```
delay 4
```

waitfor " *<string>*"

This statement causes the script to pause until it receives the specified string of characters. The waitfor statement is case-sensitive.

Example to wait for the string "Select menu item: ":

```
waitfor "Select menu item: "
```

transmit " *<string>*" | $USERID | $PASSWORD

This statement transmits a string to the server. You also can use transmit to send your user name and password as defined by the $USERID and $PASSWORD keywords. These keywords correspond to the user name and password stored with the Dial-Up Networking connection's properties.

Example to transmit the string "3" and a carriage return, followed by your password:

```
transmit "3^M"
transmit $PASSWORD
```

 Note Windows 95 appends a carriage return to the $USERID and $PASSWORD variables when it transmits them.

set port databits *<integer>*

This statement sets the number of data bits in each data word (byte), and can be set to a value from 5 to 8. If you don't specify a value for data bits, Dial-Up Networking uses the setting specified by the Dial-Up Networking connection's properties.

Example to specify 7 data bits:

```
set port databits 7
```

set port stopbits *<integer>*

This statement changes the number of stop bits for the port, and can be 1 or 2. If you don't specify the number of stop bits with the set port stopbits statement, Dial-Up Networking uses the port settings specified by the Dial-Up Networking connection's properties.

Example to specify 2 stop bits:

```
set port stopbits 2
```

set port parity none | odd | even | mark | space

This statement specifies the type of parity checking used for the connection. If you don't specify the parity method, Dial-Up Networking uses the parity method defined in the Dial-Up Networking connection's properties.

Example to specify odd parity:

```
set port parity odd
```

set ipaddr

This statement specifies the IP address of your node for the session. You generally use this statement after you use the getip statement to retrieve your computer's assigned IP address from the server. In other words, you use the getip statement to retrieve your IP address from the server, then use set ipaddr to tell Dial-Up Networking to use that IP address for the session.

getip *"<delimiter>"*

This statement reads an IP address from the server. For *delimiter,* specify the character that separates the IP address from the characters that surround it to enable Dial-Up Networking to parse the IP address from the field.

Example to retrieve the IP address when a comma is used to separate the address from other text:

```
set ipaddr getip ","
```

; (comments)

Text on a line preceded by a semicolon acts as a comment, which the script processor ignores. To create a comment, therefore, start the line with a semicolon.

Example:

```
; This is a comment
```

Note   To transmit a carriage return, include ^M or <cr> in the transmit string, such as **transmit "CIS^M"** or **transmit "CIS<cr>"**. To send only a linefeed character, use <lf> in the string, such as **transmit "<lf>"**. To transmit a carriage return and linefeed, use <cr><lf>, as in **transmit "<cr><lf>"**.

Setting Up a Windows 95 RAS Server

Microsoft Plus! for Windows 95 includes the components necessary for you to config-ure your Windows 95 workstation as a remote access server. When you install Plus, choose <u>C</u>ustom to enable you to select the items to install, then select the Dial-Up Networking Server item from the <u>O</u>ptions list. Follow the instructions Plus Setup provides to install your Plus options. For detailed information about Microsoft Plus for Windows 95, refer to Chapter 16, "Using Microsoft Plus! for Windows 95."

After you install the Dial-Up Networking Server, your Windows 95 workstation can act as a RAS server for Windows 95, Windows NT, Windows for Workgroups, and other clients that use the PPP or asynchronous NetBEUI RAS protocols. Windows 95 also can act as a gateway for IPX/SPX and NetBEUI network transports, enabling dial-in users to access the LAN to which the Windows 95 RAS server is connected. A Windows 95 RAS server cannot serve as a gateway for TCP/IP, however. If you want to dial into a remote network to gain access to the Internet or perform IP routing on the remote LAN, the RAS server must be capable of IP routing, as are Windows NT, Shiva LanRover, and other RAS servers.

Tip   Dial-Up Networking Server does not support SLIP or CSLIP as a server, nor does it support the NetWare NRN protocol for dial-in. Dial-Up Networking Server supports only the PPP and asynchronous NetBEUI protocols for dial-in clients.

How you configure your Windows 95 RAS server depends on the type of access you want users to have. You cannot prevent access to the LAN by specifically limiting access to the dial-in server. If a user dials into the server using the proper network and RAS protocols and has the necessary permissions to access resources on the network, the user can do so through the RAS server. Therefore, you need to config-ure the Windows 95 RAS server to use share-level or user-level security if you want to be able to restrict access to resources on the server and on the LAN. You can imple-ment share-level security without requiring a security server, because Windows 95 directly supports share-level security. To employ user-level security, however, the network must include a NetWare or Windows NT server that can act as the security server, authenticating accounts, passwords, and permissions. For detailed information on share-level and user-level security, refer to Chapter 35, "Sharing Resources in Windows 95."

Whichever method of security you choose, remember that you must configure the
Windows 95 RAS server for that type of security before you can configure it as a RAS
server. To specify share-level or user-level security, choose the Network object in the
Control Panel and use the Access Control property page to specify the security
method.

Configuring the Dial-Up Networking Server

Configuring your Windows 95 computer to act as a RAS server is easy. After you install
Dial-Up Networking Server from Microsoft Plus, a new menu item appears in the
Connection menu of the Dial-Up Networking folder. To configure the Dial-Up
Networking Server, open the Dial-Up Networking folder and choose Connections,
then Dial-Up Server. Windows 95 displays a Dial-Up Server property sheet similar to
the one shown in figure 33.19.

Figure 33.19

*The Dial-Up
Server property
sheet with share-
level security
enabled.*

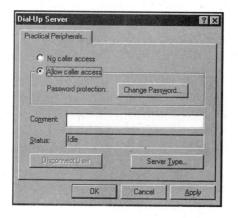

The appearance of the Dial-Up Server property sheet depends on whether you use
share-level security or user-level security on the RAS server. If the server uses share-
level security, the property sheet appears as shown in figure 33.19. If the server
employs user-level security, the property page appears similar to the one shown in
figure 33.20.

To enable dial-in access, choose the Allow caller access option button. If you use
share-level security, choose the Change Password button to open a dialog box in
which you can specify a password for dial-in access to the server. The password you
specify applies to all users who dial in to the server. If the server employs user-level
security, choose the Add button to add user names and permissions from the security
server. If you need help configuring user permissions, refer to Chapter 35, "Sharing
Resources in Windows 95."

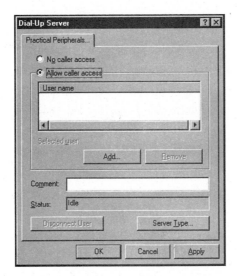

Figure 33.20

The Dial-Up Server property page with user-level security enabled.

After you specify the password or user-access list, choose the Server Type button to open the Server Types dialog box. If you choose Default from the Type of Dial-Up Server drop-down list, the Dial-Up Networking Server attempts to use the PPP protocol to establish the connection, and if the connection fails, it attempts to use the asynchronous NetBEUI protocol. If you select a specific protocol from the Dial-Up Networking Server drop-down list, the Dial-Up Networking Server only tries the selected protocol and terminates the connection if the protocol fails.

If you want the server to allow software compression for transferring data, place a check in the Enable software compression check box. If you want to require encrypted passwords for added security, place a check in the Require encrypted password check box. After you specify the necessary settings in the Server Types dialog box, choose OK. Then, in the Dial-Up Server property page, choose OK to initiate the RAS server.

Tip While the RAS server waits for calls, the **S**tatus text box on the Dial-Up Server property page displays the message Monitoring to indicate that Dial-Up Networking is monitoring the modem line for incoming calls. When dial-in access is turned off, the **S**tatus box displays the message Idle. As a connection is being negotiated, other messages appear in the **S**tatus text box to indicate the status of the connection.

Occasionally, you might need to terminate a caller's access to the Windows 95 RAS server. If the user forgot to log off before leaving his computer, for example, you can terminate the call from the server. Or, you might need to terminate connections for security reasons. To terminate the current connection, open the Dial-Up Networking folder and choose Connections, Dial-Up Server to bring up the Dial-Up Server property page. Choose the Disconnect User button to disconnect the current connection.

Disabling dial-in connections is equally easy. Simply call the Dial-Up Server property page and choose the No caller access option button. When you choose OK, the Dial-Up Networking Server stops monitoring the modem for incoming calls, and users cannot dial into the server.

Part VII

Sharing Resources and Using the Internet

New Riders Publishing
INSIDE SERIES

Network Concepts and Configuration

L ike Windows for Workgroups, Windows 95 includes built-in peer-to-peer networking and additional features for enhancing connectivity with a variety of server and client network operating systems. This chapter examines network issues in Windows 95 from two perspectives: the new network user's and the network administrator's. Because Windows 95 makes installing and administering a network relatively simple, you might fall into both categories: you might be new to networking but also need to install and manage a Windows 95 network.

This chapter examines general issues, such as general networking concepts, as well as more advanced issues, such as network driver models. Therefore, this chapter offers tips for new and advanced network users alike, covering the following topics:

- ◆ Understanding basic LAN concepts
- ◆ Understanding the physical network
- ◆ Understanding networking in Windows 95
- ◆ Structuring the network

◆ Managing resources and resource availability

◆ Using Windows 95 on Windows NT networks

◆ Using Windows 95 on Novell NetWare networks

Chapter 2 explains how to add adapters, protocols, and other services for your network, as well as how to configure those services. This book also covers many additional networking topics. Chapter 33 explains how to configure and use remote access services, also referred to as *Dial-Up Networking* in Windows 95. Chapter 35 explains how to share resources such as disks and printers in Windows 95. Chapter 36 explains the Internet and TCP/IP. Chapter 37 explains how to use the Internet utilities included with Windows 95, and also explains how to use Exchange to send and receive Internet e-mail.

Before you read through some of the following chapters, however, you should have a basic understanding of network issues. The following section provides an overview of networking.

Understanding Basic LAN Concepts

As many different network operating systems exist as ways to implement networking, which can easily confuse the novice about networks and their operations. If you just want to use a network, you don't need to understand the protocols that control the flow of data packets from one computer to another. If you understand some basic network terms and concepts, however, you can put the network to better use. Furthermore, understanding some basic points of network operation and etiquette can ensure that the network functions as well for others as it does for you. A peer-to-peer network such as Windows 95 requires that you follow a few essential rules if you want to successfully implement the network.

But what is a peer-to-peer network? To understand the network capabilities Windows 95 offers, you first must understand networks in general.

Local Area Networks Defined

The term *local area* refers to computers connected together within a small geographic area, such as a department, office, or building. In small installations, the entire company might be served by a single local area network, or LAN. You can connect LANs to other LANs in the same building or in other buildings by using direct connections called *gateways*. Your company's overall network might consist of a number of LANs connected by gateways.

Another network term to understand is *WAN*, which stands for *wide area network*, and refers to networks linked by long-distance telephone connections, satellite links, microwave transmissions, or other long-distance carrier methods. A LAN connected via satellite link to another LAN effectively belongs to a wide area network.

A LAN is not a mysterious thing; rather, a LAN simply amounts to a collection of hardware and software that enables you to use common computing resources (see fig. 34.1) located elsewhere rather than on your PC. These resources—which can include disks, printers, modems, and other peripherals—can be across the room, in another building, or across the world. Networks generally enable many users to perform the following types of computing tasks:

◆ Share common applications and data

◆ Access commonly used peripherals, such as printers, modems, plotters, and media storage devices such as disk drives

◆ Communicate with other users using e-mail and other communication services

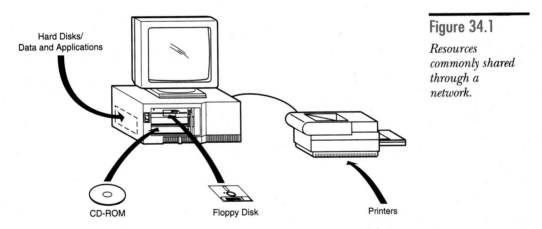

Figure 34.1

Resources commonly shared through a network.

Hard Disks/
Data and Applications

CD-ROM   Floppy Disk   Printers

Before you can understand how computers can share resources across a network, you need to understand the relationship between the computers connected to the network. Later, in the section "Understanding the Physical Network," you learn about the physical connections between computers on the network. The following section explains the logical connections between systems.

LAN Relationships

The primary purpose of any network is to provide certain services to its users. A computer that provides service is called a *server,* and a computer that uses those services is called a *client.* The term *client/server* refers to interaction between two computers in which one computer provides services to another.

A network server might provide access to data files and applications, or it might provide access to peripherals such as printers, modems, and plotters. Servers often are referred to by the type of service they perform. A *file server,* for example, provides access to files. *Modem servers,* or *communications servers,* provide access to modems. *Print servers* provide printing services.

The file server usually includes large-capacity storage devices, such as hard drives and CD-ROM devices, and provides access to programs and data files that the network's users commonly use. The file server often provides other services, such as access to printers and other peripherals.

The terms *local* and *remote* describe the types of resources you can access from a network workstation. Peripherals, applications, and data located on your workstation are *local resources.* Resources connected to other workstations or to a dedicated server are called *remote resources,* because they are remote from your workstation. In Windows 95, the shared resources on your workstation are remote resources to other users on the network, and vice versa; hence, *peer-to-peer network.*

Dedicated versus Peer-to-Peer LANs

You can loosely classify networks into two categories: dedicated and peer-to-peer. The server in a *dedicated network* performs only server-related tasks—you cannot use it for general computing. You can't run a spreadsheet or word processing application on a dedicated file server. That computer's sole task is to provide access to its disks, CD-ROMs, and other data peripherals.

Dedicated Networks

A dedicated network file server often looks much like the other computers on the network, but the server has additional hardware and software that enable it to share resources. The file server often is no more powerful (sometimes less powerful) than the computers it serves.

 Note Some network operating systems enable you to take a server out of server mode and use it as a workstation, but it can't act as a server until you again place it in server mode.

Some networks use a single file server, but others use many, depending on the size of the network and the number of users. Networks that have multiple dedicated file servers often are referred to as *distributed networks.* Some users have access to one file server, other users have access to a different server, and still others have access to more than one server. This arrangement reduces the load on any one server and improves overall network performance. It also facilitates network security by enabling

the network administrator to place security-sensitive data and applications on particular servers. The administrator then can give users access to those resources only if they need them.

Peer-to-Peer Networks

In contrast to dedicated networks, Windows 95 is a *peer-to-peer* network operating system. A peer-to-peer network does not use a dedicated server. Any workstation on the network can act as a nondedicated server. On a peer-to-peer network, a workstation not only gives other uses access to its data and peripherals, but also functions as a workstation, running applications for its own user.

Peer-to-peer networks offer a number of advantages over dedicated networks. In a peer-to-peer network, for example, any workstation can access any other workstation's disk. Suppose that your workstation doesn't include a 5 1/4-inch floppy disk drive, but you need to install some software from a 5 1/4-inch disk. You can place the disk in another workstation that does have a 5 1/4-inch floppy drive, share the disk, then attach to the disk from your workstation to install the software, using the disk drive as if it were connected directly to your own computer.

Users on a peer-to-peer network also can easily share their data across the network. If you are responsible for creating and maintaining certain data, such as monthly reports, you don't have to place the data on a dedicated server. Other users can simply attach to your hard disk across the network and access its files. For security purposes, you can control the level of access that other users have to one another's data. You can make your data available in read-only form, which lets other users view but not modify the data. You also can give users the ability to change the data. Access to any workstation's shared resources can be password-protected, enabling some users access to them while preventing other users from using or altering the resource.

Peer-to-peer networks also change the way users share peripherals, such as printers. In a dedicated network, two or three printers usually are connected to a single dedicated print server, and all users must access the server when they want to print. In a peer-to-peer network, any user can access a printer connected to any workstation, provided the user has access to that resource. If you have to print two important documents, you can print one on your own printer and the other on the printer in the office next door. By the same token, other users can use your printer.

Because Windows 95 offers peer-to-peer networking, it might change the way you work in one of the following three ways:

◆ If you currently use no network and install Windows 95 as your only network, you bring users together and give them a wide range of tools, which they can use to share data and hardware, and communicate with one another.

◆ If you switch from a dedicated network to Windows 95, you decentralize your network administration and potentially provide access to a much wider range of resources than previously available on your old network.

◆ If you install Windows 95 on workstations that another network operating system serves—such as Novell NetWare or Windows NT—you enhance the network interface, making it easier for users to access and use network resources.

Hybrid Networks

Until a few years ago, most networks were what you would call dedicated networks. Today, many companies are opting for a hybrid approach, combining the security and administrative advantages of a dedicated network with the flexibility of a peer-to-peer network. The network might include one or more Windows NT or Novell NetWare servers to provide access to shared secured resources and security authentication, for example, while Windows 95 or Windows for Workgroups provides peer-to-peer network features.

Understanding the Physical Network

Although wireless LANs are becoming increasingly available, a typical LAN generally consists of a given number of workstations connected by cables. On the network, each workstation is called a *node*. You can consider nodes to be just access points to data, or "doorways" that you use to access the network. It doesn't matter to you which node you use to access the network, because the computer is nothing more than a tool you use to manipulate data. The distinction between nodes is important only to the network operating system so that it can distinguish one request from another and provide services when a specific user requests them from a given node. In other words, the network operating system must be able to identify the doorway from which you make your request.

Network Interface Cards

Each node requires special hardware to enable it to connect to the network and access the network's resources. This hardware consists of a *network interface card (NIC)* that sends and receives messages across the network. Each NIC uses a unique network address to enable messages to be directed specifically to it, in much the same way you send mail to a specific postal address. The network card monitors all the packets of data (a *packet* is data that has been encapsulated in some way) that travel across the

network, and acts on the packet accordingly. If the packet is meant for another node, the network card passes it on. Otherwise, the network card passes the data on to the node's network drivers for processing.

To a large extent, the network card determines the network's performance. It serves as a two-way communications link with other computers on the network. Generally, the network card processes data more slowly than the network can carry it, and more slowly than the computer can send or process data. The card, therefore, must *buffer* the data, or hold it in temporary storage until the card can process it. For this reason, a slow network card can become a performance bottleneck, and a fast network card can improve network performance significantly.

Media

The network requires a means to enable data packets to move between nodes. These connections between nodes often are called the network *media*. Common network media include twisted-pair cable, coaxial cable (also called coax), fiber-optic cable, and free space. Twisted-pair, coax, and fiber-optic cable are physical connections, often referred to as *bounded* media. The term *free space* refers to wireless network connections achieved by radio or light (as in infrared networks). These kinds of media are often referred to as *unbounded* media.

Twisted-Pair Cable

Twisted-pair cable is the most commonly used form of network media. Twisted-pair cable is similar to the cabling used for standard telephone lines. Usually, networks use a considerably sturdier form of twisted-pair wiring that is much more resistant to electrical noise than standard phone lines. This special type of twisted-pair cable contains pairs of wires enclosed by metallic-foil shielding, with the entire bundle shielded by metallic braid. Other types of twisted-pair wire with less shielding also are commonly used, and some types of twisted-pair wiring contain additional twisted pairs, fiber-optic cable, or voice/data lines in the same bundle. You often hear twisted-pair cabling referred to as *10BASE-T*, which references a common standard that defines twisted-pair wire specifications.

 Tip Sometimes you can use existing phone lines for twisted-pair network media, but the quality of the lines limits the distance between nodes and the number of nodes that you can connect to the network. If you install new twisted-pair cabling for a network, consider using Category 5 or better cabling, which is designed to support higher speeds.

Coaxial Cable

Coaxial cable is another commonly used network medium. Coaxial cable used in networks is similar (but not identical) to the coaxial cable used for cable television. Coax generally offers higher data-transfer rates over longer distances than does twisted-pair, owing to lower signal loss and interference. Coaxial cable uses standard BNC connectors to connect cables together, and to connect the cable to the NIC (see fig. 34.2). You often hear coaxial cable referred to as *10BASE2*, which references a common standard for coaxial network cable.

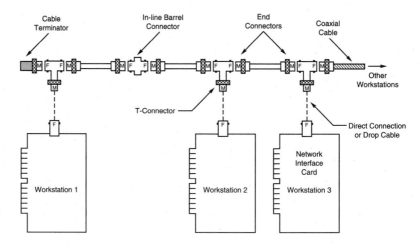

Figure 34.2

Typical coaxial cable connections.

Fiber-Optic Cabling

Although typically the most expensive form of network cabling, fiber-optic cabling provides the highest transmission rates and most signal security. Fiber-optic network adapters, though not commonplace, are becoming more common all the time. Fiber-optic cabling now often is used as a backbone to connect other network media. If you have two buildings you have to network, for example, a fiber-optic connection between the buildings can serve as a high-speed link. A special transducer connects the fiber to the local network media, such as twisted-pair or coax.

Unbounded Media

Radio networks have been used to connect systems for which a physical connection could not be made. The latest spin on unbounded media is the wireless infrared network. These networks use infrared transceivers to send data through open spaces (such as a large open office) without cabling. The primary benefit of this type of network is the elimination of planning or installation of cable or special construction

to accommodate the cables. The NICs and transceivers required for a wireless network typically are more expensive than those for bounded-media networks, but eliminating the cost of cabling can more than make up the price difference.

Network Topology

The term *network topology* sounds more imposing than what it really names. The term refers to the way in which a network's nodes are physically connected to one another. Common topologies in use today are star, ring, and bus topologies.

A simple star topology network consists of a hub to which workstations are connected, much like the points of a star connect to its center. Figure 34.3 illustrates both simple star topology and distributed star topology. A *distributed star topology* network essentially is a number of stars with hubs connected together. Star topology offers easy fault detection (detecting faulty cables and other components) and an easy means for expanding the network in multifloor installations.

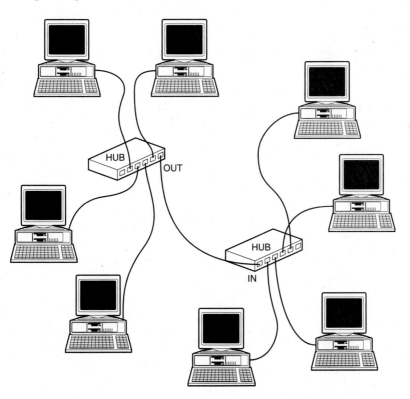

Figure 34.3

Two simple stars in a distributed star topology network.

The hubs in a star topology network (also called *concentrators*) control network communication, serving to control transmission errors, boost the signal, and route data packets. Although star topology networks might appear similar in configuration, the hub's function varies not only across different networks, but also within the same network. ARCnet networks, for example, use both passive and active hubs. Passive hubs route data packets without performing any other processing, such as signal boosting, on the packet. Active hubs also amplify and retime the signals.

A *bus topology* network uses one or more linear bus segments to which nodes or subnetworks are connected (see fig. 34.4). The nodes are connected in a series along the main, or *backbone*, cable. Nodes often are connected to the backbone using drop cables. Bus topology makes it a simple matter to add nodes linearly, such as in the same office or on the same floor of a building, but complicates adding nodes on different floors. The primary drawback of using a bus topology is that cable failure affects the entire network. In a star topology, a cable failure affects only the node to which that cable is connected.

Figure 34.4

A bus topology network.

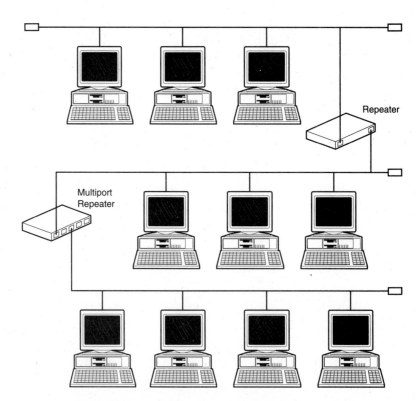

Network Layers

Most networks follow a standard network-layering scheme that separates the various parts of the network into logical layers. The standard, defined as the OSI Reference Model, is illustrated in figure 34.5.

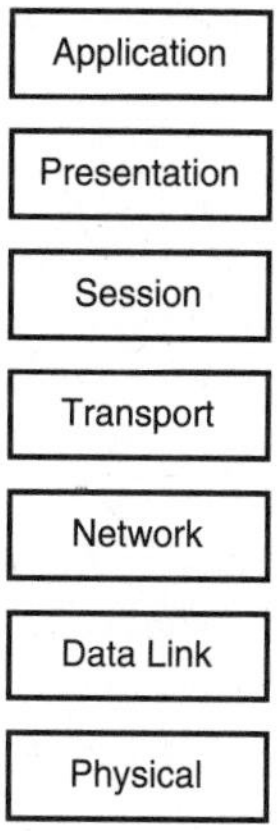

Application
Presentation
Session
Transport
Network
Data Link
Physical

Figure 34.5

The OSI Reference Model.

The layers in the OSI Reference Model are explained in the following list:

◆ **The application layer.** This layer represents the level at which applications access network services. These services support user applications, such as file transfers, database access, and e-mail.

◆ **The presentation layer.** This layer translates data from the application layer into an intermediate format. This layer also provides data encryption for security and data compression for increased throughput.

◆ **The session layer.** This layer enables applications on different computers to establish, maintain, and end a session (communication between two nodes). This layer enables the applications to regulate which side transmits, as well as when and how long the side transmits.

◆ **The transport layer.** This layer handles error recognition and recovery, and also handles encoding and decoding data packets. The transport layer at the receiving computer also transmits receipt acknowledgments.

◆ **The network layer.** This layer translates logical addresses into physical addresses, and also addresses messages. This layer also handles routing data on the network.

◆ **The data link layer.** This layer packages raw data from the underlying physical layer into frames, which are logical, structured packets. This layer transmits the frames between destinations and verifies receipt by the destination node.

◆ **The physical layer.** This layer handles the physical connection to the network, including how the cable is attached to the network adapter and the transmission method for sending data.

This layering of the network enables the use of different types of hardware and software on a single LAN. Your network can, for example, mix workstations that use different operating systems. Some workstations might run Unix, others Windows 95 or Windows NT, and yet others might run DOS or Macintosh operating systems. The network also can employ different network transport systems, with some workstations running IPX, others running NetBEUI, and still others using TCP/IP (transport systems are discussed later in the section "Network Protocols"). Figure 34.6 illustrates the OSI Reference Model as it is applied to the Windows 95 networking structure.

Figure 34.6

The Windows 95 layered networking structure.

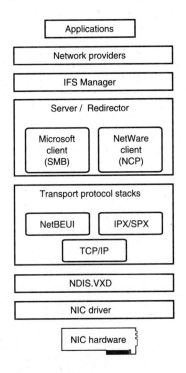

The network operating system doesn't care which type of network interface card you use, because the network operating system does not interact with the network at that low a level. The transport layers take care of communicating with the network

adapter. When the data comes in, it filters through the layers, eliminating the need for the network operating system to interpret the data at the hardware level. By the time the data reaches the network operating system, the intervening layers have converted the data to the necessary format.

Network Architectures

Various networks use different methods and rules to transfer data along the network. These different data-transfer methods are called the network's *architecture.* Common network architectures include Ethernet, ARCnet, and Token Ring. These architectures control the method by which data passes physically between nodes.

Ethernet started as a de facto standard, but has become an officially recognized international standard. Ethernet is a *contention architecture* because it handles contention between two or more nodes that try to access the network at the same time (in this context, *network* refers to the cabling connecting the nodes). When two nodes have data on the network at the same time, a collision occurs.

With the Ethernet architecture, the physical network layer senses the presence of a carrier signal, which indicates data moving on the network. If data is traveling on the network, the physical layer signals the data link layer not to transmit data. If the physical layer does not detect a carrier, it signals the link layer that it can transmit data.

If the physical layer detects a data collision, it signals the network that a collision has occurred. All other nodes then fall back to receive mode. The transmitting node then waits a random amount of time before it attempts to retransmit the data packet. This random wait time helps ensure that the two nodes that caused the collision do not attempt to retransmit at the same time and thereby cause another collision.

The Token Ring and ARCnet architectures operate differently from the Ethernet architecture. Token Ring and ARCnet both represent noncontention architectures. These types of networks are called *token-passing networks,* which function by passing a special data frame, called a *token,* around the network. If a node has data to send, it captures the token and appends its data to the token. The packet is retransmitted across the network. The receiving node strips its intended data from the token and passes the token around the network again. Because only a single token is being passed around the network, data collisions can't happen.

Although Token Ring and ARCnet architecture both employ token passing, they differ in the way the token passes from node to node. In Token Ring, the token passes from node to node in sequence around the ring. In ARCnet, the token passes from node to node from the lowest to the highest network address.

Network Redirectors

A key part of any network operating system is the redirector. A redirector does much what its name implies—it redirects network resources, providing functions for file I/O (copying, reading, deleting, and so forth) and printing. In fact, printing provides an excellent example of redirection. You can associate a local printer port with a remote printer. An application sends a print job to the printer port, and the redirector redirects the print job out on the network and to the destination printer. A network redirector typically functions at the application and presentation layers of the network model.

Windows 95 includes two network redirectors as part of two network clients:

◆ **Client for Microsoft Networks.** This network client supports communication with Microsoft-based (and compatible) networks, which operate using the Server Message Block (SMB) file-sharing protocol. The redirector resides in the virtual device driver Vredir.vxd.

◆ **Client for NetWare Networks.** This network client supports communication with NetWare-based networks, which use the NetWare Core Protocol (NCP) file-sharing protocol. The redirector resides in the virtual device driver Nwredir.vxd.

 Note   In addition to the Microsoft and NetWare redirectors, Windows 95 also supports other redirectors from other network vendors.

In Windows 95, redirectors are implemented as file system drivers. Therefore, the Installable File System (IFS) Manager manages any redirector(s). The IFS Manager determines whether a calling application needs access to a remote resource or local resource and handles mapping local resource names to remote network resources.

Network Protocols (Stacks)

The layers that translate the data coming from the media-access layers (the physical LAN connection) are called the *link control layers*. These layers implement different transport methods to convert the data into a form that the higher layers of the network (the node's operating system) can interpret. In reverse, the transport layers convert data coming from the node's operating system into a form that can be passed on to the physical network. The different transport protocols used also are referred to as *transport stacks*.

The NetBIOS (network basic input/output system) serves as a link between the computer's operating system and the network protocol stacks. NetBIOS is a set of

software routines that provide basic network access services, just as a computer's BIOS (basic input/output system) provides basic hardware services to applications running on the computer (see fig. 34.7).

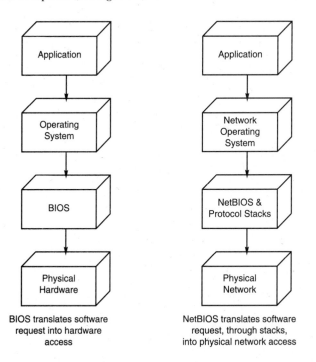

Figure 34.7

Functions of the BIOS and NetBIOS.

When the operating system requests network resources, the request goes to the NetBIOS. The NetBIOS then translates the request to the appropriate transport stack, which then translates the request to the LAN's physical layers.

Common network transport protocols include NetBEUI, TCP/IP, and IPX. NetBEUI stands for NetBIOS Extended User Interface. NetBEUI was originally developed by IBM to use on Token Ring networks, but now is common on other types of networks, including Ethernet.

TCP/IP stands for Transmission Control Protocol/Internet Protocol and was developed by the Department of Defense. TCP/IP is commonly used to connect different types of computer systems. You can use TCP/IP in Windows 95, for example, to communicate with Unix-based systems. TCP/IP is the protocol used to communicate with computers on the Internet.

If you use Windows 95 in a Novell NetWare environment, you probably will choose the IPX/SPX protocol, a variation of the original NetWare IPX protocol.

The important point to remember about transport protocol stacks is that you can use more than one protocol at a time, which enables you to connect to different systems from a single Windows 95 session. You can read a file from another Windows 95 workstation using NetBEUI, read from a NetWare server using IPX/SPX, and communicate with a computer on the Internet using TCP/IP.

You use the Network object in the Control Panel to add and configure network protocols. Adding and configuring a network protocol is explained in Chapter 2, "Setting Up and Booting Windows 95," as part of the Setup process. Chapter 33, "Using Remote Access Services," explains adding and configuring the dial-up networking adapter. Chapter 36, "TCP/IP and the Internet Connection," covers installation and configuration of the TCP/IP protocol.

Structuring the Network

If you set up a Windows 95 peer-to-peer network, you need a basic understanding of some key issues that enable you to create an effective and useful network structure. This section provides an overview of these key issues. Even if you don't have to set up or maintain the network, this section can help illustrate your relationship to other users on the network. The first step is to understand workgroups.

An Overview of Workgroups

Workgroups do not represent a new concept; if you work with other people toward a common goal, you are part of a workgroup. Your softball team, the PTA, your department at work, and your family all represent different kinds of workgroups. In essence, a workgroup simply is a group (large or small) that comprises people who share common responsibilities, tasks, and goals.

In a networked computer environment such as Windows 95, a workgroup usually consists of a group of users who share job responsibilities. In the average organization, people often belong to more than one workgroup (see fig. 34.8). You might be part of a department, for example, that represents a workgroup. In addition, you might also share tasks and responsibilities with a few other individuals in the department. Perhaps you are a group supervisor, part of a design team, or one of the department's secretaries. In any case, you might share a job title or a specific set of duties with other members of your department. These people who share your job title or duties often form a workgroup, of which you are a part. As a result, you belong to two workgroups—this smaller group of individuals and the entire department.

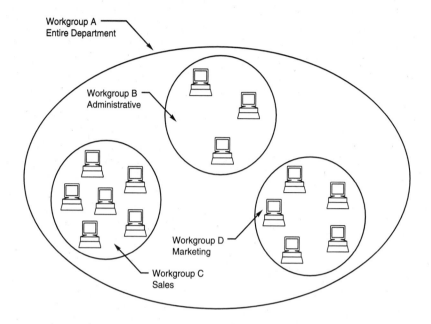

Figure 34.8

Examples of workgroups within a department.

But how do workgroups relate to the network? A network's primary function is to connect users and enable them to share resources, access common data and applications, and communicate with one another. Because they generally work on the same project or goal, the workgroup's members need to communicate with one another and share information. The network serves as a link between these users by enabling them to share data that relates to a common project and to communicate by using e-mail.

Workgroups in Windows 95

In Windows 95, a workgroup is really nothing more than a logical grouping of users. Workgroups, instead of offering any real physical separation or organization of users, primarily offer a means of organizing the way resources appear to users. Workgroups essentially enable you to view the overall network as a collection of smaller logical entities, which are the workgroups themselves.

Picture it this way: Assume that your traditional network comprises 200 workstations. To access a resource (such as a directory or printer) on another workstation, you must specify its machine name, which is assigned to the workstation when it boots. Next, you must specify the resource name, which is assigned by the user of the workstation that contains the shared resource. If you know the name of the workstation that you want to access as well as the resource share name, you simply can type the name where appropriate to access the resource, such as in a File Open or Map Network Drive dialog box (see fig. 34.9).

Figure 34.9

*You can use a
Map Network
Drive dialog box
to access other
workstations.*

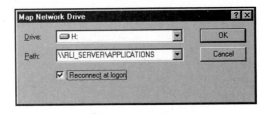

But what if you forget the machine name or the share name? Or, what if you need to connect to a directory that you have never accessed? You probably don't know the name of the resource to which you want to connect. If the network consists of 200 workstations, and each one offers three or four different shared resources, you must browse through 600 to 800 different items to find the resource you want. Workgroups provide a means of grouping resources into different categories, making them easier to locate.

Organizing Users

Workgroups do not offer any real physical organization or separation of users. A member of any workgroup potentially can share resources and communicate over the network with members of any workgroup. You don't need to belong to the same workgroup as another user if you want to access that user's disk or printer; nor do other users have to belong to your workgroup to use resources your node shares.

If workgroups don't separate users, what purpose do they serve? Workgroups in Windows 95 primarily offer a means of displaying resources in an organized and easily digestible way. Instead of showing you 200 workstations and 600 to 800 resources, for example, Windows 95 enables you to break the network into logical groups—workgroups.

The following list describes a few examples of how workgroups organize information in Windows 95:

◆ **Network Neighborhood folder.** The Network Neighborhood folder (see fig. 34.10) contains icons for each of the workstations in your workgroup, which includes servers in your domain. Instead of hunting through a list of all the workstations and servers on the network, the folder displays only the resources you are most likely to need.

◆ **Entire Network folder.** The Network Neighborhood folder (see fig. 34.11) contains an Entire Network icon. Click on that icon to display a folder that contains icons for each of the workgroups (and domains) on your network. Selecting an icon displays the computers contained in the selected workgroup.

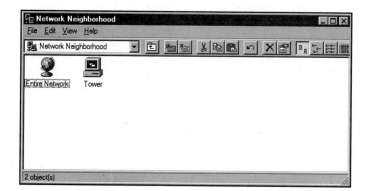

Figure 34.10

The Network Neighborhood folder.

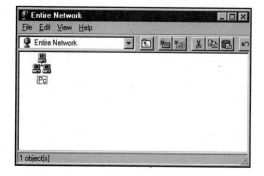

Figure 34.11

The Entire Network folder.

Defining Workgroups

When you install networking for Windows 95, one item of information you must specify is the name of your computer and the workgroup in which it belongs. The computer name and workgroup name are stored in the Registry and read from the Registry at startup. Therefore, you can't dynamically change your computer name or workgroup within a Windows 95 session. You must reboot Windows 95 after you change the computer name and workgroup.

To specify the computer name and workgroup for a computer, open the Control Panel and choose the Network object. From the Network property sheet, click on the Identification tab to display the Identification property page, shown in figure 34.12.

Enter the name by which you want your computer to be recognized on the network in the Computer name text box. The computer name is limited to 15 characters, no spaces. Use an underscore character or dash in place of a space.

Figure 34.12

*The Identification
property page.*

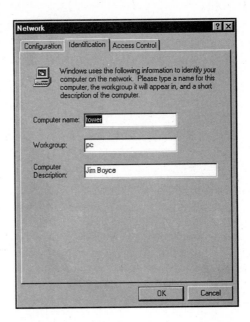

Enter the name of the workgroup to which you want your PC to belong in the Workgroup text box. Like the computer name, the workgroup name is limited to 15 characters and no spaces. To join an existing workgroup, you must specify the exact name of the existing workgroup. To create a new workgroup, simply enter a new workgroup name in the Workgroup text box.

The Computer Description field is optional. This comment string appears in a property page for a computer. You can right-click on a workstation icon in the Network Neighborhood to display its context menu, then choose Properties to display the computer's property sheet, similar to the one shown in figure 34.13. The Computer Description string appears as the Comment property on the computer's property page.

After you specify the settings in the Identification page, choose OK. Windows 95 prompts you to restart the computer. You must restart the computer before your changes can take effect.

Note   As users log on to the network, their computers begin to show up in the Network Neighborhood folder. A user's computer does not necessarily appear immediately. It can take as long as 15 minutes after a computer connects to a busy network before it appears in the Network Neighborhood folder.

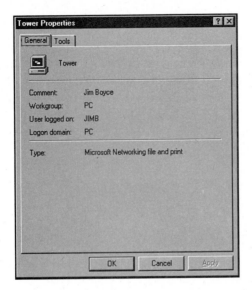

Figure 34.13

A Comment field on a computer's property page.

In addition to configuring workgroups, you should plan how to share resources on your network. The following section offers tips on configuring and managing shared resources in Windows 95. Chapter 35, "Sharing Resources in Windows 95," explains the actual mechanics of sharing those resources.

Managing Resources and Resource Availability

As you plan your network, you also should consider whether it should include primary servers. *Primary servers* are much like nondedicated servers on networks that do not offer peer-to-peer capability. These servers house the majority of shared resources, such as printers and file systems, but you also can use them as workstations. Nodes that function primarily as workstations and not servers but that also can share some of their local resources are called *secondary servers*.

Windows 95 does not require primary servers. You can scatter resources across the network nearly anywhere you like; resources do not have to reside on just a handful of primary servers. The word *scatter*, however, is a good indication that this is not the best option. By locating resources such as applications and sensitive data on a single node, you simplify network administration and provide greater network security.

If Windows 95 is your only network operating system, consider allocating as few computers as necessary as primary servers. These computers house the majority of common applications to which the network's users need access. Applications that only one workgroup uses (or which only a few members of a particular workgroup use) can reside on one of that workgroup's nodes rather than on the primary server. This arrangement enables the workgroup or person most familiar with the application to be responsible for maintaining it. Figure 34.14 illustrates this concept.

Figure 34.14

Primary and secondary servers in Windows 95.

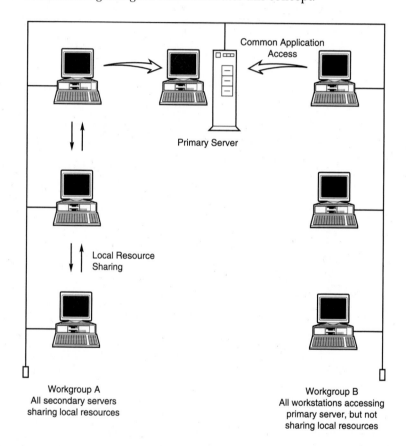

The primary servers also house sensitive data that requires more security than data stored on secondary servers. Increased security includes access security as well as file maintenance. If you want to control which users have physical access to sensitive data (other than across the network), place it on a primary server. If your network includes data that you back up regularly, place the data on a primary server where the system administrator can easily include it in automated backups.

Tip You can back up data on any computer on the network across the network, provided the folder in which the data is located is shared. Backups across the network degrade network performance, so you should consider backing up during off-hours.

If you run Windows 95 on top of another network operating system, you probably already have at least one dedicated server that contains your users' applications. This dedicated server might also contain much of your users' data. The applications and data should remain on the server for security.

 Tip If you have DOS workstations that you want to be able to access the Windows 95 network, you can install Microsoft Workgroup Connection, a DOS-based network client, on each DOS machine. Microsoft offers Workgroup Connection for free (you can find it at ftp.microsoft.com and in Microsoft forums on CompuServe). Workgroup Connection is a client-only network product—it does not enable DOS PCs to share their resources on the network.

After you decide how to allocate resources on the network, you can set up those resources to be shared. You can set up resource sharing of a node's resources only at the node; you cannot set up resource sharing across the network. After you establish the shared resource, however, the resource can be shared *persistently*, or each time Windows 95 is started on the node. This ensures that the resource is always available to other users.

 Note Generally, you share resources through My Computer or through the Printers folder. For more information on sharing resources, refer to Chapter 35, "Sharing Resources in Windows 95."

After resources are shared, you want to ensure that they are always available so that users can count on data and applications being available. This is particularly important with a primary server, which a number of users access. It is less important that secondary servers always be accessible, but important nonetheless.

 Tip To ensure that resources are always available, consider leaving the workstations running nonstop. When users leave for the day, have them log off from the network, but leave Windows 95 running on their workstations. Tell them to turn off only the monitor, not the computer.

In general, leaving a computer turned on is less damaging that turning it on and off every day. Hard disk head damage, when it occurs, often happens when the disk is powered down (the heads fly over the surface of the disk, and "land" on the disk when the disk is powered down). By always leaving the system on, you can actually increase the life of its hard disk.

You should provide surge protection for your workstations whether you leave them on all the time or turn them off periodically. In addition, you might want to add uninterruptible power supplies to the most critical servers.

To log off of Windows 95 but leave Windows 95 running, choose Start, Shut Down, then Close all programs and log on as a different user.

Tips for Windows 95 on Windows NT Networks

As you might expect, Windows 95 includes good support for Microsoft-based network environments, such as Windows NT Server provides. Windows 95 is an excellent client for Windows NT servers when you don't need the added performance of Windows NT Workstation. This section of the chapter provides a few tips on using Windows 95 as a client operating system in Windows NT networks. For more specific information on using Windows 95 in Windows NT networks, consult the *Microsoft Windows 95 Resource Kit.*

Protocol Support in Windows 95

Part of the support in Windows 95 for Microsoft-based networks is the Client for Microsoft Networks included with Windows 95. The Client for Microsoft Networks is a 32-bit protected-mode network client that provides network connectivity for networks that employ Server Message Block (SMB) servers. These include Windows 95, Windows NT, and LAN Manager. The Client for Microsoft Networks also offers limited support for connectivity to networks based on IBM LAN Server, DEC PATHWORKS, AT&T StarLAN, and LAN Manager for Unix Systems.

The Client for Microsoft Networks supports three protocols included with Windows 95—NetBEUI, TCP/IP, and IPX/SPX—and also supports NDIS 3.1-compliant network drivers.

 Note Before Windows 95 clients can connect to and access the resources on a Windows NT server, the server and clients must run the same protocol, although they also can run other protocols. The Windows NT server, for example, might run TCP/IP and NetBEUI. The client, however, might only run NetBEUI. In this situation, the two computers use NetBEUI to communicate.

Understanding Logon Validation

Using Windows 95 as clients for Windows NT servers offers a number of advantages. A Windows NT server can provide user logon and validation and pass-through security to workstations running Windows 95. Because both Windows 95 and Windows NT use the same long file name structure, you can view long file names that reside on a Windows NT server from a Windows 95 client. Windows 95 workstations can boot from a floppy disk or local hard disk and run a shared copy of Windows 95 located on a Windows NT server. Diskless workstations can boot Windows 95 from a Windows NT server, although you might need to upgrade your version of Windows NT Server to support boot of remote diskless workstations.

Windows 95 workgroups do not share security validation with one another. Each computer in a workgroup controls access to the resources it is sharing, without relying on another computer to provide user security validation. In a Windows NT environment however, computers can be grouped into domains. A *domain* is a group of computers that are grouped together to facilitate administration and management of the computers in the group, including security validation. A *domain controller* in a Windows NT environment acts as the controller for the domain, validating user logon.

If you want a client to have its logon validated by a Windows NT domain controller, you can configure it to do so. To configure the client, open the Control Panel and choose the Network object, then select the Client for Microsoft Networks and choose Properties to display the property sheet shown in figure 34.15.

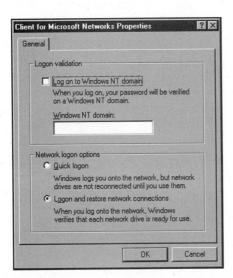

Figure 34.15

The property sheet for the Client for Microsoft Networks.

The Logon Validation group controls whether a Windows NT domain server validates logon from the Windows 95 client. To validate logon, the user must specify a valid account and user password for the domain. This user account can be located on the Windows NT domain server or any other Windows NT server within the domain. The domain controller for the domain validates the account, however, not other servers in the domain.

 Tip   A LAN Manager domain controller can provide logon validation, but it does not support pass-through security for the Windows 95 client. You must use a Windows NT domain to support pass-through security.

Enable the Log on to Windows NT domain check box if you want the domain controller to validate the Windows 95 client. You also must specify the name of the domain in the Windows NT domain text box, or the name of a Windows NT computer on which you have an account.

You also can specify in the Client for Microsoft Networks property page the way in which persistent connections are reestablished when you log on to the network. Two option buttons in the Network logon options group control how persistent connections are handled:

◆ **Quick logon.** Choose this option if you want Windows 95 to create and initialize the data structures necessary to accommodate remote resource mappings, but do not want the connections to be established. For example, if you have drive letter M associated with a remote resource, Windows 95 allocates drive ID M to the resource, but doesn't establish a connection to it. This option is useful if resources are not always available when you log on. By not waiting for the resource to become available, you can reduce logon time considerably. Windows 95 cannot establish a connection to the resource until you attempt to use the resource.

◆ **Logon and restore network connections.** If you want persistent connections to be verified when you log on, choose this option button. Windows 95 attempts to reestablish a connection to the resource as soon as you log on to the network.

Tips for Windows 95 on Novell NetWare Networks

In addition to working well as a client for Windows NT environments, Windows 95 also serves as an excellent client for Novell NetWare environments. Windows 95 can

operate on NetWare versions 2.15, 2.2, 3.*x*, and 4.*x*, and you can use one of three different NetWare clients in Windows 95 to access a NetWare server: Microsoft Client for NetWare Networks, NETX (Novell's real-mode network client for NetWare 3.*x*), and VLM (Novell's real-mode network client for NetWare 3.*x* and 4.*x*).

In many cases, the best choice of NetWare clients is the Microsoft Client for NetWare Networks that is included with Windows 95. The Microsoft Client for NetWare Networks is a 32-bit, protected-mode driver that reduces memory overhead and provides enhanced performance by enabling network requests to be handled in protected mode, rather than requiring the processor to switch to real mode. Windows 95 also includes a NetWare-compatible IPX/SPX protocol. A client can access all the same features offered by the NetWare server, including accessing resources on the server and printing to NetWare-controlled printers. Most of these features are implemented using the Windows 95 interface; for example, you can use point and print (explained in Chapter 8, "Printing and Managing Printers") to print to a NetWare print queue. If you prefer, you also can use many of the standard NetWare utilities for printing and other services.

Tip
If you want network client nodes to be able to share resources on a peer-to-peer basis while also enabling them to connect to a NetWare server, you don't have to use the NetBEUI protocol. Instead, you can use IPX/SPX for connectivity to both types of servers. If you prefer, however, you can use both protocols.

The Microsoft Client for NetWare Networks is not the ideal client in all cases, however. This client does not support the use of NetWare domains, nor does it support NetWare Naming Service (NSS), which requires domains. The following list describes situations in which you might need to use NETX or VLM instead of the client provided with Windows 95:

◆ **NetWare NCP Packet Signature.** NCP provides enhanced security in a NetWare environment, and requires VLM. The NetWare client provided with Windows 95 doesn't support this feature.

◆ **NetWare IP.** You should use NETX or VLM if you need to use NetWare IP. The NetWare client in Windows 95 doesn't support connectivity to NetWare servers running NetWare IP. Also, the Microsoft TCP/IP protocol provided with Windows 95 does not enable the Windows 95 client to communicate with a server that runs NetWare IP.

◆ **Custom VLM.** If you use utilities such as NWADMIN or NETADMIN, or use VLM components such as PNW, you must use VLM.

◆ **NetWare Directory Service (NDS).** The NetWare client provided with Windows 95 doesn't support NDS. If you need to use NDS, you must use VLM.

Note   Future releases of Windows 95 probably will support some of the features described above—including NetWare domains, NSS, and NDS—through 32-bit protected-mode clients.

The issues examined in this section cover only a few of the issues you face when you run Windows 95 in NetWare environments. For additional information on integrating Windows 95 and NetWare, refer to *Windows 95 for Network Administrators,* from New Riders Publishing, and to the *Microsoft Windows 95 Resource Kit,* which is contained on the Windows 95 CD and available separately from Microsoft.

Sharing Resources in Windows 95

As a peer-to-peer network operating system, Windows 95 enables you to share resources such as disks, printers, and fax modems on your PC with other users on the network. Windows 95 can serve as your entire network operating system, or it can function in concert with another network operating system, such as Novell NetWare. Even if you use another network operating system, however, you still can take advantage of the peer-to-peer networking in Windows 95.

This chapter explains how to share resources in Windows 95, as well as how to access and use shared resources across the network. The chapter covers the following topics:

◆ Understanding and configuring resource sharing

◆ Sharing and using disk resources

◆ Sharing and using printer resources

Before you begin sharing and accessing shared resources, you need to understand how Windows 95 makes resources available and secures access to shared resources. The following section begins with a discussion of how the logon process works in Windows 95.

Understanding and Configuring Resource Sharing

You must be logged on to the network before you can use resources shared on the network. Sharing your local resources, however, does not require that you be logged on, although your computer must be running Windows 95 with at least the Enter Network Password dialog box showing (shown later in figure 35.1). The following section explains the logon process to help you understand how network logon affects resource sharing.

Logging On to the Network

To understand the logon process for Windows 95, you must understand how Windows 95 maintains passwords and security. Unlike other network operating systems that require you to have an account on a network server before you can log on to the network, Windows 95 does not require that you already have an existing user account. Windows 95 allows you to log on to the network simply by providing a user name and password. This enables users to, in essence, create their own passwords.

 Note   The lack of a requirement for a preexisting user name applies to Windows 95-only networks and Windows for Workgroups, but not to most other network environments. In a mixed environment with Windows NT, NetWare, or other server types, you must have valid network accounts on the servers or on a domain server before you can access shared network resources.

When you start Windows 95, a logon dialog box similar to the one shown in figure 35.1 appears, prompting you for a user name and password. If your computer is configured to log on to a Windows NT domain, the dialog box contains an additional text box in which you specify the name of the domain. The first time you log on to a NetWare network, the dialog box prompts you for the name of your preferred server.

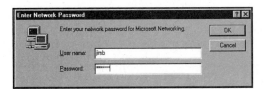

Figure 35.1

*Enter your name
and password to
log on.*

Tip   If you click on Cancel or press Esc in the Enter Network Password dialog box, a common desktop appears and you can use the PC, but you do not have access to network resources until you log on.

When you log on to the network, Windows 95 checks the user name you provide to determine if it matches an existing password cache on your workstation, or in your home directory if you boot Windows 95 from a server. If the user name you specify matches an existing password cache and you enter a valid password, Windows 95 logs you on to the network and unlocks the password cache, giving you access to the passwords it contains (explained shortly). If the password you specify doesn't match the one stored in the password cache for the account name you enter, Windows 95 displays an error message and requires you to reenter the password.

Note   Your password cache contains passwords that you use to log on to the network and access shared resources. The password cache uses your logon name as a file name. The password cache for jimb, for example, would be Jimb.pwl. The password cache is in your Windows folder or home directory.

If the user name you specify doesn't match any password cache in your Windows folder or home folder, Windows 95 displays a message that you have never logged on to the network from this PC, and asks if you want Windows 95 to save your settings. If you choose Yes, Windows 95 creates a password cache for you. Windows 95 also prompts you to verify your password (fig. 35.2).

Figure 35.2

*Windows 95
prompts you to
verify your
password.*

When you access new resources from Windows 95, the name of the resource and its password are stored in the password cache. The next time Windows 95 connects to the resource, it checks the password cache for the appropriate password. If the password matches the one the resource requires, the connection is reestablished. If not, Windows 95 prompts you for a new password (see fig. 35.3). When you enter the correct password, Windows 95 stores the new password in your password cache for your next Windows 95 session.

Figure 35.3

Windows 95 prompts for a new password.

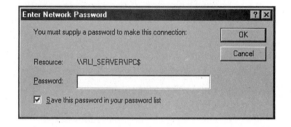

```
┌─ Enter Network Password ──────────────────────┤?│X│
│                                                       │
│   You must supply a password to make this connection:  ┌────────┐ │
│                                                       │   OK   │ │
│                                                       └────────┘ │
│                                                       ┌────────┐ │
│   Resource:    \\RLI_SERVER\IPC$                       │ Cancel │ │
│                                                       └────────┘ │
│   Password:    [                              ]        │
│                                                       │
│   ☑ Save this password in your password list           │
│                                                       │
└───────────────────────────────────────────────────────┘
```

Logging On under NetWare

Under NetWare 3.*x* and 4.*x*, Windows 95 provides a dialog box you can use to log on to a NetWare server if the network is configured for bindery emulation. Windows 95 also includes a NetWare script processor, which enables Windows 95 to process NetWare logon scripts. This enables you to use your existing NetWare logon script with little or no modification when you upgrade to Windows 95.

Tip   The Windows 95 NetWare logon script processor can handle most statements in a NetWare logon script. If the script loads TSRs, however, you must move the statements for the TSRs to the workstation's Autoexec.bat file. Because the NetWare client in Windows 95 works in protected mode, it can't load TSRs for global use.

Controlling the Logon Process

You can configure your PC to log on to the network in one of two ways: Windows 95 logon or network client logon. You select the logon option through the Network object in the Control Panel. After you choose the Network object, the Configuration property page for the network appears (see fig. 35.4). The Primary Network Logon drop-down list contains a list of the network clients installed, as well as Windows Logon.

If you select Windows Logon, Windows 95 doesn't try to validate your user name or password, but you do gain access to Windows 95. You should use this option if network resources are often unavailable, such as when your computer is not connected to the network. If you want Windows 95 to validate your user name and password, you should select your primary network client from the Primary Network Logon drop-down list. If you use a Microsoft-based network (Windows NT or LAN Manager), select the Client for Microsoft Networks. If you work with a NetWare network, select the Client for NetWare Networks.

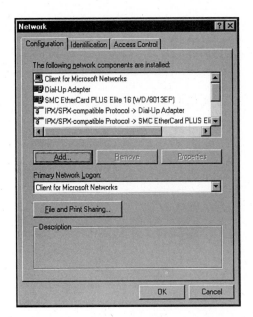

Figure 35.4

The Configuration property page for the network.

Tip   The very first time you log on to Windows 95, Windows 95 prompts you for your user name and password to log on to Windows 95 and access your password cache. Then, Windows 95 prompts you for user names and passwords for each network you want to use. If you work in a mixed environment with a NetWare server and Windows NT server, for example, Windows 95 prompts you to log on to each one with separate logon dialog boxes. If the passwords for your accounts on the servers match the password for your Windows 95 logon, subsequent logon attempts require you to enter only one user name and password. This unified password handling simplifies network logon and access, but requires the presence of a Windows NT domain server or NetWare preferred server on the network.

Configuring NetWare Logon

If you use the Client for NetWare Networks, logon occurs in protected mode after you start Windows 95. The first time you log on to Windows 95, you receive two logon dialog boxes: the first prompts you to log on to Windows 95, and the second prompts you to log on to your preferred NetWare server. If your Windows 95 logon and NetWare logon passwords match, subsequent Windows 95 sessions prompt you for only one password, and Windows 95's unified logon logs you on to Windows 95 and to your network server(s).

Note If you use a real-mode NetWare redirector rather than the Client for NetWare Networks that Windows 95 provides, you must log on to the network in real mode before you start the Windows 95 GUI. Generally, you can use your Autoexec.bat or Startnet.bat files to do so. You should not need to make any changes to your existing real-mode NetWare logon process after you upgrade to Windows 95. You still have to log on to Windows 95 separately after you start the GUI.

To configure your logon options if you run the Client for NetWare Networks, use the Control Panel. Choose the Network object, then choose the Client for NetWare Networks from the list of installed network components and choose Properties to display the property page shown in figure 35.5.

Figure 35.5

The NetWare client property page.

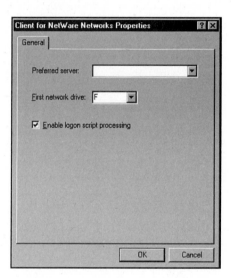

The following list explains the settings on the Client for NetWare Networks property page:

◆ **Preferred server.** Type or select the name of the NetWare server to which you want to log on when Windows 95 starts. Windows 95 reads your logon script from this server and uses this server to store user profiles and policies.

◆ **First network drive.** Select the drive letter you want assigned to your first network drive.

◆ **Enable logon script processing.** Enable this check box if you want the client to process logon scripts when you attempt to log on to a NetWare server.

Logging On and Off

Occasionally you might need to log off, then log on again using the same or a different user name. You might be logged on as a regular user, for example, but need to log on using an administrative name and password. Or, you might want to log on with a different user name so that you can work with a different desktop configuration.

To log off of Windows 95, choose Start, Shut Down, then Close all programs and log on as a different user. Windows 95 closes all running programs, resets the Windows 95 environment, and presents you with a logon dialog box. Enter the user name and password under which you want to log on.

Changing Your Password

You should change your Windows 95 and network passwords periodically for security. In fact, most networks provide a means by which the network administrator can cause your password to age and eventually expire. When the password expires, the network operating system prompts you to specify a new password (but you must also provide your old password for authentication).

To change your passwords in Windows 95, open the Control Panel and choose the Passwords object. Windows 95 displays a dialog box similar to the one shown in figure 35.6. To change your Windows 95 logon password, choose the Change Windows Password button. Windows 95 displays a simple dialog box in which you enter your old password and new password.

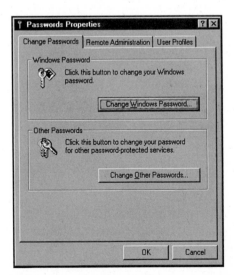

Figure 35.6

The Change Passwords property page.

You also can change the passwords for other network resources, such as servers, through the Passwords object. To do so, choose the Change Other Passwords button, which opens the Select Password dialog box shown in figure 35.7. Select the resource for which you want to change the password, then click on Change. Windows 95 prompts you for the old password and a new password.

Figure 35.7

The Select Password dialog box.

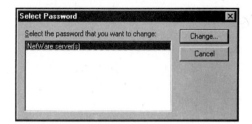

Sharing and Using Disk Resources

One of the primary functions of any network is to enable users to share folders and files. Windows 95 enables you, not only to access folders and files on a network file server, but also to share your local disks and access disks shared by other Windows 95 users. This section of the chapter explains how to share your local disk resources and how to access disk resources shared by other users.

Setting Up for Sharing

Before you can share your resources with other users, you must enable resource sharing on your computer. To do so, open the Control Panel and choose the Network object. From the Configuration property page, choose the File and Print Sharing button to open the File and Print Sharing dialog box shown in figure 35.8.

Figure 35.8

The File and Print Sharing dialog box.

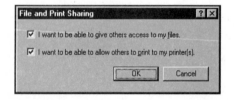

The check boxes on the File and Print Sharing dialog box enable you to control whether you can share your local resources with other users. Enable the check boxes as appropriate for your situation.

Sharing Disks, Folders, and CDs

You can use Windows 95 to share an entire disk (hard disk or floppy disk), one or more directories, or a CD. If you have used Windows for Workgroups, you're familiar with the process; the primary difference is that Windows 95 makes it much easier. Rather than use the File Manager to share a disk resource as you would in Windows for Workgroups, you can share the resource from My Computer, Explorer, or any folder window.

To share an entire disk, simply share its root directory. Open My Computer, then right-click on the icon of the disk you want to share to display its context menu. Choose Sharing to open the Sharing property page for the disk as shown in figure 35.9.

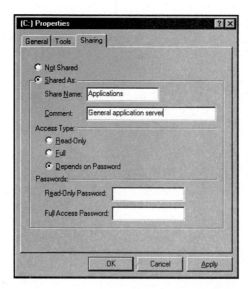

Figure 35.9

The Sharing property page.

Tip You can share a disk from Explorer. Select the disk, then choose File, Properties, or press Alt+Enter, to display its property sheet (including the Sharing page). If the property sheet doesn't include a Sharing page, your computer is not configured for sharing. Use the Network object in the Control Panel to enable sharing on your computer.

Choose the Shared As option button to enable the sharing controls on the property page. In the Share Name text box, enter the name by which you want the resource shared. By default, Windows 95 suggests the drive's logical ID, such as C or D, as the share name. You can accept the default name or enter your own. For example, you might share the disk using a name such as Applications. Another user browsing the network for resources sees a folder named Applications on the computer sharing the disk. Opening the Applications folder displays icons for all of the directories on the shared disk.

Tip

Share names can be up to 12 characters in length and can contain letters, numbers, and the following special characters:

! # $ % & ( ) - . @ ^ _ ' { } ~

You should choose a share name that makes sense to users who browse the network. Whereas the name QR2RPTS might make sense to you, Reports_2ndQ might make more sense to others.

You also can enter an optional comment string in the Comment text box. If a user browses from a Windows NT or Windows for Workgroups node, the comment appears next to the resource name in the user's Browse dialog box. If the user browses from a Windows 95 node, the comment appears in the property page for the resource (which only appears if the user selects the resource's icon, then displays its properties). The comment also appears in folder windows and other Windows 95 browse-related objects (such as common File Open and Save dialog boxes) if these objects are configured to show a detailed list rather than icons or a simple list.

Controlling Access

Also on the Sharing property page is a group of controls that enable you to specify share-level access rights and passwords for the shared resource. You can configure to share the resource as read-only, which enables other users to read but not modify the objects in the share. Or, you can grant full access to the resource, which enables other users to read and modify the objects in the share. If you prefer, you can parcel out access based on the user-supplied password, enabling some users to gain read-only access and others full access to the resource. To grant full or read-only access based on password, choose the Depends on Password option button. A user who supplies the read-only password gets read-only access to the share; a user who supplies the full access password gets full access to the share.

Stop

If you share an entire disk (by sharing its root directory), and grant full access to the share, other users can modify every file and directory on the disk. Therefore, you should use some form of password protection.

After you specify the access method by which you want to share the resource, enter a password in the appropriate text box. Choosing Depends on Password as the access method enables both the Read-Only Password and Full Access Password text boxes. Enter different passwords in each one, then choose OK to begin sharing the resource.

Tip You can create a hidden share that does not show up in browse lists or the share window of the computer that shares the resource. Refer to the section "Creating a Hidden Share" later in this chapter to learn how to create hidden shares. To learn how to share resources on a user-basis rather than share-basis, refer to "Using Pass-Through Security" later in this chapter.

Sharing One or More Directories

In general, you probably don't want to share an entire disk. Sharing individual directories enables you to share part of your disk and prevent access to the rest. When you share a directory under Windows 95, however, any subdirectories in the shared directory also are shared. Unlike Windows NT, NetWare, and other network operating systems, Windows 95 does not enable you to control access to subdirectories separate from a shared parent directory.

To share a directory rather than an entire disk, open Explorer or a folder window to the directory's parent. Select the icon of the directory you want to share, then display its property sheet. Use the Sharing property page to share the directory as explained previously.

Sharing a Floppy Disk

You can share a floppy disk just as you can any other disk. You do so the same way you share a hard disk, except you can easily remove the floppy disk, whereas you can't so easily remove most hard disks.

Sharing a CD

You can share CD-ROMs in the same manner you share hard disks, including sharing only a selection of directories on the CD if necessary. The 32-bit CD file system in Windows 95 enables sharing CDs without any special configuration. Generally, all you have to do to share the CD is open My Computer or Explorer, select the CD's drive letter, then use its Sharing property page to share the CD. Because CD-ROMs are read-only devices, users can't gain full access to the CD. They can, however, read the CD. If necessary, you can password-protect the CD just as you can any other shared resource.

Tip Normally, you don't need to use Mscdex in Windows 95 to access a CD-ROM drive on your system. Mscdex is the real-mode CD-ROM driver supplied with DOS. If Windows 95 does not support your CD-ROM drive's host adapter, however, you might have to use Mscdex to access your CD-ROM drive. If so, add the /S switch to the end of the Mscdex command line in your Autoexec.bat file to enable Mscdex to support CD-ROM sharing.

Creating a Hidden Share

Sometimes it's useful to create *hidden shares*, which do not appear in the browse list or folder windows when users browse your computer for shared resources. To access a hidden share, the user must specify the hidden share name directly in a UNC path or when mapping one of the local drive IDs to the hidden share (see fig. 35.10). This means that the user must know, not only the password for the hidden share, but also its name, which the user has no means of determining on his own.

Figure 35.10

Connecting to a hidden share.

To create a hidden share, just add a dollar sign ($) character to the end of the share name. To share drive C as a hidden share, for example, you could use the share name C$. Or, you could use any other valid share name that ends with the $ character.

Using a Shared Disk Resource

One of the most useful and welcome changes in Windows 95 is the changes in the presentation of network resources. These changes make it extremely simple for you to access shared network resources, and eliminates the need for you to map local drive IDs to remote network resources to use. The key to these improvements are the Network Neighborhood and UNC path names.

The Network Neighborhood is a typical folder that you open to display icons for each of the computers in your workgroup (see fig. 35.11). Selecting a computer's icon from the Network Neighborhood displays all the resources that computer shares, including disks, printers, and Microsoft Fax directories (used for sharing a fax modem, as explained in Chapter 29, "Installing and Configuring Exchange"). Figure 35.12 shows a typical folder for a remote computer's shared resources.

If a shared resource is not password-protected, or your password cache already contains the correct password for the resource, you can begin using it just as you do local disks, folders, and files. If you double-click on a shared folder icon, for example, Windows 95 opens a folder window showing the contents of the folder, including its files and other folders. You can open a network folder and start an application by double-clicking on its icon. Or, you can open a document file the same way. If you want to copy files from the remote computer to your own, you simply select the files and drag them to a local folder or to your desktop.

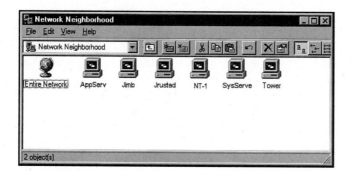

Figure 35.11

The Network Neighborhood folder.

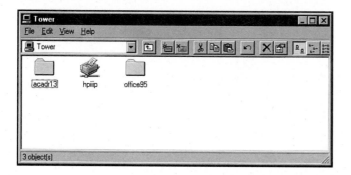

Figure 35.12

Resources shared by a remote node.

You also can work with the Network Neighborhood in Windows 95 applications' File Open dialog boxes. This common Open dialog box (fig. 35.13) works much like a mini-Explorer window, enabling you to open the Network Neighborhood like a local folder, drilling down through its objects until you locate the file you want to open. The Save and Save As dialog boxes also work in the same way. By enabling you to open a remote network computer's shared resources as if they were stored in a local folder, Windows 95 eliminates the need for mapping those resources to a local drive ID.

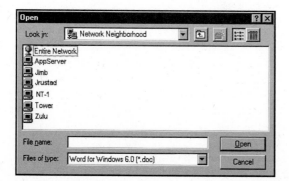

Figure 35.13

The Network Neighborhood in a typical Open dialog box.

You also can use UNC (Universal Naming Convention) path names to access remote shared folders and files. A UNC path name consists of the name of the computer sharing the resource, the resource's share name, and optionally, a file name. To open the file named Third Quarter Report.doc in a shared folder named QtrReports on a server named Sales, for example, you would enter \\Sales\QtrReports\Third Quarter Report.Doc in the Open dialog box. Being able to access folders and files in this way enables you to navigate very quickly to shared network resources.

Tip   One very useful tool is the capability to create folders from within the Save and Save As (and Open) dialog boxes. If you want to create a new folder, on a local or remote disk, you can simply right-click in the folder/file list in the dialog box, and choose Ne**w**, **F**older. After you create the folder, you can rename it if necessary, then select it to store files in it without leaving the dialog box.

Browsing on Microsoft Networks

If you use the Client for Microsoft Networks, your primary mechanism for browsing the network is the Network Neighborhood. When you browse the network, you see the following types of computers in the Network Neighborhood (and Entire Network):

◆ Computers running Windows 95, Windows NT Workstation, and Windows for Workgroups

◆ Windows NT Server domains and servers

◆ Windows 95, Windows for Workgroups, and Windows NT workgroups

◆ Computers running Workgroup Add-On for MS-DOS as peer servers

◆ LAN Manager 2.*x* domains and servers

Note   If your network contains NetWare servers and you also run the Client for NetWare Networks, NetWare servers and computers running the File and Printer Sharing for NetWare Networks service also appear in your Entire Network folder. Note, however, that you can't run the File and Printer Sharing for NetWare Networks and the File and Printer Sharing for Microsoft Networks services on the same computer. You can, however, use both the Microsoft and NetWare clients to access Microsoft- and NetWare-based servers.

To provide a structure to the browse mechanism, Microsoft networks such as Windows 95 employ *master browse servers*. The master browse server maintains the master

list of computers in a workgroup, domains, and workgroups, with one master browse server for each protocol used. Backup browse servers also serve to offload some of the overhead. Generally, there is one master browse server for every 15 computers in the workgroup. When you open the Network Neighborhood, your computer communicates with the browse server(s) to obtain a list of computers, workgroups, and domains.

The master browse server is assigned automatically by the network. When a computer first starts up, it checks the workgroup to determine if a browse server is available. If one is not available, a master browse server is elected. The master browse server then designates backup browse servers as necessary.

Although designation of master and backup browse servers usually happens automatically, you can control whether your computer can become a browse server. Typically, the only reason to change the browse server status of your computer would be to control network performance. If your computer is slow or has little available RAM, you should exclude your computer from acting as a browse server. If your computer is one of the faster ones on the network and has plenty of available RAM, you should consider allocating it as the master browse server.

To control browse services for your computer, open the Network object in Control Panel and choose File and printer sharing for Microsoft Networks, then choose Properties. The Advanced property page appears, as shown in figure 35.14.

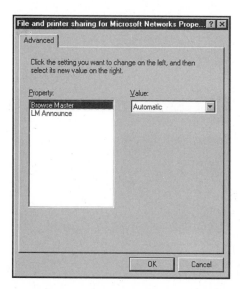

Figure 35.14

Use the Advanced property page to control browsing.

The Property list in the Advanced property page contains two settings, explained in the following list:

◆ **Browse Master.** This setting determines whether your PC acts as a browse server. Select Automatic to enable your PC to be elected as master browse server or designated as backup browse server. Select Enabled to designate your PC as the browse server for your workgroup. Select Disabled to prevent your PC from acting as a browse server.

Note At least one computer in each workgroup must use a setting of Automatic or Enabled for browsing to function normally. Windows 95 does not designate computers connected to the network by a RAS connection as browse servers.

◆ **LM Announce.** This setting determines whether your PC announces its presence in the workgroup for LAN Manager 2.x domains. If your network contains a LAN Manager 2.x domain, select Yes. If your network doesn't contain a LAN Manager 2.x domain, set this to No. Setting LM Announce to No does not prevent Windows 95 Windows NT, or Windows for Workgroups clients from seeing your computer on the network. LAN Manager clients, however, cannot see your computer on the network, but can access and connect to your computer using UNC path names.

Adding and Removing Computers from the Browse List

When a PC starts Windows 95, the .computer announces itself to the master browse server for its workgroup. The master browse server notifies the backup browse servers that an updated list is available, and the backup browse servers then request an update as network traffic and their own CPU load allows. For this reason, a computer appearing in a workgroup browse list can take as long as 15 minutes, although the time span generally is much shorter unless the workgroup has considerable network traffic or numerous computers. Even though a computer doesn't appear in the workgroup, users can connect to it through UNC path names or previously configured persistent connections.

When you shut down computers in a workgroup, their names eventually disappear from the browse list. If you shut down the computer normally (choose Start, then Shut Down), the computer announces to the browse master that it is shutting down. The browse master updates its browse list and advertises to the backup browse servers that an update is available. Again, it can take time for a computer to be removed from all browse lists. If the computer hangs or shuts down improperly for some reason, the computer doesn't have an opportunity to announce its shutdown. For this reason, the computer might continue to show up in the browse list until its name entry times out, which can be as long as 45 minutes.

Browsing on TCP/IP Subnetworks

The browsing mechanism in Windows 95 supports browsing on TCP/IP subnetworks. To enable browsing for TCP/IP, the network must include a WINS server (such as provided by Windows NT), or the Lmhosts file(s) must include #DOM entries. #DOM is a special keyword used in Lmhosts to control how browse and logon services function in a TCP/IP network. For information on configuring browsing and setting up Hosts and Lmhosts files, refer to Chapter 36, "TCP/IP and the Internet Connection."

LAN Manager Compatibility in Other Networks

Some third-party network operating systems are compatible with Microsoft LAN Manager. These network operating systems include IBM LAN Server and Microsoft LAN Manager for Unix. On these network operating systems, resources on Windows 95, Windows for Workgroups, and Windows NT computers appear in the browse list.

Note   As with Windows 95, Windows NT, and Windows for Workgroups, you can use the Windows 95 GUI interface (Network Neighborhood) or the NET VIEW command from a command prompt to browse for resources on LAN Manager-compatible networks.

Other LAN Manager-based networks, such as DEC PATHWORKS, and Microsoft-compatible networks, such as AT&T StarLAN, do not support browsing. You can, however, connect to resources on these networks using their normal connection interfaces.

Browsing on NetWare Networks

If you use Windows 95 on a NetWare network, you use the Network Neighborhood to browse NetWare servers, regardless of whether you use the protected mode Client for NetWare Networks, VLM, or NETX. If you connect to a Windows 95 computer running the File and Printer Sharing for NetWare Networks service, you can use common drag-and-drop methods to copy files from the remote server.

When you open the Network Neighborhood folder on a Windows 95 computer connected to a NetWare network (running a NetWare-compatible client), the Network Neighborhood displays all the NetWare bindery-based servers to which your PC is connected. In addition, any computers in your workgroup running File and Printer Sharing for NetWare Networks also appear in the Network Neighborhood folder. The Entire Network folder contains all the NetWare servers on the network, as well as workgroups in which the File and Printer Sharing for NetWare Networks service is being used.

Tip   If your PC is running the Client for Microsoft Networks and a NetWare-compatible client, your Network Neighborhood folder displays the Microsoft network-compatible nodes in your workgroup. NetWare servers still appear at the top of the list in the Entire Network folder.

As with the Microsoft network client, you can use disk resources on a NetWare server or computer running File and Printer Sharing for NetWare Networks without mapping a local drive ID to the resource. You simply select the computer's icon in the Network Neighborhood or Entire Network folder, then drill down through its folders to locate the object you want to use. If the resource requires a password not contained in your password cache, you are prompted to supply the correct password. You can store the password in your password cache for subsequent connections.

Connecting to a NetWare Server

You can use the Network Neighborhood folder to connect to a NetWare server. Connecting to the server enables you to use the resources on the server. To connect to a NetWare server, select the server's icon in the Network Neighborhood or Entire Network folder, then open the server's context menu. From the context menu, choose **A**ttach As, which opens an Enter Network Password dialog box similar to the one shown in figure 35.15.

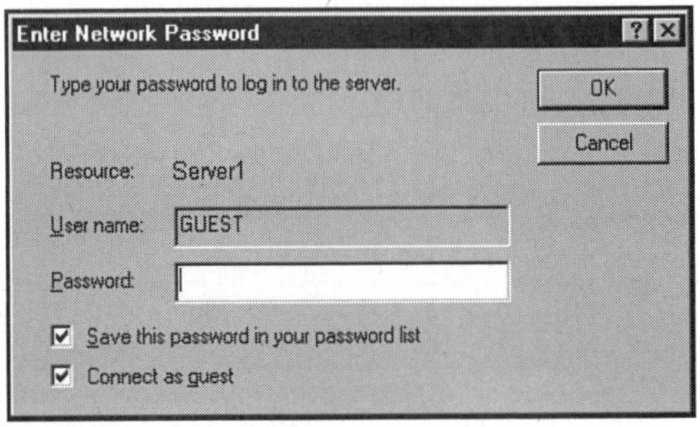

Figure 35.15

The Enter Network Password dialog box for a NetWare server.

Enter Network Password	? X
Type your password to log in to the server.	OK
	Cancel
Resource: Server1	
User name: GUEST	
Password:	
☑ Save this password in your password list	
☑ Connect as guest	

In the **U**ser name text box, enter the user name under which you want to attach to the server, then enter the appropriate password in the **P**assword text box. If you want to connect as Guest, enable the Connect as **g**uest check box. To store the password for the resource in your password cache, enable the **S**ave this password in your password list check box. After you set the settings, choose OK to attach to the server.

Tip   The context menu of a NetWare server includes other commands that enable you to log off of the server and view a list of users attached to the server.

Mapping Drives to Remote Resources

Although you can easily use disk resources through UNC path names without associating (mapping) local drive IDs with those resources, you still can map those drive letters if necessary. If you have a Windows 3.*x* program that doesn't support UNC path names, for example, mapping to the remote resource offers the only means of accessing the resource from that program. Or, your computer might require specific mappings to remote drives for configuring a mail server, file server, or other reason.

Generally, you can map drive letters through any folder window for the resource, such as Network Neighborhood, Explorer, or Entire Network. To map a local drive letter to a remote disk resource, display the folder that contains the resource, select the object to which you want to connect, and open its context menu. From the context menu, choose Map Network Drive. If you prefer not to use the context menu, choose File, Map Network Drive, or click on the Map Network Drive button in the toolbar, which opens a Map Network Drive dialog box similar to the one shown in figure 35.16.

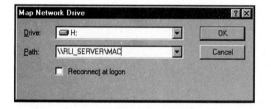

Figure 35.16

The Map Network Drive dialog box.

To map a local drive ID to a remote resource, select the drive ID you want to use from the Drive drop-down list, then enter the path to the server in the Path combo box. You can select the drop-down button to select from previously used connections, or type a new path name. You can specify a UNC path name or a NetWare-style path name (such as SERVER/SYS).

If you want the drive association to last only as long as your current Windows 95 session, clear the Reconnect at logon check box. If you want the connection to persist, so that it reconnects for each of your Windows 95 sessions, enable this check box. The connection to the resource uses the same drive letter in each Windows 95 session.

Note Persistent connections are not permanent. You can disconnect a network resource, which prevents it from being mapped on subsequent Windows 95 sessions.

If you associate a local drive ID with a directory on a NetWare server, the Map Network Drive dialog box contains an additional check box, the Connect as root of the drive check box. You enable this check box to map the selected directory as the root directory of the selected drive. This corresponds to the NetWare MAP ROOT command.

Creating Shortcuts to Remote Resources

Although the Network Neighborhood makes browsing for resources easy, drilling down through a list of workgroups, servers, and resources to find a resource you use often can prove time-consuming. A great solution is to create a shortcut to the resource, in a folder you create or on your desktop. Then, you can access the resource just by double-clicking on its shortcut icon.

You create a shortcut to a remote resource in the same way you create shortcuts to local objects. Open the Network Neighborhood folder and locate the object to which you want to create a shortcut. Then, right-drag the resource's icon to the desktop and choose Create Shortcut(s) Here. When you double-click on the shortcut icon, Windows 95 determines whether the password for the resource is stored in your password cache. If so, Windows 95 opens a folder on the desktop for the resource. If not, Windows 95 prompts you for the correct password.

Using Pass-Through Security

In addition to allowing you to use share-level security to protect shared resources, Windows 95 also enables you to use *pass-through security*, also referred to as *user-level security*. Rather than validate user access based solely on the passwords assigned to the shared resource, pass-through security relies on user validation by a security server such as Windows NT or NetWare servers. If you run the File and Printer Sharing for Microsoft Networks service, you must specify the name of a Windows NT domain or Windows NT workstation as your security server. If you run the File and Printer Sharing for NetWare Networks service, the security server must be a NetWare server or NetWare 4.*x* server running bindery emulation.

Here is how pass-through security works: A user attempts to connect to a shared resource on your computer. Windows 95 sends a message to the security server asking for verification of the user's right to access the resource. The security server validates the user's account and password, and if both are valid, sends confirmation of the user to your computer. Your computer then grants access to the resource based on the rights assigned to the user.

 Tip   You can't use share-level security if you use only the File and Printer Sharing for NetWare Networks service; then you must use pass-through security or use a Microsoft network client and sharing service.

The list of users who can access the resource and their access levels is stored on your computer. The user accounts and passwords, however, are stored on the security server. You can add user accounts and passwords to the security server only by running the account management utility the server provides (such as User Manager on Windows NT, or SYSCON or NETADMIN on NetWare), but you can run these utilities from your Windows 95 workstation if you have sufficient access rights on the server and access to the management utility. Regardless of your security level on the server, you can add names to the share list for resources you share on your PC. The following section explains how to share a resource with user-level security.

Sharing Resources with User-Level Security

To employ user-level security on your computer, you first must enable user-level security through the Control Panel. Open the Network object in the Control Panel, then click on the Access Control tab to open the Access Control property page shown in figure 35.17.

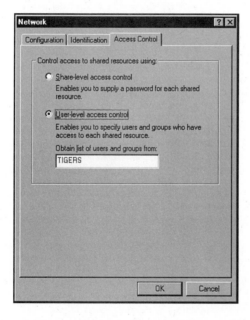

Figure 35.17

The Access Control property page.

On the Access Control property page, choose the User-level access control option button. In the Obtain list text box, type the name of a Windows NT domain, a Windows NT workstation, or NetWare server that you want to act as security server. Choose OK, and Windows 95 prompts you to restart the computer to make the change take effect.

Note   Any directories your computer currently shares are removed from sharing when you enable user-level security. You must reshare the directories after Windows 95 restarts. Also, Windows 95 doesn't support the use of NetWare domains or NetWare Name Service to support user-level security, although it does support NetWare 4.x with bindery emulation.

After you configure your computer for user-level security and restart Windows 95, you can share directories with user-level access. To do so, open a folder or Explorer window that contains the folder you want to share, or choose a disk you want to share, then open the object's context menu. Choose Sharing to display the Sharing property page shown in figure 35.18. Notice that this Sharing property page differs from the Sharing page you see during share-level access (refer to figure 35.9).

Figure 35.18

The Sharing property page with user-level security enabled.

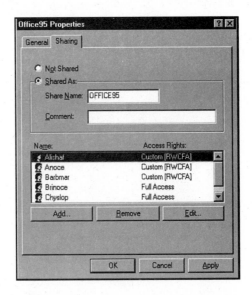

Choose the Shared As option button, then enter the share name and optional comment in the Share Name and Comment text boxes. Then, you must add account names to the list of users who can access the shared resource. To do so, choose the Add button to open the Add Users dialog box. Figure 35.19 shows the Add Users dialog box you see if you use a Windows NT domain for security services.

You can assign read-only, full, or custom access to the shared directory. To assign an access type to a user or group of users, select the user or group name from the list and choose the Read-Only, Full Access, or Custom buttons. Windows 95 adds the selected names to their respective groups. After you add all the groups or users to whom you need to give access to the directory, choose OK. If you have specified Custom for any of the users or groups, the Change Access Rights dialog box (see fig. 35.20) appears.

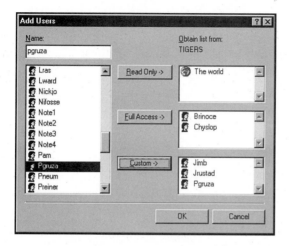

Figure 35.19

The Add Users dialog box.

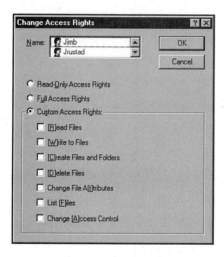

Figure 35.20

The Change Access Rights dialog box.

Tip

If you use the **C**ustom button to add multiple user or group names, all those groups and users share the same custom access rights (explained next). If you want to assign different custom rights to specific users or groups, choose OK to add the current selection of users, then choose the **A**dd button to select other users and assign a different set of custom access rights. After you assign rights to a selection of users and/or groups, you can edit individual group or user access rights without affecting the rights of any other users or groups you might have added at the same time as the one you're editing.

Unlike share-level security, which enables you to share a directory only as read-only or full access, user-level security enables you to apply a fine degree of control over the types of access users and groups have to your shared resources. The check boxes in the Change Access Rights dialog box enable you to specify one or more access rights for each user to whom you assign custom access rights. Table 35.1 lists common file operations and the access rights required to enable those operations.

TABLE 35.1
File Operations and Access Rights

File Operation	Access Rights Required
Change access rights	Change access control
Change directory or file attributes	Change file attributes
Copy files from a directory	Read, list files
Copy files to a directory	Write, create, list files
Create and write to a file	Create files
Delete a file	Delete files
Make a new directory	Create files
Read from a closed file	Read files
Remove a directory	Delete files
Rename a file or directory	Change file attributes
Run an executable file	Read, list files
Search a directory for files	List files
See a file name	List files
Write to a closed file	Write, create, delete, change file attributes

Enable or clear the appropriate check boxes to assign the necessary access rights to the selected users and groups. Then, choose OK to apply the access rights. After you apply access rights, the Sharing property page lists the users and groups and their respective rights.

To edit a user's or group's access rights, select the user or group from the Sharing property page and choose Edit. To remove a user or group from the access list, select the user or group and choose Remove.

Tip Windows NT and NetWare both enable you to set access rights on individual files on the server. Because Windows 95 relies on the FAT file system, you can't assign access rights to individual files—you can assign access rights only at the directory level. Access rights for a shared directory also pass down to its subdirectories.

Configuring Security under NetWare

User accounts, groups, passwords, and access rights are stored under NetWare 3.*x* on a NetWare server in a database called the *bindery*. NetWare 4.*x* uses bindery emulation to make it appear that each NetWare server contains a bindery. Each server contains a separate bindery.

If you use more than one NetWare server in your network environment, you might experience problems with user-level security because your Windows 95 workstation can use only one server as the security server. The solution is to add all user accounts and related information to one NetWare server on the network, then use this server as the security server for all user-level access security by all Windows 95 workstations on the network.

Sharing and Using Printer Resources

Windows 95 enables you to share printers with other users on the network in much the same way you share disks and directories. Shared printers appear in a remote computer's folder when you access the folder through the Network Neighborhood or Entire Network folders. Unlike Windows for Workgroups and other network operating environments, you don't have to map a local printer port to a remote printer before you can print it: you can just use the printer's UNC path name to print. Or, you can associate a remote printer with a local printer port if you need to support printing from DOS and Windows 3.*x* applications.

Sharing a Local Printer

The Sharing page of a printer's property sheet enables you to share the printer with other users on the network. To share a printer, first configure all its other settings and print a test page to verify that the printer works properly. Then, display the Sharing page of the printer's property sheet. Choose the Shared As option button to enable sharing, then enter a name for the printer in the Share Name text box. This is the name that other users see when they browse the network for resources. You also can add an optional comment in the Comment text box. This comment appears as additional information in the Network Neighborhood folder if the user configures the folder for a detailed view.

Tip   To password-protect the printer to restrict its use, enter a password in the **P**assword text box. Users are to enter the password when they attempt to access the printer. Note that the **P**assword text box appears on the property page only if you are employing share-level security.

Printers offer no varying levels of access rights—a user either can print to a printer or cannot. If you use share-level security, you can specify a single password in the printer's Sharing property page to protect access to the printer. If you use user-level access, you can add groups and users to the access list for the printer, assigning full access to each. Applying user-level security and configuring the user list is nearly the same for printers as for disks. Simply open the printer's Sharing property page, then use the same methods described in the section "Sharing Resources with User-Level Security" earlier in this chapter.

Chapter 8, "Printing and Managing Printers," explains how to install a network printer so that you can access it across the network. For help capturing a local printer port and associating the port with a remote network printer, refer to the section "Capturing and Releasing Ports" in Chapter 8.

TCP/IP and the Internet Connection

Although the Internet has existed for many years, only recently has it become widely popular outside academic, government, and military circles. The Internet's explosive growth in the year leading up to the release of Windows 95 has stimulated a strong demand for support of TCP/IP and Internet-related utilities and programs. Windows 95 offers a set of foundational components and general utilities that make it an excellent platform for TCP/IP internetworking.

This chapter helps you understand, configure, and use TCP/IP to provide connectivity between computers on your LAN as well as a connection to the Internet. The chapter covers the following topics:

- ◆ An overview of TCP/IP and the Internet

- ◆ Understanding TCP/IP

- ◆ Installing and configuring TCP/IP in Windows 95

- ◆ Using Hosts and Lmhosts files for name resolution

This chapter helps you configure and use TCP/IP and begin connecting to the Internet. To learn about the TCP/IP and Internet utilities included with Windows 95, refer to Chapter 37, "Using Internet Utilities."

Note   This chapter provides a general overview of Microsoft TCP/IP to help you understand how to configure and use TCP/IP. If you require a more technical description of how TCP/IP works, consult the *Microsoft Windows NT Resource Kit*, *Microsoft Windows 95 Resource Kit*, one of the many resources and FAQs (Frequently Asked Question documents) available on the Internet, or *Inside TCP/IP*, by New Riders Publishing.

For information on how to use PPP and SLIP protocols through the Dial-Up Networking service in Windows 95 to connect to the Internet, refer to Chapter 33, "Using Remote Access Services," which explains PPP and SLIP in detail.

An Overview of TCP/IP and the Internet

The two primary topics in this chapter—TCP/IP and the Internet—generally are closely related; you need the TCP/IP protocol to connect to and use the Internet. But even if you don't need to access the Internet, TCP/IP still offers an excellent means of interconnecting disparate operating systems on a single network. This section of the chapter provides a brief overview of TCP/IP and the Internet.

TCP/IP

TCP/IP stands for Transmission Control Protocol/Internet Protocol. TCP/IP is a network transport protocol widely supported by a majority of operating systems, including all versions of Unix, Windows NT, Windows 95, Novell NetWare, Macintosh, Open VMS, and others. TCP/IP originally was developed through the Defense Advanced Research Projects Agency to support defense-related projects. TCP/IP offers a number of advantages that make it an excellent network transport protocol, particularly for connecting dissimilar computers and for enabling wide-area networking.

The TCP/IP protocol included with Windows 95, dubbed Microsoft TCP/IP, operates as a 32-bit, protected-mode transport that you can use as your only network protocol or in conjunction with another protocol. You might use NetBEUI within your LAN, for example, and use TCP/IP to connect to the Internet through a router or dial-up

connection. The following list describes some of Microsoft TCP/IP's features and advantages.

◆ **32-bit protocol.** As a 32-bit, protected-mode network protocol, Microsoft TCP/IP uses no conventional memory. You also can use Microsoft TCP/IP in conjunction with other network protocols, enabling your computer to connect to a variety of systems.

◆ **WinSock 1.1.** Microsoft TCP/IP supports the Windows Sockets (WinSock) 1.1 specification, which enables you to use WinSock-based TCP/IP programs without requiring an additional WinSock driver.

◆ **DHCP.** Microsoft TCP/IP supports Dynamic Host Configuration Protocol (DHCP), which enables a DHCP server, such as a Windows NT server, to automatically assign IP addresses to workstations on the network, including computers that connect to the network through a dial-up connection. DHCP enables you to more efficiently manage a pool of IP addresses for a given set of workstations.

◆ **WINS.** Microsoft TCP/IP supports Windows Internet Naming Service (WINS), which provides automatic resolution of IP addresses into logical computer names (such as resolving tigers.k12.cfa.org into 198.87.118.2).

◆ **Protocol support.** Microsoft TCP/IP supports Point-to-Point (PPP) and Serial Line IP (SLIP), enabling remote access to TCP/IP-based servers through dial-up connections.

◆ **Core TCP/IP utilities.** Windows 95 includes a number of TCP/IP applications for file transfer, terminal emulation, troubleshooting, and other general tasks.

Although setting up TCP/IP is not difficult per se, it can prove to be a complex task. The section "Understanding TCP/IP" later in this chapter provides more information about the technical aspects of TCP/IP.

The Internet

The Internet began as a small group of interconnected LANs and has grown into a world-wide network that spans many thousands of networks and millions of computers. Although the Internet began primarily as a defense- and education-related network, it has grown to encompass government and commercial networks and users, as well as individual users. The Internet really is nothing more than a huge wide area network. On that network, however, you can access an amazing variety of services and data. You can send and receive e-mail around the globe, transfer files, query enormous databases, participate in special-interest groups, and much more.

Many ways exist to access the Internet. If you have a user account on one of the popular online services, such as CompuServe or America Online, or are a member of the Microsoft Network (MSN), you can gain access to the Internet through those services. Or, your network at work might be connected to the Internet through a dedicated or dial-up connection. You might connect from your computer to an Internet service provider through a dial-up connection. Regardless of the method you use to connect to the Internet, you can't do it without TCP/IP. Understanding TCP/IP is critical to configuring and initiating your Internet connection. The next section provides an examination of some key issues for TCP/IP networking.

Understanding TCP/IP

TCP/IP is versatile, but also complex. Before you can set up a TCP/IP network and correctly configure the computers and other devices on the network, you must understand many key issues. The following sections explain these issues, beginning with IP addressing.

Understanding IP Addressing

On a TCP/IP network, a *host* is any device on the network that uses TCP/IP to communicate, including computers, routers, and other devices. Each host must have a unique address, called an *IP address* (IP stands for Internet Protocol). An IP address identifies the host on the network so that IP data packets can be properly routed to the host. IP data packets are simply data encapsulated in IP format for transmission using TCP/IP. Every IP address on the network must be unique; conflicting (identical) IP addresses on two or more computers prevents those computers from correctly accessing and using the network.

An IP address is a 32-bit value usually represented in *dotted-decimal notation,* in which four octets (eight bits each) are separated by decimals, as in 198.87.118.1. The IP address actually contains two items of information: the address of the network and the address of the host on the network. How the network and address are defined within the address depends on the class of the IP address.

IP addresses are grouped into three classes, A, B, and C. These classes are designed to accommodate networks of varying sizes. Table 36.1 describes the IP address classes, where the variables w.x.y.z designate the octets in the address structure.

Table 36.1
IP Address Classes

Class	w	Network ID	Host ID	Available Networks	Available Hosts Per Network
A	1–126	w	x.y.z	126	16,777,214
B	128–191	w.x	y.z	16,384	65,534
C	192–223	w.x.y	z	2,097,151	254

Tip

The address 127 is reserved on the local computer for loopback testing and interprocess communication, and therefore is not a valid network address. Addresses 224 and higher are reserved for special protocols, such as IGMP multicast, and can't be used as host addresses. Host addresses 0 and 255 are used as broadcast addresses and should not be assigned to computers.

As table 36.1 shows, class A networks are potentially quite large, encompassing as many as 16,777,214 hosts. If you set up your own TCP/IP network, yours most likely falls into the class C network category, which is limited to 254 hosts.

You might wonder what's so important about an IP address. Routing data packets between computers is impossible without an IP address. By referencing the network portion of your IP address, a sending computer can route packets (with the help of intermediate routers and networks) to your network. The host portion of your IP address then routes the packet to your computer when the packet finally reaches the network.

Using Subnet Masks

A *subnet mask* is a 32-bit value expressed as a series of four octets separated by periods, just like an IP address. The subnet mask enables the recipient of an IP data packet to strip *(mask)* the IP address to which the IP packet is being sent into network ID and host ID. Basically, the subnet mask enables the IP address to be broken into its two component parts. Table 36.2 shows the default subnet masks for standard class A, B, and C networks, with each subnet mask shown in binary and dotted-decimal forms.

TABLE 36.2
Default Subnet Masks

Class	Bit Value	Subnet Mask
A	11111111 00000000 00000000 00000000	255.0.0.0
B	11111111 11111111 00000000 00000000	255.255.0.0
C	11111111 11111111 11111111 00000000	255.255.255.0

In addition to enabling an IP address to be resolved into its network and host components, subnet masks also serve to segment a single network ID into multiple local networks. Assume that your large company has been assigned a class B IP network address of 191.100. The corporate network comprises 10 different local networks with 200 hosts on each. By applying a subnet mask of 255.255.0.0, the network is divided into 254 separate subnetworks, 191.100.1 through 191.100.254. Each of the 254 subnetworks can contain 254 hosts.

Tip   The subnet masks described in table 36.2 are not the only masks you can use. Sometimes you have to mask only some of the bits in an octet. The network address and subnet mask must match, however, for every host on a local network.

Acquiring an IP Address

Although theoretically you could arbitrarily assign your own IP network address for your network, any address you might choose probably would already be assigned to someone else's network. If your network is self-contained and not connected to the Internet, duplicate addressing shouldn't cause any problems. If your network is connected to the Internet or you decide to connect it in the future, however, duplicate addressing causes serious routing problems for both networks.

To assure uniqueness of network addresses, a governing organization known as InterNIC (Internet Network Information Center) is responsible for assigning and maintaining IP addresses. If you set up a TCP/IP network, you should contact InterNIC to obtain a unique network IP address for your network. You can contact InterNIC at the following address or phone number. You also can register through the Internet by sending a registration request to hostmaster@internic.net. If you want more information about InterNIC and IP addressing, connect through the Internet to is.internic.net, log on as anonymous, and browse the directory /INFOSOURCE/FAQ for more information. To contact InterNIC through standard mail, phone, or fax, use the following information:

Network Solutions
InterNIC Registration Services
505 Huntmar Park Drive
Herndon, VA 22070
703-742-4777
Fax 703-742-4811

Understanding Gateways and Routing

To interconnect and provide routing of data packets, TCP/IP subnetworks interconnected with one another or connected to the Internet use gateways (routers). A
default gateway generally is a computer or router that maintains IP address information of remote networks (networks outside its own network). Default gateways are
required only on interconnected networks—stand-alone TCP/IP subnets do not
require default gateways.

Before a host transmits an IP packet, IP inserts the originating and destination IP
addresses into the packet. It then checks the destination address to determine
whether the packet is destined for the same local network as the originating host. If
the network addresses match (based on the subnet mask), the packet is routed
directly to the destination host on the same subnet. If the network addresses don't
match, the packet is sent to the subnet's default gateway, which then handles routing
of the packet. The default gateway maintains a list of other gateways and network
addresses, and routes the packet accordingly. Although the packet might pass
through many gateways, it eventually reaches its destination.

If yours is a stand-alone subnet, you don't need a default gateway. Otherwise, you
need at least one functioning default gateway to communicate outside of your subnet.
If for some reason your default gateway becomes inoperative (a router fails, for
example), you can't communicate outside your subnet, but you still can work within
your subnet. If you need to ensure a connection, you might want to consider using
multiple default gateways.

Tip
You can use the route utility from the command prompt to specify a static route and
override the default gateway. For more information on using route, refer to Chapter
37, "Using Internet Utilities."

Using Dynamic Address Assignment

In TCP/IP networks that comprise relatively few nodes, or in which the network
configuration is static (computers do not access the network remotely and the

number of hosts doesn't fluctuate), IP address administration is relatively easy. The network administrator simply assigns specific IP addresses to each host.

On large or dynamic networks, however, administering IP addresses can be difficult and time-consuming. To help overcome this problem, Windows 95 supports Dynamic Host Configuration Protocol, or DHCP, which enables a host to automatically obtain an IP address from a DHCP server when the host logs on to the network. When you move a host from one subnet to another on your network, the host automatically receives a new IP address, and its original IP address is released, making it available for other connecting hosts.

By providing dynamic addressing, DHCP enables you to manage a pool of IP addresses for a group of hosts. Assume that your company has 100 employees who often dial into your subnet from remote locations, but not at the same time. At any one time, 25 to 30 remote users might be connected to the network, but your subnet has only 50 available subnet host addresses. If you assign IP addresses manually, you can accommodate only 50 of the remote users. You can't assign the same IP address to 2 users, because if they both connect to the network at the same time, routing problems prevent them from using the network.

Through DHCP, you can allocate a pool of 50 IP addresses to be assigned automatically to the dial-in users. When a user dials in and connects, DHCP assigns its host a unique IP address from the pool. As long as no more than 50 users attempt to log on to the network remotely and acquire IP addresses, you can accommodate all 50 with unique addresses. If the number of users who need to connect exceed the number of available addresses, the only solution is to expand your pool of available addresses or modify the subnet mask to accommodate more than 50 addresses.

DHCP in Windows 95 relies on a Windows NT DHCP server that can assign IP addresses to hosts on the local subnet when the hosts start Windows 95, and can assign IP addresses to hosts that connect to the network remotely. Later in the section "Installing and Configuring TCP/IP in Windows 95" you learn how to configure your computer to use a static IP address or a DHCP address assignment.

In addition to using DHCP, Windows 95 can request an IP address from a PPP (Point-to-Point Protocol) dial-up router. Whether you use DHCP or connect to a PPP dial-up router, you use the same configuration option to configure dynamic address assignment. The section "Configuring IP Addressing" later in this chapter explains how to configure TCP/IP for dynamic addressing.

Understanding Domains and Name Resolution

Computers have no problems using IP addresses to locate other networks and hosts. The average user, however, can have trouble remembering those dotted-decimal addresses. Domain names and computer names make specifying the addresses or other networks or hosts much easier.

A *domain name* is a unique named formatted much like an IP address, except that the domain name uses words rather than numbers. The domain name identifies your network and is associated with your network's IP address. If your company is Foo Fang Foods, Inc., for example, your departmental subnet might be known as sales.foofang.com. The first portion, sales, identifies your subnet. The second portion, foofang, identifies your corporate network. The last portion, com, specifies the type of organization, and in this example, indicates a commercial network. Other common designators are gov for government, edu for education, mil for military, org for noncommercial organizations, and net for networking organizations.

Tip   As with your IP address, your domain must be unique. If you connect your network to other networks or to the Internet, contact the InterNIC to apply for a unique domain name.

A *computer name* specifies a host on the subnet. Your host computer name is combined with your domain to derive your Internet address. Your host name doesn't have to match your computer's name that identifies it in its workgroup, but it can. By default, Windows 95 uses as your host name the NetBIOS computer name you specify during setup, but you can specify a different name when you configure TCP/IP. Whatever name you specify as the computer name in the TCP/IP configuration is registered with the network when Windows 95 starts.

Note   The computer name you specify for your computer when you install Windows 95 is its NetBIOS name. A computer's NetBIOS name bears no relationship to its host name under TCP/IP. The two names can be different or the same.

No direct translation or correlation exists between IP addresses and domain names and host names. Some method, therefore, is required to enable computers to look up the correct IP address when a user specifies a name rather than an IP address. Your Windows 95 host can use one of two methods: DNS or WINS.

Note   For a technical discussion of DNS and WINS, you can consult volume 2 of the *Microsoft Windows NT Resource Kit*, "Windows NT Networking Guide," or consult the *Windows 95 Resource Kit* on the Windows 95 CD.

Understanding DNS

DNS stands for Domain Name System. *DNS* is a distributed database system that enables a computer to look up a computer name and resolve the name to an IP address. A DNS name server maintains the database of domain names and their corresponding IP addresses. The DNS name server stores records that describe all hosts in the name server's zone.

If you use DNS for your Windows 95 workstation, you specify the IP address of one or more DNS servers in your TCP/IP configuration. When your workstation needs to resolve a name into an IP address, it queries the DNS servers. If the server doesn't have an entry for the your specified name, the name server returns a list of other name servers that might contain the entry you need. The workstation then can query these additional name servers to resolve the name.

Tip   You can define multiple DNS servers in your Windows 95 TCP/IP configuration.

Besides a DNS server, you can use the Hosts file to resolve host.domain-formatted names to IP addresses. For an explanation of the Hosts file, refer to the section "Using Hosts and Lmhosts Files" later in this chapter.

Understanding WINS

WINS stands for Windows Internet Name Service. WINS provides a dynamic database for managing name resolution. WINS relies on a Windows NT server to act as a WINS server. When you install TCP/IP on your workstation, the client software necessary to connect to a WINS server is installed automatically.

One advantage of using WINS is that it's dynamic, rather than static like DNS. If you use DHCP to assign network addresses, WINS automatically updates the name database to incorporate DHCP IP address assignments. As computers move from one place (and address) to another on the network, the WINS server automatically updates and maintains their addresses.

Another advantage of using WINS is that it includes NetBIOS name space, which enables it to resolve NetBIOS names into IP addresses. Assume that your computer's NetBIOS name is joeblow, your computer's TCP/IP host name is JoeB, and your domain name is bozos.are.us. A DNS server could only resolve JoeB.bozos.are.us, but a WINS server could resolve JoeB.bozos.are.us *and* joeblow.bozos.are.us into the correct IP address.

Tip   The *Microsoft Windows NT Resource Kit* contains a good technical explanation of other advantages WINS offers.

When you configure TCP/IP in Windows 95, you can specify the IP addresses of up to two WINS servers to handle name resolution. If your network uses DHCP, you can configure your workstation to resolve the addresses of WINS servers dynamically using DHCP.

If you don't have a WINS server available to provide name resolution of NetBIOS computer names to IP addresses (such as resolving your computer's name to its IP

address), you can use the Lmhosts file to resolve NetBIOS names. For an explanation of how to use Lmhosts, refer to the section "Using Hosts and Lmhosts Files" later in this chapter.

Issues for NetWare

The NetWare client provided with Windows 95, Client for NetWare Networks, supports the IPX/SPX protocol also included with Windows 95. The IPX/SPX protocol provides full compatibility with NetWare networks and replaces the NetWare IP protocol. The Client for NetWare Networks, however, doesn't support NetWare IP protocol. Also, the Microsoft TCP/IP protocol stack that comes with Windows 95 does not support any NetWare clients owing to differences in the protocol implementations of TCP/IP and NetWare IP. Therefore, you must use the IPX/SPX protocol or a NetWare-supplied protocol for NetWare connectivity.

Even though you can't use Microsoft TCP/IP for NetWare connectivity, you can use Microsoft TCP/IP to provide internetworking for other clients and services. You might use IPX/SPX for connectivity with NetWare servers on the network, for example, and use Microsoft TCP/IP for connectivity and resource sharing with Microsoft- or Unix-based servers. Or, you might use Microsoft TCP/IP for Internet connectivity through a router or a dial-up networking connection.

If you use only a NetWare client (because you have a homogeneous NetWare environment with no other server types), and want to use Microsoft TCP/IP for connectivity through a router or dial-up connection to the Internet, you don't have to install any other networking clients or services to enable that TCP/IP connection. TCP/IP connectivity to the Internet does not require a network client or service of its own.

Preparing to Install TCP/IP

Now that you have a little background in how TCP/IP works, you're almost ready to install, configure, and begin using TCP/IP on your Windows 95 workstation. Before you begin the installation procedure, however, you need to gather together the information you must provide when you configure TCP/IP. In particular, you need to know the following information:

◆ **Network address and domain.** If you set up a new TCP/IP network that you intend to eventually connect to the Internet, you must register with InterNIC for a unique domain name and network IP address. Even if you do not plan at this time to connect the network to the Internet, you still should acquire a unique domain name and network address from InterNIC for future compatibility.

◆ **IP address.** Determine whether your workstation will use static IP addressing or will obtain an IP address from a DHCP server. If you require a static address, contact your system administrator for an address, or if you are the administrator, assign an available address for the workstation. If you plan to use DHCP to acquire an IP address dynamically, or you dynamically acquire an IP address from a PPP dial-up router, you do not need to know the IP address of the DHCP server or router.

◆ **Subnet mask.** You must know the appropriate subnet mask for your subnet. If yours is a standard class C network with fewer than 256 hosts, your subnet mask should be 255.255.255.0. If you're not sure what your subnet mask should be, contact your system administrator.

◆ **WINS.** Determine whether your network provides one or more WINS servers for name resolution. If so, you need to know the IP address of the primary WINS server, as well as the IP address of a secondary WINS server if you choose to use a secondary server. If your workstation uses DHCP, however, you need not know the IP addresses of the WINS servers—DHCP automatically resolves them. If your network uses NetBIOS over TCP/IP, you might need a scope ID. If you're not sure, check with your system administrator.

◆ **Default gateway(s).** If your subnet is connected to other networks or to the Internet, you need to know the IP address of the gateway (router) through which IP routing is accomplished. If your network has access to multiple gateways, you can specify multiple gateways to provide fault tolerance and alternative routing.

◆ **Domain name resolution.** You must know the domain name of your network, as well as the host name you use. The host name defaults to the computer name assigned to the computer at startup, which you specify through the Identification property page for your Network settings. If you use DNS for name resolution, you must know the IP addresses of the DNS servers you use.

◆ **Bindings.** You must know which clients and services use the TCP/IP protocol. If you dial into a server for TCP/IP access (such as dialing into an Internet service provider or an NT Server) to gain Internet access, you do not need to bind TCP/IP to any clients or services. If you use TCP/IP as your only protocol and want to dial into a server to access files and other shared resources, or you want to share your resources, you must bind TCP/IP to the appropriate client and service, such as Client for Microsoft Networks and the File and Printer Sharing for Microsoft Networks (or corresponding client and service for NetWare networks). If you use TCP/IP over a LAN, and no other protocol provides sharing services, you need to bind TCP/IP to your network client and sharing service.

Installing and Configuring TCP/IP in Windows 95

Before you can begin taking advantage of TCP/IP, you naturally have to install it. Of all network protocols, TCP/IP is the most complex to install and configure owing to its many settings and options. This section explains those settings and options, beginning with the installation process.

 Note If you have not read the previous section of this chapter, you should do so to learn what items of information you need before you install and configure TCP/IP.

Installing Microsoft TCP/IP

Microsoft TCP/IP installs like any other network transport protocol—through the Control Panel. To install TCP/IP, open the Control Panel and choose the Network object. From the Configuration property page, choose the <u>A</u>dd button. Windows 95 displays a Select Network Component Type dialog box from which you can choose the type of network component you want to install. Select Protocol from the supplied list, then choose <u>A</u>dd. Windows 95 displays a Select Network Protocol dialog box similar to the one shown in figure 36.1. From the <u>M</u>anufacturers list, select Microsoft. Then, from the Network Protocols list, select TCP/IP.

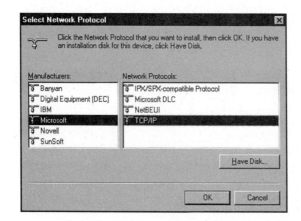

Figure 36.1

The Select Network Protocol dialog box.

After you choose OK, Windows 95 adds the TCP/IP protocol to your PC, copying files as necessary from the Windows 95 distribution disks or CD. After it copies the files, the TCP/IP protocol appears in the installed components list on the Configuration property page. If you have more than one adapter, Windows 95 adds TCP/IP to each one. If your workstation contains a network adapter, for example, and you also use the Dial-Up Adapter for remote access, Windows 95 binds TCP/IP to both adapters. If you need TCP/IP on only one adapter, select the instance of the TCP/IP protocol that you don't need, then choose **R**emove.

Next, you need to specify a number of settings to properly configure TCP/IP, beginning with the IP address. To do so, select the TCP/IP protocol from the Configuration property page, then choose P**r**operties to open the TCP/IP property sheet. The following sections explain how to set the values on the property pages for the TCP/IP protocol.

 Tip You can configure and use multiple sets of TCP/IP settings. You can use one configuration for your LAN TCP/IP connection, for example, and specify different settings for each dial-up connection you use. For information on using TCP/IP over a dial-up networking connection, refer to Chapter 33, "Using Remote Access Services."

Configuring IP Addressing

When Windows 95 first displays the property sheet for the TCP/IP protocol, the IP Address page appears (see fig. 36.2). If you use a static IP address for your workstation, choose the **S**pecify an IP address option button, then enter the IP address and subnet mask for your workstation in the **I**P address and S**u**bnet mask fields. If you want to rely on a DHCP server or PPP server to assign an IP address automatically for your workstation, choose the **O**btain an IP address automatically option button. You do not have to specify the IP address of the DHCP server.

If you specify an explicit IP address, take the time to verify that you have entered the correct address and subnet mask before you continue to the other configuration steps.

Configuring a Gateway

If your subnet is connected to other subnets, to other networks, or to the Internet, you must specify at least one default gateway. To do so, choose the Gateway tab to open the Gateway property page (see fig. 36.3).

 **Tip** Your network's router typically is the default gateway.

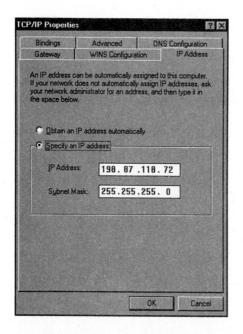

Figure 36.2

The IP Address property page.

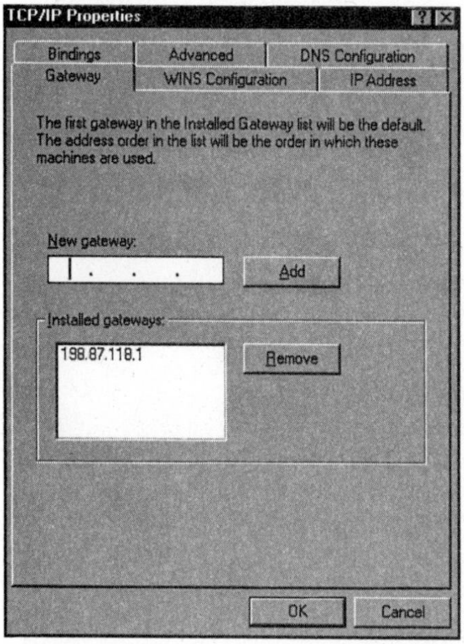

Figure 36.3

The Gateway property page.

If your network is connected to multiple gateways, you can specify as many gateways as necessary to allow for fault tolerance if one gateway becomes unavailable. To add a gateway, enter its IP address in the New gateway field, then choose Add. Windows 95 adds the gateway's IP address to the Installed gateways list. If you add multiple gateways to the list, the IP address at the top of the list serves as the default gateway. Other gateways in the list are used only if the default gateway is inaccessible. Unfortunately, you can't simply drag the IP addresses in the Installed gateways list to prioritize them. Instead, the gateway addresses are placed in the list in the order in which you add them. To prioritize a set of gateways, write down the gateway addresses, remove the addresses, and add them back in using your preferred order of priority, adding the default gateway first.

Using DNS

If your workstation requires Domain Name System (DNS) services, click on the DNS Configuration tab to open the DNS Configuration property page shown in figure 36.4. To enable DNS, choose the Enable DNS option button.

Figure 36.4

The DNS Configuration property page.

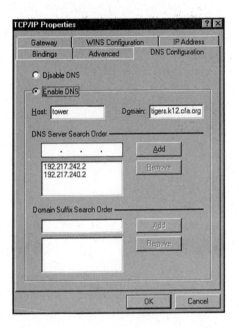

 Tip If your computer needs to use Lmhosts to resolve network names, you must enable DNS.

Specifying Host and Domain Names

After you enable DNS, you need to specify some additional items of information. First, you need to specify the host name for your computer in the Host text box. By default, the host name is your computer's name as specified in the Identification property page of the Network property sheet. You can use any host name, however; you might use your name as the host name, for example. You can use any combination of letters and numbers, a dash, or a period, but not a space or underscore character, in the host name.

Next, specify the domain name for your network in the D_omain text box. TCP/IP combines the host name you specify with the domain name you specify to derive a Fully Qualified Domain Name (FQDN) for your computer. If your host name is JimB and your domain name is newriders.mcp.com, the FQDN for your computer is JimB.newriders.mcp.com.

 Note Some TCP/IP utilities use your host name, domain name, and FQDN to authenticate your computer name. Note that a computer's FQDN is not the same as a user's e-mail address. Although the FQDN might be JimB.newriders.mcp.com, the e-mail address might be jboyce@newriders.mcp.com. Also, a DNS domain name and a Windows NT or LAN Manager domain name are in no way related.

Specifying DNS Server IP Addresses

If you do not use DHCP to define IP addresses, you must provide the IP addresses of the DNS servers you use. If you do use DHCP, the DHCP server can automatically provide the IP addresses of the DNS servers.

You can specify up to three DNS server addresses in the DNS Server Search Order group of controls. First, determine the IP address of the DNS server you want to use by default. Then, enter the server's IP address in the IP address text box and choose A_dd. Enter a second IP address if you want, then choose A_dd. Enter a third IP address in the same manner if you have a third DNS server.

 Note The DNS server IP addresses are placed in the list in the order in which you add them. Therefore, you should enter the DNS server with the highest priority first, followed by any other servers in descending order of priority. To change priority of DNS servers in the list, you must remove and re-add the IP addresses. Windows 95 uses the secondary and tertiary DNS servers only if the primary DNS server does not respond. If the primary DNS server responds that the requested name is not recognized, Windows 95 does not query the secondary or tertiary DNS servers. If you know the name is correct, you can use the Hosts file to enable proper resolution of the name, as explained later in the section "Using Hosts and Lmhosts Files."

Adding Domain Suffix Entries

Normally, DNS appends the domain name specified in the D_omain text box to your host name to resolve the FQDN of your computer. You can specify up to five additional domain suffixes that DNS can use if it can't resolve the FQDN using the default domain name. A DNS server attempts to resolve the FQDN using these additional suffixes in alphabetical order (which is how they appear in the list after you add them).

To add additional domain suffixes, enter a domain name in the Domain Suffix Search Order text box, then choose **A**dd. Repeat the process to add up to five domain names.

Using WINS

If your network includes one or more Windows NT servers configured as WINS servers, or access to WINS servers, you can configure your Windows 95 TCP/IP stack to use WINS to resolve names. WINS offers numerous advantages over DNS, particularly in conjunction with DHCP. To configure WINS, click on the WINS Configuration tab to display the WINS Configuration property page shown in figure 36.5.

Figure 36.5

The WINS Configuration property page.

TCP/IP Properties		

| Bindings | Advanced | DNS Configuration |
| Gateway | WINS Configuration | IP Address |

Contact your network administrator to find out if you need to configure your computer for WINS.

○ **D**isable WINS Resolution

⦿ **E**nable WINS Resolution

Primary WINS Server: [. . .]

Secondary WINS Server: [. . .]

S**c**ope ID: [   ]

○ Use D**H**CP for WINS Resolution

[OK]   [Cancel]

To enable WINS for your computer, choose the **E**nable WINS Resolution option button. You can specify a primary and a secondary WINS server by entering their IP addresses in the fields provided for that purpose on the property page. If your computer uses DHCP to resolve names, however, you can leave the IP address fields blank and choose the Use D**H**CP for WINS Resolution option button, and Windows 95 queries the DHCP server for the WINS server addresses.

New Riders Publishing
INSIDE
SERIES

Binding the TCP/IP Protocol

If you use TCP/IP for resource access and/or resource sharing, you must bind the protocol to the necessary network client and/or resource sharing service. To do so, click on the Bindings tab to open the Bindings property page (see fig. 36.6). Enable the check box beside the client or service to bind the protocol to the client or service.

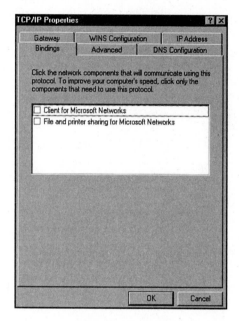

Figure 36.6

The Bindings property page.

 Note   If you use TCP/IP only to provide access to the Internet, and use a different network protocol to provide local resource sharing, you don't have to bind TCP/IP to your clients or services.

Using Hosts and Lmhosts Files

DNS name servers resolve FQDN names provided in the host.domain format to IP addresses. A WINS server can resolve IP host.domain names to IP addresses, and it also can resolve a computer's NetBIOS name into its address name. Sometimes, however, being able to resolve names locally without relying on a DNS or WINS name server comes in handy. You might not have a DNS or WINS name server available to you, for example, or the server might be temporarily unavailable.

Windows 95 provides two methods for resolving names to IP addresses locally, which you can use in conjunction with or in place of DNS and WINS name resolution. Both methods rely on simple ASCII files to store database entries for names and corresponding IP addresses. The first of these files, Hosts, resolves DNS-formatted names, and works with or in place of DNS. The second file, Lmhosts, resolves NetBIOS names into IP addresses, and works with or in place of WINS.

The following section explains the Hosts file. The Lmhosts file is explained in the section after that one.

Using the Hosts File for Name Resolution

If you can't access a DNS server, or you want to supplement a DNS server with your own entries, you can use the Hosts file to maintain a database of host names and their corresponding IP addresses. The Hosts file is called a *host table* because it contains a table of host names and their IP addresses. Windows 95 can look up entries in the Hosts file to resolve names.

When you install Microsoft TCP/IP, Windows 95 creates a sample Hosts file named Hosts.sam in the Windows folder. The Hosts.sam file is an ASCII file that you can edit using Notepad, WordPad, Edit, or any other ASCII editor. You should copy Hosts.sam to Hosts (omitting a file extension) and retain the sample file for future reference in case your Hosts file becomes corrupted or is accidentally deleted. The following lists the contents of the Hosts.sam file:

```
# Copyright (c) 1994 Microsoft Corp.
#
# This is a sample HOSTS file used by Microsoft TCP/IP for Chicago
#
# This file contains the mappings of IP addresses to host names. Each
# entry should be kept on an individual line. The IP address should
# be placed in the first column followed by the corresponding host name.
# The IP address and the host name should be separated by at least one
# space.
#
# Additionally, comments (such as these) may be inserted on individual
# lines or following the machine name denoted by a '#' symbol.
#
# For example:
#
#      102.54.94.97     tools.acme.com          # source server
#       38.25.63.10     x.acme.com              # x client host

127.0.0.1       localhost
```

The Hosts file uses the same format as the hosts file used on 4.3 BSD Unix, stored in the /etc/hosts file. The Hosts.sam file contains comments identified by a leading # character and a single address entry for localhost. The localhost entry is always 127.0.0.1 and is used for loopback testing. You should not change the IP address for localhost or remove it from the Hosts file.

To add an entry to the Hosts file, enter the IP address, then tab to the second column and enter the host name. You can specify more than one host name for an IP address, but you must use multiple entries for the different domains, each with the same IP address, as in the following example:

```
102.54.94.97      tools.acme.com
102.54.94.97      TOOLS.ACME.COM
102.54.94.97      fooyang.gruel.com
```

Entries in the Hosts file are case-sensitive. The two entries for tools.acme.com and TOOLS.ACME.COM would enable the correct host name resolution if you specified the host name in lowercase or uppercase.

You can include a single host name for each entry or specify multiple host names for a single IP address. The following, for example, are valid entries:

```
198.87.118.72   me            theboss        tower.tigers.k12.cfa.org
198.87.118.50   TheServer     theserver      THESERVER
```

Each of the entries in this example specify three host names for each IP address.

Windows 95 parses the entries in the Hosts file in sequential order until it finds a match. If you have a large Hosts file, you can speed up lookup time by placing the most often-used host name entries at the top of the file.

Using the Lmhosts File for Name Resolution

If you want Windows 95 to be able to resolve NetBIOS computer names to IP addresses, you need to use a WINS or Lmhosts file. NetBIOS names are the computer names assigned to computers on Microsoft-based networks, such as the name you assigned to your computer through the Identification page of the Network property sheet. As explained previously, your computer's NetBIOS name is not equivalent to your TCP/IP host name, although the two can use the same name.

Windows 95 automatically resolves NetBIOS names for computers running TCP/IP on a local network. To resolve IP addresses of computers on other networks to which yours is connected by a gateway (when a WINS server is not available), you need to use Lmhosts.

Note   Like Hosts, Lmhosts is an ASCII file, and the format of an entry is similar to entries in a Hosts file. The Lmhosts file, however, supports special keywords, which are explained later in this chapter. Windows 95 includes a sample Lmhosts file named Lmhosts.sam, located in the Windows folder. To use Lmhosts, copy Lmhosts.sam to Lmhosts without a file extension, then modify Lmhosts to add entries.

Microsoft TCP/IP reads the Lmhosts file when you start the computer. As it does the Hosts file, Windows 95 parses each line sequentially, which means you should place often-accessed names at the top of the file for best performance. You also need to place entries that contain special keywords at specific locations in the file (these placement rules are explained later in the chapter). First, here are a few rules for structuring a Lmhosts file:

◆ Each entry must begin with the IP address in the first column, followed by its computer name in the second column. Any additional keywords appear in subsequent columns. Columns must be separated by at least one space or tab character. Some Lmhosts keywords follow entries, while others appear on their own lines (explained later).

◆ Place each entry on a separate line.

◆ Comments must begin with the pound (#) character, but special Lmhosts keywords also begin with the # character. Keeping comments to a minimum improves parsing performance. Place often-accessed entries near the top of the file for best performance.

◆ The Lmhosts file is static, so you must manually update the file you need to create new entries or modify existing entries.

Tip   Although Microsoft TCP/IP reads the Lmhosts file at system startup, only entries designated as preloaded by the #PRE keyword are read into the name cache at startup. Other entries are read only after broadcast name resolution queries fail.

You can use any or all of six special keywords (described in the following list) in a Lmhosts file:

◆ **#PRE.** This keyword causes the associated entry to be preloaded into the name cache, rather than read-only after broadcast resolution queries fail. If you want names stored in a remote Lmhosts file to be added to the name cache at startup, use the #INCLUDE and #PRE statements in combination, such as the following:

```
#INCLUDE      \\server\pub\lmhosts      #PRE
```

◆ **#DOM:<*domain*>.** This keyword designates a remote domain controller and enables you to identify Windows NT domain controllers located across one or more routers. Entries that use the #DOM keyword are added to a special internetwork group name cache that causes Microsoft TCP/IP to forward requests for domain controllers to remote domain controllers as well as local domain controllers. The following example identifies a domain controller named appserver in a domain named thedomain, and also causes the entry to be preloaded into the name cache at startup:

```
184.121.214.2  appserver  #PRE  #DOM:thedomain    #This is a comment
```

◆ **#INCLUDE<*filename*>.** Use this keyword to include entries from a separate Lmhosts file. You can use #INCLUDE to include your own set of entries stored on your own computer, but you most commonly would use #INCLUDE to enable use of a centralized, shared Lmhosts file for multiple users. The following example includes a Lmhosts file from a local drive and directory:

```
#INCLUDE  c:\mystuff\Lmhosts       #Includes local file
```

Note   If you reference a remote Lmhosts file on a server outside of your network in a #INCLUDE statement, you must include an entry for the IP address of the remote server in the Lmhosts file. The server's entry must be inserted in the Lmhosts file before the #INCLUDE statement that references it. You also should not use #INCLUDE to reference a Lmhosts file on a redirected network drive, because your drive mappings might be different from one session to another. Use the UNC path for the file instead. Centralized Lmhosts files should never use drive-referenced entries, because the drive mappings in the file probably will not apply to all users who might use the file.

◆ **#BEGIN_ALTERNATE.** This statement signals the beginning of a block of multiple #INCLUDE statements (called a *block inclusion*). The statements within the block designate a primary and alternate locations for the included file. The alternate locations are checked if the primary file is unavailable. The successful loading of any one entry in the block causes the block to succeed, and any subsequent entries in the block are not parsed. You can include multiple block inclusions within a Lmhosts file. The following is an example of a block inclusion:

```
#BEGIN_ALTERNATE
#INCLUDE         \\server\pub\lmhosts          #Primary source
#INCLUDE         \\othersrvr\pub\lmhosts        #Alternate source
#INCLUDE         \\somewhere\pub\lmhosts        #Alternate source
#END_ALTERNATE
```

- **#END_ALTERNATE.** This statement signals the end of a block of multiple #INCLUDE statements.

- **\0x*nn*.** This keyword enables you to specify nonprinting characters in NetBIOS names. You must enclose the NetBIOS name in quotation marks and use the \0x*nn* keyword to specify the hexadecimal value of the nonprinting character. The hexadecimal notation applies to only one character in the name. The name must be padded to a total of 16 characters, with the hexadecimal notation as the 16th character. Example:

```
109.88.120.45    "thename    \0x14"        #Uses special character
```

Adding an Entry to Lmhosts

NetBIOS computer names of computers on your LAN are resolved automatically. To resolve remote names when a WINS server is not available, add the NetBIOS names and their corresponding IP addresses to the Lmhosts file. To add an entry, use Notepad, WordPad, Edit, or any other text editor that enables you to edit and save ASCII files.

Each line consists of the IP address and NetBIOS name, and also can contain optional keywords and comments as explained previously. The following are examples of Lmhosts entries:

```
192.214.240.2     me                              #Alias for my computer
198.87.118.72     tower                           #Fred's computer
198.87.118.50     rli-server  #PRE                #Application server
120.89.101.70     server      #PRE    #DOM:tigers #Some comment here
182.212.242.2     sourcesrvr  #PRE                #Source for shared Lmhosts
182.212.242.3     source2     #PRE                #Source for shared Lmhosts
182.212.242.4     source3     #PRE                #Source for shared Lmhosts
187.52.122.188    images                          #Imaging server


#INCLUDE           c:\mystuff\lmhosts             #My private Lmhosts file


#BEGIN_ALTERNATE
#INCLUDE           \\sourcesrvr\pub\Lmhosts       #Primary central Lmhosts
#INCLUDE           \\source2\pub\Lmhosts          #Alternate source
#INCLUDE           \\source3\pub\Lmhosts          #Alternate source
#END_ALTERNATE
```

In the preceding example, only the rli-server, server, sourcesrvr, source2, and source3 entries are preloaded into the name cache at system startup, because only they include the #PRE keyword. Other entries are parsed only after broadcast name resolution requests fail.

Tip   The addresses of servers you specify in a block inclusion must be preloaded through entries earlier in the file. Any entries not preloaded are ignored.

Using Internet Utilities

Windows 95 offers a good selection of tools to enable you to connect to and use the Internet. Windows 95 provides built-in support for TCP/IP and TCP/IP-related utilities, such as ftp, telnet, and others. The Microsoft Plus! for Windows 95 product includes additional utilities, including easier installation and configuration of Internet tools and an Internet Mail provider for Exchange.

This chapter explores the command-line and Windows 95-based tools and utilities provided with Windows 95 for accessing and using the Internet. The chapter covers the following topics:

- ◆ Using ftp
- ◆ Using netstat
- ◆ Using ping
- ◆ Using telnet
- ◆ Using Winipcfg

Note   Windows 95 also includes the arp, nbtstat, route, and tracert diagnostic commands. Because few users need to run these commands, this chapter doesn't cover them. For an explanation of these commands, consult the *Windows 95 Resource Kit* or telnet to a Unix host and use the man command to view the manual pages for the commands (such as man route).

This chapter doesn't cover Internet front-end applications, such as Mosaic or NetScape, nor does it cover general Internet use topics, such as gopher, WAIS, or the World Wide Web. If you need help using these types of applications and Internet services, refer to one of the many Internet books available, including *Inside the World Wide Web* from New Riders Publishing. For more information about installing Internet support in Windows 95, refer to Chapter 16, "Using Microsoft Plus! for Windows 95." For tips on configuring and using the Internet Mail provider for Exchange, refer to Chapter 30, "Using Microsoft Exchange." For help setting up TCP/IP and your Internet connection, refer to Chapter 36, "TCP/IP and the Internet Connection," and Chapter 33, "Using Remote Access Services."

Tip   The Windows 95 TCP/IP utilities are installed automatically when you install the TCP/IP protocol. If you have not yet installed TCP/IP, you must do so before you can use the utilities this chapter describes.

Using ftp

Although browsing Web pages is rapidly becoming the mode of choice for gathering information from the Internet, file transfer remains a major use for the Internet. The primary means by which you transfer files across the Internet is ftp (File Transfer Protocol). The Windows 95 ftp command-line utility enables you to connect to remote hosts and send and receive files.

To use ftp to upload or download a file on the Internet, you first must connect to the ftp host. You then can use many different ftp commands to change your current directory, specify the type of transfer, initiate the transfer, and so on.

Tip   You can open multiple ftp connections at one time by opening multiple DOS sessions in Windows 95, then starting ftp and connecting to a different server in each one. Naturally, connecting to multiple ftp sites and transferring files to and from each reduces the transfer rate for each session.

The syntax of the ftp command is as follows:

```
ftp [-v] [-n] [-i] [-d] [-g] [host] [-s: filename]
```

The command parameters you can use to start ftp are explained in the following list:

◆ **-v.** Suppresses the display of responses from the remote ftp server. Use the verbose command to turn on or off server response display after you start ftp.

◆ **-n.** Suppresses autologon for the initial connection.

◆ **-i.** Starts ftp in noninteractive mode, turning off interactive prompting. Use the prompt command to turn on or off interactive prompting if ftp is already running.

◆ **-d.** Turns on debugging, which causes all ftp commands passed between the client and server to appear on-screen.

◆ **-g.** Disables file-name globbing, which enables you to use wild-card characters in local file and path names. Use the glob command to turn on or off file-name globbing if ftp is already running.

◆ ***host.*** Specifies the host name of the remote ftp server. You can enter a DNS-format name or IP address.

◆ **-s:** ***filename.*** Specifies a script file to execute after ftp starts. You can use the script to automate ftp transfers.

The ftp utility is an interactive program. After you start ftp, you can enter a number of different commands to connect to a server, access files, control file transfer options, and much more. If you specify a host with which to connect when you issue the ftp command, ftp establishes a connection with the host, prompting you for a password if necessary. If you don't specify a host name when you start ftp, the program starts its command interpreter and waits for you to enter commands to configure ftp, run scripts, and perform other setup options. You then can use the open command to establish a connection to a host.

 Note You enter the previously discussed parameters at the command prompt with the ftp command when you invoke the program. You enter the following commands at the ftp command prompt after you start ftp. During ftp, you have an ftp> prompt, indicating that ftp is waiting for command input.

The following sections explain each of the ftp commands.

! [command [args]]

The ! command invokes an interactive shell on your computer. If you specify command arguments, ftp interprets the first argument as the command to run directly

and any subsequent parameters as arguments for that command. In essence, the !
command without any additional parameters drops you out to the Windows 95
command line so that you can execute DOS and Windows 95 commands. The ftp
program is still running, however, even after a standard Windows 95 command-line
prompt (such as `C:\WINDOWS`) replaces the `ftp>` prompt. To close the shell and return
to the `ftp>` prompt, type **exit** and press Enter.

If you include arguments with the ! command, ftp executes the command and returns
you to the `ftp>` prompt. The following example would display the text files in the
current directory on the local computer and then return to the `ftp>` prompt:

```
ftp>! dir *.txt
```

Tip   The Windows 95 ftp utility does not support two commands that Unix ftp supports—
macdef and $, which enable you to create and run ftp macros.

append *local-file* [*remote-file*]

This command appends a local file to a file on the remote host. The current file
settings (type, format, mode, and structure) are used for the operation. You must
specify the local file name, but the remote file name is optional. If you omit the
remote file name, ftp uses the local file name.

The following example appends the local file Endstuff.txt to the remote file
Begstuff.txt:

```
ftp>append Endstuff.txt Begstuff.txt
```

Note   You must have write permission in the remote ftp directory before you can append
or perform other file creation actions in the remote directory.

ascii

This command sets the file transfer type to ASCII, which is the default type. Files you
transfer when the ASCII file type is in effect transfer as ASCII files. You would use the
ascii command to reset the file type if it were set to a different type, such as binary.

bell

The bell command causes a tone to play at the end of each file transfer. By default,
the bell is off. The bell command acts as a toggle, turning the bell on or off. Turning

on the bell helps if you perform a long file transfer or series of transfers, and want the computer to notify you when the transfers are completed.

binary

The binary command sets the file type to binary, which enables transfer of binary files. If you transfer exe, com, zip, arc, or other binary file types, you must enter the binary command so that the files can transfer correctly.

bye

The bye command closes the connection to the remote host and terminates the ftp program. If you want to close the connection but keep ftp running (to connect to a different host, for example), use the close command. You also can use the quit command to close a connection and terminate ftp.

cd [*directory*]

The cd command changes the current directory on the remote host. On Unix systems, a forward slash separates directory names and file names. On DOS and Windows 95 systems, a backslash separates directory names and file names. You also can use the dot (.) and double-dot (..) entries to specify the current and parent directories.

The following example changes the current directory on the remote Unix host to the directory ftp-file, which is located in the current directory's parent directory:

```
ftp>cd ../ftp-file
```

Tip   If you are connected to a Windows NT ftp host, you can use the / or \ character to separate directory names. Unix hosts require the / character to separate directory names. Also, directory and file names on Unix systems are case-sensitive.

close

The close command terminates the ftp session with the remote host and returns to the ftp command interpreter. The close command does not terminate the ftp program. You can connect to only one host at a time, so you must use the close command before you can establish a connection to another host.

debug

The debug command turns debugging on and off. If debugging is turned on, ftp echoes each command sent to the remote host to the local screen, preceded by the characters - - ->. Debugging is turned off by default.

delete [*file*]

The delete command deletes files on the remote host. You can specify a single file name for the deletion—you cannot use wild-card characters to delete multiple files with one delete command. You must have the necessary permissions in the directory on the remote host before you can delete files. Also, remember that file names on Unix hosts are case-sensitive, so you must use the same case when you specify a file name on a Unix host.

dir [*filespec*]

The ftp dir command functions much like the DOS DIR command; it displays a listing of the files and directories on the remote host. You can use the dir command without optional file or directory specifications, or you can use file names, directories, and wild cards to display directory listings. The dir command produces output similar to the Unix ls -l command, as shown in the following example:

```
ftp> dir
200 PORT command successful.
150 Opening ASCII mode data connection for /bin/ls.
total 35
drwxr-xr-x  3 jimb     members      1024 Mar 13 21:36 .NeXT
-r--r--r--  1 jimb     members       240 Mar  4  1992 .commanddict
-rw-r--r--  1 jimb     members       477 Sep 13  1993 .cshrc
-r--r--r--  1 jimb     members       885 Jul 15  1991 .indent.pro
-rw-r--r--  1 jimb     members     16384 Nov  7  1994 .index.store
-rw-r--r--  1 jimb     members       180 Sep 13  1993 .login
-rw-r--r--  1 jimb     members         6 Sep 13  1993 .logout
-rw-r--r--  1 jimb     members        19 Sep 13  1993 .mailrc
-r--r--r--  1 jimb     members        49 Jul 15  1991 .pipedict
-rw-r--r--  1 jimb     members       257 Sep 13  1993 .plan
-rw-r--r--  1 jimb     members       236 Sep 13  1993 .profile
drwxr-xr-x  2 jimb     members      1024 Sep 13  1993 Apps
-rw-r--r--  1 jimb     members       194 Feb 11 19:39 LIST.TXT
drwxr-xr-x  5 jimb     members      1024 Nov  7  1994 Library
drwx------  3 jimb     members      1024 Oct 20  1993 Mail
```

```
drwxr-xr-x  3 jimb      members      1024 Oct 22  1993 Mailboxes
-rw-r--r--  1 jimb      members        13 Jun 10 13:08 ftpscrip.txt
-rw-r--r--  1 jimb      members      2420 Apr  3 09:41 readme.txt
226 Transfer complete.
1142 bytes received in 0.77 seconds (1.48 Kbytes/sec)
```

 Note Refer to the ls command for an explanation of the information the dir command displays.

disconnect

The disconnect command terminates the connection to the remote host and returns to the ftp command prompt. It's identical to the close command. Although the connection to the remote host is terminated, ftp continues running, and you can use the open command to connect to a different host.

get [*file*] [*newname*]

The get command directs ftp to retrieve the file specified by *file* from the remote host. The transfer takes place using the current file type (binary or ASCII). The file is placed in the current directory on the local computer. If you specify a file name for *newname,* ftp renames the file as it copies. The following example retrieves the file Readme.txt and renames it Readme.now:

```
ftp> get readme.txt readme.now
```

 Note The Windows 95 ftp command supports long file names. If you want to rename a file using a long file name as it copies, enclose the long file name in quotes, such as **get readme.txt "This is a long file name"**. Also, file names on Unix hosts are case-sensitive.

The recv command is synonymous with the get command.

glob

The glob command turns on or off file globbing. *Globbing* enables you to use wild-card characters in local file and path names. When globbing is turned on, ftp interprets wild-card characters in the file and directory names as wild-card characters. If you turn off globbing, ftp treats the file and directory names literally and does not expand them. The glob command applies primarily to the mdelete, mget, and mput commands.

hash

The hash command turns on or off printing of hash marks (the # symbol) to indicate the status of a file transfer. If hash marks are turned on, ftp prints one # symbol to the screen for each 2,048 bytes transferred. Turning on hash marks is useful for monitoring the status of a long file transfer. If hash marks are turned off, you generally have no indication of whether the transfer has stalled or is continuing normally (or occurring very slowly). By default, hash marks are turned off.

Tip   Whether hash marks are turned on or off, you can monitor the progress of the file transfer by double-clicking on the modem icon in the tray, which activates the modem status dialog box shown in figure 37.1.

Figure 37.1

The modem status dialog box.

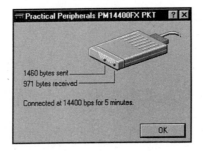

help

This command displays a list of ftp commands. The following is an example of help command output:

```
ftp> help
Commands may be abbreviated.  Commands are:

!            delete       literal      prompt       send
?            debug        ls           put          status
append       dir          mdelete      pwd          trace
ascii        disconnect   mdir         quit         type
bell         get          mget         quote        user
binary       glob         mkdir        recv         verbose
bye          hash         mls          remotehelp
cd           help         mput         rename
close        lcd          open         rmdir
```

lcd

The lcd command changes the current working directory on the local computer. If you want to place a file you are about to transfer into a different directory from the current directory, use lcd to change the current directory. The lcd command functions much like the DOS CD command. By default, the Windows folder (in which the ftp.exe program file is located) acts as the current directory.

literal or quote

The literal command sends command-line arguments to the remote ftp host verbatim, without interpreting the content of the command line. The remote ftp host returns a reply code in response. The quote command is synonymous with literal.

ls [-acdfgilqrstu1ACLFR] [*filespec*]

The ls command corresponds to the Unix ls command and produces an abbreviated list of directory contents based on the file pattern you specify with *filespec*. You can use a number of different command-line options with ls, as indicated. The most useful of these command options are described in the following list:

◆ **-l.** Displays a list in long format, giving mode, number of links, owner, size in bytes, and time of last modification for each file. If the file is a special file, the size field contains the major and minor device numbers. If the file is a symbolic link, the path name of the linked-to file prints preceded by ->.

◆ **-g.** Causes the output to include the group ownership of the file.

◆ **-t.** Sorts the listing by time modified (latest first) rather than by name.

◆ **-s.** Lists size in KB of each file.

◆ **-r.** Reverses the sort order for reverse alphabetic or oldest first as appropriate.

◆ **-u.** Gives the time of last access rather than last modification, for sorting with the -t option and/or displaying with the -l option.

◆ **-i.** Causes the output to include the i-number of each file in the first column of the report.

◆ **-F.** Causes directories to be marked with a trailing /, sockets with a trailing =, executable files with a trailing *, and symbolic links to files with a trailing @. Symbolic links to directories are marked with a trailing / unless you also use the -l option.

◆ **-R.** Recursively lists subdirectories (lists the contents of all subdirectories encountered during the file list).

◆ **-1.** (the default) Forces output to one entry per line.

◆ **-C.** Forces multicolumn output.

The mode listed with the -l option for each entry contains 11 characters. The first character can be any one of the following 6 characters:

d	directory
b	block-type special file
c	character-type special file
l	symbolic link
s	socket
-	a plain file

The remaining 9 characters in an entry's mode are interpreted as 3 sets of 3 bytes each. The first set describes owner permissions. The second set describes permissions to others in the same user group. The last set describes permissions for all others. The 3 characters in each set indicate permission to read, write, or execute the file as a program, respectively. For a directory, execute permission provides the capability to search the directory. The permissions are indicated as follows (refer to the sample ls command output earlier in the chapter):

r	read
w	write
x	execute
-	indicated permission is not granted

mdelete [*filespec*]

This command deletes multiple files on the remote host. You must have the necessary permission in the remote directory before you can delete the files. If you want to delete a single file, use the delete command. Use the glob command to turn on or off file globbing as necessary to specify file names. Remember to match file name case when you delete files on Unix hosts.

mdir [*filespec*] [*filespec*]...[*localfile*]

The mdir command displays a list of a remote directory's files and subdirectories, enabling you to specify multiple files. The last parameter is interpreted as the name of a local file in which to store the directory output. If interactive mode is on, ftp prompts you to verify that the file specified by *localfile* is to be used to store the output. The following example lists the files in the Library, pub, Mail, and Files directories and places the output in a local file name dirout.txt:

```
ftp> mdir Library pub Mail Files dirout.txt
output to local-file: dirout.txt? Y
```

mget [*filespec*]

The mget command retrieves multiple files from the remote host with a single command using the current file transfer type. You can use wild-card matching to specify the multiple files. If interactive prompting is turned on, mget prompts you to verify the receipt of each file. If you want to use mget to retrieve a large number of files while you are away from the computer, turn off interactive mode by starting ftp using the -i option, or by entering the prompt command at the ftp> prompt. The following example turns off interactive prompting and retrieves all files in the current directory on the host:

```
ftp> prompt
Interactive mode Off
ftp> mget *.*
```

mkdir [*dirname*]

The mkdir command creates the remote directory specified by the *dirname* parameter. You must have the necessary permissions in the remote host directory to create the new directory.

mls [*filespec*] [*localfile*]

This command displays an abbreviated list of the subdirectory and file names in the remote host's current directory. The output of the command is placed in the file on your computer specified by the *localfile* name.

mput

The mput command copies multiple files from your computer to the remote host using the current file transfer type. If interactive prompting is turned on, ftp prompts you to verify the transfer of each file. If you want to transfer the files without any interaction, start ftp with the -i parameter, or use the prompt command to turn off interactive prompting. The following example would copy all the files in the current directory on the local computer to the current directory on the remote host without interaction:

```
ftp> prompt
Interactive mode Off
ftp> mput *.*
```

open [[*host.domain*] or [*ipaddress*]]

The open command establishes a connection to a remote ftp server (host). You can specify a DNS-format name or enter the IP address of the remote host. If the remote host requires a logon, a logon prompt appears and you must enter a valid user name and password.

Tip   On many ftp servers, you can use the user name anonymous to log on, and your e-mail address as the password.

The following example opens a connection to Microsoft's ftp server, logging on as anonymous (to try this example, first enter **ftp** to start the ftp utility):

```
ftp> open ftp.microsoft.com
Connected to ftp.microsoft.com.
220 ftp Windows NT FTP Server (Version 3.5 DEBUG).
User (ftp.microsoft.com:(none)): anonymous
331 Anonymous access allowed, send identity (e-mail name) as password.
Password: ******
230-¦
¦ Welcome to ftp.microsoft.com (a.k.a gowinnt.microsoft.com)!
¦
¦ Please enter your "full e-mail name" as your password.
¦    Report any problems to ftp@microsoft.com
¦
¦ Refer to the index.txt file for further information
¦
230 Anonymous user logged in as anonymous (guest access).
```

prompt

The prompt command turns on and off interactive prompting. By default, prompting is turned on. If you use mget, mput, and mdir, you might want to turn off prompting so that file transfers can occur without interaction on your part. If prompting is on, you must verify the transfer of each file.

put [*file*] [*newfile*]

The put command copies a file from your computer to the remote host, using the current file transfer type. If you want to copy multiple files, use the mget command. If you specify a new file name for *newfile,* ftp renames the file as it copies. The following example copies the file Readme.txt from the local computer to the host, renaming the file to Readme.now:

```
ftp> put Readme.txt Readme.now
```

The send command is synonymous with put.

pwd

This command prints the name of the current directory on the remote host. The following is a sample output of the pwd command:

```
ftp> pwd
257 "/Users/staff/jimb/test" is current directory.
```

remotehelp [*command*]

Without a *command* parameter, this command displays a list of commands that the remote ftp host recognizes. If you enter a command name, the remote host responds with a syntax description of the command. The following example shows the output that results from using the remotehelp command without any additional command modifiers:

```
ftp> remotehelp
214-The following commands are recognized (* =>'s unimplemented).
    USER    PORT    STOR    MSAM*   RNTO    NLST    MKD     CDUP
    PASS    PASV    APPE    MRSQ*   ABOR    SITE    XMKD    XCUP
    ACCT*   TYPE    MLFL*   MRCP*   DELE    SYST    RMD     STOU
    SMNT*   STRU    MAIL*   ALLO    CWD     STAT    XRMD    SIZE
    REIN*   MODE    MSND*   REST    XCWD    HELP    PWD     MDTM
    QUIT    RETR    MSOM*   RNFR    LIST    NOOP    XPWD
214 Direct comments to ftp-bugs@tigers.
```

rename [*oldfile*] [*newfile*]

The rename command renames a file on the remote host from *oldfile* to *newfile*. The following example renames the file Readme.now on the host to Readme.txt:

```
ftp> rename Readme.now Readme.txt
```

rmdir [*dirname*]

The rmdir command removes a directory on the remote host. The remote directory must be empty, and you must have the necessary privileges to remove the directory.

status

The status command displays the current status of the ftp connection and parameters. The following is a sample output of the status command:

```
ftp> status
Connected to ftp.microsoft.com
Type: ascii; Verbose: On; Bell: Off; Prompting: On; Globbing: On
Debugging: Off; Hash mark printing: Off
```

trace

The trace command turns on and off packet tracing. *Packet tracing* displays the route and status of each packet when you run an ftp command. Generally, trace is useful only for debugging, and you should seldom, if ever, need to use it.

type [*filetype*]

The type command sets or displays the current file transfer type. If you omit *filetype* (such as ascii or binary), the type command displays the current file transfer type:

```
ftp> type
Using binary mode to transfer files.
```

 Tip   You can use the ascii and binary commands to set file transfer type, or you can enter **type ascii** or **type binary** to set the transfer type.

user [*username*]

The user command specifies the user name by which you want to log on to the remote host. If you start ftp with autologon disabled (ftp -n), ftp doesn't automatically initiate the logon process. You can configure ftp using a variety of commands, and when you're ready to log on, enter the user command to log on to the ftp server. If a password is required for the logon name you specify, the remote ftp server prompts you for a password, as in the following example:

```
C:\WINDOWS>ftp -n ftp.microsoft.com
Connected to ftp.microsoft.com.
220 ftp Windows NT FTP Server (Version 3.5 DEBUG).
ftp> user anonymous
331 Anonymous access allowed, send identity (e-mail name) as password.
Password: ******
230-¦
 ¦ Welcome to ftp.microsoft.com (a.k.a gowinnt.microsoft.com)!
 ¦
 ¦ Please enter your "full e-mail name" as your password.
 ¦    Report any problems to ftp@microsoft.com
 ¦
 ¦ Refer to the index.txt file for further information
 ¦
230 Anonymous user logged in as anonymous (guest access).
```

If you omit the *username* parameter, the ftp server prompts you to enter a user name.

verbose

The verbose command turns on and off verbose mode. If verbose mode is on, all responses from the ftp server appear on-screen, and file transfer statistics appear after a file transfer. Verbose mode is turned on by default.

Using netstat

The netstat utility is a diagnostic tool you can use to monitor your connections to remote hosts and protocol statistics for the connections. The netstat utility also is useful for extracting the IP addresses of hosts to which you have connected using domain names. The syntax of the netstat command is as follows:

```
netstat [-a] [-ens] [-p protocol] [-r] [interval]
```

The following list describes the parameters you can use with the netstat command:

◆ **-a.** Causes netstat to displays all connections. Normally, netstat does not display server connections.

◆ **-e.** Causes netstat to display Ethernet statistics. You can use the -e parameter in conjunction with the -s parameter (explained later).

◆ **-n.** Causes netstat to display addresses and port numbers in numerical format instead of listing the names in host.domain format.

◆ **-s.** Causes netstat to display statistics on a per-protocol basis. By default, nestat displays statistics for the TCP, UDP, ICMP, and IP protocols.

◆ **-p protocol.** Displays connections for the protocol specified by the *protocol* parameter.

◆ **-r.** Causes netstat to display the contents of the routing table.

◆ **interval.** You can specify an interval, in seconds, at which netstat displays the requested information. To terminate netstat's output, press Ctrl+C. If you don't include a value for *interval*, netstat displays the requested data only once, then terminates.

Tip

If you want to derive the IP address of a remote host to which you're connected, use the -n parameter with netstat. The following example uses netstat without any parameters to list the connected hosts, then issues netstat again with the -n parameter to derive the IP addresses. You can tell from the second output that the IP address of Microsoft's ftp server is 198.105.232.1.

```
C:\WINDOWS>netstat

Active Connections
   Proto  Local Address    Foreign Address        State
   TCP    tower:1283       ftp.microsoft.com:ftp  ESTABLISHED

C:\WINDOWS>netstat -n

Active Connections
   Proto  Local Address         Foreign Address       State
   TCP    198.87.118.72:1283    198.105.232.1:21      ESTABLISHED
```

Besides using netstat for deriving an IP address from a host.domain name, you can use a host's IP address to derive its host.domain name.

Using ping

ping is another TCP/IP diagnostic utility included with Windows 95 that hearkens from the Unix world. ping is a lot like sonar—you send a packet to a remote host and it bounces the packet back to you. If the packet doesn't come back, something is wrong with your connection or the host is not available. ping is the single most useful command for testing connections quickly and easily.

ping works by transmitting Internet Control Message Protocol (ICMP) packets to a remote host and then waits to receive response packets from the host. ping waits for as long as one second for the packets to be returned and prints the results of each packet transmission. By default, ping sends four packets, but you can direct ping to transmit any number of packets, or transmit continuously until you terminate the command. The following shows a sample ping command and its output:

```
C:\WINDOWS>ping 198.87.118.1

Pinging 198.87.118.1 with 32 bytes of data:

Reply from 198.87.118.1: bytes=32 time=224ms TTL=14
Reply from 198.87.118.1: bytes=32 time=213ms TTL=14
Reply from 198.87.118.1: bytes=32 time=198ms TTL=14
Reply from 198.87.118.1: bytes=32 time=170ms TTL=14
```

In addition to helping determine when a host is not available and testing connections to routers and other hosts, ping enables you to test for routing problems. If you ping a host's IP address but ping fails to reach the host when you use the host name, the host probably is not listed in your DNS server or in your local Hosts file, you have specified an invalid DNS server, or the DNS server is unavailable. You can enter the remote host's name and IP address (which you're trying to ping) to the Hosts file to alleviate the problem.

Before you begin pinging remote hosts to troubleshoot connection or routing problems, you should ping your own computer to verify that its network interface is functioning properly. To ping your own machine, use any of the following commands (substitute your computer's IP address in place of *yourIPaddress*):

```
ping localhost
ping 127.0.0.1

ping yourIPaddress
```

Tip You can use ping to determine the route taken by a packet to the remote host by using the -r parameter (explained later).

The following is the syntax of the ping command:

```
ping [-t] [-a] [-n count] [-l length] [-f] [-i ttl] [-v tos] [-r count]
➥[-s count] [[-j host-list] ¦ [-k host-list]] [-w timeout] destination-list
```

The parameters you can use with the ping command are described in the following list:

- **-t.** Directs ping to continue pinging the remote host until you interrupt the command by pressing Ctrl+C.

- **-a.** Directs ping not to resolve IP addresses to host names, useful for trouble-shooting DNS and Hosts file problems.

- **-n count.** By default, ping sends four ICMP packets to the remote host. You can use the -n parameter to specify a different number of packets to be sent.

- **-l length.** Use the -l parameter to specify the length of the ICMP packets that ping transmits to the remote host. By default, ping sends packets of 64 bytes, but you can specify up to a maximum of 8,192 bytes.

- **-f.** Causes ping to include a Do Not Fragment flag in each packet, which prevents gateways through which the packet passes from fragmenting the packet.

- **-i ttl.** Sets the Time To Live field to the value specified by *ttl*.

- **-v tos.** Sets the Type Of Service field to the value specified by *tos*.

- **-r count.** Records the route of the outgoing packet and the return packet. You must specify from one to nine hosts using the *count* value.

- **-s count.** Specifies the timestamp for the number of hops specified by *count*.

- **-j host-list.** Enables you to use a route list to route the packets. You can separate consecutive hosts by intermediate gateways. The maximum number of hosts supported by IP is nine.

- **-k host-list.** Enables you to route packets by means of the list of hosts specified by *host-list*. You cannot separate consecutive hosts by intermediate gateways. The maximum number of hosts supported by IP is nine.

◆ **-w timeout.** Specifies the time-out value in milliseconds for packet transmission.

◆ **destination-list.** Specifies the host to ping.

Using telnet

The telnet utility is one of only two Windows-based TCP/IP utility programs included with Windows 95 (the other is Winipcfg). telnet is a remote terminal emulator that enables you to log on to a remote host and perform tasks on the remote hosts such as starting and running programs (see fig. 37.2). You can use telnet across your network, for example, to log on to a Unix host and execute programs on the remote host. Or, you can use Dial-Up Networking to dial in to a Unix host or a remote LAN that contains a Unix host, then use telnet across the Dial-Up Networking connection to log on to the host.

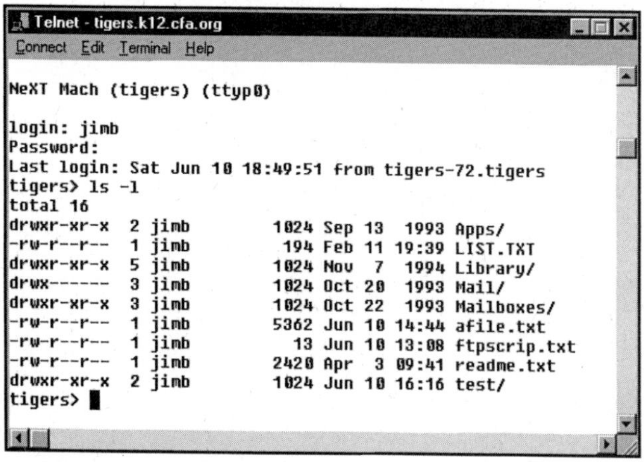

Figure 37.2

telnet enables you to connect to remote hosts.

The telnet program is located in the Windows folder as the file Telnet.exe. The syntax for starting the telnet program is as follows:

```
telnet [host] [port]
```

The *host* parameter specifies the name or IP address of the host to which you want to connect. The *port* parameter specifies the port number to which you want to connect on the remote host. If you don't supply a port value, the default value of 23 is used. The *port* parameter is included primarily for compatibility with utilities such as gopher and Mosaic that require specific port connections.

Tip If you want to create telnet shortcuts to a selection of hosts, first create the shortcuts to the telnet program. Then, open the property sheet for the shortcut and display the Shortcut property page. In the **T**arget text box, enter the name of the host after the path to the telnet program file, such as **c:\windows\telnet.exe myhost.mydomain.com**.

If you specify a host name, telnet attempts the connection to the host, and if successful, displays the remote host's logon prompt. If you don't specify a host name or IP address on the telnet command line, the telnet window opens without a connection. You then can choose **C**onnect, **R**emote System to open the Connect dialog box (see fig. 37.3). In the **H**ost Name combo box, enter the name or IP address of the host to which you want to connect, or select a previous connection from the drop-down list. Use the **P**ort combo box to enter or select a connection port. Use the **T**ermType combo box to enter or select a terminal type.

Figure 37.3

The Connect dialog box.

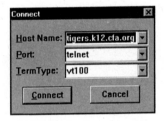

 Tip To backspace over characters that you enter on the remote host's command line, use Ctrl+backspace. Backspace is interpreted as a local key and does not cause the characters on the remote system to be deleted.

Setting Preferences

telnet supports a small number of preferences you can set to control the way the program functions. To set these preference, choose **T**erminal, **P**references to open the Terminal Preferences dialog box (see fig. 37.4).

The options in the Terminal Preferences dialog box are explained in the following list:

◆ **Local Echo.** Enable this check box to cause all keyboard input to echo to the terminal window.

◆ **Blinking Cursor.** Enable this check box if you want the cursor to blink, which can make locating the cursor easier.

Figure 37.4

The Terminal Preferences dialog box.

◆ **Block Cursor.** Enable this check box to use a block cursor rather than an underline cursor.

◆ **VT100 Arrows.** If you enable this check box, cursor key entries are treated as terminal keystrokes and sent to the remote host. Disable this check box if you want the cursor keys to be treated as local application keys.

◆ **Emulation.** Select the correct terminal type based on the requirements of the remote system.

◆ **Buffer Size.** Use this setting to specify the number of lines telnet maintains in its line buffer.

Using a Log File

You can maintain a log file of your terminal session, which logs all input and output. To turn on logging, choose Terminal, Start Logging. telnet displays an Open log file dialog box you can use to specify a file name for the log file. After you choose Open, telnet begins to echo all input and output to the log file. To turn off logging, choose Terminal, Stop Logging.

Using Winipcfg

The Winipcfg utility enables you to view information about your Ethernet adapter and TCP/IP protocol settings. Winipcfg is a Windows-based program, located in the Windows directory in the file Winipcfg.exe. To run Winipcfg, choose Start, Run, enter **winipcfg** in the Open text box, then choose OK. A Winipcfg window similar to the one shown in figure 37.5 appears.

The Winipcfg window shows the physical address, IP address, subnet mask, and default gateway settings of your primary TCP/IP adapter. If your computer contains multiple adapters to which TCP/IP is bound, you can select the other adapter(s) from the drop-down list to view their settings. To view additional information about the adapter and protocol settings, choose the More Info button to expand the dialog box to resemble the one shown in figure 37.6.

Figure 37.5

*The Winipcfg
initial window.*

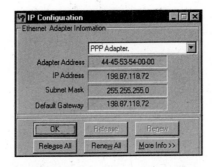

Figure 37.6

*The expanded
Winipcfg window.*

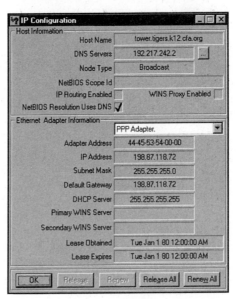

As you can see in figure 37.6, Winipcfg displays additional information, such as your computer's host name, addresses of DHCP and WINS servers (if used), and other data. If you want to copy the data to use for troubleshooting or to place in a hardware log, open Winipcfg's control menu and choose <u>C</u>opy. Winipcfg copies the information in the Winipcfg window to the Clipboard, enabling you to paste the data into Notepad or another application to print or save. The following is a sample output copied from Winipcfg:

```
Windows 95 IP Configuration
     Host Name . . . . . . . . . : tower.tigers.k12.cfa.org
     DNS Servers . . . . . . . . : 192.217.242.2
                                   192.217.240.2
     Node Type . . . . . . . . . : Broadcast
```

```
      NetBIOS Scope ID. . . . . . :
      IP Routing Enabled. . . . . : No
      WINS Proxy Enabled. . . . . : No
      NetBIOS Resolution Uses DNS : Yes
Ethernet adapter :
      Description . . . . . . . . : PPP Adapter.
      Physical Address. . . . . . : 44-45-53-54-00-00
      DHCP Enabled. . . . . . . . : No
      IP Address. . . . . . . . . : 198.87.118.72
      Subnet Mask . . . . . . . . : 255.255.255.0
      Default Gateway . . . . . . : 198.87.118.1
      Primary WINS Server . . . . :
      Secondary WINS Server . . . :
      Lease Obtained. . . . . . . :
      Lease Expires . . . . . . . :
```

If your computer uses DHCP to receive an IP address from a host, the Release and Renew buttons enable you to release and renew the IP address, respectively. For more information on DHCP and TCP/IP, refer to Chapter 36, "TCP/IP and the Internet Connection."

Part VIII

Appendix

Other Sources of Information

Although *Inside Windows 95* can answer the majority of your questions regarding Windows 95, many other sources of information exist that will provide additional information and resources to help you make the most of Windows 95. This appendix describes a selection of resources you can use to gain further information and experience with Windows 95 and related topics.

WinNews

WinNews is an online news service devoted to Windows 95. You can locate WinNews on a variety of popular online services:

◆ **America Online.** Use the keyword **winnews** to locate the WinNews area.

◆ **CompuServe.** GO WINNEWS.

◆ **FTP through the Internet.** Connect to ftp.microsoft.com and access the /PerOpSys/Win_News directory.

◆ **GEnie.** Check the WinNews area under the Windows 95 RTC.

◆ **Prodigy.** jump winnews.

◆ **World Wide Web.** Connect to http://www.microsoft.com.

Microsoft Web Site

Microsoft offers a selection of information services through its World Wide Web site at http://www.microsoft.com. The web sites offers information on Microsoft and its products, and provides access to the Microsoft Technet, Microsoft Knowledge Base, and software library (fig. A.1).

Figure A.1

Microsoft's web site.

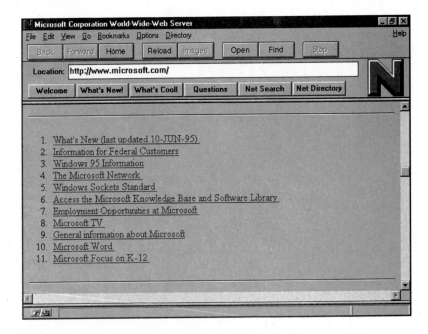

Microsoft Knowledge Base

The Microsoft Knowledge Base provides many thousands of technical articles about Microsoft products and operating systems. You can access the Knowledge Base through a variety of means, including the following:

- ◆ **Microsoft Web Site.** http://www.microsoft.com.

- ◆ **CompuServe.** GO MSKB.

CompuServe Forums

Many forums on CompuServe directly and indirectly provide information and support for Windows users. To move to the Microsoft-supported forums, enter **GO MICROSOFT**. To find other Windows-related forums, **GO TOPIC** and search using the keyword Windows.

Microsoft Download Service

The Microsoft Download Service (MSDL) is a BBS maintained by Microsoft that contains drivers and other files for Microsoft operating systems and applications. You can access the MSDL through Microsoft's web site on the Internet (http://www.microsoft.com), through Microsoft's FTP site on the Internet (ftp.microsoft.com), the Microsoft Network, CompuServe (GO MSL), and through a direct dial-in connection. The direct connection to the MSDL BBS is through (206) 936-6735 using 8-1-N.

Index

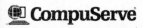

PLUG YOURSELF INTO...

THE MACMILLAN INFORMATION SUPERLIBRARY™

Free information and vast computer resources from the world's leading computer book publisher—online!

FIND THE BOOKS THAT ARE RIGHT FOR YOU!

A complete online catalog, plus sample chapters and tables of contents give you an in-depth look at *all* of our books, including hard-to-find titles. It's the best way to find the books you need!

- **STAY INFORMED** with the latest computer industry news through our online newsletter, press releases, and customized Information SuperLibrary Reports.

- **GET FAST ANSWERS** to your questions about MCP books and software.

- **VISIT** our online bookstore for the latest information and editions!

- **COMMUNICATE** with our expert authors through e-mail and conferences.

- **DOWNLOAD SOFTWARE** from the immense MCP library:
  - Source code and files from MCP books
  - The best shareware, freeware, and demos

- **DISCOVER HOT SPOTS** on other parts of the Internet.

- **WIN BOOKS** in ongoing contests and giveaways!

TO PLUG INTO MCP: ➔ WORLD WIDE WEB: **http://www.mcp.com**

GOPHER: gopher.mcp.com

FTP: ftp.mcp.com

WANT MORE INFORMATION?

CHECK OUT THESE RELATED TOPICS OR SEE YOUR LOCAL BOOKSTORE

CAD and 3D Studio

As the number one CAD publisher in the world, and as a Registered Publisher of Autodesk, New Riders Publishing provides unequaled content on this complex topic. Industry-leading products include AutoCAD and 3D Studio.

Networking

As the leading Novell NetWare publisher, New Riders Publishing delivers cutting-edge products for network professionals. We publish books for all levels of users, from those wanting to gain NetWare Certification, to those administering or installing a network. Leading books in this category include *Inside NetWare 3.12*, *CNE Training Guide: Managing NetWare Systems*, *Inside TCP/IP*, and *NetWare: The Professional Reference*.

Graphics

New Riders provides readers with the most comprehensive product tutorials and references available for the graphics market. Best-sellers include *Inside CorelDRAW! 5*, *Inside Photoshop 3*, and *Adobe Photoshop NOW!*

Internet and Communications

As one of the fastest growing publishers in the communications market, New Riders provides unparalleled information and detail on this ever-changing topic area. We publish international best-sellers such as *New Riders' Official Internet Yellow Pages, 2nd Edition*, a directory of over 10,000 listings of Internet sites and resources from around the world, and *Riding the Internet Highway, Deluxe Edition*.

Operating Systems

Expanding off our expertise in technical markets, and driven by the needs of the computing and business professional, New Riders offers comprehensive references for experienced and advanced users of today's most popular operating systems, including *Understanding Windows 95*, *Inside Unix*, *Inside Windows 3.11 Platinum Edition*, *Inside OS/2 Warp Version 3*, and *Inside MS-DOS 6.22*.

Other Markets

Professionals looking to increase productivity and maximize the potential of their software and hardware should spend time discovering our line of products for Word, Excel, and Lotus 1-2-3. These titles include *Inside Word 6 for Windows*, *Inside Excel 5 for Windows*, *Inside 1-2-3 Release 5*, and *Inside WordPerfect for Windows*.

Orders/Customer Service **1-800-653-6156**   Source Code **NRP95**

New Riders Publishing   201 West 103rd Street ◆ Indianapolis, Indiana 46290 USA